# SURVEILLANCE STUDIES

# SURVEILLANCE STUDIES

A READER

Edited by

TORIN MONAHAN

DAVID MURAKAMI WOOD

OXFORD

UNIVERSITY PRESS

# OXFORD
UNIVERSITY PRESS

Oxford University Press is a department of the University of Oxford. It furthers
the University's objective of excellence in research, scholarship, and education
by publishing worldwide. Oxford is a registered trade mark of Oxford University
Press in the UK and certain other countries.

Published in the United States of America by Oxford University Press
198 Madison Avenue, New York, NY 10016, United States of America.

CIP data is on file at the Library of Congress
ISBN 978–0–19–029782–4 (pbk.)
ISBN 978–0–19–029781–7 (hbk.)

9 8 7 6 5 4 3 2 1

Paperback printed by WebCom, Inc., Canada
Hardback printed by Bridgeport National Bindery, Inc., United States of America

# CONTENTS

# LIST OF FIGURES AND TABLES

## Figures

## Table

# ACKNOWLEDGMENTS

This book was made possible through generous financial assistance from our universities. The Department of Communication at the University of North Carolina at Chapel Hill provided support through a Kenneth and Mary Lowe Challenge Fund/Faculty Excellence Grant. The Department of Sociology and the Surveillance Studies Centre at Queen's University provided support with the aid of the Canada Research Chairs Program.

# RIGHTS AND PERMISSIONS

## SECTION 1: OPENINGS AND DEFINITIONS

James B. Rule. *Private Lives and Public Surveillance: Social Control in the Computer Age.* London: Allen Lane, 1973 [19, 22–23, 37–40, 350–52, 354–55, 357]. Reprinted with permission.

Oscar H. Gandy, Jr. *The Panoptic Sort: A Political Economy of Personal Information.* Boulder, CO: Westview, 1993 [1–2, 15–18]. Reprinted with permission.

William G. Staples. *Everyday Surveillance: Vigilance and Visibility in Postmodern Life.* Lanham, MD: Rowan & Littlefield Publishers, 2000 [3–7]. Reprinted with permission.

David Lyon. *Surveillance Studies: An Overview.* Cambridge, UK: Polity, 2007 [13–16, 25–27]. Reprinted with permission.

Gary T. Marx. "What's New about the 'New Surveillance?': Classifying for Change and Continuity." *Surveillance and Society* 1 (1):9–29. 2002. Reprinted with permission.

## SECTION 2: SOCIETY AND SUBJECTIVITY

Jeremy Bentham. *The Works of Jeremy Bentham, vol 4.* Edited by J. Bowring. Ann Arbor: University of Michigan Library, (1843) 2009 [40–41, 44–46]. Reprinted with permission.

Michel Foucault. *Discipline and Punish: The Birth of the Prison,* translated by Alan Sheridan, translation copyright © 1977 by Alan Sheridan [200–209]. Used by permission of Pantheon Books, an imprint of the Knopf Doubleday Publishing Group, a division of Penguin Random House LLC. All rights reserved.

Gilles Deleuze. "Postscript on the Societies of Control." *October* 59:3–7. 1992 [3–7]. Reprinted with permission.

Kevin D. Haggerty and Richard V. Ericson. "The Surveillant Assemblage." *British Journal of Sociology* 51 (4):605–22. 2000 [606, 608–14, 617–19]. Reprinted with permission.

Thomas Mathiesen. "The Viewer Society: Michel Foucault's 'Panopticon' Revisited." *Theoretical Criminology* 1 (2):215–35. 1997 [216–23, 225–26, 228–31]. Reprinted with permission.

David Armstrong. "The Rise of Surveillance Medicine." *Sociology of Health & Illness* 17 (3): 393–404. 1995 [393–97, 399–401, 403]. Reprinted with permission.

Irus Braverman. *Zooland: The Institution of Captivity.* Stanford: Stanford University Press, 2013 [75–79, 82–83, 86–90]. Reprinted with the permission.

## SECTION 3: STATE AND AUTHORITY

Johann Gottlieb Fichte. *Foundations of Natural Right.* Cambridge, UK: Cambridge University Press. Edited by Frederick Neuhouser, translated by Michael Baur, (1796/97) 2000 [254, 257–58, 261–63]. Reprinted with permission.

Anthony Giddens. *The Nation-State and Violence (Critique of Historical Materialism Vol. II).* Cambridge, UK: Polity, 1985 [1, 146, 159, 184–85, 189, 192, 311–13, 327, 345]. Reprinted with permission.

Geoffrey C. Bowker and Susan Leigh Star. *Sorting Things Out: Classification and Its Consequences.* Cambridge, MA: MIT Press, 1999 [196–97, 199–201, 212, 225]. Reprinted with permission.

Maria Los. "The Technologies of Total Domination." *Surveillance & Society* 2 (1):15–38. 2004. Reprinted with permission.

Anna Funder. *Stasiland: Stories from behind the Berlin Wall.* Melbourne: Text Publishing, 2002 [106–110]. Reprinted with permission.

Cindi Katz. "The State Goes Home: Local Hyper-Vigilance of Children and the Global Retreat from Social Reproduction." *Social Justice* 28 (3):47–56. 2001 [47–49, 50–51, 55]. Reprinted with permission.

## SECTION 4: IDENTITY AND IDENTIFICATION

Valentin Groebner. *Who Are You? Identification, Deception, and Surveillance in Early Modern Europe.* Translated by M. Kyburz and J. Peck. Cambridge, MA: Zone Books, 2007 [25–27, 200–202, 218–19, 257–58]. Reprinted with permission.

John C. Torpey. *The Invention of the Passport: Surveillance, Citizenship, and the State.* Cambridge, UK: Cambridge University Press, 2000 [1, 4, 6–13, 17]. Reprinted with permission.

Allan Sekula. "The Body and the Archive." *October* 39:3–64. 1986 [5–7, 10, 16–19, 62]. Cambridge, MA: MIT Press. Reprinted with permission.

Dorothy Nelkin and Lori Andrews. "DNA Identification and Surveillance Creep." *Sociology of Health & Illness* 21 (5):689–706. 1999 [689–99, 701, 703]. Reprinted with permission.

Shoshana Amielle Magnet. *When Biometrics Fail: Gender, Race, and the Technology of Identity.* Durham, NC: Duke University Press, 2011 [2–3, 5–7, 47–50]. Reprinted with permission.

## SECTION 5: BORDERS AND MOBILITIES

Louise Amoore. "Biometric Borders: Governing Mobilities in the War on Terror." *Political Geography* 25 (3):336–51. 2006 [337–38, 341–43]. Reprinted with permission.

Mark B. Salter. "Passports, Mobility, and Security: How Smart Can the Border Be?" *International Studies Perspectives* 5 (1):71–91. 2004 [78–80, 85]. Reprinted with permission.

Stephen Graham and David Wood. "Digitizing Surveillance: Categorization, Space, Inequality." *Critical Social Policy* 23 (2):227–48. 2003 [228–35, 242]. Reprinted with permission.

Katja Franko Aas. "'Crimmigrant' Bodies and Bona Fide Travelers: Surveillance, Citizenship and Global Governance." *Theoretical Criminology* 15 (3):331–46. 2011 [337–42]. Reprinted with permission.

Didier Bigo. "Security, Exception, Ban and Surveillance." *Theorizing Surveillance: The Panopticon and Beyond,* edited by D. Lyon, 46–68. Devon: Willan Publishing, 2006 [47–49, 55, 63]. Reprinted with permission.

## SECTION 6: INTELLIGENCE AND SECURITY

James Bamford. *The Puzzle Palace: Inside the National Security Agency, America's Most Secret Intelligence Organization.* Copyright © 1982, 1983 [15–16, 19, 317–20, 461–63, 468–69, 475–76]. Reprinted by permission of Houghton Mifflin Harcourt Publishing Company and Penguin Books. All rights reserved.

Alfred W. McCoy. *Policing America's Empire: The United States, the Philippines, and the Rise of the Surveillance State.* Madison: University of Wisconsin Press, 2009 [15–19]. Reprinted with permission.

Ahmad H. Sa'di. *Thorough Surveillance: The Genesis of Israeli Policies of Population Management, Surveillance, and Political Control towards the Palestinian Minority.* Manchester, UK: Manchester University Press, 2013 [52–55, 58–61, 63, 67]. Reprinted with permission.

Glenn Greenwald. *No Place to Hide: Edward Snowden, the NSA, and the US Surveillance State.* New York: Metropolitan Books, 2014 [91–96, 98–101, 118–19, 151, 153]. Reprinted with permission.

## SECTION 7: CRIME AND POLICING

Clive Norris and Gary Armstrong. "CCTV and the Social Structuring of Surveillance." In *Surveillance of Public Space: CCTV, Street Lighting, and Crime Prevention,* edited by Kate Painter and Nick Tilley, 157–78. Copyright © 1999 by Lynne Rienner Publishers, Inc. Reprinted with permission.

Mike McCahill. *The Surveillance Web: The Rise of Visual Surveillance in an English City.* Collumpton, Devon, UK: Willan Publishing, 2002 [95–98]. Reprinted with permission.

Philip Boyle and Kevin D. Haggerty. "Spectacular Security: Mega-Events and the Security Complex." *International Political Sociology* 3 (3):257–74. 2009 [267–70]. Reprinted with permission.

Pete Fussey, Jon Coaffee, Gary Armstrong, and Dick Hobbs. "The Regeneration Games: Purity and Security in the Olympic City." *British Journal of Sociology* 63 (2):260–84. 2012 [261–62, 264, 268, 273–74, 276]. Reprinted with permission.

Hille Koskela. "'The Gaze without Eyes': Video-Surveillance and the Changing Nature of Urban Space." *Progress in Human Geography* 24 (2):243–65. 2000 [246, 248–50, 255, 258–59]. Reprinted with permission.

Andrew John Goldsmith. "Policing's New Visibility." *British Journal of Criminology* 50 (5):914–34. 2010 [917–22, 931]. Reprinted with permission.

Torin Monahan and Rodolfo D. Torres. "Introduction." In *Schools under Surveillance: Cultures of Control in Public Education,* 1–18. New Brunswick, NJ: Rutgers University Press, 2010 [1–4, 6, 13–14]. Reprinted with permission.

## SECTION 8: PRIVACY AND AUTONOMY

Priscilla M. Regan. *Legislating Privacy: Technology, Social Values, and Public Policy.* Chapel Hill: University of North Carolina Press, 1995 [212–21]. Reprinted with permission.

Jean-François Blanchette and Deborah G. Johnson. "Data Retention and the Panoptic Society: The Social Benefits of Forgetfulness." *The Information Society* 18 (1):33–45. 2002 [33–39, 43]. Reprinted with permission.

Helen Fay Nissenbaum. *Privacy in Context: Technology, Policy, and the Integrity of Social Life.* Stanford, CA: Stanford Law Books, 2010 [1–3, 231–36]. Reprinted with permission.

Julie E. Cohen. *Configuring the Networked Self: Law, Code, and the Play of Everyday Practice.* New Haven, CT: Yale University Press, 2012 [148–52]. Reprinted with permission.

John Gilliom. *Overseers of the Poor: Surveillance, Resistance, and the Limits of Privacy.*

Chicago: University of Chicago Press, 2001 [2–7, 9–10, 43–44, 67–68]. Reprinted with permission.

Colin J. Bennett. "In Defense of Privacy: The Concept and the Regime." *Surveillance and Society* 8 (4):485–96. 2011. Reprinted with permission.

## SECTION 9: UBIQUITOUS SURVEILLANCE

Roger Clarke. "Information Technology and Dataveillance." *Communications of the ACM* 31 (5):498–512. 1988 [499, 502–508]. Reprinted with permission.

Dana Cuff. "Immanent Domain: Pervasive Computing and the Public Realm." *Journal of Architectural Education* 57 (1):43–49. 2003 [43–48]. Reprinted with permission.

Mike Crang and Stephen Graham. "Sentient Cities: Ambient Intelligence and the Politics of Urban Space." *Information, Communication & Society* 10 (6):789–817. 2007 [791–97, 811–14]. Reprinted with permission.

Mark Andrejevic. "Surveillance in the Big Data Era." In *Emerging Pervasive Information and Communication Technologies (PICT)*, edited by K. D. Pimple, 55–69. New York: Springer, 2014 [58–64]. Reprinted with permission.

## SECTION 10: WORK AND ORGANIZATION

Graham Sewell and Barry Wilkinson. "Someone to Watch over Me: Surveillance, Discipline, and the Just-in-Time Labour Process." *Sociology* 26 (2):271–89. 1992 [271–81, 283–84]. Reprinted with permission.

Kirstie Ball. "Workplace Surveillance: An Overview." *Labor History* 51 (1):87–106. 2010 [89, 91–94, 98–101]. Reprinted with permission.

Gavin J. D. Smith. "Behind the Screens: Examining Constructions of Deviance and Informal Practices among CCTV Control Room Operators in the UK." *Surveillance & Society* 2 (2/3):376–95. 2004. Reprinted with permission.

Christian Fuchs. "Web 2.0, Prosumption, and Surveillance." *Surveillance & Society* 8 (3):288–309. 2011. Reprinted with permission.

## SECTION 11: POLITICAL ECONOMY

Adam Arvidsson. "On the 'Pre-History of the Panoptic Sort': Mobility in Market Research." *Surveillance & Society* 1 (4):456–74. 2004. Reprinted with permission.

David Murakami Wood and Kirstie Ball. "Brandscapes of Control? Surveillance, Marketing and the Co-construction of Subjectivity and Space in Neo-Liberal Capitalism." *Marketing Theory* 13 (1):47–67. 2013 [47, 49–52, 54–55, 57, 60–62]. Reprinted with permission.

Anthony Amicelle. "Towards a 'New' Political Anatomy of Financial Surveillance." *Security Dialogue* 42 (2):161–78. 2011 [161–64, 167–69]. Reprinted with permission.

Nicole S. Cohen. "The Valorization of Surveillance: Towards a Political Economy of Facebook." *Democratic Communiqué* 22 (1):5–22. 2008 [7–15, 18]. Reprinted with permission.

Shoshana Zuboff. "Big Other: Surveillance Capitalism and the Prospects of an Information Civilization." *Journal of Information Technology* 30 (1):75–89. 2015 [77, 80–85]. Reprinted with permission.

## SECTION 12: PARTICIPATION AND SOCIAL MEDIA

Mark Andrejevic. "The Work of Being Watched: Interactive Media and the Exploitation of Self-Disclosure." *Critical Studies in Media Communication* 19 (2):230–48. 2002 [231–32, 238–39, 243–45]. Reprinted with permission.

Hille Koskela. "Webcams, TV Shows, and Mobile Phones: Empowering Exhibitionism." *Surveillance & Society* 2 (2/3):199–215. 2004. Reprinted with permission.

Anders Albrechtslund. "Online Social Networking as Participatory Surveillance." *First Monday* 13 (3). 2008. Reprinted with permission.

Priscilla Regan and Valerie Steeves. "Kids R Us: Online Social Networking and the Potential for Empowerment." *Surveillance & Society* 8 (2):151–65. 2010. Reprinted with permission.

Alice E. Marwick. "The Public Domain: Social Surveillance in Everyday Life." *Surveillance & Society* 9 (4):378–93. 2012. Reprinted with permission.

## SECTION 13: RESISTANCE AND OPPOSITION

Colin J. Bennett. *The Privacy Advocates: Resisting the Spread of Surveillance*. Cambridge, MA: MIT Press, 2008 [ix, 199, 210–11, 217, 220–22, 225]. Reprinted with permission.

Laura Huey, Kevin Walby, and Aaron Doyle. "Cop Watching in the Downtown Eastside: Exploring the Use of (Counter) Surveillance as a Tool of Resistance." In *Surveillance and Society: Technological Power in Everyday Life*, edited by T. Monahan, 149–65. New York: Routledge, 2006 [149–50, 152–54, 156–57, 161–65]. Reprinted with permission.

Finn Brunton and Helen Nissenbaum. "Vernacular Resistance to Data Collection and Analysis: A Political Theory of Obfuscation." *First Monday* 16 (5). 2011. Reprinted with permission.

Steve Mann, Jason Nolan, and Barry Wellman. "Sousveillance: Inventing and Using Wearable Computing Devices for Data Collection in Surveillance Environments." *Surveillance & Society* 1 (3):331–55. 2003. Reprinted with permission.

Torin Monahan. "The Right to Hide? Anti-Surveillance Camouflage and the

Aestheticization of Resistance." *Communication and Critical/Cultural Studies* 12 (2):159–78. 2015 [159–65, 169–71]. Reprinted with permission.

## SECTION 14: MARGINALITY AND DIFFERENCE

Oscar H. Gandy, Jr. *Coming to Terms with Chance: Engaging Rational Discrimination and Cumulative Disadvantage.* Burlington, VT: Ashgate, 2009 [1–3, 5, 10–15]. Reprinted with permission.

Jasbir K. Puar. *Terrorist Assemblages: Homonationalism in Queer Times.* Durham, NC: Duke University Press, 2007 [152, 154–56, 160–62, 164–65]. Reprinted with permission.

Corrine Mason and Shoshana Magnet. "Surveillance Studies and Violence against Women." *Surveillance & Society* 10 (2):105–18. 2012. Reprinted with permission.

Simone Browne. *Dark Matters: On the Surveillance of Blackness.* Durham, NC: Duke University Press, 2015 [7–9, 16–17, 21–22, 24, 77–79, 128]. Reprinted with permission.

## SECTION 15: ART AND CULTURE

John E. McGrath. *Loving Big Brother: Performance, Privacy, and Surveillance Space.* New York: Routledge, 2004 [2–3, 5–7, 10–11, 14, 166–68]. Reprinted with permission.

David Rosen and Aaron Santesso. *The Watchman in Pieces: Surveillance, Literature, and Liberal Personhood.* New Haven, CT: Yale University Press, 2013 [56–59, 100–104]. Reprinted with permission.

Andrea Mubi Brighenti. "Artveillance: At the Crossroads of Art and Surveillance." *Surveillance & Society* 7 (2):137–48. 2010. Reprinted with permission.

Mike Nellis. "Since *Nineteen Eighty Four*: Representations of Surveillance in Literary Fiction." In *New Directions in Surveillance and Privacy*, edited by B. J. Goold and D. Neyland, 178–204. Portland, OR: Willan Publishing, 2009 [178, 197–200]. Reprinted with permission.

Catherine Zimmer. *Surveillance Cinema.* New York: New York University Press, 2015 [18–24]. Reprinted with permission.

Jennifer R. Whitson. "Gaming the Quantified Self." *Surveillance & Society* 11 (1/2):163–76. 2013. Reprinted with permission.

# TORIN MONAHAN AND
# DAVID MURAKAMI WOOD

## INTRODUCTION

### Surveillance Studies as a Transdisciplinary Endeavor

Surveillance studies is a dynamic field of scholarly inquiry. It emerges, in large part, from recognition of the ways in which pervasive information systems increasingly regulate all aspects of social life. Whether with workplaces monitoring the performance of employees, social media sites tracking clicks and uploads, financial institutions logging transactions, advertisers amassing fine-grained data on customers, or security agencies siphoning up everyone's telecommunications activities, surveillance practices—although often hidden—have come to define the way modern institutions operate. This development indicates more than just the adoption of information-based technological systems by organizations; rather, it represents a larger transformation in how people and organizations perceive and engage with the world. It now seems completely reasonable and responsible to collect data by default and base decisions on those data. It seems rational to use data to sort people into categories according to their anticipated risk or value and to treat people differently based on their categorization. These are surveillance logics that transcend any particular technological system, and indeed they do not require technological

mediation at all. Face-to-face surveillance, of people watching and controlling others, is certainly not rendered obsolete by new technologies.

Although definitions of surveillance vary, most scholars stress that surveillance is about more than just watching; it depends also on some capacity to control, regulate, or modulate behavior. This reading draws upon the French origins of the word *surveillance*, which means "watching from above." It implies a power relationship. It is not just passive looking but is instead a form of oversight that judges and intervenes to shape behavior. Importantly, one does not need to be aware of such control dynamics for them to be effective; these dynamics can perhaps have greater force if they are felt as natural and their politics are hidden. The excerpts in this book sketch a number of definitions with different accents and nuances, but as a starting point, surveillance can be understood as "monitoring people in order to regulate or govern their behavior" (Gilliom and Monahan 2013: 2). While academics may agree, more or less, with general definitions, the term "surveillance" invites a range of interpretations. For some it is restricted to specific technologies or legal designations, whereas for others it signals any form of systematic monitoring that exerts an influence or has a tangible outcome. Additionally, because of its negative connotations, practitioners on the ground often disagree about whether surveillance is taking place. For instance, social scientists who conduct empirical work with policing agencies have found that most law-enforcement personnel do not see their work in that way, even as they describe their professional functions in terms that researchers would label as surveillance.

Surveillance may be ubiquitous, but it acquires different forms, functions, and meanings across social settings. Broadly, one could say that all formations of capital, nation, and state—three aspects that constitute the structure of contemporary societies (Karatani 2014)—depend on mechanisms of surveillance to control markets, regulate bodies, and protect institutions. Recently, these processes were illuminated in the arena of national security and state intelligence, where the public gained newfound awareness of the extent of state surveillance operations with the trove of US National Security Agency (NSA) documents released by Edward Snowden in 2013. Clearly, surveillance flourishes in other spheres too, beyond explicit state operations or formal governance structures. For instance, public interest in surveillance has likewise been piqued by revelations about peer and corporate monitoring on social media sites like Facebook, which are platforms that also engage in the robust collection, analysis, and sharing of data, sometimes even running undisclosed "experiments" on users to see how they respond to different types of content.

Across domains, from state security agencies to social media sites, surveillance regulates boundaries and relations. It reinforces separation and different treatment along lines of class, race, gender, sexuality, age, and so on. Regardless of the context, surveillance is never a neutral process. There are always value judgments and power imbalances, and they usually reproduce social inequalities. Because of growing awareness of the central role of surveillance in shaping power relations and knowledge across social and cultural contexts, scholars from many different academic disciplines have gravitated to surveillance studies and contributed to its solidification as a field.

But academic fields do not develop entirely on their own, just from a set of shared ideas or concerns. Rather, they depend on the concerted efforts of individuals to pull and hold people together, to initiate and sustain conversations over time, and, ultimately, to institutionalize the field in a set of organizational practices and artifacts (Mullins 1972). For surveillance studies, those practices entailed workshops beginning in the early 1990s and continuing with greater frequency in the 2000s; the formation of the international Surveillance Studies Network (SSN)[1] in 2006; and the hosting of international conferences every two years, starting in 2004. The artifacts include numerous edited volumes, many of them outgrowths of the aforementioned workshops, and, crucially, the founding of the open-access online journal *Surveillance & Society*[2] in 2002. Many of the people involved in these activities, including the editors of this Reader, are represented in this book, but special mention must be made of sociologist David Lyon, who was instrumental early on in organizing workshops and conference panels and producing edited volumes that drew scholars into dialogue, thus helping to constitute the field.

Clearly this is an "origin story," and such stories are always political: they set the parameters for who and what counts or should be counted. As a collection of curated materials, Readers, such as this one, are similarly political and necessarily exclusionary, if only because there simply is not sufficient room to include everything that one would like to—or should—include. Although such politics and exclusions are unavoidable, we choose to be self-reflexive about our standpoints and the choices we are making. We are interdisciplinary scholars with backgrounds and direct experience in surveillance studies, science and technology studies (STS), geography, sociology, communication, and history. Indirectly, through conferences, publications, and collaborations, we participate in many other fields: anthropology, political science, law and society, criminology, American studies, gender studies, cultural studies, and others.

This interdisciplinary orientation inflects the explicit and implicit arguments of this Reader. Instead of overemphasizing the contributions of one discipline, for instance, we seek to illustrate how different disciplinary perspectives bring different concerns, methods, and theoretical positions to the study of surveillance in society. We feel that this is an empirically accurate representation of the field, as well, in that there are many voices and disciplines represented in the conversations of the field, as any perusal of conference programs will bear out. More than being a static "snapshot," however, there is a deeper and ongoing story here about a correspondence between the field's institutionalization and its increasing interdisciplinarity. The two have occurred, and continue to occur, together. Perhaps the field's defining feature is its search for commonalities among tensions in disciplinary approaches to surveillance. This is the reason we prefer to call surveillance studies a "transdisciplinary field." It draws its strength and forms its identity from shared general concerns and productive frictions among disciplines, all the while fostering departures and innovations. It has achieved cohesion as a bona fide new field with shared concepts, "citation classics," and forms of institutionalization (e.g., a journal and conferences), but it also invites, and often seems to embrace, critiques.

This should not be read as a romanticization of the field. Certainly not every surveillance studies scholar welcomes being challenged from a disciplinary perspective other than her or his own. That said, as the field as a whole has been forced to grapple with such challenges, and continues to do so, the general tone has not been one of defensiveness but rather appreciation. Not of exclusion and ostracism, but of inclusion and acceptance. These are the norms that characterize the field for many participants, and they are ones we try to reproduce with our selection, grouping, and framing of excerpts in this book.

## Histories of Surveillance and Surveillance Studies

There may be an allure to seeing surveillance as novel, but there are important historical contexts and lineages that inform and shape the present. Some of the earliest influential work in the field, by pioneers like James B. Rule and Michel Foucault, came out of a 1960s and 1970s context of state surveillance that included the monitoring, disruption, and repression of progressive groups by both totalitarian and democratic states (Murakami Wood 2009b). At this time, as is still the case today, state actors were emboldened by new technologies that afforded the collection and analysis of information on an unprecedented scale. Rule's book *Private Lives and Public Surveillance* (1973) delved into these trends with a focus on the implications of government agencies and corporations adopting new computer databases as central tools of governance and customer management. Rule saw these changes as introducing the threat of a "total surveillance society" that could lead to diminished autonomy, curtailed rights, and political repression.

Foucault (1977), on the other hand, cast his eye backward to illustrate how surveillance became a central method for governance and the construction of modern subjects. Foucault's observations about the emergence of distributed methods of rule and self-disciplining forms of subjectivity were incredibly generative and explain his substantial and sustained influence in the field, however much scholars might question the specifics of his historical analysis or particular aspects of his theory. Ironically, as Gilles Deleuze (1992) later pointed out, the combined technological transformations and sociopolitical crises of the 1960s and 1970s presaged the end of the modern surveillance regime described by Foucault in *Discipline and Punish*, leading to today's more machinic, automated, and inhuman late-capitalist regime.

The history of surveillance, of course, goes back much further. As David Lyon's *The Electronic Eye* (1994) described, surveillance can be detected in population documents from ancient Egypt and also in records of English landholding with the Domesday Book from 1086. Interestingly, the word "eavesdrop," which had its first printed use in 1606, originally referred to someone who literally stood within the space next to a house where rainwater dripped from the eaves, where one could secretly listen to what was said inside (OED Online 2016). These historical references reveal a mixture of hierarchical politics, technological affordances (writing itself and the vernacular architecture of wooden houses, respectively), and local social practices, which come together to produce particular forms of surveillance. It is not accurate in most cases to make an arbitrary distinction between "technological" and "non-technological" surveillance. However, it is certainly true that the earlier the form of surveillance, the greater and more obvious the role that people played in the process. The actual or suspected presence of spies, informers, watchmen, and guards looms larger in social imaginaries about surveillance in the premodern and early modern periods than it does today.

The biggest historical transformations were associated not so much with the development of new technologies as they were with the social functions and goals of surveillance. In early modern Europe, states sought to discover commonalities in *groups* and codify descriptions of them in bureaucratic archives, thus creating identities against which individuals were measured (Groebner 2007). By the end of the eighteenth century, however, rulers became increasingly interested in identifying *specific* people, both in nation-states and their colonies, to effectively create "police states" of well-governed and transparent societies (Fichte 2000 [1796/97]). By the late nineteenth century, this identification imperative reached crisis levels, fueled by concerns about anonymous individuals—perhaps with criminal inclinations—circulating in newly industrialized cities and challenging established social hierarchies (Cole 2001; Torpey 2000). Identification regimes were combined with generalized surveillance and mass enforcement, which were often supplemented by spectacular and exemplary punishments to deter criminal behavior by others.

Modern surveillance also concerned itself increasingly with individual subjectivity and the management of populations in ways that generated compliance, productivity, and even health and happiness (Foucault 1978). In this, surveillance was always associated with scientific advances, particularly with the new science of numbers, statistics (Hacking 1990; Porter 1995; Scott 1998). As Ian Hacking shows in *The Taming of Chance* (1990), throughout the nineteenth century, a general belief in determinism gradually gave way to regimes of probability. The quantification of everything (grain, forests, people, suicides, and so on) gave rise to statistical bureaus and allowed states to invoke scientific rationality in governance decisions.

At the same time, the science of the body—in terms of both the broad picture of biology and evolution and the development of physiology and kinetics (movement)—was inspired by and provided the basis for a new kind of efficient and compliant workforce. Typically, these efforts mobilized surveillance to extract as much labor from bodies as was physically possible. Frederick Winslow Taylor (1911) is well known in this regard, due to his efforts to implement a system of "scientific management" of factory workers. This early form of workplace surveillance relied on close observation, segmentation of tasks, and division of labor, all overseen by a new class of managerial elites whose technocratic functions would, in Taylor's view, advance the social and economic prosperity of the nation.

Whereas Taylor believed in a voluntary system where incentives and effective management would compel heightened productivity, brutal forms of involuntary labor extraction—as with slavery in the United States, Brazil, Haiti, and elsewhere—also depended on surveillance innovations. As Nicholas Mirzoeff (2011) explains, state visuality regimes, including those used in the institutional management of slaves, rely on techniques of classification, separation, and aestheticization, such that people are reduced to governable units and represented in bureaucratic systems that obscure the symbolic and real violence of dehumanizing complexes. In the case of slavery in the United States, especially as the institution started to unravel, surveillance took the form of hot-iron branding, slave passes and "lantern laws" to regulate movement, and wanted posters encouraging the apprehension of runaway slaves (Browne 2015). In her important work on the surveillance of blackness, Simone Browne reveals how forms of agency and resistance were always a part of the slave experience and that exercises of resistance continue today in people's confrontations with discriminatory and racist surveillance apparatuses (see Section 14).

In the late nineteenth century, biological theories of racial inferiority fused with new identification techniques like physiognomy, photography, and fingerprinting—the early systems of biometric measurement (Cole 2001; Sekula 1986). These were policing technologies deployed in an effort to catalogue offenders and make criminality legible, and perhaps even predictable, through scientific means. In tandem with the rise of the eugenics movement of the Progressive Era in the United States, these scientific schemes drew upon narratives of biological difference to justify unequal treatment of supposedly inferior groups: immigrants, racial minorities, the poor, the illiterate, or the cognitively impaired (Kevles 1995). Behind the facade of objective science, discriminatory practices were institutionalized through such identification systems, and social hierarchies were reinforced in a time of heightened migration and social mobility.

The period at the end of the nineteenth century saw the creation of new rights and freedoms. The modern legal concept of privacy arose in the context of polite New England society and the frustrations of the American bourgeoisie with an increasingly intrusive media, in particular popular newspapers in their reporting of society functions. Louis Brandeis and Samuel Warren's (1890) famous line about the "right to be let alone" comes from this context, where privacy was mobilized as a right of the privileged. Perhaps awareness of unequal access to privacy rights, even during its emergence as a legal construct over a century ago, helps explain the general reservations that many surveillance studies scholars have about privacy discourses today. As we develop in Section 8, there are clearly disciplinary reasons as well for one's commitment to—or suspicion of—privacy protections as responses to surveillance. However, for better or worse, within policy arenas and liberal academia, privacy and the "private life" remain both tactically and ideologically the dominant forms of response to surveillance. This is true even as scholars search for more comprehensive, powerful, and flexible ways of responding to surveillance encroachments and abuses.

Before the field of surveillance studies started to coalesce in the late 1990s, scholars largely followed the thread of the early 1970s critiques of centralized computer databases, state surveillance, and policing. For example, Gary Marx's classic book *Undercover* (1988) connected the use of older forms of human surveillance with police informants and undercover operations to the emergence of new technologies, such as infrared cameras, that could circumvent privacy expectations without concomitant increases in legal protections. Likewise, Roger Clarke (1988) described dangers brought about by forms of "dataveillance" that allowed for the large-scale combination of data points and the construction of profiles that could be used to discriminate against people even in advance of any wrongdoing. David Lyon (1988) echoed these anxieties as well in his first major work to deal with surveillance, where he concluded by developing the ominous figure of the "carceral computer." With greater attention to racial inequalities and corporate profiling of customers, Oscar Gandy (1993) similarly noted how information systems were acting politically to sort people in unequal ways while obscuring the inherent biases of the systems in question. As a culminating point, of sorts, in 1987 a number of significant players in the emergent field (e.g., Priscilla Regan, Gary Marx, Andrew Clement, and James Rule) contributed to an influential report by the US Office of Technology Assessment (1987) on workplace surveillance; this report rearticulated some of the above critiques but also, perhaps more important for this discussion of field formation, served as an early and explicit articulation of shared concerns.

In the early 1990s, a conceptual change began with consideration of new technological innovations in conjunction with popular theorizations about postmodernism. In addition to the aforementioned Gilles Deleuze (1992) and Oscar Gandy (1993), Mark Poster (1990) described surveillance operations in new media technologies and human-machine interfaces, which simultaneously deterritorialized subjectivity and dispersed control mechanisms. David Lyon (2001, 1994) synthesized many of these themes by explicating the ways in which "information societies" are necessarily "surveillance societies" because the automatic collection of data by information systems affords the classification of individuals and groups, behaviors and risks, leading to differential treatment of people. Kevin Haggerty and Richard Ericson (2000) developed these foundations further, describing the role of the individual's "data double" in a larger "surveillant assemblage," an amorphous network of public and private systems where individuals have little recourse to alter or contest the surveillance that is taking place. More than that, almost all organizations engage in such acts of data collection, analysis, and intervention (Staples 2000), meaning—among other things—that surveillance has become one of the dominant modes of ordering in the postmodern era.

## Conceptual Challenges

As scholars from a variety of disciplines engaged with surveillance studies, they relied upon a common set of concepts to advance collective knowledge. In particular, Foucault's interpretation of Jeremy Bentham's Panopticon, the legal and moral concept of privacy, and George Orwell's figure of Big Brother were quite productive in sparking analysis. Over time, however, these concepts became strained and seemed dissonant with the empirical conditions described by researchers or the field's growing theoretical interests.

To start with, the allure of Foucault's (1977) writings on Bentham's Panopticon prison design was that he transformed it into a powerful metaphor for the ways in which institutions could provide scripts for people to internalize the surveillant gaze and police themselves into social conformity (see Section 2). There has been increasing dissatisfaction with the concept, though, perhaps because of the way people feel compelled to modify it and devise clunky spin-off terms (e.g., "superpanopticon," "synopticon," "ban-opticon") to match new phenomena rather than invent something altogether new. Foucault intended the Panopticon to serve as an illustration of a particular historical moment in the development of modern thinking about subjectivity and social control (Murakami Wood 2009), but it has become an almost hegemonic construct in the field. It is often applied or intoned as if it has some kind of universal explanatory value but, if used this way, it lacks empirical validity. Rather than being rational, centralized, and totalizing, surveillance is more often particularistic, multi-sited, and highly specialized, leading Bruno Latour (2005) to refer to contemporary surveillance—using another derivative neologism—as oligoptic, that is, narrow and focused rather than broad and distributed. Of course, the focus and intensity is not random. It varies according to one's social address (Monahan 2010) and is more likely to sort, exclude, and marginalize populations, not homogenize people and shape them into uniform docile bodies (see Section 14).

The concept of privacy remains salient in the field, as well as in legal, policy, and popular discourses. Along with data protection concerns, privacy resonates deeply with many people and provides something to organize around. That said, whereas the concept's universalizing and individualizing tendencies undoubtedly lend it force in legal and policymaking arenas, these have been seen as deficiencies as well, especially by academics trained to be suspicious or critical of such discourses. We have already observed, for example, that although perceived threats to privacy may be a clarion call to arms for civil-society groups and progressives more generally (Bennett 2008; Regan 1995), whether in its origins or today, privacy has never truly been a universal human right. Some other limitations of the concept might be its difficulty in overcoming the individualistic frame to assist with understanding encroachments on social groups or public spaces (Patton 2000); tensions between its presentation as an easily identifiable universal value and its remarkable messiness in practice (Nippert-Eng 2010); or the empirical reality that some of the targets of the most intrusive forms of surveillance are more concerned with issues of domination and power, not abstract notions like privacy (Gilliom 2001).

Finally, George Orwell's (1949) exceedingly disturbing fictional portrayal of a totalitarian society (in *Nineteen Eighty-Four*), with the human face forever crushed under the boot of Big Brother, has similarly made it difficult to escape motifs of all-powerful, centralized state surveillance. Notwithstanding the resilience of the Big Brother figure in the media or common parlance, the field continues to stress the heterogeneous mix of surveillance flows, even with state surveillance (e.g., Guzik 2016; Hayes 2009; Monahan and Regan 2012; Walby and Monaghan 2011). Edward Snowden's revelations about NSA surveillance programs, for instance, reveal that private companies are the source of much data analyzed by state agencies and that private contractors, just as Snowden was, are essential to the state surveillance apparatus. In other words, state surveillance is only part of the picture. Across many arenas, the blend of state, corporate, and social surveillance shapes life chances in concrete ways: whether someone gets health insurance or a bank loan, gets fired because of a Facebook posting or discriminated against because of their credit score, gets targeted for police scrutiny because she lives in a crime "hot spot," or spied upon as a potential "terrorist" because he protests environmental polluters. Thus, even within surveillant assemblages, as Sean Hier and Josh Greenberg (2009) note, hierarchies of visibility persist, such that descriptions of exposure alone are insufficient to account for the uneven politics of surveillance.

On the other end of the spectrum, many people would find Orwell's dystopian vision bizarre today because they see surveillance—especially social networking and media-based surveillance—as fun, convenient, or inconsequential (Albrechtslund 2008; Ellerbrok 2011; McGrath 2004). It is worth mentioning here that scholars doing literary analyses of surveillance have long observed that Orwell's vision was highly derivative of earlier writing by the Russian author Yevgeny Zamyatin (1972 [1921]). It also seems that Aldous Huxley's *Brave New World* (1932)—in which control is exercised through a combination of eugenics, pleasure, drugs, and peer pressure—provides a far more convincing set of metaphors for the contemporary situation (Marks 2005; Murakami Wood 2009a).

With the exception of the concept of privacy, which remains central for many scholars in surveillance studies, the field has largely departed from these generative concepts. Nonetheless, they have profoundly shaped the field's discourses and remain useful as symbols of the extremes of universal or totalizing forms of surveillance. As the next section will show, the field's topical and conceptual apparatuses have exploded as the field has grown, adding complexity, nuance, and renewed vigor to what came before.

## Book Overview

There are many possible ways to organize a Reader such as this one. It could be divided into sections based on historical periods, geographical focus, conceptual frameworks, topical areas, or disciplinary perspectives, among other options. Following from our earlier observation that surveillance studies is a transdisciplinary field defined by its search for commonalities among tensions in disciplinary approaches to surveillance, we have chosen a hybrid organizational approach that seeks to triangulate, somewhat loosely, topical areas, disciplinary perspectives, and the field's chronological development. Thus, each section concentrates primarily on a topical area, but this often reflects disciplinary preferences, and those preferences have changed over time as scholars from different disciplines have joined the conversation. So, by reading the sections in order, one can also get a sense of how the field has mutated over time.

Emphatically, the order of sections does not represent a neat evolutionary development but instead a fascinating iterative process, where scholars studying in one area are oftentimes influenced by the contributions of those in an entirely different area, leading to recombinant knowledge for the *collective* advancement of the field. For instance, while criminological studies of police video surveillance were some of the earliest and most formative empirical projects in surveillance studies, researchers did not cease to investigate police video surveillance once others drew the field toward explorations of resistance, ubiquitous surveillance, or the political economy; instead, scholars folded these lines of inquiry into their projects, making their findings both unpredictable and refreshing, all the while furthering the dialogue with others (e.g., Coaffee and Fussey 2015; McCahill and Finn 2014; Smith 2015). Likewise, world events can suddenly rekindle interest in older areas of investigation, as can be observed with terrorist attacks drawing attention back to national security, Snowden's leaks foregrounding state intelligence operations, or police killing of unarmed black men raising interest in the documentary evidence that video surveillance might provide, albeit with an emphasis on police accountability, not citizen wrongdoing. This iterative process is represented *within* most of the sections too, where we include excerpts from older and newer explorations of the area and note the influences in our section introductions so that these iterations and cross-fertilizations can be appreciated.

It should be mentioned that some of the excerpts are by scholars who would not necessarily identify with the field of surveillance studies. This is to be expected with foundational theoretical works that predate the formation of the field, but there are other instances of more contemporary selections by people working in aligned fields. We chose to include such pieces if they were exemplary works in new areas or they challenged the status quo in ways we found productive. Given that we valorize the relative porousness and inclusiveness of the field, it seemed appropriate that we would not exclude significant publications simply because of how an author positioned themself.

The Reader's first content section, "Openings and Definitions," offers a presentation of originary works that helped constitute surveillance studies. The authors wrestle with different definitions of surveillance, illustrating a lack of consensus at the incipient stages of the field. Some position the target of surveillance as an individual person whose freedoms are infringed upon, while others question the larger effects on subject populations or society as a whole. There is general agreement, however, that surveillance is widespread, facilitated by information systems used by most organizations, and permeating down to the capillary level of society—that is, on the level of everyday interactions in most arenas of public and private life. This movement between the macro and the micro is indicative of authors working to develop what C. Wright Mills (1959) called "the sociological imagination," situating everyday practices within larger systems of power and influence. This makes sense given that with the exception of Oscar Gandy, who is a communication scholar, each of the other authors in this section would identify as a sociologist.

Section 2, "Society and Subjectivity," provides excerpts from some of the key theoretical texts that shaped the field. These include Bentham's and Foucault's writings on the Panopticon prison design, Deleuze's delineations of the emergence of control dynamics replacing the disciplinary ones outlined by Foucault, and others exploring how such control might manifest in decentralized networks or articulate with powerful media institutions that are characterized more by the many watching the few. Because the emphasis is on how subjectivity is produced through exposure to surveillance, especially in or by institutions, we also include selections that illustrate how public health campaigns inform medical imaginaries and surveillance-based zoo designs cultivate conservationist values in zoogoers.

The next two sections, "State and Authority" (Section 3) and "Identity and Identification" (Section 4), explore the ways in which surveillance was a critical part of the rise of the modern nation-state, especially pertaining to the identification and governance of people at borders and within state territories. The authors analyze incarnations of state surveillance in the service of totalitarian and postcolonial regimes, such as Cold War–era East Germany and apartheid-era South Africa, respectively, and question the extent to which totalitarian tendencies are present in all modern nation-states. When states define themselves by territorial demarcations, then the regulation of movement, through passports or other identity documents, effectively conjures "citizens" into being as identifiable representatives of the state. Unfortunately, identification efforts cannot be divorced from the prejudices of their cultural contexts, so they usually reproduce those prejudices in technological form.

The section on "Borders and Mobilities" (Section 5) picks up these themes and places them within more of a contemporary national-security context. The identification and sorting of populations is increasingly embedded in computer algorithms, facilitating social exclusion through automated means. This is perhaps most apparent with border control systems that are effectively distributed across geographic territories and temporalities, as anywhere or anytime that someone is identified and assessed against software-encoded risk profiles. As a few of the excerpts in this section reveal, these functions are delegated not only to computer systems, but also to individual travelers and the general public, who are responsibilized to submit voluntarily to security demands and inform on others who seem suspicious in some way, usually due to their racial or ethnic identity markers. Given this focus on territory, mobility, and risk management, it is not surprising that the main disciplines represented in this section are geography, political science, and criminology.

National security and policing are two of the most prevalent areas of concern in non-academic discussions of surveillance. The sections on "Intelligence and Security" (Section 6) and "Crime and Policing" (Section 7) offer a sampling of critical academic and journalistic works in these areas. Some of it details the mind-boggling extent of the NSA's telecommunications surveillance systems, while other pieces allow us to situate these intelligence practices in a longer history of state overreach, with illegal targeted spying on activists, journalists, international allies, and others. Importantly, as other excerpts show, internal state surveillance is almost always coupled with and informed by similar applications in distant war zones and occupied territories.

When it comes to domestic policing (Section 7), video surveillance—or closed-circuit television (CCTV)—is the most obvious focal point. Criminologists, who conducted the first empirical research on police video surveillance, largely found that it was not effective at preventing most crimes, just for displacing criminal activity to areas under less overt observation or, at best, assisting with the identification of suspects after the fact. While not entirely absent from these criminological accounts, other excerpts advance an explicit gender critique of surveillance, seeing technological systems as potentially adding layers of harassment while not mitigating violence against women. Additional pieces investigate the ways in which police and security schemes connect to the political economy—securing places of commerce, advancing the security industry, and enforcing an actuarial form of risk management that invariably punishes poor and racialized populations. Of course, with the spread of camera-equipped mobile phones, the power dynamics between the police and the public may be open, at least partially, to renegotiation.

We turn next to "Privacy and Autonomy" (Section 8), with a number of treatments that address the field's apprehensions with the privacy concept. These selections add complexity to the concept, showing both how it is a dynamic social norm and how theorizations of it have advanced well beyond many of the depictions of its critics. Technological developments seem to produce the greatest threats to privacy, at least from the perspective of surveillance studies, especially as information gathering and sharing become routine. Privacy scholars—who tend to come from the disciplines of political science, philosophy, and legal studies—point out that as long as privacy is presented solely as an individual good, it is destined to be compromised and eroded in policy realms that, fairly or not, tend to view any other concerns as advancing public interests. Thus, persuasive arguments are needed about the *social good* provided by privacy protections. A few of the excerpts offer just such arguments, while others concentrate on the importance of respecting the context of information generation or of safeguarding opportunities for boundary negotiation between individuals and information systems. Finally, to flesh out the surveillance-studies debate a bit further, we offer both a critique of privacy and a more general response in defense of the concept.

Privacy concerns are so pressing, in part, because surveillance is becoming routine, pervasive, and increasingly *hidden*. The next section, "Ubiquitous Surveillance" (Section 9), brings together insights from scholars with backgrounds in information studies, communication, geography, and architecture to document this move toward invisible, automated control in built environments and data practices. The excerpts show how information-rich environments—characterized by embedded sensors, mobile computing, and algorithmic processes—are fundamentally surveillant. Their logic is that all data elements (objects, people, conditions) must be "addressable" and subject to remote or automated management. This can be seen with what has been called the "Internet of things," with networked appliances like refrigerators or with "smart cities" that use embedded sensors and other technologies to regulate transportation systems, electricity usage, and sewage treatment in "real time." Whether integrated with urban infrastructure or occurring in abstract "big data" practices, ubiquitous surveillance depends on decisions about data priorities and values that are clearly political in their effects.

The next two sections, "Work and Organization" (Section 10) and "Political Economy" (Section 11), are closely related, as two sides of the same coin. From a largely sociological perspective, analyses of workplace surveillance show how early techniques of scientific management and performance monitoring have mutated into managerial strategies to cultivate

self-discipline on the part of workers, for instance through team-based projects where peers depend on one's reliability. Information technologies facilitate the reach of workplace surveillance too. On one hand, mobile technologies lead to a condition that Melissa Gregg (2011) refers to as "presence bleed," where one is expected to be always available to work and to be monitored, even at home. On the other hand, the very systems of commerce or communication (e.g., cashier checkout systems or social media sites) are fundamentally ones of surveillance: either of employee performance or of user activity, where, in the case of social media, users effectively engage in "free labor" to generate value for companies. Then again, it is important to remember that those charged with surveilling others are themselves engaged in mostly tedious and unrewarding *work*.

This brings us to closer scrutiny of the relationship between surveillance and the political economy (Section 11). In the service of company profits, customer surveillance takes many forms, ranging from the development of customer categories to facilitate effective advertising throughout the twentieth century to the hidden screening of customers by financial industries charged with implementing risk-management techniques to block potential money launderers or terrorists. The emphasis on company brands also compels technological innovations in surreptitiously "reading" customers' physiological responses to products and shaping their affective attachment to brands. Finally, several excerpts enumerate the ways that Internet giants such as Facebook and Google have made value extraction through information systems a science, creating new information ecologies that threaten to become totalizing systems of control. In these selections, one can see the convergence of historical, sociological, criminological, and communication approaches to the political economy of surveillance.

Operating in more of a communication and media studies register, the next section, "Participation and Social Media" (Section 12), problematizes the dominant surveillance-studies paradigm of top-down control by institutions or institutional actors. On the whole, the excerpts recognize that such institutional surveillance persists in online environments, but rather than jump to quick conclusions about the totalizing capacities of Internet platforms, they pose questions about the cultural meanings or practices that exceed those systems of control. Perhaps forms of peer or lateral surveillance (e.g., social media users following each other's posts or profiles) introduce the possibility for empowerment by fostering experimentation with self-presentation or developing relationships of trust and intimacy. Then again, these exchanges could trap individuals in what Mark Andrejevic (2007) has called "digital enclosures," where people derive social value but can never achieve robust forms of democratic empowerment. These two conclusions are not mutually exclusive, of course. Vitally, the questions posed by the excerpts in this section invite the field to reconsider fundamentally its understandings of and value judgments about surveillance.

Section 13, "Resistance and Opposition," presents excerpts from scholars intrigued by the potentials for contesting surveillance, for "fighting back" in some way. These selections offer a diverse array of disciplinary perspectives, informed by political science, criminology, information studies, engineering, philosophy, and cultural studies. Some countersurveillance techniques covered here include attempts to turn surveillance against institutional agents, such as the police, by filming their activities; organizing through coalitions of civil society groups, policymakers, and activists to implement or maintain privacy protections; or using technological tools or masking techniques to obfuscate and temporarily evade surveillance

systems. With perhaps the exception of Steve Mann's work on *sousveillance*, or surveillance from "below," the work in this area is generally measured and pragmatic. On one hand, it is eager to find solutions to power asymmetries, but, on the other, it recognizes the limitations and sometimes even the dangers (or risks to others) of trying to do so.

The next section, "Marginality and Difference" (Section 14), turns further toward humanities-inflected critiques of surveillance. The selections highlight how surveillance imbricates with intersectional forms of oppression, exposing marginalized populations to differential and often augmented forms of violence and control. This can manifest in abstract ways, such as with discriminatory actuarial assessments by financial institutions, contributing to tangible "cumulative disadvantage" (Gandy Jr. 2009) for poor and racialized groups. It could also take the form of violent encounters with armed police, stalkers and domestic partners, or racist citizens concerned about terrorist threats. In order to confront surveillance that materializes or reinforces unequal conditions of marginality, one must come to terms with the fact that "threatening" racialized bodies are always constructed in opposition to normative "white" bodies that are seen as symbolically stable, compliant, and transparent (Hall 2015). If the history of surveillance is inseparable from the history of racism, as Simone Browne (2015) contends, then exposure to surveillance can never be neutral and scholarship on surveillance should reject, once and for all, any universalist claims about it.

The final section in the Reader, "Art and Culture" (Section 15), emphasizes performance theory, literary analysis, visual studies, and game studies in its consideration of surveillance-themed cultural products and practices. Representations of surveillance in literature and film, for instance, are hugely influential in shaping popular perceptions and understandings of surveillance, yet until recently there has been surprisingly little sustained academic discussion of them in the field. This is rapidly changing with a flurry of new books on these and related subjects (e.g., Lefait 2013; Rosen and Santesso 2013; Wise 2016; Zimmer 2015). The excerpts in this section offer sophisticated critical interpretations of various cultural works, thereby correcting deficiencies in the field and suggesting directions for future investigation.

## Conclusion

The thing that holds most of surveillance studies' areas together is a general agreement that surveillance is central to the functioning of contemporary societies, from the level of state practices all the way down to interpersonal exchanges among family members and friends. While some may not agree that surveillance is *the most important* social process or cultural logic, it is difficult to contest its pervasiveness and influence. It is how organizations and people make sense of and manage the world. It is also how power relations are established and reproduced. For scholars, surveillance offers a rich approach to investigating social and cultural phenomena and detecting the power relations inherent in them.

As represented in the organization of this Reader's sections, the field started out with more of an institutional focus, questioning the increasing influence of state and corporate actors over others. Technology was central in facilitating this influence, whether with architectural embodiments of control with panoptic designs or with databases and video-camera systems. The early institutional focus makes sense in that hierarchical relationships and power differentials—the roots of surveillance—are more apparent when there are extreme disparities between parties, such as between institutions and individuals. Moreover, this initial framing of

the problems of surveillance reflects classic sociological concerns about the place of individuals in society and the relationship of structure to agency. As others sought to flesh out these concerns, they did so with empirical research on people in context, classically of workplaces or police departments, where the latest surveillance systems, such as computer keystroke tracking or CCTV, were used to monitor others from a distance. Such sociological and criminological framings were formative for the field, establishing the initial parameters for the study of surveillance, and because these framings resonate with conventional understandings of surveillance (e.g., Big Brother), they continue to exert a force on new scholarship. This can be seen, for instance, with the impulse of scholars to study the next big organizational incarnation of surveillance (e.g., Google, Uber, the Department of Homeland Security), whatever it might be.

As the field expanded, this interest in institutions and technological systems persisted, but it shifted to reflect a wider range of disciplinary concerns and approaches. Privacy scholars, for instance, framed the issues in terms of rights, values, and legislative processes. The focus remained on institutional abuses facilitated by technology, but privacy scholars also outlined pragmatic solutions that might be achieved through legislative changes or technological designs (e.g., with encryption). Geographers stressed how the integration of surveillance systems into urban infrastructure was actualizing new regimes of governance and fueling neoliberal capitalism, which benefited corporations and the military but aggravated social inequalities. Communication scholars similarly situated surveillant media systems in the context of the political economy, describing how large media and technology companies shape ideologies while profiting from the labor of viewers or users.

The latest "cultural turn" in surveillance studies is significant in that it largely breaks from the institutional framework, at least as a necessary element, in order to trace power relations in the production and circulation of cultural meanings, many of which rely on representations of people and narratives about their identities (Monahan 2011). Thus, feminist studies, queer studies, and critical race studies scholars might draw attention to depictions of threats or worthiness, showing how those markers are encoded in surveillance systems and practices, propagating violence against marginalized groups. Those studying cinema, literature, media, or art often highlight the ways in which cultural products form perception and a sense of personhood, normalizing the idea of being a surveillance subject, while also presenting avenues for resistance and critique. Performance studies scholars interrogate and contest, sometimes through performance, the meaning and politics of the many surveillance routines that characterize daily life. Finally, communication scholars and others seek to understand the participatory trend in self- and peer-surveillance (e.g., through the "Quantified Self" movement or social media use), often by starting from the perspective of users themselves.[3]

This Reader provides one possible mapping of the field of surveillance studies. We take our inspiration from the field's many generous participants—our mentors, colleagues, and students—who have brought, and continue to bring, this vibrant field into being. Importantly, this book does not aspire to be a final representation of what the field is or what counts in it, but instead a provisional sketch of a dynamic and exciting process of mutation. Foremost, it is an invitation for others to explore, delve deeper into full texts that are only partially reproduced here, and participate in the ongoing conversations and debates.

## NOTES

1. http://www.surveillance-studies.net/.
2. http://www.surveillance-and-society.org/.

3. Obviously, these are broad brushstrokes that occlude much of the nuance and do not represent all contributions to the field. The aim of this summary is to offer a general sense of the arc of the field's development.

## REFERENCES

Albrechtslund, Anders. 2008. Online Social Networking as Participatory Surveillance. *First Monday* 13 (3). Available from http://firstmonday.org/htbin/cgiwrap/bin/ojs/index.php/fm/article/viewArticle/2142/1949 [accessed December 26, 2010].

Andrejevic, Mark. 2007. *iSpy: Surveillance and Power in the Interactive Era*. Lawrence: University Press of Kansas.

Bennett, Colin J. 2008. *The Privacy Advocates: Resisting the Spread of Surveillance*. Cambridge, MA: MIT Press.

Brandeis, Louis D., and Samuel D. Warren. 1890. The Right to Privacy. *Harvard Law Review* 4 (5):193, 195–97.

Browne, Simone. 2015. *Dark Matters: On the Surveillance of Blackness*. Durham, NC: Duke University Press.

Clarke, Roger. 1988. Information Technology and Dataveillance. *Communications of the ACM* 31 (5):498–512.

Coaffee, Jon, and Pete Fussey. 2015. Constructing Resilience through Security and Surveillance: The Politics, Practices, and Tensions of Security-Driven Resilience. *Security Dialogue* 46 (1):86–105.

Cole, Simon A. 2001. *Suspect Identities: A History of Fingerprinting and Criminal Identification*. Cambridge, MA: Harvard University Press.

Deleuze, Gilles. 1992. Postscript on the Societies of Control. *October* 59:3–7.

Ellerbrok, Ariane. 2011. Playful Biometrics: Controversial Technology through the Lens of Play. *The Sociological Quarterly* 52 (4):528–47.

Fichte, Johann Gottlieb. 2000 [1796/97]. *Foundations of Natural Right*. Translated by M. Baur. Cambridge, UK: Cambridge University Press.

Foucault, Michel. 1977. *Discipline and Punish: The Birth of the Prison*. New York: Vintage.

———. 1978. *The History of Sexuality: An Introduction*. Vol. 1. New York: Vintage.

Gandy, Oscar H. 1993. *The Panoptic Sort: A Political Economy of Personal Information*. Boulder, CO: Westview.

Gandy Jr., Oscar H. 2009. *Coming to Terms with Chance: Engaging Rational Discrimination and Cumulative Disadvantage*. Burlington, VT: Ashgate.

Gilliom, John. 2001. *Overseers of the Poor: Surveillance, Resistance, and the Limits of Privacy*. Chicago: University of Chicago Press.

Gilliom, John, and Torin Monahan. 2013. *SuperVision: An Introduction to the Surveillance Society*. Chicago: University of Chicago Press.

Gregg, Melissa. 2011. *Work's Intimacy*. Malden, MA: Polity.

Groebner, Valentin. 2007. *Who Are You? Identification, Deception, and Surveillance in Early Modern Europe*. Translated by M. Kyburz and J. Peck. Cambridge, MA: Zone Books.

Guzik, Keith. 2016. *Making Things Stick: Surveillance Technologies and Mexico's War on Crime*. Oakland: University of California Press.

Hacking, Ian. 1990. *The Taming of Chance*. Cambridge, UK: Cambridge University Press.

Haggerty, Kevin D., and Richard V. Ericson. 2000. The Surveillant Assemblage. *British Journal of Sociology* 51 (4):605–22.

Hall, Rachel. 2015. *The Transparent Traveler: The Performance and Culture of Airport Security*. Durham, NC: Duke University Press.

Hayes, Ben. 2009. Neoconopticon: The EU Security-Industrial Complex: Statewatch and the Transnational Institute. Available from http://www.tni.org/sites/www.tni.org/files/download/neoconopticon_0.pdf [accessed May 17, 2013].

Hier, Sean P., and Josh Greenberg. 2009. The Politics of Surveillance: Power, Paradigms, and the Field of Visibility. In *Surveillance: Power, Problems, and Politics*, edited by S. P. Hier and J. Greenberg, 14–29. Vancouver: UBC Press.

Huxley, Aldous. 2006 [1932]. *Brave New World*. Reprint ed. New York: Harper Perennial.

Karatani, Kojin. 2014. *The Structure of World History: From Modes of Production to Modes of Exchange*. Translated by M. K. Bourdaghs. Durham, NC: Duke University Press.

Kevles, Daniel J. 1995. *In the Name of Eugenics: Genetics and the Uses of Human Heredity*. Cambridge, MA: Harvard University Press.

Latour, Bruno. 2005. *Reassembling the Social: An Introduction to Actor-Network-Theory*. Oxford: Oxford University Press.

Lefait, Sébastien. 2013. *Surveillance on Screen: Monitoring Contemporary Films and Television Programs*. Lanham, MD: Scarecrow Press, Inc.

Lyon, David. 1988. *The Information Society: Issues and Illusions*. Cambridge, UK: Polity.

———. 1994. *The Electronic Eye: The Rise of Surveillance Society*. Minneapolis: University of Minnesota Press.

———. 2001. *Surveillance Society: Monitoring Everyday Life*. Buckingham, UK: Open University.

Marks, Peter. 2005. Imagining Surveillance: Utopian Visions and Surveillance Studies. *Surveillance & Society* 3 (2/3):222–39.

Marx, Gary T. 1988. *Undercover: Police Surveillance in America*. Berkeley: University of California Press.

McCahill, Michael, and Rachel L. Finn. 2014. *Surveillance, Capital, and Resistance: Theorizing the Surveillance Subject*. New York: Routledge.

McGrath, John E. 2004. *Loving Big Brother: Performance, Privacy, and Surveillance Space*. New York: Routledge.

Mills, C. Wright. 1959. *The Sociological Imagination*. New York: Oxford University Press.

Mirzoeff, Nicholas. 2011. *The Right to Look: A Counterhistory of Visuality*. Durham, NC: Duke University Press.

Monahan, Torin. 2010. *Surveillance in the Time of Insecurity*. New Brunswick, NJ: Rutgers University Press.

———. 2011. Surveillance as Cultural Practice. *The Sociological Quarterly* 52 (4):495–508.

Monahan, Torin, and Priscilla M. Regan. 2012. Zones of Opacity: Data Fusion in Post-9/11 Security Organizations. *Canadian Journal of Law and Society* 27 (3):301–17.

Mullins, Nicholas C. 1972. The Development of a Scientific Specialty: The Phage Group and the Origins of Molecular Biology. *Minerva* 10:52–82.

Murakami Wood, David. 2009a. Can a Scanner See the Soul? Philip K. Dick against the Surveillance Society. *Review of International American Studies* 3 (3)–4 (1):46–59.

———. 2009b. The 'Surveillance Society': Questions of History, Place and Culture. *European Journal of Criminology* 6 (2):179–94.

Nippert-Eng, Christena E. 2010. *Islands of Privacy*. Chicago: University of Chicago Press.

OED Online. 2016. "eavesdrop, v." Available from http://www.oed.com/view/Entry/59159?rskey=elS7Jf&result=2&isAdvanced=false [accessed August 19, 2016].

Orwell, George. 1949. *Nineteen Eighty-Four*. Centennial ed. New York: Harcourt Brace.

Patton, Jason W. 2000. Protecting Privacy in Public?: Surveillance Technologies and the Value of Public Places. *Ethics and Information Technology* 2:181–87.

Porter, Theodore M. 1995. *Trust in Numbers: The Pursuit of Objectivity in Science and Public Life*. Princeton, NJ: Princeton University Press.

Poster, Mark. 1990. *The Mode of Information: Poststructuralism and Social Context*. Chicago: University of Chicago Press.

Regan, Priscilla M. 1995. *Legislating Privacy: Technology, Social Values, and Public Policy*. Chapel Hill: University of North Carolina Press.

Rosen, David, and Aaron Santesso. 2013. *The Watchman in Pieces: Surveillance, Literature, and Liberal Personhood*. New Haven, CT: Yale University Press.

Rule, James B. 1973. *Private Lives and Public Surveillance: Social Control in the Computer Age*. London: Allen Lane.

Scott, James C. 1998. *Seeing Like a State: How Certain Schemes to Improve the Human Condition Have Failed*. New Haven, CT: Yale University Press.

Sekula, Allan. 1986. The Body and the Archive. *October* 39:3–64.

Smith, Gavin J. D. 2015. *Opening the Black Box: The Work of Watching*. New York: Routledge.

Staples, William G. 2000. *Everyday Surveillance: Vigilance and Visibility in Postmodern Life*. Lanham, MD: Rowman & Littlefield Publishers.

Taylor, Frederick Winslow. 1911. *The Principles of Scientific Management*. New York: Harper & Brothers.

Torpey, John C. 2000. *The Invention of the Passport: Surveillance, Citizenship, and the State.* Cambridge, UK: Cambridge University Press.

U.S. Office of Technology Assessment. 1987. The Electronic Supervisor: New Technology, New Tensions, OTA-CIT-333. Washington, DC: U.S. Office of Technology Assessment.

Walby, Kevin, and Jeffrey Monaghan. 2011. Private Eyes and Public Order: Policing and Surveillance in the Suppression of Animal Rights Activists in Canada. *Social Movement Studies* 10 (1):21–37.

Wise, J. Macgregor. 2016. *Surveillance and Film.* New York: Bloomsbury.

Zamyatin, Yevgeny. 1972 [1921]. *We.* Translated by M. Ginsburg. New York: Viking.

Zimmer, Catherine. 2015. *Surveillance Cinema.* New York: New York University Press.

# SECTION 1

# OPENINGS AND DEFINITIONS

///////////////////////////////////////////////////////////////////////////////////////////////////////////////////

How one defines surveillance is vital. Definitions inform the types of research one does and claims one can make. Although it may be true that the specific interests of scholars, which are disciplinarily conditioned, lead them to prefer some definitions over others, the early years of the field saw greater variation in definitions than is typically the case today. This is probably because scholars were dispersed and mostly working in separate areas with few opportunities to form a consensus about key definitions or concepts. With a few exceptions, though, participants in the field quickly agreed that surveillance signified more than passive observation; it was instead, or additionally, about the production of power relations.

One of the first scholars to consider surveillance as a singular phenomenon was James B. Rule (excerpted in Chapter 1). He and his colleagues defined surveillance as "any systematic attention to a person's life aimed at exerting influence over it" (Rule et al. 1983: 223). This sociologically inflected definition depends on a liberal conception of personhood that sees individuals as sovereign agents shaped by external influences and interactions. Concerns emerge when these external forces might be destructive, unwanted, or unaccountable—as with the bureaucratic surveillance analyzed by Rule. Because this definition derives its potency from a view of individuals' essential rights

under attack, this framing logically leads to appeals to the law to mitigate such harms.

The modifications that have been made to this type of definition have been predominately influenced by a Foucauldian conception of power that decenters the individual and emphasizes the ways in which all people are caught in webs of power relations. So, instead of placing the individual human subject at the center, the focus of analysis could be on groups, societies, or even nonhumans. The introduction of the possibility of the nonhuman subject of surveillance has several implications. The first is that nonhuman creatures might be under surveillance, which has been considered at greater length by both Irus Braverman (see Section 2) and Kevin Haggerty and Daniel Trottier (2015). The second implication is that it might not be human beings directly who are under surveillance, but rather situations, events, or a person's indirect traces in data, which are the details of one's "life" in Rule's sense. This attention to information and personal data is at the heart of Rule's book *Private Lives and Public Surveillance*, which was published in 1973—a few years before Foucault's *Discipline and Punish*—at the beginning of what was then being called the "database society," so clearly Rule was negotiating a few different approaches to power. Scholars such as Roger Clarke (see Section 9) and Oscar Gandy (excerpted in Chapter 2) would later pick up this focus on surveillance through data (or "dataveillance") and develop it further. Even today, information and data remain central to most contemporary definitions of surveillance and to the field more broadly, as the selections in this reader testify.

By crafting definitions to emphasize populations or groups as the targets, one can focus analytic attention on issues of governance. For instance, in his influential book *Surveillance, Power, and Modernity* (1990), Christopher Dandeker defines surveillance as "the gathering of information about and the supervision of subject populations in organizations" (Dandeker 1990: vii). This definition seems to offer a rather wider sense of who or what is under surveillance—the term "subject populations" both strips out the requirement for the subject of surveillance to be an individual or even to be human at all. Through its explicit reference to subjection, it also draws attention to power, and with the last phrase of the definition, "in organizations," provides an institutional framework for that power. In some ways, one could argue that surveillance is about making and remaking both subject populations and organizations, often at the same time. William Staples (excerpted in Chapter 3) emphasizes this co-constitutive relationship in his investigation and theorization of "everyday surveillance."

Likewise, David Lyon's oft-quoted definition of surveillance—as "the focused, systematic and routine attention to personal details for purposes of influence, management, protection or direction" (excerpted in Chapter 4)—retains a focus on the person, but his analysis is further concerned with "sites" of surveillance (both actual and metaphorical) and with processes. Beyond simply "watching," Lyon's definition explicitly considers the purposes and qualities of attention that are needed for something to be "surveillance." One of the dangers inherent in a new transdisciplinary field like surveillance studies is the "imperial urge" to redefine everything as surveillance, and while some, like Gary Marx (2016), do indeed argue for a maximalist definition that recasts casual observation or just "looking" as somewhere on a continuum of surveillance, a primary purpose of definitions is to clarify the object of study, as well as its social context. Lyon's highlighting of the "focused, systematic and routine" nature of surveillance separates out surveillance from other, more casual, occasional, and disorganized forms of attention. It does not, of course, say anything about the social significance or morality of either, merely that they are not the same. Gary Marx's own modus operandi, as demonstrated by his excerpt in this section, is to produce comprehensive lists of features and characteristics of surveillance, against which any particular thing can be assessed. He stresses key differences between earlier modes of surveillance and "new" digital surveillance.

These definitions offer different prisms for thinking about the various sites, forms, targets, and functions of surveillance. Some mechanism of control or regulation may be seen as necessary for surveillance to be taking place, but the theoretical frames adopted by scholars color their views of what else matters most (e.g., individuals, groups, contexts). While the goals of those implementing surveillance systems may seem like an obvious focal point, for some time the field has been concentrating instead on conditions, contexts, experiences, and negotiations of surveillance (e.g., Ball 2009; McCahill and Finn 2014; Saulnier 2016). Perhaps with the advent of big data and automated analytics, definitions will have to shift to emphasize the construction of *emergent* purposes in a society in which surveillance is ubiquitous and all data are collected as a matter of course.

## REFERENCES

Ball, Kirstie S. 2009. Exposure: Exploring the Subject of Surveillance. *Information, Communication & Society* 12 (5):639–57.

Dandeker, Christopher. 1990. *Surveillance, Power, and Modernity: Bureaucracy and Discipline from 1700 to the Present Day.* Cambridge, UK: Polity.

Haggerty, Kevin D., and Daniel Trottier. 2015. Surveillance and/of Nature: Monitoring beyond the Human. *Society & Animals* 23 (4):400–20.

Marx, Gary T. 2016. *Windows into the Soul: Surveillance and Society in an Age of High Technology.* Chicago: University of Chicago Press.

McCahill, Michael, and Rachel L. Finn. 2014. *Surveillance, Capital, and Resistance: Theorizing the Surveillance Subject.* New York: Routledge.

Rule, James B., Douglas McAdam, Linda Stearns, and David Uglow. 1983. Documentary identification and mass surveillance in the United States. *Social Problems* 31 (2):222–34.

Saulnier, Alana. 2016. *Surveillance Studies and the Surveilled Subject.* Doctoral dissertation, Department of Sociology, Queen's University, Kingston, ON.

# 1

# JAMES B. RULE

## PRIVATE LIVES AND PUBLIC SURVEILLANCE

Social Control in the Computer Age

In a work that predates Foucault's recasting of Bentham's Panopticon, James Rule anticipates a comprehensive system of surveillance that amasses data on all individuals, stores those data indefinitely, has predictive capabilities for advance intervention, and fosters social control by eliminating possibilities for disobedience. He calls this system a "total surveillance society." While Rule is explicit in mobilizing the concept of a total surveillance society as a heuristic for analysis—against which to compare existing surveillance systems—and as a cautionary figure, today's emerging capabilities in predictive analytics and data fusion show just how prescient he was.

\*\*\*

Why do we find the world of *1984* so harrowing? Certainly one reason is its vision of life totally robbed of personal privacy, but there is more to it than that. For the ugliest and most frightening thing about that world was its vision of total *control* of men's lives by a monolithic, authoritarian state. Indeed, the destruction of privacy was a means to this end, a tool for enforcing instant obedience to the dictates of the authorities.

And yet, such thoroughgoing, relentless social control represents nothing other than an extreme manifestation of one of the ubiquitous processes of social life. Ubiquitous, and actually vital. . . .

Those who seek to maintain social control must accomplish two sorts of things. First, they must maintain what one might call *powers of control*. This means, for one thing, that they need to be able to apply sanctions, or inducements sufficient to discourage the sanctioned person from repeating his disobedient acts. . . . Second, if the system is not to rely only on reward or punishment after the fact, it must possess means of excluding would-be rule-breakers from the opportunity to disobey, for example, by refusing in some way to deal with them. . . .

Neither of these two powers does any good, however, without . . . a system of *surveillance.* In the first place, surveillance entails a means of knowing when rules are being obeyed, when they are broken, and, most importantly, who is responsible for which. In some instances these things may be easy to accomplish, e.g., a flagrant armed robbery by notorious criminals. In the case of other forms of disobedience, such as income tax evasion, it may be extremely difficult. A second element of surveillance, also indispensable, is the ability to locate and identify those responsible for misdeeds of some kind. Again, this may be simple in many cases . . . however, it may be the most difficult condition of all to fulfil.

In practice, it is often very difficult to draw boundaries between processes of surveillance and the application of what has been termed the powers of control . . . the same people and the same bodies are often engaged in the collection of information and in the application of sanctions. Nevertheless, when I want to emphasize those activities having to do with collecting and maintaining information, I speak of *systems of surveillance.* Where the concern lies more with the actual management of behaviour, through sanctioning or exclusion, I refer to *systems of control.* . . .

[L]et me sketch a model of the most extreme possible development of mass surveillance, an ideal type of a social order resembling the one portrayed by Orwell, though perhaps even more extreme. This I call a *total surveillance society.*

In such a world, first of all, there would be but a single system of surveillance and control, and its clientele would consist of everyone. This system would work to enforce compliance with a uniform set of norms governing every aspect of everyone's behaviour. Every action of every client would be scrutinized, recorded and evaluated, both at the moment of occurrence and for ever afterwards. The system would collate all information at a single point, making it impossible for anyone to evade responsibility for his past by fleeing from the scene

of earlier behaviour. Nor would the single master agency compartmentalize information which it collected, keeping certain data for use only in certain kinds of decisions. Instead, it would bring the whole fund of its information to bear on every decision it made about everyone. Any sign of disobedience—present or anticipated—would result in corrective action. The fact that the system kept everyone under constant monitoring would mean that, in the event of misbehaviour, apprehension and sanctioning would occur immediately. By making detection and retaliation inevitable, such a system would make disobedience almost unthinkable.

One should never expect to encounter a real system like the one just described. That is just the point. The only usefulness of this paradigm is as a foil for comparison to real systems, as a case guaranteed to be more extreme than the real world could ever produce. True, some agencies may develop something like systems of total surveillance over very limited numbers of people, for short periods of time. Police may keep constant watch over a small group of conspirators, or the staff of a hospital may exercise something like total surveillance over those in the intensive care ward. But difficulties of staging, and especially prohibitive costs, rule out such techniques for larger clienteles over longer periods of time. No, the usefulness of the paradigm lies in its making it possible to compare systems of surveillance and control now in existence to this theoretical extreme and to one another in terms of their proximity to this extreme. . . .

[A]ny real surveillance system is limited in *size.* This means, for one thing, limitation to the numbers of persons whom it can depict in its files. Second, there is always a limitation in the amount of information with which a system can cope, the amount which it can meaningfully use in its decision-making on each person. Indeed, . . . the amount of *usable* information is often less than that which is theoretically available on file. And such limitations on the amount of usable data kept per person correspond in turn to limitations in the amount of the subject's life depicted in the files. Third, surveillance systems also face limitations in what one might term the *subtlety* of their decision-making based on filed data. In the world of *1984* the authorities seemed to use information cunningly enough to know what their people were going to do even before they themselves did. . . .

Second, real surveillance systems are limited in the *centralization* of their files . . . some are more centralized than others. Centralization of data is extremely important in the staging of social control, in that it prevents clients from escaping the effects of their past by moving from one place to another. If the single central record can be applied wherever the fugitive goes, such movement does no good. Thus, to be fully effective, any system of surveillance should be able to collect information on a person's behaviour from any point in a society, and use it to enact measures of control on the same person at any other point.

Third, real systems fall short of the total surveillance extreme, and vary considerably among themselves, in terms of the *speed* of *information-flow* and *decision-making* which they exhibit. In Orwell's world, all misbehaviour presumably was registered with the authorities immediately, and resulted in immediate retribution when necessary. The systems studied here, by contrast, are not nearly so sophisticated. They are slow, for one thing, in their intake of information: relevant facts may be available for some time before the system can bestir itself to incorporate them in usable form. Moreover, these systems vary in the speed of movement of data once it is incorporated in their files, and in the application of such data to decision-making about people. Limitations like these make it easier for the individual to escape the effects of his past, for example, in cases where the agency of surveillance and control cannot bring its

data to bear on a client quickly enough to act against him.

Fourth, and finally, real systems of mass surveillance and control are limited to varying degrees in what I term their *points of contact* with their clienteles. This again involves several things. First, existing systems are limited in the numbers of points at which they can incorporate information on the people with whom they must deal. Whereas in *1984* the authorities could 'tune in' on virtually every moment of every person's life, real surveillance systems restrict themselves to limited points of intake—for example, through the courts and a few other junctures in the case of police surveillance, and through credit-granting institutions, in the instance of consumer credit reporting. Similarly, existing systems are limited in terms of their ability to 'get back at'—to locate, accost and apprehend—those who have broken the rules. Unlike Orwell's world, modern societies provide many opportunities for those who wish to avoid the attention of the authorities simply to drop out of sight. To be sure, systems of mass control have their own ways of countervailing against these opportunities. . . .

A final and equally important element of contact between system and clientele is the ability of the former to identify individual clients. . . . [T]he position of the agency of control suffers unless it can quickly and unerringly link any single client to his record. Since clients themselves often wish to avoid such linkage, the strength of identification systems represents one of the important elements of the hold of the system on those with whom it deals. . . .

There are several distinct reasons for mistrusting the continuing growth of mass surveillance. One is simply the repressive potential which they confer upon the corporate agencies maintaining the surveillance, or upon whoever controls those agencies . . . any over-all response to these systems must take into account not only their present impact, but also their future prospects. And this means accepting the possibility that, in the course of other political changes, the intent and political disposition of those who control these systems may change. . . .

Another objection to the extension even of 'just' discrimination based on mass surveillance has to do with their effects on those discriminated *against*. The object of discriminations like those discussed here, after all, is to achieve the cheapest possible identification of those who have not or will not obey the rules. Often the idea is to exclude these people in advance. . . . [W]ith sophisticated manipulations of aggregate data, even tiny and seemingly irrelevant facts can represent significant predictors. The use of such discrimination procedures thus raises the question of what sorts of data should legitimately be usable in decision-making which may, after all, weigh very heavily upon the clients concerned. . . .

What if, by collecting data on some extremely private area of people's behaviour, one could predict with virtual certainty the likelihood of their causing a fatal traffic accident in the near future? The predictive behaviour, presumably, would involve no direct and obvious connection with motoring, and obviously would not itself represent an infraction against motoring laws. To this extent, one would be inclined to resist compulsory surveillance over the behaviour in question. On the other hand, if prediction were really virtually perfect, the cost of forgoing it, in terms of lives, would be excruciatingly obvious. At present such discrimination represents nothing more than

another heuristic, hypothetical case. But there is no guarantee that this will always be true. The growing sophistication of predictive techniques promises to make the choices implicit in these situations increasingly dramatic and difficult. . . .

There is a final reservation about the growth of mass surveillance, more subtle than the preceding ones, but no less compelling. It has to do with the inherent value of choice in responding to the strictures of control imposed by the social world. . . . Total surveillance could theoretically provide limitless benefits in the way of compliance, but only at the expense of watching and controlling people so closely and constantly as to render misbehaviour out of the question. . . . Corporate participation in every moment of every individual's life, no matter how fair or how discreet or how benign, is simply too great a price to pay for obedience. Life in a highly imperfect social world is still infinitely preferable to life in a world offering no opportunities for imperfection. . . .

Because of the beguiling appeal of fine-grained decision-making, it is hard to hope for any sweeping curtailment of mass surveillance and control. Certainly it is reasonable to expect public opinion to oppose measures seen as repressive or coercive towards the public at large. Certainly, too, one can realistically hope for the acceptance of reform measures like those already proposed, to make mass surveillance more open, accountable and just. Whether one can expect people to renounce altogether the benefit of practices felt to provide essential personal services is another matter.

# 2

# OSCAR H. GANDY, JR.

## THE PANOPTIC SORT

A Political Economy of Personal Information

Oscar Gandy's lifework has been in understanding systems of sorting and classification, particularly in regard to racial and other inequalities. He is one of the few scholars from whom we have two excerpts in this Reader because his work is both foundational and of direct ongoing contemporary relevance. This excerpt is from *The Panoptic Sort*, one of the books that defined what surveillance studies was to become both in its objects of study (the social and political consequences of contemporary systems of data gathering and analysis) and its theoretical influences, combining political economy (Marx), sociology (Weber, Giddens), the history of ideas (Foucault), and critical approaches to technology (Ellul).

***

In 1934, the Spiegel corporation was an industry leader in the development of a pointing system, which it used to evaluate applications for credit. Spiegel developed what it called the "vital question system," which gathered data in four critical areas that were then used as the primary factors in the decision to grant credit. The four questions were (1) amount of the order, (2) occupation of the applicant, (3) marital status, and (4) race of the applicant. Other data gathered in the rating process included an assessment of the importance of the geographic territory to the overall marketing plan. Although race and marital status are no longer legally permissible components of the credit authorization process, the evidence is clear that a similar discriminatory process that sorts individuals on the basis of their estimated value or worth has become even more important today and reaches into every aspect of individuals lives in their roles as citizens, employees, and consumers.

I refer to this process as the "panoptic sort," the all-seeing eye of the difference machine that guides the global capitalist system. Kevin Robins and Frank Webster have coined the phrase "cybernetic capitalism" to underscore the nature of the totalizing system of social control that depends on the ability of state and corporate bureaucracies to collect, process, and share massive amounts of personal information to track, command, coordinate, and control each and every one of us to an extent we would not have considered possible. Other descriptive terms appeared over the years as I have gathered examples and insights about the nature of this process. One that still holds an attraction is the notion of triage. The popular understanding of the term is that associated with medical decision making: "the sorting and allocation of treatment to patients, especially battle and disaster victims, according to a system of priorities designed to maximize the number of survivors." The original meaning of the term, however, is derived from the French *trier*, meaning to pick or to cull, but the word emerged into the English language as having to do with the "grading of marketable produce," and more specifically, referring to "the lowest grade of coffee berries, consisting of broken material." Although some metaphors speak for themselves, let me be clear. I see the panoptic sort as a kind of high-tech, cybernetic triage through which individuals and groups of people are being sorted according to their presumed economic or political value. The poor, especially poor people of color, are increasingly being treated as broken material or damaged goods to be discarded or sold at bargain prices to scavengers in the marketplace. . . .

In my view, this sorting mechanism cannot help but exacerbate the massive and destructive inequalities that characterize the U.S. political economy as it moves forward into the information age. It is a process that feeds on itself. Although there are already some signs of resistance that have emerged in some quarters, the response of the panoptic system is very much like that of a child's straw finger puzzle: Once you have placed your fingers in either end of the tube, the more you struggle to escape, the more it tightens its grip. I would like to suggest that these inequalities are emerging in an area that is critical to the maintenance of a democratic polity and to the operation

of an efficient market. These inequalities have to do with differential access to information that is necessary for informed decision making.

The operation of the panoptic sort increases the ability of organized interests, whether they are selling shoes, toothpaste, or political platforms, to identify, isolate, and communicate differentially with individuals in order to increase their influence over how consumers make selections among these options. At the same time that the panoptic sort operates to increase the precision with which individuals are classified according to their perceived value in the marketplace and their susceptibility to particular appeals, the commoditization of information increases the dependence of these interests on subsidized information. To the extent that the panoptic sort, as an extension of technical rationalization into the social realm of consumer and political behavior, depends on a reduction of the skills of individuals in the same way that automation reduces the skills of laborers in the factory or the modern office, the market and the political or public sphere as we understand them are transformed and are placed at risk.

As the panoptic sort matures and increases in scale and scope, a number of contradictory developments seem likely. First, because the sorting mechanism utilizes data about past behaviors, it tends to limit the options that are presented for individuals to choose. When the options concern choices about information, this tendency has the potential to increase the knowledge and information gap between the haves and the have nots. Also, to the extent that these conservative models aim at the lowest common denominator, the panoptic sort will contribute to a generalized lowering of the average level of public understanding. Second, because the sorting mechanism is based on theoretical models that reflect quite transitory fads or trends in social, economic, and political thought, increasing instability in markets and political action will become the rule rather than the exception. Third, as people's awareness of the panoptic machine grows, some will find ways to resist, and others will attempt to withdraw. Both responses will invite further attempts at inclusion and containment within the panoptic sphere. The same technology that threatens the autonomy of the individual seems destined to frustrate attempts to reestablish community and shared responsibility because it destroys the essential components of trust and accountability. . . .

The panoptic sort is the name I have assigned to the complex technology that involves the collection, processing, and sharing of information about individuals and groups that is generated through their daily lives as citizens, employees, and consumers and is used to coordinate and control their access to the goods and services that define life in the modern capitalist economy.

The panoptic sort is a system of disciplinary surveillance that is widespread but continues to expand its reach. The operation of the panoptic system is guided by a generalized concern with rationalization of social, economic, and political systems. The panoptic sort is a difference machine that sorts individuals into categories and classes on the basis of routine measurements. It is a discriminatory technology that allocates options and opportunities on the basis of those measures and the administrative models that they inform. The panoptic sort has been institutionalized. It is standard operating procedure. It is expected. It has its place. Its operation is even required by law. And where it is not, people call out for its installation. Its work is never done. Each use generates new uses. Each application justifies another. It is efficient, having largely been automated. Like a voice-activated recorder, it moves into action

solely in response to an action by the object of its control. The panoptic sort is a system of actions that governs other actions. The panoptic sort is a system of power.

## Identification

The panoptic sort can be understood to involve three integrated functions or processes: identification, classification, and assessment. Although its operation is by no means limited to identifiable individuals, it depends to a large part on the ability of its users to reliably identify the objects to be controlled. The identification will never move to the level of personhood as we may understand the person as the subject of religion, philosophy, and idealized systems of justice. The attention of the panoptic sort moves only to levels of identification that have administrative and instrumental relevance. Here we refer to the identification of persons with histories, records, and resources when those persons or agents of those persons present a card, form, signature, claim, or response, or when they present themselves at a particular place or time. Identification is associated with authorization and authentication of claims. Identification is associated with the assumption of responsibility for actions, transactions, interactions, and reactions, which may be recorded by the panoptic system. The level of identification required by the panoptic system is indicated by the importance of the transaction that is about to take place. As the level of risk increases, more sophisticated technologies are called into play. The signature gives way to the physical description, which gives way to the photograph, which gives way to the fingerprint, or the voice print, or the retinal scan. But that is not enough.

The panoptic sort frequently requires third-party validation. You may be who you say you are, but we need verification that you are what you say you are. Are you old enough? Are you, perhaps, too old? Are you trained and certified; is your license currently in force? Are you creditworthy, reliable, stable, honest, entitled? Are you one of us? This form of identification, more often than not, involves some form of classification.

## Classification

Classification involves the assignment of individuals to conceptual groups on the basis of identifying information. Class membership is based on measurement of one or more attributes of an individual's identifying array of attributes. As we have suggested with regard to identification, the data matrix may be infinitely complex, depending on the requirements and resources of the panoptic system brought into play at any given point of interaction. The identification of class membership will always be made on the basis of less information than is at hand or is readily available. As we have suggested with regard to preprocessing, information is thrown away so that more efficient means of control may be put in place. . . .

The panoptic sort institutionalizes bias because the blind spots in its visual field are compensated for by a common tendency to fill in the missing with the familiar or with that which is expected. When the paradigmatic vision of the panoptic machine is linked with the futures of bureaucratic organizations and the individuals who stand at their helms, the incentive to find precisely what has been predicted is often too powerful to resist. A disciplinary profession that depends on treating a particular kind of problem has every incentive to calibrate its instruments to find ever more cases of the dysfunction that are in need of expert attention. The discovery of epidemics is very difficult to

separate from the interests of the agencies whose responsibility it is to keep them under control. Bureaucratic records reflect the local custom. The definition of what is a crime depends as much on the social status of the perpetrator and the victim as it does on the actions that have allegedly taken place. Troy Duster notes that "if one looks at the record in 250 years of U.S. history, no white man ever committed the crime of rape on a black woman in twelve southern states." Is this a statement about the violent sexual behavior of southern white males, or is it a statement about a racially biased system of classification? There are no objective standards; classification always includes an assessment, whether expressed or not.

## Assessment

Assessment represents a particular form of comparative classification. Individuals are compared with others. Individuals are compared with hundreds and thousands of others whose measured attributes help to establish norms and the bounds of reasonableness and acceptability. Assessment involves the use of standards and assumptions about the normality and the independence of distributions. Social distributions are often highly skewed rather than normal. Social distributions are often highly correlated, because they share a common cause, rather than being independent.

Once classification has occurred, assessment frequently involves the examination of probabilities—that is, the likelihood that a person will act, react, or interact in a particular way to a situation or circumstance. Individuals may be classed and evaluated on the basis of the responses they give, as well as on estimates of how likely similar responses are to occur. As with the requirement for precision in identification, the demand for precision in assessment is based on an assessment of the consequentiality of error. Given the tendency of humans to be risk averse, the privileging of avoidance over gain is not without a basis in fact. . . .

The panoptic sort victimizes because it decontextualizes. Status is divorced from circumstance. The circumstance cannot be recaptured; an assessment will always be incomplete. However, the ways in which context is misrepresented are not randomly distributed but reflect an institutionalized bias; a bias established by race, gender, age, class, culture, and consciousness.

Just as capitalism as a form of social organization has neither fully matured nor been extended to the same degree in all areas of social existence in even the most advanced industrial societies, the spread of panoptic technology is uneven and incomplete.

# 3

# WILLIAM G. STAPLES

## EVERYDAY SURVEILLANCE

Vigilance and Visibility in Postmodern Life

William Staples has been specifically concerned with everyday practices of surveillance and social control, neither the soft forms of social control that saturate our corporate-dominated urban environments nor the hard forms of access control and targeted surveillance of suspected criminals and terrorists, but that which is in between, which constructs our "normality." He argues that the "meticulous rituals of power" that characterize contemporary life are increasingly impersonal in nature, methodical, and technologically mediated, leading to more universal exposure to surveillance, even as forms of discrimination and inequality persist.

*** 

Between . . . soft and hard types of social control lies a vast array of techniques and technologies—exercised on and by people both inside and outside the justice system—that are designed to watch our bodies, to regulate and monitor our activities, habits, and movements, and, ultimately, to shape or change our behavior. These procedures are often undertaken in the name of law and order, public safety, the protection of private property, or simply "sound business practice"; other procedures are initiated for an individual's "own good" or benefit. But no matter what the stated motivation, the intent of social control is to mold, shape, and modify actions and behaviors.

[These] cultural practices . . . I will call "meticulous rituals of power." Most generally, I include those microtechniques of social monitoring and control that are enhanced by the use of new information, communications, and medical technologies. These are knowledge-gathering activities that involve surveillance, information and evidence collection, and analysis. I call them meticulous because they are "small" procedures and techniques that are precisely and thoroughly exercised. I see them as ritualistic because they are faithfully repeated and are often quickly accepted and routinely practiced with little question. And they are about power because they are intended to discipline people into acting in ways that others have deemed to be lawful or have defined as appropriate or simply "normal." In this way, meticulous rituals are the specific, concrete mechanisms that operate to maintain unbalanced and unequal authority relationships. These relationships exist between specific clusters of individuals (e.g., between managers and workers, police officers and suspects, probation officials and offenders, teachers and students, parents and children, and the like) and, in a larger sense, between individuals and the public and private organizations where these rituals take place.

Surveillance and social control of this type are not orchestrated by a few individuals; they are not part of a master plan that is simply imposed on us. Rather, in my view, *we are all involved and enmeshed within a matrix of power relations that are highly intentional and purposeful; arrangements that can be more or less unequal but are never simply one-directional. . . .*

I see at least four defining characteristics that set these practices apart from more traditional methods. In the first place, consider the following. In the past, the watchful eyes of a small shopkeeper may have deterred a would-be shoplifter; her surveillance was personal, not terribly systematic, and her memory, of course, was fallible. She was more likely to know her customers (and they her), to keep a "closer eye" on strangers, and to "look the other way" when she saw fit (and to make a call to the offending juvenile's parents later). This kind of "personal" social control was once typical of small communities or close-knit societies where people certainly watched one another very closely and where fear of ridicule or exclusion was a powerful inducement to conformity. By contrast, the part-time, non-owning employees of the large corporate bookstore where I sat with my friend have less interest in watching for thieves; their huge number of customers is an anonymous crowd. So here, the store management relies on the hidden, faceless,

and ever-ready video security camera. The videocam—one of the defining features of postmodern society—projects a hyper-vigilant "gaze," randomly scanning the entire store day or night, recording every event, and watching *all* the customers, not just the "suspicious ones." The cameras are also positioned to watch the vast number of employees, who must now be monitored both as "productive" workers and as potential thieves. In this way, surveillance and discipline have become oddly democratic; everyone is watched, and no one is trusted.

So the first characteristic of postmodern social control is that it tends to be systematic, methodical, and automatic in operation. It is likely to be impersonal in that the observer is rarely seen and is anonymous; further, the "observer" is likely to be a computer system, a videocam, a drug-testing kit, or an electronic scanner of some kind. Once more, the data that these devices collect may become part of a permanent record in the form of a videotape, a computer file, or some other digital format. In fact, the role played by efficient and inexpensive digital databases is crucial. Corporate personnel files, hospital, mental health, and substance abuse agency records, as well as insurance company data banks, join all those demographic, financial, credit, and consumer habits data to create "virtual" database identities of all of us. Once created, these representations are, as Mark Poster suggests, "*capable* of being acted upon by computers at many social locations without the least awareness by the individual concerned yet just as surely as if the individual were present somehow inside the computer." For example, credit ratings can be destroyed, loan applications rejected, or medical benefits denied, without personal notice, input, or influence.

Second, these new meticulous rituals of power often involve our bodies in new and important ways, and I want to distinguish two primary tactics of bodily social control. I agree with Donald Lowe when he states: "As living beings, we are more than body and mind, more than the representations and images of our body. We lead a bodily life in the world." These bodily lives are shaped, manipulated, and controlled by a set of ongoing practices that compose our daily lives as workers, consumers, and community members.

The first tactic I want to distinguish has to do with types of monitoring and surveillance that enhance our visibility to others. We seem to be entering a state of permanent visibility where attempts to control and shape our behavior, in essence our bodies, are accomplished not so much by the threat of punishment and physical force but by the act of being watched—continuously, anonymously, and automatically. This kind of watching happens when people engage in such diverse activities as clipping on a company beeper, using a credit card to purchase something at a store, or parking their car in a garage with a security camera. These instances signify different forms of "visibility"; the beeper enables an employer to remotely "check up" on and monitor an employee; the credit card purchase leaves an electronic paper trail of a person's activities and whereabouts; and the security camera identifies to the police, or anyone else who gains access to the tape, that a particular individual was indeed parked in that garage on a particular day at a certain time. The methodical, technology-driven, impersonal gaze, I argue, is quickly becoming a primary mechanism of surveillance and, by extension, social control in our society, and it is fixed on our bodies and their movements.

A second tactic of bodily surveillance and social control relates to new developments in science, technology, and medicine. These intersecting fields are making the human body infinitely more accessible to official scrutiny and assessment. This means that the ability of organizations to monitor, judge, or even regulate our actions and behaviors through our bodies is significantly enhanced. It also means that it becomes less important to trust suspects to "speak the truth" or convicted offenders to "mend their ways." Rather, it is the individual's body that will "tell us what we need to know," as in indicating that someone is using drugs or was at the scene of a crime or even has "deviant desires." In this way, the body is treated as an "object" that contains the evidence of any possible deviance. For example, on the soft side of our spectrum of social control, we see that corporations are using medical data collected on employees in their "wellness" and exercise clinics to confront the "unhealthy lifestyles" of those not conforming to prevailing standards (about, for example, tobacco use or obesity). Meanwhile, on the hard side, DNA samples are being systematically collected and stored and are increasingly presented as evidence in courtroom proceedings. The body, I contend, is a central target of many postmodern surveillance techniques and rituals.

The third defining characteristic of postmodern social control relates to a shift in the location of social control and surveillance and which behaviors are the subject of it. Since the early nineteenth century, our primary method of dealing with lawbreakers, those thought to be insane, other deviants, and even the poor has been to isolate them from everyday life—as in the case of the modern prison, mental asylum, poorhouse, and reformatory. Yet the kinds of practices I am most concerned with here attempt to impose a framework of accountability on an individual in everyday life. While, obviously, removing "troublesome" people from society is still a significant means of formal social control (after all, in the United States, we institutionalize more people than any other Western country does), this approach is increasingly considered, by various experts, to be an inefficient, ineffective, and undesirable practice. This is particularly true if we consider the idea that as a society we seem to be engaged in a far-reaching attempt to regulate not only the traditional crimes of person and property but also the behaviors, conditions, and "lifestyles" of substance (ab)use, alcohol and tobacco consumption, "eating disorders," forms of sexual expression and sexual "promiscuity" and "deviance," teenage pregnancy, out-of-marriage births, domestic violence, child abuse, "dysfunctional" families, various psychological or psychiatric disorders and other "medical" conditions such as "attention deficit disorder," and such diseases as AIDS. How can we possibly institutionalize and control everyone that falls into these rapidly expanding categories of "troublesome" individuals?

Given these conditions, it would appear that the segregative or quarantine models of social control of the nineteenth century are an invention whose time has simply passed. The incentive now is to develop new ways to control and "keep an eye on" what appears to be an increasing number of "deviants" through an expanding network of formal "community corrections" programs; regulatory welfare, health, and social service agencies; and even schools, workplaces, and other community institutions. New developments in the forensic, medical, and computer and information sciences—generated by corporate research and development departments and the post–Cold War military-industrial complex (which I believe is being converted rapidly into a "security-industrial complex")—are creating more remote, more flexible, and more efficient ways of making this happen.

Finally, as new forms of social control are localized in everyday life, they are capable of bringing wide-ranging populations, not just the official "deviant," under their watchful gaze. As I indicated earlier, trust is becoming a rare commodity in our culture. The notion of "innocent until proven guilty" seems like a cliché these days, when people are apt to be subjected to disciplinary rituals and surveillance ceremonies simply because statistics indicate that they have the potential for being offenders (for example the police tactic known as "racial profiling" as a justification

for stopping motorists). Data generated through surveillance techniques produce "types" or whole classes of individuals who are deemed "at risk" for behavior, whether any particular individual has engaged in such behavior or not. These data, of course, are then used to justify even closer surveillance and scrutiny of this group, thereby increasing the likelihood of uncovering more offenses; and so it goes. In the context of these changes, social control becomes more about predicting and preventing deviance—always assuming that it will, indeed, happen—rather than responding to a violation after it has occurred. Therefore, when put in place, ritualistic monitoring and surveillance ceremonies often blur the distinction between the official "deviant" and the "likely" or even "possible" offender. Indeed, what separates the convicted felon, the college athlete, or the discount store cashier if each is subjected to random drug screening? One consequence of this blurring is that we may be witnessing a historical shift from the specific punishment of the individual deviant to the generalized surveillance of us all.

But by implying that social control is becoming more universal and thus oddly more democratic, I am not suggesting that we are all necessarily subject to the same quantity or quality of social control. Historically and cross-culturally, the amount and character of monitoring, discipline, and punishment that individuals are afforded have varied considerably by such defining characteristics as race, ethnicity, class, and gender. Without question, this continues today. My point is that there are more impersonal, more methodical, and more technology-driven forms of surveillance and social control in our society than ever before, and today's forms—and their sheer volume—are enveloping even those who might have been previously exempt. For those who have traditionally been the target of monitoring and control, these developments serve only to intensify and increase the amount of formal regulation already in their daily lives.

**4**

# DAVID LYON

## SURVEILLANCE STUDIES

An Overview

David Lyon is probably the scholar most directly responsible for the growth of surveillance studies as a field. His seminal work, *The Electronic Eye* (1994), placed surveillance in a larger historical trajectory and presented the concept of the "surveillance society" as important for sociological investigation. Lyon's definitions, here expressed in his introductory book, *Surveillance Studies*, remain a necessary starting point for any scholarly inquiry into surveillance.

\*\*\*

Although the word 'surveillance' often has connotations of surreptitious cloak-and-dagger or undercover investigations into individual activities, it also has some fairly straightforward meanings that refer to routine and everyday activity. Rooted in the French verb *surveiller*, literally to 'watch over', surveillance refers to processes in which special note is taken of certain human behaviours that go well beyond idle curiosity. You can 'watch over' (or, more clumsily, 'surveill') others because you are concerned for their safety; lifeguards at the edge of the swimming pool might be an example. Or you can watch over those whose activities are in some way dubious or suspect; police officers watching someone loitering in a parking lot would be an example of this kind of surveillance.

Surveillance always has some ambiguity, and that is one of the things that make it both intriguing and highly sensitive. For example, parental concern and care for children may lead to the adoption of some surveillance technologies in order to express this. But at what point does this become an unacceptable form of control? Does the answer depend on whether or not the offspring in question are aware that they are being tracked, or is the practice itself unethical by some standards? At the same time, putting the question this way assumes that people in general are wary, if not positively spooked, when they learn that others may be noting their movements, listening to their conversations or profiling their purchase patterns. But this assumption is not always sound. Many seem content to be surveilled, for example by street cameras, and some appear so to relish being watched that they will put on a display for the overhead lenses, or disclose the most intimate details about themselves in blogs or on webcams.

So what is surveillance? For the sake of argument, we may start by saying that it is the focused, systematic and routine attention to personal details for purposes of influence, management, protection or direction. Surveillance directs its attention in the end to individuals (even though aggregate data, such as those available in the public domain, may be used to build up a background picture). It is focused. By systematic, I mean that this attention to personal details is not random, occasional or spontaneous; it is deliberate and depends on certain protocols and techniques. Beyond this, surveillance is routine; it occurs as a 'normal' part of everyday life in all societies that depend on bureaucratic administration and some kinds of information technology. Everyday surveillance is endemic to modern societies. It is one of those major social processes that actually constitute modernity as such.

Having said that, there are exceptions. Anyone who tries to present an 'overview' has to admit that particular circumstances make a difference. The big picture may seem over-simplified but, equally, the tiny details can easily lose a sense of significance. For example, not all surveillance is necessarily focused. Some police surveillance, for instance, may be quite general—a 'dragnet'—in an attempt somehow to narrow down a search for some likely suspects. And by the same token, such surveillance may be fairly random. Again, surveillance may occur in relation to non-human phenomena that have only a secondary relevance to 'personal details'. Satellite images may be used to seek signs of mass graves where genocide is suspected or birds may be tagged to discover how avian flu is spread. Such exceptions are important, and add nuance to our understanding of the big picture. By looking at various sites of surveillance, and exploring surveillance in both 'top-down' and 'bottom-up' ways, I hope to illustrate how such variations make a difference to how surveillance is understood in different contexts.

The above definition makes reference to 'information technology', but digital devices only increase the capacities of surveillance or, sometimes, help to foster particular kinds of surveillance or help to alter its character. Surveillance also occurs in down-to-earth, face-to-face ways. Such human surveillance draws on time-honoured practices of direct supervision, or of looking out for unusual people or behaviours, which might be seen in the factory overseer or in neighbourhood watch schemes. Indeed, to accompany the most high-tech systems invented, the US Department of Homeland Security still conscripts ordinary people to be the 'eyes and ears' of government, and some non-professional citizen-observers in Durban, South Africa have been described by a security manager (without irony) as 'living cameras'.

But to return to the definition: it is crucial to remember that surveillance is always hinged to some specific purposes. The marketer wishes to influence the consumer, the high school seeks efficient ways of managing diverse students and the security company wishes to insert certain control mechanisms—such as PIN (personal identification number) entry into buildings or sectors. So each will garner and manipulate data for those purposes. At the same time, it should not be imagined that the influence, management or control is necessarily malign or unsocial, despite the frequently negative connotations of the word 'surveillance'. It may involve incentives or reminders about legal requirements; the management may exist to ensure that certain entitlements—to benefits or services—are correctly honoured and the control may limit harmful occurrences.

On the one hand, then, surveillance is a set of practices, while, on the other, it connects with purposes. It usually involves relations of power in which watchers are privileged. But surveillance often involves participation in which the watched play a role. It is about vision, but not one-sidedly so; surveillance is also about visibility. Contexts and cultures are important, too. For instance, infra-red technologies that reveal what is otherwise shrouded in darkness help to alter power relations. But the willing self-exposure of blog-writers also helps to change the contours of visibility. To use infra-red devices to see into blog-writers' rooms at night would infringe personal rights and invade private spaces. But for blog-writers to describe their nocturnal activities online may be seen as an unexceptional right to free expression. . . .

At first glance, as it were, surveillance seems to be about watching. One person watches others in order to check for inappropriate or abnormal behaviour. The pole-mounted camera in the street keeps watch for potential deviance, from criminal acts to 'undesirable' activities. But surveillance may also be about listening, from eavesdropping to phone-tapping. What is heard may in certain circumstances be used as evidence, and in the context of global fears about terrorism fairly flimsy references to violent action may count for something. Already these examples include some technological mediation, whether closed-circuit television (CCTV), wiretaps or whatever. But once we consider the range of possible mediations, the surveillance picture enlarges significantly. . . .

Concepts such as 'surveillance society' draw our attention to the ways in which our whole way of life in the contemporary world is suffused with surveillance. In this perspective, the gaze is ubiquitous, constant, inescapable. What once was experienced only in specific contexts such as voter registration, tax files or medical records, in each of which personal records are held by an impersonal organization, has spilled over into every dimension of daily life. Whether travelling, eating, shopping, telephoning,

working, walking in the street or working out at the gym, some check occurs, some record is made or some image is captured. As Robert O'Harrow's book title says, there's 'no place to hide'. But such terms as 'surveillance society', while useful, are also potentially misleading because they suggest merely a total, homogeneous situation of 'being under surveillance' when the reality is much more nuanced, varying in intensity and often quite subtle.

Rather than thinking only of 'surveillance societies', it is helpful to think of specific surveillance sites, as they have developed historically in the modern world. Theoretically, this is a more institutional approach that separates surveillance strands out into different domains of social life such as work and leisure. This gives us a sense of the variety of surveillance situations that we might encounter, a sense of how one system gave rise to or facilitated another, and at the same time a sense of how one system may overlap with another or several others. Eventually, however, we are obliged to see that contemporary surveillance is very much influenced by the apparent imperative to be joined-up. The desire to create assemblages is strong, even if these are not always matched by the reality, which may be technically deficient or may encounter user resistance, or both.

Separate strands do still exist but increasingly, using electronic information and communication networks, they are or can be connected. . . . There are also some common threads, which help us to analyse similarities and differences between different sites of surveillance. Such threads include processes basic to modernity, such as the following:

*Rationalization.* This describes the process whereby standardized techniques are sought and reason (rather than tradition, emotion or common-sense knowledge) is prized as the guide to social, political and economic life. Whether or not surveillance

LYON: SURVEILLANCE STUDIES    21

systems (or any other ones) that owe their peculiar traits to the modern quest for rationalization actually work well, or better than what preceded them, is an open question. Because in the case of surveillance personal information gathering is rationalized, there are bound to be tensions.

*Technology.* The application of science and technology to organizational practices, in order to support and reinforce rationalization and to speed up processes, is clearly visible in surveillance sites. Surveillance, which for most of human history has been a matter of face-to-face oversight augmented with some methods of recording basic information, is now also characterized by high-technology applications. As these become embedded in surveillance systems they sometimes help to alter the very character of those systems.

*Sorting.* The classification of groups—workers, prisoners, customers and so on—into categories to facilitate management and control through differential treatment of those groups is also central to surveillance. Those who have the capacity to influence how people are classified and categorized tend to be in positions of greater power than those who do not. This process is now somewhat occluded, especially in the present context, by the use of computer software to accomplish the sorting processes.

This simply pushes the question back, however, to ask how the highly consequential coding is done that distinguishes between one group and another.

*Knowledgeability.* The different levels of knowledgeability and willing participation on the part of those whose life-details are under scrutiny make a difference to how well surveillance works. Surveillance works best with the cooperation of those who are subject to it. Of course, the Iraqi soldier caught in a remote satellite image or the supermarket shopper whose preferences are sold to a third-party marketing company can hardly be thought to be involved in their surveillance. But what they do know and what they do with what they know makes a difference . . . at a micro-level all sorts of strategies and subterfuges on the part of knowing subjects make a difference to how surveillance works.

*Urgency.* A fifth thread that has become increasingly prominent within the safety-and-security-oriented world of the present, especially since 9/11, is what might be called obsessive risk aversion and media-amplified public panic. This tends to prompt the adoption of surveillance measures of many kinds, even if already-existing measures do the same job. Some national ID card proposals fall within this category.

# 5

# GARY T. MARX

## WHAT'S NEW ABOUT THE "NEW SURVEILLANCE?" CLASSIFYING FOR CHANGE AND CONTINUITY

Continuing an exploration he began in his book *Undercover: Police Surveillance in America* (1988), in this excerpt Gary Marx outlines key dimensions of what he calls "the new surveillance." Some notable changes are that the new surveillance is technologically mediated, largely undetectable, involuntary, and often automated. By systematizing differences (between "old" and "new"), Marx seeks to provide a framework for careful and rigorous analysis on the part of other researchers.

*** 

One indicator of rapid change is the failure of dictionary definitions to capture current understandings of surveillance. For example in the *Concise Oxford Dictionary* surveillance is defined as "close observation, especially of a suspected person." Yet today many of the new surveillance technologies are not "especially" applied to "a suspected person." They are commonly applied categorically. In broadening the range of suspects the term "a suspected person" takes on a different meaning. In a striking innovation, surveillance is also applied to contexts (geographical places and spaces, particular time periods, networks, systems and categories of person), not just to a particular person whose identity is known beforehand.

The dictionary definition also implies a clear distinction between the object of surveillance and the person carrying it out. In an age of servants listening behind closed doors, binoculars and telegraphic interceptions, that separation made sense. It was easy to separate the watcher from the person watched. Yet self-monitoring has emerged as an important theme, independent of the surveilling of another. In the hope of creating self-restraint, threats of social control (i.e.: the possibility of getting caught) are well-publicized with mass media techniques.

A general ethos of self-surveillance is also encouraged by the availability of home products such as those that test for alcohol level, pregnancy, menopause and AIDS. Self-surveillance merges the line between the surveilled and the surveillant. In some cases we see parallel or co-monitoring, involving the subject and an external agent. The differentiation of surveillance into ever more specialized roles is sometimes matched by a rarely studied de-differentiation or generalization of surveillance to non-specialized roles. For example regardless of their job, retail store employees are trained to identify shoplifters and outdoor utility workers are trained to look for signs of drug manufacturing.

The term "close observation" also fails to capture contemporary practices. Surveillance may be carried out from afar, as with satellite images or the remote monitoring of communications and work. Nor need it be close as in detailed—much initial surveillance involves superficial scans looking for patterns of interest to be pursued later in greater detail.

The dated nature of the definition is further illustrated in its seeming restriction to visual means as implied in "observation." The eyes do contain the vast majority of the body's sense receptors and the visual is a master metaphor for the other senses (e.g., saying "I see" for understanding or being able to "see through people"). Indeed "seeing through" is a convenient short hand for the new surveillance.

To be sure the visual is usually an element of surveillance, even when it is not the primary means of data collection (e.g., written accounts of observations, events and conversations, or the conversion to text or images of measurements from heat, sound or movement). Yet to "observe" a text or a printout is in many ways different from a detective or supervisor directly observing behavior. The eye as the major means of direct surveillance is increasingly joined or replaced by hearing, touching and smelling. The use of multiple senses and sources of data is an important characteristic of much of the new surveillance.

A better definition of the new surveillance is the use of technical means to extract or create personal data. This may be taken from individuals or contexts. In this definition the use of "technical means" to extract and create the information implies the ability to go beyond what is offered to the unaided senses or voluntarily reported. Many of the examples extend the senses by using material artifacts or software of some kind, but the technical means for rooting out can also be deception, as with informers and undercover police. The use of "contexts" along with "individuals" recognizes that much modern surveillance also looks at settings and patterns of relationships. Meaning may reside in cross classifying discrete sources of data (as with computer matching and profiling) that in and of themselves are not that revealing. Systems as well as persons are of interest.

This definition of the new surveillance excludes the routine, non-technological surveillance that is a part of everyday life such as looking before crossing the street or seeking the source of a sudden noise or of smoke. An observer on a nude beach or police interrogating a cooperative suspect would also be excluded, because in these cases the information is volunteered and the unaided senses are sufficient. . . .

For simplicity I have arranged this largely in a series of discrete either/or possibilities (e.g., visible or invisible, gathered by a human or a machine). But there may be continuous gradations between the extreme values (e.g., between visible and invisible). Some dimensions involve mutually exclusive values (e.g., single vs. multiple measures) but many do not (e.g., the hybrid case of a guard dog wearing a tiny video camera).

In some cases classification reflects an inherent property of the technology (e.g., infra-red and sound transmission devices go beyond the unaided senses). In other cases where a means is classified depends on how it is used. A technology may seem to lend itself well to a value (e.g., video lens can be used invisibly relative to the traditional bulky 35mm camera), but a policy announcing that a video camera is in use would lead to its being classified as visible.

The differences between traditional and new surveillance can be approached in terms of the categories in Table 1. Traditional surveillance tends to be characterized by the left side of the table. The traditional means have certainly not disappeared. They have however been supplemented by the new forms which tend to fall on the right side of the table. . . .

The new surveillance relative to traditional surveillance extends the senses and has low visibility or is invisible. It is more likely to be involuntary. Data collection is often integrated into routine activity. It is more likely to involve manipulation than direct coercion. Data collection is more likely to be automated involving machines rather than (or in addition to) involving humans. It is relatively inexpensive per unit of data collected. Data collection is often mediated through remote means rather than on scene and the data often resides with third parties. Data is available in real time and data collection can be continuous and offer information on the past, present and future (à la statistical predictions). The subject of data collection goes beyond the individual suspect to categories of interest. The individual as a subject of data collection may also become the object of an intervention. There may be only a short interval between the discovery of the information and the taking of action.

The new surveillance is more comprehensive often involving multiple measures. But since it is often mediated by physical and social distance (being more likely to be acontextual) it is not necessarily more valid. It is more intensive and extensive. The ratio of what the individual knows about him or herself relative to what the surveilling person knows is lower than in the past, even if objectively much more is known. Relative to the past the objects of surveillance are more likely to be an anonymous individual, a mass or an aggregate. The emphasis is expanded beyond the individual to systems and networks. The data often goes beyond direct representation to simulation and from narrative or numerical form to also include video and audio records. The monitoring of specialists is often accompanied (or even replaced) by self-monitoring. It is easy to combine visual, auditory, text and numerical data and to send and receive it. It is relatively easier to organize, store, retrieve and analyze data. Traditional surveillance is the reverse of the above. . . .

Given the nature of perception, lists imply an egalitarianism among terms that is often unwarranted. The dimensions in Table 1 are hardly of equal significance. They can be clustered or ranked in various ways. Among those on the new surveillance side with the clearest social implications are extending the senses, low visibility, involuntary nature, remoteness, and lesser cost. These create a potential for a very different kind of society and call for stringent vigilance. In extending the senses (the ability to see in the dark, into bodies, through walls and over vast distances etc.) they challenge fundamental assumptions about personal and social borders (these after all have been maintained not only by values and norms and social organization, but by the limits of technology to cross them). Low visibility and the involuntary and remote nature of much contemporary surveillance may mean more secrecy and lessened

TABLE 1 Surveillance Dimensions

| DIMENSION | A. Traditional Surveillance | B. The New Surveillance |
|---|---|---|
| Senses | unaided senses | extends senses |
| Visibility (of the actual collection, who does it, where, on whose behalf) | visible | less visible or invisible |
| Consent | lower proportion involuntary | higher proportion involuntary |
| Cost (per unit of data) | expensive | inexpensive |
| Location of data collectors/ analyzers | on scene | remote |
| Ethos | harder (more coercive) | softer (less coercive) |
| Integration | data collection as separate activity | data collection folded into routine activity |
| Data collector | human, animal | machine (wholly or partly automated) |
| Data resides | with the collector, stays local | with 3rd parties, often migrates |
| Timing | single point or intermittent | continuous (omnipresent) |
| Time period | present | past, present, future |
| Data availability | frequent time lags | real time availability |
| Availability of technology | disproportionately available to elites | more democratized, some forms widely available |
| Object of data collection | individual | individual, categories of interest |
| Comprehensiveness | single measure | multiple measures |
| Context | contextual | acontextual |
| Depth | less intensive | more intensive |
| Breadth | less extensive | more extensive |
| Ratio of self to surveillant knowledge | higher (what the surveillant knows, the subject probably knows as well) | lower (surveillant knows things the subject doesn't) |
| Identifiability of object of surveillance | emphasis on known individuals | emphasis also on anonymous individuals, masses |
| Emphasis on | individuals | individual, networks systems |
| Realism | direct representation | direct and simulation |
| Form | single media (likely or narrative or numerical) | multiple media (including video and/ or audio) |
| Who collects data | specialists | specialists, role dispersal, self-monitoring |
| Data analysis | more difficult to organize, store, retrieve, analyze | easier to organize, store, retrieve, analyze |
| Data merging | discrete non-combinable data (whether because of different format or location) | easy to combine visual, auditory, text, numerical data |
| Data communication | more difficult to send, receive | easier to send, receive |

accountability, less need for consent and less possibility of reciprocity. Lesser costs create a temptation to both widen the net and thin the mesh of surveillance. For example what if brain scan technology lives up to the claims of its advocates to identify what people feel, know or are thinking? In the interest of preventing terrible things from happening (which after all it would be irresponsible not to do, not to mention legal liability), the sacred value traditionally placed on interior life would be eroded.

# SECTION 2

# SOCIETY AND SUBJECTIVITY

///////////////////////////////////////////////////////////////////////////////////////////////////////////////////////////////

How are subjectivities produced by and governed through surveillance? If modern society and its institutions are organized around surveillance, as the previous section claimed, then surveillance encounters infuse all interactions individuals have with institutions, whether direct or indirect. One's individual identity, social relations, and life chances are shaped by such interactions, whether with government agencies, schools, healthcare systems, places of employment, or any of the other institutions that pervade society. More than that, to the extent that such surveillance operates in the background, as part of the largely invisible, rational functioning of society, its politics are insulated and obscured, making them difficult to detect or challenge. Some of the most influential work in the field of surveillance studies has explored and theorized these very dynamics.

The figure of the Panopticon—or "all-seeing" prison—is one of the most potent representations of such institutional power. As conceived of by philosopher Jeremy Bentham in the eighteenth century,[1] and then popularized by Michel Foucault's expansive analysis in his book *Discipline and Punish: The Birth of the Prison* (1977), this prison design afforded the efficient control of people by delegating governance

functions to the architecture, to the very material and bureaucratic system of managing individuals in space. The excerpts in this section sketch the Panopticon in great detail, but, in brief, the prison design was that of a circular building with cells along the outer walls and a guard tower in the center. Inmates were housed individually in backlit cells, which facilitated their easy monitoring by guards or others. The vitally important design element of window blinds in the guard tower prevented inmates from knowing exactly when they were under observation, leading—it is argued—to prisoners' internalization of discipline such that they could be rehabilitated and introduced back into society as law-abiding citizens.

For both Bentham and Foucault, the Panopticon model was something that could be, or was in Foucault's reading, replicated in other institutions throughout society. The principles of comprehensive and individualizing surveillance could be found also in schools, hospitals, factories, military barracks, and so on. Across these settings, Foucault argued, control was achieved through complete visibility and legibility of subjects. In large part, the impetus for these transformations was the perceived instability caused by revolution, industrialization, and class mobility in Europe in the eighteenth century. If older social hierarchies (guaranteed by monarchies or feudalism) could not be counted on to provide stability, this created a pressing need for new ways to regulate society and maintain order. At the same time, the Enlightenment provided a philosophical justification for such changes. Principles of reason, equality, and transparency were viewed as having the capacity to transform society positively. Thus, the Panopticon model was intended to reverse the logic of the dungeon by spreading light and reason to the dark space where evil might flourish; to eradicate physical and moral disease by intervening on the level of the soul, not the body; and to reform and rehabilitate prisoners for the larger social good.

The functioning of this panoptic design is predicated not necessarily on its efficiency, of many being watched by a few, but instead on its ability to instill in subjects the power of the gaze and of becoming self-disciplining "docile bodies" (Foucault 1977). As Foucault explains: "There is no need for arms, physical violence, material constraints. Just a gaze. An inspecting gaze, a gaze which each individual under its weight will end by interiorising to the point that he is his own overseer, each individual thus exercising this surveillance over, and against, himself" (Foucault 1980: 155). Over time, subjected to meticulous bureaucratic procedures and continuous inspection, one ostensibly loses the very desire to deviate from social norms.

Embedded in such articulations is a particular conception of power that differs radically from classic understandings of power as something possessed by people and used to exert influence over others. For Foucault, as his analysis of the Panopticon illustrates, power is a distributed social machine in which all are caught and shaped. It is not simply a *repressive* force, although it may have those elements, but is also *productive* of social relations, subjectivities, and materialities. While hierarchies may persist,

power does not originate from the topmost position but rather from the larger system of relations. As Gilles Deleuze explains: "Power has no essence; it is simply operational. It is not an attribute but a relation: the power-relation is the set of possible relations between forces, which passes through the dominated forces no less than through the dominating" (Deleuze 1988: 27).

Although surveillance studies scholars have drawn heavily on the idea of the Panopticon and on Foucault's notions of disciplinary power, the field reached something of a consensus in the early 2000s that the concept of the Panopticon—as an almost obligatory invocation in writings on surveillance—was impeding theoretical innovation. As a result, a number of spirited critiques emerged, particularly questioning the empirical accuracy and utility of the concept for describing contemporary surveillance regimes (Haggerty 2006; Murakami Wood 2007). Some scholars challenged the implied separation of control functions by institution, when in fact data flow among institutions and individuals are subjected to multiple, overlapping articulations of surveillance simultaneously (Haggerty and Ericson 2000). Others focused on the difficulty in ascribing panoptic functions to digital technologies (Lyon 1993), the mass media (Mathiesen 1997), or unenclosed spaces (Norris and Armstrong 1999). Others noted that contemporary surveillance most often does not engender uniformity, but instead creates differences and sorts populations unequally based upon assessments of risk or value (Gandy 1993; Lyon 2003; Simon 2005). Others questioned the applicability of the panoptic model for describing consumer surveillance, which can prioritize pleasurable rewards and incentives over interdictions (Elmer 2003). Still others observed that surveillance is not used exclusively to govern people but also to monitor abstract data, organizations, and even the environment (Haggerty 2006). Finally, instead of accepting the passivity of so-called docile bodies, others emphasized the agency of individuals to resist or appropriate surveillance or use it for pleasurable or empowering ends (Gilliom 2001; Koskela 2004; Monahan, Phillips, and Murakami Wood 2010). Clearly, there were cracks in the foundations of the Panopticon metaphor, leading some to call for the field to "tear down the walls" (Haggerty 2006) and move on to more descriptively accurate concepts.

Notwithstanding these frustrations with the limitations of the Panopticon concept, Foucault's writings on biopolitical power offer a much more inclusive and perhaps more relevant explanation of the broader molding of society through surveillance. If sovereign power represented a single, arbitrary system of punishment that acted on the body, and disciplinary power accounted for multiple closed systems of rational control that trained individuals' "souls," biopolitical power concerned itself with the creating and governing of populations through mechanisms of categorizing and controlling people in aggregate (Foucault 2003: 1978). Some of the most obvious instantiations of biopolitical power are public health programs, migration control, insurance schemes, or the census, but it can be witnessed with just about any efforts to classify, sort, and regulate populations or groups, whether by state or nonstate institutions. Obviously, scholars concerned with issues of surveillance and inequality can fruitfully draw upon these insights, even if the Panopticon, as such, is less helpful. It is important to note that Foucault was careful to say that even by Bentham's time, disciplinary power was mutating into, or being transcended by, mechanisms of biopolitical power, so he clearly did not view disciplinary power, or the internalization of discipline by individuals, as the culminating form of social control in modern society (Foucault 1980).

Moreover, Foucault not only acknowledged that there were plenty of overlaps among these regimes, and no clear breaks, he also observed that disciplinary power could be put in the service of biopolitical efforts (see excerpt). Therefore, for a field interested in surveillance's role in the shaping of modern society and subjectivity, Foucault's influence will surely endure.

This section begins with excerpts of Jeremy Bentham's original eighteenth-century letters explicating the Panopticon design and extolling its utilitarian efficiencies. An excerpt from Michel Foucault's *Discipline and Punish* follows, wherein he describes the Panopticon schema as a generalizable model of disciplinary power that penetrates society, allowing for an "automatic functioning of power" without direct force. An excerpt from Gilles Deleuze's "Postscript on the Societies of Control" builds upon Foucault's analysis to argue that a new regime of power has taken hold—one characterized by corporate interests achieved through divisions, abstract codes, fluidity, and the production of insecurity. Kevin Haggerty and Richard Ericson's piece echoes some of Deleuze's themes, while also arguing that much contemporary surveillance operates more like an assemblage, allowing for the ready exchange of data and the convergence of control functions that act upon partial representations, or "data doubles," of individuals for instrumental aims.

Thomas Mathiesen's excerpt focuses on what he views to be a shortcoming of panoptic explanatory frameworks: their inability to account for the persistent role of spectacle, and particularly the mass media, in maintaining ideological control over society in the late twentieth century. Rather than the few watching the many with the Panopticon, he claims that significant ideological control is achieved by the many watching the few, such as news reporters, which is a relationship he labels "synopticism." Given the discussion of Foucault's work above, it is worth questioning Mathiesen's emphasis on the panoptic efficiency of watching, when *Discipline and Punish* was certainly making a much broader argument about spread of disciplinary mechanisms throughout society and the internalization of discipline by people. That said, synopticism is undoubtedly a relevant area of investigation for surveillance studies today, especially in respect to celebrity culture and the dynamics of cultivated publicity on social media.

The excerpt by David Armstrong brings us back to a focus on population, with particular attention given to the construction of a modern medical imaginary that normalizes things like health screening and public health campaigns (see also French 2009). For Armstrong, "surveillance medicine" depends on the systematic measurement of entire populations, not just sick ones, which is a process that provides a comparative baseline for healthfulness while also changing the way people understand their bodies, risk, and care. The final excerpt, by Irus Braverman, demonstrates how social values and identities can be intentionally constructed—or disciplined—through experiences of observing nonhuman animals in painstakingly designed zoos. The presumed objects of surveillance in zoos may be nonhuman animals, but the audiences are zoogoers who are trained to embrace conservationist values through exposure to contrived scenes of "wildness."

## NOTE

1. The Panopticon idea was initially conceived of by Jeremy Bentham's brother, Samuel, as an efficient means of overseeing workers (Semple 1993).

## REFERENCES

Deleuze, Gilles. 1988. *Foucault.* Translated by S. Hand. Minneapolis: University of Minnesota Press.

Elmer, Greg. 2003. A Diagram of Panoptic Surveillance. *New Media & Society* 5 (2):231–47.

Foucault, Michel. 1977. *Discipline and Punish: The Birth of the Prison.* New York: Vintage.

———. 1978. *The History of Sexuality: An Introduction.* Vol. 1. New York: Vintage.

———. 1980. *Power/Knowledge: Selected Interviews and Other Writings, 1972–1977.* Brighton, Sussex: Harvester Press.

———. 2003. *"Society Must Be Defended": Lectures at the College de France, 1975–76.* Translated by D. Macey. New York: Picador.

French, Martin A. 2009. Woven of War-Time Fabrics: The Globalization of Public Health Surveillance. *Surveillance & Society* 6 (2):101–15.

Gandy, Oscar H. 1993. *The Panoptic Sort: A Political Economy of Personal Information.* Boulder, CO: Westview.

Gilliom, John. 2001. *Overseers of the Poor: Surveillance, Resistance, and the Limits of Privacy.* Chicago: University of Chicago Press.

Haggerty, Kevin D. 2006. Tear Down the Walls: On Demolishing the Panopticon. In *Theorizing Surveillance: The Panopticon and Beyond,* edited by D. Lyon, 23–45. Cullompton, Devon: Willan Publishing.

Haggerty, Kevin D., and Richard V. Ericson. 2000. The Surveillant Assemblage. *British Journal of Sociology* 51 (4):605–22.

Koskela, Hille. 2004. Webcams, TV Shows and Mobile Phones: Empowering Exhibitionism. *Surveillance & Society* 2 (2/3):199–215.

Lyon, David. 1993. An Electronic Panopticon? A Sociological Critique of Surveillance Theory. *The Sociological Review* 41 (4):653–78.

———, ed. 2003. *Surveillance as Social Sorting: Privacy, Risk, and Digital Discrimination.* New York: Routledge.

Mathiesen, Thomas. 1997. The Viewer Society: Michel Foucault's 'Panopticon' Revisited. *Theoretical Criminology* 1 (2):215–34.

Monahan, Torin, David J. Phillips, and David Murakami Wood. 2010. Editorial: Surveillance and Empowerment. *Surveillance & Society* 8 (2):106–12.

Murakami Wood, David. 2007. Beyond the Panopticon? Foucault and Surveillance Studies. In *Space, Knowledge and Power: Foucault and Geography,* edited by J. W. Crampton and S. Elden, 245–63. Burlington, VT: Ashgate.

Norris, Clive, and Gary Armstrong. 1999. *The Maximum Surveillance Society: The Rise of CCTV.* Oxford: Berg.

Semple, Janet. 1993. *Bentham's Prison: A Study of the Panopticon Penitentiary.* Oxford: Clarendon Press.

Simon, Bart. 2005. The Return of Panopticism: Supervision, Subjection, and the New Surveillance. *Surveillance & Society* 3 (1):1–20.

# 6

# JEREMY BENTHAM

## THE PANOPTICON

The Utilitarian philosopher Jeremy Bentham's plans for Panopticon reformatories, derived from his brother Samuel's original conception, became a touchstone of surveillance theory largely through Michel Foucault's analysis. However, the original plan, created in numerous letters and papers written over many years, speaks for itself and goes much further than Foucault's description, covering aspects as diverse as food, clothing, segregation by sex and class, reflections on the economy of imprisonment and on the corruption of guards, and much more. In these excerpts from Bentham's early letters, we concentrate on the surveillant intent of panoptic institutions.

***

## From Letter I

Dear * * * *,—I observed t'other day in one of your English papers, an advertisement relative to a HOUSE OF CORRECTION therein spoken of, as intended for * * * * * * *. It occurred to me, that the plan of a building, lately contrived by my brother, for purposes in some respects similar, and which, under the name of the *Inspection House,* or the *Elaboratory,* he is about erecting here, might afford some hints for the above establishment. I have accordingly obtained some drawings relative to it, which I here inclose. Indeed I look upon it as capable of applications of the most extensive nature; and that for reasons which you will soon perceive.

To say all in one word, it will be found applicable, I think, without exception, to all establishments whatsoever, in which, within a space not too large to be covered or commanded by buildings, a number of persons are meant to be kept under inspection. No matter how different, or even opposite the purpose: whether it be that of *punishing the incorrigible, guarding the insane, reforming the vicious, confining the suspected, employing the idle, maintaining the helpless, curing the sick, instructing the willing* in any branch of industry, or *training the rising race* in the path of *education:* in a word, whether it be applied to the purposes of *perpetual prisons* in the room of death, or *prisons for confinement* before trial, or *penitentiary-houses,* or *houses of correction,* or *work-houses,* or *manufactories*, or *mad-houses*, or *hospitals*, or *schools*.

It is obvious that, in all these instances, the more constantly the persons to be inspected are under the eyes of the persons who should inspect them, the more perfectly will the purpose of the establishment have been attained. Ideal perfection, if that were the object, would require that each person should actually be in that predicament, during every instant of time. This being impossible, the next thing to be wished for is, that, at every instant, seeing reason to believe as much, and not being able to satisfy himself to the contrary, he should conceive himself to be so. This point, you will immediately see, is most completely secured by my brother's plan; and, I think, it will appear equally manifest, that it cannot be compassed by any other, or to speak more properly, that if it be compassed by any other, it can only be in proportion as such other may approach to this.

## From Letter V

The essence of it consists, then, in the centrality of the inspector's situation, combined with the well-known and most effectual contrivances for seeing without being seen. As to the general form of the building, the most commodious for most purposes seems to be the circular: but this is not an absolutely essential circumstance. Of all figures, however, this, you will observe, is the only one that affords a perfect view, and the same view, of an indefinite number of apartments of the same dimensions: that affords a spot from which, without any change of situation, a man may survey, in the same perfection, the whole

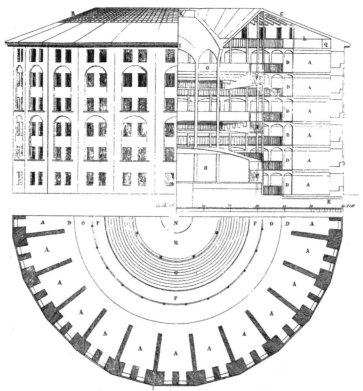

Jeremy Bentham's Panopticon prison design, 1791, Willey Reveley.

number, and without so much as a change of posture, the half of the whole number, at the same time: that, within a boundary of a given extent, contains the greatest quantity of room:—that places the centre at the least distance from the light:—that gives the cells most width, at the part where, on account of the light, most light may, for the purposes of work, be wanted:—and that reduces to the greatest possible shortness the path taken by the inspector, in passing from each part of the field of inspection to every other.

You will please to observe, that though perhaps it is the most important point, that the persons to be inspected should always feel themselves as if under inspection, at least as standing a great chance of being so, yet it is not by any means the only one. If it were, the same advantage might be given to buildings of almost any form. What is also of importance is, that for the greatest proportion of time possible, each man should actually be under inspection. This is material in all cases, that the inspector may have the satisfaction of knowing, that the discipline actually has the effect which it is designed to have: and it is more particularly material in such cases where the inspector, besides seeing that they conform to such standing rules as are prescribed, has more or less frequent occasion to give them such transient and incidental directions as will require to be given and enforced, at the commencement at least of every course of industry. And I think, it needs not much argument to prove, that the business of inspection, like every other, will be performed to a greater degree of perfection, the less trouble the performance of it requires.

Not only so, but the greater chance there is, of a given person's being at a given time actually under inspection, the more strong will be the persuasion—the more intense, if I may say so, the feeling, he has of his being so. How little turn soever the greater number of persons so circumstanced may be supposed to have for calculation, some rough sort of calculation can scarcely, under such circumstances, avoid forcing itself upon the rudest mind. Experiment, venturing first upon slight transgressions, and so on, in proportion to success, upon more and more considerable ones, will not fail to teach him the difference between a loose inspection and a strict one.

It is for these reasons, that I cannot help looking upon every form as less and less eligible, in proportion as it deviates from the circular.

## From Letter VI

I FLATTER myself there can now be little doubt of the plan's possessing the fundamental advantages I have been attributing to it: I mean, the *apparent omnipresence* of the inspector (if divines will allow me the expression,) combined with the extreme facility of his *real presence*.

A collateral advantage it possesses, and on the score of frugality a very material one, is that which respects the *number* of the inspectors requisite. If this plan required more than another, the additional number would form an objection, which, were the difference to a certain degree considerable, might rise so high as to be conclusive: so far from it, that a greater multitude than ever were yet lodged in one house might be inspected by a single person; for the trouble of inspection is diminished in no less proportion than the strictness of inspection is increased.

Another very important advantage, whatever purposes the plan may be applied to, particularly where it is applied to the severest and most coercive purposes, is, that the *under* keepers or inspectors, the servants and subordinates of every kind, will be under the same irresistible controul with respect to the *head* keeper or inspector, as the prisoners or other persons to be governed are with respect to *them*. On the common plans, what means, what possibility, has the prisoner, of appealing to the humanity of the principal for redress against the neglect or oppression of subordinates in that rigid sphere, but the *few* opportunities which, in a crowded prison, the most conscientious keeper *can* afford—but the none at all which many a keeper *thinks* fit to give them? How different would their lot be upon this plan!

In no instance could his subordinates either perform or depart from their duty, but he must know the time and degree and manner of their doing so. It presents an answer, and that a satisfactory one, to one of the most puzzling of political questions—*quis custodiet ipsos custodes* [Who will guard the guards themselves]? And, as the fulfilling of his, as well as their, duty would be rendered so much easier, than it can ever have been hitherto, so might, and so should, any departure from it be punished with the more inflexible severity. It is this circumstance that renders the influence of this plan not less beneficial to what is called *liberty*, than to necessary coercion; not less powerful as a controul upon subordinate power, than as a curb to delinquency; as a shield to innocence, than as a scourge to guilt.

Another advantage, still operating to the same ends, is the great load of trouble and disgust which it takes off the shoulders of those occasional inspectors of a higher order, such as *judges* and other *magistrates*, who, called down to this irksome task from the superior ranks of life, cannot but feel a proportionable repugnance to the discharge of it. Think how it is with them upon the present plans, and how it still must be upon the best plans that have been hitherto devised! The cells or apartments, however constructed, must, if there be nine hundred of them (as there were to have been upon the penitentiary-house plan,) be opened to the visitors, one by one. To do their business to any purpose, they must approach near to, and come almost in contact with each inhabitant; whose situation being watched over according to no other than the loose methods of inspection at present practicable, will on that account require the more minute and troublesome investigation on the part of these occasional superintendents. By this new plan, the disgust is entirely removed, and the trouble of going into such a room as the lodge, is no more than the trouble of going into any other. . . .

Among the other causes of that reluctance, none at present so forcible, none so unhappily well grounded, none which affords so natural an excuse, nor so strong a reason against accepting of any excuse, as the danger of *infection*—a circumstance which carries death, in one of its most tremendous forms, from the seat of guilt to the seat of justice, involving in one common catast'rophe the violator and the upholder of the laws. But in a spot so constructed, and under a course of discipline so insured, how should infection ever arise? or how should it continue? Against every danger of this kind, what private house of the poor, one might almost say, or even of the most opulent, can be equally secure?

Nor is the disagreeableness of the task of superintendence diminished by this plan, in a much greater degree than the efficacy of it is increased. On all others, be the superintendent's visit ever so unexpected, and his motions ever so quick, time there must always be for preparations blinding the real state of things. Out of nine hundred cells, he can visit but one at a time, and, in the meanwhile, the worst of the others may be arranged, and the inhabitants threatened, and tutored how to receive him. On this plan, no sooner is the superintendent announced, than the whole scene opens instantaneously to his view. . . .

You see, I take for granted as a matter of course, that under the necessary regulations for preventing interruption and disturbance, the doors of these establishments will be, as, without very special reasons to the contrary, the doors of all public establishments ought to be, thrown wide open to the body of the curious at large—the great *open committee* of the tribunal of the world. And who ever objects to such publicity, where it is practicable, but those whose motives for objection afford the strongest reasons for it?

# 7

# MICHEL FOUCAULT

## DISCIPLINE AND PUNISH

The Birth of the Prison

The figure of the Panopticon, as theorized by Michel Foucault, has had a profound influence on surveillance studies. By illustrating how architectures of surveillance have spread throughout societies, Foucault developed a new theory of power as pervasive, operating on a capillary level of social relations, and not dependent on individual actors asserting control over others. The Panopticon serves as an influential metaphor for the ways in which subjectivity can be transformed through exposure to surveillance, such that people voluntarily regulate their behaviour even in the absence of verifiable external observation.

\*\*\*

Bentham's *Panopticon* is the architectural figure of this composition. We know the principle on which it was based: at the periphery, an annular building; at the centre, a tower; this tower is pierced with wide windows that open onto the inner side of the ring; the peripheric building is divided into cells, each of which extends the whole width of the building; they have two windows, one on the inside, corresponding to the windows of the tower; the other, on the outside, allows the light to cross the cell from one end to the other. All that is needed, then, is to place a supervisor in a central tower and to shut up in each cell a madman, a patient, a condemned man, a worker or a schoolboy. By the effect of backlighting, one can observe from the tower, standing out precisely against the light, the small captive shadows in the cells of the periphery. They are like so many cages, so many small theatres, in which each actor is alone, perfectly individualized and constantly visible. The panoptic mechanism arranges spatial unities that make it possible to see constantly and to recognize immediately. In short, it reverses the principle of the dungeon; or rather of its three functions—to enclose, to deprive of light and to hide—it preserves only the first and eliminates the other two. Full lighting and the eye of a supervisor capture better than darkness, which ultimately protected. Visibility is a trap.

To begin with, this made it possible—as a negative effect—to avoid those compact, swarming, howling masses that were to be found in places of confinement, those painted by Goya or described by Howard. Each individual, in his place, is securely confined to a cell from which he is seen from the front by the supervisor; but the side walls prevent him from coming into contact with his companions. He is seen, but he does not see; he is the object of information, never a subject in communication. The arrangement of his room, opposite the central tower, imposes on him an axial visibility; but the divisions of the ring, those separated cells, imply a lateral invisibility. And this invisibility is a guarantee of order. If the inmates are convicts, there is no danger of a plot, an attempt at collective escape, the planning of new crimes for the future, bad reciprocal influences; if they are patients, there is no danger of contagion; if they are madmen there is no risk of their committing violence upon one another; if they are schoolchildren, there is no copying, no noise, no chatter, no waste of time; if they are workers, there are no disorders, no theft, no coalitions, none of those distractions that slow down the rate of work, make it less perfect or cause accidents. The crowd, a compact mass, a locus of multiple exchanges, individualities merging together, a collective effect, is abolished and replaced by a collection of separated individualities. From the point of view of the guardian, it is replaced by a multiplicity that can be numbered and supervised; from the point of view of the inmates, by a sequestered and observed solitude.

Hence the major effect of the Panopticon: to induce in the inmate a state of conscious and permanent visibility that assures the automatic functioning of power. So to arrange things that the surveillance is permanent in its effects, even if it is discontinuous in its action; that the perfection of power should tend to render its actual exercise unnecessary; that this architectural apparatus should be a machine for creating and sustaining a power relation independent of the person who exercises it;

in short, that the inmates should be caught up in a power situation of which they are themselves the bearers. To achieve this, it is at once too much and too little that the prisoner should be constantly observed by an inspector: too little, for what matters is that he knows himself to be observed; too much, because he has no need in fact of being so. In view of this, Bentham laid down the principle that power should be visible and unverifiable. Visible: the inmate will constantly have before his eyes the tall outline of the central tower from which he is spied upon. Unverifiable: the inmate must never know whether he is being looked at at any one moment; but he must be sure that he may always be so. In order to make the presence or absence of the inspector unverifiable, so that the prisoners, in their cells, cannot even see a shadow, Bentham envisaged not only venetian blinds on the windows of the central observation hall, but, on the inside, partitions that intersected the hall at right angles and, in order to pass from one quarter to the other, not doors but zig-zag openings; for the slightest noise, a gleam of light, a brightness in a half-opened door would betray the presence of the guardian. The Panopticon is a machine for dissociating the see/being seen dyad: in the peripheric ring, one is totally seen, without ever seeing; in the central tower, one sees everything without ever being seen.

It is an important mechanism, for it automatizes and disindividualizes power. Power has its principle not so much in a person as in a certain concerted distribution of bodies, surfaces, lights, gazes; in an arrangement whose internal mechanisms produce the relation in which individuals are caught up. The ceremonies, the rituals, the marks by which the sovereign's surplus power was manifested are useless. There is a machinery that assures dissymmetry, disequilibrium, difference. . . . The Panopticon is a marvelous machine which, whatever use one may wish to put it to, produces homogeneous effects of power.

A real subjection is born mechanically from a fictitious relation. So it is not necessary to use force to constrain the convict to good behaviour, the madman to calm, the worker to work, the schoolboy to application, the patient to the observation of the regulations. Bentham was surprised that panoptic institutions could be so light: there were no more bars, no more chains, no more heavy locks; all that was needed was that the separations should be clear and the openings well arranged. The heaviness of the old 'houses of security', with their fortress-like architecture, could be replaced by the simple, economic geometry of a 'house of certainty'. The efficiency of power, its constraining force have, in a sense, passed over to the other side—to the side of its surface of application. He who is subjected to a field of visibility, and who knows it, assumes responsibility for the constraints of power; he makes them play spontaneously upon himself; he inscribes in himself the power relation in which he simultaneously plays both roles; he becomes the principle of his own subjection. By this very fact, the external power may throw off its physical weight; it tends to the noncorporal; and, the more it approaches this limit, the more constant, profound and permanent are its effects: it is a perpetual victory that avoids any physical confrontation and which is always decided in advance. . . .

The Panopticon is a royal menagerie; the animal is replaced by man, individual distribution by specific grouping and the king by the machinery of a furtive power. With this exception, the Panopticon also does the work of a naturalist. It makes it possible to draw up differences: among patients, to observe the symptoms of each individual, without the proximity of beds, the circulation of miasmas, the effects of contagion confusing the clinical tables; among schoolchildren, it makes it possible to observe performances (without there being any imitation or copying), to map aptitudes, to assess characters, to draw up rigorous

classifications and, in relation to normal development, to distinguish 'laziness and stubbornness' from 'incurable imbecility'; among workers, it makes it possible to note the aptitudes of each worker, compare the time he takes to perform a task, and if they are paid by the day, to calculate their wages. . . .

The Panopticon is a privileged place for experiments on men, and for analysing with complete certainty the transformations that may be obtained from them. The Panopticon may even provide an apparatus for supervising its own mechanisms. In this central tower, the director may spy on all the employees that he has under his orders: nurses, doctors, foremen, teachers, warders; he will be able to judge them continuously, alter their behaviour, impose upon them the methods he thinks best; and it will even be possible to observe the director himself. An inspector arriving unexpectedly at the centre of the Panopticon will be able to judge at a glance, without anything being concealed from him, how the entire establishment is functioning. And, in any case, enclosed as he is in the middle of this architectural mechanism, is not the director's own fate entirely bound up with it? The incompetent physician who has allowed contagion to spread, the incompetent prison governor or workshop manager will be the first victims of an epidemic or a revolt. ' "By every tie I could devise", said the master of the Panopticon, "my own fate had been bound up by me with theirs" '. The Panopticon functions as a kind of laboratory of power. Thanks to its mechanisms of observation, it gains in efficiency and in the ability to penetrate into men's behaviour; knowledge follows the advances of power, discovering new objects of knowledge over all the surfaces on which power is exercised. . . .

The Panopticon . . . must be understood as a generalizable model of functioning; a way of defining power relations in terms of the everyday life of men. No doubt Bentham presents it as a particular institution, closed in upon itself. Utopias, perfectly closed in upon themselves, are common enough. As opposed to the ruined prisons, littered with mechanisms of torture, to be seen in Piranese's engravings, the Panopticon presents a cruel, ingenious cage. The fact that it should have given rise, even in our own time, to so many variations, projected or realized, is evidence of the imaginary intensity that it has possessed for almost two hundred years. But the Panopticon must not be understood as a dream building: it is the diagram of a mechanism of power reduced to its ideal form; its functioning, abstracted from any obstacle, resistance or friction, must be represented as a pure architectural and optical system: it is in fact a figure of political technology that may and must be detached from any specific use.

It is polyvalent in its applications; it serves to reform prisoners, but also to treat patients, to instruct schoolchildren, to confine the insane, to supervise workers, to put beggars and idlers to work. It is a type of location of bodies in space, of distribution of individuals in relation to one another, of hierarchical organization, of disposition of centres and channels of power, of definition of the instruments and modes of intervention of power, which can be implemented in hospitals, workshops, schools, prisons. Whenever one is dealing with a multiplicity of individuals on whom a task or a particular form of behaviour must be imposed, the panoptic schema may be used. . . .

In each of its applications, it makes it possible to perfect the exercise of power. It does this in several ways: because it can reduce the number of those who exercise it, while increasing the number of those on whom it is exercised. Because it is possible to intervene at any moment and because the constant pressure acts even before the offences, mistakes or crimes have been committed. Because, in these conditions, its strength is that it never intervenes, it is exercised spontaneously and without noise, it constitutes

a mechanism whose effects follow from one another. Because, without any physical instrument other than architecture and geometry, it acts directly on individuals; it gives 'power of mind over mind'. The panoptic schema makes any apparatus of power more intense: it assures its economy (in material, in personnel, in time); it assures its efficacity by its preventative character, its continuous functioning and its automatic mechanisms. . . .

In short, it arranges things in such a way that the exercise of power is not added on from the outside, like a rigid, heavy constraint, to the functions it invests, but is so subtly present in them as to increase their efficiency by itself increasing its own points of contact. The panoptic mechanism is not simply a hinge, a point of exchange between a mechanism of power and a function; it is a way of making power relations function in a function, and of making a function function through these power relations. Bentham's Preface to Panopticon opens with a list of the benefits to be obtained from his 'inspection-house': *Morals reformed—health preserved— industry invigorated—instruction diffused— public burthens lightened—Economy seated, as it were, upon a rock—the gordian knot of the Poor-Laws not cut, but untied—all by a simple idea in architecture!*.

Furthermore, the arrangement of this machine is such that its enclosed nature does not preclude a permanent presence from the outside: we have seen that anyone may come and exercise in the central tower the functions of surveillance, and that, this being the case, he can gain a clear idea of the way in which the surveillance is practised. In fact, any panoptic institution, even if it is as rigorously closed as a penitentiary, may without difficulty be subjected to such irregular and constant inspections: and not only by the appointed inspectors, but also by the public; any member of society will have the right to come and see with his own eyes how the schools, hospitals, factories, prisons function. There is no risk, therefore, that the increase of power created by the panoptic machine may degenerate into tyranny; the disciplinary mechanism will be democratically controlled, since it will be constantly accessible 'to the great tribunal committee of the world'. This Panopticon, subtly arranged so that an observer may observe, at a glance, so many different individuals, also enables everyone to come and observe any of the observers. The seeing machine was once a sort of dark room into which individuals spied; it has become a transparent building in which the exercise of power may be supervised by society as a whole.

The panoptic schema, without disappearing as such or losing any of its properties, was destined to spread throughout the social body; its vocation was to become a generalized function. The plague-stricken town provided an exceptional disciplinary model: perfect, but absolutely violent; to the disease that brought death, power opposed its perpetual threat of death; life inside it was reduced to its simplest expression; it was, against the power of death, the meticulous exercise of the right of the sword. The Panopticon, on the other hand, has a role of amplification; although it arranges power, although it is intended to make it more economic and more effective, it does so not for power itself, nor for the immediate salvation of a threatened society: its aim is to strengthen the social forces—to increase production, to develop the economy, spread education, raise the level of public morality; to increase and multiply.

How is power to be strengthened in such a way that, far from impeding progress, far from weighing upon it with its rules and regulations, it actually facilitates such progress? What intensificator of power will be able at the same time to be a multiplicator of production? How will power, by increasing its forces, be able to increase those of society instead of confiscating them or impeding them? The Panopticon's solution to this problem is that the productive increase of power can be assured only if, on the one hand, it can be exercised continuously in the very foundations of society, in the subtlest possible way, and if, on the other hand, it functions outside these sudden, violent, discontinuous forms that are bound up with the exercise of sovereignty. The body of the king, with its strange material and physical presence, with the force that he himself deploys or transmits to some few others, is at the opposite extreme of this new physics of power represented by panopticism; the domain of panopticism is, on the contrary, that whole lower region, that region of irregular bodies, with their details, their multiple movements, their heterogeneous forces, their spatial relations; what are required are mechanisms that analyse distributions, gaps, series, combinations, and which use instruments that render visible, record, differentiate and compare: a physics of a relational and multiple power, which has its maximum intensity not in the person of the king, but in the bodies that can be individualized by these relations. At the theoretical level, Bentham defines another way of analysing the social body and the power relations that traverse it; in terms of practice, he defines a procedure of subordination of bodies and forces that must increase the utility of power while practising the economy of the prince. Panopticism is the general principle of a new 'political anatomy' whose object and end are not the relations of sovereignty but the relations of discipline.

The celebrated, transparent, circular cage, with its high tower, powerful and knowing, may have been for Bentham a project of a perfect disciplinary institution; but he also set out to show how one may 'unlock' the disciplines and get them to function in a multiple, polyvalent way throughout the whole social body. These disciplines, which the classical age had elaborated in specific, relatively enclosed places—barracks, schools, workshops—and whose total implementation had been imagined only at the limited and temporary scale of a plague-stricken town, Bentham dreamt of transforming into a network of mechanisms that would be everywhere and always alert, running through society without interruption in space or in time. The panoptic arrangement provides the formula for this generalization. It programmes, at the level of an elementary and easily transferable mechanism, the basic functioning of a society penetrated through and through with disciplinary mechanisms.

8

# GILLES DELEUZE

## POSTSCRIPT ON THE SOCIETIES OF CONTROL

The figure of the Panopticon and the disciplinary societies it epitomized have been productive but also enormously constraining constructs in surveillance studies. In this influential
essay, Gilles Deleuze outlines a new regime emerging in the twentieth century: societies
of control. If disciplinary societies emphasized institutional molds and cultivated uniform
subjects, the new regime is characterized by modulations and the production of fluid, insecure, and atomized "dividuals."

\*\*\*

### 1. Historical

Foucault located the *disciplinary societies* in
the eighteenth and nineteenth centuries;
they reach their height at the outset of the
twentieth. They initiate the organization
of vast spaces of enclosure. The individual
never ceases passing from one closed environment to another, each having its own
laws: first, the family; then the school ("you
are no longer in your family"); then the
barracks ("you are no longer at school");
then the factory; from time to time the hospital; possibly the prison, the preeminent
instance of the enclosed environment. . . .
Foucault has brilliantly analyzed the ideal
project of these environments of enclosure,

particularly visible within the factory: to concentrate; to distribute in space; to order in
time; to compose a productive force within
the dimension of space-time whose effect
will be greater than the sum of its component forces. But what Foucault recognized
as well was the transience of this model: it
succeeded that of the *societies of sovereignty*,
the goal and functions of which were something quite different (to tax rather than to
organize production, to rule on death rather
than to administer life); the transition took
place over time, and Napoleon seemed to
effect the large-scale conversion from one
society to the other. But in their turn the
disciplines underwent a crisis to the benefit
of new forces that were gradually instituted

and which accelerated after World War II: a disciplinary society was what we already no longer were, what we had ceased to be.

We are in a generalized crisis in relation to all the environments of enclosure—prison, hospital, factory, school, family. The family is an "interior," in crisis like all other interiors—scholarly, professional, etc. The administrations in charge never cease announcing supposedly necessary reforms: to reform schools, to reform industries, hospitals, the armed forces, prisons. But everyone knows that these institutions are finished, whatever the length of their expiration periods. It's only a matter of administering their last rites and of keeping people employed until the installation of the new forces knocking at the door. These are the *societies of control*, which are in the process of replacing the disciplinary societies. . . . There is no need to ask which is the toughest or most tolerable regime, for it's within each of them that liberating and enslaving forces confront one another. For example, in the crisis of the hospital as environment of enclosure, neighborhood clinics, hospices, and day care could at first express new freedom, but they could participate as well in mechanisms of control that are equal to the harshest of confinements. There is no need to fear or hope, but only to look for new weapons.

## 2. Logic

The different internments or spaces of enclosure through which the individual passes are independent variables: each time one is supposed to start from zero, and although a common language for all these places exists, it is *analogical*. On the other hand, the different control mechanisms are inseparable variations, forming a system of variable geometry the language of which is numerical (which doesn't necessarily mean binary). Enclosures are *molds*, distinct castings, but controls are a *modulation*, like a self-deforming cast that will continuously change from one moment to the other, or like a sieve whose mesh will transmute from point to point.

This is obvious in the matter of salaries: the factory was a body that contained its internal forces at a level of equilibrium, the highest possible in terms of production, the lowest possible in terms of wages; but in a society of control, the corporation has replaced the factory, and the corporation is a spirit, a gas. Of course the factory was already familiar with the system of bonuses, but the corporation works more deeply to impose a modulation of each salary, in states of perpetual metastability that operate through challenges, contests, and highly comic group sessions. If the most idiotic television game shows are so successful, it's because they express the corporate situation with great precision. The factory constituted individuals as a single body to the double advantage of the boss who surveyed each element within the mass and the unions who mobilized a mass resistance; but the corporation constantly presents the brashest rivalry as a healthy form of emulation, an excellent motivational force that opposes individuals against one another and runs through each, dividing each within. The modulating principle of "salary according to merit" has not failed to tempt national education itself. Indeed, just as the corporation replaces the factory, *perpetual training* tends to replace the *school*, and continuous control to replace the examination. Which is the surest way of delivering the school over to the corporation.

In the disciplinary societies one was always starting again (from school to the barracks, from the barracks to the factory), while in the societies of control one is never finished with anything—the corporation, the educational system, the armed services being metastable states coexisting in one and the same modulation, like a universal system of deformation. . . . The disciplinary societies have two poles: the signature that designates the *individual*, and the number or administrative numeration that indicates his or her position within a *mass*. This is be-cause the disciplines never saw any incompatibility between these two, and because at the same time power individualizes and masses together, that is, constitutes those over whom it exercises power into a body and molds the individuality of each member of that body. (Foucault saw the origin of this double charge in the pastoral power of the priest—the flock and each of its animals—but civil power moves in turn and by other means to make itself lay "priest.") In the societies of control, on the other hand, what is important is no longer either a signature or a number, but a code: the code is a *password*, while on the other hand the disciplinary societies are regulated by *watchwords* (as much from the point of view of integration as from that of resistance). The numerical language of control is made of codes that mark access to information, or reject it. We no longer find ourselves dealing with the mass/individual pair. Individuals have become "*dividuals*," and masses, samples, data, markets, or "*banks*." Perhaps it is money that expresses the distinction between the two societies best, since discipline always referred back to minted money that locks gold in as numerical standard, while control relates to floating rates of exchange, modulated according to a rate established by a set of standard currencies. The old monetary mole is the animal of the spaces of enclosure, but the serpent is that of the societies of control. We have passed from one animal to the other, from the mole to the serpent, in the system under which we live, but also in our manner of living and in our relations with others. The disciplinary man was a discontinuous producer of energy, but the man of control is undulatory, in orbit, in a continuous network. Everywhere *surfing* has already replaced the older *sports*.

Types of machines are easily matched with each type of society—not that machines are determining, but because they express those social forms capable of generating them and using them. The old societies of sovereignty made use of simple machines—levers, pulleys, clocks; but the recent disciplinary societies equipped themselves with machines involving energy, with the passive danger of entropy and the active danger of sabotage; the societies of control operate with machines of a third type, computers, whose passive danger is jamming and whose active one is piracy and the introduction of viruses. This technological evolution must be, even more profoundly, a mutation of capitalism, an already well-known or familiar mutation that can be summed up as follows: nineteenth-century capitalism is a capitalism of concentration, for production and for property. It therefore erects the factory as a space of enclosure, the capitalist being the owner of the means of production but also, progressively, the owner of other spaces conceived through analogy (the worker's familial house, the school). As for markets, they are conquered sometimes by specialization, sometimes by colonization, sometimes by lowering the costs of production. But, in the present situation, capitalism is no longer involved in production, which it often relegates to the Third World, even for the complex forms of textiles, metallurgy, or oil production. It's a capitalism of higher-order production. It no longer buys raw materials and no longer sells the finished products: it buys the finished products or assembles parts. What it wants to sell is services and what it wants to buy is stocks. This is no longer a capitalism for production but for the product, which is to say, for being sold or marketed. Thus it is essentially dispersive, and the factory has given way to the corporation. The family, the school, the army, the factory are no longer the distinct analogical spaces that converge towards an owner—state or private power—but coded figures—deformable and transformable—of a single corporation that now has only stockholders. Even art has left the spaces of enclosure in order to enter into the open circuits of the bank. The conquests of the market are made by grabbing control and no longer by disciplinary training, by fixing the exchange rate much more than by lowering costs, by transformation of the product more than by specialization of production. Corruption thereby gains a new power. Marketing has become the center or the "soul" of the corporation. We are taught that corporations have a soul, which is the most terrifying news in the world. The operation of markets is now the instrument of social control and forms the impudent breed of our masters. Control is short-term and of rapid rates of turnover, but also continuous and without limit, while discipline was of long duration, infinite and discontinuous. Man is no longer man enclosed, but man in debt. It is true that capitalism has retained as a constant the extreme poverty of three quarters of humanity, too poor for debt, too numerous for confinement: control will not only have to deal with erosions of frontiers but with the explosions within shanty towns or ghettos.

## 3. Program

The conception of a control mechanism, giving the position of any element within an open environment at any given instant (whether animal in a reserve or human in a corporation, as with an electronic collar), is not necessarily one of science fiction. Félix Guattari has imagined a city where one would be able to leave one's apartment, one's street, one's neighborhood, thanks to one's (dividual) electronic card that raises a given barrier; but the card could just as easily be rejected on a given day or between certain hours; what counts is not the barrier but the computer that tracks each person's position—licit or illicit—and effects a universal modulation.

The socio-technological study of the mechanisms of control, grasped at their inception, would have to be categorical and to describe what is already in the process of substitution for the disciplinary sites of enclosure, whose crisis is everywhere proclaimed. It may be that older methods, borrowed from the former societies of sovereignty, will return to the fore, but with the necessary modifications. What counts is that we are at the beginning of something. In the *prison system*: the attempt to find penalties of "substitution," at least for petty crimes, and the use of electronic collars that force the convicted person to stay at home during certain hours. For the *school system*: continuous forms of control, and the effect on the school of perpetual training, the corresponding abandonment of all university research, the introduction of the "corporation" at all levels of schooling. For the *hospital system*: the new medicine "without doctor or patient" that singles out potential sick people and subjects at risk, which in no way attests to individuation—as they say—but substitutes for the individual or numerical body the code of a "dividual" material to be controlled. In the *corporate system*: new ways of handling money, profits, and humans that no longer pass through the old factory form. These are very small examples, but ones that will allow for better understanding of what is meant by the crisis of the institutions, which is to say, the progressive and dispersed installation of a new system of domination. One of the most important questions will concern the ineptitude of the unions: tied to the whole of their history of struggle against the disciplines or within the spaces of enclosure, will they be able to adapt themselves or will they give way to new forms of resistance against the societies of control? Can we already grasp the rough outlines of these coming forms, capable of threatening the joys of marketing? Many young people strangely boast of being "motivated"; they re-request apprenticeships and permanent training. It's up to them to discover what they're being made to serve, just as their elders discovered, not without difficulty, the telos of the disciplines. The coils of a serpent are even more complex than the burrows of a molehill.

# 9

# KEVIN D. HAGGERTY AND RICHARD V. ERICSON

## THE SURVEILLANT ASSEMBLAGE

In this field-shaping article, Kevin Haggerty and Richard Ericson borrow from assemblage theory to make sense of new configurations of surveillance. "The surveillant assemblage," as they describe it, links the surveillance capacities of multiple systems throughout society, allowing for the convergence of control functions, potentially capturing everyone in its decentralized and distributed web. The authors further develop the concept of "data doubles" to account for the ways that this assemblage abstracts bodies into discrete, deterritorialized data elements, as pragmatic rather than accurate representations, which can be acted upon to achieve instrumental aims.

*** 

[W]e are witnessing a convergence of what were once discrete surveillance systems to the point that we can now speak of an emerging 'surveillant assemblage'. This assemblage operates by abstracting human bodies from their territorial settings and separating them into a series of discrete flows. These flows are then reassembled into distinct 'data doubles' which can be scrutinized and targeted for intervention. In the process, we are witnessing a rhizomatic leveling of the hierarchy of surveillance, such that groups which were previously exempt from routine surveillance are now increasingly being monitored. . . .

The philosopher Gilles Deleuze only occasionally wrote directly on the topic of surveillance, usually in the context of his commentaries on Foucault's work. In conjunction with his colleague Félix Guattari, however, he has provided us with a set of conceptual tools that allow us to re-think the operation of the emergent surveillance system, a system we call the 'surveillant assemblage'. . . .

Deleuze and Guattari introduce a radical notion of multiplicity into phenomena which we traditionally approach as being discretely bounded, structured and stable. 'Assemblages' consist of a 'multiplicity of heterogeneous objects, whose unity comes solely from the fact that these items function together, that they "work" together as a functional entity'. They comprise discrete flows of an essentially limitless range of other phenomena such as people, signs, chemicals, knowledge and institutions. To dig beneath the surface stability of any entity is to encounter a host of different phenomena and processes working in concert. The radical nature of this vision becomes more apparent when one realizes how any particular assemblage is itself composed of different discrete assemblages which are themselves multiple.

Assemblages, for Deleuze and Guattari, are part of the state form. However, this notion of the state form should not be confused with those traditional apparatuses of governmental rule studied by political scientists. Instead, the state form is distinguished by virtue of its own characteristic set of operations; the tendency to create bounded physical and cognitive spaces, and introduce processes designed to capture flows. The state seeks to 'striate the space over which it reigns', a process which involves introducing breaks and divisions into otherwise free-flowing phenomena. To do so requires the creation of both spaces of comparison where flows can be rendered alike and centres of appropriation where these flows can be captured.

Flows exist prior to any particular assemblage, and are fixed temporarily and spatially by the assemblage. In this distinction between flows and assemblages, Deleuze and Guattari also articulate a distinction between forces and power. Forces consist of more primary and fluid phenomena, and it is from such phenomena that power derives as it captures and striates such flows. These processes coalesce into systems of domination when otherwise fluid and mobile states become fixed into more or less stable and asymmetrical arrangements which allow for some to direct or govern the actions of others. . . .

Some caution is needed, however, at this point. To speak of *the* surveillant assemblage risks fostering the impression that we are concerned with a stable entity with its own fixed boundaries. In contrast, to the extent that the surveillant assemblage exists, it does so as a potentiality, one that resides at the intersections of various media that can be connected for diverse purposes. Such linkages can themselves be differentiated according to the degree to which they are *ad hoc* or institutionalized. By accentuating the emergent and unstable characteristic of the surveillant assemblage we also draw attention to the limitations of traditional political strategies that seek to confront the quantitative increase in surveillance. As it is multiple, unstable and lacks discernible boundaries or responsible governmental departments, the surveillant assemblage cannot be dismantled by prohibiting a particularly unpalatable technology. Nor can it be attacked by focusing criticism on a single bureaucracy or institution. In the face of multiple connections across myriad technologies and practices, struggles against particular manifestations of surveillance, as important as they might be, are akin to efforts to keep the ocean's tide back with a broom—a frantic focus on a particular unpalatable technology or practice while the general tide of surveillance washes over us all. . . .

The analysis of surveillance tends to focus on the capabilities of a number of discrete technologies or social practices. Analysts typically highlight the proliferation of such phenomena and emphasize how they cumulatively pose a threat to civil liberties. We are only now beginning to appreciate that surveillance is driven by the desire to bring systems together, to combine practices and technologies and integrate them into a larger whole. It is this tendency which allows us to speak of surveillance as an assemblage, with such combinations providing for exponential increases in the degree of surveillance capacity. Rather than exemplifying Orwell's totalitarian state-centred Oceana, this assemblage operates across both state and extra-state institutions. . . .

A great deal of surveillance is directed toward the human body. The observed body is of a distinctively hybrid composition. First it is broken down by being abstracted from its territorial setting. It is then reassembled in different settings through a series of data flows. The result is a decorporealized body, a 'data double' of pure virtuality.

The monitored body is increasingly a cyborg; a flesh-technology-information amalgam. Surveillance now involves an interface of technology and corporeality and is comprised of those 'surfaces of contact or interfaces between organic and non-organic orders, between life forms and webs of information, or between organs/body parts and entry/projection systems (e.g., keyboards, screens)'. These hybrids can involve something as direct as tagging the human body so that its movements through space can be recorded, to the more refined reconstruction of a person's habits, preferences, and lifestyle from the trails of information which have become the detritus of contemporary life. The surveillant assemblage is a visualizing device that brings into the visual register a host of heretofore opaque flows of auditory, scent, chemical, visual, ultraviolet and informational stimuli. Much of the visualization pertains to the human body, and exists beyond our normal range of perception. . . .

The surveillant assemblage does not approach the body in the first instance as a single entity to be molded, punished, or controlled. First it must be known, and to do so it is broken down into a series of discrete signifying flows. Surveillance commences with the creation of a space of comparison and the introduction of breaks in the flows that emanate from, or circulate within, the human body. For example, drug testing striates flows of chemicals, photography captures flows of reflected lightwaves, and lie detectors align and compare assorted flows of respiration, pulse and electricity. The body is itself, then, an assemblage comprised of myriad component parts and processes which are broken-down for purposes of observation. . . .

Such processes are put into operation from a host of scattered centres of calculation where ruptures are co-ordinated and toward which the subsequent information is directed. Such centres of calculation can include forensic laboratories, statistical institutions, police stations, financial institutions, and corporate and military headquarters. In these sites the information derived from flows of the surveillant assemblage are reassembled and scrutinized in the hope of developing strategies of governance, commerce and control. . . .

Today, however, we are witnessing the formation and coalescence of a new type of body, a form of becoming which transcends human corporeality and reduces flesh to pure information. Culled from the tentacles of the surveillant assemblage, this new body is our 'data double', a double which involves 'the multiplication of the individual, the constitution of an additional self'. Data doubles circulate in a host of different centres of calculation and serve as markers for access to resources, services and power in ways which are often unknown to its referent. They are also increasingly the objects toward which governmental and marketing practices are directed. And while such doubles ostensibly refer back to particular individuals, they transcend a purely representational idiom. Rather than being accurate or inaccurate portrayals of real individuals, they are a form of pragmatics: differentiated according to how useful they are in allowing institutions to make discriminations among populations. Hence, while the surveillant assemblage is directed toward a particular cyborg flesh/technology amalgamation, it is productive of a new type of individual, one comprised of pure information. . . .

For both Orwell and Foucault, surveillance is part of a regime where comparatively few powerful individuals or groups watch the many, in a form of top-down scrutiny. Contemporary studies of surveillance continue to emphasize this hierarchical aspect of observation. For example,

Fiske concludes his insightful analysis of the surveillance of American Blacks (particularly Black men), by proclaiming that 'although surveillance is penetrating deeply throughout our society, its penetration is differential. The lives of the white mainstream are still comparatively untouched by it'. And while the targeting of surveillance is indeed differential, we take exception to the idea that the mainstream is 'untouched' by surveillance. Surveillance has become rhizomatic, it has transformed hierarchies of observation, and allows for the scrutiny of the powerful by both institutions and the general population.

All contemporary institutions subject their members to forms of bureaucratic surveillance. Individuals with different financial practices, education and lifestyle will come into contact with different institutions and hence be subject to unique combinations of surveillance. The classifications and profiles that are entered into these disparate systems correspond with, and reinforce, differential levels of access, treatment and mobility. Hence, while poor individuals may be in regular contact with the surveillance systems associated with social assistance or criminal justice, the middle and upper classes are increasingly subject to their own forms of routine observation, documentation and analysis. The more institutions they are in contact with, the greater the level of scrutiny to which they are subjected. In the case of the powerful, this can include the regular monitoring of consumption habits, health profile, occupational performance, financial transactions, communication patterns, Internet use, credit history, transportation patterns, and physical access controls. . . .

Premodern living arrangements typically consisted of individuals residing in rural villages where they knew and were known by their neighbours. The mass movements of individuals into cities ruptured these long-standing neighbourly and familial bonds. Individuals in cities became surrounded by streams of unknown strangers. Sociologists have drawn a wide range of implications from this social transformation. Anonymity allowed for new possibilities in self-creation: the freedom to partake in experiments with identities and life projects. . . . Others have accentuated the darker side of these possibilities for self-creation, cautioning how this new found 'freedom' could also be experienced as a daunting obligation, as modern individuals are now compelled to be free, to establish identities and life projects in the face of radical uncertainty about correct courses of action. . . .

From the beginning, however, this general narrative of anonymity and invisibility contained a subplot, one which involved countervailing efforts by institutions. The rise in credentials and surveillance systems was a way to create institutional reputations and provide for ways to differentiate among unknown strangers. These new forms of reputation lack the deep subjective nuances which characterized familial and neighbourly relations in the idealized premodern rural village. Instead, knowledge of the population is now manifest in discrete bits of information which break the individual down into flows for purposes of management, profit and entertainment. While such efforts were originally a footnote to the historical rise of urban anonymity, they now constitute an important force in their own right. The coalescence of such practices into the surveillant assemblage marks the progressive 'disappearance of disappearance'—a process whereby it is increasingly difficult for individuals to maintain their anonymity, or to escape the monitoring of social institutions.

# 10

# THOMAS MATHIESEN

## THE VIEWER SOCIETY

### Michel Foucault's "Panopticon" Revisited

In this early critique of the Panopticon model of surveillance-based discipline, Thomas Mathiesen explores the influence of the mass media—and persistent forms of "spectacle"—in controlling individuals. If the Panopticon operated on the principle of the few watching the many, it is complemented by a media-facilitated formation of the many watching the few, or what Mathiesen calls the "synopticon." The power of the mass media to shape ideology offers a disturbing counterpart to the various forms of "soul" training described by Foucault.

\*\*\*

The opening chapter of *Discipline and Punish* gives a dramatic and terrifying account of an execution in Paris. The year was 1757, and the man who was executed was a certain Robert Francois Damiens, who had attempted to murder the King of France, Louis XV. . . . The execution was brutal to say the least, Damiens was kept alive for a long time and tortured in the most painful manner, and finally torn apart by horses tied to his arms and legs. The horses had to be helped by the executioner to complete the task. The spectacle was attended by large crowds. . . . The next account in Foucault's presentation . . . implies a complete change of scene. Three-quarters of a century has past. The year is 1838, and Foucault's source now is the rules for 'the house of young prisoners in Paris'. The life of the young prisoners is regulated by rules down to the most minute details, from the first drum roll in the morning, making the prisoners rise and dress in silence, through prayer, working hours, meals, education, rest, the washing of hands, the inspection of clothes, and finally order, silence and sleep 'at half-past seven in the summer, half-past eight in the winter'. Gone is the open brutality and uncontrolled infliction of physical pain so characteristic of Damiens' execution; instead, there is a carefully developed system of rules regulating life in full and complete detail.

What does Foucault want to illustrate by contrasting the two scenes? First, he wants to say something about the change in the nature of punishment, from physical punishment to prison. Second, and more importantly, he wants to say something about a change in the content of punishment, from the torture of the body to the transformation of the soul. . . . Third, Foucault wants to say something about a broad historical change of social order. . . . To Foucault, panopticism represents a fundamental movement or transformation *from the situation where the many see the few to the situation where the few see the many.* . . . It is the normalizing gaze of panopticism which presumably produces that subjectivity, that self-control, which disciplines people to fit into a democratic capitalist society. . . .

Synopticism . . .

We certainly live in a society where the few see the many. Yet, something of crucial importance is missing. . . . As a striking parallel to the panoptical process, and concurring in detail with its historical development, we have seen the development of a unique and enormously extensive system enabling *the many to see and contemplate the few,* so that the tendency for the few to see and supervise the many is contextualized by a highly significant counterpart.

I am thinking, of course, of the development of the total system of the modern mass media. It is, to put it mildly, puzzling that Michel Foucault, in a large volume which explicitly or implicitly sensitizes us inter alia to surveillance in modern society, does not mention television—or any other mass media—with a single word. It is more than just an omission; its inclusion in the analysis would necessarily in a basic way have changed his whole image of society as far as surveillance goes.

Corresponding to panopticism, imbued with certain basic parallels in structure, vested with certain reciprocal supplementary functions, and—during the past few years—merged with panopticism through a common technology, the system of modern mass media has been going through a most significant and accelerating development. The total time span of this development—the past 150 to 200 years—coincides most remarkably with the period of the modern growth of panopticism. Increasingly, the few have been able to see the many, but also increasingly, the many have been enabled to see the few—to see the VIPs, the reporters, the stars, almost a new class in the public sphere.

Formulated in bold terms, it is possible to say that not only panopticism, but also *synopticism* characterizes our society, and characterized the transition to modernity. The concept is composed of the Greek word *syn* which stands for 'together' or 'at the same time', and *opticon*, which, again, has to do with the visual. It may be used to represent the situation where a large number focuses on something in common which is condensed. In other words, it may stand for the *opposite* of the situation where the few see the many. In a two-way and significant double sense of the word we thus live in a *viewer society.* . . .

In our own time, television, video, satellites, cables and modern computer development are joint technological features. In his book *1984* George Orwell described panopticism and synopticism in their ultimate form as completely merged: through a screen in your living room you saw Big Brother, just as Big Brother saw you. We have not come this far, but we clearly see tendencies for panopticism and synopticism to merge into one. . . .

What about power? . . .

[A]n elaboration is necessary as far as synopticism goes: is *power* actually represented in the media? This is an important question. To repeat, Foucault wrote that 'the pomp of sovereignty, the necessarily spectacular manifestations of power', have today gradually yielded to 'the daily exercise of surveillance, in a panopticism in which the vigilance of the intersecting gazes was soon to render useless both the eagle and the sun'.

The power of visible and concrete rulers was and is fading away. This perspective fits nicely with Foucault's view of power in modern society: the visible actors' power in central institutions of state and society is blurred, indistinct and even unimportant; instead, power is a phenomenon permeating society as invisible micropower.

If this is true, and if those we meet and see in the media are just ornamental figures without power, Foucault's omission of synopticism might not be so serious.

I do not think it is true, and find reason to give an affirmative answer to the question of whether power—indeed, great power—is located in concrete individuals and concrete delimited groups as represented in our mass media. The eagle and the sun have not been extinguished, but are expressed in a different way. This is probably especially so in the most visible media. It does not mean that Foucault's micropower, which cannot be delimited to definite performers but which silently permeates the social fabric, is unimportant. Both perspectives, the perspective of micropower but also that of *the actor's* power, are necessary.

In synoptic space, particular news reporters, more or less brilliant media personalities and commentators who are continuously visible and seen are of particular importance. To understand them just as ornamental figures is to underestimate them. They actively filter and shape information; as has been widely documented in media research, they produce news . . . ; they place topics on the agenda and avoid placing topics on the agenda. To be sure, all of this is performed within the context of a broader hidden agenda of political or economic interests, so to speak behind the media. But this does not detract from the importance and role of the visible actors, on the stage. . . .

## Control functions

Finally, I arrive at the question of control functions. I use the concept here in its simplest possible form, as change in behaviour or attitude in a wide sense, following from the influence of others. 'Control', then, is something more than 'surveillance'; it implies the regulation of behaviour or attitude which may follow for example from surveillance. I use the concept of 'discipline', Foucault's term, as a synonym.

There is an ongoing discussion of whether panopticism and synopticism, surveillance and the media, in fact have the effect of control or discipline. The discussion should be taken beyond the effects of isolated, single measures or messages, which have characterized media research in particular. The question is the effects of the total pattern of surveillance measures or media messages. Thus, with regard to the media, the total Gestalt produced by the messages of television is much more important than the individual programme or even type of programme. . . .

The question is, then, the control or discipline of behaviour and attitude. That aspect of *panopticism* which consists of the growth of a modern veiled and secret surveillance industry, and which preoccupies us here, first of all controls or disciplines our *behaviour*. In this respect the modern surveillance systems are very different from the old panoptical prisons, which are also growing by leaps and bounds. The latter inflict great pain on those who inhabit them. But a vast amount of research shows that they have no effect, or at most a marginal effect, in terms of controlled behaviour. Rather, I am thinking of the vast hidden apparatus, and the effect of this apparatus on people in usual or unusual political situations. Well aware of 'the intersecting gazes' of panopticism, but unable to point concretely to them—this is the nature of their secrecy—we arrange our affairs accordingly, perhaps without being fully aware of it. We remain, in our attitude, communists, left-oriented, or what have you, but adjust in terms of behaviour. . . .

What I have said here is, as far as it goes, in line with Foucault: to him, the fact that the torture of the docile body came to an end did not mean that the body ceased to be an object of attention. It just took place in a different way: 'The human body was entering a machinery of power that explores it, breaks it down and rearranges it'. But at the same time, as I have said before, he saw his book as 'a correlative history of the modern soul'. To repeat, by the control of the soul, vis-a-vis the control of the body, I understand him to mean the creation of human beings who control themselves through self-control.

My guess is that the souls in our time, and precisely in Foucault's sense as I understand it, above all belong to the other machinery, that of *synopticism* . . . . My point is that synopticism, through the modern mass media in general and television in particular, first of all directs and controls or disciplines our *consciousness*. . . .

To repeat, it is the total pattern or Gestalt rather than the individual programme or type of programmes which functions this way. . . . The total message inculcates or produces a general understanding of the world, a *world paradigm* if you like, which emphasizes personal and individual, the deviant, the shuddering, the titillating— as alluded to already, the entertaining in a wide sense. The paradigm is successful because it is received in the context of a need—satisfies a need—for escape from the concrete misery of the world, very much like the Church which offered rescue and salvation in the hereafter. It is by satisfying the need for escape that people are made to acquiesce, accept and fit into the requirements of our society. In this sense, the Church and television are real functional alternatives. . . .

In bold relief: surveillance, panopticon, makes us silent about that which breaks fundamentally with the taken-for-granted because we are made afraid to break with it. Modern television, synopticon, makes us silent because we do not have anything to talk about that might initiate the break. . . .

Taken as a whole, things are much *worse* than Michel Foucault imagined. The total situation clearly calls for political resistance. But to muster such double resistance is a difficult task, because the call for resistance may—in line with what I have argued in this article—be silenced by the very panopticon and synopticon which we wish to counteract.

# 11

# DAVID ARMSTRONG

# THE RISE OF SURVEILLANCE MEDICINE

Whereas one might imagine today's fervor for active lifestyles and self-screening for health risks to be completely reasonable, these practices emerge from a relatively recent medical imaginary. In this excerpt, David Armstrong argues that the dominant contemporary regime of "surveillance medicine," which arose in the twentieth century, depends on constructions of normalcy that can only be obtained through programs monitoring entire populations, not just sick ones. One's personal health comes to be understood as always in relation to others and along a continuum—from healthy to ill. Under such a regime, one is responsibilized to track risks vigilantly and mitigate them quickly.

\*\*\*

Perhaps the most important contribution for understanding the advent of modern medicine has been the work of the medical historian Ackerknecht, who described the emergence of a number of distinct medical perspectives during the early and late eighteenth century. In brief, he identified an earlier phase of Library Medicine in which the classical learning of the physician seemed more important than any specific knowledge of illness. This gave way to Bedside Medicine when physicians began to address the problems of the practical management of illness, particularly in terms of the classification of the patient's symptoms. In its turn Bedside Medicine was replaced by Hospital Medicine with the advent of hospitals in Paris at the end of the eighteenth century.

Hospital Medicine was clearly an important revolution in medical thinking. Also known as the Clinic, pathological medicine, Western medicine and biomedicine, it has survived and extended itself over the last two centuries to become the dominant model of medicine in the modern world. . . . [With Hospital Medicine] the relationship of symptoms and illness was reconfigured into a three-dimensional framework involving symptom, sign and pathology. In this new arrangement, the symptom, as of old, was a marker of illness as experienced by the patient, but to this indicator was added the sign—an intimation of disease as elicited by the attentive physician through the clinical examination. For example, the patient's symptom of abdominal pain might be linked to the sign of abdominal tenderness that the physician could discover; but neither symptom nor sign in itself constituted illness: both pointed to an underlying lesion that was the disease. In contrast to the previous regime of Bedside Medicine in which the overt symptom was the illness, the 'clinical picture' as drawn by both symptom and sign enabled the pathology that existed beneath experience to be inferred. . . .

Despite the clear hegemony of Hospital Medicine over the last two centuries, it is the contention of this paper that a new medicine based on the surveillance of normal populations can be identified as beginning to emerge early in the twentieth century. This new Surveillance Medicine involves a fundamental remapping of the spaces of illness. Not only is the relationship between symptom, sign and illness redrawn but the very nature of illness is reconstrued. And illness begins to leave the three-dimensional confine of the volume of the human body to inhabit a novel extracorporal space. . . .

Hospital Medicine was only concerned with the ill patient in whom a lesion might be identified, but a cardinal feature of Surveillance Medicine is its targeting of everyone. Surveillance Medicine requires the dissolution of the distinct clinical categories of healthy and ill as it attempts to bring everyone within its network of visibility. Therefore one of the earliest expressions of Surveillance Medicine—and a vital precondition for its continuing proliferation—was the problematisation of the normal. . . .

[I]t was the child in the twentieth century that became the first target of the full deployment of the concept. The significance of the child was that it underwent growth and development: there was therefore a constant threat that proper stages might not be negotiated that in its turn justified close medical observation. The establishment

and wide provision of antenatal care, birth notification, baby clinics, milk depots, infant welfare clinics, day nurseries, health visiting and nursery schools ensured that the early years of child development could be closely monitored. . . .

In parallel with the intensive surveillance of the body of the infant during the early twentieth century, the new medical gaze also turned to focus on the unformed mind of the child. As with physical development, psychological growth was construed as inherently problematic, precariously normal. The initial solution was for psychological well-being to be monitored and its abnormal forms identified. . . .

If there is one image that captures the nature of the machinery of observation that surrounded the child in those early decades of the twentieth century, it might well be the height and weight growth chart. Such charts contain a series of gently curving lines, each one representing the growth trajectory of a population of children. Each line marked the 'normal' experience of a child who started his or her development at the beginning of the line. Thus, every child could be assigned a place on the chart and, with successive plots, given a personal trajectory. But the individual trajectory only existed in a context of general population trajectories: the child was unique yet uniqueness could only be read from a composition which summed the unique features of all children. . . . Abnormality was a relative phenomenon. A child was abnormal with reference to other children, and even then only by degrees. In effect, the growth charts were significant for distributing the body of the child in a field delineated not by the absolute categories of physiology and pathology, but by the characteristics of the normal population. . . .

The socio-medical survey, first introduced during World War II to assess the perceived health status of the population, represented the recruitment to medicine of an efficient technical tool that both measured and reaffirmed the extensiveness of morbidity. The survey revealed the ubiquity of illness, that health was simply a precarious state. . . . [T]he patient was inseparable from the person because all persons were becoming patients. . . . The referent external to the population under study, which had for almost two centuries governed the analysis of bodies, was replaced by the relative positions of all bodies. Surveillance Medicine fixed on these gaps between people to establish that everyone was normal yet no-one was truly healthy. . . .

The process through which the older techniques of hygiene were transformed into the newer strategy of health promotion occurred over several decades during the twentieth century. But perhaps one of the earliest experiments that attempted the transition was the collaborative venture between the city of Fargo in North Dakota and the Commonwealth Fund in 1923. . . . While the classroom was the focus for a systematic campaign of health behaviour, a periodic medical and dental examination both justified and monitored the educational intervention. In effect 'health teaching, health supervision and their effective coordination' were linked together. In Fargo 'health teaching departed from the hygiene textbook, and after a vitalizing change, found its way back to the textbook'. From its insistence on four hours of physical exercises a day—two of them outdoors—to its concern with the mental maturation of the child, Fargo represented the realisation of a new public health dream of surveillance in which everyone is brought into the vision of the benevolent eye of medicine through the medicalisation of everyday life.

After World War II this approach began to be deployed with more vigour in terms of a strategy of health promotion. Concerns with diet, exercise, stress, sex, etc., become the vehicles for encouraging the community to survey itself. The ultimate triumph of Surveillance Medicine would be its internalisation by all the population.

The tactics of Hospital Medicine have been those of exile and enclosure. The lesion marked out those who were different in a great binary system of illness and health, and processed them (in the hospital) in an attempt to rejoin them to the healthy. The tactics of the new Surveillance Medicine, on the other hand, have been pathologisation and vigilance. The techniques of health promotion recognise that health no longer exists 'in a strict binary relationship to illness, rather health and illness belong to an ordinal scale in which the healthy can become healthier, and health can co-exist with illness; there is now nothing incongruous in having cancer yet believing oneself to be essentially healthy. But such a trajectory towards the healthy state can only be achieved if the whole population comes within the purview of surveillance: a world in which everything is normal and at the same time precariously abnormal, and in which a future that can be transformed remains a constant possibility. . . .

Symptoms and signs are only important for Surveillance Medicine to the extent that they can be re-read as risk factors. Equally, the illness in the form of the disease or lesion that had been the end-point of clinical inference under Hospital Medicine is also deciphered as a risk factor in as much as one illness becomes a risk factor for another. Symptom, sign, investigation and disease thereby become conflated into an infinite chain of risks. A headache may be a risk factor for high blood pressure (hypertension), but high blood pressure is simply a risk factor for another illness (stroke). And whereas symptoms, signs and diseases were located in the body, the risk factor encompasses any state or event from which a probability of illness can be calculated. This means that Surveillance Medicine turns increasingly to an extracorporal space—often represented by the notion of 'lifestyle'—to identify the precursors of future illness. Lack of exercise and a high fat diet therefore can be joined with angina, high blood cholesterol and diabetes as risk factors for heart disease. Symptoms, signs, illnesses, and health behaviours simply become indicators for yet other symptoms, signs, illnesses and health behaviours. Each illness of Hospital Medicine existed as the discrete endpoint in the chain of clinical discovery: in Surveillance Medicine each illness is simply a nodal point in a network of health status monitoring. The problem is less illness *per se* but the semi-pathological pre-illness at-risk state. . . .

[T]he risk factor network of Surveillance Medicine is read across an extracorporal and temporal space. In part, the new space of illness is the community. Community space incorporates the physical agglomeration of buildings and homes and their concomitant risks to health, though risks from the physical environment reflect more on nineteenth century concerns with sanitation and hygiene. Twentieth century surveillance begins to focus more on the grid of interactions between people in the community. . . .

Risk factors, above all else, are pointers to a potential, yet unformed, eventuality. For example, the abnormal cells discovered in cervical cytology screening do not in themselves signify the existence of disease, but only indicate its future possibility. The techniques of Surveillance Medicine—screening, surveys, and public health campaigns—would all address this problem in terms of searching for temporal regularities, offering anticipatory care, and attempting to transform the future by changing the health attitudes and health behaviours of the present. Illness therefore comes to inhabit a temporal space. . . .

Surveillance Medicine maps a different form of identity as its monitoring gaze sweeps across innovative spaces of illness potential. The new dimensionality of identity is to be found in the shift from a three-dimensional body as the locus of illness to the four-dimensional space of the time-community. Its boundaries are the permeable lines that separate a precarious normality from a threat of illness. Its experiences are inscribed in the progressive realignments implied by emphases on symptoms in the eighteenth century, signs in the nineteenth and early twentieth, and risk factors in the late twentieth century. Its calculability is given in the never-ending computation of multiple and interrelated risks. Its subject and object is the 'risky self'.

# 12

# IRUS BRAVERMAN

## ZOOLAND

### The Institution of Captivity

Sometimes public sentiment and action can be shaped by surveillance practices even if the objects of scrutiny are not humans. In her book *Zooland*, Irus Braverman explores zoos as highly bureaucratic and intentionally designed sites committed to cultivating conservationist values in wider society. The following excerpt draws attention to some of the contradictions of zoos' manufacturing a sense of proximity to "wildness" through artificial and often manipulative means.

\*\*\*

The visual display of nonhuman animals is central to the zoo's construction of nature. This visual display also exposes an inherent contradiction in the mission of contemporary American zoos: in contrast to the old-style cage exhibits, where animals were fully and constantly exposed to the gaze of the public, a convincing nature display inevitably renders less control over the animal and thus over what zoogoers will see. Moreover, the very act of seeing animals, which is an essential component of the zoo's mission, already undermines the animal's wildness and thus the authenticity of the zoo's message.

In light of the near-consensus among zoo professionals about zoo animals being wild, how do they explain that wild animals can actually be seen in zoo exhibits? According to Tom Mason, Toronto Zoo's curator of birds and invertebrates: "The animals here allow themselves to be seen. They wouldn't allow themselves to be seen by humans, their number one predators, in the wild. But here they feel safe to show themselves. Otherwise, there would be much less sense in keeping them in captivity." In other words, Mason assigns agency to the zoo animal by describing its willingness to submit itself to human inspection. Ironically, then, the animal's choice to expose itself to humans is what reifies its wildness. . . .

Zoo designers have come up with an array of spatial tricks to bridge the inherent contradiction posed by the fact that seeing wild animals undermines their wildness. . . . The glass panel is a central feature of the Louisville exhibit and one of the more common tricks used by contemporary North American zoo designers.

Adapted from aquarium design, glass panels enable visitors to get "real close, literally face-to-face, with the animal." The glass also enables a variety of vantage points and a level of visual domination that could never be achieved with the old-fashioned barred cage. Animals can now be viewed from the front, side, and back, topside and bottom, thus creating a controlled intimacy between observer and observed. . . .

Vanishing mesh is yet another trick used at zoo exhibits to enable heightened vision. . . . While permitting an unobstructed view for zoogoers, the mesh also maintains a physical barrier to movement between various animal species and between animals and humans.

An additional tactic for the enhancement of seeing involves the placement of temperature-controlled places at strategic viewing points. This tactic attracts animals to use these spaces, in turn exposing them to the eyes of visitors. For example, exhibit designers use light to attract lizards to high visibility locations and comfortably heated resting spots for certain primates and large cats where they can be seen by visitors. Additionally, the animals' hiding places—secure and nesting spots—are often designed to be near windows and viewing points. According to Gwen Howard, "it's really a kind of staged reality. You force them to do the thing they would naturally do, [but to do it] in a prime viewing spot."

But there is more to exhibit design than the closeness and convenience of seeing. Zoo designers create some exhibits with the intention of fostering a sense of awe and respect toward zoo animals, especially primates. This is achieved by elevating the exhibit spaces so that the human gaze is directed upward rather than downward. . . . The visual dynamics between humans and animals at the zoo are designed to promote a sense of wonder toward a remote nature that cannot be touched nor looked directly in the eye, a nature that can only be known through managed observation. . . .

Whereas the zoo's publicly visible spaces have transformed over time to exhibit naturalistic features, its invisible holding areas have arguably not changed much since the turn of the century. . . . An American Zoological Association conference paper dated 1995 states . . . that, "It is still the rule rather than the exception for most zoo animals to spend the greater part of each day in concrete cubes of cages." A bifurcated space is thereby constructed: a visible stage outdoors, which follows a naturalistic design that hides human features, and an invisible backstage indoors, which does nothing to conceal such human management. . . .

The most intense form of human management that occurs in the holding areas is animal training by zoo staff. . . . Animals holding their tail out of a cage for a shot [of medicine] to win a positive reward in the form of a blueberry muffin are not exactly the image of wild nature that visitors expect to see at the zoo. Indeed, such everyday scenes of animal training are made invisible to the eyes of the zoo-going public. [The director of the Minnesota Zoo] explains that "all the management facilities—the holding areas, and the spaces for keepers—are parts that distract from the message of an animal in the environment. So I think it's basically about emphasizing the message of animals as a part of a habitat that leads to the desire to hide the infrastructure." . . .

In his article "Zoos and Eyes," Ralph Acampora compares the project of seeing animals at the zoo to pornography. Zoo and porn participants, he argues provocatively, are both visual objects whose meaning is shaped predominantly by the perversions of a patriarchal gaze. In Acampora's words, "Zoos are pornographic in that they make the nature of their subjects disappear precisely by overexposing them." For Acampora, the wildness of animals is negated by their observation in captivity, where their wildness cannot be expressed.

One need not adopt such a radical approach to recognize the importance of the gaze at the zoo. Michel Foucault situates the gaze at the nexus of knowledge and power. He famously applies Jeremy Bentham's panoptic design of a model prison to various institutions that practice order and power over human bodies—for instance, the military base, the asylum, the hospital, and the school—demonstrating how these institutions use the gaze to discipline their subjects. The gaze, Foucault asserts, is embedded within the institutional architecture so that it may function automatically. . . . Curiously, Bentham's architectural model was inspired by the design of Louis XIV's menagerie at Versailles, where animal stalls were enclosed by three walls, with bars facing a central pavilion from which the animals could be viewed.

Is the panopticon a relevant lens through which to look at the zoo? Is the zoo yet another institution—alongside prisons and asylums—that practices power through panoptic design? Many scholars believe that the answer to both questions is no. Some even claim that vision at the zoo triggers the opposite effects of those sought by the panopticon model: through being exposed to the human gaze, animals are disciplined to ignore the gaze rather than to internalize it. Moreover, scholars suggest that zoos make an effort to display their animals as if they were not in captivity, so that they may engage in behaviors that spectators imagine them performing in the wild. The ultimate goal of the zoo gaze, these scholars believe, is to acculturate animals sufficiently to ignore their human spectators. At the same time, the inward-focused gaze established by the panopticon might seem meaningless in the context of animals, since, unlike humans, they purportedly cannot ever be the full, realized subjects of discipline.

The rhetoric of punishment associated with human prisons, too, does not fit so well in the context of zoos. "Do you think we like seeing wild animals held in captivity?" curator Mason asks me in an interview. "The animals are deprived of their individual freedom in order to save the rest of their species and even their entire habitat," he says. The animals are, in other words, subject to a collective form of incarceration: collective not in the usual sense, but in the sense that they are individually imprisoned in the name of their particular animal collective and for actions performed by another collective: humans. This form of sacrifice recalls the essential paradox of Foucault's pastoral power: the shepherd who must mediate between the needs of the individual and those of the entire flock. Finally, unlike human prisoners, who are disciplined to act normatively and rewarded when they do so, the behavior of zoo animals typically does not make a difference for the course of their captivity. As ambassadors for their species, the animals have no say in the process of their incarceration.

For these reasons, some have suggested moving beyond the paradigm of the panopticon into that of the "zoopticon"—namely, "a kind of panopticon turned inside out." Others have suggested using a different framework altogether: the exhibition. The exhibition model entails the transfer of bodies and objects from restricted private domains into progressively more open and public arenas. Through the exercise of power to command and arrange things and bodies for public display, exhibitionary technologies seek to enable people, en masse rather than individually, to see rather than to be seen and to know rather than to be known. At the exhibition, then, the focus is on the observer instead of on the observed. Tony Bennett further articulates this idea: "Not, then, a history of confinement but one of the opening up of objects to more public contexts of inspection and visibility: this is the direction of movement embodied in the formation of the exhibitionary complex. A movement which simultaneously helped to form a new public and inscribe it in new relations of sight and vision." The exhibitionary gaze is panoramic: it focuses on how those who gaze are influenced and disciplined. Instead of the many being inspected by the few, the panoramic gaze affords the inspection of the few by the many. Thomas Mathiesen refers to this system of control of the few by the many as a "synopticon."

Although both the panopticon and the exhibition (or the synopticon) models tell important parts of the story, neither fully accounts for the complexity of the human-animal gazes at the zoo. Rather than juxtaposing the panoptic and the exhibition, zoos demonstrate their interconnectivity. At the zoo, the two gazes work simultaneously. First, the traditional Foucauldian (or panoptic) gaze focuses on the body of the animal for the purpose of governing it. At the same time, the gaze is also panoramic, reflecting back upon the human masses that visit the zoo. In the context of accredited zoos in North America, the exhibitionary technology (or the synopticon) enables 175 million zoo visitors to observe 751,931 zoo animals every year. . . .

Whereas the traditional focus by the vast majority of panopticon scholars has been on disciplining the subject of the gaze, the zoo brings to the forefront the public education of the masses and their disciplining into a certain philosophy of nature and conservation. In the case of the prison, the public's gaze upon the panopticon functions through the power of deterrence and shame. By contrast, the spectacle of the zoo is meant to be powered by care and sympathy for the animals. . . . Whereas once zoos were in the business of entertainment through taxonomic exhibitions, now they discipline the public into caring about nature. . . .

At the zoo, heightened vision is a tool for disciplining zoogoers into a particular conservation etiquette that relies on carefully drawn associations between zoo and wild animals, and between the conduct of zoogoers and that of an abstract human collective. By inspiring their visitors to care for wildlife, zoos also delegate their own power of care to the public. And as care by zoos is bestowed upon both individual animals and the flock, the public, too, is educated to care for both the single animal subject and the entire flock. Human zoogoers are thus disciplined by the zoo's institutional gaze to become caregivers—or, in Foucauldian terms, shepherds.

# SECTION 3

# STATE AND AUTHORITY

///////////////////////////////////////////////////////////////////////////////////////////////////////////////////////////////////

Concerns with questions of power and authority are at the very heart of surveillance studies. State power, in particular, has been a persistent focus for scholars from across the many disciplines that contribute to this field. Although surveillance has existed in some form throughout history, there are good reasons for its association with the rise of the modern nation-state. The function of the "the police," broadly understood in the eighteenth century as what Foucault (1991) would later call governmentality (or the "conduct of conduct"), was theorized in emerging nation-states in Europe as the role the state should have in providing protection to its citizens. Thus, the first excerpt in this section—by the preeminent Prussian liberal jurist Johann Gottlieb Fichte—provides us with a description of ideal police states as well-ordered societies. Fichte concentrated, for example, as much on the role of police in making sure that unscrupulous medical practitioners did not prescribe fake treatments to patients as he did on questions of state control of citizens. Nevertheless, Fichte clearly argues that the efficient functioning of the state depends on identification (see more on this in Section 4) and the continuous surveillance of the population—ostensibly for the benefit of all. "No one," says Fichte, "must remain unknown to the police" (Fichte 1869: 378).

To present-day sensibilities, the construct of the police state might seem antithetical to modern democracies, but this is not necessarily the case. For example, Anthony Giddens (excerpted here) posits in *The Nation-State and Violence*, "aspects of totalitarian rule are a threat in all modern states, even if not all are threatened equally or in exactly the same ways" (Giddens 1985: 310). The expansion of surveillance supports such latent totalitarianism. Democracies have always depended on management of populations and limits to freedom. However, one of the key functions of the police has always been political policing, that is, the controlling of the boundaries of acceptable discourse and activity, and as Agamben (2005) argues, there is often a particular erosion of democracy at times of crisis. Finally, many liberal democratic states draw upon their imperialist histories to act in international arenas in ways that are contrary to their supposed democratic principles: waging illegal wars, depriving the citizens of other nation-states of their rights and freedoms, and supporting undemocratic regimes in other parts of the world when it suits their strategic aims.

The excerpt from Geoffrey Bowker and Susan Leigh Star's *Sorting Things Out* situates such imperial-colonial ordering practices in the context of identity schemes in apartheid South Africa. The authors consider the ways in which the state created, maintained, and changed pseudoscientific classifications in its efforts to establish and police racial hierarchies. Here we see how arbitrary forms of racial surveillance were codified in infamous bureaucratic systems and "passbooks." Symbolic violence of forceful, arbitrary categorization merged with—and supported—physical violence of territorial displacement, containment, and policing that could lead to punishment or death. Thus, colonial and postcolonial systems often provide extreme cases of state surveillance that are later modified and applied to domestic populations as well.

In the first half of the twentieth century, the liberality of the nation-state system in Europe—but also in places like Japan, which had deliberately set out to imitate and improve on the Western model—came under threat from contradictions within itself. These arose from two opposing wings of the conventional political spectrum: first from the left with the communist revolution in Russia and then from the right with Benito Mussolini's Fascists in Italy, Francisco Franco's Falangists in Spain, and Adolf Hitler's Nazi Party in Germany. Each of these developments spawned state surveillance practices that today serve as cautionary tales of the dangerous endpoints societies must avoid (e.g., concentration camps, gulags, Stasi police).

Because surveillance critics are perhaps too quick—and often inaccurate—in declaring that the latest state surveillance programs are authoritarian or totalitarian, it is worth exploring what these terms signify and the distinctions between them. Basic authoritarianism or autocracy is government by authority, and often by violence. Such authority tends to be directed to contingent and corrupt ends. Generalized surveillance can be unnecessary in such states, but the threat of surveillance, along with disappearances and violence, creates a climate of fear and intimidation. One can see examples of this in some of the military "juntas" in Latin America in the 1970s and 1980s. While these articulations of authoritarianism varied in their level of individual surveillance and degree of violence, they also varied in their stated political ideologies.

Totalitarianism, on the other hand, is a specific form of authoritarianism that imposes total control over society for ideological, even supposedly morally justifiable, ends. Totalitarianism implies total knowledge. First, this includes the production of knowledge, often with an intense state propaganda machine and control of media, cultural, and academic institutions. Second, it involves the collection of information through surveillance, usually overseen by secret police and a large bureaucracy of internal espionage. Related to this, totalitarian states often implement systems of terror, wherein people may be imprisoned, tortured, or killed for political—or even arbitrary—reasons. In part because of these shared characteristics, Hannah Arendt, in *The Origins of Totalitarianism* (1966), argued that Stalinism and Nazism had common roots and were similar in operation—for example, in giving priority to the needs of the state over society (as Agamben [2005] later argued of Nazi Germany, the state was founded on exception from the law). In this section, the excerpt by Maria Los, who was herself a refugee from Soviet-era Poland, takes these insights further with an unflinching portrayal of the reality of surveillance in totalitarian states.

To further illustrate this coupling of surveillance and totalitarianism, the next excerpt comes from *Stasiland*, Anna Funder's brilliant series of linked interviews with both state agents and those put under surveillance in former East Germany, the German Democratic Republic (GDR). In the GDR, perhaps the apex of state surveillance in the twentieth century, internal control was the business of the Ministry for State Security (Stasi). Its operations were characterized by an intensely paranoid style, particularly based around the recruitment and mobilization of legions of informers. By some estimates, the Stasi had 1 informer for every 6.5 people (Koehler 1999), leading to the development of a unique "Stasi consciousness" (Darnton 1993: 132)—or a justified concern that one might be watched or listened to anywhere, at anytime, and by anyone, even by family members. Funder draws attention to the numerous paradoxes of the rules that governed the Stasi, which seem to have been a combination of the visions of Franz Kafka and George Orwell; for example, surveillance was only permitted of "enemies," but investigation itself meant that the target must, de facto, be an enemy.

The relationship of states to populations shifted significantly in the final decades of the twentieth century, catalyzing transformations in surveillance too. On one hand, there have been sustained trends in the privatization of government, deregulation of industry, and responsibilization of people to meet their basic needs (Bourdieu 1998; Brown 2006; Harvey 2005; Wacquant 2009). This process is furthered through cultural shifts that normalize the commodification of all aspects of life, effectively establishing new forms of governmentality organized around market-based freedoms (Rose 1999). On the other hand, the state has reaffirmed its role in security provision, military campaigns, and internal policing of racialized minorities and the poor (e.g., through the prison-industrial complex), all of which are heavily supported by private companies and contractors. In the final excerpt in this section, Cindi Katz analyzes some of the implications of neoliberal responsibilization, where individuals are called upon to ensure social reproduction—particularly, in her examples, with child safety

Stasi smell samples for dog tracking, undated, John Steer, courtesy of the Stasi-Museum, Berlin, ASTAK.

and care—in the absence of state programs. As parents turn to surveillance technologies to do so, homes become mini-states that aggravate racial and class tensions more broadly, while leaving fundamental causes of inequality and need unchallenged.

## REFERENCES

Agamben, Giorgio. 2005. *State of Exception.* Chicago: University of Chicago Press.

Arendt, Hannah. 1966. *The Origins of Totalitarianism.* New York: Harvest.

Bourdieu, Pierre. 1998. The Essence of Neoliberalism. *Le monde diplomatique,* December. Available from http://mondediplo.com/1998/12/08bourdieu [accessed July 24, 2016].

Brown, Wendy. 2006. American Nightmare: Neoliberalism, Neoconservatism, and De-Democratization. *Political Theory* 34 (6):690–714.

Darnton, Robert. 1993. *Berlin Journal, 1989–1990.* New York: W. W. Norton.

Fichte, Johann Gottlieb. 1869. *The Science of Rights.* Translated by A. E. Kroeger. Philadelphia: J. B. Lippincott.

Foucault, Michel. 1991. Governmentality. In *The Foucault Effect: Studies in Governmentality,* edited by G. Burchell, C. Gordon, and P. Miller, 87–104. Chicago: University of Chicago Press.

Giddens, Anthony. 1985. *The Nation-State and Violence (Critique of Historical Materialism Vol. II).* Cambridge, UK: Polity.

Harvey, David. 2005. *A Brief History of Neoliberalism.* Oxford: Oxford University Press.

Koehler, John O. 1999. *Stasi: The Untold Story of the East German Secret Police.* Boulder, CO: Westview.

Rose, Nikolas S. 1999. *Powers of Freedom: Reframing Political Thought.* New York: Cambridge University Press.

Wacquant, Loïc. 2009. *Punishing the Poor: The Neoliberal Government of Social Insecurity.* Durham, NC: Duke University Press.

# 13

# JOHANN GOTTLIEB FICHTE

## FOUNDATIONS OF NATURAL RIGHT

The principles of the modern European nation-state were set down by the liberal Prussian jurist Johann Gottlieb Fichte in the late eighteenth century. The application of these principles relies heavily on the institution of the "police," a broad term that includes all agents of the state concerned with the monitoring of people and enforcement of laws, including issues as diverse as fire prevention, fraud, and medical malpractice, in addition to security. Surveillance is essential to this. The implied contract was that citizens would be known to the police at all times, and, in return, the police would protect citizens' bodies, property, and rights, including the protection of women from rape. However, very importantly, Fichte argued that this police surveillance must be open and not secret. Secret surveillance, in his view, undermines the relationship between citizens and the state.

\*\*\*

It is through the police that the mutual influence, the ongoing reciprocal interaction, between the state and its subjects first becomes possible. Accordingly, the police is one of the absolutely necessary requirements of a state, and an account of the police in general belongs to a pure doctrine of natural right.

The state has a twofold relation to its subjects. On the one hand, it has duties to them, namely the duty to protect them as per its contract with them; on the other hand, it has rights, namely the right to require that they fulfill their duties as citizens and obey the laws. Instances where such duties or rights arise are mediated by the police; in both cases it is the mediating link between the state and its subjects. Just as a judicial verdict relates to positive law in connection with citizens, so the police relates to the positive law in connection with state authority. The police power makes it possible for the law to be applied. . . .

If there were a prohibition against being on the street at certain hours of the night without a light, that would be a police law, and its intention would be to make it easier for everyone to be seen at night. No one is harmed if a person happens to be on the street without a light; but in the darkness it would be quite easy for that person to cause harm, and it is just this possibility that ought to be eliminated. If someone violates a police law, he has only himself to blame for the troubles that might befall him as a result, and he may be punished for it as well.

The principal maxim of every well-constituted police power must be the following: *every citizen must be readily identifiable, wherever necessary, as this or that particular person.* Police officers must be able to establish the identity of every citizen, which can only be accomplished as follows. Everyone must always carry an identity card with him, issued by the nearest authority and containing a precise description of his person; this applies to everyone, regardless of class or rank. Since merely verbal descriptions of a person always remain ambiguous, it might be good if important persons (who therefore can afford it as well) were to carry accurate portraits in their identity cards, rather than descriptions. No one will be allowed to take up residence in any place without first disclosing, by means of his identity card, his identity and last place of residence. Below we shall see a remarkable example of what can be achieved with the use of such identity cards. But in order not to prevent citizens from enjoying even the innocent pleasure of remaining anonymous, police officers must be prohibited—on pain of punishment—from demanding to see identity cards out of mere whim or curiosity, but may do so only when it is necessary to verify the person's identity; in which case—if it should become an issue—they must be required to justify why it was necessary.

The state does not know what goes on inside a person's house; but it does have the authority to supervise what happens on the street that a person must, after all, traverse in order to enter his house. Therefore citizens cannot assemble inside a house without the police knowing about it; and the police have the power, as well as the right (since the street is subject to their authority), to prevent such an assembly, if it arouses their suspicion. If so many people assemble that public security is threatened—and any assembly can pose such a threat if it is strong enough to resist the armed power of local authorities—then the police shall demand an explanation of their intentions, and watch to make sure that they actually do what they claim to be doing. In such a situation, a person's right over his house ceases to exist; or, if the owner of the house does not want that to happen, then the group must assemble in a public building. The situation is the same when people gather in the streets, in marketplaces, and so on: the police have the right to prevent, or to oversee, such gatherings. And so the state must issue laws saying that, depending on the circumstances, not more than a certain number of people may assemble without first having announced their assembly and its purpose to the police, so that the police may take the appropriate measures. . . .

In addition to the duties of protection noted above, the executive authority also has the right to see to it that the laws (both civil and police laws) are obeyed. It must take responsibility for any offense committed within the state's territory, and it must apprehend the offender. But in order to oversee the laws in this way, it is obvious that the state does not need any special institutions; rather these functions must be included in the protective institutions we have been describing. For if someone is *acting unjustly* and overstepping the law, it follows that someone else is in need of *being protected.*

The exclusive condition of the law's effectiveness and of the entire apparatus of the state is that every citizen know in advance and with absolute certainty that, if he violates the law, he will be discovered and punished in the manner clearly prescribed. If a criminal can count on a high degree of possibility that his crime will not be discovered and punished, what will deter him from committing it? And then—even though we might have the wisest of laws—wouldn't we still be living in the previous state of nature, where everyone does as he pleases and we remain dependent on the good will of others? And then it would also be manifestly unjust to punish with the law's full rigor the few who happen to get caught. For in seeing others around them go unpunished, did they not have reason to think that they, too, would escape punishment? How could they be deterred by a law that they couldn't help but regard as invalid? The derisive observation made by ordinary people everywhere concerning our state constitutions—that a person is punished not because of his crime, but because he was caught—is fitting and just. The requirement that the police, as servant of the law, apprehend every guilty party without exception is absolutely necessary. . . .

The sole source of every evil in our makeshift states . . . is *disorder* and the impossibility of bringing about order in them. In our states the only reason why finding a guilty party often involves such great and insurmountable difficulties, is that there are so many people the state fails to care for, and who have no determinate status . . . within it. In a state with the kind of constitution we have established here, every citizen has his own determinate status, and the police know fairly well where each one is at every hour of the day, and what he is doing. Everyone must work and has, if he works, enough to live on: there are no vagabonds . . . , for they are not tolerated anywhere within the state. With the help of the identity cards described above, every citizen can be identified on the spot. In such a state crime is highly unusual and is preceded by a certain unusual activity. In a state where everything is ordered and runs according to plan, the police will observe any unusual activity and take notice immediately; and so, for my part, I do not see how either the crime or the criminal can remain hidden.

It should also be noted here that the police power, as we have been describing it, requires neither spies nor secret agents. Secrecy is always petty, base, and immoral. If someone dares to do something, he must dare to do it before the eyes of the whole world. Besides, *to whom* is the state to give such a dishonorable task? Should the state itself encourage dishonor and immorality and make them into a duty? For once the state authorizes some of its citizens to act in secrecy, who can guarantee that these citizens will not make use of that secrecy to commit crimes?

Besides, why should the state want to observe its citizens secretly? So that the citizens will not realize that they are being observed. And why should they not realize that they are being observed? Either, so that they will reveal without inhibition what they think about the government and what they are planning against it, and thus become their own traitors; or, so that they will reveal what they know of other secret, illegal activities. The first is necessary only where the government and its subjects live in constant war with one another, where the subjects are unjustly oppressed and are striving to regain their freedom (as they have a right to do in a state of war). The second is necessary only where the police in general are so insufficiently watchful that something could have been kept secret from them. Neither reason applies in the state we have been describing here. The chief of police in Paris, who wanted his secret police to wear uniforms, became the laughing stock of a corrupt people. . . . In my opinion, he showed healthy, uncorrupted judgment. In the state we have been describing here, police officers can wear uniforms. They are just as much honorable witnesses to innocence as they are accusers in the event of a crime. How could rectitude possibly fear and hate the eye of such watchfulness?

# 14

# ANTHONY GIDDENS

# THE NATION-STATE AND VIOLENCE

Anthony Giddens is one of the most prominent living sociologists. He is the author of several general theoretical texts and, in the mid-1980s, a large multivolume project called *A Contemporary Critique of Historical Materialism*, which aimed to correct what he saw as several deficiencies in Marxist analysis and extend other aspects. Key to this was both a focus on the nation-state and on information and surveillance as inescapable elements of the power of both the nation-state and capital. The following excerpt, which comes from Volume 2 of the work, *The Nation-State and Violence*, investigates some of the many ways that the state depends upon and mobilizes surveillance to govern populations.

*** 

Historical materialism connects the emergence of both traditional and modern states with the development of material production . . . But equally significant, and very often the main means whereby such material wealth is generated, is the collection and storage of information, used to coordinate subject populations. Information storage is central to the role of 'authoritative resources' in the structuring of social systems spanning larger ranges of space and time than tribal cultures. Surveillance—control of information and the superintendence of the activities of some groups by others—is in turn the key to the expansion of such resources. . . .

Four clusterings of institutions can be distinguished in the conjunctions between capitalism, industrialism and the nation-state in the European societies [namely, Private property (Class), Surveillance, Transformation of nature (created environment), and Means of violence (military power)]. . . .

[A] very considerable development in modes of surveillance in the work-place is a primary feature of the emergence of industrial capitalism. But surveillance activities also expand the realm of the state itself, both within its borders and externally, as states begin to monitor the character of 'international relations'. . . . [S]urveillance is a medium of power which, whatever its ties to the ownership of private property, does not derive directly from it. The same comment applies to control of the means of violence.

My main thesis runs as follows. In industrial capitalism there develops a novel type of class system, one in which class struggle is rife but also in which the dominant class—those who own or control large capital assets—do not have or require direct access to the means of violence to sustain their rule. Unlike previous systems of class domination, production involves close and continuous relations between the major class groupings. This presumes a 'doubling-up' of surveillance, modes of surveillance becoming a key feature of economic organizations and of the state itself. The process of what . . . can be called the internal pacification of states is an inherent part of the expanding administrative co-ordination which marks the transition from the absolutist state to the nation-state. It is this internal pacification, which coincided historically with a prolonged period of absence of major wars between the European powers, that is the backdrop against which those in the 'classic traditions' of liberalism and socialism developed their views of the intrinsically pacific nature of industrial capitalism. . . .

Surveillance as the mobilizing of administrative power—through the storage and control of information—is the primary means of the concentration of authoritative resources involved in the formation of the nation-state. But it is accompanied by large-scale processes of internal transformation which have their origins in substantial part in the development of industrial capitalism and which essentially can be represented as producing internal pacification. The meaning of 'internal pacification' needs to be carefully understood and interpreted against the backdrop of the character of the internal administration of traditional states. . . .

'Disciplinary power' as described by Foucault depends perhaps primarily upon surveillance in the sense of information-keeping, especially in the form of personal records of life-histories held by the administrative authorities. But it also involves surveillance in the sense of direct supervision. In this sense, prisons and asylums share some of the generalized characteristics of modern organizations, including the capitalistic work-place, but a range of other organizations as well. All involve the concentration of activities either for a period of the day, or for a period in individuals' lives, within specially constructed locales. We may regard disciplinary power as a sub-type of administrative power in general. It is administrative power that derives from disciplinary procedures, from the use of regularized supervision, in order either to inculcate or to attempt to maintain certain traits of behaviour in those subject to it. Since, in previous eras, the monastery was one of the few locales in which large portions of people's lives could be concentrated, it is not surprising that some of the main features of disciplinary power originate there.

Disciplinary power is built around the time-table just like other more spatially diffuse aspects of modern organizations. But in this case time-tables are used to organize the time-space sequencing of settings of action within physically restricted locales, in which the regularity of activities can be enforced by supervision of individuals who might not otherwise acquiesce. Supervision demands either continued observation (as, for example, in the case of a teacher confronting a classroom of pupils) or ready access to such observation when it is thought necessary (as in the instance of devices that can be used to keep a watch upon prisoners when they are in their cells). In the sense that disciplinary power involves observation, Foucault is right to take Bentham's panopticon as its epitome, regardless of how far it was actually used as a model by those who designed or operated prisons or other organizational locales. But Foucault is mistaken in so far as he regards 'maximized' disciplinary power of this sort as expressing the general nature of administrative power within the modern state. Prisons, asylums and other locales in which individuals are kept entirely sequestered from the outside, as Goffman has made clear, have to be regarded as having special characteristics that separate them off rather distinctively from other modern organizations. In virtue of the fact that it is 'total' in its effects upon inmates, the former type of organization specifically disrupts the ordinary routines through which human agents live their lives. Goffman's notion of 'total institution' may or may not have been consciously coined in awareness of its affinities to 'totalitarianism' but certainly the concentration camp is, in recent times, the most dramatic and frightful example of enforced sequestration. The use of techniques of surveillance in such enclosed and brutally time-tabled settings undeniably has set a malign stamp on the modern era. One can see from this regard why Foucault chooses to accentuate the implications of those forms of disciplinary power that were perhaps often first established for essentially humanitarian motives. But we still have to insist that it is the work-place or, more generally, the specialized locale within which administrative power is concentrated, that is prototypical of the Western nation-state.

Characteristic of the work-place setting of the business firm or of the school, and most other modern organizations, is that the individual only spends part of the day within their walls; and that during that segment of the day the application of disciplinary power is more diffuse than in 'total institutions'. In all organizations, in virtue of the dialectic of control, there is some sort of 'effort bargain' that is explicitly or implicitly concluded by participants. But outside locales of forcible sequestration, this is one which both de jure and de facto acknowledges strict limits to the degree to which activities can be forcibly constrained to fit designated or desired patterns. . . .

This suggests that there are two substantive features of the association of disciplinary power with the modern state that should be distinguished. On the one hand, there takes place a marked impetus towards the expansion of this form of power, made possible by the establishment of locales in which the regularized observation of activities can be carried on in order to seek to control them. This is important for the nature of the modern workplace and, thereby, is a major tie connecting industrial capitalism (as a mode of economic enterprise) to the nation-state (as an administratively coordinated unit). It is not, as such, part of the directive influence of the state apparatus, but a generalized phenomenon enhancing internal pacification through promoting the discipline of potentially recalcitrant groups at major points of tension, especially in the sphere of production. This is distinguishable from a growth in disciplinary power linked to, and expressive of, the sanctions that those in the state apparatus are able to wield in respect of 'deviance'. It is this second aspect that is most closely meshed with the development of surveillance as the policing of the routine activities of the mass of the population, by specialized agencies separate from the main body of the armed forces.

Another aspect of internal pacification is of quite elemental importance. . . . This is the eradication of violence, and the capability to use the means of violence, from the labour contract—the axis of the class system. . . . In industrial capitalism—in contrast to pre-existing class systems— employers do not possess direct access to the means of violence in order to secure the economic returns they seek from the subordinate class. Marx entirely correctly laid considerable emphasis upon this, even if he did not pursue its implications. 'Dull economic compulsion', plus the surveillance made possible by the concentration of labour within the capitalistic work-place, replaces the direct possibility of coercion by the use of force. Of course, employers did not relinquish the use of sanctions of violence without some reluctance and the class struggles waged by workers have often involved violence. But these facts do not compromise the key importance of 'bourgeois rights' in the formation of a 'demilitarized' system of production. This is one of the most significant elements of the liberal-democratic state—that the rights of freedom of disposal of labour-power, for which the bourgeoisie actively fought, carry with them the intrinsic limitation of the power of employers in the work-place to hiring and firing workers and to supervising 'management'. These are not in any way negligible sources of control. However they are only possible in a society which has been internally pacified in other ways. . . .

A final characteristic of internal pacification . . . is the withdrawal of the military from direct participation in the internal affairs of state. It is this which seemed to many nineteenth-century thinkers to confirm the thesis of the essentially pacific character of industrial capitalism. What it involves, however, is not the decline of war but a concentration of military power 'pointing outwards' towards other states in the nation-state system. The consolidation of the internal administrative resources of the state dislocates administrative power from its strong and necessary base in the coercive sanctions of armed force. I do not want this statement to be misunderstood. In the nation-state, as in other states, the claim to effective control of the means of violence is quite basic to state power. But the registering of the more or less complete success of this claim, made possible by the expansion of surveillance capabilities and internal pacification, radically lessens the dependence of the state apparatus upon the wielding of military force as the means of its rule. . . .

Surveillance is an independent source of institutional clustering in all class-divided as well as modern societies. In its two aspects, surveillance is fundamental to social organizations of all types, the state being historically the most consequential form of organization, but nevertheless only being one organization among many others. In nation-states surveillance reaches an intensity quite unmatched in previous types of societal order, made possible through the generation and control of information, and developments in communication and transportation, plus forms of supervisory control of 'deviance'. These are in various ways quite decisively influenced by the expansion of capitalism, although again they are neither reducible nor inevitably tied to it once they come into existence. In stimulating the development of a class system not based upon the direct control of the means of violence on the part of the dominant class, in which violence becomes extruded from the labour contract, the emergence of capitalism serves to accentuate some key trends in the modern state. The successful monopoly of control of the means of violence in the hands of the state authorities is the other face of surveillance in the work-place and the control of deviance.

Once constituted in this way, in the context of the state system the nation-state increasingly becomes the pre-eminent form of political organization. Control of the means of violence becomes bound up with the role of professional armed forces, within a framework of industrialized war, while system integration depends in an essential way upon surveillance. This latter development, of course, does not render unimportant the control of the means of violence, particularly given the close connections that exist between industrialism and war. Nonetheless, the potential for military rule is thereby restricted, since in a modern state 'government' involves specialized administration and the participation of the population within a polyarchic dialectic of control.

Movements oriented to the enlargement of democratic participation within the polity should be seen as always . . . oriented towards redressing imbalances of power involved in surveillance. What 'democracy' means here has to be understood as inherently involved in the very contestations such movements promote. There is a basic flaw, however, in the thesis . . . that the expansion of organizations inevitably supplants 'democracy' with 'oligarchy'. The intensification of surveillance, which is the basis of the development of organizations in modern societies and in the world system as a whole is, on the contrary, the condition of the emergence of tendencies and pressures towards democratic participation. In each of its aspects surveillance promotes the possibility of the consolidation of power in the hands of dominant classes or elites. At the very same time, however, this process is accompanied by counter-influences brought to bear in the dialectic of control. . . .

The governability of a modern state concerns the success of the surveillance operations it is able to sustain, these in turn however only having some relevance in so far as they allow control over aspects of the day-to-day lives of the populace. What is important here is not so much the level of legitimacy a government can generate in respect of the mass of the population, as how far established patterns of social conduct are malleable in respect of state policies. . . .

Understood as the reflexive monitoring of social reproduction, surveillance has been important both to the consolidation of the world system in modern times and to the internal ordering of states. The questions raised by its role as a source of power can only increase in importance in the forseeable future. Intensified surveillance and totalitarian tendencies are intimately linked. This is not something which should lead us to despair, for administrative power and polyarchy are equally closely connected. There is not a direct relation between the expansion of the administrative power of states and political oppression. The more effectively states seek to 'govern', the more there is the likelihood of counter-balance in the form of polyarchic involvement.

# 15

# GEOFFREY C. BOWKER AND SUSAN LEIGH STAR

## SORTING THINGS OUT

### Classification and Its Consequences

As the authors say, the situation of South Africa under the apartheid system was an extreme one. Nonetheless, it is also a key case for understanding how states deploy surveillance to create categories and police the boundaries of those categories, regardless of their arbitrary nature. Geoffrey Bowker and Susan Leigh Star show how such categorizations are extremely consequential for the lives and life chances of people subjected to them.

\*\*\*

From the early days of Dutch settlement of South Africa, the de jure separation and inequality of people coexisted with interracial relationships. In the mid-nineteenth century charter of the Union, it was simply stated that "equality between White and coloured persons would not be tolerated." Various laws were enacted that reinforced this stance. When the Nationalists came to power in 1948, however, a much more detailed and restrictive policy, apartheid, was put into place. In 1950 two key pieces of legislation, the Population Registration Act and the Group Areas Act[,] were passed. These required that people be strictly classified by racial group, and that those classifications determine where they could live and work. Other areas controlled de jure by apartheid laws included political rights, voting, freedom of movement and settlement, property rights, right to choose the nature of one's work, education, criminal law, social rights including the right to drink alcohol, use of public services including transport, social security, taxation, and immigration. The brutal cruelty, of which these laws were the scaffolding, continued for more than four decades. Millions of people were dislocated, jailed, murdered, and exiled.

The racial classification that was so structured in the 1950s sought to divide people into four basic groups: Europeans, Asiatics, persons of mixed race or coloureds, and "natives" or "pure-blooded individuals of the Bantu race." The Bantu classification was subdivided into eight main groups, with Xhosa and Zulu the most numerous. The coloured classification was also complexly subdivided, partially by ethnic criteria. The terribly fraught (and anthropologically inaccurate) word Bantu was chosen in preference to African (or black African), partly to underscore Nationalist desires to be recognized as "really African."

State authorities, touching every aspect of work, leisure, and education obsessively enforced apartheid. In a bitter volume detailing his visit to South Africa, Kahn notes:

> Apartheid can be inconvenient, and even dangerous: Ambulances are segregated. A so-called European injured in an automobile accident may not be picked up by a non-European ambulance (nor may a non-European by a European one), and if a white man has the misfortune to bleed to death before an appropriate mercy vehicle materializes, he can comfort himself in extremis by reflecting that he will most assuredly be buried in an all-white cemetery. (Nonwhite South African doctors may not perform autopsies on white South African corpses.)

"Separate development" was the euphemism used by the Nationalist party to justify the apartheid system. It argued from a loose eugenic basis that each race must develop separately along its natural pathway, and that race mingling was unnatural. This ideology was presented in state-sanctioned media as a common-sense policy. Despite that fact that it was required by law, it often took months or years for blacks to acquire passbooks, during which time they were in danger of jail or being deported to one of the black homelands. . . .

Any form of interracial sexuality was strictly forbidden by a series of immorality laws, some of which predated apartheid.

Ormond states that "Between 1950 and the end of 1980 more than 11,500 people were convicted of interracial sex; anything from a kiss on up". . . . These sexual borders were vigorously patrolled by police. Ormond continues, "Special Force Order 025A/69 detailed use of binoculars, tape recorders, cameras, and two-way radios to trap offenders. It also spelled out that bedsheets should be felt for warmth and examined for stains. Police were also reported to have examined the private parts of couples and taken people to district surgeons for examination." . . .

For black South Africans, the system of segregation included a legal requirement to carry a pass book, a compilation of documents attesting to birth, education, employment history, marriage, and other life events. . . . The books were over fifty pages long. No black was allowed to be in a white area for more than seventy-two hours without special permission, including government authorization for a work contract (such as that for a live-in servant). The consequences of transgression were severe, as Frankel notes. "The inestimable number of 'illegals' in the urban areas live a life of harassment that is Kafkaesque in its proportions, yet even those fortunate enough to qualify for urban status are faced with a harsh and insecure daily existence. . . .

A Foucauldian system of control of all people except whites ensued (although by law the restrictions applied to whites entering proscribed areas, this was rarely enforced and whites did not carry pass books). Blacks were the major targets of scrutiny, and the pass book system allowed for comprehensive surveillance of their actions. "The whole system has been extended and rationalised over the years by widening the categories of officials who can formally demand the production of passes, and by linking this up with sophisticated computer technology centred on the reference book bureau of the Department of Plural Relations in Pretoria."

These data were entered into a centralized database that was cross-referenced across the different domains. Kahn notes:

> Every African over sixteen must have on his person what is called a reference book. . . . His pass book must contain particulars about every job he has had, every tax he has paid, and every x-ray he had taken. . . .

In addition to the pass book system regulating the lives of black South Africans, the state attempted to enforce many other forms of segregation. Christopher Hope, in his novel *A Separate Development*, writes of petty apartheid such as the segregation of buses and benches:

> One lived, of course, surrounded by such signs and notices. Most of them, however, served some clear purpose, the point of which everyone recognized as being essential for their survival: WHITES ONLY on park benches; BANTU MEN HERE on nonwhite lavatories; or INDIAN BENCH; or DEFENSE FORCE PROPERTY: PHOTOGRAPHS FORBIDDEN; or SECOND CLASS TAXI; or THIS PLAYGROUND IS RESERVED FOR CHILDREN OF THE WHITE GROUP. And, of course, people were forever being prosecuted for disobeying one or other of these instructions.

For apartheid to function at this level of detail, people had to be unambiguously categorizable by race. Despite the legal requirement for certainty in race identification, however, this task was not to prove so easy. Many people did not conform to the typologies constructed under the

law: especially people whose appearance differed from their assigned category, or who lived with those of another race, spoke a different language from the assigned group, or had some other historical deviation from the pure type. New laws and amendments were constantly being debated and passed. . . . By 1985, the corpus of racial law in South Africa exceeded 3,000 pages.

Both the scientific theories about race and the street sense of terms were confused. . . . The original official sorting by race after the 1950 Population Registration Act derived from the categories checked on the 1951 census returns. An identity number was given to each individual at that time. The census director was in charge of deciding everyone's racial classification, on the basis of the census data, and, where necessary, other records of vital statistics. Horrell notes, "But this classification is by no means formal. Section *Five(3)* of the Population Registration Act provides that if *at any time* it appears to the Director that the classification of a person is incorrect, after giving notice to the person concerned, specifying in which respect the classification is incorrect, and affording him or her an opportunity of being heard, he may alter the classification in the register." . . .

So in the case of apartheid, we see the scientistic belief in race difference on the everyday level and an elaborate formal legal apparatus enforcing separation. At the same time, a much less formal, more prototypical approach uses an amalgam of appearance and acceptance and the on-the-spot visual judgments of everyone from police and tram drivers to judges—to perform the sorting process on the street. . . .

Apart from the categories themselves, the technology associated with the reclassification process was crude. Combs were sometimes used to test how curly a person's hair was. Horrell notes that barbers were sometimes called as witnesses to testify about the texture of the person's hair.

One source mentioned expert testimony from the South African Trichological Institute (presumably an organization for the scientific study of hair). Affidavits were taken from employers, clergy, neighbors, and others to establish a general acceptance or repute. . . . Complexion, eyes, facial features, and bone structure were examined by board officials, and they could summon any relative and examine them in this way as well. . . . Horrell notes, "It is reported that some were even asked 'Do you eat porridge? Do you sleep on the floor or in a bed?' Some Coloured people said that they had been told to turn sideways so that the officials could study their profiles." Folk theories about race abounded; differences in cheekbones, even the notion that blacks have softer earlobes than whites, were taken seriously. . . .

The "pencil test" was recounted by many who had undergone the reclassification ordeal. Sowden gives us the following passage, quoting at first from an old black woman describing apartheid to him:

> "If you're black and pretend you're
>   Coloured, the police has the
>   pencil test."

"The pencil test?"

"Oh, yes, sir. They sticks a pencil in your hair and you has to bend down, and if your hair holds the pencil, that shows it's too woolly, too thick. You can't be Coloured with woolly hair like that. You got to stay black, you see." . . .

Not all systems attempt to classify people as globally, or as consequentially, as did apartheid; yet many systems classify users by age, location, or expertise. Many are used to build up subtle (and not-so-subtle) profiles of individuals based on their filiations to a myriad of categories. In the process of making people and categories converge, there can be tremendous torque of individual biographies. The advantaged are those whose place in a set of classification systems is a powerful one and for whom powerful sets of classifications of knowledge appear natural. For these people the infrastructures that together support and construct their identities operate particularly smoothly (though never fully so). For others, the fitting process of being able to use the infrastructures takes a terrible toll. To "act naturally," they have to reclassify and be reclassified socially.

# 16

# MARIA LOS

# THE TECHNOLOGIES OF TOTAL DOMINATION

Maria Los, like the more widely known Zygmunt Bauman, was a scholar who lived under communist Poland's totalitarian regime and was forced to flee the country. The following excerpt draws upon that experience and combines with it an analysis based heavily on Hannah Arendt's work on totalitarianism. As Los explains, whereas the Panopticon might produce order through extreme visibility and clear expectations for behavior, totalitarian societies thrive on inscrutable bureaucratic processes and uncertain consequences for infractions. In such societies, domination over people is achieved through the cultivation of terror (e.g., concentration camps) and the amassing of knowledge (e.g., through a vast network of informants). Such an environment creates a culture of fear, suspicion, and collective guilt, transforming everyone into a *potential* informant for the state.

\*\*\*

In so far as Foucault's generalized Panoptical-disciplinary mechanism secures stable predictability of social arrangements and a good fit between the formation of the individual and realistic opportunities for advancement and stabilization, it has no place in the totalitarian movement-state. Accordingly, any references to normal standards, practical learning sequences and natural/temporal limits to human capabilities contradict the totalitarian assumption of *tabula rasa* and infinite malleability of human beings. A discourse of life goals, career planning, qualifications and recognized credentials is alien and antithetical to the totalitarian project. . . .

To pursue total, monistic domination, the [totalitarian] ruling structure cannot be itself monolithic and coherent, yet it must generate a belief in a menacing deeper unity, hidden underneath and perpetuated behind the scenes. The ambiguity of the power arrangement between the movement (the Party) and the administration (the State) is deliberate and inherent in the project of total domination and its globalization. While the former rules with no formal legal basis, the latter is a façade trapped over a legal frame. The lack of clear hierarchy, the vagueness, shapelessness and duplication of functions and services prevents establishment of a stable government that might lose revolutionary zeal and start to perceive the masses not as an expandable matter but a *population* to govern. The masses need to acquire a Kafkaesque sense that the true power structure does not lie in the visible maze of offices, but is deeply hidden and profoundly secret. . . .

All this produces a sense of conspiracy and the type of mentality that [Hannah Arendt said] "sees every conceivable action as an instrument for something entirely different." Nothing can be taken at its face value. There are, therefore, no valid criteria for pragmatic action or even for positioning oneself within the maze. This unique type of Panopticon serves to confuse and immobilize the masses without giving them practical programs for stability and advancement. . . .

Within the opaque power maze, Supreme Leader's role has some affinity to Bentham's vision of the hidden but seemingly all-knowing Inspector. What counts is social awareness of his watchful presence behind the scenes—his *apparent,* God-like omnipresence. The Inspector is not a fiction, he must really exist, but to maintain the fiction of his divine qualities he should only sporadically reveal himself in person. His power "over the prisoners derives from his invisibility, or more precisely, his 'invisible omnipresence'." The effectiveness of the Panoptical surveillance hinges on an image, a fiction, a state of mind. There is, however, an added mechanism at work in a totalitarian Panopticon, which is possible because of the prevailing *conspiracy consciousness.* It allows people to simultaneously view the Leader as an omnipotent, all-seeing god (or monster) and place blame for many hated policies and atrocities on his underlings, who are believed to have somehow escaped his gaze.

The executive power is concentrated in the hands of the political secret police whose quasi-invisible presence is felt everywhere. Yet secret services themselves have to be multiplied and set against each other for mutual supervision, surveillance and vigilance. Beyond the initial phase, when they focus on crashing the actual opposition, their main functions centre on spreading terror and compiling knowledge. Total domination cannot be achieved without terror and the particular knowledge it produces and requires. It starts as a tool for suppression of strife, but evolves into a complex power technology calculated to achieve such long-term goals as interiorization of fear, breaking of social bonds, destruction of predictability and creation of new categories of *objective enemies.* . . .

The entire institutional regime machinery is geared to prevention and sanitation of any forms of knowledge that may emerge spontaneously or through professional efforts. All sectors and agencies of the totalitarian regime, such as the statistical office, education, health, penal system, industrial complex, army and police, are generating an enormous amount of information selectively tailored to meet specific political expectation, propaganda effects, censorship criteria and economic quota. Endless forms are filled with streams of data contrived in anticipation of the centre's wishes. A paper reality is created that takes life of its own. It is geared to negation of problems and fabrication of success. It also serves to create in subjects a surreal sense of being oppressed by make-believe reality. *The constant tension between the (Weberian) logic of bureaucracy and the (il)logic of the ideologically-driven party results in de-rationalization of bureaucracy and bureaucratization of ideology and, therefore, routinization and normalization of fiction.* The bureaucratized ideology substitutes a fiction for reality and reproduces it in ever more inclusive domains.

Amidst this huge machinery, bent on producing diverse types of deliberately manipulated knowledge, secret police services are practically the only agency expected to maintain a firm grip on reality. While various university departments are being closed or decimated, secret services hire or secure collaboration of experts to assist them in their diagnostic tasks. They have to be careful, however, not to pass to the Leader findings he does not want to hear. They continuously collect and process information about individuals, families, communities, organizations, agencies, industries and all other social and economic entities. This heavily guarded secret knowledge—which is only selectively shared with the top political leadership—is conditioned and structured according to the logic and mission of the security apparatus. It consists of two main types of knowledge: the operational surveillance knowledge (contained in individual/group/site files) and aggregated, diagnostic knowledge about various spheres and sectors of society. The latter may and occasionally does inform policy-making/ implementation processes.

The concentration camp is at the core of the secret knowledge-production processes and their rationality is measured by the progress in mastering the logistics of mass transportation, slave labour and extermination machinery ostensibly in the service of ideological purity. Both Soviet and German authorities kept detailed records of prisoners, the categories they fell into as well as other particulars, such as their movements, family ties, [beliefs] or creed, tasks and fate. Both regimes experimented and perfected their techniques. They used either hardened violent criminals or prisoner-functionaries selected from among the political prisoners to control the general inmate population; they multiplied camp categories; revised selection, segregation and distribution techniques; synchronized the intake of new prisoners with fluctuation in demand for slave labour, and constantly searched for more efficient ways of killing and of eliminating corpses. They conducted pseudo-scientific experiments on the captive populations in order to develop and test new techniques of surveillance, brain-washing, genetic engineering or chemical and biological warfare. . . .

According to Bentham, the ingenuity of his Inspection House lies in its double effect, whereby the inmates appear "to the keeper, as a *multitude*, though not, a *crowd*; [while] to themselves they are solitary and sequestered individuals." Social atomization precludes rebellion. Totalitarian projects strive to achieve social atomization through forced collectivization and total surveillance of the society at large. The role of mass movements is not to bring people together as individuals but rather as insignificant particles, assembled together to assume appearance of *masses* following the leader. All eyes are supposed to be turned first of all towards the Leader (or his image) and only then towards those around them in order to make sure that they do not deviate from the path. *The strength of the masses rests on the feeling of insignificance by individuals. The totalitarian technology of the self must strive to purge the self and replace it with indivisible "we."* . . .

In a totalitarian Panopticon, judgement is based on the individual's *interconnected appearance* (with whom one may be connected) and on the secret police reports. This arrangement fosters self/other control, guilt by association (collective responsibility) and dissolution of the self. *It totalizes through atomization, both of which are essentially objectifying.* It works to erase the possibility of individual resistance. Through a simple device known as "guilt by association," family, friends and acquaintances of the accused are automatically considered suspect or contaminated. To save their skin, they are prone to be transformed into the doomed person's enemies by volunteering information, denouncing and berating the accused. . . .

In his comments on the Greco-Roman civilization, Foucault draws attention to the theme of care of the self that permeated moral reflection of the time. To willingly relate to oneself, know oneself, care for oneself, improve oneself, master one's appetites, were all imperatives around which *ethics as a conscious practice of freedom* revolved. It can be argued that there is some, even if tenuous, affinity between these moral techniques of antiquity and the surreptitious cultivation of the self under the totalitarian regime. While the former acquired meaning through the contrast to slavery, the latter represents a form of resistance against massive political technologies of eradication of the self. This is evident in the extraordinary importance of the true, tested, *self*-nourishing friendship, the constant practicing of self control, separation of public acting and private living (if any privacy still remains) and conscious efforts to know (while also denying or rationalizing) the limits of one's courage, humanity or even sheer physical fortitude.

Yet, moral strategies to salvage (and nourish) the self are inevitably combined with and often compromised by strategies of survival that require betrayal of the ethical self. In extreme situations of total domination, a radical detachment from one's self may be the best available strategy. Some concentration camp survivors testify that only by separating themselves from their selves could they distance themselves from the dehumanization visited upon them. They became strangers to themselves, sometimes to the point of identifying with the oppressor.

On a different level, the memoirs of Tadeusz Grygier, Polish lawyer-psychologist, survivor of the Soviet gulag, offer remarkable insights into his predicament. A man well tutored and experienced in powers of self-care/knowledge, he found them invaluable in achieving a state of self-detachment and a willful conversion from a victim into researcher. "Instead of seeing myself as a prisoner destined to die in the camp, I redefined myself as a lucky scientist who had penetrated the forbidden zone of the gulags . . ., and who was able to observe the effects of oppression on other prisoners, myself and our guards." He morally neutralized the brutal regime and learned to deal with arising issues by using his understanding of the working of the system, its representatives and its victims, thereby testing his hypotheses in practice.

Cultivating and displaying powers of observation is not a strategy of survival commonly adopted in totalitarian societies, however. There is always danger of seeing too much or appearing to be seeing too much. The surveillance principle typical for these regimes may be viewed as an enhanced version of the classical Panopticon. In this form of surveillance, *each member of the society is also aware of being turned into a potential policeman for others, a secret eye of the system.* Since the totalitarian secret security complex recruits and cultivates a web of secret informers, who are obliged to spy and report on their family, friends, neighbours, co-workers, strangers, etc., everyone must be suspected of being one. It is prudent to do so. Consequently, not only are people constantly and acutely aware that they are watched by dispersed, unidentified secret surveillance agents, but they are also conscious that others view them as potential agents of secret police. *In addition to becoming agents of their own subjection, they are thus turned into objects used as tools in policing others.* This happens without their participation, simply by virtue of being in the orbit of totalitarian control.

Within such a double-edged Panoptical arrangement, 'inmates' have no way of verifying who is a secret agent and have no way of preventing others from suspecting them of being spies. As a result, people try to reduce not just their visibility but also their appearance of *being, seeing and knowing.* This mechanism reinforces one of the key premises and effects of the totalitarian project— the erosion of citizenship, trust and basic social solidarity. The terror-induced fear is transformed into a normalized fear, which leads to elaborate conformity-projecting strategies. Their effect is the formation of psychological and mental straightjacket in the form of a set of taboos and magical lines one should never cross.

# 17

# ANNA FUNDER

## STASILAND

Stories from behind the Berlin Wall

During the Cold War, the Ministry for State Security (Stasi) in East Germany was a key force in transforming the country into a police state. Through its technological surveillance (e.g., wiretapping phones), intelligence apparatus, and extensive network of citizen spies, it grew by spreading fear, forever enlisting more citizens into its ranks. Anna Funder's book *Stasiland* documents the stories of citizens—as well as of informers and Stasi agents—shortly after the fall of the Berlin Wall in 1989, noting the palpable terror people felt, but also their impressive efforts to resist the Stasi. The following excerpt details the story of one woman's encounter with a Stasi agent trying to recruit her as a spy.

*** 

Major N.

Then a card came in the letterbox. 'It seemed normal enough—a standard printed card as if I had to report to the police to have my ID renewed. It had spaces in it for them to handwrite my name, and the date and time of the appointment.'

She's not looking at me. She's hardly talking to me. Her eyes move around the room although there's not much to see: behind me the hot-water cistern over the sink with its little blue flame, to my left the door to the hall. Candlelight catches her face, etches cheekbone and chin. She is remembering as I watch, summoning presences more real than mine.

'There are some things—' she stops. 'I don't think I'll be able to remember this. I haven't remembered this.' I stick to small facts. 'Did you know what the card was about?'

'I thought I had overstayed my visa in Hungary. Usually they would just restamp your ID at the border and let you back in. I started preparing excuses in my mind. At the same time I said to myself: look, it can't be that bad! What can they do to me? I mean I wasn't afraid they'd collect me in the night and lock me up and torture me.'

Julia analysed the situation from every angle. In its later stages the regime stopped, for the most part, direct action (arrest, in-carceration, torture) against its people. It opted instead for other ways of silencing them, methods that Amnesty would find harder to chronicle. 'The typical thing that could happen to you in my day in the GDR [German Democratic Republic]—that your career was broken before it was begun—that had already happened to me! And now that I didn't even have the Italian boyfriend any more—what else could they want?'

The police station had a vast waiting hall. People stood silently in two long queues curled around the room, each one joined to a counter. The lines hardly moved. 'I took a number but then I realised I didn't know which queue was the right one,' she says. 'So I went up to the policewoman who was overseeing things. She looked at my card and said straight away:

"Ah Miss Behrend. You don't need to queue at all. You are to go directly to Room 118." '

Julia laughs at herself. 'I was pleased at first! I thought I had got out of standing in line.' Then she noticed that all the people in the queues were going into one of two rooms behind the counters, but neither of those was Room 118.

'I had to go by myself up several flights of stairs and down a long corridor, left around a corner and then left again. There were no other people around. I saw no-one enter or leave any of the rooms I passed. Room 118 was way over on the other side of the building.'

She knocked.

'Come in.'

There was a man alone behind a desk. The first thing she noticed was that he wore a western suit and a good tie. He stood up straight away, a small nod, his feet clicking together.

'Miss Behrend, I am N., Major,' he smiled and extended his hand.

And then, clear as a bell, 'Ministry of State Security.'

She felt fear, she says, 'like a worm in my belly.'

The man was not yet forty, with a wide face, and receding hair. He wore small round eyeglasses. He had a glowing suntan. He was friendly, in fact for GDR standards, exaggeratedly polite.

'Please,' he said, 'do sit down.' They sat. She thought it might still, perhaps, be about the overstayed visa.

But N. began, 'Such an attractive, intelligent young woman as yourself, Miss Behrend, perhaps you could explain to me why it is,' he smiled, 'that you are not working.'

This was it. Up until this moment it could all have been a product of her imagination: the boarding school, the headmaster's visit, the constant street searches, the failed exam, the 'friend's' warning, the cruising Lada, the extraordinary unemployment.

She was in shock. She spoke slowly.

'You must know why I have no job,' she said.

His voice was soft. He did not stop smiling. 'How would I know that, Miss Behrend?'

Her mind flew. She could see where this was going: she was going to be kicked out of the country. 'I thought it was my last chance to stay home,' she says. So she told him, straight out, 'Look, please, I don't want—I don't want to go to the west. But I think you people are forcing me out.' She realised she was imploring him. 'I must work somewhere. I am, after all, unemployed.'

'But Miss Behrend,' he said, 'how can that be?' He laced his fingers together on the desk. 'There is no unemployment in the German Democratic Republic.'

She could not answer.

He reached across his desk to a pile of papers and pulled them to him.

'First, I have some questions,' he said, 'about these letters.'

Julia looked at his hand and saw, under it, her own handwriting. She was confused. She looked closer. They were copies of her letters to the Italian boyfriend.

Julia had imagined all along that her mail might be being read. Sometimes letters she received from overseas had been brutally torn and taped back together with a sticker: 'Damaged in Transit.' 'It was ridiculous really,' she says. But, like all the other things, she had never thought about it for long.

Major N. laid the first letter flat on the desk and smoothed it out with both hands. He cleared his throat. To Julia's horror, he started to read it aloud. I think of the shame I would feel sitting opposite Major So-and-So in his office with these intimate things in his fingers. Shame at hearing your words turn into the universal banalities of love in his mouth. Julia and her boyfriend wrote to one another in English. Major N. had underlined in each letter the words he had not been able to find in his German-English dictionary.

'He sat there and he—' Julia stops and takes a sip of tea. It must be cold by now. It goes down the wrong way. She coughs and coughs, but puts her hand out to stop me helping, '—and he asked me,' she says in a choked voice, 'what they meant.'

The hairs on my forearms stand up. I have stopped looking at Julia now because in this dimness she ceased addressing her words to me some time ago. I am humbled for reasons I cannot at this moment unravel. I am outraged for her, and vaguely guilty about my relative luck in life.

Major N. took his time perfecting his translation. The words that were not in the dictionary were, mostly, the words of their private lovers' language. He asked her, 'what is the meaning of this?' and again, 'would you mind, please, explaining this term?' One long forefinger on her handwriting, or her lovers'. 'What about this?' he asked, touching the word *cocoriza* in a letter from her boyfriend.

'*Cocoriza*,' Julia told him, 'is the Hungarian word for corn.'

'What does this mean then, Miss Behrend, when your friend writes, "I want my little *cocoriza*"?'

She had to explain. On their holidays her hair had lightened to the colour of corn. *Cocoriza* was his pet name for her.

'Thank you, Miss Behrend.' Then, in his western suit, with his foreign manners and his exaggerated courtesy, Major N. proceeded through her relationship, one letter at a time.

'It took quite a while,' Julia says in a faraway voice. Her eyes are fixed in the middle distance. Major N. was thorough. There was a pile of her letters to the Italian. There was a pile of his letters back to her. This man knew everything. He could see when she had had doubts, he could see by what sweet-talking she had let herself be placated. He could see the Italian boyfriend's longing laid bare, and his invention, for his own pleasure, of his faraway girl.

N. insinuated he knew—as Julia surely also realized—that the Italian had an image of her that didn't quite hit the mark. He flattered her. 'You are more complex, I think Miss Behrend, and much more intelligent than he gives you credit for.' When he was done reading, pointing, probing, he straightened the two piles of letters and put them back to the side of the desk. 'Let us discuss your friend for a moment now,' he said, 'shall we?'

He started to tell Julia about her boyfriend. 'They weren't particularly spectacular things,' she says. 'But they were things I could not have known because I couldn't go to Italy and see for myself.' Julia assumes that the Stasi had people in Italy. 'He was even sort of witty about it, drawing me in as if we could both have a chuckle about aspects of my boyfriend's life, as if we were both on the same side, and it was my friend not I who was the object of observation.'

'As we know,' N. said, 'our friend is in the computer business.'

Julia nodded. 'I'd never understood much about the sort of business he was in,' she says, 'and with my East German mindset not at all! He had told me it was trade in computer components.'

N. specified it for her. 'He is a sales manager for the regional branch of the firm.' Then he described the boyfriend's family house in Umbria. He told her the make of car he drove. When he saw that this meant nothing to Julia, he interpreted it for her: in N's estimation it was a 'middle class' sort of car, 'so there's no thinking he's rich or anything.'

Julia wondered where this was going.

He opened his desk drawer and brought out a thick manila folder which he put, closed, on the desk.

'Now Miss Behrend,' he said, 'we come to you.'

He evaluated her life-in-progress. 'He knew everything about me,' she says. 'He knew all the subjects I'd taken and how I did in them. He knew all about each of my sisters, my parents. He knew my youngest sister wanted to study piano at the conservatory.' Major N. felt sufficiently informed to make some psychological assessments. He told her that there were clearly issues her father did not understand, that Dieter was 'problematic'. Irene, by contrast, was much more loyal to the state.

'It is clear to us on the evidence, Miss Behrend, that you take after your mother,' he said. 'Which, if I may be so bold as to say so, is a good thing.'

'He was showing me that he had me in the palm of his hand,' she says. Julia draws her knees up to her chest and places her heels on the seat. She stretches her jumper over the knees, making herself into a small black ball. 'The only thing—' she says, '—it's ironic but the only thing that they seemed not to know, was that I'd broken up with my boyfriend!' Since their split in Hungary, the Italian boyfriend had written several imploring letters. Julia had replied to the first one but then stopped writing.

'Or at least the Major acted as if he didn't know that we'd broken up,' she says. 'I thought it was strange that he didn't know. Maybe he'd been on holidays and had missed the last couple of letters.'

Or, I think, he might have known, and thought his prospects with her then were better.

N. put the manila folder to one side next to the love letters. He joined the tips of his fingers together and leant forward. 'As I'm sure you will have picked up, we are interested in your friend.'

And then it came. 'We would propose,' he said, 'if you would assist us, that we meet every now and again. For a chat.'

Julia says, 'I thought it was absurd. I thought: what on earth could interest them in him?' She could not imagine that the Italian boyfriend was in any way a bigwig. 'He did not have any high-up connections he ever mentioned, or any special expertise or training at all.' It did not occur to her until she got home that it could have been her they wanted.

There was no question for Julia. She would not inform on him, or at all. 'I am terribly sorry,' she told Major N., 'but I can't help you because we split up on this last trip to Hungary. I want nothing more to do with him. He wanted to own me. I knew if I stayed with him I would not be able to determine my own life.' She added, 'I never want to see him again, even as a friend.'

N. smiled. 'If,' he said, 'after giving the matter some further thought you reach a different decision, you should not hesitate to call at any time.'

He gave her his card with his phone number on it. 'Oh and Miss Behrend,' he said, 'one more thing. You must not discuss our little talk with anyone, not your parents, not your sisters, not your closest friends. If you do, we will know about it. This afternoon has not occurred. You have never been to Room 118. If you see me on the street you are not to acknowledge me, you must walk on past. All this for obvious reasons, as I'm sure you will have understood long ago.'

She nodded.

And that was it. He had shown her that with one phone call to him she could be in, or she could be out. She could be with them, or she could be gone.

'And then he let me leave.' The street was another world, the daylight bright and unnatural. Julia watched a class of small children being herded along the pavement. She felt sundered, suddenly and irrevocably, from life. 'It was as though all at once I was on the other side,' she says, 'separate from everybody.'

# 18

# CINDI KATZ

## THE STATE GOES HOME

Local Hyper-Vigilance of Children and
the Global Retreat from Social Reproduction

In the face of neoliberal reductions in state support for basic social needs, forms of privatized surveillance become a seemingly logical response to insecurities. In this excerpt, Cindi Katz illustrates this trend with the emergence of the "child protection industry." Parents increasingly embrace surveillance devices as a corrective to the anxiety and guilt they feel about their children and their absentee parenting. In the process, parents are prone to demonize caregivers, while ignoring the profound absence of state or corporate support for safe and nurturing environments for everyone.

***

In an early scene in *The Terminator*, the cyborgian Arnold Schwarzenegger walks into an L.A. gun shop and asks to see the wares. The shopkeeper lays out Uzis, submachine guns, rocket launchers, and other sophisticated means of overkill, nervously understating, "Any one of these will suit you for home defense purposes." The situation is likewise in the growing child protection industry. In keeping with the shopkeeper's sly comment, these businesses feast on an all-pervasive culture of fear, while creating a mockery, alibi, and distraction out of what they are really about—to remake the home as a citadel through the peddling of private protective technologies that reinforce it against various forms of intrusion.

These industries offer utterly inappropriate technocratic solutions for broad social problems. More important, the growth of the child protection industry is yet another response to the venomous and slippery fear-of-crime discourse that has become one of the key stocks in trade of the neoliberal state. Retrenching on its commitments to the social wage, the contemporary state has not reneged at all, of course, on its commitments to social order.

The commitment to order is legitimated through a tedium of pronouncements concerning crime that creates an aura of fearfulness and distrust while naturalizing increasingly virulent policing, stepped-up prison construction, stricter sentencing policies, and the like, as responses. As the circular discourse of crime, fear, law, and order—propounded at all scales of the US state and largely unquestioned in conventional media—has burgeoned, there has been little willingness to address whether these measures actually have any impact on crime or the creation of genuine public safety. But one thing is certain: the discourse of fear has provoked an increasingly serious domestic response to the perceived dangers in our midst. It is no small irony, then, that as the state pumps up fear to legitimate itself and its skewed expenditures, the loathing it simultaneously produces and the distrust it stokes have encouraged the proliferation of privatized strategies of coping. From the explosion in the production of household armaments to the alarming of all personal property, many Americans seem intent on taking the law into their own hands. This tendency, coupled with the sort of precious concern for children's well-being that has become prevalent in the US since the late 1970s, have created the ideal conditions for the emergence and growth of the child protection industry.

The child protection industry is part of the $1.1 billion home surveillance industry brought about by the migration of spy technologies and logics across the domestic frontier. Its products enable parents to monitor from afar their children, childcare workers, and others interacting with their kids. Selling technologies such as "nanny cams" and child-watch monitors, among an arsenal of home security accessories— tazers, pepper spray, maces (including "child size mace with a mini alarm"), stun guns, crossbows, animal repellents, electronic barking dogs, door braces, telephone voice changers, all manner of safes, infrared alarms, wrist rockets—these businesses render something like a burglar alarm almost quaint, to say nothing of the notion that technologies appropriate for the home should encompass things like vacuum cleaners.

The child protection industry markets its products by tapping into a great and growing anxiety that children can and should be protected from everything. But the anxiety is papered over with disingenuous claims about family life. For instance, "at Securityke we are intent upon reducing the amount of child abuse in America by empowering parents with the appropriate equipment needed to survey your child's surroundings." This claim neatly glides over the fact that nearly all child abuse is perpetrated by members of the child's family. . . . Other businesses invoke consumer sovereignty as a selling point for getting daycare-based cameras, exclaiming that since parents pay so much for childcare and their children's educations, they deserve to know whether they are getting good value for the money. No matter what they claim in their materials, however, virtually all of these businesses are willing to prey upon parental fears and use sensationalized accounts of children putatively abused by nonfamilial care providers to sell their wares. The murderous nanny Louise Woodward is never far from the scene.

None of these technologies—no matter how strange or impractical—offer anything more than micro-scale and private solutions to what are social and political-economic problems. Of course, in the contemporary neoliberal climate, that is precisely their allure. Rather than agitating for safer public environments or socially provided childcare, individual households can purchase or rent an array of technologies designed to reassure them that their private strategies for minding their children are at the very least doing them no harm. Such privatized strategies sidestep the social issues of social reproduction in the contemporary US, including the lack of public or corporate support for childcare or other social benefits, and the largely unaltered gender division of household labor that continues to hold women responsible for childcare whether they provide it themselves or organize and schedule others to do so. They also take for granted the enormous gaps between wealthy and poor households, both nationally and internationally, that enable households of one class to employ members of another. Yet it is in part these inequalities that foster the distrust and animosity that lead to investments in surveillance technologies.

Among the technologies for sale or rent are "nanny cams," miniature wireless or wired devices that can be mounted in the home or come concealed in teddy bears, air purifiers, lamps, clocks, and the like. The cameras enable parents to produce a covert tape or live video of their child and his or her minder. Some systems are motion-activated and some record sound as well as image, but most provide a simple visual record of the scene. Most of those who deploy these technologies do not like what they see. Of course, these parents are a suspicious lot to begin with, but according to one purveyor of nanny cams in the US, 70% of users fire their nanny. They rarely find evidence of abuse, but rather degrees of benign neglect—nannies who let children watch television rather than playing with them, who talk on the telephone rather than with their charges, who let children cry rather than attend to them, or who nap while kids are left to their own devices. Although these issues can be serious, they often are not, and taking such extreme action as firing the caregiver rather than clarifying expectations begs the question of how most parents would fare under the disciplining gaze of such scrutiny. Perhaps after breaching the trust one might expect in such an intimate employer-employee relationship, there is no going back to a discussion of work expectations. . . .

The latest child monitoring technologies are electronic tracking systems. These systems, which involve the use of a chip that can be located with global positioning systems (GPS), were initially developed for tracing merchandise in warehouses or on delivery routes. They have begun to be used in some large private parks for keeping a watch on children "freely" wandering on the grounds, and recently came on the market for individual use. In parks, parents rent a wrist or ankle band with an embedded chip that can only be removed from their child with a special device. Child minders can then visit kiosks outfitted with video monitors that reveal their child's location anywhere on the property. The next iteration of this technology, already dubbed *Digital Angel*, involves placing the chip subcutaneously in the child for constant vigilance. Marketing has been stalled by the legal privacy issues raised by embedding a chip in another person, even one's own child.

Any one of these technologies is suitable for "home defense purposes." What is being defended against? For one, guilt and anxiety are frequently the prime emotions of two-career couples, but evidence suggests that they affect women more deeply than is the case with their male partners. The technologies also "defend" against the absence of state- or business-subsidized high-quality daycare in either neighborhood or work settings, because they offer a way to ensure that whatever childcare services are purchased by those who can afford them are high quality. Such individualized strategies sidestep the question of why these issues are so vexed in the US. Not coincidentally, the struggle for widely available and affordable childcare is no longer much on the agenda of middle-class and professional people, who have come to take care of their childcare needs through private means, and then invest in surveillance technologies to assure their quality. These technologies are also a defense against the scattering of the extended family and the increased hours of parental work outside the home that characterized the latter 20th century. . . .

It must be noted how privileged it is to fetishize certain children's well-being, while at the same time—thanks to broad retreats in social reproduction—other children are vulnerable to risks of an entirely different order. These risks, such as homelessness, poor schools, lack of health care, and unsafe and understimulating public environments, not only go largely unremarked, but are also largely made invisible by the resolutely narrow focus of hypervigilance, as if individual issues of children's safety are the only ones that matter. Moreover, part of the anxiety that drives hypervigilance is the result of hiring childcare workers across the income gap created by uneven capitalist development and nourished by globalized capitalist production. Children are vulnerable, north, south, east, and west, because of the crumbling of the social wage and the retreat from social reproduction enabled by the globalization of capitalist production. This is much more dangerous than an understimulating nanny, even a murderous one. . . .

The technologies on offer may give parents and children a sense of control and reassurance and may indeed respond to the twin plagues of anxiety and guilt. However, I argue that the problems are of a different order. It is not possible to protect children from everything— as anxious parents in the global North seem to want to do—with all the micromanagement in the world (including the children's own defiance and the stubborn fact that most of the dangers to children come from the family itself). Most significantly, the problems are social, political, and economic, and so, too, must be the means to redress them. The shrunken state under our beds cannot redress the problems produced by the broad retreats from the social wage resulting from the globalization of capitalist production, by the enduring inequalities of class, race, and nation that foster lopsided domestic exchanges of money, love, and care, or by the gendered division of household labor and the unwillingness of most employees to recognize this in workplace rules that might provide for schedule flexibility, if not work-based care arrangements. All that little state can do is monitor what happens in the riven domestic field that is produced by these problems. The proliferation of child protection technologies and the broadening of surveillance across the domestic frontier mark an enormous retreat from politics. Exposing the issues that have provoked this shift provides fertile grounds for broad-based organizing and action.

# IDENTITY AND IDENTIFICATION

The desire for bureaucratic or scientific identification techniques is typically fueled by anxieties surrounding unknown others. This problem of unverifiability has a long history, dating back at least to early modern Europe, but was amplified by increasing social and geographical mobility—and the circulation of anonymous individuals in industrializing cities—in the late nineteenth century. The concern was that criminals or vagrants could become imposters or pass undetected, threatening both social stability and the well-being of people who supposedly belonged to a place. As Simon Cole relates in his impressive history of fingerprinting, the story of Jekyll and Hyde is emblematic of these nineteenth-century apprehensions "that criminals, far from exhibiting their villainy on their faces, were invisible, concealed beneath an inconspicuous facade. Criminals, it was said, exploited the anonymity of modern society, melting into the urban crowd, and this made them all the more dangerous" (Cole 2001: 2). Thus, early identification schemes began with a study of known "criminal" bodies with the goals of *detecting* previously labeled criminals and arriving at a scientific means of *predicting* criminality by mapping a set of shared characteristics.

From its outset, therefore, the science of identification began with racialized, classed, and gendered assumptions about who was considered dangerous or suspect. As a rule, the known criminal bodies were those already stigmatized in some way. They were people of color, migrants, the poor, beggars, prostitutes, or others deemed undesirable (Cole 2001; Sekula, excerpted in Chapter 21). Under the aura of scientific objectivity, a raft of early biometric techniques emerged to read biological difference and predisposition from the body: photography and physiognomy (measuring facial features), phrenology (measuring cranial size and shape), dactyloscopy (identifying fingerprints), and others. Unsurprisingly, white and relatively affluent bodies were found to be superior, whereas racialized bodies were found to be degenerate. Clearly, eugenic aspirations, of purifying society by gradually eliminating deficient traits and people, inflected these projects, such that racial prejudices were fused with scientific practice (Harding 1993). Over time, at least for criminal identification, explicitly racist agendas were muted, but the taint of racist origins remains and can be seen with the discriminatory functions and uses of newer biometric systems today (Magnet, excerpted in Chapter 23).

State identification projects offer the most glaring examples of how discrimination may become encoded in—and reproduced through—abstraction. While the origins of many internal state identification schemes may have been to manage taxation and provide benefits for citizens, some of the worst atrocities against people have been facilitated by identification systems. As David Lyon writes, "In the mid-twentieth century, infamous systems of internal passport were developed under the Nazi regime in Germany, in South Africa under apartheid, and in the Soviet Union. In Germany, where . . . the administration of the Holocaust represents the apogee of modernist rationality, International Business Machines (IBM) was recruited to provide the technical infrastructure for genocidal identification" (Lyon 2009: 46). In colonial Rwanda, the strict codification of the categories *Hutu, Tutsi*, and *Twa* by Belgian authorities in the 1930s artificially fixed ethnic identities and created rifts between groups, which later contributed to civil war and genocide in the 1990s (Lyon 2009). State identification systems have also played a crucial role in the identification and management of slaves, refugees, prisoners, welfare recipients, and more. As new identification systems come into being, such as India's massive biometric identity card scheme for its entire population or the United Nations' biometric system for tracking refugees, it is worth asking questions about their discriminatory potential.

The politics of surveillance reside in the tangled relationship between identity and identification. Whereas identity is colloquially thought of as one's core sense of self, as a self-fashioned personhood that one carries throughout the world of others, identification is a process of verification—of matching one's claims of identity to representations in

abstract systems (Barnard-Wills 2012). From this perspective, surveillance occurs through exposure to identification processes, where one is verified, categorized, and governed based upon her or his fit (or lack thereof) with the system in question, be that a passport control checkpoint, an online shopping site, or a college classroom. This narrative, however, paints over the socially constructed nature of identity to begin with. As Valentin Groebner (excerpted in Chapter 19) explains, identity historically "denoted not uniqueness, but the features that the various elements of a group had in common." The significance of group elements, physical traits, or individual abilities depends on a historically contingent system of social relations. As identification categories become codified in bureaucratic apparatuses and technological systems, the formation of identity through the negotiation of such categories can undermine any strong sense of self-ascription (van der Ploeg and Pridmore 2016). Tensions between identity and identification can be a good place to investigate the politics of surveillance, but the two formations coproduce each other and resist differentiation.

The excerpts in this section offer a window to the productive and repressive character of identification systems. Valentin Groebner traces the history of state identification systems in Western Europe, illustrating how they functioned to create the social world in their image but, also, inadvertently generated con men and imposters who could exploit the vulnerabilities of paper documents and records. John Torpey shows in his history of the passport that as countries asserted a monopoly on the legitimate means of movement, they effectively brought both "citizens" and the contemporary "nation-state" into being through the process of demarcating state territory and membership. Allan Sekula posits that the nineteenth-century use of photography to identify social deviance should be understood in relation to the simultaneous circulation of photographic portraits of moral leaders; together, they constituted a larger archive that communicated a social and moral hierarchy. Dorothy Nelkin and Lori Andrews explore controversies over compulsory DNA testing of military personnel and prisoners to underscore how such ostensibly objective identification techniques are value-laden, fallible, and prone to abusive forms of "surveillance creep." Finally, Shoshana Magnet problematizes contemporary biometric systems and reveals their propensity to reproduce and augment historical forms of discrimination.

## REFERENCES

Barnard-Wills, David. 2012. *Surveillance and Identity: Discourse, Subjectivity, and the State.* Burlington, VT: Ashgate.

Cole, Simon A. 2001. *Suspect Identities: A History of Fingerprinting and Criminal Identification.* Cambridge, MA: Harvard University Press.

Harding, Sandra G., ed. 1993. *The "Racial" Economy of Science: Toward a Democratic Future.* Bloomington: Indiana University Press.

Lyon, David. 2009. Identification Practices: State Formation, Crime Control, Colonialism and War. In *Technologies of InSecurity: The Surveillance of Everyday Life*, edited by K. F. Aas, H. O. Gundhus, and H. M. Lomell, 42–58. New York: Routledge-Cavendish.

van der Ploeg, Irma, and Jason Pridmore, eds. 2016. *Digitizing Identities: Doing Identity in a Networked World.* New York: Routledge.

# 19

# VALENTIN GROEBNER

## WHO ARE YOU?

Identification, Deception, and Surveillance
in Early Modern Europe

The following excerpt comes from Valentin Groebner's ambitious history of identification from the fifteenth through the seventeenth century in Western Europe. He argues that identification was achieved not by the documents one carried but by matching such documents with an official register or archive. These systems did not reflect existing identities but instead imposed administrative representations upon people in efforts to align the larger world to its bureaucratic image. Ultimately, the bureaucratic *fiction* of comprehensive registration and control generated possibilities for resistance, giving rise to new figures—the con man and the imposter—who exploited the systems.

\*\*\*

"Identity" is a medieval coinage. It was in common use in its Latin form *idemptitas* or *identitas* in medieval logic. Derived from *idem*, "the same," or *identidem*, "time and again," it denoted not uniqueness, but the features that the various elements of a group had in common. (In proper New Latin, a person's uniqueness would not be referred to as *identitas*, but as *ipseitas*.) In the past thirty years, "identity" has made headway and become a power word of sorts in cultural studies across a much wider range of meanings, not least, it seems, because of its ambiguity. "Identity" thus refers today to several things at once. First, it refers to an individual's subjective self-definition, that is, to the identity of the self. Second, it stands for the heteronymous or external description of a second-person singular, that is, a person's distinguishing marks and classification. Finally, "identity" is used to assign an individual to a particular group, to a set of collective features that the individual either represents or would like to represent. Notably, all three uses of the term tend to converge in common academic usage.

It is this very vagueness that makes "identity" such a ubiquitous and irresistible term these days. It covers the waterfront. For one thing, it blurs the boundaries between self-definition and external definition and implies coherence in substance and through time. Between the covers of one book, "identity" can refer to membership in a collective as much as a postulate of self-perfection that can never quite be realized. One and the same term can indicate "structured representation" (but what kind of representation is not structured?) as well as internalized physical experience as a core of the self. . . . The term lends itself splendidly to every cause, whether it be emblazoning some far-reaching conference proceedings, making a grant application, or mobilizing support for a political cause.

However effective it may be as a prolific and polymorphous formula, the term seems useless for analysis. In the following, I will be talking about "identification," and not identities. The distinction is deliberate, because identification is always a process that involves more than one person. It seems to me that the various agents and authorities involved in naming and keeping individuals distinct cannot be brought into view otherwise, for they are always present, . . . if not in plain view, then out of sight, or in the bureaucracy.

If identity is not intrinsic to individuals, but stands, as in medieval *identitas*, for a set of collectively used signs whose specific combination enables identification, we can . . . renounce the term. . . . With our renunciation, the apparent contrast between the "collectivizing" Middle Ages and the "individualizing" Renaissance to which older surveys cling so tenaciously simply dissolves. When the older categories crumble, matters usually get interesting. If individuals were recognized by their signs, then those signs must already have been disseminated in the collective, and their meanings must have remained stable. Only in exceptional cases, however, can individuals decide for themselves what combination of signs (name, description, insignia) is to refer to them for the long term. . . . Whatever a specific personal, individual, and unmistakable combination of information about a person might look like, it must resemble other, comparable signs in order to gain acceptance as a proof of identity. Welcome to the kingdom of small distinctions. . . .

During the course of the sixteenth century . . . a utopian slogan was formulated that was to determine the discourse on individuality and identification in Europe from then on: "Register everyone and everything." Now it was not only royal officers, inquisitors, and border guards who would act as supervisory authorities; from the mid-sixteenth century on, municipal directives instructed innkeepers to submit a tally sheet of all newly arrived aliens to the authorities every day. In Leipzig and other German cities, poorer tenants living in the cheaper suburbs were referred to as *Zettelbürger* (literally "paper citizens"), because they were required to have paper permits bearing their landlord's surety ready at hand when moving around inside the city. In 1563, the Council of Trent adopted the famous *Decretum tametsi*, which commanded all Catholic parishes to keep written records of all baptisms and marriages in order to monitor their congregations more effectively. Such registers were intended to prevent clandestine name changes and marriages and to facilitate the persecution and punishment of bigamists. Moreover, a recording system of this kind, in principle adopted from Reformation books, promised greater scope to safeguard religious discipline. In 1567, the Council of Constance obliged priests to keep even more detailed records of their parishes by entering baptisms, Holy Communions, marriages, and deaths in separate registers; confessions made before Easter were to be recorded in yet another register. Two years later, the provincial synod of Salzburg required three general registers to be compiled: the first to contain the first and surnames of all parish members, together with their ages and status; the second to record all decedents and everyone who had moved away; and the third to list all new-born babies and immigrants. In France, where the council's resolutions were not fully recognized, birth, marriage, and death records were introduced in 1579.

All registration and administration systems established in Europe during the sixteenth and seventeenth centuries were based on a premise that was as powerful as it was utopian. They were drawn up on the assumption that all personal data had been previously recorded somewhere. Identification thus involved tracing the officially registered information in the records and comparing it with an individual's details to verify that information—verify it in the true sense of "verify." In his *Six Livres sur la Republique* (1576), the French jurist Jean Bodin proposed population censuses as the appropriate administrative means to dispose of all parasites encumbering the commonwealth as beggars and dangerous idlers. All royal subjects had to be registered by name, status, and place of residence, Bodin argued, to "detect the wolves among the sheep." A few years later, in 1571, Spanish jurists specified an *entera notizia de las cosas* in the *Nueva ordenanzas* (New regulations) for the New World, a comprehensive population register that was compiled to monitor the overseas dominions. In 1623 and 1669, the French king enacted laws prohibiting anyone from leaving France without explicit permission.

In short, identification and furnishing proof of a person's authenticity would no longer be rendered possible by the official signs of absent authorities adorning documents that an individual produced. Instead, authenticity in identification was to be achieved by matching such documents with internal registers, replete with information supposedly readily on hand in official archives. In the turn to the modern period, identity documents became more and more closely bound up with area-wide, exhaustive registration systems, at least in official theory. Such is the large historical

narrative of expanding control, tightening administration, and "disciplining" in a period that is said to begin in the fifteenth century and whose fruition is commonly dated in the sixteenth and seventeenth centuries. It is this period that is construed as the past perfect of modernity, as *the* origin of modern administration—a conception to which surveys of modern nationhood cling adamantly to this day.

Yet just how accurately were these papers and registers checked, and how accurate could such checks be? It is worth noting that contemporary comments on enforcing administration on a larger scale were low key. On his journey to Italy in 1580–81, Montaigne noted curtly that while the mandatory *bollette di sanità* were ubiquitous, they had nothing to do with fighting disease, but were rather a means of relieving travelers of their money. . . .

The rise of the impostor and simulator as a generic literary figure coincided with unrelenting efforts to establish systems of description, recording, and surveillance designed to render possible the unfailing identification of an individual. Furthermore, aspects of fiction (or of administrative abstraction, for want of a different term) were inherent in systems that endeavored not only to record real historical beings on paper, but also to replicate them through the same material. Seen from this angle, the rise of the impressive administrative institutions in early modern Europe that were to become the basis for modern statehood was not necessarily due to their efficiency in adjusting themselves to existing realities. On the contrary. These institutions became what they were because they boldly exaggerated their own efficacy. Creating the fiction of a world registered on and allegedly controlled through paper, they imposed their own criteria on reality, thereby altering it.

From the mid-fifteenth century on, as we have noted, increasingly larger social groups of travelers were obliged to carry personal identity papers. The introduction of such documents was accompanied—at least in theory—by stricter control mechanisms and tighter feedback loops into other recording systems and registers that collected personal data. The portable documents that individuals produced on demand were thus meant to be made verifiable against records kept about them elsewhere. Within the bureaucratic procedures, these passports declared themselves valid and genuine by displaying official signs, the duplicated insignia of authenticity. It was reproduction that literally created the proofs of a person's individuality: an individual had to be doubled by an identity document plus an official internal record on the document issued.

The history of identification I have traced from the mid-fifteenth to the end of the seventeenth century leads to an unequivocal conclusion. After two centuries of regulations, laws, and ever newer forms of official documents declared compulsory, after two centuries of bureaucratic orders—"Register everyone and everything!"—and of repeated admonitions that stricter attention should be paid to recording and checking individuals, what was the outcome of all these endeavors? The rise of the con man and the impostor, together with their official counterparts, the diplomat and the spy equipped with authentic counterfeit papers. Their careers in dissimulation took place not in spite of, but through the expanding systems of bureaucratic control.

In their urge to register everything, the scribes of early modern Europe produced mountains of paper abounding with forged attestations, false details, and invented names. At the turn of the sixteenth century to the seventeenth, we have encountered travelers who made condescending or self-indulgent comments on the bureaucratic efforts to have them identified by their real names and selves. Others even proudly recorded how they used official documents to have their name, creed, or origin changed through the magic words that allegedly proved who they were. Identity papers worked because they overstated the case, promising control and comprehensive registration. It was this effectiveness—or rather, the fiction of control and authenticity—that also led to their being used even more frequently as a means for undermining surveillance. . . .

If a person's identity can be anything at all other than a mere terminological trick of arbitrary, user-defined applicability, it can be nothing that "belongs" to a person, nothing but a battleground. Identity constitutes the attempt to control how others define us—as anyone who has ever lost their papers in an unfriendly environment knows all too well. Identity operates as authorization to access resources and private property or as an opportunity to receive apportionments of collectively administered assets. It is coupled with strictly defined and particularly exclusionary prohibitive legal instruments. Assigning and attributing identity are therefore not dispassionate, neutral processes, but sites of contention over representation where opportunities to discuss one's capacity of transformation and dissimulation are far from equal. Those whose rights are safeguarded dispose of much greater liberties in their self-representation and their social role playing than groups with lower social status.

# 20

# JOHN C. TORPEY

## THE INVENTION OF
## THE PASSPORT

Surveillance, Citizenship, and the State

According to John Torpey, modern nation-states were constituted—in large part—through bureaucratic practices of identifying and regulating the movement of people across and within their territories. As states claimed a "monopoly of the legitimate means of movement," the necessary demarcation of territory and membership institutionalized the state. Meanwhile, passports and other portable identification documents served to fabricate identities for citizens and others, transforming individuals into representatives of their respective states within a larger international system.

***

[I]n the course of the past few centuries, states have successfully usurped from rival claimants such as churches and private enterprises the "monopoly of the legitimate means of movement"—that is, their development as states has depended on effectively distinguishing between citizens/subjects and possible interlopers, and regulating the movements of each. This process of "monopolization" is associated with the fact that states must develop the capacity to "embrace" their own citizens in order to extract from them the resources they need to reproduce themselves over time. States' ability to "embrace" their own subjects and to make distinctions between nationals and

non-nationals and to track the movements of persons in order to sustain the boundary between these two groups (whether at the border or not), has depended to a considerable extent on the creation of documents that make the relevant differences knowable and thus enforceable. Passports, as well as identification cards of various kinds, have been central to these processes, although documentary controls on movement and identification have been more or less stringently developed and enforced in different countries at various times. . . .

The result . . . has been to deprive people of the freedom to move across certain spaces and to render them dependent on states and the state system for the authorization to do so—an authority widely held in private hands theretofore. A critical aspect of this process has been that people have also become dependent on states for the possession of an "identity" from which they can escape only with difficulty and which may significantly shape their access to various spaces. There are, of course, virtues to this system—principally of a diplomatic nature—just as the expropriation of workers by capitalists allows propertyless workers to survive as wage laborers and the expropriation of the means of violence by states tends to pacify everyday life. Yet in the course of each of these transformations, workers, aggressors, and travelers, respectively, have each been subjected to a form of dependency they had not previously known. . . .

States have sought to monopolize the capacity to authorize the movements of persons—and unambiguously to establish their identities in order to enforce this authority—for a great variety of reasons which reflect the ambiguous nature of modern states, which are at once sheltering and dominating. These reasons include such objectives as the extraction of military service, taxes, and labor; the facilitation of law enforcement; the control of "brain drain" (i.e., limitation of departure in order to forestall the loss of workers with particularly valued skills); the restriction of access to areas deemed "off-limits" by the state, whether for "security" reasons or to protect people from unexpected or unacknowledged harms; the exclusion, surveillance, and containment of "undesirable elements," whether these are of an ethnic, national, racial, economic, religious, ideological, or medical character; and the supervision of the growth, spatial distribution, and social composition of populations within their territories.

States' efforts to monopolize the legitimate means of movement have involved a number of mutually reinforcing aspects: the (gradual) definition of states everywhere—at least from the point of view of the international system—as "national" (i.e., as "nation-states" comprising members understood as nationals); the codification of laws establishing which types of persons may move within or cross their borders, and determining how, when, and where they may do so; the stimulation of the worldwide development of techniques for uniquely and unambiguously identifying each and every person on the face of the globe, from birth to death; the construction of bureaucracies designed to implement this regime of identification and to scrutinize persons and documents in order to verify identities; and the creation of a body of legal norms designed to adjudicate claims by individuals to entry into particular spaces and territories. Only recently have states actually developed the capacities necessary to monopolize the authority to regulate movement.

To be sure, despotisms everywhere frequently asserted controls on movement before the modern period, but these states generally lacked the extensive administrative infrastructure necessary to carry out such regulation in a pervasive and systematic fashion. The *successful* monopolization of the legitimate means of movement by states and the state system required the creation of elaborate bureaucracies and technologies that only gradually came into existence, a trend that intensified dramatically toward the end of the nineteenth century. The process decisively depended on what Gerard Noiriel has called the *"révolution identificatoire,"* the development of "cards" and "codes" that identified people (more or less) unambiguously and distinguished among them for administrative purposes. Such documents had existed previously, of course, but their uniform dissemination throughout whole societies, not to mention their worldwide spread as the international passport with which we are familiar today, would be some time in coming. Once they became available to (almost) anyone, however, they also became a requirement for legitimate movement across territorial spaces. . . .

The transition from private to state control over movement was an essential aspect of the transition from feudalism to capitalism. . . . The process also paralleled the rationalization and nationalization of poor relief, for communal obligations to provide such relief were an important source of the desire for controls on movement. Previously in the domain of private and religious organizations, the administration of poor relief gradually came to be removed from their purview and lodged in that of states. As European states declined in number, grew in size, and fostered large-scale markets for wage labor outside the reach of landowners and against the traditional constraints imposed by localities, the provision of poor relief also moved from the local to the national arena. These processes, in turn, helped to expand "outward" to the "national" borders the areas in which persons could expect to move freely and without authorization. Eventually, the principal boundaries that counted were those not of municipalities, but of nation-states.

The process took place unevenly in different places, following the line where modern states replaced non-territorial forms of political organization and "free" wage labor replaced various forms of servitude. Then, as people from all levels of society came to find themselves in a more nearly equal position relative to the state, state controls on movement among local spaces within their domains subsided and were replaced by restrictions that concerned the outer "national" boundaries of states. Ultimately, the authority to regulate movement came to be primarily a property of the international system as a whole—that is, of nation-states acting in concert to enforce their interests in controlling who comes and goes. Where pronounced state controls on movement operate *within* a state today, especially when these are to the detriment

of particular "negatively privileged" status groups, we can reliably expect to find an authoritarian state (or worse). The cases of the Soviet Union, Nazi Germany, apartheid-era South Africa, and Communist China (at least before the 1980s) bear witness to this generalization.

The creation of the modern passport system and the use of similar systems in the interior of a variety of countries—the product of centuries-long labors of slow, painstaking bureaucratic construction—thus signaled the dawn of a new era in human affairs, in which individual states and the international state system as a whole successfully monopolized the legitimate authority to permit movement within and across their jurisdictions. The point here is obviously not that there is no unauthorized (international) migration, but rather that such movement is specifically "illegal"; that is, we speak of "illegal" (often indeed, of "undocumented") migration as a result of states, monopolization of the legitimate means of movement. What we now think of as "internal" movement—a meaningless and anachronistic notion before the development of modern states and the state system—has come to mean movement within national or "nation-states." Historical evidence indicates clearly that, well into the nineteenth century, people routinely regarded as "foreign" those from the next province every bit as much as those who came from other "countries." . . .

Systems of registration, censuses, and the like—along with documents such as passports and identity cards that amount to mobile versions of the "files" states use to store knowledge about their subjects—have been crucial in states' efforts to achieve these aims. Though not without flaws and loopholes, of course, such registration systems have gone a long way toward allowing states successfully to "embrace" their populations and thus to acquire from them the resources they need to survive, as well as to exclude from among the beneficiaries of state largesse those groups deemed ineligible for benefits. . . .

This . . . has a special relevance with regard to identities. Too frequently in recent academic writing, identities have been discussed in purely subjective terms, without reference to the ways in which identities are anchored in law and policy. This subjectivistic approach, given powerful impetus by the wide and much-deserved attention given to Benedict Anderson's notion of "imagined communities," tends to ignore the extent to which identities must become codified and institutionalized in order to become socially significant. . . . The cases of "Hispanics" (as opposed to Caribbeans or South or Central Americans, for example) or "Asian Americans" (as opposed to Japanese-Americans, Korean-Americans, etc.) in the United States, categories designed for the use of census-takers and policy-makers with little in the way of subjective correlates at the time of their creation, are here very much to the point. Whether substantial numbers of people think about themselves subjectively in these terms is an open, empirical question; that they would not be likely to do so without the institutional foundation provided by the prior legal codification of the terms seems beyond doubt. . . .

[S]tates with a rising interest in embracing their populations had to develop less invasive means to identify people. The approach they adopted employs roughly the same principle that underlies ju-jitsu: the person's body is used *against* him or her, in this case as evidence of identity. Techniques for "reading off the body" have become more and more sophisticated over time, shifting from unreliable subjective descriptions and anthropometric measurements to photographs (themselves at first often considered unreliable by police), fingerprinting, electronically scanned palmprints, DNA fingerprinting, and the retina scans dramatized in the recent film version of *Mission: Impossible*. The persistent tinkering with these techniques indicates that states (and other entities, of course) have a powerful and enduring interest in identifying persons, both their own subjects and those of other countries. The ability of states uniquely and unambiguously to identify persons, whether "their own" or others, is at the heart of the process whereby states, and the international state system, have succeeded over time in monopolizing the legitimate means of movement in the modern world.

# 21

# ALLAN SEKULA

## THE BODY AND THE ARCHIVE

In this excerpt, Allan Sekula discusses the emergence of nineteenth-century photography used, ostensibly, to identify criminals and predict criminality. He connects applications of photography for the regulation of social deviance to the simultaneous circulation of honorific photographic portraits of moral leaders. Together, these images comprised a generalized archive that served the twin purposes of social regulation and cultural edification, of situating people within a social and moral hierarchy. In terms of surveillance, rather than signifying a complete embrace of photographic realism, of using images alone to read one's character, the messiness of optical methods was seen as needing taming through complementary methods of filing and filtering images as part of a larger bureaucratic system.

***

Although photographic documentation of prisoners was not at all common until the 1860s, the potential for a new juridical photographic realism was widely recognized in the 1840s, in the general context of these systematic efforts to regulate the growing urban presence of the "dangerous classes," of a chronically unemployed subproletariat. . . . [A] new *instrumental* potential in photography [was recognized]: a silence that silences. The protean oral "texts" of the criminal and pauper yield to a "mute testimony" that "takes down" (that diminishes in credibility, that transcribes) and unmasks the disguises, the alibis, the excuses and multiple biographies of those who find or place themselves on the wrong side of the law. This battle between the presumed denotative univocality of the legal image and the multiplicity and presumed duplicity of the criminal voice is played out during the remainder of the nineteenth century. In the course of this battle a new object is defined—the criminal body—and, as a result, a more extensive "social body" is invented.

We are confronting, then, a double system: a system of representation capable of functioning both *honorifically* and *repressively*. This double operation is most evident in the workings of photographic portraiture. On the one hand, the photographic portrait extends, accelerates, popularizes, and degrades a traditional function. This function, which can be said to have taken its early modern form in the seventeenth century, is that of providing for the ceremonial presentation of the bourgeois self. Photography subverted the privileges inherent in portraiture, but without any more extensive leveling of social relationships, these privileges could be reconstructed on a new basis. That is, photography could be assigned a proper role within a new hierarchy of taste. Honorific conventions were thus able to proliferate downward. At the same time, photographic portraiture began to perform a role no painted portrait could have performed in the same thorough and rigorous fashion. This role derived, not from any honorific portrait tradition, but from the imperatives of medical and anatomical illustration. Thus photography came to establish and delimit the terrain of the other, to define both the *generalized look*—the typology—and the contingent instance of deviance and social pathology.

Michel Foucault has argued, quite crucially, that it is a mistake to describe the new regulatory sciences directed at the body in the early nineteenth century as exercises in a wholly negative, repressive power. Rather, social power operates by virtue of a positive therapeutic or reformative channeling of the body. Still, we need to understand those modes of instrumental realism that do in fact operate according to a very explicit deterrent or repressive logic. These modes constitute the lower limit or "zero degree" of socially instrumental realism. Criminal identification photographs are a case in point, since they are designed quite literally to facilitate the *arrest* of their referent. . . . [T]he semantic refinement and rationalization of precisely this sort of realism was central to the process of defining and regulating the criminal.

But first, what general connections can be charted between the honorific and repressive poles of portrait practice? To the extent that bourgeois order depends upon the systematic defense of social relations based on private property, to the extent that the legal basis of the self lies in the model of property rights, in what has been termed "possessive individualism," every proper portrait has its lurking, objectifying inverse in the files of the police. . . .

Notwithstanding the standard liberal accounts of the history of photography, the new medium did not simply inherit and "democratize" the honorific functions of bourgeois portraiture. Nor did police photography simply function repressively, although it is foolish to argue that the immediate function of police photographs was somehow more ideological or positively instrumental than negatively instrumental. But in a more general, dispersed fashion, in serving to introduce the panoptic principle into daily life, photography welded the honorific and repressive functions together. Every portrait implicitly took its place within a social and moral hierarchy. The *private* moment of sentimental individuation, the look at the frozen gaze-of-the-loved-one, was shadowed by two other more *public* looks: a look up, at one's "betters," and a look down, at one's "inferiors." Especially in the United States, photography could sustain an imaginary mobility on this vertical scale, thus provoking both ambition and fear, and interpellating, in class terms, a characteristically "petit-bourgeois" subject.

We can speak then of a generalized, inclusive *archive*, a *shadow archive* that encompasses an entire social terrain while positioning individuals within that terrain. This archive contains subordinate, territorialized archives: archives whose semantic interdependence is normally obscured by the "coherence" and "mutual exclusivity" of the social groups registered within each. The general, all-inclusive archive necessarily contains both the traces of the visible bodies of heroes, leaders, moral exemplars, celebrities, and those of the poor, the diseased, the insane, the criminal, the nonwhite, the female, and all other embodiments of the unworthy. The clearest indication of the essential unity of this archive of images of the body lies in the fact that by the mid-nineteenth century a single hermeneutic paradigm had gained widespread prestige. This paradigm had two tightly entwined branches, physiognomy and phrenology. Both shared the belief that the surface of the body, and especially the face and head, bore the outward signs of inner character. . . .

A physiognomic code of visual interpretation of the body's signs—specifically the signs of the head—and a technique of mechanized visual representation intersected in the 1840s. This unified system of representation and interpretation promised a vast taxonomic ordering of images of the body. This was an archival promise. Its realization would seem to be grounded primarily in the technical refinement of strictly optical means. This turns out not to be the case. . . . If we examine the manner in which photography was made useful by the late-nineteenth-century police, we find plentiful evidence of a crisis of faith in optical empiricism. In short, we need to describe the emergence of a truth-apparatus that cannot be adequately reduced to the optical model provided by the camera. The camera is integrated into a larger ensemble: a bureaucratic-clerical-statistical system of "intelligence." This system can be described as a sophisticated form of the archive. The central artifact of this system is not the camera but the filing cabinet. . . .

The institution of the photographic archive received its most thorough early articulation in precise conjunction with an increasingly professionalized and technological mode of police work and an emerging social science of criminology. This occurred in the 1880s and 1890s. Why was the model of the archive of such import for these linked disciplines?

In structural terms, the archive is both an abstract paradigmatic entity and a concrete institution. In both senses, the archive is a vast substitution set, providing for a relation of general equivalence between images. . . . The capacity of the archive to reduce all possible sights to a single code of equivalence was grounded in the metrical accuracy of the camera. Here was a medium from which exact mathematical data could be extracted. . . . For nineteenth-century positivists, photography doubly fulfilled the Enlightenment dream of a universal language: the universal mimetic language of the camera yielded up a higher, more cerebral truth, a truth that could be uttered in the universal abstract language of mathematics. . . . Photography promised more than a wealth of detail; it promised to reduce nature to its geometrical essence. Presumably then, the archive could provide a standard physiognomic gauge of the criminal, could assign each criminal body a relative and quantitative position within a larger ensemble.

This archival promise was frustrated, however, both by the messy contingency of the photograph and by the sheer quantity of images. The photographic archive's components are not conventional lexical units, but rather are subject to the circumstantial character of all that is photographable. Thus it is absurd to imagine a dictionary of photographs, unless one is willing to disregard the specificity of individual images in favor of some model of typicality. . . . Clearly, one way of "taming" photography is by means of this transformation of the circumstantial and idiosyncratic into the typical and emblematic. This is usually achieved by stylistic or interpretive fiat, or by a sampling of the archive's offerings for a "representative" instance. Another way is to invent a machine, or rather a clerical apparatus, a filing system, which allows the operator/researcher/editor to retrieve the individual instance from the huge quantity of images contained within the archive. Here the photograph is not regarded as necessarily typical or emblematic of anything, but only as a particular image which has been isolated for purposes of inspection. These two semantic paths are so fundamental to the culture of photographic realism that their very existence is usually ignored. . . .

Contrary to the commonplace understanding of the "mug shot" as the very exemplar of a powerful, artless, and wholly denotative visual empiricism, these early instrumental uses of photographic realism were systematized on the basis of an acute recognition of the *inadequacies* and limitations of ordinary visual empiricism. Thus two systems of description of the criminal body were deployed in the 1880s; both sought to ground photographic evidence in more abstract statistical methods. This merger of optics and statistics was fundamental to a broader integration of the discourses of visual representation and those of the social sciences in the nineteenth century. Despite a common theoretical source, the intersection of photography and statistics led to strikingly different results in the work of two different men: Alphonse Bertillon and Francis Galton.

The Paris police official Alphonse Bertillon invented the first effective modern system of *criminal identification*. His was a bipartite system, positioning a "microscopic" individual record within a "macroscopic" aggregate. First, he combined photographic portraiture, anthropometric description, and highly standardized and abbreviated written notes on a single fiche, or card. Second, he organized these cards within a comprehensive, statistically based filing system.

The English statistician and founder of eugenics, Francis Galton, invented a method of composite portraiture. Galton operated on the periphery of criminology. Nonetheless, his interest in heredity and racial "betterment" led him to join in the search for a biologically determined "criminal type." Through one of his several applications of composite portraiture, Galton attempted to construct a *purely optical* apparition of the criminal type. This photographic impression of an abstract,

statistically defined, and empirically non-existent criminal face was both the most bizarre and the most sophisticated of many concurrent attempts to marshall photographic evidence in the search for the essence of crime.

The projects of Bertillon and Galton constitute two methodological poles of the positivist attempts to define and regulate social deviance. Bertillon sought to individuate. His aims were practical and operational, a response to the demands of urban police work and the politics of fragmented class struggle during the Third Republic. Galton sought to visualize the generic evidence of hereditarian laws. His aims were theoretical, the result of eclectic but ultimately single-minded curiosities of one of the last Victorian gentleman-amateur scientists. Nonetheless, Bertillon's work had its own theoretical context and implications, just as Galton's grimly playful research realized its practical implications in the ideological and political program of the international eugenics movement. Both men were committed to technologies of demographic regulation. Bertillon's system of criminal identification was integral to the efforts to quarantine permanently a class of habitual or professional criminals. Galton sought to intervene in human reproduction by means of public policy, encouraging the propagation of the "fit," and discouraging or preventing outright that of the "unfit."

The idealist proclivities, territorialism, and status consciousness of intellectual history have prevented us from recognizing Bertillon and Galton's shared ground. While Galton has been considered a proper, if somewhat eccentric, object of the history of science, Bertillon remains an ignored mechanic and clerk, commemorated mostly by anecdotal historians of the police. . . .

Unfortunately, Bertillon and Galton are still with us. "Bertillon" survives in the operations of the national security state, in the condition of intensive and

# Forme générale de la tête vue de profil.

1._Nègre à prognathisme moyen.

2._Type D'Européen prognathe.

3._Prognathisme limité aux os de la base du nez (prognathisme nasal).

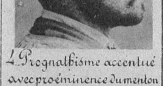

4._Prognathisme accentué avec proéminence du menton

5._Type D'orthognathe.

6._Profil fronto-nasal rectiligne.

7._Tête en bonnet à poils (acrocéphale).

8._Tête en carène (scaphocéphale).

9._Tête en besace (cymbocéphale).

Plate 41 from *Identification anthropométrique*, 1893, Alphonse Bertillon.

extensive surveillance that characterizes both everyday life and the geopolitical sphere. "Galton" lives in the renewed authority of biological determinism, founded in the increased hegemony of the political Right in the Western democracies. That is, Galton lives quite specifically in the neo-Spencerian pronouncements of Reaganism, Thatcherism, and the French National Front. Galton's spirit also survives in the neoeugenicist implications of some of the new biotechnologies.

# 22

# DOROTHY NELKIN
# AND LORI ANDREWS

## DNA IDENTIFICATION
## AND SURVEILLANCE CREEP

Identification techniques using DNA samples may seem less prone to bias, but—as with their predecessors—these techniques are driven by institutional agendas and infused with the prejudices of their social contexts. The following excerpt analyzes a few failed efforts to contest compulsory DNA testing of military personnel and prisoners. The authors draw attention to the likelihood of DNA identification to lend itself to surveillance creep, particularly given that it is generally seen as noninvasive yet can reveal much more than just one's identity.

\*\*\*

A wad of spit, a spot of blood, a semen stain, or a single hair is all that is necessary to create a DNA 'fingerprint'. DNA profiles can be extracted not only from blood or sperm at a crime scene, but also from objects touched by a person's hands, and from saliva used to lick stamps. From a tiny sample of body tissue, a forensic laboratory can create an image on an autoradiogram; a cluster of horizontal bands form a pattern, resembling a bar code. Despite its imperfect accuracy rate, law enforcement officials argue that DNA fingerprinting can be a unique way of identifying people and thus should be used as the gold standard.

DNA analysis had been developed in a medical context as a technique to identify the markers that indicate familial disorders. But in 1983, a British geneticist used the technique to identify a rapist. Subsequently, DNA testing spread out of the medical sphere into the sphere of public surveillance. As a non-intrusive and easy procedure, DNA fingerprinting has been used in many nonmedical contexts. It appeals to military, law enforcement and other governmental authorities: those seeking evidence to establish the identity of a dead body, a missing person, a biological relative, or the perpetrator of a crime. In 1990, the US Congress authorised and funded a military programme mandating the collection of blood and tissue for DNA testing of all military personnel. The FBI and the law enforcement agencies in every state require convicted felons to have a sample of their body tissue banked and tested for purposes of future identification. In some states, non-violent offenders and misdemeanants are included. Some countries require immigrants to provide a DNA sample as a condition of entry. . . . The collection of body fluids for DNA identification is an expanding enterprise.

There are, of course, many reasonable purposes for DNA identification. Why not facilitate crime control by having records of recidivists? Why not develop accurate means of identifying missing persons or the remains of soldiers killed in war? To the military and law enforcement officials who collect body fluids for DNA identification, body material is an efficient means to implement legitimate policy goals. But the expanding use of DNA identification also reinforces a pervasive trend towards increased surveillance. . . .

## The military DNA collection programme

In January 1995, Corporal Joseph Vlacovsky and Lance Corporal John Mayfield III, two Marines stationed at the Kaneohe base near Honolulu, were ordered to provide blood and cheek epithelial cell samples as part of the military's mandatory genetic testing programme. Their DNA samples would be stored at the Department of Defense DNA Repository in order to facilitate the efficient identification of the remains of soldiers killed in battle. They refused to comply and were court-martialled for violating an order from their superior officer (Mayfield v. Dalton 1995). They became 'the first DNA conscientious objectors'.

The Department of Defense (DOD) began collecting blood and tissue from every person in the military services in 1992. Included in this programme are all active duty and reserve personnel as well as

civilian employees and contractors. . . . By 2001, over 4 million tissue samples from military personnel will be in the Maryland repository. It is the largest DNA bank in the world. . . .

Vlacovsky and Mayfield cared less about the identification of their dead bodies than their ability to control the integrity of their living bodies. Explaining his willingness to risk a court-martial, Vlacovsky said: 'This won't destroy the rest of my life. When this is over, I will still have control over my DNA'.

The Marines argued in court that the taking of their tissue violated their Fourth Amendment right to privacy. They regarded the requirement as unreasonable search and seizure: 'I expected to give up some privacy when I joined the military', said Mayfield. 'But,' he added, 'It doesn't say we hereby waive our constitutional rights'. 'It is our God-given right to maintain possession of our genes'. . . .

The Council for Responsible Genetics and a clinician, Paul Billings, submitted affidavits supporting the objecting Marines. They documented cases where access to genetic information revealing predisposition to genetic disease had resulted in discrimination. 'Thousands of tests could be done on these samples', Billings said: 'The military may have kept the door open as a way to counteract rising benefits costs by excluding coverage for those with pre-existing conditions that can be discovered in DNA samples'.

[The programme manager of the Armed Forces DNA Identification Laboratory] dismissed such concerns: 'When you've licked a stamp on your tax return you've sent the government a DNA sample'. . . . Questioned about the initial DOD policy of keeping specimens after service members were discharged from the military . . . [the programme manager] called for greater trust; he said he would not abuse the information in the DNA files. . . .

The court held that the taking of a blood sample was not unreasonable seizure and thus did not violate the Fourth Amendment. Taking blood was, after all, legally considered a minimal intrusion. And, because there was no immediate plan to use the specimens for research, the Nuremberg Code's requirements for informed consent were not relevant. . . .

Other cases quickly followed. In April 1996, Sgt. Warren Sinclair, age 33, a 14-year Air Force veteran and medical equipment repairman, refused to submit blood samples for genetic testing. Vlacovsky and Mayfield generally mistrusted military motives, but Sinclair, an African American, had specific political concerns about the use of his body tissue. . . . Sinclair recalled the use of genetic testing in the 1970s when blacks in the Navy were tested for sickle cell carrier status. Though no scientific evidence suggests this would affect a person's health (only reproductive decisions), those found to be carriers were disqualified from certain jobs. Black servicemen interpreted the exclusion as one more way to restrict their opportunities. The Air Force court ruled against Sinclair, arguing that the interest of the government in assuring the identification of remains outweighed the intrusiveness of taking blood. Sinclair was convicted by court-martial on 10 May 1996 and sentenced to 14 days of hard labour and a two-grade reduction in rank. . . .

Those who refused to comply with mandatory genetic testing were challenging longstanding assumptions about the authority of the military over the bodies of its men. . . . Moreover, the Marines mistrusted the promises of confidentiality; they believed that their samples would become a useful and efficient resource not just for identification purposes, but for decisions about promotion, health insurance, and law enforcement. . . .

## DNA Dragnets . . .

In 1968, President Johnson's Commission on Law Enforcement and the Administration of Justice declared that information and systems technology was the most important tool for controlling crime. The Commission also proposed the creation of a national computerised criminal history repository. But the efforts to implement a system faced public opposition. . . . Critics emerged to warn of the potential for abuse, the unwarranted tracking of 'suspicious' persons, the selective surveillance of particular groups, the harassment of political activists, and the leakage of information to private organisations seeking information for employment or credit ratings. . . .

In 1991, six inmates from Virginia's Tazewell Correctional Unit Number 31 challenged the state's mandatory DNA testing programme. . . . The inmates claimed that the Virginia programme was unconstitutional; that in the absence of individualised suspicion, mandatory extraction of DNA samples violated their Fourth Amendment right against search and seizure. Also, they argued, imposing blood test requirements as a condition of release would impose additional punishment for their crimes and interfere with the right to due process by putting extra conditions on possibilities of parole.

Like soldiers, prisoners relinquish certain rights. But the prisoners defined their right to bodily integrity in a distinctive category; their body fluids, their genetic blueprint, should not be violated even in the context of the prison system. The Virginia Court disagreed. . . . Convicted felons, said the court, already lose the right to privacy from routine searches of the cavities of their bodies and their prison cells. Most searches, however, are conducted to determine whether the inmates present a current danger—by, for example, concealing weapons. In contrast, the collection of DNA is to protect against a remote future risk. . . .

[A]ll 50 states have adopted laws requiring specified offenders to provide blood samples for forensic DNA testing. . . . Once in place, the DNA programmes expanded to cover a range of both violent and nonviolent crimes. . . . Maintaining confidentiality is also problematic: there are over 19,000 law enforcement agencies in the US and over 51,000 additional criminal justice agencies worldwide, which means 'over 600,000 employees have direct access to the National Crime Information Center maintained by the FBI.

Law enforcement agencies also enjoy access to many other DNA sources. The military had admitted it is willing to release its data to law enforcement officials. A proposed federal law, the Human Genome Privacy Act, would allow police officers to have access to hospital diagnostic DNA collections without patient authorization. . . .

There is increased discussion in the popular and policy media about predicting and preventing crime by identifying those people thought to have 'criminal genes'. . . . But the attraction of efficiency has also encouraged a wider use of DNA fingerprinting as DNA dragnets are used to search for suspects in serious crimes. These may involve many innocent people. In 1990, the San Diego police department collected blood samples from 800 men during a search for a serial killer. They selected men who matched the description of a 'dark-skinned male'. . . .

Refusal to comply with requests to submit a blood sample in a DNA dragnet is bound to imply guilt. Submission to testing is not necessarily voluntary. In addition, the collection of body tissue for DNA testing presents a distinctive set of problems, for unlike fingerprints, tissue samples expose individuals to the risk that the cells will be used for purposes other than identification. They can reveal information about predisposition to disease or physical traits, a fact that becomes increasingly problematic as public authorities responsible for social control in an expanding range of situations—such as immigration—are attracted to DNA testing as a means to extend surveillance and facilitate investigations. . . .

## Possibilities of error

DNA fingerprinting has been called the 'gold standard' of identification. The technology is premised on the assumption that DNA fingerprints are unique for each individual. Indeed, a printout of a person's entire genome of more than three billion base pairs would be a unique identifier, except for identical twins. However, forensic tests look at only a small subset of a person's genome, and segments may be shared by other individuals especially within an ethnic group. Statistically, the chances that DNA from a crime scene actually comes from a particular suspect depends on how many other individuals could share that DNA pattern. . . .

In addition, there is potential for laboratory error. . . . In a 1993 study, 45 laboratories were asked whether particular DNA samples matched. The labs were undoubtedly using their best techniques since they knew they were being tested. Yet, in the 223 tests performed, the study identified matches in 18 cases where matches did not exist. If these had been real trials, innocent people would have been convicted. . . .

The interpretation of DNA fingerprints is also prone to bias. . . . Forensic scientists have professional incentives to adopt the goals of their clients and this may compromise scientific detachment. . . .

## Potentials for abuse . . .

If genetic predispositions were identified for antisocial acts, social interests could encourage measures to prevent crime by circumscribing the rights of people thought to have criminal genes. This might include identifying those with antisocial genes, keeping them under surveillance, or preventively detaining them. . . .

Concerns about such misuse of surveillance technologies are not without basis. In the 1960s and 1970s the FBI and local law enforcement officials kept tabs on thousands of citizens who were active in the civil rights and anti-war movements, and in some cases harassed innocent people. Today, the tools of surveillance are improving with the growing capacity of central data banks that include DNA.

# 23

# SHOSHANA AMIELLE MAGNET

## WHEN BIOMETRICS FAIL

### Gender, Race, and the Technology of Identity

Contemporary biometric technologies, such as fingerprinting or iris scanning, typically work by translating body measurements into digital code, which can then be matched against future scans to confirm one's identity. While biometric systems might be thought of as being more accurate and less prone to bias than older forms of identification, Shoshana Magnet illustrates some of the many ways that this is not the case. Rather, as prejudices are encoded into seemingly neutral biometric systems, mechanisms of discrimination may be less apparent and therefore more pernicious.

*\*\*\**

Despite the multibillion-dollar investments in [biometric] technologies, investments that depend upon the assumption that bodies can be easily rendered into biometric code, they cannot. Biometric science presupposes the human body to be a stable, unchanging repository of personal information from which we can collect data about identity. Biometric failures, encompassing mechanical failure, failures to meet basic standards of objectivity and neutrality in their application, and the failure to adequately conceive of the human subjects and identities that are their purported objects, necessarily call these claims into question. Yet despite persistent mechanical failures, biometric technologies still accomplish a great deal for state and commercial actors whose interests are tied to contemporary cultures of security and fear. In this sense biometric technologies succeed even when they fail. On the other hand, even when they function technically, biometrics do real damage to vulnerable people and groups, to the fabric of democracy, and to the possibility of a better understanding of the bodies and identities these technologies are supposedly intended to protect. In this sense biometric technologies fail even when they succeed. . . . In examining those instances when biometrics break down, we see that the real-world deployment of biometric technologies depends upon practices of inscription, reading, and interpretation that are assumed to be transparent and self-evident and yet remain complex, ambiguous, and, as a result, inherently problematic. . . .

Bodies rendered biometric become a particular kind of capital. For example, biometric maps of the body help to spin the bodies of prisoners, welfare recipients, and travelers into valuable data. Biometric representations of the body also produce new forms of identity, including unbiometrifiable bodies that cannot be recognized by these new identification technologies, a subject identity that has profound implications for individuals' ability to work, to collect benefits, and to travel across borders.

Biometric failures are wide-ranging. They occur across biometric technologies and consistently plague the introduction and application of these technologies to any institutional setting or marketing program. These new identification technologies suffer from "demographic failures," in which they reliably fail to identify particular segments of the population. That is, even though they are sold as able to target markets and sell products to people specifically identified on the basis of their gender and race identities, instead these technologies regularly overtarget, fail to identify, and exclude particular communities. For example, biometric fingerprint scanners are consistently reported to have difficulty scanning the hands of Asian women, a category not problematized in the scientific literature. Iris scanners exclude wheelchair users and those with visual impairments. More generally, "worn down or sticky fingertips for fingerprints, medicine intake in iris identification (atropine), hoarseness in voice recognition, or a broken arm for signature" all give rise to temporary biometric failures. More durable failures include "cataracts, which makes retina identification impossible or rare skin diseases, which permanently destroy a fingerprint." This broad range of biometric failures to identify some subjects and to overselect others has given rise to questions by the media and privacy advocates as to whom exactly biometric technologies reliably can identify. . . .

Although biometric failures are wide-ranging, knowledge of them is limited. The reasons for this are complicated. Biometric failures are often treated as aberrations, as exceptions, or as caused by a few incompetent scientists who did not fully refine their technological products before releasing them onto the market. And yet in examining the application of these new identification technologies to a broad range of institutions and programs, I find that rather than a small minority, biometric errors are endemic to their technological functioning. . . .

We have limited ways of speaking about scientific errors. In studying the reasons for the silence around medical errors, [Marianne] Paget found that the denial of failure and the use of technical terms to mask the subjectivity of medical errors came in part from the norms of masculine, scientific culture as well as from individual longings for a high-stakes science that would get it right every time. In addition a relentless quest for "mechanical objectivity" in which science is imagined to exist outside culture—including outside cultures of racism, sexism, and economic inequality—provides part of the motivation to deny failure related to systemic forms of discrimination. We continue to see the perpetuation of scientific norms that uphold a scientific practice free from cultural assumptions about identity as a vaunted scientific goal. Developed in a culture deeply divided by interlocking oppressions and with the aim of being able to reliably identify othered bodies, biometrics fail to work on particular communities in ways connected to race, class, gender, sexuality, and disability. I argue that we need to think beyond the "few bad apples" theory of failure and think about structural failures related to systemic inequalities more broadly. . . .

## Racial Profiling

It is no accident that biometrics play a significant role in racial profiling after 9/11. Held up by industry and government proponents as objective and free from the forms of systemic discrimination that plague real life, biometric technologies are represented as particularly useful because they will help to eliminate racial profiling. Biometric technologies, which claim to eliminate racial profiling through mechanical objectivity, simultaneously are explicitly based upon assumptions that categorize individuals into groups based on phenotypical markers of racialization and used in the implementation of programs specifically aimed at racial profiling. Moreover biometric technologies result in new forms of technologized racial profiling as people may not be allowed to travel as a result of how the scanners work. Clearly biometrics allow the state to both implicitly and explicitly engage in racial profiling while using the rhetoric of technological neutrality and mechanical objectivity to obscure this fact.

## Queer Renderings of the Body . . .

[O]ld assumptions about the ways that sex may be read off the body, from hair length to clothing, are assertions about the absolute nature of the divide between men and women. Those bodies that do not fit the inflexible criteria defined for men and women regularly are discounted, as we saw in the Yang, Li, and Haizhou study, which deemed any face that had a "strange" hairstyle to be unclassifiable. These studies are reminiscent of earlier research attempts to read sexual variance and sexual deviance off the body, as in the case of the medical doctors who attempted to identify lesbianism by measuring vulva size and nipple length. With respect to biometrics, we might imagine discounted bodies to regularly include those of butch women and femme men as well as transgendered persons. . . . In general people who cannot easily be categorized as either men or women are interpreted as biometric system failures. Showing a naïve belief in the assumption that low-cut blouses and long hair can be used to distinguish women from men with beards and ties, the scientists conducting these studies rely on narrow definitions of sex and gender in which both are collapsed, and in which those who do not easily fit these categories are erased altogether. As Paula Treichler commented, these scientists appear to be immune to even the most basic tenets of fashion; even one season of *Project Runway* might make a world of difference to their attempts at classification.

Although biological understandings of race and gender have long been analyzed by cultural theorists and scientists, their findings have largely failed to make it into the labs of scientists designing biometric systems. Biometrically producing reified racialized and gendered identities can have severe material ramifications. Most at risk from having their race, sex, and gender identities biometrically codified are those who refuse neat categorizations as well as those whose bodies the state believes to be a threat.

What are the implications of biometric techniques of verification for vulnerable bodies? What happens when biometrics fail? Given that the studies I've discussed assume neat bifurcations of gender into the mutually exclusive categories of male and female, the transsexual and transgendered community in particular faces significant risks from biometric forms of identification. For example, the U.S. Real ID Act of 2005 calls for the development of a national database of information and the creation of national identification cards equipped with chips that would carry both biometric data and information about biological sex. The Act poses grave risks for transgendered people living in the United

States and was identified as one of the most pressing issues facing transgendered people today by Mara Keisling, the executive director of the National Center for Transgender Equality. Any form of identification that contains biometric information could easily endanger trans folks if it was used to link them to a history of name changes or spotlight discrepancies in legal names and gender markers. In particular it could publicly identify people by making visible connections to outdated gender designations. In this way the representation of biometrics as able to stain identity onto the body—especially given the essentialized notions of gender upon which they are based—makes this community vulnerable to the prying eyes of the state. Mobilization also is occurring in the U.K. to address difficulties created by British plans for biometric IDs and for a national identification card. It remains unclear whether British ID cards will compare a person's biometric profile with his or her "birth gender" or "chosen gender." . . .

Scientific studies that rely upon biological understandings of gender and race represent some of the most egregious failures of biometric technologies. Any technology that takes as its premise the assumption that bodies are stable entities that can be reliably quantified is problematic. Relying upon erroneous biological understandings of race and gender in the development of biometric technologies has a number of ramifications, from the marginalization of transgendered bodies to facilitating forms of mechanized racial profiling. Like other identification technologies before them, biometric technologies are deployed in ways that remind us of other racist regimes premised on similar strategies of racialized and gendered classification.

Using technology to tell us "truths" about the body never reveals the stable narratives we are hoping for. Biometric technologies cannot be counted on

effectively and definitively to identify any bodies. However, as these technologies are specifically deployed to identify suspect bodies, the impact of technological failure manifests itself most consistently in othered communities. Representing these new identification technologies as able to circumvent cultural assumptions and subjective human judgment does not make it so. Rather biometric technologies are always already inflected by the cultural context in which they were produced. Biometrics are marketed as able to eliminate systemic forms of discrimination at the same time as they are produced in a context marked by the persistence of problematic assumptions about difference. That is, the rhetoric of scientific neutrality masks their racist, sexist, homophobic, ableist, and classist practices. Given the context for which they were developed, it is unsurprising that biometric technologies are imagined as able definitively to identify suspect bodies. Nor is it surprising, given cultural assumptions about othered bodies, that these assumptions are both explicitly and implicitly coded into the technologies. Biometrics fail precisely at the task which they have been set: to read the body perfectly, and in doing so tattoo permanent identities onto deviant bodies. Thus biometrics fail most often and most spectacularly at the very objective they are marketed as able to accomplish. Race and gender identities are not nearly as invisible to new identification technologies as is claimed. The technological fallibility of biometrics manifests itself practically in their disproportionate failure at the intersection of racialized, queered, gendered, classed, and disabled bodies, as they represent the latest attempt to definitively tie identity to the body. Rather than telling stories of mechanical objectivity, race neutrality, and the guaranteed detection of formerly invisible bodies, biometric technologies continue to tell stories heavily inflected by the intersection of bodily identities.

# SECTION 5

# BORDERS AND MOBILITIES

/////////////////////////////////////////////////////////////////////////////////////////////////////////////////////////////////////

The border is everywhere. This evocative and apt phrase conveys a complex social truth about life in the twenty-first century. As scholars in surveillance studies and beyond have noted (e.g., Balibar 2002; Lyon 2005), a world that is economically globalizing is also one in which boundaries, walls, fences, and borders are becoming more, not less, important. It is a world with systems designed to facilitate and regulate flows—on one hand, ensuring unencumbered transit for commercial goods, capital, and the relatively affluent who present low security risks, while, on the other, slowing down or stopping altogether flows that might threaten economic stability, social exclusivity, or security (Cowen 2014).

Surveillance is essential to these processes. It affords the rapid, and often automated, differentiation of flows on multiple scales. Thus, identification schemes try to fix the identities of known and unknown bodies so that they can be assessed and sorted either in real time or in advance, in an anticipatory way, so that screening at borders or checkpoints becomes largely perfunctory for elite (white) travelers, while it remains an anxiety-producing, unpredictable ordeal for (racialized) others. While the criteria used to assess risk might be arbitrary or prejudicial, thereby engendering different experiences and outcomes for different people, there is also differential exposure to *types* of systems. On one end of the spectrum, for instance, elite travelers might enroll in pre-screening systems (or use dedicated toll roads in non-border settings), whereas on the other end of the spectrum, refugees seeking to relocate in Europe from North Africa and the Middle East are rigorously questioned about their backgrounds and then entered into various identification systems, some using iris scans, to assess their level of threat or need, apportion benefits, and track them across territories (Monahan 2017). Such risk-management approaches to the social sorting of mobilities are the norm, and whereas the emphasis in this section is on systems that regulate the mobility of people, parallel systems exist for assessing and regulating the flows of goods and capital across the world.

These developments partly correspond with Gilles Deleuze's (1992) influential observations about "control societies," where the modulation of flows occurs in the service of neoliberal capitalism—or "the corporation," in his framing—which segments society and shapes it to conform to markets. As the excerpts in this section show, however, articulations of biopolitical and disciplinary power persist and mutate within control societies (see Section 2). This process puts the resources of the nation-state, including for border control, into the service of the market. Wendy Brown (2010) has famously argued that this embrace of border control by states is also a sign of the contemporary weakness of the nation-state: having already been effectively deprived of its ability to regulate economies, the border becomes one of the few sites available for the excessive display of national security power. Some of the nuances of this situation are explored by Louise Amoore (excerpted in Chapter 24), who uses the case of biometric systems at US borders to illustrate how such systems materialize biopolitical power through regimes of risk management and risk profiling (see also Mueller 2010). Yet, as Mark Salter shows in his paper on the post-9/11 US border regime (excerpted in Chapter 25), screening systems, like all technological systems, are fallible, so the state also cultivates a disciplinary culture of self-regulation and conformity to achieve its ends. It further seeks to enlist citizens in the process of monitoring for suspicious-looking people or activities, which is a process that could spread fear and exacerbate discriminatory conditions for others. His concluding question is perhaps the key one: "Who pays the cost of freedom for the mobility of others?"

This brings us to surveillance studies' strongest contribution to the study of mobility: sustained analysis of the ways in which differential mobilities are established or reproduced by technological systems in specific socio-spatial contexts (e.g., cities, borders). As David Murakami Wood and Stephen Graham (2006: 177) note: "Differential mobility is in no way a new phenomenon; from the moment some people rode or were carried while others walked, there have existed differences in mobility which reflect and reinforce existing social structures." As with most forms of privilege, the mobility of a new transnational upper class, or "kinetic elite" (Sloterdijk 1987), may benefit from this system in ways that are, or might become, imperceptible (e.g., not needing to obtain a visa to visit another country, having traffic signals optimized to accelerate vehicle throughput as opposed to pedestrian traffic). Social inequality is aggravated by technological forms of social sorting that gradual "unbundle" utilities and services from urban and other environments, such that equal access is not guaranteed to public goods like water, electricity, or transportation (Graham and Marvin 2001). The excerpt by Stephen Graham and David Murakami Wood pursues this line of thinking, underscoring how forms of automated social exclusion could be enacted by digital systems in urban settings or elsewhere. Crucially, they explain, there is always a social component to the regulation of access or mobility; it is present in the design process that embeds values into the systems, the context of deployment and use that lends meaning to them, and the human mediation of the systems by operators (see also Monahan 2007).

The final two excerpts in this section probe the ramifications of surveillance-supported differential mobilities for people on the margins. Katja Franko Aas describes how the collision of people in dire circumstances (e.g., refugees) with state mechanisms of crime control and immigration enforcement brings about a new subject for state regulation: the "crimmigrant." She reads the plight of crimmigrants through the lens of Giorgio Agamben's (1998) concept of "bare life," where unlike citizens to be governed through biopolitical means, these outsiders are subjected to an entirely different logic (and different surveillance systems too), where they may face death through exclusion. Thus, for some people, intimidating borders, boundaries, walls, and fences are a daily and consequential reality. Didier Bigo extends this mode of analysis to include holding camps and internment facilities, which prevent the mobility of people deemed (potentially) dangerous. By framing the problem of terrorism as a global threat and an exceptional state of emergency, the US government and others have been able to assert the need for interlinked global security networks and extralegal measures. These support the de-differentiation of surveillance systems and practices, as well as the blurring of police and intelligence functions. The banalization and institutionalization of such exceptions suggests, among other things, that racist or xenophobic beliefs will continue to inform security applications and that the mobility and life chances of the most needy will remain threatened.

## REFERENCES

Agamben, Giorgio. 1998. *Homo Sacer: Sovereign Power and Bare Life*. Stanford, CA: Stanford University Press.

Balibar, Etienne. 2002. *Politics and the Other Scene*. New York: Verso.

Brown, Wendy. 2010. *Walled States, Waning Sovereignty*. New York: Zone Books.

Cowen, Deborah. 2014. *The Deadly Life of Logistics: Mapping Violence in Global Trade*. Minneapolis: University of Minnesota Press.

Deleuze, Gilles. 1992. Postscript on the Societies of Control. *October* 59:3–7.

Graham, Stephen, and Simon Marvin. 2001. *Splintering Urbanism: Networked Infrastructures, Technological Mobilities, and the Urban Condition*. New York: Routledge.

Lyon, David. 2005. The Border Is Everywhere: ID Cards, Surveillance, and the Other. In *Global Surveillance and Policing: Borders, Security, Identity*, edited by Elia Zureik and Mark Salter, 66–82. Cullompton, Devon: Willan Publishing.

Monahan, Torin. 2007. "War Rooms" of the Street: Surveillance Practices in Transportation Control Centers. *The Communication Review* 10 (4):367–89.

———. 2017. Regulating Belonging: Surveillance, Inequality, and the Cultural Production of Abjection. *Journal of Cultural Economy* 10 (2):191–206.

Mueller, Benjamin J. 2010. *Security, Risk, and the Biometric State: Governing Borders and Bodies*. New York: Routledge.

Murakami Wood, David, and Stephen Graham. 2006. Permeable Boundaries in the Software-sorted Society: Surveillance and Differentiations of Mobility. In *Mobile Technologies of the City*, edited by M. Sheller and J. Urry, 177–91. New York: Routledge.

Sloterdijk, Peter. 1987. *Critique of Cynical Reason*. Minneapolis: University of Minnesota Press.

# 24

# LOUISE AMOORE

## BIOMETRIC BORDERS

### Governing Mobilities in the War on Terror

Louise Amoore has been one of the most consistent and persistent academic critics of the post-9/11 transformations of governance toward a model of risk management and what she has called, more recently, "the politics of possibility." In this piece she considers the ways in which biometric technologies have been deployed in United States border security.

\*\*\*

At a United States House subcommittee hearing in February 2002, a panel of commercial information technology experts and management consultants were asked to give technical advice on how the war on terror might be fought using risk profiling techniques. The hearing concluded that technologies designed to classify populations according to their degree of threat—long available in the private commercial sector—should be deployed at the service of border security. Indeed, the invited panel of experts stated clearly that 'our enemies are hiding in open and available information' and that, had surveillance and profiling techniques been in place, the events of 9/11 'could have been predicted and averted'. In the immediate months following September 11, the dilemmas of the war on terror were being framed as problems of risk management, clearing the

path for a burgeoning homeland security market that was to have implications far beyond the US 'homeland'.

Two years on from the initial hearings, the US Department of Homeland Security (DHS) announced the *Smart Border Alliance*, headed up by management consultants *Accenture*, as the prime contractors for US VISIT, a $US10 billion project to restructure and manage all aspects of US air, land and sea port of entry security. The US VISIT programme . . . represents one discrete example of a more prevalent phenomenon in the contemporary war on terror: the proliferation of risk management techniques as a means of governing mobilities. *Accenture*'s self-styled 'virtual border', they promise, 'is designed to operate far beyond US boundaries', enabling the DHS to 'assess the security risks of all US-bound travellers and prevent potential threats from reaching US borders'. Under US VISIT, the management of the border cannot be understood simply as a matter of the geopolitical policing and disciplining of the movement of bodies across mapped space. Rather, it is more appropriately understood as a matter of biopolitics, as a mobile regulatory site through which people's everyday lives can be made amenable to intervention and management. . . .

I develop the concept of the biometric border in order to signal a dual-faced phenomenon in the contemporary war on terror: the turn to digital technologies, data integration and managerial expertise in the politics of border management; and the exercise of biopower such that the body itself is inscribed with, and demarcates, a continual crossing of multiple encoded borders—social, legal, gendered, racialized and so on. The term biometric border, now part of the lingua franca of the risk consultants and the government departments charged with fighting the war on terror, has yet to be analysed critically in terms of how it is being deployed. . . . [B]iometric borders extend the governing of mobility into domains that regulate multiple aspects of daily life. Subject to biopower, the crossing of a physical territorial border is only one border crossing in a limitless series of journeys that traverse and inscribe the boundaries of safe/dangerous, civil/uncivil, legitimate traveller/illegal migrant. . . .

In effect, the biometric border is the portable border par excellence, carried by mobile bodies at the very same time as it is deployed to divide bodies at international boundaries, airports, railway stations, on subways or city streets, in the office or the neighbourhood. The work of the biometric border is thus the work of redefining what [Didier] Bigo calls the 'Möbius ribbon' of internal and external security, such that 'internal and external security become embedded in the figure of the "enemy within", of the outsider inside, increasingly labeled with the catchphrase "immigrant"'. Read through Bigo's lens of a

governmentality that combines 'technological sophistication with the old disciplines of the body', immigration and the terrorist threat become combined as a problem 'not because there is a threat to the survival of society' but because 'scenes from everyday life are politicized, because day-to-day living is securitized'. Thus, the governing of mobility through US VISIT's biometric borders is categorically not about new border threats in a post-9/11 world, but rather a means of identifying and designating the safe from the dangerous at multiple borders of daily life. US VISIT, then, is but one element of a liberal mode of governmentality that sees risk profiling in the war on terror pervade and claim every aspect of species life itself, or something akin to a shift from geopolitics to biopolitics.

Certainly such biopolitical and governmental techniques and technologies capture a crucial aspect of what is at stake politically in the extension of the biometric border into multiple realms of social life. . . . Yet, here I am also seeking to sound a note of caution lest, when we advance a critique of biopolitical systems in the war on terror, we inadvertently reproduce the certainties and assurances of the technical matrix that has become the mainstay of the homeland security programmes. The authority of risk profiling in the war on terror precisely relies upon the representation of a world that would be safer if only ambiguity, ambivalence and uncertainty could be controlled. In effect, the place of science and technology in fighting the war on terror is ever more secured if we overstate the coherence of the grip it has on life itself. . . .

The deployment of electronic personal data in order to classify and govern the movement of people across borders has become a key feature of the contemporary war on terror. The US VISIT programme, though, extends the use of integrated personal data into biometrics. . . . The allure of biometrics derives from the human body being seen as an indisputable anchor to which data can be safely secured. What [Irma] van der Ploeg has observed as a gradually extending intertwinement of individual physical characteristics with information systems' has served to deepen faith in data as a means of risk management and the body as a source of absolute identification.

Biometric technologies are perhaps best understood as techniques that govern both the mobility and enclosure of bodies, or what David Lyon has termed surveillance as 'social sorting'. In January 2005, for example, the then Secretary of the Department of Homeland Security, Tom Ridge, completed a number of agreements with the Dutch government to deploy biometric systems to accelerate the movement of 'trusted travellers' whilst restricting the movement of higher risk groups. Opening the new registered traveller programmes at Schiphol airport, Secretary Ridge emphasized the possibilities for the categorization of air passengers via biometrics: 'we can design border security initiatives to both enhance homeland security and facilitate global commerce and travel'. Within these programmes, we see not only the intertwinement of physical identifiers with information systems, but the annexing of patterns of behaviour, and their associated identities, that can be afforded smooth movement across borders. The use of air miles databases, for example, is coupled to the biometric submission of an iris scan to produce the identity of a 'trusted traveller'. Of course, Secretary Ridge himself qualifies for the programme:

> A fingerprint or iris scan is all that is needed for quick passenger identification and expedited processing through security. I've enrolled in the program myself, and I can tell you that it is a great tool that helps move low risk travellers more efficiently so that resources can be focused elsewhere, where the need is greater.

In a sense, the US Air Transportation Association's registered traveller projects, together with the Netherlands' Privium Plus, have much in common with the historical practices of what is called 'risk pooling' in studies of the insurance industry. By categorizing patterns of behaviour as 'low risk' (whether in the profiling of claims history in insurance, or via frequent flier history in airline security), authorities group together for common treatment individuals who are classified and encoded with a similar category of risk—in this case expedited passage through security checks. Indeed, the trusted traveller is called into being through an array of self-governing techniques. The US VISIT in-flight video has an animated Tom Ridge warning that the traveller has the responsibility to record their own electronic fingerprint at exit kiosks in the departure lounges. Rather as a credit rating is derived from past patterns of responsible financial borrowing, the trusted traveller is the individual who governs his own mobility and establishes a low risk mobility rating.

In populations targeted for higher risk pools, of course, the electronic enmeshment of data with bodies is more invasive, and the degree of surveillance intensified. Whereas the *trusted traveller biometrics* tend to emphasize membership of (or inclusion in) a group based on pre-screening checks such as citizenship and past travel patterns, what I will call *immigrant biometrics* are based on ongoing surveillance and checks on patterns of behaviour. While for the trusted traveller the biometric submission is usually the end of the matter, the passport to 'borders lite' (if not to a borderless world), the risky traveller's biometric submission is only the beginning of a world of perennial dataveillance where the border looms large. Regular travellers across the US-Mexico and US-Canada border, for example, can submit biometric data in order to fast-track the security checkpoint. Unlike Mr. Ridge's frequent flier experience, though, on trial at the US-Mexico border are radio frequency identification (RFID) enabled smart cards, enabling the tracking of the holder's whereabouts within the US.

In terms of what is at stake politically, the emerging contests around biometric borders centre on the question of the verification of identity. Biometric technologies are represented as infallible and unchallengeable verifiers of the truth about a person—the ultimate guarantors of identity. As such, they are increasingly being seen as the smart scientific solution to the problem of fighting the war on terror without impeding globalization—the means of managing risk by embracing risk or ... of fighting liberal war whilst securing the liberal peace.

# 25

# MARK B. SALTER

## PASSPORTS, MOBILITY, AND SECURITY

How Smart Can the Border Be?

Mark Salter is perhaps the most significant international relations scholar working on surveillance and, like Didier Bigo, one who creates important links between surveillance studies and critical security studies. He is known for work on air travel, airports, borders, and smart technologies, but also, more recently, pioneering theoretical work on the place of non-human "things" in international relations (IR). In this excerpt, written just a few years after the terrorist attacks of 9/11, Salter describes how the inability of states to discern all threats in advance motivates the adoption of risk-management approaches to border security, which—we would point out—invariably lead to forms of racial, ethnic, and religious profiling.

\*\*\*

At the border, all visitors, including Americans, have a greatly circumscribed set of rights. Border officials have wide powers of search, seizure, detention, and of course, the ability to exclude travelers from the country. Once admitted into the country, however, one's rights, including the right to due process, come into effect. Under this system, the intense application of state power through the examination at the border substitutes for wider police powers of surveillance once inside American territory. Simply, an examination at the border cannot deter or detect a motivated criminal. Limits in intelligence-gathering and information-sharing will inevitably lead to the admission of more terrorists. The openness on which America prides itself proves to be a weakness in terms of terrorist activities. Thus, controls have been tightened at the border and the surveillance of "high-risk" nationals will be extended domestically. Because the examination of the 9/11 terrorists failed, the Homeland Security Department and other federal law enforcement agencies aim to continue the surveillance of "high-risk" individuals within American territory. The transition from "undesirable" visitors to "high-risk" marks a significant shift in discourse. The exclusion of undesirable visitors indicates knowledge of the individual, if only as undesirable. However, defining individuals as "high-risk" indicates a lack of precise knowledge, suggesting only suspicions based on statistics, sociology, and narratives. As the government defines individuals as "high-risk," it encourages a cycle of insecurity that leads to the increase of police powers and bureaucratic structures of control. [Didier] Bigo has made this argument in the European context, but we believe that it can be extended to the post-9/11 American context also. For example, after the capture of Abdullah Al Muhajir (born Jose Padilla), Attorney General John Ashcroft said, "Al Qaeda officials knew that as a citizen of the United States holding a valid U.S. passport, Al Muhajir would be able to travel freely in the U.S. without drawing attention to himself." Al Muhajir was "high-risk" precisely because of his mobility, not because of something that had been proven in court. Ashcroft petitioned to have Al Muhajir declared an enemy combatant, leading to a severe circumscription of his rights, which would normally be unconceivable.

Whereas previous border security regimes focused on the actual examination between the agent of the government and the traveler, the surveillance regime aims to make the agents of the government present but invisible so that travelers police themselves. By surveillance we invoke the work of Foucault who describes an architecture of power and authority by which individuals come to police themselves in addition to being policed from outside. This surveillance strategy operates most efficiently when "surveillance is permanent in its effects, even if it is discontinuous in its action [consequently] the perfection of power should tend to render its actual exercise unnecessary." . . . This surveillance system applies to the border security regime, and in the case of the US-VISIT, to the entire mobile population of border-crossers.

In addition to an extended examination at the border, the US-VISIT special registration program continues the work of domestic monitoring of high-risk visitors. Aliens are initially fingerprinted and photographed at the border. They must report any change in their employment, schooling, or residence details to the government within ten days, and must also report in person to a BCIS [Bureau of Citizenship and Immigration Services] official after one month and one year, where they are interviewed and are compared to the records of their fingerprints and photograph, after which they are also recorded. The function of the program is to define, regulate, and identify foreign visitors in the country. While the extended examination strengthens the discernment functions of the contemporary border regime, the collection and verification of biometric information and residence details indicate a shift in the mode of policing from examination to surveillance.

This surveillance regime imitates the 1994 Californian Proposition 187 that required all state employees to act as de facto immigration inspectors and the Illegal Immigration Reform and Immigrant Responsibility Act of 1996 that offered a mechanism by which anyone could report illegal immigrants or their employers. The proposed Terrorist Information and Prevention System (TIPS) creates a national neighborhood watch program. Through a toll-free telephone number American transportation workers, truckers, letter carriers, train conductors, ship captains, utility employees, and other members of the USA Citizen Corps may identify suspected terrorists, who will then be questioned by authorities.

Tom Ridge, the head of Homeland Security, has also launched a public awareness campaign. *The Citizens' Preparedness Guide* encourages every citizen to be "vigilant" toward suspicious individuals, packages, and situations. The guide enlists all 280 million Americans into the war on terror. For example, Shiels reported programs that trained airline passengers to restrain hijackers; and *USA Today* ran a feature "Here's what to do if you're hijacked," in which an expert on terrorist attacks suggested: "You want to take a good look at who's getting on board. Do your own screening and profiling. You want to look into their eyes. You can tell a lot about people by looking in their eyes. Are they shifty? Are they nervous?" This is epitomized in the campaign slogan: "Don't be afraid, be ready." We would argue that the campaign in fact urges citizens to be afraid in an "economy of danger." Simply put, buying duct tape and extra water does not attack the roots of global terrorism rather it places American citizens in the position of continuous threat against which they can only be ready to be victims. The primary functions of this public campaign are to distract the populace from the external war on terror . . . and to enlist the populace's help in policing the national population. Reinforcing the notion that all citizens are watching each other leads each individual to attempt to appear as "normal" as possible. Examination has been supplanted by a surveillance regime, in which every citizen is both watched and a watcher. . . .

In addition to the deepening of border examination at the physical limits of America and increasing surveillance of high-risk nationals within the territory of America, several new programs attempt to make "up-stream" surveillance more rigorous. These policies, which especially relate to the visa and passport system, affect visitors before they arrive on American soil. This delocalization of the border is necessary because the border exists not only at the physical limits of the state, but also at the points of entry/exit to the state such as airports, ports, and train stations. The border is not just a line, but a network of POE (ports of entry) that accommodate the global transportation grid. It is better to speak of the "border function" than of lines in the sand.

The Enhanced Border Security and Visa Reform Act of 2002 (EBSVRA) was passed by Congress in March 2002 to increase the security of the American border. In addition to more funding for the Border Patrol, specifically targeting the Northern border, the EBSVRA modifies the Visa-Waiver Program to make machine-readable passports mandatory and attempts to increase information exchange between states and governmental agencies. The majority of its provisions relate to increasing security at the border, however, the EBSVRA also expands the US-VISIT program to the visa system. Nationals from identified terrorist sponsoring countries, for example, North Korea, Cuba, Syria, Sudan, Iran, Iraq, and Libya, are interviewed by an officer and fill out an additional form. Some of the additional information DS-157 requests is: tribe or clan, "all professional, social and charitable organizations to which you belong or contribute or with which you work," participation in military conflict, details of any military service, "specialized skills or training, including firearms, explosive, nuclear, biological, or chemical experience? If YES, please explain." Applicants are also asked to provide their full name in native alphabet, and all possible spellings of their full name. This additional form attempts to remedy the problem of differing spellings and transliterations of non-Western names. By listing the organizations and communities with which the applicant is related, American consular authorities hope to connect their foreign intelligence to specific individuals. The function of the EBSVRA is to extend the discriminatory function of the border to American embassies abroad—thus controlling immigration and access to the American border from "up-stream." . . .

Borders are permeable, even when the full capabilities of a national security state are applied on the control of movement of persons. Passports can be authenticated, but only to the degree that they rely on other identity documents. Border examinations cannot detect intentions, but rely on policies and practices that are formulated in terms of low- and high-risk populations. The weaknesses of the U.S. border security regime stem in part from the radical power of the terrorist. A terrorist's advantage stems from his or her willingness both to kill and to die for the cause and such devotion cannot be detected or deterred by any of the governmental means above. As recent attacks in America, Israel, and Russia have illustrated, the use of nonstate violence against civilians is nearly impossible to prevent. The question thus becomes, what kind of policies may be implemented to minimize the insecurity of borders? In the European case . . ., a scholarly and public debate has been spawned that evaluates the price of the freedom of mobility. For more precisely, who pays the cost of freedom for the mobility of others?

# 26

# STEPHEN GRAHAM AND DAVID MURAKAMI WOOD

## DIGITIZING SURVEILLANCE

Categorization, Space, Inequality

Stephen Graham and David Murakami Wood both came out of the Centre for Urban Technology (CUT) at Newcastle University in the United Kingdom, whose importance in critical geographical and planning studies of urban infrastructure, including surveillance, belied its relatively short life. Graham was one of the first scholars to conduct extensive studies of video surveillance in British cities, and—together and apart—the two authors have written several influential pieces on digital and algorithmic surveillance. This excerpt is from one of the first of those pieces. It explores the politics of digital surveillance systems that are increasingly embedded in material infrastructures. Such systems may have the capacity to increase access or equality, but they are shaped by the biases of their design and use contexts. Thus, they are more likely to individualize people and commodify data in ways that unequally sort populations.

\*\*\*

Bureaucratic and electromechanical surveillance systems (a foundation for the modern nation state, public health and welfare) are being supplemented and increasingly replaced by digital technologies and techniques, enabling what [Richard] Jones calls 'digital rule'. Digitization is significant for two reasons: first, it enables monitoring, prioritization and judgement to occur across widening geographical distances and with little time delay; second, it allows the active sorting, identification, prioritization and tracking of bodies, behaviours and characteristics of subject populations on a continuous, real-time basis. Thus, digitization encourages a tendency towards automation. Crucially, the work of human operators shifts from direct mediation and discretion to the design, programming, supervision and maintenance of automated or semi-automatic surveillance systems.

Digitization facilitates a step change in the power, intensity and scope of surveillance. Surveillance is everywhere.

Computers are everywhere. Their combination already has that air of inevitability that can attach itself to the history of technology. Computer technology certainly is . . . a player in social policy processes, but it is crucial not to read social and policy implications and effects of digital surveillance deterministically from the intrinsic capabilities of the technologies involved. . . . [S]uch techniques are mediated, at all levels, by social practices that interact with all aspects of the making and functioning of the technological system. Even apparently automated systems, far from being inhuman domains, involve continuous complex social practices and decisions that do much to shape digital surveillance in practice.

This is important because a characteristic of digital surveillance technologies is their extreme flexibility and ambivalence. On the one hand, systems can be designed to socially exclude, based on automated judgements of social or economic worth; on the other hand, the same systems can be programmed to help overcome social barriers and processes of marginalization. The broad social effects and policy implications of digital surveillance are thus contingent and, while flexible, are likely to be strongly biased by the political, economic and social conditions that shape the principles embedded in their design and implementation.

Currently, these conditions are marked by the widespread liberalization and privatization of public services and spaces. This reflects a movement from free, universal public services and spaces, based on notions of citizenship, to markets and quasi-markets based on consumerism. These markets continually differentiate between users based on ability to pay, risk or eligibility of access. While there is clearly much variation and detail in particular cases, this broad political-economic bias means that digital surveillance is likely to be geared overwhelmingly towards supporting the processes of individualization, commodification and consumerization that

are necessary to support broader political-economic shifts towards markets, quasi-markets and prioritized public services and spaces. . . .

Digital encoding works by reducing information to the minimum necessary for accurate reconstruction: the binary code of 1s and 0s. In contrast, analogue forms aim at perfect reproduction of the original. Digital surveillance thus makes the information more amenable to storage, transmission and computation. But is it sufficiently different from analogue forms to merit rethinking and retheorization? . . .

The obvious differences between digital surveillance and analogue surveillance are quantitative: computer hard drives can store far more information more conveniently and faster than analogue systems. However, the fundamental differences lie in what can be done with the information gathered. There are two basic processes.

[Clive] Norris and [Gary] Armstrong, in their study of closed circuit television (CCTV) in Britain, argue that what is of most concern is the linking of cameras to databases and the integration of different databases. Digitization facilitates interconnection within and between surveillance points and systems. To be truly effective, linkage is often required so that captured and stored data can be compared. Technological reasons will always be found to integrate. However, political and economic arguments are not always either presented, heard or assigned equivalent importance, and thus a covert process of 'surveillance creep' occurs, whereby integration is presented as necessary or inevitable.

Importantly, digital systems also allow the application of automated processes: algorithmic surveillance. An algorithm is a mathematical term for a set of instructions: algorithms are the foundation of mathematics and computing. However, algorithms need to be translated into a form that computers are programmed to understand, namely software—essentially many coded algorithms linked together. Algorithmic surveillance refers to surveillance systems using software to extend raw data: from classification (sensor + database 1); through comparison (sensor + database 1 + software + database 2); to prediction or even reaction (sensor + database 1 + software + database 2 + alarm/weapon).

Many of the latest surveillance technologies have embedded digital and algorithmic features. A city centre CCTV system providing images that are watched and analysed by human operators may be digitally recorded and stored, but is not algorithmic. If the system includes software that compares the faces of the people observed with those in a database of suspects, it becomes algorithmic. Patient records in a health service computer are digital and are algorithmic to the extent that software determines the format of the information entered. However, the process becomes algorithmic surveillance when, for example, software compares patient records against signs of particular disease risk factors and categorizes patients automatically.

Some have claimed that algorithmic systems improve on conventional systems. [Gary] Marx argues that algorithmic surveillance provides the possibility of eliminating the potential for corruption and discrimination. For example, a racist police officer cannot decide to arrest any black male when a facial recognition system can decide categorically whether a particular individual is the wanted man. However, algorithmic surveillance can also intensify problems of conventional surveillance and of computerization. . . . Algorithmic systems also pose new questions, particularly relating to the removal of human discretion. In the most extreme cases, such as the development of movement recognition software linked to an automatic lethal response in certain commercially available perimeter defence systems, this can lead to death without explanation or appeal. Even in less immediately vital situations, for example one

person's Internet traffic secretly bypassing another's because of algorithmic prioritization, the consequences can nevertheless be serious and exclusionary.

It is critical to stress here the subtle and stealthy quality of the ongoing social prioritizations and judgements that digital surveillance systems make possible. This means that critical social policy research must work to expose the ways in which these systems are being used to prioritize certain people's mobilities, service quality and life chances, while simultaneously reducing those of less favoured groups. Importantly, both beneficiaries and losers may, in practice, be utterly unaware that digital prioritization has actually occurred. This gives many of these crucial processes a curiously invisible and opaque quality that is a major challenge to researchers and policy makers alike. . . .

Social, commercial and state definitions of norms of behaviour within the various contexts of the city are thus increasingly automatically policed by assemblages of digital technology and software. These are less and less mediated by human discretion. Normative notions of good behaviour and transgression within the complex space–time fabrics of cities are embedded into software codes. So, increasingly, are stipulations and punishments (for example, electronic tagging).

Increasingly, the encoding of software to automatically stipulate eligibility of access, entitlement of service or punishment is often done far away in time and space from the point of application. Software is coded across the world: call centres that monitor the gaze of automated cameras of electronic tags are switched to low-cost labour locations. Digital surveillance therefore promotes a new round of space–time distanciation, which moves us ever further from modern notions of discipline based on the gaze of supervisors within the same space–time as the disciplined subject. Efforts are then made to enforce such norms and boundaries on the ground on a continuing, real-time basis through the withdrawal of electronic or physical access privileges, the detailed stipulation and monitoring of acceptable behaviours and the automated tracking of individuals' space–time paths.

Within contemporary political-economic contexts marked by privatization and consumerization, this proliferation of automatic systems raises clear concerns that social exclusion itself will be automated. Rather than being based exclusively on uneven access to the Internet, the digital divide in contemporary societies is based on the broader disconnections of certain groups from IT hardware and the growing use of automated surveillance and information systems to digitally red-line their life chances within automated regimes of service provision. Such systems actively facilitate mobility, access, services and life chances for those judged electronically to have the correct credentials and exclude or relationally push away others. They thereby accelerate the trend away from persons towards data subjects. As [Clive] Norris [and colleagues] suggest, the problem with automated systems is that 'they aim to facilitate exclusionary rather than inclusionary goals'. Algorithmic systems thus have a strong potential to fix identities as deviant and criminal—what Norris calls the technological mediation of suspicion. [Michalis] Lianos and [Mary] Douglas note that this also means that challenging these identifications becomes harder because what they term 'Automated Socio-Technical Environments' (ASTEs) 'radically transform the cultural register of the societies in which they operate by introducing non-negotiable contexts of interaction'.

Digital surveillance techniques therefore make possible the widening commodification of urban space and the erection within cities of myriad exclusionary boundaries and access controls. These range from the electronic tagging of

offenders within their defined space–time domains to gated communities with pin number entry systems and shopping malls with intense video surveillance. Digital surveillance systems also provide essential supports to the electronically priced commodification of road spaces; to digitally mediated consumption systems; and to smartcard-based public services—all of which allow user behaviours to be closely scrutinized. Crucially, the new digital surveillance assemblage is being shaped in a biased way to neatly dovetail with and support a new political economy of consumer citizenship and individualized mobility and consumption which would otherwise not be possible.

This is especially important within a context marked by the increasing privatization of public services, infrastructures and domains (with a growing emphasis on treating users differently based on assessments of their direct profitability). Digital surveillance also provides a new range of management techniques to address the widening fear of crime and the entrenchment of entrepreneurial efforts to make (certain parts of) towns and city spaces more competitive in attracting investors and (selected) consumers. . . .

As digital surveillance proliferates, the politics of surveillance are increasingly the politics of code. The processes through which algorithms and software are constructed are often now the only parts of the disciplinary chain completely open to human discretion and shaping. Once switched on, many digital systems become supervised agents that continually help to determine ongoing social outcomes in space and time.

The research challenges raised here are clear. Software for surveillance is often bought off the shelf from transnational suppliers. Critical researchers into digital algorithmic systems practices face an imperative to 'get inside' the production and implementation of code. This might mean switching the focus of research to the social and political assumptions that software producers embed (unconsciously or consciously) into their algorithms years before and thousands of miles away from the site of application. Research is required to systematically track the sourcing, implementation and implications of digital surveillance in practice, across multiple spaces, as the code moves from inception to application. Such research also needs to address time, as another implication of digital surveillance is its use in decreasing the ability of people to escape deemed offences in the distant past.

The policy implications of such research are complex and problematic. Digital surveillance systems tend to be developed, designed and deployed in ways that hide the social judgements that such systems perpetuate. Rates of technological innovation are rapid and policy makers face serious problems in simply understanding the esoteric and technical worlds of the new surveillance. Policy makers also face geographical and jurisdictional problems. Efforts to regulate and control digital surveillance are necessarily bound by the geographical jurisdictions that give them political legitimacy and power.

# 27

# KATJA FRANKO AAS

## "CRIMMIGRANT" BODIES AND BONA FIDE TRAVELERS

### Surveillance, Citizenship, and Global Governance

Katja Aas, one of many brilliant feminist scholars in the Faculty of Law at Oslo University, is far from the only scholar to have drawn on Giorgio Agamben's version of biopolitics to analyze border control and migration, but this piece is one of the clearest statements about both the theory and practice of surveillance at the contemporary border.

\*\*\*

Crime control has become particularly important in defining contemporary systems of governance, including issues of border control and global governance. Preventing cross-border crime (i.e. terrorism, human trafficking, drug smuggling and illicit arms traffic) has been, at least on the discursive level of policy formation, the main driving force and justification for systems such as the Schengen Information System and Eurosur. However whether it is these forms of illicitness which end up being the main target of surveillance is another question. Judging from the recorded activity of the Schengen system, illegal migration is its main practical preoccupation. About 80 percent of entries in the Schengen database refer to article 96 which deals with illegal aliens. The illegalities produced through definitions of unauthorized mobility as a criminal matter are thus proving to be the major target of EU surveillance systems, and thereby also a vital motor of day-to-day EU police cooperation.

The intertwining of crime control and migration control is also evident in several other databases such as the VIS [Visa Information System], Entry/Exit and Eurodac systems. VIS is particularly interesting given its sheer size, administrative nature, openness to police and security agencies and the potential synergies it may have with other police databases. This convergence of crime control and immigration enforcement has been dubbed in the US context 'crimmigration law'. These two previously distinct legal spheres are increasingly converging and overlapping, particularly through the progressive criminalization of immigration offenses and through the growing similarities in how they are enforced. The two systems are united by a similar social function of 'acting as gatekeepers of membership' and defining the terms of social inclusion and exclusion.

On the other hand, systems such as Automated Border Crossings, the planned Registered Travelers System, IRIS and FLUX [frequent traveler programs], seem to be driven by a different logic. Although crime figures in the pre-vetting procedures, the primary objective of these systems appears to be *gate opening*. Surveillance paraphernalia is used to speed up the process and to make travel 'a seamless experience' for so-called bona fide travelers. These two groups of passengers—crimmigrants and bona fide travelers—may not always be clearly distinguishable; the EU's ambition is, after all, to make the various systems interoperable and connected to one integrated border management system. Nevertheless, there are clear lines of distinction since it is precisely the time savings resulting from more lax controls of bona fide travelers which would 'allow border authorities to focus their resources on those groups of third country nationals that require more attention'.

One marker used to differentiate between the so-called crimmigrants and bona fide travelers is, naturally, citizenship. The explicit purpose of systems such as Automatic Border Crossings, IRIS and FLUX, is to ease travel burdens for citizens of their respective states. Moreover, by virtue of signing the Schengen Agreement mobility has become one of the main benefits of European integration for EU citizens. However, while citizenship is the most salient marker between who is to be subjected to 'gate closing' and 'gate opening' forms of surveillance, it is not the only one. The privilege of high mobility is not reserved only for EU citizens and, importantly, it is not a privilege

enjoyed by all EU citizens. The purpose of programs such as Frequent Travelers and IRIS is to carve out from the long lists of third country nationals the ones which are trustworthy (the use of the term bona fide implies good faith, sincerity and genuineness; the opposite of being deceitful, false and bogus).

The main EU police database, the Schengen Information system, also includes in its categories of alerts EU citizens who can be put under surveillance, checked and have their mobility restricted. One category, article 99, has been open to considerable debate because of its potential for broad interpretation. The article refers to persons or vehicles to be placed under surveillance or subjected to specific checks in relation to serious criminal offenses. Questions have been raised about whether groups of so-called 'violent troublemakers' (related primarily to mass gatherings such as international sports and cultural events, European summits and G8 meetings) should fall under this category. . . .

Although enjoying formal citizenship, the freedom of these groups has been restricted because of their allegedly criminal status, as was evident in recent debates about en masse deportation of Roma from France and other EU countries. The citizenship status of these groups is irregular or 'flawed' and comes close to what [Lucia] Zedner terms 'probationary citizenship', which although developed in respect of immigrants, 'is extended to all those whose standing as full citizens is in doubt'. Consequently, the 'crimmigration' policies are directed not only towards the exclusion of undesirable non-citizens but also 'seep into domestic crime control'. . . .

Even though the markers of citizenship are the primary lines of distinction between gate closing and gate opening, it is evident from the discussion above that the picture is more complex and requires additional attention. According to [Willem] Schinkel, citizenship represents a focal point of two interrelated, but distinct, forms of social control: zoepolitics and biopolitics. Building on the works of Agamben and Foucault, he suggests that zoepolitics is 'primarily *externally* directed towards persons outside the state, as becomes visible, for instance, in the reduction to bare life of those detained in Guantanamo Bay and in the administrative detention of "illegal aliens"'. Biopolitics, on the other hand, 'is *internally* directed and aims at the control of populations occupying the state's territory but which are discursively placed outside the domain of hegemony marked as "society"'. . . .

According to Agamben the main preoccupation of zoepolitics is to establish the distinction between the human and the citizen; or the often cited Schmittian discrimination between friend and enemy. This is close to the traditional task of border control which is to determine who is a member of the polity and who is not. Several of the surveillance systems presented in this article, such as the SIS, Eurosur and Eurodac, operate according to this logic by targeting unwanted aliens (i.e. aliens to be denied entry), bogus asylum seekers and 'asylum shoppers'. Here, through the figure of the *homo sacer* (the banned person), Agamben establishes an explicit connection between the state's protection of human life and the possibility of its destruction as 'bare life'. Refugees and those subjected to various types of administrative and extra-legal detention tend to be described as contemporary homines sacri. And although the contention has been open to critique because of its overly pessimistic and passive image of these groups, Agamben brings attention to one important aspect of state politics: the ability to kill by expelling life from the sphere of legal protection. . . .

While the main concern of zoepolitics is with banishment and exclusion (which nevertheless is, according to Agamben, an inclusive exclusion), biopolitics, on the other hand, is concerned with classifying the life of the social body. Its primary objective is the 'internal differentiation *inside* the bios' and control of populations already occupying the state's territory. It is, as Foucault eloquently put it, 'power to make live'; a 'technology of power over the population as such, over men insofar as they are living beings'. Biopolitical surveillance is thus directed at the (already established) social body, its health and productivity. While zoepolitics creates precarious life conditions, biopolitics finds its sphere of application within a normatively and legally regulated territorial space, where the objective is to multiply life and incorporate it into the political sphere. . . . Consequently, biopolitical surveillance internally differentiates the bios, and its forms of exclusion are primarily scientific and moral, rather than territorial exclusion from the polity as such. This process is exemplified by the heated debates about home grown terrorists, other types of 'crimmigrants' and integrating immigrant populations. This type of politics creates groups of subcitizens—or what might be termed 'outsiders inside'—who, although territorially included, find their citizenship status securitized and substantially depleted. Here, systems such as the PNR [Passenger Name Records], Schengen and Entry/Exit, enable the authorities to uncover the potentially risky and untrustworthy individuals, overstayers and 'troublemakers' mentioned above, who are (no longer) deemed worthy of freedom of movement. Unlike noncitizens, who are subjected to zoepolitics, these groups can be described as irregular or 'flawed citizens'; they belong formally, but their inclusion is morally in question.

It would be misleading, however, to suggest that these forms of control can be found in their pure, or extreme, forms in the surveillance systems described in this article. Rather, what we often see is symbiosis, hybridity and mutual interaction. For example, preserving life plays an important role in justifying the Eurosur system (at least at the discursive level), while the practical consequences of Frontex's actions may be to increase migrant vulnerability and even mortality. Moreover, normalizing, panoptic forms of control, have a long history of incorporating elements of banishment and territorial exclusion, exemplified by prisons and other closed institutions. . . .

However, we need an additional caveat if we are to understand gate-opening forms of surveillance which are afforded to privileged non-citizens. These are exemplified by IRIS and the Registered Traveler program, which create an internal differentiation in the zoe by letting in life which, in a sense, should be bare, yet it is not. Termed, in a different context, by [Jennifer] Hyndman as 'supracitizens', such individuals enjoy higher forms of mobility and privilege compared to other groups of foreigners, 'usually on the basis of the resources—economic, educational and cultural—which they bring with them'. This includes not only foreign business, diplomatic and cultural elites, frequent flyers (from visa white-listed and occasionally also from visa black-listed countries), but also those 'humanitarian internationals', such as staff of international relief agencies, academics, consultants, lobbyists and international human rights workers. Although their position evades easy categorization, one might say that they inhabit the global biopolitical rooms which have been carved out of the zoe. This inclusion into the global bios is, importantly, not primarily connected to citizenship but most often to private forms of economic, cultural and social capital.

This development has prompted some observers to ask 'what is left of citizenship'. The question suggests a process of decomposition, where the original 'citizen' or 'sovereign' or 'authority' has decayed. According to [Benjamin] Muller, in western societies citizenship is being decomposed into 'identity management'. The shift is exemplified by a change in focus from questions of entitlement and rights, and attendant cultural and ethnic attributes of citizenship, to questions of 'verifying/authenticating "identity" for the purpose of access to rights, bodies, spaces, and so forth'. To understand this development demands a thorough analysis of one of the central techniques for constructing safe identities in contemporary societies: biometric technology. Biometrics (predominantly fingerprinting, but also facial and iris recognition) are, with the exception of the PNR and the first edition of the SIS, employed in all of the databases described above. Biometrics are used both to detect illegal migrants and so-called asylum shoppers through the EURODAC system, overstayers in the planned Entry/Exit system, and to speed up movement and open gates at Automated Border Crossings, for IRIS, FLUX and Registered Travelers. . . .

These two types of surveillance must be analysed in relation to each other. . . . Although a growing strata of the population is captured by this surveillance of mobility (as evidenced by the sheer potential size of systems such as VIS and Entry/Exit), we should nevertheless be careful not to normalize the experience and to identify its socially stratified qualities which are directed only at certain populations. The often heard refrain about the mundane nature of surveillance and the erosion of citizenship, as well as Agamben's prediction about all life potentially becoming bare life, should be therefore balanced by taking into account the exceptional exclusionary and inclusionary nature of surveillance. Rather than exception becoming the norm, and citizenship dissolving into bare life, the examples discussed in this article show that citizenship is still a highly relevant analytical and political category, albeit one containing important exceptions. So, while EU surveillance systems are increasingly directed toward EU citizens, these practices are predominantly directed at specific groups of 'crimmigrant' others who form a class of subcitizens, where crime control objectives define the terms of their exclusion from the bios. The flip side of this negative exceptionalism is the positive exceptionalism directed at bona fide foreign citizens who, although treated as potential crimmigrants in the vetting procedures, are nevertheless empowered by surveillance, to open gates that remain closed to the vast majority of the world's less privileged populations.

# 28

# DIDIER BIGO

# SECURITY, EXCEPTION, BAN, AND SURVEILLANCE

Didier Bigo, along with his extended team of researchers, has been crucial to bridging the gap between international relations (IR) and critical security studies, on one hand, and surveillance studies, on the other. His development of the concept of the "ban-opticon" (or the exclusionary logics of surveillance) has been accompanied and supported by rigorous and detailed institutional research mapping the new "landscape" of intelligence, surveillance, and security. His work has largely addressed the context of the European Union, although its connections to the United States in the post-9/11 period are clear.

\*\*\*

The notion of 'ban' originates from international relations (IR) and critical security studies and is on a parallel track with surveillance studies. The ban-opticon deconstructs some of the post-September 11 analysis as a 'permanent state of emergency' or as a 'generalized state of exception', which reinstates the question of who decides about the exception in the heart of the IR debate: who is sovereign, and who can legitimately name the public enemy. The ban-opticon dispositif is established in relation to a state of unease created by the United States and its allies. The United States has propagated the idea that there is a global 'in-security', which is attributed to the development of threats of mass destruction, thought to be derived from terrorist and other criminal organizations and governments that support them. This has led the US to assert the need for a globalized security that would render national borders obsolete and pressure other international actors to collaborate. These developments have created the field of 'unease management', which is the formation of global police networks, policing military functions of combat and criminalizing the notion of war. The governmentality of unease is characterized by practices of exceptionalism, acts of profiling and containing foreigners, and a normative imperative of mobility.

The ban attempts to show how the role of routines and acceptance of everyday life protects some over others, or how the protection of these others against themselves as the profound structure which explains the 'moment' of the declaration of exception. It also attempts to reveal the judicial illusion that a specific moment declares the sovereign borders of the political, which is so favoured in many analyses. This view needs to be amended by a sociological stance that takes into account long-term social processes and public acceptance of the routines of surveillance. . . .

In relation to the framing of the ban-opticon, the underlying argument emerging from discussions about September 11 and the notion of the state of exception and the detention of foreigners, is to try to understand that exceptionalism is not only linked with derogatory measures and special laws against presumed terrorists, but also with a specific form of governmentality. The governmentality of unease increases the exception and banalizes it. The declaration of an emergency in security by the US, United Kingdom and Australian authorities, and with some nuances in some countries of the European Union, is not the central element of the ban-opticon. Even if these declarations of emergency attempt to change the way we are governed, they do not have the ability to upset the rule of law. A large majority of countries have not 'declared' a 'state of exception', they have merely implemented old and new surveillance technologies, and reinforced control over foreigners without citing any emergency or terrorism activities. Many countries like Austria, Italy, and France have also equated the notion of the criminalization of migration, radical Islam and clandestine organizations with arguments of a struggle against terrorism, organized crime and illegal migration, using the same techniques of dataveillance, of increased checks of identity by different means.

In the US, the 'emergency' has been a way to justify a war against Afghanistan and at the same moment, a militarization of internal security, an enlargement of the role of external intelligence services inside, and a downsizing of the role

of police, judges, parliament, and international agreements. . . .

The 'unanimism' of the professionals of politics after September 11 created a specific period for the enunciation of a discourse of necessity of war against terrorism and suspicion against foreigners, ethnic and religious minorities, but it was rooted in previous practices. These previous 'routines' enable the executive, in so-called time of emergency, to use the justification of prolonged derogatory measures (such as indefinite detention, the demand for longer retention of telecommunications traffic data, introduction of new biometric identifiers in visas, passports and ID cards, as well as the use of transnational exchange of passenger name records) with the argument that it is necessary to act to protect people and to reassure the task of collective survival. This political move is embedded in the expansion of resources for control and monitoring opened by the combination of new technologies reconfiguring the relation between space, time, speed and distance and the will of the bureaucracies of control to use them at their maximum. . . .

All these derogatory and emergency measures are supposed to answer the questions haunting security services and politicians. How will it be possible to find the boundaries again, the distinctions between those who are hostile and the 'others' when everybody is inside the country? How can people be protected against those wanting to get in and how can they clarify their motivations? How can somebody anticipate their actions? How can somebody control the fear of others, of all others, including their relatives? It is clear that classical control procedures and the indiscriminate use of IT linked to other identification technologies using digital imprints, photo-numerical systems, iris or genetic imprints, is not the solution. Nevertheless, the narratives of the professionals of politics in the US and Europe, the discourses of the main international bodies and the main world companies repeat again and again that technologies of control are not a solution, but that the solution to terror is in its capacity to trace the movement of people, to recognize patterns of behaviour and to prevent the suspected terrorists or criminals to act. . . .

From September 11, the transnationalization of the bureaucracies of surveillance is seen as the alternative to the Sisyphean task to seal the borders at a national level. Global surveillance by coordination of the different services inside and by the different nodes of coordination at the Western Level is seen as an 'imperative' which cannot be delayed by any consideration of privacy. Every politician, either in favour of the war or for a more judicial approach, agrees on this view; more centralized and globalized intelligence about people on the move is the key to success against all the evils generated by the freedom of movement of persons.

The main narrative starts with the security of airplanes and the request for air marshals inside planes. The security of airplanes depends on knowing that nobody has brought arms onto the plane under a false name; thus the security of airports relies on the reinforcement of the control of luggage and of the identity of the people travelling abroad. . . .

The goal is to control identities in the most invisible manner possible, and [the advertisements of security companies] signal that this is the best way 'due to the fact that this society of individuals does not like to be affected or slowed down when controlled, but as long as they do not register the act of control, they do not protest'. One can therefore think of generalizing the system in the future not only in airports but in any collective place, in the name of transparency (not to hide from the police) and fear of the future.

The discussion about airport security and safety shows the extent of the US government's unease. The discourse is moving toward more control by the state and public agents in airports and for systematic control over everyone, but social practices are moving massively in the other direction. Privatization is one factor; so is the desire of the rich not to be targeted. If surveillance practices become private, the multiplicity of actors will limit any attempt to have a good system of data protection. In short, controls are always differentiated and carried out under different logic. They articulate more than they integrate. They are unequal and do not target the same people in the same way. They reinforce the advantages of some and the disadvantages of others, even if sometimes they have contradictory and unpredictable effects. These effects come also from multiple technologies and disciplines and are not only confined to border technologies and their locus, but are concentrated there.

It is not the proliferation of these technologies that is surprising, it is the will to de-differentiate them, to interconnect databases and to enlarge their possible use, especially those of police and intelligence services. The development of all these technologies is correlated with the rise of surveillance, from the mid-1980s and especially after the end of bipolarity. These technologies are not at all new, but they are now intensified and globalized. For example, the Schengen Information System (SIS) manages individual dossiers, and functions as a file preventing illegal migrants from returning to the EU. This system is not very effective at managing criminality, but Schengen is now seen as the cornerstone of all security in Europe. . . .

[T]o focus on governmental antiterrorist policies alone, on Guantanamo Bay and torture in Iraq or elsewhere, without seeing the relationship to the daily treatment of foreigners at the borders and the suspicion concerning any deviant behaviour, is misleading. We need to insist on this normalization of emergency as a technique of government by unease, and on the success of the differentiation between a normalized population which is pleased to be monitored 'against danger' and an 'alienation' of some groups of people considered as dangerous 'others'.

The surveillance and monitoring of the movement of each individual is growing, but effective controls and coercive restrictions of freedom are concentrated on specific targets. These targets are constructed as 'invisible and powerful enemies in networks' and the narratives concerning these threats predate September 11 and even the end of bipolarity. Nevertheless, September 11 has reinforced the idea that the struggle against these threats justifies the profiling of certain people's potential behaviours, especially if they are 'on the move'. The political reaction to September 11 justifies a proactive and pre-emptive strategy, which has the ambition to know, and to monitor the 'future'. The call for preventive action creates uncertainty and gathers, inside large transnational databases, to control the judiciary protection of privacy, both solid information about the past, and rumours collected by different sources. They are used to create profiles and trends in order to anticipate the events through social sciences and psychological bodies of knowledge. But in fact, this new technique is mixing the newest technologies (biometrics, databases, DNA analysis) with a kind of astrological discourse of intelligence agencies and of some professionals of politics concerning their capacity to know the future with some certainty. It is driven by a faith in the truth of the body identification as a sign for a predictable pattern of behaviour. And it fails.

# SECTION 6

# INTELLIGENCE AND SECURITY
/////////////////////////////////////////////////////////////////////////////////////////////////////////////////

Edward Snowden rekindled interest in the murky world of state and military intelligence when he leaked US National Security Agency (NSA) documents in 2013. Two of the excerpts in this section concentrate on this agency: one from veteran journalist James Bamford's early 1980s account of the then little-known agency, and the other from journalist Glenn Greenwald, who was Snowden's initial contact. It is worth bearing in mind that however extensive the NSA's networks and programs, and however impressive its technologies, it remains just one powerful intelligence agency in a larger global network of allied national intelligence agencies.

Military interests intersect with and often motivate state intelligence operations. Although some of the writers who strongly influenced the direction of surveillance studies placed the development of surveillance within a broader context of militarism (e.g., Dandeker 1990; Giddens 1987), the military remained underemphasized until well after 9/11. In addition, studies of intelligence were largely carried out within a narrow, not very central subfield of international relations (IR) and security studies, and, reflecting the conservatism of IR more generally, were regarded with some skepticism if they deviated from official sources.

There are three interweaving streams of military surveillance development: warfare, occupation, and espionage. In the first stream, surveillance is concerned with knowing "the enemy" and the situation ("terrain"). Warfare overlaps with the history of many sociotechnical fields; for example, almost all technologies of flight have a military surveillance purpose or early adaptation (Adey 2010; Packer and Reeves 2013). Hot-air balloons were used to surveil troop deployments and defenses during nineteenth-century conflicts, including the US Civil War, and during the Cold War, supersonic and high-flying aircraft were used for military espionage, for example, America's U2 and SR-71 Blackbird planes. Now, new generations of drones or Unmanned Aerial Vehicles (UAVs) of all sizes operate from the edge of space right down to the battlefield (Parks and Kaplan 2017; Wall and Monahan 2011). The history of military camouflage, or art of evading surveillance, grew alongside these developments in verticality and optics (Shell 2012). The changing situation of conflict, in particular the renewed emphasis in the 1990s on fighting in cities (Military Operations in Urban Terrain—MOUT), has led to a military embrace of video surveillance and research and development of smaller, disguised sensors, many drawing from natural inspirations (so-called biomimetic devices), as well as of surveillance and combat robots. But, just as in Bentham's Panopticon where it was not only the inmates who were watched but also the guards, in warfare, it is not just the "enemy" who is watched but also one's own soldiers. Military discipline was an early indicator of modern surveillance described in Foucault's (1977) *Discipline and Punish*. Perhaps the main reasons for such management are that soldiers are expensive but unreliable "assets": they are often reluctant to kill others; they suffer from fatigue; and they use illicit substances to stay awake, improve performance, or overcome combat boredom. The monitoring of troops has become increasingly technologized and intimate. For example, the US military research program "Objective Force Warrior" has attempted to develop real-time body sensors and automated medical systems— *somatic surveillance* (Monahan and Wall 2007)—incorporated into light-weight armored bodysuits for soldiers.

The second stream of military surveillance, as described in Alfred McCoy's *Policing America's Empire* (excerpted in Chapter 30), relates to the development of surveillance as a mode of counterinsurgency in imperial policing. McCoy's study is of US neo-imperialism in the Philippines and how the techniques devised there were not only developed into a whole strategic field of counterinsurgency that was widely used elsewhere, but were also "brought home" to the United States and drawn upon for internal political policing. Similar stories have been told of the United Kingdom, where techniques developed in the later period of the British Empire, such as fingerprinting in India, spread to other parts of the Empire, like Ireland, as well as to major English cities like London. These patterns can be witnessed in contemporary colonial situations too, as in the

AeroVironment Nano-Hummingbird, 2011, sponsored by US Defense Advanced Research Projects Agency (DARPA).

Israel-Palestine conflict described in the excerpt by Ahmad Sa'di, which presents a distillation of the bleeding edge of contemporary counterinsurgency surveillance techniques (see also Zureik, Lyon, and Abu-Laban 2011).

The final stream is the more conventional story of espionage. It was during the twentieth century that international espionage moved from being a rather intermittently used tool of government—very much subsidiary to diplomacy, as it had been, for example, since the formation of a small agency under Francis Walsingham during the reign of Elizabeth I of England in the sixteenth century—to being a key part of what former US president Eisenhower would call the "military-industrial complex." The foundation of early formal intelligence agencies took place largely during and after the First World War, with the Naval Intelligence division of the British Admiralty, then the most powerful military force in the world. The institutionalization and professionalization of state intelligence apparatuses accelerated in the decades after the war, with the forming of the US Central Intelligence Agency (CIA) in 1947 and the NSA in 1952, among others.

Although new technologies did not determine the direction of military and other surveillance practices, the synergy of perceived need, institutional commitment, postwar interdisciplinary experiments in cybernetics, and new technologies catalyzed a new formation of state intelligence. Technological developments in this environment were underpinned by new military-academic research fields—in particular, cybernetics and space science—and massively funded military research organizations, including the Advanced Research Projects Agency (ARPA—later, with the addition of "Defense," DARPA). The first consequential innovation was the computer, with its accelerated development occurring largely in response to sophisticated mechanical encryption deployed by German forces in the Second World

War. The second, also an indirect product of that war, was the communications satellite, which US intelligence agencies began to operate from 1959 onward. And the third innovation was the growth of telecommunications technologies more generally. Each of these innovations would facilitate military espionage and surveillance more broadly.

These technological developments supported a massive global surveillance network. The United States solidified its dominance in this field by the end of World War II with the signing of agreements like the Britain-USA (BRUSA) agreement, relating to signals intelligence sharing, which was succeeded in the immediate postwar period by the UKUSA agreement. This agreement became the basis for what is now known as the "Five Eyes" network, with ex-British colonies Canada, Australia, and New Zealand added to the original partnership. As the excerpt reproduced here from Glenn Greenwald's book on the Snowden revelations shows, the spy network has greatly expanded to include many other willing and reluctant allies of the United States. Additionally, postwar Europe was saturated by a multiplicity of US counterinsurgency and intelligence operations, from the Gladio network of anti-Nazi agents, to cultural programs, which included the promotion of European political unification and anti-communist cultural initiatives. Similar networked intelligence efforts also occurred in the Soviet Union and the Warsaw Pact nations, as well as in several other countries, particularly France, which remained outside NATO and therefore developed an independent intelligence and satellite surveillance capability.

The potential for comprehensive forms of military surveillance was realized relatively early, with American military strategists in the Cold War period working toward what they conceived of as a "closed world" of total information control (Edwards 1996), which combined cybernetics and surveillance to recreate the globe as a defensible, secure space. Along with the creation of multiple orbital satellite surveillance systems, this closed-world impulse also led in the late 1960s to the combination of computing and telecommunications into a secure, distributed packet-switching electronic communications system, ARPAnet, which would form the foundations for the Internet.

By the early 1990s, Manuel DeLanda (1991) could write without irony in his groundbreaking work, *War in the Age of Intelligent Machines*, of the emergence of a US military "panspectron," extending the logic of the Panopticon beyond the simply visible to all frequencies of the electromagnetic spectrum. At this time, in the immediate post–Cold War period, there were some briefly expressed hopes for a peace dividend and even a post-military society, but the so-called military-industrial complex rapidly diversified to cultivate civilian markets for surveillance and dataveillance products, as well as to maintain purely military production. This enabled the growth of an even larger, military-*security* complex, or a "neoconopticon" that emphasized private-sector involvement coupled with conservative political ideologies (Hayes 2009). Besides technological production, a variety of other indicators characterize this arena. These include, first, the transfer of discourse between civil and military fields: while the business world increasingly makes reference to "threat assessments," "information warfare," and "disruption," the military deploys business terminology, such as "core competencies" and "solutions," to describe its internal operations. This sharing of discourse is also part of a more profound shift in public-private partnerships among security organizations, seen for instance with the outsourcing of state intelligence work to private contractors. Roughly 70 percent of the US intelligence budget goes to private

companies (Halchin 2015), and one should not forget that Snowden was an employee of one such company, Booz Allen Hamilton, when he accessed the NSA documents he would later leak. Another change is the increasing similarity of militaries and police forces. As the US military acts as a "global police," US military techniques and equipment have also infiltrated domestic police forces, as seen with military-like raids and the purchase and use of body armor, helmet-cams, and both lethal and "less lethal" weaponry. Military style intelligence programs have also "come home" in the post-9/11 period, with some examples being the growth of the Homeland Security field in the United States and the development of Fusion Centers and Domain Awareness Centers in cities across the country (Monahan 2011).

## NOTE

It is worth outlining briefly the different types of security intelligence surveillance. The first is human intelligence (HUMINT), what one might call old-fashioned spying through contacts, informers, etc. This is traditionally what the US Central Intelligence Agency or Britain's MI6 do. With the growth of social media, a subdivision of HUMINT called open-source intelligence (OSINT) or social media intelligence (SOCMINT) has emerged. OSINT originally referred to conventional media monitoring, but now encompasses social media too. Signals intelligence (SIGINT) agencies deal with information that contains (either individually or in combination) communications intelligence (COMINT), electronic intelligence (ELINT), and foreign instrumentation signals intelligence (FISINT). COMINT refers to information obtained for intelligence purposes from (foreign) communications interception and could thus be interpreted as including SOCMINT. Finally, another very important domain is imagery intelligence (IMINT) or photographic intelligence (PHOTINT).

## REFERENCES

Adey, Peter. 2010. *Aerial Life: Spaces, Mobilities, Affects.* Malden, MA: Wiley-Blackwell.

Bauman, Zygmunt. 1995. *Life in Fragments: Essays in Postmodern Morality.* Oxford: Blackwell.

Dandeker, Christopher. 1990. *Surveillance, Power, and Modernity: Bureaucracy and Discipline from 1700 to the Present Day*. Cambridge, UK: Polity.

DeLanda, Manuel. 1991. *War in the Age of Intelligent Machines*. New York: Zone Books.

Edwards, Paul N. 1996. *The Closed World: Computers and the Politics of Discourse in Cold War America*. Cambridge, MA: MIT Press.

Foucault, Michel. 1977. *Discipline and Punish: The Birth of the Prison*. New York: Vintage.

Giddens, Anthony. 1987. *The Nation-State and Violence: Volume 2 of A Contemporary Critique of Historical Materialism*. Berkeley: University of California Press.

Halchin, L. Elaine. 2015. The Intelligence Community and Its Use of Contractors: Congressional Oversight Issues. Congressional Research Service, August 18. Available from https://www.fas.org/sgp/crs/intel/R44157.pdf [accessed July 15, 2016].

Hayes, Ben. 2009. *Neoconopticon: The EU Security-Industrial Complex*. Statewatch and the Transnational Institute. Available from http://www.tni.org/sites/www.tni.org/files/download/neoconopticon_0.pdf [accessed May 17, 2013].

Monahan, Torin. 2011. The Future of Security? Surveillance Operations at Homeland Security Fusion Centers. *Social Justice* 37 (2–3):84–98.

Monahan, Torin, and Tyler Wall. 2007. Somatic Surveillance: Corporeal Control through Information Networks. *Surveillance & Society* 4 (3):154–73.

Packer, Jeremy, and Joshua Reeves. 2013. Romancing the Drone: Military Desire and Anthropophobia from SAGE to Swarm. *Canadian Journal of Communication* 38 (3):309–31.

Parks, Lisa, and Caren Kaplan, eds. 2017. *Life in the Age of Drone Warfare*. Durham, NC: Duke University Press.

Shell, Hanna Rose. 2012. *Hide and Seek: Camouflage, Photography, and the Media of Reconnaissance*. New York: Zone Books.

Wall, Tyler, and Torin Monahan. 2011. Surveillance and Violence from Afar: The Politics of Drones and Liminal Security-Scapes. *Theoretical Criminology* 15 (3):239–54.

Zureik, Elia, David Lyon, and Yasmeen Abu-Laban, eds. 2011. *Surveillance and Control in Israel/Palestine: Population, Territory and Power*. New York: Routledge.

# 29

# JAMES BAMFORD

## THE PUZZLE PALACE

Inside the National Security Agency,
America's Most Secret Intelligence Organization

As an early whistleblower, in the 1970s, of domestic surveillance by the United States National Security Agency, James Bamford was threatened with espionage charges. His findings informed congressional investigation into domestic surveillance, by the "Church Committee," leading to the establishment of the Foreign Intelligence Surveillance Court— which is an oversight court that Bamford criticizes for being largely ineffective. Although Bamford has since written two further accounts of the NSA, his first, *The Puzzle Palace*, remains notable for having been the first book-length account of the world's largest signals intelligence (SIGINT) organization.

*** 

At 12:01 on the morning of November 4, 1952, a new federal agency was born. Unlike other such bureaucratic births, however, this one arrived in silence. No news coverage, no congressional debate, no press announcement, not even the whisper of a rumor. Nor could any mention of the new organization be found in the Government Organization Manual or the Federal Register or the Congressional Record. Equally invisible were the new agency's director, its numerous buildings, and its ten thousand employees.

Eleven days earlier, on October 24, President Harry S Truman scratched his signature on the bottom of a seven-page presidential memorandum addressed to Secretary of State Dean G. Acheson and Secretary of Defense Robert A. Lovett. Classified top secret and stamped with a code word that was itself classified, the order directed the establishment of an agency to be known as the National Security Agency....

Thirty years later Mr. Truman's memorandum is still one of Washington's most closely guarded secrets. Those seven pages remain "the foundation upon which all past and current communications intelligence activities of the United States government are based," according to a senior official of the National Security Council. And in its defense against a 1976 lawsuit seeking access to the memorandum, the NSA argued successfully against the release of even one word: "The Memorandum remains the principal charter of the National Security Agency and is the basis of a number of other classified documents governing the conduct of communications intelligence activities and operations, functions [and] activities of the National Security Agency." Even a congressional committee was forced to issue a subpoena in order to obtain a copy of the directive that implemented the memorandum. . . .

Despite its size and power, however, no law has ever been enacted prohibiting the NSA from engaging in any activity. There are only laws to prohibit the release of any information about the Agency. "No statute establishes the NSA," former Senate Intelligence Committee chairman Frank Church reported, "or defines the permissible scope of its responsibilities." The CIA, on the other hand, was established by Congress under a public law, the National Security Act of 1947, setting out that agency's legal mandate as well as the restrictions on its activities. In addition to being free of legal restrictions, the NSA has technological capabilities for eavesdropping beyond imagination. Such capabilities once led former Senate Intelligence Committee member Walter F. Mondale to point to the NSA as "possibly the most single important source of intelligence for this nation."

Yet the very same capabilities that provide the United States with its greatest intelligence resource also provide the nation with one of its greatest potential dangers. Noted Senator Church: "That capability at any time could be turned around on the American people and no American would have any privacy left, such is the capability to monitor everything: telephone conversations, telegrams, it doesn't matter. There would be no place to hide." . . .

The systematic inclusion of American names and organizations in NSA's watch lists, which began in 1962, took a major swing upward in 1967. On October 20 of that year, Major General William P. Yarborough, the Army's assistant chief of staff for Intelligence, sent a TOP SECRET COMINT CHANNELS ONLY message to NSA director Marshall Carter, requesting that NSA provide any available information about possible foreign influence on civil disturbances in the United States.

I would appreciate any information [the Yarborough message said] on a continuing basis covering the following:

A. Indications that foreign governments or individuals or organizations acting as agents of foreign governments are controlling or attempting to control or influence the activities of U.S. "peace" groups and "Black Power" organizations.
B. Identities of foreign agencies exerting control or influence on U.S. organizations.
C. Identities of individuals and organizations in the U.S. in contact with agents of foreign governments.
D. Instructions or advice being given to U.S. groups by agents of foreign governments.

To one senior NSA official, the receipt of such a request was "unprecedented. . . . It is kind of a landmark in my memory; it stands out as a first." . . .

As the Army began sending over its pages of protesters' names, other agencies did the same—some individually, some on preprinted forms, and some simply on the telephone.

The Secret Service delivered a watch list containing names of individuals and organizations active in the antiwar and civil rights movements, presumably believing that picking up their phone calls and messages might in some way help protect the President.

The CIA was interested in "the activities of U.S. individuals in either civil disorder, radical student or youth activities, racial militant activities, radical antiwar activities, draft evasion/deserter support activities, or in radical related media activities where such individuals have some foreign connection." The FBI and the DIA followed suit.

The names on the various watch lists ranged from member of radical political groups to celebrities to ordinary citizens involved in protest against their government. Included were such well-known figures as Jane Fonda, Joan Baez, Dr. Benjamin Spock, Dr. Martin Luther King, Jr., the Reverend Ralph Abernathy, Black Panther leader Eldridge Cleaver, and Chicago Seven defendants Abbie Hoffman and David T. Dillinger.

A frightening side effect of the watch list program was the tendency of most lists to grow expanding far beyond their original intent. The multiplier effect was caused by the inclusion of names of people who came in contact with those persons and organizations already on the list. Because of NSA's vacuum cleaner approach to intelligence collection—whereby it sucks into its system the maximum amount of telecommunications and then filters it through an enormous screen of "trigger words"—analysts end up reviewing telephone calls, telegrams, and telex messages to and from thousands of innocent persons having little or nothing to do with the actual focus of the effort. Thus if an organization is targeted, all its members' communications may be intercepted; if an individual is listed on a watch list, all communications to, from, or even mentioning that individual are scooped up. Captured in NSA's net were communications about a peace concert, a communication mentioning the wife of a U.S. senator, a correspondent's report from Southeast Asia to his magazine in New York, and a pro–Vietnam War activist's invitations to speakers for a rally. . . .

One of the oldest, and probably most strictly followed, internal NSA guidelines was the prohibition against entirely domestic eavesdropping—where both terminals were located within the United States. It was possibly the rule that caused the most consternation, since it eliminated the possibility of collecting the communications between the

foreign embassies in Washington and their consulates and UN missions in New York. "If the Russian [consulate] in New York calls the Russian embassy in Washington, that's domestic intelligence," complained Frank Raven. "If it's going to South America, it's all right . . . but if it's going between New York and Washington, you can't touch it."

For twenty-five years the NSA struggled in total secrecy over the questions of foreign versus domestic intelligence collection. Its power to eavesdrop, the Agency had always insisted, came under no earthly laws but rather emanated from some celestial "inherent presidential authority" reposed in the chief executive by the Constitution. . . .

[T]he FISA [Foreign Intelligence Surveillance Act] was finally signed into law by President Jimmy Carter, who also backed the bill, on October 25, 1978. For decades the technology of espionage had greatly outpaced the law. Now, with the FISA, the lawmakers were attempting to catch up. The statute would at last bring under the rule of law an area of surveillance that had heretofore been considered far too sensitive even to discuss with another branch of government: electronic eavesdropping within the United States on foreign embassies, diplomats, and agents of foreign powers.

The key to the legislation could have been dreamed up by Franz Kafka: the establishment of a supersecret federal court. Sealed away behind a cipher-locked door in a windowless room on the top floor of the Justice Department building, the Foreign Intelligence Surveillance Court is most certainly the strangest creation in the history of the federal Judiciary. Its establishment was the product of compromises between legislators who wanted the NSA and FBI, the only agencies affected by the FISA, to follow the standard procedure of obtaining a court order required in criminal investigations, and legislators who felt the agencies should have no regulation whatsoever in their foreign intelligence surveillances. . . .

Given the fact that the top secret court has never said no to the government, it would be difficult to conclude that it has become anything other than a rubber stamp. . . . Even more disturbing than the apparent evolution of the surveillance court into an Executive Branch rubber stamp are the gaping holes and clever wording of the FISA statute, which nearly void it of usefulness. Such language, intentional as well as unintentional, permits the NSA to rummage at will through the nation's international telecommunications network and to target or watch-list any American who happens to step foot out of the country.

Once an American leaves the United States, he or she is stripped of any protection from the NSA. The Agency is permitted to target, record, transcribe, and disseminate any and all of his or her communications the same way it would the communications of the Red Brigades. There is no statutory requirement to seek approval from the surveillance court, the Attorney General, or any other authority. . . .

The major advantage of the FISA statute is that NSA is no longer permitted to target or watch-list Americans by name without an FISA warrant, even in international communications as long as the person happens to be located on U.S. soil. Yet even this welcome reform appears to be undermined by what may be the Agency's most sinister loophole.

"Electronic surveillance," the statute reads, means "the acquisition by an electronic, mechanical, or other surveillance device" of the approved targets. But nowhere does the statute define the meaning of the key word acquisition. Rather, it is left to NSA to define—which it does in a top secret document. "Acquisition," according to the document, "means the interception by the National Security Agency through electronic means of a communication to which it is not an intended party and the processing of the contents of that communication into an intelligible form intended for human inspection."

By carefully inserting the words "by the National Security Agency," the Agency has skillfully excluded from the coverage of the FISA statute as well as the surveillance court all interceptions received from the British GCHQ or any other non-NSA source. Thus it is possible for GCHQ to monitor the necessary domestic or foreign circuits of interest and pass them on to NSA through the UKUSA Agreement. Once they were received, NSA could process the communications through its own computers and analysts, targeting and watch-listing Americans with impunity, since the action would not be covered under the FISA statute or any other law. . . .

Then there is the last, and possibly most intriguing, part of the definition, which stipulates that NSA has not "acquired" anything until the communication has been processed "into an intelligible form intended for human inspection." NSA is therefore free to intercept all communications, domestic as well as foreign, without ever coming under the law. Only when it selects the "contents" of a particular communication for further "processing" does the FISA take effect. . . .

The major problem with the two revolutions, the tremendous advances in the use of satellite and microwave technology and the enormous growth of SIGINT, is that they have left a void where there should have been a third revolution: the law. Three decades after its creation, the NSA is still without a formal, statutory charter, the first reform called for by the Church Committee.

Instead, there is a super hush-hush surveillance court that is virtually impotent; the FISA, which has enough loopholes and exceptions to render it nearly useless; and an executive order that was designed more to protect the intelligence community from the citizens than citizens from the agencies. In addition, because it is an executive order, it can be changed any time at the whim of a President, without so much as a nod toward Congress.

Like an ever-widening sinkhole, NSA's surveillance technology will continue to expand, quietly pulling in more and more communications and gradually eliminating more and more privacy.

# 30

# ALFRED W. MCCOY

## POLICING AMERICA'S EMPIRE

### The United States, the Philippines, and the Rise of the Surveillance State

Alfred McCoy's book traces one path of what Stephen Graham has called "Foucault's boomerang"—the way in which colonial states used colonized countries as test beds for new forms of surveillance and military pacification technologies that they could then deploy at home—in this case, through a history of United States neo-imperialism in the Philippines and an exploration of its ramifications for both countries. It is a large, detailed book, to which a short excerpt cannot do justice, yet this, from the opening chapter, gives some of the flavor of the argument.

\*\*\*

At the dawn of the twentieth century, Commodore George Dewey of the U.S. Navy arrayed his squadron of steel-hulled warships at the edge of Asia. Steaming across Manila Bay at first light on May 1, 1898, his rapid-fire guns sank the aging Spanish fleet and cleared the way for an attack on Manila. After transports arrived three months later, U.S. Army troops stormed Manila's massive battlements and seized a city Spain had ruled for 350 years. At the cost of just 121 casualties in a single day of sporadic fighting, the United States had become, for the first time in its history, an imperial power.

Yet even in this hour of glory, the U.S. Army faced the immediate threat of a second and far more violent war. Only hours after occupying the city, the Provost Guard was charged with maintaining order in what its commander called "this revolutionary and insurrectionary city of . . . 250,000 inhabitants of the most diverse nationality and . . . [with] an unusually large proportion of the criminal classes . . . , gamblers and speculators, toughs and the blackguards." And ringing the city were trench works bristling with the guns of fifteen thousand Filipino soldiers, the army of a revolutionary republic poised to rise in revolt.

At the dawn of the twenty-first century, Chief Superintendent Florencio Fianza of the Philippine National Police (PNP) arrayed his squads of helmeted riot police before the gates of Manila's presidential palace. Fighting desperately from first light on May 1, 2001, police armed with shotguns and water cannons scattered a mob of fifty thousand urban poor, their bodies marked with gang tattoos and fortified with drugs. At the cost of just 117 civilian casualties in six hours of hand-to-hand fighting, Philippine police had saved the presidency of Gloria Arroyo.

Yet even in its hour of victory the Arroyo administration faced volatile instability. Millions of urban poor filled the fetid slums that ringed Manila, ready to spill into the streets in anger over miserable lives plagued by endemic disease and endless unemployment. Armed with special powers, Arroyo's police would struggle to prevent a recurrence of mass violence by "hoodlums and criminals" hidden in the back alleys of a metropolis swollen to some twenty million inhabitants.

The juxtaposition of these two battles separated by a century reveals the Philippines as the site of a protracted social experiment in the use of police as an instrument of state power. In the late nineteenth century at this edge of empire, freed of the constraints of constitution, courts, and civil society, the U.S. regime deployed its information technologies to form what was arguably the world's first surveillance state. True, [there were precedents and similar formations elsewhere, but] . . . none of these could match the synthesis of legal repression, incessant patrolling, and suffocating surveillance found in the colonial Philippines. During the first decade of U.S. rule, the colonial security services, particularly the multifaceted Philippines Constabulary, succeeded in demobilizing a deeply rooted national revolution and advancing a conservative elite to fill the political void. Hence this study's first

substantive conclusion: the creation of sophisticated modern policing was crucial to the U.S. pacification of the Philippines.

After creating a formidable counterinsurgency force, the U.S. regime installed this coercive apparatus within the Philippine colonial state, making the constabulary central to both its administration and popular perception. With strong links to the executive and minimal checks and balances, the police quickly emerged as a major factor in the country's politics. Moreover, by enacting stringent laws against personal vices such as gambling and drugs, the colonial government inadvertently amplified the role of police as would-be guardians of public morality. After Philippine independence in 1946, the national police remained as a key instrument of both legal and extralegal presidential power. Simultaneously, a symbiosis of police power, political corruption, and vice prohibition soon metastasized into something akin to a social cancer that persisted long after colonial rule, fomenting iconic incidents of abuse and violence. Through corruption and excessive force, the police became the source of the country's recurring legitimation crises, from the electoral violence of the early 1950s through the latest "people power" uprising of 2001. In a nation with countless sources of social conflict, it seems significant that police scandals, often petty or even sordid, should raise such profound issues of political legitimacy. Thus a second major conclusion: the U.S. colonial regime's reliance on police for pacification and political control embedded this security apparatus within an emerging Philippine state, contributing ultimately to an unstable excess of executive power after independence.

Not only did colonial policing influence Philippine state formation, but it also helped transform the U.S. federal government. Indeed, security techniques bred in the tropical hothouse of colonial governance were not contained at this periphery of American power. Through the invisible capillaries of empire, these innovations percolated home-ward to implant both personnel and policies inside the Federal bureaucracy for the for-mation of a new internal security apparatus. During the social crisis surrounding World War I, a small cadre of colonial police vet-erans created a clandestine capacity within the U.S. Army, establishing Military Police for the occupation of a war-torn Europe as well as Military Intelligence for both sur-veillance at home and espionage abroad. Once established under the pressures of wartime mobilization, this federal surveil-lance effort persisted in various forms for the next fifty years, as a sub rosa matrix that honeycombed U.S. society with active informers, secretive civilian organiza-tions, and government counterintelligence agencies.

This exploration of colonial policing thus reveals an important facet of state forma-tion not only in the Philippines but also in the United States. Though generally ignored by U.S. historians as a regrettable, even forgettable episode in the course of American progress, when viewed through the prism of policing the conquest of the Philippines emerges as an event of seminal import. Viewed conservatively, it was a bell-wether, a significant manifestation of the repressive potential of America's first infor-mation revolution, discussed below. Viewed more boldly, it arguably accelerated these changes, making the Philippine Islands a social laboratory at a critical juncture in U.S. history and producing a virtual blue-print for the perfection of American state power. From the time its troops landed at Manila in 1898, the U.S. Army applied the nation's advanced information technology for combat operations and colonial pacifi-cation, merging Spanish police structures with its own data management to create powerful new security agencies. Unchecked by constitutional constraints, American colonials developed innovative counterintel-ligence techniques that expanded the state's ability to monitor its Filipino subjects.

Indeed, the first U.S. federal agency with a fully developed covert capacity was not the Federal Bureau of Investigation (FBI) or the Office of Naval Intelligence (ONI) but the Philippines Constabulary (PC).

These colonial origins were no mere cat-alyst for a process that might have produced the same preordained outcome; instead, through a congruence of motive and oppor-tunity, this imperial influence left a distinc-tive imprint on the character of America's domestic security apparatus. These secret service methods, whether broad infor-mation systems or specific interrogation techniques, have a specific institutional genealogy, a gestational continuity, that requires the historian to track personnel, policies, and precedents, not assuming that they somehow arrive axiomatically with the advent of modernity. While Europe's highly evolved state security services, colonial and national, contributed obliquely to the de-velopment of U.S. intelligence doctrines, the occupation of the Philippines provided a particularly favorable environment for cultivating covert techniques, institutional networks, and systematic surveillance. These security procedures, bred like trop-ical hybrids, were antithetical to American political traditions. But empire provided a vehicle for introducing them into a deeply democratic society. Hence a third conclu-sion: innovative colonial policing in the Philippines influenced the formation of the American state, contributing to the devel-opment of a sophisticated internal security apparatus.

The flow of security personnel and practices coursing through these capillaries of empire was neither unilat-eral nor confined to a particular period. Once their roots were planted in the first decade of colonial rule, the circulation of ideas would continue unabated for an-other century, first westward from Manila to Washington, where they shaped U.S. in-ternal security operations during World War I, and then eastward back across the Pacific, where they strengthened the repressive capacities of the postcolonial Philippine state. Whenever the Philippines has been shaken by insurgency in the last sixty years, Washington has intervened to shore up its security services with an infusion of military aid, first under the Republic (1946–72), then under President Marcos's martial law regime (1972–86), and most recently through President Arroyo's role in the global war on terror (2001–9). Viewed from Manila, these recurring contacts with U.S. security agencies have made police power a key facet of the Philippine state. The Philippines has become a major battleground in the war on terror—another protracted foreign adventure whose security innovations are slowly migrating homeward silently to spread surveillance and curtail civil liberties inside the United States. Thus a fourth conclusion: by collaborating in the refinement of covert techniques for internal security, these two states have forged powerful instruments to fortify themselves against the processes of political change, slowing progress toward civil rights in America and social justice in the Philippines. . . .

In the postcolonial era . . . , the constant U.S. presence in the Philippines exemplified Washington's global reach through overseas bases, military alliances, and CIA covert operations whose sum has been the integration of this and other sovereign nations into a nonterritorial American imperium. For nearly half a century, from 1947 to 1992, the massive air and naval bases near Manila were the largest among hundreds of U.S. military facilities in operation overseas. While nuclear armadas contained communist armies behind the Iron Curtain, a mix of covert intervention and counterinsurgency suppressed any dissidence inside the allied nations that lay on America's side of this global divide. At the dawn of the cold war during the 1950s, the CIA tested new counterinsurgency doctrines against peasant guerrillas in the Philippines. A decade later, as Washington trained anticommunist police worldwide, American advisers helped build a massive antiriot force for metropolitan Manila, laying the foundations for martial rule. When Washington embraced third-world dictators during the 1970s, President Marcos and his first lady were toasted at a White House state dinner. After the United States reversed its policy and began advocating democracy worldwide, the Philippines again led the way with its famed 1986 "people power" revolution against Marcos, a televised uprising that inspired imitation along the Iron Curtain from Beijing to Berlin. Its newly elected president, Corazon Aquino, addressed the U.S. Congress to thunderous applause and graced the cover of Time as the magazine's woman of the year. Since September 2001, President Bush has spoken before the Philippine Congress and U.S. Special Forces have become a constant presence in the Islamic isles of the southern Philippines. Thus, the study of the twentieth-century Philippines reveals much about the changing character of U.S. global power.

# 31

# AHMAD H. SA'DI

## THOROUGH SURVEILLANCE

The Genesis of Israeli Policies of Population
Management, Surveillance, and Political Control
towards the Palestinian Minority

Ahmad Sa'di's work details the methods of surveillance and control deployed against the Palestinians by the State of Israel since its foundation in 1948. As he points out, many of these derive from "emergency" regulations and measures devised by the Military Government after the war following the founding of Israel, and which have never been repealed despite the return to "normal" civilian government.

\*\*\*

The objectives of the Military Government were not confined to surveillance and normalization as in the case of Bentham's panopticon prison; rather, they stemmed from a generalized conception of state security. In 1958, Mishal Shoham, the head of the Military Government, made a distinction between two conceptions of state security: overt/direct and covert/accumulative. The first includes the aims of preventing the return of the refugees, smuggling and espionage, preventing the establishment of Palestinian organizations deemed hostile to the state and the seizure of Palestinian lands for military training (when it was necessary and when it was not, he stated).

The second, the accumulative conception of security, encompassed five goals, which did not have immediate effect on security, but their accumulation, according to Shoham, bolstered it:

(A) To prevent the rehabilitation of deserted villages by their inhabitants who became internal refugees and who lived in nearby localities. . . .

(B) To stop the Palestinian workforce from reaching the labor market in the cities and Jewish settlements in order to keep the available jobs for Jewish migrants.

(C) To prevent Palestinians from moving in 'security-sensitive areas.' . . .

(D) To limit the seizure of state-declared lands. . . .

(E) To protect newly established Jewish settlements that were physically and organizationally weak by preventing Palestinians from passing through their lands. . . .

Shoham used a canonized conception of security, which means—in the words of [David] Kretzmer:

> Security of the state is synonymous with security of the Jewish collective, and that is often seen as being dependent on promoting 'Jewish national goals'. Acts that strengthen the Jewish collective are perceived as acts that promote security. On the other hand, acts that tend to strengthen Arab national aspirations among Israeli Arabs are regarded threatening to the Jewish collective.

Given these goals, it might be misleading to evaluate the Military Government according to its success in perfecting surveillance. Rather, it should be analysed in accordance with the political plans and schemes of the regime.

The second difference between the Military Government and the panopticon metaphor relates to the way in which power was practised. The Military Government was not based on routinized procedures or sets of rules and rituals as in the institutions described by Foucault; rather, in representing a state of exception, it was based on unrestricted arbitrary power. Indeed, the emergency regulations gave the military governors unlimited authority that was subject neither to administrative nor to judicial reviews. . . .

In governing the Palestinians, the Military Government was aided by various bodies which were in charge of surveillance and security directly as well as with organizations employing subtle forms of power. These

organizations include first and foremost the Shin Bet (General Security Services—*Sherut Bitachon Klali*). Established in the summer of 1950, the Shin Bet's main assignment has been the prevention of sabotage and espionage activities. Yet, it had engaged in wide-ranging surveillance of the various aspects of Palestinian lives: it monitored Palestinians in classes, offices, mosques, public spaces and social gatherings to learn about their political attitudes. . . . Such activities were conducted besides the usual practices that such agencies commonly undertake including wiretappings, interception of mail and bugging communication systems. Additionally, the Shin Bet screened, and in many cases continues to screen, Palestinian candidates for positions in state and public sectors such as teachers, headmasters, inspectors, bureaucrats in state . . . bodies and functionaries in Islamic religious institutions. Its recommendations, which are decisive, would be passed in the discussed period, to the Office of the Advisor on Arab Affairs. Additionally, the Shin Bet gave advice to policy-making bodies regarding the policy options towards the Palestinians available to them.

The second agency is the police. Besides its duty of maintaining law and order, it had additional assignments in the Palestinian-populated areas, including political surveillance and control. The police, particularly 'the department for special assignments' (*Matam*), was entrusted with surveillance over the Palestinians as well as coordinating police activities with the Shin Bet and the Military Government. The *Matam* operated sections at the district and the regional levels, known as *Latam*.

These three organizations—the Military Government, the Shin Bet and the police (*Matam*)—along with the Prime Minister's Advisor coordinated the running of Palestinians' everyday lives. . . .

In three aspects, the Military Government could be compared to the panopticon: its fixing of the population to specific spaces, its use of polarities as bases for judgement and its close and continual surveillance and registration.

The majority of Palestinians lived in closed areas, where movement in or out required passes. The three regions under the Military Government were divided and subdivided into smaller units, which in many cases formed the boundaries of a single locality. . . .

These spatial divisions were used as the criteria according to which the military commanders made decisions with regard to the allocations of permits, supplies, transportation and services. The social communications and relationships between the residents were consequently confined to their areas of residence, thus giving rise to localism. Moreover, such divisions made it easier to control Palestinians through state-sponsored programmes. . . .

In line with this objective . . . , various measures were taken to concentrate Palestinians in small areas. For example, on Ben-Gurion's [Israel's first Prime Minister] request to settle Palestinian commute workers in Haifa, Abba Hushi set up a housing company with the bishop Hakim to build and market apartments, yet not much came out of it. Palestinian workers preferred to commute rather than be packed up in dense neighbourhoods. . . .

Yet the idea of having these subdivisions was intended to prevail after the end of the Military Government. The policies towards the Negev Bedouins and the plans for their forced settlement represent perhaps one of the clearest examples of this principle of fixing and concentrating Palestinians. . . .

The second similarity between the Military Government and the panopticon is the employment of a binary classification. It is obvious from the previous two sections that a binary division of the population into Jews and non-Jews comprised a cornerstone in Israeli policy. . . .

The imposition of the Military Government on Palestinian-populated areas meant, in the legal sphere, the establishment of two legal systems: one for Palestinians and another largely for Jews. Although the emergency regulations are stated in universalistic terms, their application was almost confined to Palestinians. For example, Military Governor Shoham stated in 1958 that the areas under the Military Government were drawn in such a way as to be imposed on Palestinian localities only. . . . The discrimination in the application of the law was not only on spatial criteria but on ethnic grounds as well. Indeed, the state comptroller stated in his 1957/8 report:

> An order from the military governor declaring an area closed is, in theory, applicable to all citizens without exception, whether living in the area or outside it. Thus anyone who enters or leaves a closed area without a permit from the military governor is in fact committing a criminal offense. In practice, however, Jews are not expected to carry such permits and in general are not prosecuted for breaking the regulations in article 125.

Another dimension of the legal duality was the establishment of military courts alongside the civilian ones. While the emergency regulations specified the nature of offences which were tried in either of these courts, the military commanders were given discretion in deciding the choice of the court that would deal with any case. The military courts epitomized the arbitrary judicial system which was the essence of the state of emergency.

They were of two types. The first was composed of three officers (who did not necessarily have legal education) who were mandated to deal with any breach of the emergency regulations and to pass any verdict the officers deemed appropriate. The second, of a lower rank, was composed of a single officer who could pass sentences of up to two years' imprisonment and impose fines.

Until 1963, the verdicts of these courts were final. Indeed, many Palestinians passed through this legal system. For example, during March–December 1951, some 2,028 Palestinians stood in these courts. Another type of military court, the tribunal for the prevention of infiltration, was established on the basis of the Prevention of Infiltration Law, [in] 1954. It consisted of a one-officer court that was authorized to deal with all offences of this law, although an appeal could be filed to request a tribunal of three officers. This type of tribunal operated until 1959, when offences under this law were transferred to civilian courts.

To make these arrangement more effective, the police force acting in the Military Government zones was put under military authority. The implication of this duality . . . was the criminalization of Palestinians on political grounds:

> Many categories of crime are a clear 'outcome' of the political character of the law and its selective implementation on the Arab population. During the military government . . . crime in the Arab population was, to a large extent, a result of political control over it . . . the political use made of the criminal law, both in respect of its content and the methods of its enforcement, played a central role in 'creating' crime and delinquency among Arabs. . . . [Thus] a very broad area of social, economic and political activity was defined as 'crime' and was dealt with by the rhetoric and practices of crime control.

Third, intimate surveillance was sought not only through Palestinian collaborators—who passed on information which people made public in social gatherings or while travelling on public transportation—but also through their operators. The regional representatives of the Military Government were required to live in the area under their supervision in order to obtain first-hand and unfiltered information when necessary and to be in reach of the *mukhtar* and collaborators.

Moreover, they preserved what might be considered a primitive archive, a 'record of sins' in which the names and addresses of offenders and their punishments were recorded. More generally, . . . the security agencies paid special attention to the method of face-to-face interview with Palestinians, assuming that the balance of power in such encounters was in their favour as the majority of their interviewees would be anxious and shaken. Moreover, this method enabled them to use ways and means of hearsay, promises or intimidation. . . .

What characterized the state of exception was not only the suspension of the normative law but the awarding of power to officials who would render the law irrelevant and whose behaviour would turn any appeal to justice or rule of law [into] a mockery. Yet, the state of exception was not devoid of laws and regulations, but emergency laws possess different motivations and ends than normal ones. In this regard, it is worth distinguishing rule by law which is characteristic of emergency laws from the normative rule of law.

In the first instance, the rules and regulations are not universally applied and they are considered another tool of domination. Therefore, the law loses its 'objective and universal aura'. Thus, its [stature] is diminished in the eyes of both the dominant and the dominated. . . .

Although . . . abuses were not exceptional, the manner in which the Military Government managed the daily life of Palestinians was by its nature abusive. For example, the Military Governor of Jaffa was surprised by the brutality of his soldiers, complaining that 'They do not stop beating people'. The manner of getting passes was also a humbling experience and was often used as a means of exerting reward or punishment. . . .

Exceptionalism was also characterized by the absence of relevant knowledge by those who were under surveillance, a state which guaranteed their precarious position. The passes were written in Hebrew, a language that the vast majority of the population could not read, and the boundaries of the closed areas were not known to the population.

The Military Government never published the extent of the areas under its control and very rarely disclosed anything about its activities. Anyone wanting to find out which areas he/she could visit without a permit had to go to one of the few Military Government offices or to a police station, which could rarely provide the information. Anyone entering or leaving a closed area without a permit was liable to prosecution for breaking the emergency regulations, despite the fact that he/she did not, or might not, know the boundaries. Ignorance was not a valid excuse before a military court. . . .

While various surveillance methods relating to the panopticon were employed, normalization—as integration—was not sought, and the rule of law did not prevail. Palestinians had lived through a long period under a state of exception. What was the final aim of this combination of surveillance methods? It seems that it was meant to normalize the aspects of life that the state of exception engendered, that is, to condition Palestinians to stop imagining that an autonomous life was possible.

# 32

# GLENN GREENWALD

## NO PLACE TO HIDE

Edward Snowden, the NSA, and
the US Surveillance State

As one of Edward Snowden's key contacts, reporter Glenn Greenwald had unprecedented access to leaked documents on the United States National Security Agency's surveillance programs. The following excerpt, from Greenwald's book *No Place to Hide*, hints at how Snowden intentionally curated his archive of leaked documents to underscore the extent and illegality of the NSA's practices. In the organization's efforts to collect literally *all* telecommunications data throughout the world, it flagrantly transgressed legal prohibitions against wholesale surveillance, particularly—but certainly not only—of American citizens.

*** 

Snowden's files indisputably laid bare a complex web of surveillance aimed at Americans (who are explicitly beyond the NSA's mission) and non-Americans alike. The archive revealed the technical means used to intercept communications: the NSA's tapping of Internet servers, satellites, underwater fiber-optic cables, local and foreign telephone systems, and personal computers. It identified individuals targeted for extremely invasive forms of spying, a list that ranged from alleged terrorists and criminal suspects to the democratically elected leaders of the nation's allies and even ordinary American citizens. And it shed light on the NSA's overall strategies and goals.

Snowden had placed crucial, overarching documents at the front of the archive, flagging them as especially important. These files disclosed the agency's extraordinary reach, as well as its deceit and even criminality. The BOUNDLESS INFORMANT program was one of the first such revelations, showing that the NSA counts all the telephone calls and emails collected every day from around the world with mathematical exactitude. Snowden had placed these files so prominently not only because they quantified the volume of calls and emails collected and stored by the NSA—literally billions each day—but also because they proved that NSA chief Keith Alexander and other officials had lied to Congress. Repeatedly, NSA officials had claimed that they were incapable of providing specific numbers—exactly the data that BOUNDLESS INFORMANT was constructed to assemble.

For the one-month period beginning March 8, 2013, for example, a BOUNDLESS INFORMANT slide showed that a single unit of the NSA, Global Access Operations, had collected data on more than 3 billion telephone calls and emails that had passed through the US telecommunications system. . . . That exceeded the collection from the systems each of Russia, Mexico, and virtually all the countries in Europe, and was roughly equal to the collection of data from China.

Overall, in just thirty days the unit had collected data on more than 97 billion emails and 124 billion phone calls from around the world. Another BOUNDLESS INFORMANT document detailed the international data collected in a single thirty-day period from Germany (500 million), Brazil (2.3 billion), and India (13.5 billion). And yet other files showed collection of metadata in cooperation with the governments of France (70 million), Spain (60 million), Italy (47 million), the Netherlands (1.8 million), Norway (33 million), and Denmark (23 million).

Despite the NSA's statutorily defined focus on "foreign intelligence," the documents confirmed that the American public was an equally important target for the secret surveillance. Nothing made that clearer than the April 25, 2013, top secret order from the FISA [Foreign Intelligence Surveillance Act] court compelling Verizon to turn over to the NSA all information about its American customers' telephone calls, the "telephony metadata." Marked

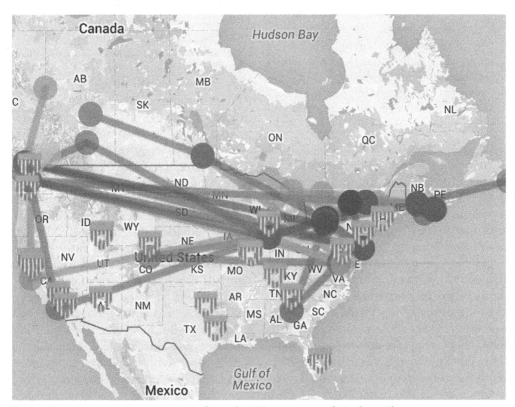

IXmaps Project tracing Internet routes through NSA servers, 2016, Andrew Clement.

"NOFORN," the language of the order was as clear as it was absolute:

> IT IS HEREBY ORDERED that, the Custodian of Records shall produce to the National Security Agency (NSA) upon service of this Order, and continue production on an ongoing daily basis thereafter for the duration of this Order, unless otherwise ordered by the Court, an electronic copy of the following tangible things: all call detail records or "telephony metadata" created by Verizon for communications (i) between the United States and abroad; or (ii) wholly within the United States, including local telephone calls. Telephony metadata includes comprehensive communications routing information, including but not limited to session identifying information (*e.g.*, originating and terminating telephone number, International Mobile Subscriber Identity (IMSI) number, International Mobile station Equipment Identity (IMEl) number, etc.), trunk identifier, telephone calling card numbers, and time and duration of call.

This bulk telephone collection program was one of the most significant discoveries in an archive suffused with all types of covert surveillance programs—from the large-scale PRISM (involving collection of data directly from the servers of the world's biggest Internet companies) and PROJECT BULLRUN, a joint effort between the NSA and its British counterpart, the Government Communications Headquarters (GCHQ), to defeat the most common forms of encryption used to safeguard online transactions, to smaller-scale enterprises with names that reflect the contemptuous and boastful spirit of supremacy behind them: EGOTISTICAL GIRAFFE, which targets the Tor browser

that is meant to enable anonymity in online browsing; MUSCULAR, a means to invade the private networks of Google and Yahoo!; and OLYMPIA, Canada's program to surveil the Brazilian Ministry of Mines and Energy.

Some of the surveillance was ostensibly devoted to terrorism suspects. But great quantities of the programs manifestly had nothing to do with national security. The documents left no doubt that the NSA was equally involved in economic espionage, diplomatic spying, and suspicionless surveillance aimed at entire populations.

Taken in its entirety, the Snowden archive led to an ultimately simple conclusion: the US government had built a system that has as its goal the complete elimination of electronic privacy worldwide. Far from hyperbole, that is the literal, explicitly stated aim of the surveillance state: to collect, store, monitor, and analyze all electronic communication by all people around the globe. The agency is devoted to one overarching mission: to prevent the slightest piece of electronic communication from evading its systemic grasp. . . .

A military branch of the Pentagon, the NSA is the largest intelligence agency in the world, with the majority of its surveillance work conducted through the Five Eyes alliance. Until the spring of 2014, when controversy over the Snowden stories became increasingly intense, the agency was headed by four-star general Keith B. Alexander, who had overseen it for the previous nine years, aggressively increasing the NSA's size and influence during his tenure. In the process, Alexander became what reporter James Bamford described as "the most powerful intelligence chief in the nation's history."

The NSA "was already a data behemoth when Alexander took over," *Foreign Policy* reporter Shane Harris noted, "but under his watch, the breadth, scale, and ambition of its mission have expanded beyond anything ever contemplated by his predecessors." Never before had "one agency of the

U.S. government had the capacity, as well as the legal authority, to collect and store so much electronic information." A former administration official who worked with the NSA chief told Harris that "Alexander's strategy" was clear: "I need to get all of the data." And, Harris added, "He wants to hang on to it for as long as he can."

Alexander's personal motto, "Collect it all," perfectly conveys the central purpose of the NSA. He first put this philosophy into practice in 2005 while collecting signals intelligence relating to the occupation of Iraq. As the *Washington Post* reported in 2013, Alexander grew dissatisfied with the limited focus of American military intelligence, which targeted only suspected insurgents and other threats to US forces, an approach that the newly appointed NSA chief viewed as too constraining. "He wanted everything: Every Iraqi text message, phone call, and e-mail that could be vacuumed up by the agency's powerful computers." So the government deployed technological methods indiscriminately to collect all communications data from the entire Iraqi population.

Alexander then conceived of applying this system of ubiquitous surveillance— originally created for a foreign population in an active war zone—to American citizens. . . .

Although some of the more extreme statements from Alexander—such as his blunt question "Why can't we collect all the signals, all the time?," which he reportedly asked during a 2008 visit to Britain's GCHQ—have been dismissed by agency spokespeople as mere lighthearted quips taken out of context, the agency's own documents demonstrate that Alexander was not joking. . . .

Far from being a frivolous quip, "collect it all" defines the NSA's aspiration, and it is a goal the NSA is increasingly closer to reaching. The quantity of telephone calls, emails, online chats, online activities, and telephonic metadata collected by the agency is staggering. Indeed, the NSA frequently, as one 2012 document put it, "collects far more content than is routinely useful to analysts." As of mid-2012, the agency was processing more than twenty billion communications events (both Internet and telephone) from around the world *each day*. . . .

The domestic total collected by the NSA is . . . stunning. Even prior to Snowden's revelations, the *Washington Post* reported in 2010 that "every day, collection systems at the National Security Agency intercept and store 1.7 billion emails, phone calls, and other types of communications" from Americans. William Binney, a mathematician who worked for the NSA for three decades and resigned in the wake of 9/11 in protest over the agency's increasing domestic focus, has likewise made numerous statements about the quantities of US data collected. In a 2012 interview with *Democracy Now!*, Binney said that "they've assembled on the order of 20 trillion transactions about U.S. citizens with other U.S. citizens."

After Snowden's revelations, the *Wall Street Journal* reported that the overall interception system of the NSA "has the capacity to reach roughly 75% of all U.S. Internet traffic in the hunt for foreign intelligence, including a wide array of communications by foreigners and Americans." Speaking anonymously, current and former NSA officials told the *Journal* that in some cases the NSA "retains the written content of emails sent between citizens within the U.S. and also filters domestic phone calls made with Internet technology." Britain's GCHQ similarly collects such a great quantity of communications data that it can barely store what it has. . . .

To collect such vast quantities of communications, the NSA relies on a multitude of methods. These include tapping directly into fiber-optic lines (including underwater cables) used to transmit international communications; redirecting messages into NSA repositories when they traverse the US system, as most worldwide communications do; and cooperating with the intelligence services in other countries. With increasing frequency, the agency also relies on Internet companies and telecoms, which indispensably pass on information they have collected about their own customers. . . .

Beyond its work with compliant telecoms and Internet companies, the NSA has also colluded with foreign governments to construct its far-reaching surveillance system. Broadly speaking, the NSA has three different categories of foreign relationships. The first is with the Five Eyes group: the US spies with these countries, but rarely on them, unless requested to by those countries' own officials. The second tier involves countries that the NSA works with for specific surveillance projects while also spying on them extensively. The third group is comprised of countries on which the United States routinely spies but with whom it virtually never cooperates.

Within the Five Eyes group, the closest NSA ally is the British GCHQ. As the *Guardian* reported, based on documents provided by Snowden, "The U.S. government has paid at least £100m to the UK spy agency GCHQ over the last three years to secure access to and influence over Britain's intelligence gathering programs." Those payments were an incentive to GCHQ to support the NSA's surveillance agenda. "GCHQ must pull its weight and be seen to pull its weight," a secret GCHQ strategy briefing said.

The Five Eyes members share most of their surveillance activities and meet each year at a Signals Development conference, where they boast of their expansion and the prior year's successes. Former NSA deputy director John Inglis has said of the Five Eyes alliance that they "practice intelligence in many regards in a combined way— essentially make sure that we leverage one another's capabilities for mutual benefit."

Many of the most invasive surveillance programs are carried out by the Five Eyes partners, a substantial number of these involving the GCHQ. Of special note are the British agency's joint efforts with the NSA to break the common encryption techniques that are used to safeguard personal Internet transactions, such as online banking and retrieval of medical records. The two agencies' success in setting up backdoor access to those encryption systems not only allowed them to peer at people's private dealings, but also weakened the systems for everyone, making them more vulnerable to malicious hackers and to other foreign intelligence agencies.

The GCHQ has also conducted mass interception of communications data from the world's underwater fiber-optic cables. Under the program name Tempora, the GCHQ developed the "ability to tap into and store huge volumes of data drawn from fibre-optic cables for up to 30 days so that it can be sifted and analysed," the *Guardian* reported, and the "GCHQ and the NSA are consequently able to access and process vast quantities of communications between entirely innocent people." The intercepted data encompass all forms of online activity, including "recordings of phone calls, the content of email messages, entries on Facebook, and the history of any internet user's access to websites." . . .

If the quantity of collection revealed was already stupefying, the NSA's mission to collect all the signals all the time has driven the agency to expand and conquer more and more ground. The amount of data it captures is so vast, in fact, that the principal challenge the agency complains about is storing the heaps of information accumulated from around the globe. . . .

To address its storage problem, the NSA began building a massive new facility in Bluffdale, Utah, that has as one of its primary purposes the retention of all that data. As reporter James Bamford noted in 2012, the Bluffdale construction will expand the agency's capacity by adding "four

25,000-square-foot halls filled with servers, complete with raised floor space for cables and storage, In addition, there will be more than 900,000 square feet for technical support and administration." Considering the size of the building and the fact that, as Bamford says, "a terabyte of data can now be stored on a flash drive the size of a man's pinky," the implications for data collection are profound.

# SECTION 7

## CRIME AND POLICING

//////////////////////////////////////////////////////////////////////////////////////////

Crime prevention and control are the covert rationales for much state and private surveillance, particularly that occurring in public, open spaces. For a long time in surveillance studies, consideration of video surveillance (or closed-circuit television, CCTV) was a dominant area of study. In many ways, this explains the prominence of British academics and studies of the United Kingdom in surveillance studies in the 1990s and early 2000s, as the United Kingdom was a pioneer of state public open-space video surveillance.

The United Kingdom remains a good—or perhaps, bad (Murakami Wood and Webster 2009)—example because it is so well studied, and there are some very good summary articles on the spread of CCTV in that country (Fussey 2004; Webster 2004). Although there were earlier experiments by police conducting undercover surveillance with movie cameras (Williams 2003; Williams et al. 2009), the main story begins in the late 1980s with a combination of factors that are shared by other nations. In general, transformations of capitalism and the restructuring of urban space generated support for surveillance, which became a mechanism for securing places of commerce and policing borders between neighborhoods (e.g., of newly formed gated communities).

During this time, urban centers were successively hollowed out and then revitalized through a combination of securitization, gentrification, and privatization. This process was well described by Mike Davis (1990) in relation to the US situation, and specifically Los Angeles, but Clive Norris and Gary Armstrong (1999) identified similar trends in the United Kingdom in their book, *The Maximum Surveillance Society*. Further, the creation of "enterprise zones" and out-of-town shopping centers and malls in the 1980s, under the pioneering neoliberal government of Margaret Thatcher, led to the decline of urban retail centers. Newly popular private commercial spaces were highly securitized with security guards and video surveillance cameras. Local authorities in the UK looked to them as an example, adopting many of the same tactics for their city centers, encouraged both by the police, who argued that video surveillance, in particular, would prevent crime, and by business initiatives like town-centre management (TCM) and business improvement districts or associations (BIDs/BIAs), where the private sector could pay for some of the costs of these systems (Coleman 2004).

These early examples of actuarialism and risk-reduction as crime-control policy were taken up at the national level by the post-Thatcher administrations of both John Major and Tony Blair, who despite being from different political parties, shared a common approach to "caring" authoritarianism (Fussey 2004; Webster 2004), reflected in a whole suite of neoliberal, surveillance-based policies (SSN 2006). As a result of substantial national funding, CCTV in the United Kingdom went through massive periods of expansion from the mid-1990s and again in the early years of the 2000s.

However, the economic drivers would never, on their own, have generated the public support for, or at least apathy towards, video surveillance. In the United Kingdom, there were a series of trigger events or moral panics, involving football hooliganism, child abduction, and terrorism, such as the attacks by the Provisional IRA on the Conservative Party conference in 1986, and then in other British cities, and particularly London in the early 1990s (Coaffee et al. 2009). One iconic event was the abduction and brutal killing of two-year-old Jamie Bulger by two ten-year-old kids in 1993. A grainy CCTV image of Bulger being led by his assailants out of a Merseyside shopping center became a focal point for the public's outrage, driving further support for video surveillance, despite its presence and lack of efficacy in preventing Bulger's death or even in assisting with the identification of the killers (Monahan 2006).

In this section, excerpts from Norris and Armstrong and Mike McCahill provide just a glimpse of the authors' detailed empirical accounts of British cities and British police, security guards, retail-store employees, and ordinary people, as they negotiate surveillance in the context of economic, political, and spatial transformations. The excerpts show adaptation to these new forces, and in many ways surveillance's effectiveness as a means of social control at some levels. That said, they also find a fair amount of cynicism, failure, and the manipulation and misuse of new technological powers for purposes of discrimination, personal amusement, and low-level corruption.

Despite the complexity of actual video surveillance deployment (Goold 2004; Smith 2015), evidence of its limited ability to prevent crime (e.g., Gill and Spriggs 2005; Welsh and Farrington 2009), and its inefficient use of public funds (Groombridge 2008), the proliferation of video surveillance provided the United Kingdom, and especially London, with the dubious distinction of being labelled the surveillance capital of the world.[1] The role of London as a global leader showed when, after 9/11, the example of London was promoted in the United States and elsewhere as having a model urban security policy (Murakami Wood and Webster 2009). The "ring of steel" established around the City of London and Docklands (Coaffee 2004) was appropriated for use in traffic control (the Congestion Charge Zone) in the early 2000s and then reintegrated into a security perimeter (Coaffee et al. 2009), which was further extended for the 2012 Olympic Games (Fussey et al. 2011). The role of sporting and other mega-events is considered in Philip Boyle and Kevin Haggerty's excerpt, which is a piece that examines the circuits of influence around policing techniques and technologies. This is followed by an excerpt from Pete Fussey and colleagues that looks explicitly at how security efforts for the 2012 London Olympics were coupled with urban rejuvenation projects that attempted to purify what were remarkably diverse neighborhoods. Minas Samatas (2004) was one of the first scholars to interrogate the political scandals and consequences of Olympic security with the 2004 Summer Olympic Games in Athens, but mega-events remain a rich and important area of study (Giulianotti and Klauser 2010). Colin Bennett and Kevin Haggerty's edited collection, *Security Games* (2011), is an excellent place to start for further exploration of this area.

The result of these trends is that in major cities around the world, public open space video surveillance seems both normal and expected (Doyle et al. 2012). Even at its extreme—for instance, with the security for the 2008 Beijing Olympics, with its networks of steel fences and gates, both "fan" and "protest zones," anti-aircraft missiles, heavy human security, biometric identification, and so on—the pattern is little different from that for the London Olympics and involved many of the same transnational corporations and experts. Similarly, China's "Safe City" project, announced in 2013, funded a massive expansion of biometric-enabled, "smart" video surveillance in cities, with around 10 million new cameras installed and integrated with transport, schools, and shopping malls. The emphasis of this project is on regions of ethnic tension and potential "terrorist" threat, which is a rationale that has been widely criticized, especially in the context of the Olympics, as effectively supporting censorship and the suppression of political dissent (Klein 2008). Nonetheless, as advanced as these systems might be, they are simply augmented versions of the systems being implemented in the United Kingdom, United States, and elsewhere.

Part of the reason for the spread of cameras has to do with the association of visibility with knowledge and accountability. Surveillance cameras are a visible manifestation of the state's concern with crime and security—they are a kind of "security theater" (Schneier 2008) that assuages fears about unknown risks (De Cauter 2004). The spread of video and other forms of surveillance also builds upon a broader culture of visibility and voyeurism, seen, for instance, with the current popularity of small amateur drones or with contemporary social media practices of "stalking" others through their profiles (see Section 12). There is furthermore a highly emotional and affective dimension to video surveillance. The excerpt by Hille Koskela explores this dimension while also problematizing the relationship of video surveillance to crimes against women. Whereas video surveillance is often not present in spaces where women are most at risk of violence (such as the home), in places where it is present (such as shopping malls), it is unlikely to prevent harassment or assault and may even make those spaces more hostile to women if CCTV control room operators act as voyeurs.

In another register, widely accessible camera technologies, especially in mobile phones, have supported attempts by activists and others to hold the state and police officers accountable through techniques of counter-surveillance or "sousveillance" (see Section 13). The excerpt by Andrew Goldsmith situates this trend within a larger regime called the "new visibility" (Thompson 2005), where people harness new technologies to become active producers, not just consumers, of visual content and evidence. There have been several responses to these developments. One has been to equip the police with body-worn cameras both so that the police perspective can be seen, but also so that the means of visual representation can be controlled (Brucato 2015; Schneider 2016). This should be seen alongside other attempts by states to limit the use of public photography or recording in the name of counterterrorism and security (Newell 2014). Once again, the United Kingdom has led the way here with the inclusion of anti-photography provisions in law, for example in Section 44 of The Terrorism Act; illegally intimidating photographers and seizing their equipment; and even making expressions of interest in video cameras itself a reasonable ground (probable cause) for police intervention.

There have likewise been other responses to the "failure" of public open space video surveillance to prevent crime. One response has been to reinvent them as vital components in a larger system of databases and algorithmic processing with the aim of achieving forms of anticipatory, preemptive policing (van Brakel and de Hert 2011). A related approach has been to integrate the cameras into multifunction, interactive security systems that augment surveillance capabilities with microphones, loudspeakers, and potentially even digital "noises," often undetectably coupled with existing urban infrastructure like streetlights. This is increasingly part of the informatization of cities through "smart city" initiatives, presented, like earlier waves of gentrification and privatization, as an unquestionable civic good. With government funding, police have also invested heavily in many cities around the world in biometrics; flying drone cameras, including micro air vehicles (MAVs); and other robotics; and there has been a general extension of military and quasi-military technology into urban space as part of global surveillance surges. Under what Stephen Graham (2010) has called the "new military urbanism," everything from terrorism through crime to mere disorder and antisocial behavior are increasingly seen as part of a spectrum of threat justifying extreme intervention.

Such policing and securitization logics infuse public institutions, while—paradoxically—also being framed as necessary reactions to the failures of such institutions. For example, the final excerpt by Torin Monahan and Rodolfo Torres shows how the contemporary American school system has become a site of paranoid monitoring of children at least as much because of the threat *from* kids (see also Taylor 2013). Surveillance in this context restructures public education around unforgiving zero-tolerance policies, relentless accountability measures, and overlapping education and criminal justice systems (for instance, with armed and uniformed police officers on school grounds). All of this disproportionately punishes poor, minority students, with disastrous consequences for their lives and life chances (Hirschfield 2010; Kupchik and Monahan 2006). From this perspective, surveillance must be understood in relation to the "prison-industrial complex"—itself a long-standing testing ground for experiments in surveillance. Schools act almost as an antechamber to a life of harsh policing, imprisonment, and the constant threat of death for some, as much as a vector of opportunity for others.

## NOTE

1. Ironically, it was the media's serial misreporting of some notional figures from Clive Norris that helped promote this idea. The two figures, which are still being used, are the presence of "4.2 million CCTV cameras in Britain," and the average person "is caught on camera 300 times daily." The first figure derives from Mike McCahill and Clive Norris's (2002) admittedly rough "guesstimate," extrapolated out from a casual count of cameras in one small ordinary neighborhood in London around 2000. The second figure comes from a little fictional vignette of a day in the life of "Thomas Kearns" in *The Maximum Surveillance Society* (Norris and Armstrong 1999), which was intended to illustrate how many cameras a person could possibly be caught by in any one day. It remains the case that no one knows exactly how many cameras there are in Britain or indeed in most countries in the world. Additionally, although media and scholarly accounts still refer to Britain as the video surveillance capital, China has likely far surpassed Britain in both numbers of cameras and their capability (Gilliom and Monahan 2013).

## REFERENCES

Bennett, Colin J., and Kevin D. Haggerty, eds. 2011. *Security Games: Surveillance and Control at Mega-Events*. New York: Routledge.
Brucato, Ben. 2015. Policing Made Visible: Mobile Technologies and the Importance of Point of View. *Surveillance & Society* 13 (3/4):455–73.
Coaffee, Jon. 2004. Rings of Steel, Rings of Concrete and Rings of Confidence: Designing Out Terrorism in Central London pre and post September 11th. *International Journal of Urban and Regional Research* 28 (1):201–11.
Coaffee, Jon, and David Murakami Wood. 2006. Security Is Coming Home: Rethinking Scale and Constructing Resilience in the Global Urban Response to Terrorist Risk. *International Relations* 20 (4):503–17.

Coaffee, J, David Murakami Wood, and Peter Rogers. 2009. *The Everyday Resilience of the City.* London: Palgrave.

Coleman, Roy, 2004. *Reclaiming the Streets: Surveillance, Social Control, and the City.* Portland, OR: Willan.

Davis, Mike. 1990. *City of Quartz: Excavating the Future in Los Angeles.* New York: Vintage Books.

De Cauter, Lieven. 2004. *The Capsular Civilization: On the City in the Age of Fear.* Rotterdam: NAi Publishers.

Doyle, Aaron, Randy K. Lippert, and David Lyon, eds. 2012. *Eyes Everywhere: The Global Growth of Camera Surveillance.* New York: Routledge.

Fussey, Pete. 2004. New Labour and New Surveillance: Theoretical and Political Ramifications of CCTV Implementation in the UK. *Surveillance & Society* 2 (2/3):251–69.

Fussey, Pete, Jon Coaffee, Gary Armstrong, and Dick Hobbs. 2011. *Securing and Sustaining the Olympic City: Reconfiguring London for 2012 and Beyond.* Burlington, VT: Ashgate.

Gill, Martin, and Angela Spriggs. 2005. *Assessing the Impacts of CCTV.* Home Office Research Study 292. Home Office (UK).

Gilliom, John, and Torin Monahan. 2013. *SuperVision: An Introduction to the Surveillance Society.* Chicago: University of Chicago Press.

Giulianotti, Richard, and Francisco Klauser. 2010. Security Governance and Sport Mega-Events: Toward an Interdisciplinary Research Agenda. *Journal of Sport & Social Issues* 34 (1):49–61.

Goold, Benjamin J. 2004. *CCTV and Policing: Public Area Surveillance and Police Practices in Britain.* Oxford: Oxford University Press.

Graham, Stephen. 2010. *Cities under Siege: The New Military Urbanism.* New York: Verso.

Groombridge, Nic. 2008. Stars of CCTV? How the Home Office Wasted Millions—A Radical 'Treasury/Audit Commission' View. *Surveillance & Society* 5 (1):73–80.

Hirschfield, Paul. 2010. School Surveillance in America: Disparate and Unequal. In *Schools under Surveillance: Cultures of Control in Public Education,* edited by T. Monahan and R. D. Torres, 38–54. New Brunswick, NJ: Rutgers University Press.

Klein, Naomi. 2008. China Unveils Frightening Futuristic Police State at Olympics. *Huffington Post,* August 8. Available from http://www.alternet.org/story/94278 [accessed August 20, 2008].

Kupchik, Aaron, and Torin Monahan. 2006. The New American School: Preparation for Post-Industrial Discipline. *British Journal of Sociology of Education* 27 (5):617–31.

McCahill, Michael, and Clive Norris. 2002. CCTV in London. Hull, UK: UrbanEye Project.

Monahan, Torin. 2006. Questioning Surveillance and Security. In *Surveillance and Security: Technological Politics and Power in Everyday Life,* 1–23, edited by T. Monahan. New York: Routledge.

Murakami Wood, David, and C. William R. Webster. 2009. Living in Surveillance Societies: The Normalisation of Surveillance in Europe and the Threat of Britain's Bad Example. *Journal of Contemporary European Research* 5 (2):259–73.

Newell, Bryce Clayton. 2014. Crossing Lenses: Policing's New Visibility and the Role of Smartphone Journalism as a Form of Freedom-Preserving Reciprocal Surveillance. *University of Illinois Journal of Law, Technology & Policy* 1:59–104.

Norris, Clive, and Gary Armstrong. 1999. *The Maximum Surveillance Society: The Rise of CCTV.* Oxford: Berg.

Samatas, Minas. 2004. *Surveillance in Greece: From Anticommunist to Consumer Surveillance.* New York: Pella Publishing Company.

Schneider, Christopher J. 2016. *Policing and Social Media: Social Control in an Era of New Media.* London: Lexington Books.

Schneier, Bruce. 2008. *Schneier on Security.* New York: Wiley.

Smith, Gavin J. D. 2015. *Opening the Black Box: The Work of Watching.* New York: Routledge.

Surveillance Studies Network (SSN). 2006. *A Report on the Surveillance Society.* Wilmslow: Information Commissioner's Office (ICO) (UK).

Taylor, Emmeline. 2013. *Surveillance Schools: Security, Discipline, and Control in Contemporary Education.* New York: Palgrave.

Thompson, John B. 2005. The New Visibility. *Theory, Culture & Society* 22 (6):31–51.

van Brakel, Rosamunde, and Paul de Hert. 2011. Policing, Surveillance and Law in a Pre-Crime Society: Understanding the Consequences of Technology Based Strategies. *Journal of Police Studies* 20 (3):163–92.

Webster, C. William R. 2004. The Diffusion, Regulation, and Governance of Closed-Circuit Television in the UK. *Surveillance & Society* 2 (2/3):230–50.

Welsh, Brandon C., and David P. Farrington. 2009. *Making Public Places Safer: Surveillance and Crime Prevention.* Oxford: Oxford University Press.

Williams, Chris A. 2003. Police Surveillance and the Emergence of CCTV in the 1960s. *Crime Prevention and Community Safety* 5 (3):27–37.

Williams, Chris A., James Patterson, and James Taylor. 2009. Police Filming English Streets in 1935: The Limits of Mediated Identification. *Surveillance & Society* 6 (1):3–9.

# 33

# CLIVE NORRIS AND GARY ARMSTRONG

## CCTV AND THE SOCIAL STRUCTURING OF SURVEILLANCE

The work of Clive Norris and Gary Armstrong in the 1990s was crucial to a growing critical understanding of open street video surveillance. Their research was based in the United Kingdom, but it inspired similar studies throughout Europe and the rest of the world, in part through the EU-funded UrbanEye project in which Norris participated. This paper, one of several that led up to Norris and Armstrong's book, *The Maximum Surveillance Society*, is based on rigorous empirical research. One of their most important findings was that technologically mediated police surveillance reproduces—in new forms—previously existing social prejudices.

***

CCTV [closed-circuit television surveillance] has been portrayed . . . as a "Friendly Eye in the Sky" benignly and impartially watching over the whole population and targeting only those deemed as acting suspiciously. . . . But this begs the question as to what, in practice, constitutes suspicious behaviour? . . .

Bombarded by a myriad of images from dozens of cameras, and faced with the possibility of tracking and zooming in on literally thousands of individuals, by what criteria can operators try to maximise the chance of choosing those with criminal intent? Camera operators and street patrol officers are at both an advantage and a disadvantage. Because the "presence" of operatives is remote and unobtrusive, there is less likelihood that people will orient their behaviour in the knowledge that they are being watched, and, by virtue of the elevated position and telescopic capacity of the camera, operators have a greater range of vision than the street-level patrol officer. However, these advantages must be offset against their remoteness, which means they are denied other sensory input—particularly sound—that can be essential in contextualising visual images.

Unlike the patrol officer, the CCTV operative is both deaf and dumb: they simply cannot ask citizens on the street for information, nor can they hear what is being said. Faced with such an avalanche of images, and a limited range of sensory data, how then does the CCTV operator selectively filter these images to decide what is worthy of more detailed attention? . . . It is . . . an occupational necessity that they develop a set of working rules to narrow down the general population to the suspect population. . . .

[S]election for targeted surveillance appears, at the outset, to be differentiated by the classic sociological variables of age, race, and gender. Nine out of ten target surveillances were on men (93%), four out of ten on teenagers (39%) and three out of ten on black people (31%). . . .

In terms of the general population, men were nearly twice as likely to be targeted than their presence in the population would suggest. Similarly, teenagers—who account for less than 20% of the population—made up [roughly] 40% of targeted surveillances. Of course, the street population (i.e., those available for targeting) is not the same as the general population. However, all three of our sites were busy commercial areas that during the day were populated by shoppers and workers, both male and female, many of whom were middle aged.

It is more difficult to estimate how a person's race affected the chance of being selected for targeting, since the proportion of ethnic minorities varied dramatically from site to site. However, we have calculated that black people were between one-and-a-half and two-and-a-half times more likely to be targeted for surveillance than their presence in the population would suggest.

On their own, however, these findings do not indicate that CCTV operators are selecting targets for surveillance on the basis of observable social characteristics, since this distribution may relate to the behaviour of those targeted that initially prompted operator suspicion. To examine this we classified each surveillance as: "crime related," "order related," occurring for "no obvious reason," or "other." . . .

Three out of ten people (30%) were surveilled for crime-related matters, two out of ten (22%) for forms of disorderly conduct, but the largest category—nearly four out of ten (36%)—were surveilled . . . for "no obvious reason." This was echoed when we examined the basis of suspicion, with one quarter (24%) of people subject to targeted surveillance because of their behaviour. But the most significant type of suspicion was categorical; one-third (31%) of people were surveilled merely on the basis of belonging to a particular social or subcultural group. . . .

[T]he reason for the surveillance and the suspicion on which it was based was also found to be highly differentiated. Thus we can see that two-thirds (65%) of teenagers—compared with only one in five (21%) of those aged over 30—were surveilled for "no obvious reason." Similarly, black people were twice as likely (68%) to be surveilled for "no obvious reason" than whites (35%), and men three times (47%) more likely than women (16%). The young, the male and the black were systematically and disproportionately targeted, not because of their involvement in crime or disorder, but for "no obvious reason" and on the basis of categorical suspicion alone. . . .

[W]earing headgear is particularly stigmatizing in the view of CCTV operators. This has two components. First baseball caps, woolly hats, and hooded parkas were seen as indicative of subcultural affiliation, and thus helped to single out respectable from "deviant" youths. Indeed, sometimes the only distinguishing feature that could justify why one youth, as opposed to another, was targeted for extended surveillance was the presence of baseball caps, particularly if worn with the peak facing backwards. But, more importantly, operators know that hats can potentially deprive them of recording a clear image of a person's face. Knowing this, they act on the assumption that citizens do as well. Operators believe they have a right to surveille any person's face who appears in their territory. Anyone who supports a visible means of denying them this opportunity immediately places himself in the category of persons of questionable intent and worthy of extended surveillance. Moreover, in the eyes of the operator, moving the headgear to deliberately obscure the face merely compounds suspicion. . . .

Racist language was not unusual to hear among CCTV operators. Although only used by a minority, the terms "Pakis," "Jungle Bunnies" and "Sooties" when used by some operatives did not produce howls of protests from their colleagues or line managers. Stereotypical negative attitudes towards ethnic minorities and black youths in particular were more widespread. These attitudes ranged from more extreme beliefs, held by a few operators, about these groups' inherent criminality to more general agreement as to their being "work-shy," or "too lazy" to get a job, and in general, "trouble." Given these assumptions, the sighting of a black face on the streets of either Metro City or County Town would almost automatically produce a targeted surveillance. . . .

Male youths, particularly if black or stereotypically associated with the underclass, represent the fodder of CCTV systems. But this overrepresentation is not justified on the basis of those subsequently arrested. While teenagers accounted for 39% of targeted surveillance they only made up 18% of those arrested, whereas those in their 20s counted for 46% of targeted surveillance but made up 82% of all arrests. Similarly, black people accounted for 32% of targeted surveillance but only 9% of those arrested. . . .

While women make up 52% of the general population they only accounted for 7% of primary persons surveilled. Women were almost invisible to the cameras unless they were reported as known shoplifters by store detectives (33%) or because of overt disorderly conduct (31%). Nor were women more likely to [become] targets by virtue of a protectional gaze. Indeed, in nearly 600 hours of observation only one woman was targeted for protectional purposes—as she walked to and from a bank cash dispenser. Moreover, there was evidence that the same attitudes that have traditionally been associated with the office occupational culture surrounding domestic violence continue to inform the operation of CCTV. . . .

[T]he essentially male gaze of CCTV has little relevance for the security of women in town centres, and may indeed undermine it by offering the rhetoric of security rather than providing the reality. CCTV also fosters a male gaze in the more conventional and voyeuristic sense: with its pan tilt and zoom facilities, the thighs and cleavages of scantily-clad women are an easy target for those male operators so motivated. Indeed, 10% of targeted surveillances on women and 15% of operator-initiated surveillances on women were for voyeuristic reasons, which outnumbered protective surveillance by five to one. . . .

The power of CCTV operators is highly discretionary as they have extraordinary latitude in determining who will be watched, for how long and whether to initiate deployment. The sum total of these individual discretionary judgments produces, as we have shown, a highly differentiated pattern of surveillance leading to a massively disproportionate targeting of young males, particularly if they are black or visibly identifiable as having subcultural affiliations. As this differentiation is not based on objective behavioural and individualised criteria, but merely on being categorised as part of a particular social group, such practices are clearly discriminatory.

Of course, it may be argued that since those officially recorded as deviant—young, male, black, and working class—are disproportionately represented, targeting such groups merely reflects the underlying reality of the distribution of criminality. Such an argument is, however, circular: the production of the official statistics is also based on pre-conceived assumptions as to the distribution of criminality, which itself leads to the particular configuration of formal and informal operational police practice. As self-report studies of crime reveal, offending is, in fact, far more evenly distributed throughout the population than reflected in the official statistics. Indeed, race and class differentials, so marked in the official statistics, disappear when self-reported offending behaviour of juveniles is examined. . . .

Another argument is that even if there is differentiation in target selection, it is irrelevant because it does not result in actual intervention and therefore no "real" discrimination occurs. As our own results clearly show, even though teenagers make up 39% of those targeted they constitute only 23% of those deployed against and 18% the arrested population. Thus, we would respond that on effectiveness measures alone, such targeting is inefficient, but we would also challenge the notion that it is irrelevant. Just because no intervention or arrest results does not mean that a significant social interaction, albeit remote and technologically mediated, has not taken place.

Imagine two youths who, on entering city centre space, are immediately picked up by the cameras. They notice the first camera moving to track them as they move through the streets and go out of range of the camera. At the same time, another camera is seen altering its position to bring them into view. In fact, wherever they go they can see the cameras being repositioned to monitor their every movement. How do these youths feel? They have done nothing wrong, they have not drawn attention to themselves by their behaviour and they are not "known offenders." But they are being treated as a threat, as people who cannot be trusted, as persons who do not belong, as unwanted outsiders. The guarantee that such systems will show no interest or engage in deliberate monitoring of people going about their daily business is empty rhetoric.

This technologically mediated and distanced social interaction is, then, loaded with meaning. Moreover, for literally thousands of black and working-class youths, however law-abiding, it transmits a wholly negative message about their position in society. But it has wider consequences than just its impact on individual psychology. The central tenet of policing by consent—that policing is viewed as legitimate by those who experience it—is undermined. If social groups experience CCTV surveillance as an extension of discriminatory and unjust policing, the consequential loss of legitimacy may have disastrous consequences for social order.

# 34

# MIKE MCCAHILL

## THE SURVEILLANCE WEB

### The Rise of Visual Surveillance in an English City

In Mike McCahill's detailed study of the use of closed-circuit television (CCTV) systems, he illustrates how surveillance technologies and social practices converge to produce a larger "surveillance web." The excerpt demonstrates the importance of human connections in this sociotechnical assemblage that spans functions of social control, crime prevention, and law enforcement.

\*\*\*

As Nigel Thrift argues, the development of electronic communications systems does not produce 'an abstract and inhuman space, strung out on the wire'; rather it produces more association, much of it face to face. . . . [T]he construction and operation of CCTV surveillance systems has given rise to a whole new range of human linkages. This has brought together the police, private security managers, department store and shopping centre manager and store detectives. These developments are increasing the integration of police and private security CCTV systems and facilitating information-sharing and liaison between those responsible for managing such systems. . . . [O]ne of the main reasons for the development of this informal network is that it allows the security personnel to deal with the problem of identification, i.e. the problem of putting names to faces, putting faces to names, and sharing information on 'known' names and faces. In the city centre, for example, police and private security personnel hold bi-monthly City Centre Security Group meetings which provides those involved in the operation of the 'shopnet' with an opportunity to share information on 'known' persons. According to the operations manager of City Centre Mall:

> We discuss particular shoplifters, you know. If you're getting one guy coming round or you may not have seen one guy for a long time and somebody might have had a tip-off through overhearing or actually observing shoplifters and a pattern may be starting to arise, or you may be getting a certain individual

behaving in a certain pattern, yes, so we just try and let each other know. So again it's the, er . . . collecting information to try and use to combat the problem basically.

Another common practice at the City Centre Security Group meetings is the exchange of photographic information between the security personnel to help with the problem of putting names to faces and faces to names:

> We used to go along with our video and say 'this is so and so, we've got a name for him'. (The security manager, department store)

> Well, it's worked in conjunction with the police and a lot of them we know from our own experience. I've actually detained them for shoptheft, the others are well known, what we call 'professional shoplifters' that are passed onto us by the police. (The security manager, City Centre Mall)

> . . . the police are quite influential in that, you know, they'll give you information, erm . . . and often photographic information to guide you as to the people that you don't particularly want in your business. (The manager, department store)

Another way of putting names to faces is through informal visits to CCTV control rooms. At Housing Estate Mall, for example, the police are regular visitors to the control room where sometimes they will just sit and chat, usually about the local 'druggies':

> We used to sit up here with 'snatch squads', didn't we, to catch the 'druggies'. We'd sit up here watching them and have officers at the exit doors waiting for them. (Ex-beat officer)

During these informal visits to CCTV control rooms the visitor will often sit and watch the monitors and try to put a name to a face. At Housing Estate Mall most of the security personnel live on the local housing estate and some of the guards went to school with many of the people who visit the shopping centre. This means that the security team have an extensive local knowledge of the people who visit the shopping centre. In the incident below Shaun (the beat officer) sits and watches the monitors with Kevin (the Security Manager) and taps into this local knowledge:

> SHAUN: 'So what do you know then?'
> KEVIN: 'Not much.'
>   Kevin sees a man on the monitors walking through the centre with no shirt on and a large tattoo on his chest.
> KEVIN: 'That's Steve Brown.'
> SHAUN: 'Who's Steve Brown?'
> KEVIN: 'Pete Brown's brother.'
> SHAUN: 'Oh yes, I know Pete Brown.'

On other occasions security officers or the police will pay informal visits to the control room because they might have a *name* but not a *face*. As Mark Railton, the former security manager, told me: 'You see, if the police get warrants with names on they haven't got the faintest idea who they are.' In this case what happens is the beat officer brings a list of bench warrants to the control room and asks the security personnel if they will contact him if any of the 'wanted' persons enter the shopping centre. During one shift Shaun (the beat officer) arrived in the control room after receiving a tip-off from the guards that a 'wanted' person would be arriving in the shopping centre between one o'clock and two o'clock to collect his methadone prescription from one of the chemists within the centre. Before he arrived in the control room Shaun paid a visit to the chemist and asked the manager of the shop to telephone the control room when the suspect arrived to collect his methadone prescription. After sitting in the control room for about half an hour Shaun received the telephone call from the chemist informing him that the suspect had arrived. The CCTV operative on duty used a camera to zoom in on the suspect through the chemist door. Shaun had a quick look at the suspect on the monitor and left the control room to arrest him.

Another way the security personnel overcome the problem of classification is by constructing 'rogues galleries' of 'shoplifters' and 'troublemakers'. Eleven of the 30 CCTV control rooms which make up the surveillance web contained hard-copy printout machines which allowed them to produce stills from the CCTV footage. The ability to store images in electronic spaces (i.e. video tape), which can then be 'lifted out' and used at some future time and place, is one of the main benefits of CCTV systems. . . .

The fact that not all of the control rooms have hard-copy printout machines means that the construction of a 'rogues gallery' depends to some extent on the development of 'face-to-face' meetings between security personnel working in different CCTV control rooms. In City Centre Mall, for example, the security officers employed by one of the stores within the shopping centre do not have the facility to produce photographs on a hard-copy printout machine. To get around this problem they would often monitor the activities of suspected shoplifters from their own CCTV control room and then bring the video recording of the suspects to the shopping centre's CCTV control room and ask the operatives to produce them a photograph.

The security personnel employed by Housing Estate Mall also relied on security officers working in other stores to help them compile their 'rogues galleries'. On my first visit to the control room at Housing Estate Mall, Kevin (the security manager) showed me a 'Banned Persons File' which contains photographs of suspects taken with the hard-copy printout machine and the date the picture was taken. He also showed me a 'Mug Shot File' which contains updated pictures of 'known persons' and 'people to watch out for', and pictures of 'troublemakers' whose identity is not yet known. As he flicked through the 'Mug Shot File' Kevin drew my attention to the quality of some of the photographs which were recorded on disc by the security officers at the local Superstore. Kevin tells me that the two security officers at Superstore used to work as guards at the shopping centre and that they help each other quite a lot with putting names to faces.

This favour was often reciprocated by the security personnel at Housing Estate Mall who helped the security officers at Superstore and other stores to put a name to a face. Also some of the security officers employed by the major department stores in the city centre have worked with Kevin in the past:

> . . . the big department stores. I know them all. We meet quite a lot . . . when we ban them they're not allowed in here for 12 months. They're still gonna do the shoplifting bit. They hit the resorts a bit in the summer, but mainly it's the town centre. And Geoff at X and Barry at Y was talking about it, and they said: 'We'll try and get some photos of people that's been hitting us hard. We've got the video evidence but we don't know the names. Can you put a name to it Kev?' Things like this.

Informal contacts with the police are also important in the construction of 'rogues galleries'. The police are regular visitors to the CCTV control room at Housing Estate Mall and, as we have already seen, are well known to the security personnel. This provides the police with a pool of information but it also means that the security personnel can ask the police for favours, including helping them to compile their 'rogues gallery'. As Dave explains:

We caught somebody in X store the other day and when Bill arrived I said: 'Bill, we want a picture of that suspect, is there any chance of bringing him through the centre?' Cos most of them [the police] leave out the back door. So Bill brought this kid out through the centre and said: 'look at that camera'.

# 35

# PHILIP BOYLE AND KEVIN D. HAGGERTY

## SPECTACULAR SECURITY

Mega-Events and the Security Complex

Philip Boyle and Kevin Haggerty's piece examines a number of aspects of sports mega-events like the Olympic Games or World Cup. Such events have become significant case studies for surveillance studies scholars, largely because they represent key spatio-temporal locations for experimentation, demonstration, and marketing around new surveillance technologies and practices. Mega-event security may produce legacy systems that shape policing practices for years to come, but they also reproduce and normalize security routines through templates, knowledge bases, and training protocols—a "pedagogy of security."

\*\*\*

Mega-events . . . foster the production and circulation of sophisticated and specialized security knowledges. While the operational security needs for different events can vary substantially, they share the common fact that they often outstrip locally available expertise and resources. As these events continue to "pop-up" around the world, there arises a comparable need for mobile "pop-up" security practices.

Canada and the United States have tried to address this problem by developing special event designations and using standardized security templates. In the American context the relevant policy is the NSSE [National Special Security Event] designation. Created by President Clinton's 1998 Presidential Decision Directive 62, an event deemed to be of national significance will automatically become the responsibility of the USSS [US Secret Service]. Of the 28 NSSE designations between 1998 and 2007, seven were sporting events (six Super Bowls and the 2002 Olympics), all of which have come after 9/11. Canada mimics such efforts with its Major Event designation. Like the NSSE classification, a major event in Canada is defined as one of national or international significance where the overall responsibility for security rests with the federal government. Also like the NSSE, the major event designation automatically centralizes all security responsibilities, a role assumed in Canada by the RCMP [Royal Canadian Mounted Police].

Both the RCMP and the USSS have internal Major Event Divisions responsible for crafting major event security policy. They also use standardized security templates to maintain continuity in security planning between events and to act as institutional memory banks for lessons learned from previous events. In the Canadian case the relevant policy is the Major Events Template, which is modeled on the Incident Command System, a crisis management tool combined with a defined set of positions, roles, and responsibilities. In an interview, one of the RCMP operational planners responsible for drafting aspects of the template describes it as

> a policy piece or a structure, a tool that someone can use who's planning an event as to how they go about it. The concepts behind it are the first steps, then how to build a team and that sort of thing. And then it gets into specifics of individuals in that planning structure. As far as a tool, it standardizes our systems so that someone who is just starting to plan can look at this and get a sense of where to start and who to talk to.

Our interviews with RCMP officials and related documentation indicate that the further development of this template will be one key outcome of the 2010 Winter [Olympic] Games. The Director of the Major Events Division described how the template is "basically the blueprint that we will follow when we coordinate major events across Canada" and that the department is "leveraging the planning process [for the 2010 Winter Games] in order to support the development of the template and our planning processes internally." Though the funding structure and size of the Games means that what works in 2010 "will not

apply uniformly in the coordination of major events across Canada in the future," the Games are seen as a "platform to learn that much more because of the amount of security that will go into it," according to the Director.

The template will develop by incorporating lessons learned and best practices gleaned from other events and real-world experience. It also relies on the tacit, experiential knowledge needed to make the template work. As MacKenzie has noted, complex technological systems consist of both formal artifacts and the practical knowledges and understanding of such artifacts. It can be exceedingly difficult to make such systems operate by relying exclusively on blueprints or manuals. One also requires the practical knowledge gained in the real world to make systems function. While formal knowledge can be stored indefinitely, tacit knowledge can be lost through decaying skills or a failure to pass along such abilities to a new generation of practitioners. Major event security, as a form of complex system, also relies on specialized training and preparation mechanisms aimed at generating stocks of experiential security knowledge and expertise. A 2005 RCMP planning document, for example, details numerous training seminars and professional conferences in other countries which personnel from the Vancouver 2010 Integrated Security Unit "have attended, reviewed, and shared best practices," including numerous IOC-sponsored knowledge transfer services, government-sponsored post-Games debriefing events, direct observation of other political summits and sporting events, and numerous FBI and USSS training conferences.

These processes culminate in a formalized body of knowledge and the tacit skills needed to make them work that can, in principle, be transposed from event to event. For Canada, one of the legacies to stem from the 2010 Games will be the further development of a mobile security diagram informed by a wide range of domestic and international experience and honed through an exceptional public event involving numerous security agencies working in an integrated fashion in what the RCMP and Canadian Forces have repeatedly characterized as a "no-fail" operation. Insofar as intra-national organizations and networks are increasingly forged surrounding these events the circulation of such expertise will continue to move beyond individual nations to become part of a multi-scalar and globalizing network of security knowledge.

There is also a flurry of indirect knowledge and technology transfers surrounding the Olympics or other mega-events that have almost nothing to do with staging comparable events. These secondary processes help circulate technologies and expertise honed for the extraordinary conditions of mega-events into wider society. A prominent example of this occurred at the 2001 Super Bowl in Tampa Bay where, for the first time, security officials deployed a large-scale assemblage of cameras, biometric software and terrorist databases to surreptitiously scan and record the facial image of every spectator at that event. Afterwards the cameras were relocated to a nearby Tampa Bay neighborhood, where the technology monitored public streets. This example underscores how major events are seen as a real-world mock-up of security initiatives that might be employed in more prosaic situations.

More broadly, 9/11 raised the question of how to secure open, complex, and infrastructurally vulnerable societies from asymmetrical attacks. Officials have looked to the models and principles of Olympic security as one way to address this problem. A post–Salt Lake Olympics security conference, for example, sought to apply lessons from the "Olympic Security Model" to US homeland security. Addressing the conference, IOC security consultant Peter Ryan noted why Olympic security preparations are relevant to national security and helped redefine the territorial dimensions of national security:

> a security plan on the Olympic scale is directly related to the national defense of any host country. . . . But the traditional national defense has been principally to defend against conventional military attack, not necessarily against internal or external terrorist attack. The security operations for the Olympics Games are in fact, exactly designed to do just that, and much more. It simply tests every plan we have for every contingency. The lessons from this for any nation must be preserved and absorbed and developed further. National security now begins on the streets of our cities, the ports and airports, and vulnerable borders which all nations have. . . .

Private firms are helping drive this process. The massive budgets and cultural capital associated with Olympic involvement makes them the security industry equivalent of what Paris or Milan is to the fashion industry. The successful pilot testing of security practices and technologies—or, more accurately, the lack of stunning failures—helps to ensure that new knowledge, practices and devices emerge as "proven" solutions to be marketed as applications suitable for other contexts. The Olympic Update supplement to the Security Industry Association's China Security Market Report identifies the 2008 Olympics as bringing "huge commercial opportunities" and an unprecedented opening that can help to build brand awareness in the world's fastest-growing security market. The SIA recommended that contractors for the 2008 Beijing Games consider the event as a platform to launch into the Chinese security market including the freshly stimulated urban public security market. Similarly, the London 2012 Olympics are hailed by the British Security Industry Association as a "sellers market" and a "fantastic showcase" for the British security industry to "demonstrate that it actually is an important resource in public reassurance and safety."

The marketable experience that comes with being involved in Olympic security also helps disperse security knowledge and practice. Olympic security experience can translate into lucrative consultation and risk management contracts with government and private firms. . . . One consequence of these knowledge transfer dynamics is the further erasure of the ostensible line between military and civilian applications of high technology. As one of the effects of 9/11 was the increased securitization of urban centers, it follows that the increased militarization of event security also means the militarization of cities. These security legacies also have a series of global implications for the future of urban spaces more generally due to the processes that inform how cities are chosen to sponsor mega-events. The competitors for such events are typically premier cites including London, Vancouver, Beijing, and New York. Such locations are, or aspire to be, models of global cities. Given that part of the legacy of mega-events appears to be a step change in the security infrastructure of each host city, the templates for what is entailed in being a global city consequently also undergo a change, increasingly appealing to urban exemplars that have been re-imagined in light of new security initiatives. . . .

[T]he transformations in security dynamics surrounding mega-events offer a palpable pedagogy of security. The undeniable physical presence of security devices and routines, combined with their spectacular media representations, familiarize individuals with the routines of high security. In addition to reducing public anxieties about terrorist attacks, the spectacle of security also attunes individuals to new security realities and helps to normalize the indignities of personal revelation associated with demands for documents and requirements to reveal oneself and one's body through assorted screening practices. The proliferating security routines characteristic of mega-events fosters a security-infused pedagogy of acceptable comportment, dress and documentation, as small lessons in security are inflated and played out before a global audience. Although largely imperceptible, it is this pedagogy in the personal routines of an advanced security assemblage that might be one of the most lasting legacies of mega-events.

# 36

# PETE FUSSEY, JON COAFFEE, GARY ARMSTRONG, AND DICK HOBBS

## THE REGENERATION GAMES

Purity and Security in the Olympic City

Although security and surveillance efforts at different mega-events may share similarities, they are also shaped profoundly by local cultures and geographies. In the following excerpt, the authors analyze the preparations leading up to the 2012 Olympic Games in London. They find that because the games were sited in an urban setting, they were coupled with—and justified by—urban rejuvenation agendas that ultimately catalyzed efforts to purify incredibly diverse neighborhoods through various forms of exclusion, including zero-tolerance policing practices.

*** 

Transformational urban regeneration has now become a key rationale for cities to be awarded the [Olympic] Games by the International Olympic Committee (IOC). In turn, hosting the Olympics is increasingly seen by urban managers as a once-in-a-lifetime opportunity for large-scale urban redevelopment and rebranding of a city to advertise particular urban geographies to an international audience. Olympic-led regeneration is also not without its critics. [Some] . . . show how Olympic regeneration schemes tend to privilege (visible) spatial form at the expense of social processes. Once international attention has moved on, grand Olympic projects often fail to fulfil their much-publicized promises to regenerate communities or to improve the environment. Less visible localized community-oriented benefits are consistently sacrificed in order to secure the more (literally) spectacular and globally oriented features of the Games. Even Barcelona 1992—often eulogized as the most successful regeneration Games in recent decades, with the 'Barcelona Model' seen as the blueprint for bids to the IOC from hopeful candidate cities—fell short in this capacity. Others have pointed to the legacy of under-used sports stadia and facilities and the resource- and energy-intensive construction programmes that belie proclaimed environmental benefits.

This article focuses on a key—and often underplayed—phenomenon: the marriage of regeneration processes with issues of safety and security. Physically, technologically and conceptually inbuilt in its regeneration programme, the London Olympic Games have shepherded in a more intensive securitization of East London: regeneration and securitization are yoked together. However, the mix of local, national and international actors and stakeholders means that no single agency can be identified as imposing any overarching plan nor is there even an unintended linear convergence. London 2012 is not witness to anything so simple as the imposition of an externally imposed global Olympic security model. The urban rather than exurban location of the 2012 Games means that blank canvas *de novo* wholesale approaches to both security and regeneration are impossible to achieve: Olympic-related interventions have to operate within an extant, complex and diverse urban milieu. In the 'Olympic borough' of Newham, for example, the industrial base of its White, Caribbean and Asian working class has been largely obliterated and, early in the twenty-first century, the borough is a fragmented, multi-ethnic enclave. Newham is consistently referred to as one of the most ethnically diverse places on the planet, with over 300 languages spoken in the borough. . . .

Unlike the post-modern proliferation of urban 'Disneyland', for example in the form of shopping malls, contrasting with the great modernist trade fairs and contrary to the general tendency to stage Olympic transformations on the fringes of the urban realm—such as the suburban Olympic 'theme parks' of Sydney 2000, Athens 2004 and Beijing 2008—much of the infrastructure of London 2012 is compressed into a brownfield site located in the heart of an existing urban milieu. In turn, East London's densely populated host geographies meet up with the complexity of Olympic-related urban governance (comprising international, national and local elements 'meshing' in a far from unified manner). For all the IOC's insistence that Olympics sporting venues be encircled by security perimeters, the Olympic park does not simply stand as a sterile, hygienized promontory in an otherwise dangerously imagined landscape. Certainly, that is indeed one vision of the Olympic process of ordering, a moment where the visions of unelected international sporting committees (in this case the IOC) of how the city should be presented coincide with long standing stereotypes of East London as a place of dangerous disorder. . . .

Siting the Games within this congested setting renders impossible the adoption of wholesale approaches to cleansing apparent in the development of other, mainly suburban, Olympic theme parks. As such, more subtle approaches have been taken towards the reconfiguration of space and the cultivation of the branded Olympic landscape. As a result, a spectrum of controlling mechanisms has been introduced into the area which, it is argued, reflect five broad and overlapping themes, and are articulated as a legacy benefit to the 'community'. The five themes are: the exclusion of specific sub-populations and behaviours, enhanced internal and external perimeters and borders, the creation of exclusive and privatized centres of consumption, intensified technological surveillance capabilities, and an extended security 'footprint' beyond the infrastructure of the Games. . . .

Similar to the Olympic Park, security measures in [the] wider Olympic neighbourhood are technological, as well as physical and conceptual. East Londoners have long been viewed as test candidates for new security technologies. In 1997 Stratford saw the world's first public space deployment of Face Recognition CCTV [closed-circuit television surveillance]. In anticipation of the Olympics, perhaps the most notable are experiments in 'extra-territorial' surveillance, such as unmanned aerial vehicles (UAVs)—similar in principle to (although not the same as) those utilized in Afghanistan—equipped with high-resolution cameras and able to survey large geographies at any given time. One of the test events involved the surveillance of crowds at the post-Beijing 'Olympic Handover Party' held in Central London in 2008. There are also proposals to deploy new, more powerful CCTV infrastructure ahead of the Games. . . .

Here, however tempting it may be to portray the Olympics as a Trojan Horse transporting the state's control assets into the local realm, such accounts should be resisted. The situation is more complex and contested and this is particularly evident in relation to surveillance cameras. Seemingly, 'Olympic borough' local authorities—faced with unprecedented government cuts that stand among the worst in the country—have limited their investment in upgrading existing surveillance systems in anticipation that equipment deployed for the Olympics would be available to them after the Games. However, policing agencies have threatened that, without advance contributions from local authorities, these legacy 'benefits' will be denied: mobile surveillance units can always be removed.

A £600 million 'envelope' (with the possibility of a further £238 million contingency funding) has been budgeted by the UK government to fund 'policing and wider security' for the Games. This goes beyond the Olympic Park itself. The potential breadth of 'wider security' raises further issues for local policing. As the Chief Superintendent responsible for policing Newham saw it,

his operational policing issue might best be described as 'a beast with two backs'. The two backs were the already high levels of crime in Newham and the perception of further crime that the Olympics could bring (as with other Olympics, such as the 2002 Salt Lake City Winter Games). Among the estimated 500,000 daily visitors to the borough, it is likely that not all of them will be there to appreciate athletic prowess or observe the Olympic Truce.

The London policing strategy for securing major events is based on the tradition of a 'layered' approach: managerial, technological and geographical. Regarding the latter, in May 2010 the OSD implemented an additional ring of control, the Olympic Coordination Zone (OCZ), which extends deep into surrounding neighbourhoods across Newham, Waltham Forest, Tower Hamlets and, to a lesser extent, Hackney. Senior police officers have stated that community engagement, intelligence gathering, prevention and enforcement in relation to potential terrorist threats and, separately, gang-related violence are OCZ priorities. However, these Olympic-related priorities contrast with (and potentially conflict with) other national and local agendas. The Olympic neighbourhood hosts the greatest intensity of counter-terrorism prosecutions in mainland Britain. Yet, at the same time as the OCZ escalation of community 'engagement', the Former Minister for Security and Counter-terrorism has intimated a nationwide reduction of similar 'Prevent' measures. Correspondingly, in a desperate attempt to protect more visible 'frontline' services from swingeing government cuts, local authorities have scaled down and offered redundancies across a range of social crime prevention initiatives focused on gangs and gang-related violence.

In sum, whilst revealing conflicts and contestations between local and wider policing around the Olympics, the extension of the territorial footprint of policing within East London, has also involved a hardening of the police response. This more intensified response can be argued to hold a range of instrumental and expressive functions similar to those articulated by Douglas above. Here, 'the social structure is credited with punitive powers' via punishment or effacement of the non-pure, which serves to publicly reaffirm the punitive structure. For both new agencies and territorial expressions of control, boundaries are classified and crystallized via such hardened expressions. . . .

Aggressive policing strategies have been a consistent feature of Olympic security for decades and feed into processes of public expressions of authority. Preceding the 1968 Mexico Games specially convened militarized 'Olympia Battalions' killed over 200 people protesting against the diversion of scarce welfare budgets towards Olympic pageantry. Whilst London 2012 also finds itself caught between commitments to Olympic grandeur and the new 'austerity' government regime, this example still stands as an extreme reaction and a single-incident centred exception. What is far more typical is the way that Olympic cities have almost unfailingly deployed low-level but geographically extensive 'zero-tolerance' models to police the Games in settings as diverse as Soviet Moscow and 'Share the Spirit' Sydney. In Sydney traditional policing roles were supplemented with controversial (for Australia) municipal by-laws to regulate behaviour and assembly that were also retained after the Games. Similarly, in Manchester, attempts to 'civilize' the city ahead of the 2002 Commonwealth Games via the stringent punishment of 'inappropriate behaviour' became an active strategy. [Neil] Gray and [Gerry] Mooney also note the 'concerted effort by the local state in conjunction with a range of central state and other agencies to "civilize" the

population of Glasgow East' in preparation for the 2014 Commonwealth Games.

In advance of London 2012 'zero tolerance' policing of specific incivilities is being played out in a number of ways that, curiously, avoid the word 'Olympics'. Over the past 12 months, the Newham police agenda has focused on both specific notifiable offences [an offense for which a crime report must be filed] and overall levels of incivility (and thus the image of the area). Here too disparities between local and central decision-making mechanisms within the police can be discerned. Newham's Chief Superintendent expressed some consternation at having local priorities 'randomly picked out by ACPO [Association of Chief Police Officers]'. Partially overlapping with the concerns about gang activity discussed above, one thematic area of law and order particularly deemed to relate to both notifiable offences and the image of Newham is in the area of serious youth violence. Prominent here is the emphasis on high-visibility policing and intensive enforcement strategies. To mobilize these strategies, Newham police have developed a Total Enforcement Team (TET), utilizing GIS profiling and hot-spotting practices, to target areas of perceived criminal concentration. Fast food 'chicken shop' outlets have received particular attention as 'crime generating' locations. At one level they have sometimes figured at the epicentre of conflict between groups of young people, while, at the opposite end of the scale, is their association with 'incivilities'. TET raids on such premises extend beyond standard policing responses and incorporate other agencies, including Trading Standards authorities, Immigration and Newham Council. Under one heading or another, the chances of finding at least some regulatory violation are multiplied.

# 37

# HILLE KOSKELA

## "THE GAZE WITHOUT EYES"

### Video-Surveillance and the Changing Nature of Urban Space

In this article, Hille Koskela deploys a rich and multipronged analysis to interrogate the presumed ease and effectiveness of video surveillance in urban settings. If surveillance is supposed to make spaces safer and therefore more open and accessible, she questions whether this is truly the case. The piece touches on many things that have since (in some cases, much later) become key areas within surveillance studies: consumption, gender, emotion, and the experiences of surveillance subjects, yet it is also fundamentally about the policing of urban space.

*** 

Despite all the policing with surveillance cameras, there is little agreement among researchers about whether surveillance cameras actually reduce crime. Studies on surveillance have produced contradictory results. There is evidence that surveillance causes the 'displacement' of crime since, whereas the areas under surveillance become safer, the areas not covered by cameras become more dangerous. Sometimes, however, cameras can 'spread' their influence so that crime rates are reduced both in areas under surveillance and in the surrounding areas. Studies suggest that the use of cameras has reduced property crime such as criminal damage, vehicle crime, theft and burglary. There is much less evidence to show that cameras would reduce *violent crime*, such as battery and sexual violence. Sexual offences, in particular, are most common in places that are rarely monitored, such as parks, suburban areas and private space. . . . An unwanted outcome of trying to guarantee as low a crime rate as possible is that it leads easily to ever-increasing surveillance and such solutions to reducing the crime rate can make the city a *less pleasant* place to live in rather than a more pleasant place. . . .

Surveillance is changing the nature of space or, in fact, is producing a new kind of space. This change can be understood in three ways: *space as a container, power-space* and *emotional space*. . . . [T]hese concepts are . . . partly overlapping, not mutually exclusive, dimensions of space—they are present simultaneously in a city that is under surveillance. . . .

[I]t is often suggested that space is not *just* a container but that many processes (production, consumption, power structures, etc.) come together to shape and create it. While generally agreeing with this, I would still like to argue that it is useful to consider space as a container. It *does* matter what kind of physical (architectural) frames space offers for social interaction, where objects in space lie (both vertically and horizontally) and how things are located in relation to each other. . . .

[F]or people under surveillance, I would argue, space as a container can be disorientating and alienating. First, what causes most mistrust about the technical ability of a camera is that a camera mainly operates backwards: it is designed to solve crime rather than to prevent it. However, . . . for a victim of violence, the help proffered by a camera may come too late. In the case of an attack, it might be possible to use the videotape to catch the offender(s), and to use the tape as evidence in court, but this response would not erase the actual experience of violence. This is a particularly serious drawback in relation to sexual violence. The prevention of sexual assault is of much greater importance than any reaction to it, and women have clearly indicated that this inability is a crucial reason for their mistrust of video-surveillance.

Secondly, even if the camera seems to look down from above, *the camera itself has no eyes*. Its lens is blind unless someone is looking through it. Similarly, a camera's location gives no indication of where the people behind the camera are situated. There is no personal contact between the security personnel and the public. One does not know whether anyone is looking and, if so, who that person is or how far away he or she is. One does not even know whether that person is *above* or *below*. Surveillance cameras have been considered as being 'literally above': they survey from 'above the crowd', 'from up there'. But quite often this is not the case. The camera seems to be looking at people from above but the monitoring room may be, for example, in the basement of a shopping mall where premises are cheaper. This makes it very difficult to ask for help through the agency of the camera—the camera *leaves its object entirely as an object*: passive, without any ability to influence the situation. . . .

What is characteristic of surveillance design is its paradoxicality: forms are at the same time transparent and opaque. While everything (and everyone) under surveillance is becoming more visible, the forces (and potential helpers) behind this surveillance are becoming less so. Forms are transparent from one side and opaque from the other—such as the mirror-like windows [used by police] in Helsinki metro stations. Although the purpose of surveillance is supposed to be an increase in safety, its design is rather, producing uncertainty. Again, this leaves the public as passive subjects in a container: they are subjects in a position of not knowing their own being. . . .

Just as the cameras and architectural forms of surveillance disturb the public, they are also disorientating and alienating to the people behind them—the police and guards. Such people have less personal contact with the public in the street. Compared to social control characterized by encounters with people, control accomplished through surveillance is faceless. . . . The use of video-surveillance can arguably be said to effect the ways in which 'reality' is conceptualized and understood. By being positioned behind a surveillance camera (where the world is seen on a TV screen) one can be tempted to believe that what is seen on the screen is real. However, this is only a restricted image of reality. It is reality seen from a particular viewpoint that has a certain ability to pan or zoom in—an image reduced to the visual.

What I wish to argue here is that surveillance actually *makes* space a container. The alienated who look from behind the camera see the space under surveillance through the monitor (simplified to two dimensions) and they look at people as if they were objects. The very absence of direct personal contact and the fact that the overseers are not themselves in the monitored space make them see the space from the outside. In the monitoring room, the two-dimensional 'virtual' space becomes more authentic than the three-dimensional reality outside. . . . People are reduced to doll-like bodies lacking personal qualities, and surveillance is reduced to the observation of bodily movements. The technical equipment that separates the two sides of surveillance makes it difficult for the space to be recognized as a lived, experienced space. . . .

[S]ince video-surveillance usually reduces everything to the visual, it is unable to identify situations where more sensitive interpretation is needed. For example, surveillance overseers can easily observe clearly visible but otherwise minor offences while ignoring situations they might regard as ambivalent, such as (verbal) sexual harassment. Most cameras are unable to interpret threatening situations that are not visually recognizable, and therefore cases of harassment often go unnoticed. Sexual harassment is more difficult to identify, and to interrupt, by surveillance camera than by the police/guards patrolling on foot. This insensitivity of the cameras—i.e., restriction within the field of vision—is an important reason for doubt and disorientation. 'The gaze' becomes gendered.

This failure could be understood as a 'passive' relationship between surveillance and harassment, but there is more to surveillance than this. There is a dimension that could be understood as an 'active'

relationship between surveillance and harassment. By this I mean it is possible to use surveillance cameras as a means of harassment. There is some voyeuristic fascination in looking, in being able to see. And scrutiny is a common and effective form of harassment. In urban space women are the ones likely to be looked at—the objects of the gaze. . . . Looking connotes power, and being looked at powerlessness. Harassment makes the gaze reproduce the embodiment and sexualization of women. . . .

The very experience of being under surveillance is ambivalent. Whatever form of surveillance is investigated—crime prevention, collection of evidence, invasion of privacy, etc.—this appears to be the case. Even if we can work out, for example, how potential criminals would react if watched (and that video-surveillance is guaranteeing our better security) this does not mean we would feel more safe. For a lone woman in an underground station subject to surveillance by a camera, the camera (as an object) could represent threat more than security or, even more interestingly, threat *as well as* security. The very same object that is reminding her of (male) power is, at the same time, supposed to protect her from male (power). In such circumstances, internal negotiation is not easy.

Although one of the aims of surveillance is to increase people's feelings of security, being the object of surveillance does not necessarily *encourage* feelings of safety. Feelings of vulnerability are related to lack of control. To be controlled by a surveillance camera—to be 'under control'—does not increase one's feeling of being 'in control'. This can perhaps be explained by comparing a surveillance camera to another familiar object: a public telephone. A public telephone in a corridor may make one feel safer than a surveillance camera even if one understood that, if something violent were to happen, it would be much more likely that the people behind the camera would inference, rather than someone on the other end of the pay-phone. This feeling emanates because, in relation to the telephone, one feels 'a subject' and thus able to control the situation whereas, in relation to the camera, one is always 'an object'. The object of a camera is in the situation of being a *potential victim*, without the opportunity to influence his or her own destiny. The object is forced to trust in someone else. This is why surveillance raises contradictions: to be placed in the position of a victim does not increase the feeling of being 'in control', but rather the feeling of being 'under control'. However, while feelings of being under control may not be pleasant, they might still ensure one's feelings of safety.

Emotional space may be difficult to understand because it cannot be described in static terms; it evades definitions and remains 'untouchable'. However, emotions such as fear of violence do, arguably, shape one's interpretation of space: the streets of fear are different in length according to the time of the day, who is passing by, how confident one feels at that moment, etc. Emotional space is 'elastic'. It is like a liquid—its nature changes according to where one is, what one does, who one is with, etc. It feels like one thing but then, all of a sudden, it changes to something else. Moreover, emotional space is essentially ambivalent. It is not logical but internally contradictory by nature. *There is no clear dynamic of power and resistance.* . . .

To be under surveillance is an ambivalent emotional event. A surveillance camera, as an object, can at the same time represent safety and danger. To be protected can feel the same as being threatened. A paradox of emotional space is that it does, indeed, make sense that surveillance cameras can make people feel both more secure and more fearful.

# 38

# ANDREW JOHN GOLDSMITH

## POLICING'S NEW VISIBILITY

The long-standing control that police had over their own "image management" has shifted radically in the past two decades. As Andrew Goldsmith explains, the spread of camera-equipped mobile phones, alongside the emergence of social media and video-sharing platforms, has afforded alternative documentation of police activities. The proliferation of alternative representations of police conduct does not necessarily lead to greater police accountability, however, as footage is interpretable and status positions may be used to discredit the images and narratives of others.

\*\*\*

Until just two decades ago, in terms of secondary visibility, police image management was closely tied to relationships between police and mass circulation newspapers and other traditional media outlets, particularly free-to-air television and radio. As these media became networked across countries and then globally, their capacity to disclose matters unfavourable to the police grew correspondingly. The Rodney King [beating] really was a threshold event, whereby the actions of a group of Californian police officers towards a citizen, Rodney King, became visible across the world in an unprecedented manner. Among other things, it allowed millions of viewers often thousands of kilometres away to form a view about the propriety or rectitude of the police officers' actions. The advent of the video camera presaged a major shift in the terms upon which even ordinary deeds became widely visible. . . .

The impact upon police image management of such changes is potentially profound. Less and less can police rely upon close relations with particular journalists, news photographers and trusted local news outlets to shape what is reported publicly about them. As well as favourable reporting, less flattering episodes of policing started to emerge within the 'mundane practices of police work which communicate . . . images of policing, and through which the social meanings of policing are produced'. The police were more and more in performances in which they not only did not control who the audience was or what they saw, but also could not predict who the critics were or what they might say and to whom.

In short, the past two decades have witnessed an increase in public capacity for surveilling the police, along with enhancements in state capacity to observe members of the public. Thomas Mathiesen noted the emergence of the synoptic age, the 'situation where a large number [of people] focuses on something in common which is condensed'. The Rodney King beating in 1991 is a classic example of synopticism in action. Another was the media coverage of the 11 September 2001 terrorist attacks in New York and Washington. These displays of synoptic capacity, while enormously powerful, relied for the most part upon the amplifying and disseminating capacity of mainstream media for their effect. . . .

The 'new visibility' refers to something beyond the kind of processes identified by Mathiesen. In part, it refers to the fact that the viewer society has also become the *media producer society* in the past decade, as the means of recording and disseminating images has become more widely held and commonly put into use. But there is more to this concept that refers to the uses made of the capability in question. Here, [John B.] Thompson has noted:

> [T]he making visible of actions and events is not just the outcome of leakage in systems of communication and information flow that are increasingly difficult to control; it is also an *explicit strategy of individuals who know very well that mediated visibility can be a weapon in the struggles they wage in their day-to-day lives.*

Thompson is pointing here to the greater willingness, as well as capability, within some sectors of the population to engage in 'disruptive disclosures' that, in the context of policing, subvert the appearance of 'normal policing'. Policing's visibility, while always contingent in some measure, is now much more contestable as a consequence of these changes. Thompson refers to the 'proliferation of mediated forms and networks of communication' that make it 'more difficult for political actors to throw a veil of secrecy around their activities' and 'much harder to control the images and information that appear in the public domain, and much harder to predict the consequences of such appearances and disclosures'. When applied to the circumstances and ascribed public responsibilities of policing, the destabilizing and destructive consequences arising from such visibility for favourable police image management become particularly grave. On the other side of the coin, it can enhance accountability. . . .

Another threshold in the visibility of policing occurred when the capacity to photograph and film policing activity became widely available in the hands of ordinary people, principally through the incorporation of camera recording capacity within mobile phones. The almost simultaneous development of video-sharing and social network sites also played a crucial role. . . .

The mobile phone camera enjoys a much wider distribution and diverse ownership and greater mobility, compared with fixed CCTV cameras or traditional television news cameras. Having achieved critical mass in the general population (as it has in many Western countries), it can go just about anywhere and capture images of just about anything, often surreptitiously given its semblance as a phone rather than as a camera. It can then be quickly linked to other flows of information through wireless transmission to sites like YouTube, unlike a traditional camera. This 'user created content' (UCC) is 'amateur media content [that is] created outside of professional routines and practices'. Once captured, the internet offers a 'generative' system that takes away a fundamental means of controlling the flow of information and images from those traditionally in charge of broadcasting.

Recording the police, 2015, unknown.

People, especially younger people, have become active participants in this 'post-broadcasting age', in which the constraints of traditional media upon what is disseminated are largely removed. The fact that this same group is also particularly prone to being targeted by police patrols in public spaces makes this a particularly potent coincidence for the police. Video-sharing platforms such as YouTube amplify the significance of mass access to mobile camera phones, providing alternative outlets to official media for mass viewing of UCC. Especially when linked to social networking sites such as Facebook, there is a dramatically increased capacity for reaching new audiences using different formats with few, if any, professional or commercial constraints upon the release of the material possessed. Looking into the future, this disruptive capability looks likely to grow very quickly. . . .

[A] greater capacity for holding the police accountable may not directly translate into more accountable policing. Within the 'new visibility' is the tendency for accounts to proliferate, often without providing ready means for resolving differences of perception and thus reaching clear judgments of propriety or impropriety. Part of the challenge in understanding these issues stems from what John Keane has called *communicative abundance*. This is a characteristic of our 'multi-media-saturated societies', those 'whose structures of power are continually "bitten" by monitory institutions operating within a new galaxy of media defined by the ethos of communicative abundance'. Monitoring in the policing context can be taken as referring to the production as well as consumption of accounts of police activities in the public sphere. Keane refers in this context to the idea of *monitory democracy*, the proliferation of forms of public scrutiny of power and its exercise, a trend driven by 'computerized media networks' that generate the 'new galaxy of communicative abundance'. Keane is thus addressing the same phenomenon as this article—the implications of new technologies for public power and accountability. The effect overall, he suggests, is to make people sceptical, if not suspicious and even cynical, about the exercise of power, especially unaccountable power. The proliferation of accessible, but also often competing and conflicting accounts is a feature of this environment, according to Keane. What this narrative material enables is questioning by ordinary people of officially presented reality.

The robustness of the material provided in many of these communications is also in doubt. Not all of it can be expected to meet evidential standards set by courts or disciplinary tribunals. This issue raises the fundamental question of the *purposes behind the new visibility* in relation to policing. When mobilized, does it reflect widespread commitment by internet users and informal media producers to new forms of political engagement, or rather broad participation in a politics of virtual connection that remains, ironically, detached and otherwise passive? While the potential is there for it to be both, we need to know more about how it is used, particularly by whom and for what agendas. . . . [N]ot all contributors to YouTube or other internet sites can be presumed to be acting in good faith as concerned citizens trying to examine the 'truth' of a particular matter. Both the technical capabilities of the new media technologies (to re-write, manipulate, etc.) and the largely uncontrolled access for persons to become producers as well as receivers of messages and images has the result that the capacity to distort or mislead through the internet is immense. Not every picture tells a true story, whether on the internet or elsewhere. Apparently credible accounts of fabricated video material on YouTube have recently emerged. This technological possibility immediately provides those represented in such material with the option of alleging that it was fabricated and hence untrue.

Without necessarily involving deliberate attempts to mislead, [Cass] Sunstein writes about the potential in the hands of internet users to produce informational and reputational *cybercascades* that are 'diverse but inconsistent'. 'Cascade' refers to a process in which people adhere, or appear to adhere, to a particular position, at least in large measure, because others they know or are aware of are doing so. This effect is made possible in large measure due to the growing linkages between viewing platforms and social network sites such as Twitter and Facebook. When these linkages exist and are used, such cascades can occur very quickly and potentially on a massive scale, producing what Sunstein has termed a 'wildfire' effect. Mapping the effects of this communicative abundance remains to be done. However, there is the risk that this material, especially where it is insubstantial or maliciously skewed, may serve merely to confirm pre-existing prejudices or opinions. This occurred in the Rodney King case, where black Americans were more likely to interpret the recorded events negatively than white Americans, reflecting at least in some measure pre-existing patterns of thought about the motives and dispositions of American police officers. . . .

Overall, the picture is a sobering one both for the police and for the established oversight and accountability mechanisms. For police, there will almost inevitably be more attention given to ways of doing 're-pair work' around the disruptions aired through the internet. While there remains uncertainty regarding the enduring effects of mass media exposure of police misconduct upon public perceptions, an expansion of this capacity as described here is likely to confirm the suspicions and negative attitudes of those already unfavourably disposed towards the police, while potentially alienating or distancing those who have not previously held such attitudes towards the police. While routinization of scandals concerning police could lead to diminishing effects, it also seems likely that the police's particular status as societal moral agent will ensure the ongoing salience of these exposures in the public eye. In the case of police, the actions of an individual can damage the standing of the organization as a whole. The risks are particularly acute in cases of police forces in high standing or historically held in such standing, such as Canada's RCMP [Royal Canadian Mounted Police].

As noted above, the capacity of these technologies to produce unfocused doubt and distrust as well as contribute to forensic accuracy leaves the police vulnerable for reasons often beyond their control. Ongoing management of these situations will become more important for police organizations. As the Rodney King case showed, it is possible to develop interpretations of events that are more favourable towards police, 'despite appearances' once interpretive work is undertaken upon those images. However, not everyone will be persuaded by such 'repair work'. Whereas, by comparison, there was once the occasional, localized performance of police impropriety achieving notoriety, we now can expect more frequent, globalized spectacles of such impropriety.

For oversight agencies, as we have already begun to see, things are only likely to get busier and the call for greater resources is likely to become more urgent among them, even if less individualized methods of complaint processing are quickly devised and find broad acceptance. A combination of measures may be required if the rate of growth of complaint and grievance increases dramatically, as seems likely. Without considerable adaptability by these institutions, they face the real risk of losing their previously substantial dominance of the oversight role due to their role in the 'institutionalization of distrust'. They will need to adapt so as to be able to accommodate the new material generated and to develop capacities to channel and credibly handle such material. This will not be easy, in large measure because the extent and implications of the phenomenon in question remain largely unknown. One can predict, though, that one effect of the 'abundance' will be even greater public scepticism towards the police investigating police and demands for more robust civilian oversight mechanisms capable of conducting independent investigations of notorious incidents, especially those involving apparent brutality, sooner and more thoroughly than in the past.

# 39

# TORIN MONAHAN AND RODOLFO D. TORRES

## SCHOOLS UNDER SURVEILLANCE

### Cultures of Control in Public Education

Educational institutions are fundamentally organized around surveillance practices. This excerpt explains the political and economic context for contemporary school surveillance, with an emphasis on public schools in the United States, and underscores the social inequalities produced by such systems. As educational and criminal justice institutions overlap, it is most often poor students of color who are funneled through the school-to-prison pipeline.

\*\*\*

The imperative to protect children is seldom questioned. It would seem degenerate to do so. But one must wonder what it means when armed police officers roam school hallways, when students line up for more than an hour before class just to get past security screening checkpoints, when fingerprinting is required for students to enter schools or use school cafeterias, or when schools look more like prisons, with barbed-wire perimeters, video surveillance, and police cars parked on campus. Sometimes public schools are even located in former prisons.

Public education is one important domain where the perceived need for greater security has given rise to new formations in school discipline, primarily for students but increasingly for teachers and administrators too. Some of the well-known mechanisms of student and teacher discipline include high-stakes standardized testing, zero-tolerance policies for violence, rigid schedules, and architectures of visibility and containment. Less obvious is the host of new institutional arrangements and technologies that augment these existing disciplinary mechanisms: on-site police officers who routinize experiences of crime control and effectively interlink public education and criminal justice systems; advanced surveillance technologies that are used to subject students to constant monitoring and to demand that they engage in ritual performances—such as submitting to metal detectors—to demonstrate their innocence; and new bureaucratic developments in so-called decision-support systems and performance audits, by which students and teachers are evaluated from afar and micromanaged or disciplined accordingly.

Most school surveillance today is of the kind just described, though it must not be forgotten that face-to-face human surveillance in schools is far from extinct. Examples of such surveillance include simple observation, watching, listening, and following; the use of human spies, undercover operatives, and informers; and mandatory drug tests and searches. Some peer-to-peer surveillance occurs when students use cell phones or social networking Web sites to find out about each other's activities, allowing for social bonding but sometimes creating distrust and violence among students. The most intensive authoritarian surveillance regimes have been constructed around not much more than these basic ingredients, usually combined with a strong sense of mistrust and fear of infiltration, persecution, or invasion of privacy. At its root, therefore, surveillance is not simply about monitoring or tracking individuals and their data—it is about the structuring of power relations through human, technical, or hybrid control mechanisms.

Perhaps not surprisingly, racial minorities are disproportionately subjected to contemporary surveillance and policing apparatuses. The emerging governance regimes may be fueled by public fears of crime, but control mechanisms are applied differentially and with different effects. Thus, students in poorer inner-city schools are subjected to more invasive hand searches and metal-detector screenings, while students in more affluent schools tend to be monitored more discreetly with video surveillance cameras. Lower-income

minority students, especially males, also get funneled more systematically into the criminal justice system by police officers on school campuses. Similarly, military recruiters enjoy a great deal of access to poorer students—mostly in urban and rural schools—and actively collect intelligence on them in order to further their mission of enlisting soldiers. Given that public education putatively supports the progressive goal of equality, the use of surveillance to target and sort students along lines of race, class, and gender deserves continued scrutiny and critique, especially as the institution of education further aligns itself with the criminal justice system, the military, and private industry.

To begin to understand the complexity of surveillance and security practices in public education, it may be useful to outline some of the factors contributing to such cultures of control. Certainly fear should not be underestimated. Tragedies of school shootings become shared media and cultural spectacles, instigating moral panics that overshadow any cold, objective assessment of risk. After all, schools continue to be perhaps *the* safest place for children; far safer than streets, cars, or homes. . . . Nonetheless, the threat of "another Columbine" (or Virginia Tech, and so on) haunts the social imaginary, leading parents, policy makers, and others to the sober conclusion that any security measure is worth whatever trade-offs are involved in order to ensure safety. Never mind the fact that an armed guard and a video surveillance system were present at Columbine, which is why many people have such vivid memories of the attack. . . .

The socio-legal landscape has shifted dramatically over the past few decades too. We have come to understand crime as that which causes fear, rather than as acts of deviance; crime is less about breaches in social acceptability than perceptions of individual vulnerability. This helps explain the furor over school violence in suburban and rural communities: crime in "good" neighborhoods elicits more moral outrage than crime in "bad" ones because it is apparently worse if people think that they are safe and then discover that they are not. At the same time, policing practices have shifted since the 1970s to stress crime containment, risk management, and outsourcing of policing responsibilities. As David Garland explains: "In the past, official criminology has usually viewed crime *retrospectively* and *individually*, in order to itemise individual wrongdoing and allocate punishment or treatment. The new criminologies tend to view crime *prospectively* and in *aggregate* terms, for the purpose of calculating risks and shaping preventative measures." Fortification and securitization epitomize such "preventative measures," whether in gated communities, malls, airports, or schools. And a host of scaled-up punitive interventions has accompanied these developments so that any instance of crime is severely punished, transforming what scholars have described as "the welfare state," predicated on ideals of rehabilitation and inclusion, into "the penal state," enforcing maximum punishments and exclusion.

In public education settings, these sociolegal changes manifest in zero-tolerance policies for the possession of weapons or drugs, for any acts of violence, and even for verbal threats. The presence of police officers on school grounds ensures that violators will be charged with crimes for infractions, such as school fights or thefts, that previously might have resulted in softer forms of punishment, such as detention, expulsion, or conferences between parents (or guardians), students, and school officials. Concentrations of "school resource officers" (SROs), who are trained police officers, are greatest in urban areas of highest poverty, and their numbers have skyrocketed in recent years so that now 68 percent of all high schools and middle schools in the United States have SROs. One inimical result of

this phenomenon is the augmentation of a "school-to-prison pipeline," disproportionately escorting low-income, minority students into prisons and contributing to astronomical levels of incarceration in the United States. . . .

Rather than surmise that the present articulation of school discipline emerged organically, one can identify specific laws, policies, and reports that catalyzed the norms and forms of school discipline today. Notably, the Safe Schools Act of 1994 provided funds for public schools if they could demonstrate an existing crime problem, which compelled schools to implement data-collection systems and categorize crimes as broadly as possible. Various grants from government agencies further supported school-police partnerships, as did an amendment to the 1968 Omnibus Crime Control and Safe Streets Act in 1998. Zero-tolerance policies for drug use were solidified in 2002, when the U.S. Supreme Court upheld the legality of mandatory drug tests for students absent any evidence of drug problems in a particular school. Under the No Child Left Behind (NCLB) Act of 2001, school districts receiving federal funds "must have a policy requiring that any student who brings a firearm or weapon to school will be referred to the criminal justice or juvenile delinquency system." The Safe School Initiative, which was a collaborative research project between the U.S. Secret Service and the Department of Education to learn from previous school shootings, released a report in 2002 advocating that schools conduct "threat assessments" in conjunction with the implementation of student profiling and security systems. And in the aftermath of 9/11 and of the deadly terrorist attack on a school in Beslan, Russia, in 2004, the U.S. Department of Homeland Security made grants available for schools to implement crisis management plans, coordinate with police, and purchase security equipment.

Our neoliberal ideological climate plays an important role in the formation of cultures of control in public education. The general distrust of public institutions and celebration of private-sector and individual solutions to social problems nourishes control mechanisms that aggravate social inequalities. This is a coupling of the so-called invisible hand of free-market solutions with the iron fist of discipline and control. Those who are unable to embody the identity of empowered consumers taking responsibility for their own needs might be understood as failed neoliberal citizens who are subsequently targeted for punitive state interventions. Neoliberal policies are typically not aimed at achieving "small government," no matter what their proponents claim. Instead, especially in the post-9/11 context, they inscribe new priorities for government bodies: to amplify security and military functions of the state on one hand and to serve the needs of industry on the other. In education, one can witness this trend with the judicious government funding for information technology (IT) and surveillance systems in schools that cannot afford books, supplies, furniture, classrooms, or even teachers. These schools then turn around and pay private vendors and contractors for those systems, effectively handing over to industry public funds that are sorely needed for other purposes. . . .

Although it makes sense to locate the social control dimensions of educational neoliberalism in security equipment, police presence, and unforgiving policies for dealing with infractions, standardized tests and audits represent the most widespread forms of surveillance and social control in public schools. Standardized tests are nothing new, but they now carry harsh penalties not only for students but also for public school teachers, administrators, and districts. As mandated by NCLB, all schools receiving federal funds must annually test students in grades three through twelve for reading and math (and science after 2007–2008). Schools must then demonstrate improvement across all subgroups of students (for example, "English language learners," "special education," or "African American") from year to year or risk being "placed on probation" and taken over by the state. Teachers and administrators are penalized if students' subgroups do not demonstrate adequate improvement, which then encourages teachers to flee from schools serving poor or immigrant students. NCLB carves out other avenues for surveillance too by requiring public schools to open their campuses to military recruiters and provide them with personal data (names, addresses, phone numbers) on all students. . . .

With audit cultures, workplaces mutate to value that which can be documented, subsequently altering workplace practices to stress the generation of reports (such as test results) and to devalue that which cannot easily be translated into documents or databases (such as mentoring students). These documents then open organizations and the people within them to heightened surveillance through software applications that can mine data and generate reports comparing performance levels of employees, students, or schools. Seemingly, having the data necessitates comparative evaluations through software applications such as decision support systems, which then compel administrative actions to discipline "underperformers" and ensure accountability. Thus, although audit mechanisms such as tests may not have the look and feel of harder surveillance technologies, they are clearly a form of surveillance and need to be understood as such. . . .

Surveillance is a privileged form of modern knowledge production, organizational management, and social control. . . . Surveillance entails much more than the use of video cameras to passively monitor people. Surveillance is a mode of governance that controls access, opportunities, and life chances and even helps to channel choices, often using personal data to determine who gets what. This is clearly evident in the context of public education, where disparate surveillance mechanisms—from metal detectors to standardized tests—overlap to enmesh school actors in a larger surveillant assemblage that thrives upon the production and exchange of data and the sorting of populations based on their perceived value, potential, or risk. In other words, education is inseparably linked to the political economy and often serves as a battleground for ideological and material conflicts over resources, values, and rights. Surveillance is not merely a weapon in those larger contests; it actively shapes the social field upon which those contests play out.

# SECTION 8

# PRIVACY AND AUTONOMY

////////////////////////////////////////////////////////////////////////////////////////////////////////////////////

Privacy is the thing that most people think of as being compromised by surveillance. If for no other reason, the concept of privacy is important because it profoundly shapes public discourse, as seen with just about any news story about a new surveillance system or program, whether it be a cell phone app to track one's children, Facebook's collection of user data, or government-level data-collection schemes. The concept of privacy also offers a way to identify tangible problems with surveillance and seek redress. Thus, an understanding of privacy as a legal right, or even a human right, animates engagements with surveillance in legal systems and in public policy. It is further laden with importance as civil society organizations—such as the American Civil Liberties Union or the Electronic Frontier Foundation—invoke it in lawsuits contesting corporate or government violations of laws surrounding information access. In short, the link between privacy and surveillance is codified in legal and policy regimes and hardwired in the contemporary social imaginary.

Privacy is classically understood as the "right to be let alone" (Brandeis and Warren 1890), which can include things like protection from scrutiny in one's home, control over personal information, or confidentiality with regard to healthcare or educational data (Allen 2007). It is important to note that

even from the time of Louis Brandeis and Samuel Warren's foundational 1890 essay on "The Right to Privacy," the orientation was toward threats from private parties and businesses, not principally from the government (Rotenberg 2007). The supposed galvanizing event for this essay was Samuel Warren's unwanted exposure to publicity, as he was outraged that tabloid publications of the time listed him as attending Boston society functions (Kersch 2004: 57). This sense of bourgeois elitism, of privacy as an individual right for the privileged, is something that later critics of privacy would revisit in questioning the utility of privacy rights discourses more broadly.

While privacy offers a vast legal and philosophical terrain for scholarly inquiry, for the field of surveillance studies, the concentration is on technology-based challenges to privacy, especially with regard to information systems used by corporate and government organizations (Kerr, Steeves, and Lucock 2009). Further, the field has directed attention to the varied responses to such challenges, such as the development of privacy-enhancing technologies or the work of civil-society groups to alter or ensure the enforcement of laws or policies (see Section 13). Perhaps more so than with other areas in surveillance studies, the work of legal and policy scholars overlaps with and often complements the efforts of civil-society groups, policymakers, and legal practitioners working to develop (or enforce) privacy laws and policies.

It may seem counterintuitive, especially given the centrality of privacy in public discourses about surveillance, but the field of surveillance studies has an uncomfortable relationship with the privacy concept, sometimes bordering on an aversion. Some of the critiques are that it is a largely individual-istic concept that is poorly suited to account for discrimination against groups (Gandy 1993; Murakami Wood et al. 2006), that it is empirically inaccurate in representing the concerns of marginalized populations with issues of domination and survival (Gilliom 2001), and that it is universalizing and there-fore unable to effectively grapple with power inequalities or differences (Monahan 2015). Colin Bennett (excerpted in Chapter 45) has suggested that the field's attack on—or dis-missal of—the concept of privacy stems from a generational difference, where "younger scholars" simply do not find it as "cool" as other things they might study. A more per-suasive explanation would be that different *disciplinary* orientations inflect the interests of scholars, making some areas of study or conceptual approaches more compelling than others. For instance, philosophy, po-litical science, and legal studies each have established track records of engaging with privacy issues. This makes sense given the importance of liberal individualism in the Western philosophical tradition—as well as in political science and legal studies—where concerns with issues of freedom, rights, and constraint are paramount. Thus, it is no acci-dent that the pieces excerpted in this section, even the one that is challenging the privacy paradigm, are authored or coauthored by scholars trained in the disciplines of philos-ophy, political science, or legal studies.

The excerpts in this section each reveal a sensitive awareness of the limitations of the privacy concept. They represent the internal tension in the field about whether privacy is the best approach to studying surveil-lance, but they also productively add com-plexity to the notion of privacy, seeing it as a dynamic social norm that is transformed through technological and institutional change. By shifting focus away from an ex-clusively individual-based privacy frame, and toward a broader understanding of privacy as a "social good," the majority of the pieces excerpted here seek to recuperate privacy as a vital area of investigation, theorization, and advocacy.

The excerpt by Priscilla Regan explains that in the policy realm, when privacy is conceived of solely as an individual interest, then any other interests, especially organiza-tional ones, are uncritically interpreted as so-cial goods, which all but ensures the erosion of privacy rights over time. Jean-François Blanchette and Deborah Johnson pick up this thread and add that the right to be forgotten, through systematically planned data expul-sion policies by institutions, will also yield valuable social benefits. Helen Nissenbaum develops a framework of privacy as "contex-tual integrity" to sidestep increasingly murky distinctions between "public" and "private" and instead to advocate for adherence to social norms about the expected purposes of data generated in specific contexts—in other words, data collection and exchange are not necessarily problematic as long as one maintains the integrity of the consen-sual context of data origination.

Julie Cohen takes a somewhat different tack, investigating the relationship between the ongoing project of personal identity construction and the less pliable identity patterns imposed by information systems; for her, "conditions for human flourishing" can emerge from the boundary management one does between these poles, so the eth-ical imperative is to keep those conditions for negotiation open. Based on his research

*Eavesdropping*, 1880, Théodore Jacques Ralli.

on the surveillance of welfare mothers, John Gilliom finds the privacy paradigm wanting; he instead draws upon the narratives of these women to illustrate how they prioritize an "ethic of care" for their families and engage in forms of everyday resistance to survive. The final excerpt by Colin Bennett defends the privacy concept and responds to the field's critiques of it. He finds that many of the detractors construct "straw man" representations of privacy to easily knock down, but that these critiques fail to engage with the theoretical developments of privacy scholars or with the actual practices of legal authorities and regulators. Privacy frames, as he puts it, are here to stay.

## REFERENCES

Allen, Anita L. 2007. Definition of Privacy. In *Encyclopedia of privacy*, edited by W. G. Staples, 393–403. Westport, CT: Greenwood Press. ·

Brandeis, Louis D., and Samuel D. Warren. 1890. The Right to Privacy. *Harvard Law Review* 4 (5):193, 195–97.

Gandy, Oscar H. 1993. *The Panoptic Sort: A Political Economy of Personal Information*. Boulder, CO: Westview.

Gilliom, John. 2001. *Overseers of the Poor: Surveillance, Resistance, and the Limits of Privacy*. Chicago: University of Chicago Press.

Kerr, Ian, Valerie Steeves, and Carole Lucock, eds. 2009. *Lessons from the Identity Trail: Anonymity, Privacy, and Identity in a Networked Society*. Oxford: Oxford University Press.

Kersch, Kenneth Ira. 2004. *Constructing Civil Liberties: Discontinuities in the Development of American Constitutional Law*. Cambridge, UK: Cambridge University Press.

Monahan, Torin. 2015. The Right to Hide? Anti-Surveillance Camouflage and the Aestheticization of Resistance. *Communication and Critical/Cultural Studies* 12 (2):159–78.

Murakami Wood, David (ed.), Kirstie Ball, David Lyon, Clive Norris, and Charles Raab. 2006. *A Report on the Surveillance Society*. Wilmslow: Office of the Information Commissioner.

Rotenberg, Marc. 2007. Louis D. Brandeis (1856–1941). In *Encyclopedia of Privacy*, edited by W. G. Staples, 72–76. Westport, CT: Greenwood Press.

# 40

# PRISCILLA M. REGAN

## LEGISLATING PRIVACY

Technology, Social Values, and Public Policy

In her influential book *Legislating Privacy*, Priscilla Regan argues that privacy rights are attenuated in the policy realm not only because of the influence of organizational actors but also because of an overreliance on an individualistic framing of privacy. Such a framing, as taken up in policy debates, spuriously presumes that privacy is an individual concern only, whereas organizational interests represent the public good. The following excerpt critiques this problematic framing and advocates instead for the *social* importance of privacy.

\*\*\*

Privacy may be close to extinction, but not because of technology or lack of public concern; the reason may be a failure to conceptualize privacy in a way that sustains public interest and support.

The philosophical basis of privacy policy overemphasizes the importance of privacy to the individual and fails to recognize the broader social importance of privacy. This emphasis on privacy as an individual right or an individual interest provides a weak basis for formulating policy to protect privacy. When privacy is defined as an individual right, policy formulation entails a balancing of the individual right to privacy against a competing interest or right. In general, the competing interest is recognized as a social interest. For example, the police interest in law enforcement, the government interest in detecting fraud, and an employer's interest in securing an honest work force are discussed and defined as societal interests. It is also assumed that the individual has a stake in these societal interests. As a result, privacy has been on the defensive, with those alleging a privacy invasion bearing the burden of proving that a certain activity does indeed invade privacy and that the "social" benefit to be gained from the privacy invasion is less important than the individual harm incurred.

Once one recognizes the sources and effects of modern threats to "individual" privacy, the notion that privacy should be considered from a social perspective rather than solely from an individual perspective becomes apparent. Database surveillance, electronic eavesdropping, and polygraph testing are generally not techniques that individuals use in relation to other individuals. These techniques do not primarily affect individuals' relationships of friendship, love, and trust. Instead, these threats come from private and governmental organizations—the police, welfare agencies, credit agencies, banks, and employers—and affect all individuals' relationships to these organizations and all individuals' ability to get a job, credit, or insurance. In modern society, then, privacy pertains to relations between individuals and corporate or government organizations as well as to relations among individuals. When these organizations are part of the public realm, privacy concerns cross the boundary between public and private.

I argue that privacy is not only of value to the individual as an individual but also to society in general, and I suggest three bases for a social importance of privacy. The first two are normative bases that were identified in some of the earlier writing on privacy but have been overshadowed by an emphasis on the importance of privacy to the individual. A reconsideration of these social bases is especially important in light of the policy experiences that resulted from focusing on the importance of privacy to the individual. Privacy is a *common value* in that all individuals value some degree of privacy and have some common perceptions about privacy. Privacy is also a *public value* in that it has value not just to the individual as an individual or to all individuals in common but also to the democratic political system. The third basis for the social importance of privacy is derived from the theoretical literature in economics. Privacy is rapidly becoming a *collective value* in that technology and market forces are making it hard for any one person to have privacy without all persons having a similar minimum level of privacy.

It may be that *all* individual interests or rights are important to both individuals and society. But in the case of privacy, its importance to society has not been pursued while its importance to the individual has received much attention. Therefore, I have attempted to make explicit the social importance of privacy. . . . Rethinking the importance of privacy in this way will change the definition of policy problems involving privacy and technology and provide a more convincing argument for formulating policy to protect privacy. . . .

But, as illustrated in congressional attempts to protect privacy, defining privacy primarily in terms of its importance to the individual and in terms of an individual right has served as a weak basis for public policy. There are three explanations for the weakness of individual privacy as a policy goal: it emphasizes the negative value of privacy; it establishes a conflict between the individual and society; and it fails to take into account the importance of large social and economic organizations. . . .

*Negative value.* . . . The view of privacy as the "right to be let alone" draws attention to the possible reasons why an individual might want to be let alone. Other than for the establishment of intimate relationships and the development of autonomy, the reason offered most often is to "hide" things the individual does not want known. In policy discussions, those opposed to privacy protections easily raise suspicions about the reasons individuals want privacy. Two possibilities seem to follow from these suspicions. First, if an individual does not have anything to hide, then privacy would not be of value to him or her. Second, if the individual does have something to hide, the question is whether it should remain private or whether others need to know about it. . . .

Policy difficulties that result from viewing privacy as a negative value can be seen in Richard Posner's analysis of privacy. . . . Posner [says] that the "case for protecting business privacy is stronger, in general, than that for protecting individual privacy," because "secrecy is an important method of appropriating social benefits to the entrepreneur who creates them, while in private life it is more likely to conceal legitimately discrediting or deceiving facts." Posner argues that business privacy is of greater value because the benefits to the entrepreneur are regarded as "social" while the value of individual privacy is not only individual rather than social but also assumed to be used largely for negative purposes. In order to gain supporters for privacy protections, this negative conception of privacy must be overcome. . . .

*Conflict with "society."* In much of the philosophical and legal literature on privacy, a conflict is established between the individual and society. Alan Westin, in his seminal work *Privacy and Freedom,* views privacy and social participation as competing desires and sees each individual establishing a balance between the two that is best for that individual. . . .

The more privacy is identified with the individual's ability to withdraw from society or establish a boundary between himself or herself and society, the more privacy is viewed as an impediment to the functioning of society. . . . [T]he philosophical thinking about privacy that establishes a tension between the individual and society often moves policy debate into a discussion of how privacy conflicts with social interests such as government efficiency, law enforcement, and an honest work force. Not only is the conflict cast as one between the individual and society, but because the other interests are defined as social interests, they can draw upon both self-interest and public interest in mobilizing support. . . .

[M]y quarrel is with the common notion that social concerns and privacy values are antithetical. Not only has this assumption not been adequately or critically explored, but framing debate in terms of an individual interest in competition with a social interest does not make for fruitful discussions of social issues. . . . The two spheres are not necessarily contradictory or in conflict; instead, a dynamic relationship exists between the two. A simple dichotomy

between the individual and society, or private and public, fails to take into account the modern reality that people operate in a range of contexts that can be more or less public or private. . . .

*Failure to acknowledge social organizations.* Related to this antithetical view of the individual and society is the absence of an examination of the constituent parts of society. . . . For example, the omission of large social and economic organizations from the individual-society dichotomy presents a serious problem when discussing privacy and technology. In both the philosophical literature and policy discussions, such organizations are assumed to operate as part of society, and their interests are considered social interests. But there is no serious analysis of the nature of social organizations . . . [and] the philosophical literature does not confront situations in which privacy is threatened by the activities of large organizations. . . .

A definition of privacy as the right of the individual to control access to himself or herself, in effect, rests upon an "exaltation of the powers of the individual." It also explains the failure to examine the interests of the organizations collecting and using personal information; instead, the individual is given the means to mediate his or her relationship with the organization. By placing the burden on the individual, there is less need to evaluate whether organizational interests are indeed social interests or whether individual privacy interests could be conceived as social interests. . . .

Because privacy has been viewed as an individual interest, because it has been conceptualized as a means of hiding something, and because the organizational interests threatening privacy have not been questioned, privacy has not generated public interest. The conceptualization of privacy has instead narrowed political support and policy options. . . .

I argue that privacy's importance does not stop with the individual and that a recognition of the social importance of privacy will clear a path for more serious policy discourse about privacy and for the formulation of more effective public policy to protect privacy. . . . Privacy has value beyond its usefulness in helping the individual maintain his or her dignity or develop personal relationships. Most privacy scholars emphasize that the individual is better off if privacy exists; I argue that society is better off as well when privacy exists. I maintain that privacy serves not just individual interests but also common, public, and collective purposes.

# 41

# JEAN-FRANÇOIS BLANCHETTE AND DEBORAH G. JOHNSON

## DATA RETENTION AND THE PANOPTIC SOCIETY

### The Social Benefits of Forgetfulness

The dominant framing of privacy as an *individual right* may contribute to its erosion, especially when it is pitted against social exigencies such as the need for national security. In this excerpt, the authors argue for the importance of viewing privacy as a *social good* that can be safeguarded by ensuring that data expulsion (or planned "institutional forgetfulness") is a core element of any approach to information management.

*** 

Control over personal information is not only affected through selective access, but also through selective retention of such information. That is, control is not only a question of who has and who does not have access to personal information (nowadays, seemingly everyone has access but its producer), but who gets to retain or discard it. Most privacy commentators focus on access and control, and address retention only as an afterthought—if at all. A central concern of this article is to make the importance of this component explicit: We argue that data retention must figure as an important element of any comprehensive account of informational privacy. . . .

Our approach to data retention begins from the insight that the endurance of data is a feature that has invisibly but powerfully changed with the shift from paper-and-ink to electronic systems of record-keeping. In the paper-and-ink world, the sheer cumbersomeness of archiving and later finding information often promoted a form of institutional forgetfulness—a situation with parallels to human memory. The forgetfulness of the paper-and-ink world was implicit in the material being of institutions, the available storage space, the budget for file cabinets, etc. Often the institution's memory/forgetfulness was not even recognized as a policy issue but dealt with as a matter of physical facilities. In many cases, as storage technologies have gained in practicality, ease of remote access, and lowered in price, the shift to an electronic medium changed the default position from one of forgetfulness to one of memory.

Whether the paper-and-ink environment or the electronic environment favors data retention, the point remains that decisions about length of retention of data may be made unintentionally or in an ad hoc manner, rather than with an eye to privacy policy or institutional memory per se. We find ourselves in a world that captures endless data on us and then decides (sometimes by failing to decide) how long to retain this data. When data are lost or deleted, our behavior is forgotten. When data endure, our behavior is not forgotten and some important values may shrink with it—values that are fundamental to democratic society. In other words, we must ask, what are the social implications of a lack of institutional forgetfulness?

We begin our investigation of this question within the U.S. context, for several reasons. First, there is a general consensus that in the United States too little is being done to stop the onslaught of personal data collection. . . . At the same time (and perhaps ironically), the United States has traditionally understood itself to be a place where individuals could get a "second chance." The idea that an American citizen can sometimes "wipe the slate clean" and start anew is, no doubt, tied to the immigrant, pioneer histories of so many Americans. Whatever its origins, the idea is in tension with current U.S. data collection and retention policies. . . .

But while . . . others have drawn attention to the value of starting over, of having a portion of the past forgotten, the issue has been cast, implicitly or explicitly, as one involving a tension between personal or individual privacy and social goods. They have portrayed the issue as a matter of balancing individual privacy against such social goods as law enforcement, government efficiency, or national security. Yet there is reason to believe that this framing of the problem is inaccurate and biased against individual privacy.

The lesson of the 1980s and early 1990s is that when personal privacy is put into a cost-benefit analysis, it generally loses. The needs of government agencies and private organizations or institutions for more accurate and efficient information systems so as to further their goals (law enforcement, national security, administrative efficiency) overpower the desire (need, interest, or right) of individuals to have information about them kept private. [Priscilla] Regan describes how this framing of the issue has led to the loss of privacy protection in several major public policy contexts. She argues against such a reductive framing of privacy on grounds that it does not recognize the social importance of personal privacy. Hence, in our analysis of institutional forgetfulness, we want to argue for forgetfulness as a social good, not just an individual good.

## The Value of Social Forgetfulness

Privacy as an individual good and privacy as a social good are inextricably tied together. To see this, one need only appreciate that the kind of world we live in makes us into certain kinds of beings and certain kinds of beings are essential for a certain kind of world. Democracy depends on individual citizens who are capable of formulating plans for their lives, taking action, thinking critically, and making decisions. Yet individuals of this kind can not develop in an environment of constant surveillance. The problem is not just that democracy is squelched when individuals live in fear of repercussions for any nonconforming behavior; it is also that the mere fact that one is being watched changes the way one behaves. . . .

The argument for privacy as a social good thus encompasses privacy as an individual good; the argument includes both. Privacy is not just something individuals want because it makes them feel good or is good for them; rather, privacy is good for society insofar as it promotes the development of the kinds of individuals who are essential for democracy. A world in which there is no forgetfulness—a world in which everything one does is recorded and never forgotten—is not a world conducive to the development of democratic citizens. It is a world in which one must hesitate over every act because every act has permanence, may be recalled and come back to haunt one, so to speak. . . .

In order to begin understanding the requirements of retention policies, we examined three policy arenas in which forgetfulness seems to play an important and explicit role: bankruptcy law, juvenile crime records, and credit reporting. . . .

## Bankruptcy Law

The first thing to note about bankruptcy law is that the discussion surrounding it does, indeed, recognize forgetfulness (and forgiveness) as a social good. . . . While the literature we examined did express the concern for forgiveness for mistakes and the good of letting individuals move on, there are reasons to believe that these values alone would not have led to the forgiveness of bankruptcy, were it not for the fact that creditor interests were also served by the forgiveness. Moreover, government (social) interests were at work insofar as there was a perceived need to respond to periodic national financial crises and to facilitate individuals (especially those involved in business) in getting back into economic activity.

The literature on the history of bankruptcy law supports Regan's idea that when policy debates are framed as a tension between individual interests and social good, individual interests do not win. In bankruptcy law, the tension between individual and social interests was finally (and perhaps, only) resolved when there was a coming together of institutional interests (creditors' interest in a noncompetitive way to obtain whatever they could), individual interests in being able to start afresh (having their mistakes forgiven and forgotten), and social interests (in responding to major economic crises and getting entrepreneurs back into the economy). . . .

## Juvenile Crime Records

Juvenile justice has evolved considerably over the last few centuries, concurrently with changing social conceptions of both children and the role of the state. Although there are many different and competing visions of how the state should intervene with regard to juvenile crime, one prominent train of thought has been the liberal (progressive) view of the state as protector of juveniles. Such a view primarily aims at rehabilitating juveniles through deemphasizing their offenses and highlighting their treatment needs. . . .

Whether one holds that a child's criminal behavior is truly criminal or rather simply "naughty," whether the child is held competent or not to understand the consequences of his or her actions, it is nevertheless understood that, following a certain purgatory, a young person's mistakes should not unduly burden his or her future goals: "For those offences that could be called 'crimes' a child should not be expected to have a criminal record for behavior that may be transient or reflect a particular stage of development." This is the justification for the special provisions within juvenile crime statutes aimed at removing the stigma of a juvenile court history. . . .

Individuals are allowed to move on beyond their juvenile criminal records not just because it is good for them, but also because society has an interest in turning juvenile offenders into law-abiding adults. Social forgetfulness serves individual and social interests. . . .

### Credit Reports

Far from being limited to financial information, the reports assembled by credit bureaus may contain information relating to convictions, suits, employment history, past addresses, family status, etc. . . . Thus, with regard to our previous discussions of bankruptcy and crime records, credit bureaus' activities would seem to go directly against the idea of granting the opportunity for a fresh start. Such past blemishes are precisely what the credit bureaus are paid to look for. . . .

In the 1960s . . . Congress felt compelled to regulate this booming industry through the Fair Credit Reporting Act (1971, revised 1997). The act was designed to cover a broad range of issues with regard to the activities of credit bureaus; its stated purpose was to protect individuals from the deleterious effects of credit reports, by establishing precise rules under which personal information can be reported. Most pertinent to our discussion, it defined certain categories of information that are subject to obsolescence: bankruptcies, suits and judgments, paid tax liens, accounts placed for collection or charged to profits or loss, and records relating to a crime. For each category, the act established precise time limits after which information must be deleted from credit reports. The FCRA thus ensured that the social forgetfulness principles established in the case of bankruptcy and juvenile crime records were not overwhelmed by the new data

collection and aggregation practices of credit bureaus. . . .

## Policy Strategies for Data Retention

We have argued, then, that social forgetfulness is an important social value that is quietly slipping away because of the increasing use of increasingly sophisticated personal data together with a neglect of data retention policies. We have also argued that privacy policy debates should not be framed as a matter of balancing the social goods of information against individual rights or interests in privacy. Rather, the issue should be understood as involving tensions between social goods, the social good of privacy (and forgetfulness), and other social goods. When the value of social forgetfulness has been recognized, such as in bankruptcy law, juvenile criminal records, and credit reporting, legislation has been developed to provide a form of forgetfulness. . . .

## Conclusion

In this article we have pointed to the importance of social forgetfulness and explored the relationship between social forgetfulness and information technologies. The nature of public/institutional memory is dramatically changing due to the evolving character of information technologies. While preserving the opportunity for a second chance might have been easily achieved in the past, it has become increasingly difficult today. The ongoing balancing of "discard and forget" and "preserve and evaluate" has been skewed in favor of the latter. Unless data retention issues are addressed explicitly as part of a comprehensive policy approach to personal privacy, we will gradually move to a panoptic society in which there is little social forgetfulness and little, if any, opportunity to move on beyond one's past and start afresh. . . .

Even in the three cases we discussed wherein social forgetfulness has been institutionalized, there are signs of this forgetfulness being eroded. More juveniles are being tried as adults; bankruptcy laws being tightened; and limitations on data retention in credit reporting are being undermined by other, nonregulated, information services. Thus, there is need for a reaffirmation of the social value of forgetfulness, along with more extensive study and focus on the topic of data retention, through empirical and cross-cultural studies.

# 42

# HELEN FAY NISSENBAUM

## PRIVACY IN CONTEXT

Technology, Policy, and the Integrity of Social Life

Helen Nissenbaum argues that a sense of privacy violation occurs when information is used for purposes that exceed the expectations of people in the context of the information's origination. To move privacy conversations beyond technical legal distinctions between "the public" and "the private," she develops a framework of "contextual integrity" to assist with identifying, anticipating, and responding to situations where informational practices might problematically transgress contextually specific social norms.

\*\*\*

Information technology is considered a major threat to privacy because it enables pervasive surveillance, massive databases, and lightning-speed distribution of information across the globe. In fact, privacy has been one of the most enduring social issues associated with digital electronic information technologies. A fixture in public discourse at least since the 1960s, when the dominant concern was massive databases of government and other large institutions housed in large stand-alone computers, concerns have multiplied in type and extent as radical transformations of the technology have yielded the remarkable range of present-day systems, including distributed networking; the World Wide Web; mobile devices; video, audio, and biometric surveillance; global positioning; ubiquitous computing; social networks; sensor networks; databases of compiled information; data mining; and more. Associated with each of these developments is a set of worries about privacy. Whether expressed in the resigned grumbles of individuals, the vocal protests of advocacy groups and eloquent politicians, or the pages of scholarly publications and popular media, the common worry time and again is that an important value is a casualty of progress driven by technologies of information.

Countless books, articles, and commentaries call for reform in law and policy to shore up defenses against the erosion of privacy due to swelling ranks of technology-based systems practices. Many of them argue that protecting privacy means strictly limiting access to personal information or assuring people's right to control information about themselves. I disagree. What people care most about is not simply *restricting* the flow of information but ensuring that it flows *appropriately*, and an account of appropriate flow is given here through the framework of contextual integrity. . . .

The framework of contextual integrity identifies the roots of bewilderment, resistance, and sometimes resignation expressed by experts and non-experts alike. According to the framework, finely calibrated systems of social norms, or rules, govern the flow of personal information in distinct social contexts (e.g., education, health care, and politics). These norms, which I call context-relative informational norms, define and sustain essential activities and key relationships and interests, protect people and groups against harm, and balance the distribution of power. Responsive to historical, cultural, and even geographic contingencies, informational norms evolve over time in distinct patterns from society to society. Information technologies alarm us when they flout these informational norms—when, in the words of the framework, they violate contextual integrity.

As troubled as we might be by technologies that diminish control over information about ourselves, even more deeply troubling are those that disregard entrenched norms because, as such, they threaten disruption to the very fabric of social life. To be sure, not all systems that alter the flow of information are cause for alarm, for there are clear cases of new information devices and systems that serve societal as well as context-based values, ends, and purposes better than those we already have in place (e.g., promoting intellectual development, health and well-being, and vibrant democracy). In such cases, the systems in question generally are and should be accepted, even celebrated. . . .

We have a right to privacy, but it is neither a right to control personal information nor a right to have access to this information restricted. Instead, it is a right to live in a world in which our expectations about the flow of personal information are, for the most part, met; expectations that are shaped not only by force of habit and convention but a general confidence in the mutual support these flows accord to key organizing principles of social life, including moral and political ones. This is the right I have called contextual integrity, achieved through the harmonious balance of social rules, or norms, with both local and general values, ends, and purposes.

This is never a static harmony, however, because over time, conditions change and contexts and norms evolve along with them. But momentous changes—war, revolution, famine—may cause asynchronicities between present practices newly jarred by such discontinuities and expectations that have been evolving incrementally and not kept apace. We are living through one such discontinuity, neither as cataclysmic nor as stark as war and famine, but disruptive nevertheless. The rapid adoption and infiltration of digital information technologies and technology-based systems and practices into virtually all aspects of life, to my mind, have resulted in a schism, many schisms, between experience and expectation.

Where a schism has resulted from radical change in the flows of personal information, it is experienced and protested as a violation of privacy.

Accepting privacy as a moral and political right, the framework of contextual integrity is a model of the structure of people's expectations in relation to the flows of information in society. It builds on the substantive thesis that more-or-less coherent, distinctive systems of norms, which shape the contours of our expectations, evolve within the distinctive contexts that make up the social. These distinctive systems of what I have called context-relative informational norms, governing flows of personal information, are finely tuned to the internal purposes of contexts and also to some degree responsive to fundamental human rights and values. In general, informational norms prescribe the principles under which personal information of certain kinds flow from one point, a sender acting in a certain capacity, to another, a recipient acting in a certain capacity. . . .

The framework of contextual integrity rejects the private/public dichotomy as a sound basis for a right to privacy and along with it the attempt to define a category of sensitive information deserving special consideration. It is time for us to lay these two ideas to rest.

Beyond the rationale, my hope has been to articulate the structure of contexts and informational norms, two of the key constructs, and to demonstrate how the framework can be used to account for many systems and practices experienced as persistently threatening to privacy. What I have identified as the descriptive use or function of the framework can account for and predict when people experience systems or practices as privacy violations. But the framework also has a normative or prescriptive dimension. Although there is a presumption in favor of entrenched norms, the framework allows that novel flows of information might trump entrenched flows when these novel flows are more effective in promoting general and context-relative values, ends, and purposes. . . .

It should be clear that the doctrine of "reasonable expectation of privacy," which has usefully served to adjudicate privacy disputes in countless court cases and policy-making settings, is conceptually closely allied to contextual integrity. As with other "reasonable person" doctrines, it has a built-in but not immediately obvious normative requirement because it calls on judges and other decision makers to determine, factually, not only that there is an expectation but that it is a reasonable one. Because we do not imagine that judges and decision makers will quickly conduct large-scale surveys or observations to determine what is reasonable in each particular case or decision before them, we assume they apply wisdom and discretion to define what is reasonable.

A judge may establish that an expectation in relation to a certain activity or practice is reasonable by pointing out that the activity in question is commonplace. Thus, a plaintiff should not be surprised that a defendant acted in a certain way because such actions are common and the plaintiff had no right to expect otherwise. In the case . . . regarding the use of thermal imaging (Kyllo v. United States 2001), since the practice had not entered the common experience (in comparison to overhead flights, which have), the plaintiff's expectation was judged reasonable. In terms of contextual integrity, the use of thermal imaging to detect heat patterns within a private residence violates informational norms in at least two ways: by altering the type of information that flows to law enforcement officers and via the transmission principle that governs the flow of information to law enforcement officers. The suggestive correspondence illustrated in the case of thermal imaging is that actions and practices seen to violate a reasonable expectation of privacy correspond to those judged to be violations of context-relative informational norms. . . .

To determine that an action under consideration violated a person's reasonable expectation of privacy, a judge must be satisfied that the action is similar enough to, or of the same type as, or analogous to, other actions that society deems a violation of privacy. Invoking terminology from the framework of contextual integrity, the judge determines that an action in question violates standing informational norms, or that the action in question is of the same type as actions deemed to violate standing informational norms. In formulating the reasonable expectation requirement in his concurring opinion in Katz v. United States, Justice Harlan argued that a phone call, even though conducted in a telephone booth, was similar enough to phone calls conducted in private residences to be governed—in terms of contextual integrity—by the same informational norms. In my view it is not philosophically obvious even in cases like this, which most people accept as clear and obvious, when such generalizing inferences are (and are not) sound. Although the framework of contextual integrity does not provide an easy formula to transform philosophically demanding questions into straightforwardly simple ones, it does offer a potentially significant resource for answering them and, at the same time, for avoiding missteps.

Of particular relevance to the central aims of this book are cases in which technical systems are employed in a manner people find disturbing, such as closed-circuit television (CCTV) introduced into public spaces, the use of thermal imaging to detect heat patterns emanating from residences, mining of large aggregated databases, and radio frequency identification (RFID) tags installed in consumer items. When the U.S. Supreme Court deemed the use of thermal imaging an unreasonable search, one might wonder at what point a court will find that uses of thermal imaging have become common enough to make *Kyllo's* expectation unreasonable, comparing this to the case in which the marijuana grower was not protected from a search of his courtyard conducted by a surveillance airplane (Florida v. Riley, 1989). For thermal imaging, one can imagine a standard progression of development where the technology is improved, production costs decrease, and (possibly) it enters the consumer market embedded in numerous handy devices. In this scenario, a judge might find a similar case does not have the same understanding of reasonable expectation as *Kyllo*.

The framework of contextual integrity, however, would caution *against* drawing this conclusion. What matters is not merely that a particular technical device or system is not overly unusual, but that its use in a particular *context*, in a particular *way* is not overly unusual. One cannot generalize from the observation that certain installations in certain contexts are commonplace, accepted, and supported to the conclusion that all installations irrespective of contexts will not violate expectations of privacy. A judge deciding whether a particular use of thermal imaging, CCTV, or facial recognition software violates expectations of privacy should not merely assess how common the technologies and how familiar people are with them, but how common and how familiar they are in context, and if this is known, whether the particular application in question violates or conforms to relevant context-relative informational norms. . . .

Incorporating key steps from the contextual integrity (CI) decision heuristic promises an approach to assessing reasonable expectations of privacy that may be less arbitrary. Judges (and other decision makers) will still need to draw on discretion and wisdom, but contextual integrity suggests where they should be looking for relevant norms, which similar cases constitute reasonable analogies and which do not. Clearly, it would be of great benefit for purposes of practical application to see these ideas developed in greater detail, particularly by reinterpreting more of the well-known cases in which establishing a reasonable privacy expectation was decisive in the outcome of a case.

# 43

# JULIE E. COHEN

## CONFIGURING THE NETWORKED SELF

Law, Code, and the Play of Everyday Practice

As Julie Cohen notes in *Configuring the Networked Self,* dominant approaches to privacy typically presume a model of liberal individualism, where the person whose privacy is threatened is understood to be a rational, autonomous, and fully formed legal subject. A more postmodern view of the self would see subjectivity as socially constructed, constantly negotiated, and always embedded in material relations. While Cohen's book is far-ranging, exploring paradoxes in the control of cultural information and personal information in the networked information society, her treatment of privacy and surveillance locates the conditions for human flourishing in the valuable—but increasingly fragile and threatened—spaces of boundary management between the socially constructed self and the identity patterns imposed by information systems.

\*\*\*

Reimagining privacy for the networked information age requires that we take account of both the processes of evolving subjectivity and the ways in which the emergence of networked space enables practices of surveillance and self-exposure to intensify. Subjectivity evolves as individuals and communities engage in practices of self-definition that are both culturally embedded and open ended. Surveillance presses against those practices and against the play of subjectivity, in ways both metaphorical and literal. The interest in privacy, which operates at the interface between evolving subjectivity and surveillance, should be understood as an interest in preserving room for socially situated processes of boundary management to operate.

The mainstream public debate about privacy typically portrays privacy as a good infinitely amenable to being traded off against other goods. That debate reflects the powerful influence of [Alan] Westin's taxonomy of individual preferences about privacy. According to the taxonomy, the production of which was funded in part by businesses that engage in direct marketing, the U.S. population consists of three groups of people: the "privacy unconcerned," "privacy pragmatists," and "privacy fundamentalists." On Westin's account, the privacy unconcerned do not care what happens to information about them, while privacy fundamentalists will not be satisfied with anything but the most stringent, and therefore unrealistic, level of privacy protection. That leaves privacy pragmatists—those willing to make reasonable compromises when the gains outweigh the costs—as the group to whom privacy policy should be targeted. The taxonomy sounds innocuous, but it does important normative work. To be a Westin-style pragmatist is to consent to the continual erosion of privacy in the name of convenience. To want more privacy than the "pragmatists" want is to be a "fundamentalist," a term tarred with myriad negative connotations.

The exploration undertaken in this chapter allows us to formulate a revised conception of what privacy is about and what purposes it serves. As in the case of copyright, the law of privacy must balance a type of fixity against a type of mobility, and the nature of that balance is widely misunderstood. Privacy law does not exist to protect fixed, exogenously constituted selves from the effects of technological and social dynamism; it exists to shelter dynamic, emergent subjectivity from informational and spatial constraint. Both sides of the balance are valuable. Subjectivity requires some stability and predictability; similarly, the development of relationships and communities requires the ability to know and remember certain facts about one another and to coexist in defined spaces. But a society that wishes to remain democratic, vibrant, and innovative cannot hope to do so based solely on practices and architectures directed toward transparency and exposure.

Choices about privacy are choices about the scope for self-articulation. They are,

therefore, choices about room to pursue the (unattainable, yet vitally important) liberal ideals of autonomy and critical independence. By this, I do not intend either to romanticize privacy or to readmit the liberal conception of privacy for fixed, autonomous selves through the back door. I mean only to make a narrower claim about the importance of some of liberalism's cultural and political aspirations. In a society committed at least to the desirability of the liberal ideal of self-determination, pervasive transparency and exposure are troubling because they constrain the range of motion for the development of subjectivity through both criticism and performance, and these conditions do not automatically cease to be troubling when the subjects of surveillance have indicated their willing surrender. Such a society values neither the docile bodies of Foucauldian theory, the assimilated denizens of Deleuzian systems of social control, nor the fragmentary, infinitely protean selves posited by performance theorists.

It follows that choices about privacy are constitutive not simply of civil society, as some privacy theorists would have it, but of a particular type of civil society that prizes particular types of activities and particular types of subjects. In this respect, privacy functions as a sort of social Rorschach test, and not simply because norms about acceptable levels of privacy vary from culture to culture. Privacy exemplifies a culture's normative, collective commitments regarding the scope of movement, both literal and metaphorical, accorded to its members.

The privacy that emerges as most important for fulfilling these commitments is best described as an interest in breathing room to engage in socially situated processes of boundary management. Privacy is not only about refusing access, visibility, or interference with particular decisions. It is also and more generally about preventing the seamless imposition of patterns predetermined by others. The privacy embedded in social practices of boundary management by situated subjects preserves room for the development of a critical, playful subjectivity that is always-already intersubjective—informed by the values of families, confidants, communities, and cultures. In a world with effective boundary management, however, there is play in the joints, and that is better than the alternative. And on this understanding, privacy implicates not only individual interests, but also collective interests in human flourishing and in the ongoing development of a vibrant culture. Privacy's goal, simply put, is to ensure that the development of subjectivity and the development of communal values do not proceed in lockstep.

This understanding of the relationship between subjectivity and boundary management dovetails well with Foucault's later statements positioning subjectivity as a sort of critical-ethics-in-operation. To the extent that the subject exists outside the framework of social shaping, it exists precisely in the possibility of change through the problematization of existing subjectivities and collectivities. That possibility always exists in the interstices of the informational and material architectures of social discipline, but it exists more fully to the extent that the interstices are larger and the linkages less complete.

Some intriguing new strands in the scholarly literature on privacy lend additional support to a definition of privacy as room for boundary management in the service of always-emergent subjectivity. Jonathan Kahn's provocative reading of the Georgia Supreme Court's decision in Pavesich v. New England Life (1905) against Plessy v. Ferguson, decided by the U.S. Supreme Court nine years earlier, shows that for the turn-of-the-century legal thinkers who developed the quintessentially American understanding of privacy as a right to be let alone, privacy and slavery were conceptual opposites. To similar effect, scholars in surveillance studies have documented the use of surveillance systems to control underprivileged populations. A conception of privacy as the opposite of subordination also underlies David Matheson's argument that privacy invasion is a "wrongful relational interference" with one's person, liberty, or property, a species of informational assault on the self.

Implicit in all these scholarly treatments of privacy, moreover, is a recognition that processes of boundary management operate along dimensions that are spatial and material as well as informational. Slavery operates by control of bodies and spaces. Modern social welfare systems operate via similar principles, albeit for rather different purposes. The systems are alike in their casual abrogation of the physical, spatial, and emotional boundary principles that ought to prevail in the state's interaction with its citizens. In Matheson's treatment, the idea of a wrongful relational interference suggests the absence of breathing space, in both the informational and the spatial sense, that deprivations of privacy can produce.

It is worth noting that the understanding of privacy as a set of boundary-management practices is intimately related to the cluster of values that I have argued should inform our understanding of copyright law. The play of culture and the play of subjectivity are inextricably intertwined; each feeds into the other. Creativity and cultural play foster the ongoing development of subjectivity. Educators in particular have long recognized that engagement with the arts promotes both cognitive development and transformative learning. Evolving subjectivity, meanwhile, fuels the ongoing production of artistic and intellectual culture, and the interactions among multiple, competing self-conceptions create cultural dynamism. But the enabling relation between privacy and creativity is even more fundamental. Privacy is an indispensable enabler of processes of creative engagement. Creative workers self-report that the ability to create boundaries and separations is an essential one at all stages of the process. Freedom of intellectual exploration similarly presupposes and requires the ability to exact a degree of intellectual privacy from one's surroundings. . . . [B]oundaries matter in creative practice as they do elsewhere, and perhaps more so. Creativity thrives on a mixture of connection and disconnection; for both creative individuals and creative collaborations, bringing creative practice to fruition requires breathing space.

To restate privacy's role in terms of ongoing processes of boundary management is to confront, once again, the insuperable difficulties of expressing privacy interests in the abstract language of rights theories. But this should not trouble scholars nearly as much as it has done. Rights theories help us articulate important aspirations that privacy serves, including the Millian liberty to develop one's convictions without fear of social tyranny. Those aspirations do not become irrelevant simply because the background assumptions of liberal political theory fail to hold. At the same time, rights theories fail privacy advocates and privacy policy in at least two ways. First, the abstract language of rights without contexts establishes an implicit baseline that is manifestly inaccurate. As we have seen, there are good reasons that privacy is so resistant to the abstractions that dominate most rights theories; it cannot be separated from the contexts and places that give it meaning. Second, "privacy" is itself an abstraction, and a potentially dangerous one. The protections necessary to safeguard processes of boundary management within the systematic, rhizomatic architectures of the surveillance society need to be conceptualized systemically and concretely if they are to be effective.

Economics and behavioral approaches to privacy, meanwhile, risk mistaking satisficing behavior for normative judgments about the socially appropriate extent of transparency and exposure. Those approaches are therefore extraordinarily useful for predicting the directions that surveillant assemblages will take, but at the same time extraordinarily useless in countering them. Measuring the costs and benefits of privacy within a framework that takes satisficing behavior as the baseline tends to elide the systemic externalities that the loss of privacy imposes. Economic insights are valuable, but only to the extent that they might inform a hybrid methodological stance. The challenge for a law and politics of privacy is to ensure that collective practices of surveillance and information processing cohere with other collective aspirations for self-development.

Finally, the conflation of human flourishing with open access to information in all its forms is far too simple and needs to be carefully reconsidered. In some contexts, human flourishing demands reduced openness; in particular, human flourishing requires a reversal of the dynamic of one-way transparency, a rethinking of the principle of exposure, and a critical, revisionist stance toward the normative underpinnings of the culture of exposure. Human flourishing requires both boundedness and some ability to manage boundedness. Respect for privacy does not require absolute secrecy for personal matters. Rather, it entails something easier to imagine but more difficult to achieve: more openness about some things and less openness about others.

# 44

# JOHN GILLIOM

## OVERSEERS OF THE POOR

Surveillance, Resistance, and the Limits of Privacy

John Gilliom's *Overseers of the Poor* was a landmark contribution to the field of surveillance studies. In the book, he drew attention to the inadequacy of privacy discourses to explain the experiences of poor mothers contending with the invasive surveillance of welfare systems. Such women were more concerned with the practicalities of survival—along with the indignities and hassle of external scrutiny—than they were with legal abstractions like privacy. The welfare mothers in Gilliom's study prioritized the ethical responsibility of meeting the needs of their families over the oftentimes opaque stipulations of welfare agencies. Gilliom views these women as engaging in political acts of everyday resistance against dehumanizing bureaucratic surveillance.

\*\*\*

By now, virtually any public or private agency handling large numbers of people is likely to have an advanced surveillance capacity as a central part of its daily operations. On the basis of these systems of information, decisions are made regarding the lives and life prospects of everyone from suspected criminals to prospective home buyers, and from students to welfare families. People have always been observed and evaluated by kin, by neighbors, by employers, and by strangers, but now both watching and being watched have become more complex, more systematic, and in some areas, far more critical in the everyday lives of families and individuals. . . . Because of this, a new politics has been created, or, rather, an old politics has changed and become more important and pervasive—the politics of surveillance.

The politics of surveillance necessarily include the dynamics of power and domination. The very idea of "surveillance"—roughly translated as *watching from above*—implies that the observer is in a position of dominance over the observed. Related terms like *supervisor*, or the one chosen for the title of this work, *overseer*, remind us that surveillance is not a mere glance exchanged between equals—it is both an expression and instrument of power. Surveillance of human behavior is in place to control human behavior, whether by limiting access to programs or institutions, monitoring and affecting behavior within those arenas, or otherwise enforcing rules and norms by observing and recording acts of compliance and deviance. It is hard to imagine a surveillance and control program being applied in a context that lacked regular efforts or tendencies to violate rules or norms; therefore struggles over power, information, exposure, and secrecy are virtually guaranteed to be part of the politics of surveillance. . . .

[W]hile we have heard much about long-standing debates over the legal concepts of "privacy" and "due process" and about policymaking concerns like effectiveness, impact, and risk, we have heard relatively little about the everyday American conversations and struggles over the actual implementation of surveillance policies. . . . I wanted to find a way to bring the voices and experiences of the surveilled into our struggles to understand what surveillance is and into the public discussions about the ongoing revolution in surveillance technology and policy. I wanted to learn how they perceived the system of surveillance, how they spoke of it, and how they coped with it in their daily lives. Therefore, in the mid-1990s, I began a research project centering on how a group of welfare mothers in Appalachian Ohio experienced the impact of a major new computerized surveillance and information system in welfare administration. The surveillance system they live with . . . gives welfare and law enforcement authorities the power to make regular data sweeps which can detect virtually any recorded income or investment-returns that an individual may receive. It also automates the case monitoring and review process that is a regular part of receiving welfare and shifts the previously unwieldy county-by-county record-keeping system into one unified matrix. With this sophisticated new "Client Information System," administrators were able to organize, enhance, and expand the various dimensions of scrutiny that have long been part of

American welfare. The system was . . . the new "overseer of the poor." In a computerized aspirant to the "panopticon"—Jeremy Bentham's name for an ideal prison in which everyone is watched, all the time— the state's power tries to be a constant presence in the lives of the poor. . . .

The stories that we heard [from welfare mothers] were diverse and multifaceted, but amid that diversity an important theme began to emerge. Although they live in a culture that is said to be overrun with rights claims and among the most litigious and law-oriented on earth, and although they were talking about a policy area that has been almost totally defined by debates over legal rights to privacy and due process, the women who are at the center of this book said very little about the idea of rights, or of privacy, or of other potentially protective or emancipatory legal claims. What emerged from these conversations was, in fact, a widely shared and principled critique of surveillance, but one that had very little to do with the ongoing mainstream legal and policy debates about rights to privacy and due process. Instead, the mothers complained about the hassle and degradation caused by surveillance and the ways that it hindered their ability to meet the needs of their families. They advanced few claims tied to the right of privacy; instead, they told particular stories about daily need and about the power of surveillance to both make their needs greater and limit their capacity to meet them. They made references not to the great claim of due process, but to their own struggles to cope and to the power of surveillance to thwart them. In their need and anger, they mounted no litigation or protest campaigns, but engaged in necessarily quiet practices of everyday resistance and evasion to beat, as best they could, the powers of surveillance.

In many ways, then, these women eschew the prevailing languages and tactics of the privacy-rights paradigm to position their critique of surveillance within a framework emphasizing their needs, their practical problems, and their duty to care for their children. In so doing, they build a critique of surveillance that is based in the realities and demands of everyday life. They also appear to give voice to what has been called the "ethic of care," a political language that centers on needs, relationships, and interdependency and may, therefore, be distinct from the more conventional liberal thinking and its emphasis on abstract principles and individualistic rights claims. In resonance with the types of claims-making found among other oppressed groups and with a long-standing though often subjugated "maternalist" ideology in American welfare, our conversations returned again and again to what was clearly, for these women, the "business at hand"—getting their families through another day.

In their struggles to get through the day, the women we talked with also engage in a widespread and little-noticed form of antisurveillance "politics"—they do things that politicians and many (but not all) welfare officials might view as fraud, evasion, or cheating, but that the welfare mothers see as some of their only options for struggling with the powers of the state. As they hide little bits of extra money, or sneak an extra boarder or family member into their home, they make no grand challenges to an invasive bureaucracy, but they do enhance their material lives and create small and necessary spaces of personal control and autonomy. And since the system of welfare surveillance is specifically designed to prevent these forbidden material improvements and to eliminate personal control and autonomy, we can only see the work of these welfare mothers as an apparently significant and widespread form of antisurveillance politics. . . .

Bureaucratic surveillance manifests a way of seeing and knowing the world that excludes much of our true complexity while moving a small cluster of characteristics to the forefront. Simplified criteria that are important to the state—such as documentation regarding income, family makeup, or evidence of unreported resources—push aside the other facets, dimensions, and complexities of the lives of the poor. . . . A surveillance system is not just a way of watching the world, it is a way of seeing and knowing the world that shapes both our understandings of reality and our capacities for action. Such systems impose an order upon the world with official declarations about what matters and what does not and, as they do this, they shape important decisions about the distribution of rewards and benefits, as well as punishment and costs. In this light, critiques of surveillance that focus just on the "invasion of privacy" may be both misguided and too limited—as bureaucratic surveillance becomes the defining administrative mode of our times, it will be far more important to account for and battle the ways in which one particular and rather bizarre view of the world becomes *the* view of the world that guides policy and politics. . . .

Today's welfare surveillance is a system of defining, implementing, and enforcing the law through which individual cases are evaluated and responded to in terms of predefined categories, in which centrally defined norms are asserted upon a complex, large, and dispersed group of people, and in which violators of the codes are actively sought out in regular computer number matches, telephone hotline programs, and other control measures. It is here that we find the most tangible source of conflict between the poor and their overseers. Because the design of a system like AFDC [Aid to Families with Dependent Children] requires families to fit closely defined categories of income, status, and need, and then remain true to those categories to continue receiving aid, welfare clients are uniformly pressured to present a version of their lives that maximizes their potential for support. And because the level of cash support under AFDC is well below a livable income, clients are also uniformly pressured to seek additional income which, necessarily, must be kept secret. Further, even if income would be allowed (which it often is), the complexity, obfuscation, and informal security surrounding the actual terms of welfare rules mean that clients can rarely be sure whether they really need to hide what they hide, so they do so as a necessary precaution.

In sum, the welfare program studied in this project could almost have been designed to ensure ongoing struggle between poor families and the welfare bureaucracy—the direct interests of the former push them to manage information about their case as effectively as they can, and the legal and political mandates of the latter push them to detect each little departure from the truth or the norm. Any withholding of information or misrepresentation of facts regarding the makeup, resources, or income of the family is a violation of code, and the information systems for modern welfare are specifically designed to catch the poor in these misrepresentations and petty crimes. . . .

The bulk of our conversations about welfare surveillance centers on the degradation and hassle of constant scrutiny and the ways in which the scrutiny that these women live with makes it more difficult for them to care for themselves and their children. Their critique of surveillance puts forth an important alternative to the traditional emphasis on the individualistic privacy rights of the abstract citizen, as it puts issues of family, care, and need to the forefront of concern. From their conditions and vantage points as mothers and needy people comes a new voice in the ongoing debate over surveillance policy—one which often sidesteps the legalist terrain of privacy, due process, and rights, and plants itself squarely in the world of everyday needs and concerns. . . .

In nearly all these stories, the women have violated the rules, particularly by doing things to bring in a little extra money. Typically, these are their secrets—the things that they need to hide from sight in their struggles with the rules and restrictions of the welfare system.

With mixtures of defiance, fear, pride, guilt, and anger, they told us about their everyday struggles to scrape up a little extra cash, or use food stamps for diapers, or hide resources which might threaten their eligibility. . . . The pervasive and often spirited nature of these everyday tactics marks a humble and widely successful pattern of opposition to the surveillance mechanisms which seek to detect them, define them as fraud, and sanction the offenders. In this way they testify both to the remarkable power and impact of an advanced surveillance regime—because there are so many fears, so many limits, so few hiding places—and to the incredible combination of need and resilience among the target population—because they continue to struggle both because of and in spite of the regime that dominates their lives.

# 45

# COLIN J. BENNETT

## IN DEFENSE OF PRIVACY

### The Concept and the Regime

Despite the centrality of privacy discourses in most public conversations about surveillance, many scholars have found the concept of privacy to be conceptually insufficient and politically limiting. In this excerpt, Colin Bennett responds to such critiques, most of which he views as being out of touch with the theoretical innovations of privacy scholars and the contemporary practices of legal authorities and regulators.

\*\*\*

The study of surveillance has now matured to the point where it embraces a wide diversity of disciplinary traditions. . . . However, there is one issue over which this broad and diverse community of surveillance scholars tends to agree: the concept of *privacy*, and the policies it generates, are inadequate. Indeed, this view has almost reached the level of a conventional wisdom. 'Privacy' and all that it entails is argued to be too narrow, too based on liberal assumptions about subjectivity, too implicated in rights-based theory and discourse, insufficiently sensitive to the social sorting and discriminatory aspects of surveillance, culturally relative, overly embroiled in spatial metaphors about 'invasion' and 'intrusion', and ultimately practically ineffective. . . .

On closer examination, however, I want to suggest that the critiques of privacy are quite diverse, and often based on some faulty assumptions about the contemporary framing of the privacy issue and about the implementation of privacy protection policy. . . . There is a good deal of overstatement and a certain extent to which 'straw men' are constructed for later demolition. . . . The purpose of this paper, therefore, is to disentangle the various critiques and to subject each to a critical analysis. . . .

### Privacy Is about Me, Me, Me . . .

At root, many surveillance scholars are troubled by the theoretical roots of modern privacy claims. Philosophically, privacy has its roots in liberal individualism, and notions of separation between the state and civil society. Privacy, in this conception, is about the protection of the self, from the state, from organizations and from other individuals. Privacy, therefore, tends to reinforce individuation, rather than community, sociability, trust and so on. . . .

Unfortunately the individualization of the issue is reinforced by some of the more prominent and influential definitions of privacy, which tend to proceed from a sort of state of nature assumption that there is a condition of perfect privacy which is violated when one enters into social relations. The frequency, for example, with which the Warren and Brandeis formulation of privacy as the 'right to be let alone' is cited has an unfortunate implication of reinforcing the notion that privacy is about seclusion and separation.

The concept of privacy has therefore been open to attack on the same grounds on which liberalism more generally is critiqued. It reifies a problematic distinction between the realms of the public and the private. . . . It negates communitarian values such as trust and the common good. It reinforces the patriarchal separation between a masculine public realm and a private female realm. And it completely misses the point of some post-modern theorists who insist that the notion of the 'self' or the 'subject' mask far deeper ontological contradictions and complexities. . . .

The individualistic conceptions of privacy, however, hardly constitute a paradigmatic understanding of the problem, and there have been a number of attempts to realign the issue in ways that perhaps hold more contemporary relevance. Most prominently, Priscilla Regan has argued that privacy should be seen as a common value, . . . a public value, . . . [and] a collective value. . . . Her analysis suggests that privacy, framed in individualistic terms, is always on the defensive against arguments for the social benefits of surveillance. . . . We must, therefore, frame the question in social terms, because society is

better off if individuals have greater levels of privacy. . . .

As the issue has matured, both nationally and internationally, we have seen an increasing recognition that the work of this policy community is directed by the larger questions about the kind of society we are building. . . . The regulators and the discourse have moved on. Whether or not an individualistic conception of 'privacy' as conceived in the 'privacy literature' effectively describes the challenges of contemporary surveillance is largely beside the point. For a long time, privacy protection has been a matter of *public policy*.

## Privacy and the 'Invasion' of Space

A related theme within the surveillance literature is a critique of the 'spatial' implications inherent in much privacy discourse. Felix Stalder critiques the concept because it is typically framed as a 'kind of a bubble that surrounds each person, and the dimensions of this bubble are determined by one's ability to control who enters and who doesn't. Privacy is a personal space; space under the exclusive control of the individual. Privacy, in a way, is the informational equivalent to the (bourgeois if you will) notion of "my home is my castle."' . . .

Again, however, it can be argued that the governance of the issue has moved beyond the popular rhetoric. The privacy literature contains several attempts to add other dimensions, or forms, of privacy to provide intellectual foundations for the more complicated relationships between the individual and modern organizations. . . .

And at the governance level, only a fraction of privacy problems that reach the desks of the regulators really relate to the protection of a private realm from 'invasion'. . . . They assume a relationship between the organization and the individual, and the regulatory problems then relate to how that relationship is managed in informational terms: how the personal information is kept secure; how access controls within the organization are managed; how disclosures are controlled; how notification and consent are communicated, and so on. Hence, the framing of the problem in terms of the conditions under which others might 'enter' one's personal space is unhelpful.

## Privacy Suffers as a Human 'Right'

A third and related set of objections rests on the notion that privacy is normally articulated as a 'right' and is therefore plagued with some of the same problems associated with the rights discourse more generally. Fundamentally, perceptions of privacy violation can be very subjective, and inseparable from wider attitudes about the institution, the program or the service.... Privacy battles also tend to pit vulnerable individuals, or poorly resourced civil liberties groups, against very powerful public or private organizations....

The argument that the rights discourse tends, therefore, to push debate toward experts and authorities and fails to serve the people most at risk, is an important and generally valid one. Individuals do find it difficult to relate their experiences of surveillance to the possibilities of legal claim. We might ask, however, about just how much of this critique is prompted by observations of privacy violations in the United States, a country that uniquely relies on the self-assertion of claims of privacy violations, and litigation through the courts? In almost every other advanced industrial state, these claims can be mediated through a privacy or data protection agency which receives and investigates complaints from individuals from all walks of life, and which attempts to act on behalf of the data subject in opposition to the large data controllers....

## The Problem is Discrimination, not Privacy

A related tack is taken by those who contend that the concept and policies of privacy never challenge the larger questions of categorical discrimination. Individuals are arguably placed at risk because of their membership in, or assignment to, certain groups, rather than on the basis of their individual identities and the personal information it generates. According to Oscar Gandy, the problem is better articulated as 'the panoptic sort—a difference machine that sorts individuals into categories and classes on the basis of routine measurements. It is a discriminatory technology that allocates options and opportunities on the basis of those measures and the administrative models they inform'....

In my reading, there are two implications of the surveillance and social sorting argument that need to be analyzed. The first is that the panoptic sort necessarily operates in secret. It relies on a level of mystification and complexity. One of the main purposes of privacy protection policy, however, is to render such processes transparent.... [M]ajor corporations can, and do, get in trouble when they are perceived to be collecting and processing personal information surreptitiously in order to build their vast marketing databases and thus enhance advertising revenue. When companies are watched, the 'panoptic sort' can be revealed.

A second implication of social sorting relates to the argument that privacy addresses the problems of discrete individuals, rather than categories of people.... At a governance level, however, there is plenty of evidence that laws and other policy instruments are being designed with sensitivity to the particular invasions and problems experienced by categories of people and the data they generate. . . . Many regulators have attempted to target their advice and assistance to particularly vulnerable subpopulations within their jurisdictions, be it aboriginal groups in Australia and Canada or immigrant groups in Europe. . . .

## Privacy Is Too 'Narrow'

Implicit in each of the above critiques is the argument that privacy is, in fact, too narrow. . . . At this level, however, the critique is more often pitched at the propensity of privacy protection policy to reduce any issue to *informational* terms and to the definition of successful privacy governance in terms of the application of the 'fair information principles (FIPS)' doctrine. Over time, national and international policy has converged around these principles, on the assumption that any surveillance must involve a moment of capture of personally identifiable data. The approach is arguably reductionist and over time a number of different critiques have emerged.

First, the problem of determining the point at which information becomes personal information is increasingly difficult to determine. . . . Secondly, the FIPS can be insensitive to the means of extraction and capture. . . . Thirdly, power relations are present between the watcher and watched even when personal information is not captured. . . .

It is in these examples that we find, I think, the crucial point at which privacy analysis ends and surveillance analysis begins. If some other structure simply does not collect personal information on the individual, it is difficult to contend that a 'privacy problem' *per se* arises. . . .

## Conclusion: Privacy Is 'Cool' Too

Privacy is not the 'antidote to surveillance' nor was it ever meant to be. But privacy has come a long way—conceptually and politically. . . . Arguably, I have summarized and categorized a complex critique which does not do justice to the richness of these arguments. My overall impression, however, is that they address a conception of privacy which is dated, and a framing of the issue which is only partially related to what privacy protection means in practice, and what privacy regulators do in their day-to-day work. Thus, each critique is an important contribution, but none really challenges the concept and regime of privacy *in toto*. And none persuasively argues for a more effective way to redress the power imbalances between the hapless subject and the large organizations employing the latest information technologies. . . .

For younger scholars in particular, perhaps privacy simply is not 'cool'; surveillance is. Poring over laws, reports, guidelines, standards or privacy policies is not 'cool' either; interpreting the latest technologies and practices through the lens of post-modern social theory is. Responding to consultative exercises, or preparing for hearings, or registering complaints is not 'cool'; resistance is. Engaging with the crucially important contemporary debates about how, practically, to make consent meaningful on the internet is not 'cool'; deconstructing the ontological assumptions behind the very notion of consent, is. Coming to grips with cookies, deep-packet inspection, cryptography, spyware, protocols, and other opaque instruments of network management is not cool either; constructing metaphors about 'cyber-surveillance' is.

In conclusion, it is obvious that for all the academic critique, 'privacy', as a concept, as a regime, as a set of policy instruments, and as a way to frame advocacy and activism, is not going to disappear. . . . Like it or not, privacy frames the ways that most ordinary people see the contemporary surveillance issues. Surveillance scholars have got to live with it.

# SECTION 9

# UBIQUITOUS SURVEILLANCE

////////////////////////////////////////////////////////////////////////////////////////////////////////////////////////

As we saw in Section 1, computers and computer databases—and their combination with telecommunications technologies—contributed to one of the most fundamental transformations in contemporary surveillance. Surveillance enabled by the analysis of abstract and often discrete data signaled a phase shift in the bureaucratic monitoring of individuals and groups, increasing the intensity of systematic observation but also adding layers of buffering that obscured such processes. These were some of the shifts described by James Rule (1973) in one of the field's earliest works, *Private Lives and Public Surveillance.*

In discussing technological changes of this sort, it is essential to consider, using the term introduced by Donald Norman (1988), the *affordances* of particular sociotechnical systems. This is neither to go down the route of technological determinism and argue that technologies create certain kinds of inevitable transformations nor to ally with extreme forms of social constructionism that can see no agency or purpose in technologies beyond their intended functions. Instead, an appreciation for affordances recognizes that, in their social and technological aspects, sociotechnical developments open up some possibilities and limit others. Within their specific cultural contexts, technologies lend themselves to certain uses in ways that can

seem natural (Pfaffenberger 1992; Winner 1986). Such is the case with the relationship between computational and telecommunications systems and surveillance.

This section starts out with Roger Clarke's classic 1988 piece on *dataveillance,* which is a term he coined to describe the process by which data—often generated from previous stages of surveillance—are acted upon to make profiles and judgments about people in the real world. When "non-obvious relationships" emerge from these processes, data analysts tend to refer to this as "knowledge discovery in databases." Data can be subjected to a second stage of processing to examine, combine, sort, match, and predict, with outcomes that ramify both on individual and group levels, which are some of the concerns that Oscar Gandy (1993) and David Lyon (1994) would later explore in further detail.

A few short years after Clarke wrote his piece, Mark Weiser (1991) of Xerox wrote another vital piece that claimed that the future of computing would be "pervasive," that is, both that computing devices would be everywhere in the world and at the same time there would be a gradual disappearance of these devices *into* the world. Weiser's highly influential vision came to be known by many names: pervasive computing, ubiquitous computing (or "ubicomp"), or ambient intelligence (AmI). The latter term, pioneered by the Philips Corporation, includes both ambient computing and ubiquitous communications, and this understanding of the combination of pervasive computing with the Internet has given rise to the idea of the "Internet of everything" or more commonly, the "Internet of things" (IoT).

In an important but largely overlooked article in the mid-1990s, Agustin Araya (1995) argued that ubiquitous computing is necessarily ubiquitous surveillance. Why is this? Briefly, this is because ubiquitous computing requires knowledge of the location and identity of anything that is networked (devices, people, etc.) and for all of these to be addressable. These are systemic impositions. In other words, if the system is to function, these parameters are basic requirements. This insight gradually spread in the social sciences, particularly in geography with articles by scholars such as Nigel Thrift and Shaun French (2002), who talked of the "automatic production" of both space and social relations, and urbanist Dana Cuff (excerpted here), who wrote of the agential "enactment"—or ongoing recreation—of pervasive-computing embedded space, along with its propensity to displace and disperse public life. As communication scholar David Phillips (2005) observed, with ubiquitous computing systems, the automatic and restrictive coding of possibilities for identity expression might also curtail the ability of people to manage the context of intentional performances of self-disclosure, such as with "coming out" by members of the gay or lesbian communities, which could reduce opportunities for the achievement of personal and political power by marginalized groups.

The fields of geography and urban studies have tended to be at the forefront of theoretical innovations in approaches to the convergence of space and surveillance, both in consideration of video surveillance (see

Section 7) and of the emerging "virtual" world. Stephen Graham and Simon Marvin are significant figures in this regard, with works like *Telecommunications and the City* (1996) and *Splintering Urbanism* (2001). In this section, we excerpt a piece by Mike Crang and Stephen Graham, which is a rich and eclectic treatment of the ways in which cities were (and are) being transformed through ambient intelligence and augmented reality (AR)—the layering of virtual information onto the physical world—leading them to suggest that the city itself comes to possess an emergent kind of sentience. Research continues to flourish in this area, with Rob Kitchin and Martin Dodge (2011) producing what remains perhaps the most sustained treatment of these themes in their book, *Code/Space*, whose title indicates both the influence of Lawrence Lessig (1999)—where code acts as a kind of law, akin to what Langdon Winner (1986) called the "politics" of technologies—and the guiding conception that the human environment is always already, to some extent, coproduced with computing software.

With the protean nature of industry and academic branding of so-called technological innovations, the digital city and cyborg city have given way to the intelligent city and the smart city. The labels change, but the proponents of these terms share a vision of combined ubiquitous computing and urban management, characterized by pervasive wireless computing networks and distributed sensor platforms, which monitor flows of anything from people and traffic to sewage and weather. Augmented reality, the Internet of things, and the smart city all assume the connection of individuals through handheld devices (or a more direct connection) to an information-rich environment and, also, the translation of bodies into information, which then becomes part of the operable environment. In these visions, more than in their actual application so far (Shelton

*Hyper-Reality* [Augmented reality city of the near future], 2016, Keiichi Matsuda.

et al. 2015), Deleuze's societies of control (see Section 2) are manifest. Information is seen as diffuse and everywhere, "in the cloud" (Mosco 2014), which tends to draw attention away from both the real physical infrastructure and the social and environmental impacts of these systems.

However, recently we seem to have returned somewhat to Clarke's warning about the perils of dataveillance. The current buzzword of "big data," which is critically unpacked in the excerpt by Mark Andrejevic, draws attention to the combination and processing of enormous quantities of data. These data are generated, of course, in large part by the forms of pervasive surveillance, mobile computing, and telecommunications discussed so far. Big data promises that Clarke's dataveillant world will finally be brought to fruition, emphasizing the possibilities of preempting and anticipating future risks and profits through automated analytics that can detect patterns that human beings cannot.

The hubris of big data brings to mind Laplace's demon, the imaginary being posited by the early modern statistician, which, because it was able to know everything in the present, could see the future. It seems that big data advocates see this as a real possibility not a metaphor (Mayer-Schönberger and Cukier 2013). However, it seems unavoidable that pervasive computing will transform not just the city or particular aspects of life but the entire planet—Benjamin Bratton's conjuring of *The Stack* (2016), the planet as computing system, seems all too plausible. And planetary computing means planetary surveillance. But few have even begun to consider what kind of affordances are offered by a truly ubiquitous surveillance. As the excerpts in this section show, the surveillance being scripted into such systems is frequently dictated by the interests of capital and tends to exacerbate existing societal divisions, tension, and inequalities. Thus, Mark Andrejevic (2014: 1674) refers to "a form of *data divide* not simply between those who generate the data and those who collect, store, and sort it, but also between the capabilities available to those two groups."

However, the affordances of ubiqui-tous surveillance need not necessarily be oppressive. There is no reason why pervasive computing could not be empowering and en-abling (Monahan et al. 2010; Monahan 2010). For example, combinations of augmented reality with universal design could allow for richer, extended sensory environments for those disabled by the current social em-phasis on the visual. And while the big data divide is exacerbated by its analytic processes being proprietary, state secrets, or just being hidden from the public gaze in the black boxes of algorithm-driven sys-tems (Pasquale 2013), big data could also be open data, with the same analytic tools and possibilities available to people as to states and corporations. These are futures worth exploring and implementing, but a neces-sary first step seems to be coming to terms with the inherent politics of all technological systems—politics that are increasingly diffi-cult to detect as the systems themselves fade from view.

## REFERENCES

Andrejevic, Mark. 2014. The Big Data Divide. *International Journal of Communication* 8:1673–89.

Araya, Agustin A. 1995. Questioning Ubiquitous Computing. In *Proceedings of the 1995 ACM 23rd Annual Conference on Computer Science*, 230–37.

Bratton, Benjamin H. 2016. *The Stack: On Software and Sovereignty*. Cambridge, MA: MIT Press.

Gandy, Oscar H. 1993. *The Panoptic Sort: A Political Economy of Personal Information*. Boulder, CO: Westview.

Graham, Stephen, and Simon Marvin. 1996. *Telecommunications and the City: Electronic Spaces, Urban Places*. New York: Routledge.

———. 2001. *Splintering Urbanism: Networked Infrastructures, Technological Mobilities, and the Urban Condition*. New York: Routledge.

Kitchin, Rob, and Martin Dodge. 2011. *Code/Space: Software and Everyday Life*. Cambridge, MA: MIT Press.

Lessig, Lawrence. 1999. *Code: And Other Laws of Cyberspace*. New York: Basic Books.

Lyon, David. 1994. *The Electronic Eye: The Rise of Surveillance Society*. Minneapolis: University of Minnesota Press.

Mayer-Schönberger, Viktor, and Kenneth Cukier. 2013. *Big Data: A Revolution That Will Transform How We Live, Work, and Think*. Boston: Houghton Mifflin Harcourt.

Monahan, Torin. 2010. Surveillance as Governance: Social Inequality and the Pursuit of Democratic Surveillance. In *Surveillance and Democracy*, edited by K. D. Haggerty and M. Samatas, 91–110. New York: Routledge.

Monahan, Torin, David J. Phillips, and David Murakami Wood. 2010. Editorial: Surveillance and Empowerment. *Surveillance & Society* 8 (2):106–12.

Mosco, Vincent. 2014. *To the Cloud: Big Data in a Turbulent World*. New York: Paradigm.

Norman, Donald A. 1988. *The Design of Everyday Things*. New York: Doubleday.

Pasquale, Frank. 2015. *The Black Box Society: The Secret Algorithms That Control Money and Information*. Cambridge, MA: Harvard University Press.

Pfaffenberger, Bryan. 1992. Technological Dramas. *Science, Technology, and Human Values* 17 (3):282–312.

Phillips, David J. 2005. From Privacy to Visibility. Context, Identity, and Power in Ubiquitous Computing Environments. *Social Text* 23 (2):95–108.

Rule, James B. 1973. *Private Lives and Public Surveillance: Social Control in the Computer Age*. London: Allen Lane.

Shelton, Taylor, Matthew Zook, and Alan Wiig. 2015. The 'Actually Existing Smart City'. *Cambridge Journal of Regions, Economy and Society* 8 (1):13–25.

Thrift, Nigel, and Shaun French. 2002. The Automatic Production of Space. *Transactions of the Institute of British Geographers* 27 (4):309–35.

Weiser, Mark 1991. The Computer for the 21st Century. *Scientific American* 265 (3):94–104.

Winner, Langdon. 1986. *The Whale and the Reactor: A Search for Limits in an Age of High Technology*. Chicago: University of Chicago Press.

# 46

# ROGER CLARKE

## INFORMATION TECHNOLOGY AND DATAVEILLANCE

Roger Clarke's 1988 piece on dataveillance, a term he coined, was prescient in its anticipation of the challenges posed by a society founded increasingly on the ubiquitous collection, sharing, and processing of data, particularly by governments—although he did not neglect the private sector. The following excerpt outlines Clarke's typology of dataveillance elements and presents his main critiques of both individual and mass dataveillance.

*** 

*Dataveillance* is the systematic use of personal data systems in the investigation or monitoring of the actions or communications of one or more persons. . . .

### Personal Dataveillance Techniques

Organizations maintain records about individuals they are concerned with (their *data subjects*). . . . Dataveillance depends on data that identify people. . . .

Given that identified records exist, a variety of dataveillance techniques are available. The most primitive technique, *record integration,* brings together all of the data an organization holds about each person. . . .

An approach adopted by most organizations is to monitor new transactions. Each transaction an organization receives (e.g., an application for employment, a loan, or a government benefit) is processed according to standard rules to determine whether the transaction is valid and acceptable. Additional rules may be applied, expressly designed to detect both inaccuracies and attempts to cheat the decision criteria. Exceptional cases are generally submitted to a more senior authority for more careful, nonroutine consideration.

Where the processing rules depend only on data already available to the organization, these practices are generally referred to as screening or authentication. . . .

*Front-end verification* of transactions represents a further development beyond screening. It involves the collection of data from other personal data systems in order to facilitate the processing of a transaction. . . .

Front-end verification is a personal-dataveillance technique when the transaction has been identified as exceptional, and the purpose of collecting the additional data is to establish whether there is any inconsistency between the various sources of data. An inconsistency may disqualify the transaction or be evidence of some wrongdoing such as providing misleading information. . . .

A broader form of personal dataveillance is what might be termed *front-end audit*. This uses the occasion of the detection of an exceptional transaction as an opportunity to further investigate other matters relating to the individual. For example, when a driver is stopped for a traffic offense, it is becoming standard practice for the police officer to initiate on-line inquiries. . . .

Intersystem and interorganizational arrangements can be pursued a step further by means of *cross-system enforcement*. This technique makes an individual's relationship with one organization dependent on his or her performance in relation to another. . . .

## Mass Dataveillance Techniques

[M]ass dataveillance is concerned with groups of people and involves a generalized suspicion that some (as yet unidentified) members of the group may be of interest. Its purposes are to identify individuals who may be worth subjecting to personal surveillance, and to constrain the group's behavior. . . .

Screening or authentication of transactions . . . is arguably a form of mass surveillance to the extent that it is routinely or automatically applied to every transaction, whether or not it appears to be exceptional. Similarly, when data are routinely sought from other internal databases or third parties in order to undertake front-end verification of all transactions, mass dataveillance is being undertaken.

The application of such techniques to existing records, rather than to new transactions, is referred to here as *file analysis*. . . .

Screening, front-end verification, front-end audit, and file analysis may all be undertaken with varying degrees of sophistication. Transaction data may be compared against a formal standard or other norm, for example, highlighting those tax returns that include deductions above a certain value or show more than, say, eight dependents. The norms against which the data are compared may be either legal or other a priori norms that have been set down in advance by some authority, possibly for good reasons, possibly quite arbitrarily. Alternatively, they may be a posteriori norms that were inferred from analysis of the collection of records.

Alternatively, transaction data may be compared against permanent data, for example, highlighting tax returns where the spouse's name does not match that on file. Or transaction data may be compared against other transaction data, for example, highlighting people whose successive tax returns show varying numbers of dependents. . . .

Judgments of any complexity must be based on multiple factors, rather than just one. *Profiling*, as it is commonly known, may be done on the basis of either a priori arbitrary or pragmatic norms, or on a posteriori norms based on empirical evidence. . . .

Sophisticated profiling techniques are claimed to hold great promise because they can detect hidden cases amid large populations. . . .

## Facilitative Mechanisms

Mass-dataveillance techniques may be successfully applied within a single personal-data system, but their power can be enhanced if they are applied to data from several. These systems might all be operated by the organization concerned or by a number of distinct organizations. In such cases a preliminary step may be undertaken:

> *Computer matching* is the expropriation of data maintained by two or more personal-data systems, in order to merge previously separate data about large numbers of individuals. . . .

Matching makes more data available about each person and also enables comparison between apparently similar data items as they are known to different organizations. Rather than relating to a single specified person for a specific reason, matching achieves indiscriminate data cross-referencing about a large number of people for no better reason than a generalized suspicion. . . .

## Benefits

Significant benefits can result from dataveillance. The physical security of people and property may be protected, and financial benefits may accrue from the detection and prevention of various forms of error, abuse, and fraud. Benefits can be foreseen both in government activity (e.g., tax and social welfare) and in the private sector (e.g., finance and insurance). . . .

Few people would contest the morality of an organization applying the more basic techniques, for example, record integration and screening. Some would go so far as to regard organizations that did not apply modern IT in such ways as failing to fulfil their responsibilities to taxpayers and shareholders. Nevertheless, dataveillance is, by its very nature, intrusive and threatening. It therefore seems reasonable that organizations should have to justify its use, rather than merely assuming its appropriateness.

## Dangers of Personal Dataveillance

The vast majority of data systems operators are quite casual about the quality of most of their data. . . . For many organizations it is cost-effective to ensure high levels of accuracy only of particular items (such as invoice amounts), with broad internal controls designed to ensure a reasonable chance of detecting errors in less vital data. Some errors are intentional on the part of the data subject, but many are accidental, and some are a result of design deficiencies such as inadequate coding schemes. Similar problems arise with other elements of data quality such as the timeliness and completeness of data. . . .

When the data are used in their original context, data quality may be sufficient to support effective and fair decision making, but when data are used outside their original context, the probability of misinterpreting them increases greatly. This is the reason why information privacy principles place such importance on relating data to the purpose for which they are collected or used, and why sociologists express concern about the "acontextual" nature of many administrative decision processes.

Much front-end verification is undertaken without the subject's knowledge. . . . Where consent is sought, the wording is often such that the person has no appreciation of the import of the consent that is being given, or the bargaining position is so disproportionately weighted in favor of the organization that the data subject has no real option but to comply. . . .

Front-end audit and cross-system enforcement give rise to additional concerns. Their moral justification is not obvious, and they create the danger of individuals being effectively blacklisted across a variety of organizations. . . . It is particularly problematic where the person is unaware that the (possibly erroneous, incomplete or out-of-date) data have been disseminated. Finally, even where individuals have brought the problems upon themselves, blacklisting tends to deny them the ability to redeem themselves for past misdemeanors.

## Dangers of Mass Dataveillance to the Individual

Mass dataveillance embodies far greater threats. In respect of each individual, mass surveillance is clearly an arbitrary action, because no prior suspicion existed. . . .

With mass dataveillance, the fundamental problems of wrong identification, unclear, inconsistent, and context-dependent meaning of data, and low data quality are more intense than with personal dataveillance. Data arising from computer matching are especially problematic. Where there is no common identifier, the proportion of spurious matches (type (1) errors) and undetected matches (type (2) errors) can be very high. . . . In addition, the meaning of the record as a whole must be properly understood. Although it might seem improper for a person to be both in employment and in receipt of a social-welfare benefit, many pensions and allowances are, in law, either independent of, or only partially dependent on, income from other sources. . . .

In the hands of the inadequately trained, insufficiently professional, or excessively enthusiastic or pressured, profiling has all the hallmarks of a modern witch-hunting tool.

Profiling is not restricted to retrospective investigation. It purports to offer the possibility of detecting undesirable classes of people before they commit an offense. . . .

It is unclear on what moral and, indeed, legal grounds profiling may be used to reach administrative determinations about individuals or discriminate between individuals. Such vague constraints may not be sufficient to stultify an attractive growth industry. With computer displays and printouts lending their (largely spurious) authority to such accusations, how will the tolerance needed in complex social environments be maintained? . . .

Some procedures are now being structured, particularly in such areas as taxation, such that a government agency makes a determination, and individuals who disagree must contest the decision. This inversion of the onus of proof exacerbates the problems of misinterpretation resulting from data merger, and uncertainty arising from correlative profiling. It is further compounded by the imbalance of power between organization and individual. . . .

Some dataveillance is undertaken with dubious legal authority or in the absence of either authority or prohibition. To avoid being subjected to public abuse and perhaps being denied the right to undertake the activity, it is natural for organizations to prefer to undertake some operations covertly. . . .

To protect the mechanism or the source, an individual may not be told that dataveillance has been undertaken, the source of the accusation, the information on which the accusation is based or even what the accusation is. . . . Dataveillance tends to compromise the individual's capacity to defend him or herself or to prosecute his or her innocence. In its most extreme form, one Kafka could not anticipate, the accuser could be a poorly understood computer program or a profile embodied in one.

## Social Dangers of Mass Dataveillance

With personal dataveillance, investigation and monitoring normally take place after reasonable grounds for suspicion have arisen. Mass surveillance dispenses with that constraint because the investigation is routinely performed and the suspicion arises from it. The organization therefore commences with a presumption of guilt on the part of at least some of the data subjects, although at the beginning of the exercise it is unknown which ones. The result is a prevailing climate of suspicion. . . .

Dataveillance encourages investigators to focus on minor offenses that can be dealt with efficiently, rather than more important crimes that are more difficult to solve. Law enforcers risk gaining a reputation for placing higher priority on pursuing amateur and occasional violators (particularly those whose records are readily accessible, like government employees and welfare recipients), rather than systematic, repetitive, and skilled professional criminals. The less equitably the law is perceived to be enforced, the greater the threat to the rule of law. . . .

In general, mass dataveillance tends to subvert individualism and the meaningfulness of human decisions and actions, and asserts the primacy of the state.

# 47

# DANA CUFF

## IMMANENT DOMAIN

### Pervasive Computing and the Public Realm

Architect Dana Cuff's essay on pervasive computing and ubiquitous surveillance was pioneering in recognizing that these two phenomena were inextricably interlinked and that together they would generate multiple social and spatial consequences. Rather like Brian Eno's remark about the Velvet Underground—that very few people bought their records but everyone who did formed a band—Cuff's essay has not been anywhere near as widely read as it should have been in surveillance studies or beyond, but almost everyone who has read it has gone on to write about ubiquitous surveillance.

\*\*\*

In 1991, the late Mark Weiser wrote a prescient essay for *Scientific American* foretelling the age of ubiquitous computing which he described as "embodied virtuality," in contrast to then cutting edge virtual reality. . . . [W]hile embodied virtuality has emerged from clear historic precedent and origins, it raises four distinct implications that hold the potential to change our ideas about space and spatial practices.

First, our environment is enacted and given life, not in the sense that robots are actuated, but the entirety of the physical environment is re-created as a potential source of coordinated, interdependent actions and reactions. Whether this enacted environment is actual or imagined, as Foucault argued in the case of the panopticon, it reformulates our notions of power and moreover, our relationship to the world around us. Second, visibility both literal and metaphorical is transformed. What was solid and opaque becomes transparent, yet what makes the hidden accessible is itself invisible. Third, further erosion of the concepts of public and private force their reconsideration. In particular, questions of surveillance, control, and exhibitionism render the distinction between public and private anew. Fourth, heightened security and surveillance possibilities hold the potential to restructure civility, or public life as we know it. . . . The consequences for the public sphere are paradoxical given the intrinsic nature of information technology to bite back, to be turned and used in ways opposed to its original intent. . . .

Although there are clear technological precedents for the emergent, pervasive technologies, they can be distinguished from past developments by the fact that this new technology can be both everywhere and nowhere (unlike the automobile that is mobile but locatable); that it acts intelligently yet fallibly, and its failure is complex (versus the thermostat, which is responsive but singular and unintelligent); and that intelligent systems operate spatially, yet they are invisible (unlike robots). For utopians like Weiser, these distinctions suggest that an environment embedded with intelligent computing can be nuanced in compelling and even more natural ways, "as refreshing as taking a walk in the woods." Embedded networks, however, are just as likely to spark dystopic views, as have all preceding technological breakthroughs. Now, as pervasive computing grows, there is a certain urgency to its critical review by all those concerned with the public sphere. . . .

Baudrillard, in an essay on "Consumer Society," says that the ecology of the human species has fundamentally mutated from a life surrounded by other human beings, to a life surrounded by objects:

> The concepts of "environment" and "ambiance" have undoubtedly become fashionable only since we have come to live in less proximity to other human beings, less in their presence and discourse, and more under the silent gaze of deceptive and obedient objects which continuously repeat the same discourse, that of our stupefied (medusée) power, of our potential affluence and of our absence from one another.

This could fundamentally mutate once again, as our objects/environment are no longer silent but active, nor are they obedient but indirectly willful.

New capabilities of pervasive computing systems will expedite the restructuring of everyday life because they permit what we considered the context to become a bona fide agent in the public arena. This is the opposite of early projections about electronic technology. In 1964, Marshall McLuhan wrote "The telephone: speech without walls. The phonograph: music hall without walls. The photograph: museum without walls. The electric light: space without walls. The movie, radio and TV: classroom without walls. Man the food-gatherer reappears incongruously as information-gatherer. In this role, electronic man is no less a nomad than his Paleolithic ancestors." Instead, speech is issued by the walls, the museum's walls present visitors its works of art according to their particular viewing habits, or any of myriad curatorial themes. Street lights monitor as well as regulate traffic by assessing variable fees and suggesting less-crowded routes; public park sensors scan for unusual behavior and known criminals, reporting each to the authorities; smart glass becomes more obscure and reflective during the hottest part of the day; stores can identify your vehicle and send drive-by messages tailored to your past consumer behavior. These new levels of information, security, conservation, and access are balanced by heightened possibilities of intrusion, tracking, classification, and exclusion.

Thus, our urban environment can be qualitatively transformed so that it occupies a new status and role in everyday life. We can be complicit with the sidewalks, rejected or embraced by a park, bombarded in the streets with advertisements. Marshall McLuhan, sometimes called the "oracle of the electronic age," argued that the content or message was not just distorted but defined by the media. Had he lived to see pervasive computing, his thesis might have extended to question the boundary between space and subject, between the advertisement, the object being advertised, and the reception of that ad. Even if we are less technological determinists than McLuhan, his analysis sets the stage for embedded virtuality. . . .

Pervasive computing enhances what we can know, where we can know it, and how immediate it will be. As when Muybridge showed stop-frame action in his time-sequence photographs, infrared sensors, microsensors, and processors can network together to build a dynamic portrayal of what otherwise could not be known. Doctors can track the real-time progress of an ingested medication or see the internal anatomical details of a surgery patient; firefighters can get critical information about the fire as it rages and their rescue efforts; the migration of endangered whales can be closely monitored.

"Visualization technologies" provide access into what was opaque, knowledge where there was previously ignorance, bringing close what had been remote—all these capabilities of pervasive computing transform our ideas about space. Now that police equipped with increasingly common thermal imaging technology (and a search warrant) can drive past a house and "peer through" the walls, our ideas about not only privacy, but the walls themselves must change. Even stranger is the use of the same imaging to see where a person has been—sensors of the past tense. This new technology goes beyond the often-mentioned collapse of distance promulgated by fax, telephone, or overnight delivery. It also represents the possibility of new knowledge that will enhance safety, inform action, and provide perspective. Publicly accessible monitors that display moment-by-moment readings of everything from water quality to activity in the public square to traffic patterns can provide a type of information previously unavailable and potentially community enhancing. Pervasive computing can open up the workings of an otherwise inaccessible mystery, whether that be the performance of a building's structure in an earthquake or the nanny's behavior while mom and dad are at work. There is an irony here: it is invisible, miniaturized sensors that make formerly inaccessible realms visible.

That irony of pervasive computing is related to long-standing critical inquiry into the relationship of seeing and being seen. For example, Roland Barthes characterized the mythical status of the Eiffel Tower explicitly in these terms: because it "transgresses this separation, this habitual divorce of *seeing* and *being seen*; it achieves a sovereign circulation between the two functions; it is a complete object which has, if one may say so, both sexes of sight." As such, it attracts meaning like a lightning rod. The digitally embedded city, strewn with sensors, pervasively monitored and actuated, is fundamentally the opposite of the Eiffel Tower. De-monumentalized, the seeing transpires with a spatial disconnect—not from a distance, but from somewhere else. The possibility of being seen, on the other hand, is everywhere. But without the identifiable point of observation (the top of the Eiffel Tower, the center of the panopticon), surveillance becomes pernicious—potentially everywhere, by any agency, for unknown purposes. Embedded systems create the opposite of monument, the opposite of geographic centeredness, the opposite of subjectivity and objectivity. . . .

In privacy debates, some take the position that signage to the effect of "camera surveillance in operation" must be required. But how far should the signage go? It could also post: "by the London Police," "your facial features will be scrambled," or "connected to Interpol database." Such signage under our current assumptions of the city is the public space equivalent of Duchamps's "Ceci n'est pas une pipe." Being watched for unclear purposes by uncertain authority contradicts basic notions of public space. The uncertainty goes hand-in-hand with nanotechnologies, with embeddedness, with surveillance and even closed-circuit

TV. Unlike Maupassant who could choose to dine in the Eiffel Tower in order to both escape its presence and reverse its relation to the city, the surveillance state is intrinsically omnipresent. There is no escape except perhaps to exhibitionism. . . .

The effect of ubiquitous surveillance cannot yet be known, but it is clear that security interests of the state have negative consequences for individual privacy. . . . We can be certain that privacy will not be the only terrain in which social impacts will result. Sociologist Anthony Giddens describes the "disembedding" mechanisms of modernity. By this he means those mechanisms that break apart social relations across space and time, that remove local control of resources, services, information, and even the mechanisms themselves. Pervasive computing used as a tool of surveillance is a disembedding, abstract mechanism, because the sensors, processors, and actuators are anonymous. Thus, although any abstract system requires trust of the anonymous (e.g. that nuclear reactors are built well enough to withstand terrorist attacks), that trust is intertwined with intrinsic doubt. The streets are surveilled by the police, yet we know that the police are not always trustworthy and that surveillance systems can be hacked. . . .

[P]ervasive computing will nudge a newly defined public life into existence. It will be part of the historical trajectory of technology's sociospatial implications for public life, as is the development of plate glass with the resultant shop window, and the television with the interiorization of residential space. In "A Manifesto for Cyborgs" (cybernetic organisms, like us), Donna Haraway argues that digital capabilities will transform everyday life: "No longer structured by the polarity of public and private, the cyborg defines a technological polis based partly on a revolution of social relations in the *oikos*, the household." Just as Haraway sees the previously

private household's restructuring, there are parallels in the public sphere where common ground grows more individuated and privatized because of wireless technology. And public space can incorporate, even publicize, that which was remote and inaccessible: a town broadcasts its emotions, or a school projects a children's collaborative art project as it develops or webcasts their music lesson.

Foucault's analysis of the panopticon captured a formal-social symbiosis, whereby a spatial model arose to typify and exemplify a complex nexus in cultural history. Koolhaas's description of the skyscraper as proximate stacking of unrelated lives captured the essence of the twentieth century. The immanent equivalent is the city of embodied virtuality: the cyburg for cyborgs. The embedding of tiny computers and their networks into the city brings promise and uncertainty. Creating a realm of dispersed displacement, surveillance aims toward a particular space or spaces. It—and we know not what or who *it* is—observes us and our actions, emotions, histories, and reactions. These observations may be known to us (screening for passenger-carried metal objects at airports), uncertain to us (visible cameras linked to unknown processors, such as face recognition systems and criminal data bases), or opaque to us (cyber-interceptions of potential terrorist communications). Thus, the actuated environment, our actuated surroundings, can now "manage" not only that which is capable of being seen and known, but also that which is not capable of being seen, and about which we remain ignorant.

In a realm of dispersed displacement, discourse about centers and margins becomes irrelevant. For lovers walking hand in hand while speaking simultaneously by cell phone to their respective spouses, spatial dislocation is crucial and unquestioned. In this they remain secure. But they cannot be certain even about the immediate other: with whom is she speaking? Is she with me, or is she elsewhere? In this context, the other is not just distracted; neither is she absent. Instead, she is both present and absent in a way that was not possible prior to wireless technologies whereby everywhere is connected. There is no spatial logic nor spatial guarantees for intimacy. Publicity likewise embodies uncertainty. Public life is spatially located, but also displaced and dispersed, requiring new logics and new physical forms.

# 48

# MIKE CRANG AND STEPHEN GRAHAM

## SENTIENT CITIES

### Ambient Intelligence and the Politics of Urban Space

Mike Crang and Stephen Graham's 2007 article is representative of widely expressed concerns in the 2000s around the "recombination" of the digital and material. The question of what happens to social relations and urban space as software increasingly forms the ground for life remains pertinent, even though the specific examples may change. In selecting the excerpt, we have concentrated on the approach of the piece rather than on its more transitory examples of military, commercial, and artistic projects. The article is framed by consideration of Michel de Certeau's fears about how transparency altered the city, illustrating a fruitful post-panoptic route to theorizing surveillance.

*** 

De Certeau saw social control and knowledge operating, like geodemographic information, by immobilizing society into a transparent text. His nightmare city was one of perfect knowledge and transparency where terror is no longer about the shadows but 'an implacable light that produces this urban text without obscurities, which is created by a technocratic power everywhere and which puts the city-dweller under control (under the control of what? No one knows)'. De Certeau's response was a celebration of opacity provided by social practices like walking. For him, consumers move in a system 'too vast to be able to fix them in one place, but too constraining for them to ever be able to escape from it' so instead the city is 'the scene of Brownian movements of invisible and innumerable tactics'. People's lives escape the dictates of official knowledge where inverting the schema of the Panopticon 'haunted places are the only habitable places'. These realms create gaps and lacunae in the gaze of knowledge. . . .

### Promises and dreams of ubiquitous computing

Software and algorithms code people, places and their data in interrelated systems that are then used to profile and drive decision-making systems. This raises a key question: What happens when the processing and not just the data is embedded in the everyday environment? . . .

To clarify some of the dimensions that concern us here, it is useful to outline a typology of the multiple ways in which urban environments might become animated through ubiquitous computing systems hidden in the background of the city. We would point to three distinct but related approaches here.

### Augmenting space

A first approach points out that the built environment has been saturated with information for centuries—from signage to adverts. . . .

The significant shift with 'augmented space' is overlaying physical space with dynamically changing information, multimedia in form and localized for each user where the data form an always connected, pervasive environment rather than necessarily appearing in our field of vision. The novelty is the real-time alteration of the data, the convergence of different forms of access and its personalization. The screen is mobilized and goes travelling, becoming embedded in our environment rather than separating us from it. The term augmentation reflects media adding to our experiential world not taking it over and speaks a language of enhancement and new capacities, alongside a sensible recognition of incremental rather than epochal changes.

### Enacting space

The vision of augmented spaces tends to produce a sense of superimposed but re-active environments—the emphasis is on the users' activity. So for a different, second, emphasis we might turn to Dana Cuff's depiction of enacted spaces composing 'Cyburgs', which are 'spatially embodied computing, or an environment

saturated with computing capability. It is the immanent stage of digital media that places computation in all things around us, from our own skin and bodies (biotechnology and nanotech medication), to our clothing, to our cars, our streets, our homes, and our wildernesses'. In enacted space, the computer moves to inhabit the most ordinary of things to produce an 'enacted environment' which is more than an enhancement of our capacities, it relocates agency into the world. . . .

### Transducting space . . .

[W]e need to think through the technological agency of ubiquitous computing more carefully. And here our third strand of approaches may help. . . .

[Martin] Dodge and [Rob] Kitchin distinguish 'coded space', where information is inscribed digitally that enhances the functioning of a particular environment, and 'code/space', where information and space are so fused that the space cannot function without the information and there is no uncoded, manual alternative. In part the enhanced 'technicity' these environments offer comes down to coded objects being networked through more codes and these enabling coded processes to organize new forms of action (transduction). Coding is about making places happen—not in specific or discrete moments but continually. . . .

## Fantasies of friction-free consumption

### Locating consumers

The fantasy of active and learning spaces has long been touted in terms of the possibility for a customized consumer paradise where goods can be found on demand—or, even better, before we realized we needed them. A variety of technologies build up profiles of preferences 'memorizing' our actions in places. Past patterns of purchase no longer need to be manually 'bookmarked' but form self-generated 'favourites' lists of goods regularly purchased (for instance in online supermarkets) and from thence it is but a short step to the lists of 'suggestions' compiled from those preferences (as in Amazon or many e-tailers). If online stores can remember their visitors, the possibilities of tags and coding mean 'real' stores and locations might also do so. In that sense spaces begin to have both a memory and anticipation of uses. . . .

First, spatial databases allow the selection of services based on location or proximity criteria. Second, mobile media offer the possibility of centring such searches on the current location of the user. Geolocation technologies offer the possibility of devices automatically knowing where they are (receiving locative data) or saying where they are (transmitting it) or both. Location starts to organize the interaction. . . .

The promises . . . are large and better than just finding a shoe shop when and where you need one. We might look at the possibilities for traffic organization and car pooling schemes. While organizations such as Zipcar have a distributed pool of cars, where you can look up a car by type, location and period available and rent it, trip sharing is yet more difficult to organize. . . . Rather than a vast central database, an augmented informational landscape would continually provide data on the location and direction of vehicles that could be picked up and sorted by those with receivers wishing to travel. Distributed sensors and computing would make it a collaborative task through ad hoc automated peer-to-peer communication. It offers the prospect of something like an electronic thumb for the twenty-first century. Of course, this in some ways offers a mythic technical fix since it does not build trust in other users in and of itself. Registering users and allowing drivers to decide what sort of people they will pick up might entail another coding and sorting of people.

## Tracking objects through the world

These locative technologies are also crucial in the production of bricks'n'clicks assemblages of electronic and material provision in an augmented retail landscape. Corporations rely on connecting demands through to supply chains and, as supply chains lengthen and increase in complexity, the smooth flow of goods in response to demand has become a key issue for global capital. In this climate we can see the rise of technologies such as the Radio Frequency Identification (RFID) chip. The various types of this device can be attached to just about anything and used to record or code its identity. . . .

Such devices mean pervasive environments may produce seamless data trails across a number of devices. We have a combination of

> technologies [that] constitute 'history-enriched' digital objects that can produce autobiographical traces some of which objects are supplemented with profiling programmes that adapt them to personal preferences . . . and thus learn or build in anticipation as well as memory. . . .

[E]nvironments are now being saturated with anticipatory technologies. These profile users in more sophisticated ways that in the end possibly pacify that user by creating a delegated agency. They also constantly use surveillance data to categorize users, a process which strongly links imaginations and anticipations of future behaviour(s) to categorical renderings from computerized memory. Such a technological politics, of course, risks delegating whole sets of decisions and, along with that, the ethics and politics of those decisions, to invisible and sentient systems. These blur seamlessly into local, urban environments, and enact and organize global and transactional flows producing an ongoing geography of distanciated, technological performance. . . .

[There is] an emerging politics of visibility as these technologies make our habits and practices visible. Technologies are shaped to recognize us and make us knowable as individuals. Military technologies are designed to render human subjects trackable and create a visual field where this can be used to distinguish friend from foe. Consumer technologies are also clearly designed to make our preferences for, uses of, and indeed thoughts about, products traceable. In the newly visible field of practices they, too, can then deploy algorithmic agency to target the most appropriate or profitable consumer. . . .

[A]rtistic works are trying to play around this visibility to make alternative worlds accessible to enrich our environment. However, we have tried to suggest that these moves risk making what was formerly protected by its opacity and transitoriness, visible and recordable. As such, there may well be an issue where rendering our tacit sociospatial practices visible is an uncomfortably close echo of commodified and surveillant systems. But these artistic endeavours in turn offer a second politics of visibility, that is these technologies themselves need to be made visible. If they simply become buried infrastructure without ever being visible to most users we shall surely miss the chance for many people to influence their development. . . .

Other emerging ubicomp [ubiquitous computing] technologies . . . are being established to try to re-enchant human links to place by recording and sustaining the personal and transient meanings of places. These artistic practices suggest that the effect of memory is not the creation of perfectly known environments. Rather, it involves a destabilization of spaces, a haunting of place with absent others. The double, indeed triple and quadruple, coding of spaces and people through narratives and

information carried in digital networks may thus actually serve to disperse our notion of both person and place. . . .

In a sense, following de Certeau, it is clear that the urban ubicomp experiments reviewed here very often involve an erotics of knowledge and a fantasy of perfect vision. We need to recall that these dreams of perfect spatial and urban transparency and omniscience are longstanding. Such dreams always remain unrealized, however, as the contradictions of urban technosocial change always render them rather naive. . . .

We want to suggest this is not just a technical issue that will be overcome through further technological refinement. What is notable is that, for capital and the military, ubicomp is being invoked as a technical fix or 'silver bullet' to somehow magically address complex and deep-seated social and political issues. Urban ubicomp clearly has a fetishistic power in appearing to finally offer solutions by rendering place and space utterly transparent in some simple, deterministic way. Indeed, we would argue that there is a danger that locative media are equally seen as a technical fix for oppositional voices and alternative histories in art projects. In this sense the myths matter and have effects. But they are only mythologies of a perfect, uniform informational landscape. . . .

Far from the pure vision of what de Certeau calls the 'concept city', we may find the production of myriads of little stories—a messy infinity of 'Little Brothers' rather than one omniscient 'Big' Brother. Some of these may be commercial, some personal, maybe some militarized. There is a real issue about proliferating knowledges circulating routinely and more or less autonomously of people. But it would seem to us that the political options are not those of rejection or romanticizing notions of disconnection. Rather, it is to work through the inevitable granularity and gaps within these systems, to find the new shadows and opacities that they produce.

# 49

# MARK ANDREJEVIC

## SURVEILLANCE IN THE BIG DATA ERA

Mark Andrejevic has been studying online surveillance and labor practices for many years. In this piece, he summarizes the ways in which the development of a "big data" paradigm tilts data practices toward impersonal mass dataveillance of the kind forecast by Clarke, and in particular with a focus on anticipatory or predictive uses of data.

\*\*\*

If, once upon a time, surveillance functioned as a strategy for catching someone in the act or for gathering evidence that could be used against a prime suspect, big data surveillance switches the order around. Rather than starting with a suspect and then monitoring him or her, the goal is to start with generalized surveillance and then generate suspects. Building on the work of Jean Baudrillard, William Bogard has described this form of monitoring as "the simulation of surveillance"—not just monitoring as deterrent (the placement of a surveillance camera in a notorious crime spot, for example) but as a strategy for intervening in the future by modeling it. . . . Modeling the future in order to prevent or favor particular outcomes requires comprehensive monitoring: ubiquitous surveillance. . . .

In the era of big data, monitoring and surveillance have the following six key characteristics. . . .

### 1. Tracking Is "Populational"

Big data makes tracking "populational" rather than targeted . . . [these forms of surveillance] rely on an inductive logic which requires tracking the entire population. This means that content is less important than pattern, and that individual data contributions gain in value to the extent that they can be aggregated, stored, sorted, and mined. In other words, data has a very different value to those with access to the computing and storage infrastructure than to those without. We might describe this as the big data version of the digital divide: Those who have access to the database, and to data generating platforms, can make sense of the data deluge and enlist it for purposes of their own devising; those without access and control are unable to make use of the data that they help generate. . . .

## 2. Correlation and Predictability Are Trump

A further corollary of the shift to "populational" surveillance is the privileging of correlation over causation, predictability over referentiality. The goal of populational surveillance, despite its ubiquity, is not so much to generate an accurate "map of the territory" as it is to generate useful, reliable correlations. This aspect gets to the question of content and comprehension. Perhaps the best description of this shift is provided by Chris Anderson's diagnosis of the fate of theory in the so-called "petabyte" era: "Out with every theory of human behavior, from linguistics to sociology. Forget taxonomy, ontology, and psychology. Who knows why people do what they do? The point is they do it, and we can track and measure it with unprecedented fidelity. With enough data, the numbers speak for themselves." We might push this formula even further: forget about trying to describe a world (and the various impasses this poses) and focus on predicting it.

Data, in this context, becomes detached from what might be described as "referentiality"—describing not the world beyond it so much as the data's own patterns of inter-relationships. There is a logic not dissimilar to that of the derivative or other "postmodern" reflexive financial instruments that, in a sense, liberate themselves from any determinate attachment to underlying economic realities (at least for a while). . . .

## 3. Monitoring Is Pre-emptive

When the emphasis of monitoring shifts from description to prediction, its goal becomes pre-emptive. As Bogard notes in his analysis of the simulation of surveillance, the goal of predictive analytics is not simply predicting outcomes, but devising ways of altering them. In policing terms, the goal of predicting the likelihood of criminal behavior is to deter it. In marketing or campaigning terms it is to deter alternatives to the desired outcome. Transposed into business jargon, as one digital marketing executive put it, "In the early days of digital marketing, analytics emerged to tell us what happened and, as analytics got better, why it happened. Then solutions emerged to make it easier to act on data and optimize results." . . . The promise of predictive analytics is to incorporate the future as a set of anticipated data points into the decision making process: "Historically all Web analytics have reflected data from the past which has been to a certain extent like driving a car using only the rear view mirror . . . for the first time we can be marketers using data in a manner that allows us to drive while facing the road ahead." It is a vision of the future in which the structure outlined by predictions is subject to modification along certain pivot points. If, for example, a credit card company can predict a scenario that might lead to losses, it can intervene in advance to attempt to minimize these. . . .

## 4. Tracking Is Interventionist

Big data surveillance does not rely simply on observation but also on forms of experimentation that generate even more data. The logic of modulation provides a second link between ubiquitous computing and predictive analytics: the ability to transform user environments in targeted and customized ways in accordance with predictions based on the ability to process big data in real time. Thus, the goal of marketers, for example is to customize the available information environment—the messages to which we are exposed, the contexts in which these appear, and so on—in ways most likely to influence consumers in accordance with the marketers' imperatives. This means an ongoing process of experimentation to discover which ads should be placed in which contexts, what types of ads work best in conjunction with which combination of search results, and so on. . . . We might describe the commercial use of predictive analytics as having several steps: First, the detection of robust patterns that can be used to identify particular categories of consumer; second, the use of controlled experiments to determine how best to influence this category of consumer; and third, the modulation of consumers' information environment in accordance with these findings.

For an indication of how predictive analytics operates in the context of retail marketing, consider the example of its use by retail giant Target to determine which of its customers might recently have become pregnant. Market research indicates that the birth of a child is a life-changing event that disrupts consumer habits and allows for interventions that might reshape them. So Target searched through its giant consumer database to determine what patterns of purchasing correlate with the eventual appearance of female consumers on its baby registry (abrupt changes in purchase behavior that include large amounts of unscented lotion, dietary supplements, scent-free soap, etc.). Then it determines what patterns of advertising generate the most sales amongst these consumers, conducting controlled experiments on its target population by creating different combinations of advertising appeals. Thanks to its proficiency in data mining, Target is able to determine personal information indirectly about consumers and use this to attempt to influence their behavior. The potentially intrusive character of this type of research was indicated by an anecdote reported to the *New York Times* about a man who complained to Target after his teenage daughter started receiving advertising for baby products: it turned out that the store knew before he did that his daughter was pregnant. . . .

## 5. All Information Is Relevant

Because predictive analytics is, as it were, model-agnostic, it does not rule out in advance the relevance of any kind of information. The result is that monitoring in the era of big data ranges across the complete spectrum of available information about the activities of humans and their environment. The proliferation of interactive applications and services doubles as a means of expanding the available range of data collection. When a company like Google, for example, offers a new range of online services, it is also creating a new category of data collection. When it stores your documents, it also learns about the ways in which you use them; when it provides email, it also learns about the details of the content of your messages and your communication patterns; when it provides you with online videos, it learns about your viewing habits and preferences, and on and on. All aspects of life that can be captured within interactive environments enter into the database—with their potential relevance to be determined by their contribution to robust patterns of correlation. The appetite of the database is, for the foreseeable future, insatiable, and there are no logical limits to the expansion of data collection for purposes ranging from marketing to health care to policing and security.

## 6. Privacy Is Irrelevant

Any attempt to build a protective bulwark against big data surveillance on the foundation of privacy must confront the fact that much of the tracking is anonymous. Data miners are not interested in the details of particular individuals so much as in the way these individuals fit into patterns of correlation. In some cases data patterns are linked to particular individuals even if these people are not identified. Determining, for example whether past behavior of some kind correlates with a subsequent event—going on a trip to France or becoming pregnant—requires the ability to track an individual over time. However, determining whether a pattern of online comments correlates with, say, the electoral success of a particular party or a fluctuation in the stock market need not require identifying who made the comments. Some forms of monitoring require that a particular individual be tracked in ways that can easily lead to identification, but others need only rely on "scraping" anonymous data off the internet. At the same time, much of the data that is personally identifiable is not generally considered particularly sensitive, in part because we are not yet cognizant of how it can be used. That is to say, its collection may not feel like the kind of intrusion that we associate with an invasion of privacy.

# WORK AND ORGANIZATION

There is a long history of workplace surveillance, dating back at least to the formal scientific management processes developed by Frederick Winslow Taylor in the early twentieth century (Taylor 1911). Although scholars have given a great deal of attention to Taylor's stopwatch-facilitated "time and motion" studies, which observed the minutiae of workers' actions and sought to optimize performance, his key contribution was a powerful argument in favor of a highly educated managerial class to oversee low-level workers in organizations. Over time, management became seen as a necessary organizational component, equated with employee supervision. Belief in the necessity of managerial oversight has only been amplified by the growth of complex organizations with heightened levels of task differentiation and geographic dispersion.

Contemporary workplace surveillance has also intensified in most employment sectors with the incorporation of information and communication technologies (ICTs), which simultaneously support employee tasks and afford degrees of Tayloristic performance monitoring by management (Andrejevic 2007). In the United States, it is estimated that roughly 75 percent of employees are electronically monitored at work, especially through computer, mobile phone, and tablet applications (Ball 2010). There is a moralistic dimension to much workplace surveillance, as demonstrated by practices of employment prescreening with credit reports, criminal background checks, drug tests, and social media reports. These mechanisms become normalized as smart "risk management" strategies, which often continue after one is hired and may be augmented by keystroke tracking, video surveillance, productivity reports, and so on (Gilliom and Monahan 2013).

Workplace surveillance can engender mixed responses from employees, with some viewing it as a meritocratic tool to maintain high performance standards and others perceiving it as instrumentally extractive and invasive (Sewell, Barker, and Nyberg 2012; Zweig and Webster 2002). Forms of lateral surveillance are increasing as well, particularly among project team members who depend on one another, effectively encouraging individuals to discipline themselves and submit to labor intensification in the interests of the team (Gregg 2011; Sewell 1998). When "function creep" occurs, where systems put into place for non-surveillance purposes are then used to monitor and discipline employees, conditions for resistance and sabotage are strongest (Ball 2010; Monahan and Fisher 2011). But even in the absence of overt forms of resistance, there is typically an ongoing negotiation of

*Modern Times*, 1936, Charlie Chaplin.

boundaries (Di Domenico and Ball 2011), wherein control and resistance dialectically constitute each other to produce organizational life (Mumby 2005).

The excerpts in this section trace these developments while emphasizing potentially counterintuitive manifestations of surveillance of and by workers. The piece by Graham Sewell and Barry Wilkinson illustrates how new managerial techniques cultivate employee self-discipline and attenuate the possibility (or desire) for resistance. Kirstie Ball's excerpt calls attention to the apparent necessity of surveillance in hierarchical organizations and the rationales used to normalize workplace surveillance practices. Gavin J. D. Smith shifts the focus to analyze the experiences of those charged with monitoring others as their primary work responsibility, not as managers but as operators in a video surveillance control room. Finally, Christian Fuchs advances a forceful argument that users of social media sites are ultimately exploited laborers submitting to electronic surveillance and generating valuable content for technology companies and advertisers. Together, these pieces problematize the power differentials and inequalities that characterize workplace and organizational surveillance.

## REFERENCES

Andrejevic, Mark. 2007. *iSpy: Surveillance and Power in the Interactive Era*. Lawrence: University Press of Kansas.

Ball, Kirstie. 2010. Workplace Surveillance: An Overview. *Labor History* 51 (1):87–106.

Di Domenico, MariaLaura, and Kirstie Ball. 2011. A Hotel Inspector Calls: Exploring Surveillance at the Home-Work Interface. *Organization* 18 (5):615–36.

Gilliom, John, and Torin Monahan. 2013. *SuperVision: An Introduction to the Surveillance Society*. Chicago: University of Chicago Press.

Gregg, Melissa. 2011. *Work's Intimacy*. Malden, MA: Polity.

Monahan, Torin, and Jill A. Fisher. 2011. Surveillance Impediments: Recognizing Obduracy with the Deployment of Hospital Information Systems. *Surveillance & Society* 9 (1/2):1–16.

Mumby, Dennis K. 2005. Theorizing Resistance in Organization Studies: A Dialectical Approach. *Management Communication Quarterly* 19 (1):19–44.

Sewell, Graham. 1998. The Discipline of Teams: The Control of Team-Based Industrial Work through Electronic and Peer Surveillance. *Administrative Science Quarterly* 43 (2):397–428.

Sewell, Graham, James R. Barker, and Daniel Nyberg. 2012. Working under Intensive Surveillance: When Does 'Measuring Everything That Moves' Become Intolerable? *Human Relations* 65 (2):189–215.

Taylor, Frederick Winslow. 1911. *The Principles of Scientific Management*. New York: Harper & Brothers.

Zweig, David, and Jane Webster. 2002. Where Is the Line between Benign and Invasive? An Examination of Psychological Barriers to the Acceptance of Awareness Monitoring Systems. *Journal of Organizational Behavior* 23 (5):605–33.

# 50

# GRAHAM SEWELL AND BARRY WILKINSON

## "SOMEONE TO WATCH OVER ME"

Surveillance, Discipline, and the Just-in-Time Labour Process

In this 1992 article, Graham Sewell and Barry Wilkinson discuss the emergence of Just-in-Time (JIT) manufacturing and Total Quality Control (TQC) as organizational techniques designed to improve efficiencies while also purportedly granting greater control to workers. The authors argue that unlike cruder forms of managerial control, such as scientific management, these new organizational developments have a panoptic effect: they compel workers to internalize discipline and direct their creative energies toward labor productivity, not workplace improvements or resistance. Responsibility may be devolved to workers, but the labor process is subject to central control and verification through surveillance.

\*\*\*

Stemming from research into the human effects of the implementation of management information systems as a superstructure of control to support Just-in-Time (JIT) manufacturing and Total Quality Control (TQC), this article addresses some issues surrounding the role of human surveillance and control in the contemporary industrial labour process. . . .

Our thoughts on the JIT/TQC labour process, centring as they do on issues of surveillance, control, discipline and obedience, have been greatly influenced by the work of Michel Foucault. At an immediately apparent level, Foucault's use of surveillance as the connective tissue in the Power/Knowledge relationship—especially in the context of the practical undertakings of control in the formalised social systems which exist in institutions such as prisons, hospitals, barracks, and, to a certain extent, factories—appears congruent with developments in management information systems that we have witnessed during our research. . . .

The similarities between the prison and the factory have never escaped radical and reformist commentators and comparisons between the two have long been drawn. Often this has been based on the force of sheer emotion rather than a sound analysis of the similarities between organisational forms which pervade each type of institution. However, such a line of analysis does have a degree of historical credibility which can be traced back to the earliest days of capitalism. . . .

The question we wish to pose is whether, despite years of reform and struggle which have changed the nature and form of both prisons and of factory-based production, there are still resonant elements within each which bear comparison. Furthermore, if there have been qualitative developments in the capitalist labour process, rendered possible or enhanced by developments in production and information technology which point to a move away from a production system dominated by 'scientific management', then what forms of surveillance and discipline, if any, characterise the new systems? . . .

The emergence of the modern factory and its supportive bureaucracy was characterised by a by-passing of the sub-contractor ('indirect rule') and a more complete system of surveillance . . . . Bureaucratic managers using the developing cost accounting techniques of machine pacing and 'scientific' management established a more direct control over the labour process. Planning departments specified fragmented work tasks in great detail and in advance of production, and armies of clerks and supervisors monitored compliance with specified work procedures and norms of output. Compliance was itself gained mostly through threat of sanction and money incentives. The domain over which the worker had a direct influence was drastically reduced, as was the extent of activity not subject to surveillance, and social interaction was limited—a sort of solitary confinement. If a contract of employment freely entered into confers a degree of legitimacy on capitalist appropriation, bureaucratic surveillance strengthens it. This is because, after Weber, the bureaucracy (managers, planners, clerks, etc.) justifies its actions (instruction, monitoring, discipline) on the grounds that they are the most rational means for achieving a given end. Bureaucratic surveillance, however, carries certain costs. . . . The pyramid (hierarchy) rather than the circle (Panopticon) became necessary to maintain the 'disciplinary gaze'; the capitalist needed relays. The armies of bureaucrats who provided the relays meant: high administrative overheads; the danger of information distortion as it passes through each relay or each level in the hierarchy (upwards or downwards); a slow process of gathering, interpreting and using information in the management of behaviour; and the problem of controlling the bureaucrats themselves, who could become concerned more with means than ends, and with their functional specialism rather than the whole enterprise. . . .

JIT/TQC regimes, on the other hand, are premised on more direct and detailed control (ideally 'total' control) and are characterised by a low degree of trust and strong management discipline. . . . JIT/TQC regimes both create and demand systems of surveillance which improve on those of the traditional bureaucracy in instilling discipline and thereby consolidating central control and making it more efficient. It will be recalled that Foucault characterised the bureaucracy of the modern factory as a pyramidal hierarchy rather than the Panoptic ideal. Our observations suggest JIT/TQC regimes are characterised by systems of surveillance which more closely approximate the Panopticon than do those characteristic of the traditional bureaucratic pyramid. . . .

Just-in-time and total quality control can be described as complimentary 'philosophies' or 'tool boxes' of techniques. As a philosophy just-in-time production means matching the production process with the market place—the ideal is the establishment of perfect symmetry between demand and supply, within and without the factory, with no shortages, no costly stockpiles, and no waste. As a philosophy total quality control means building quality (defined as satisfaction of customer requirements) into a product or service, rather than coping with the problem after the event (or suffering the consequences of customer dissatisfaction). JIT and TQC complement one another: in the absence of stocks and buffers provided by just-in-case manufacturing, JIT is dependent on total quality; TQC on the other hand is given impetus—becomes an imperative—under JIT. Stripping out stocks at the interfaces between production processes starkly exposes quality problems. Overarching these principles is the tenet of 'Continuous Improvement'. No limits to production can be allowed to remain static but should always be tested and pushed back. Once one problem has been dealt with, it will reveal other problems which must be addressed. . . .

One of the immediately striking features of a factory organised on JIT principles is the ease with which the fresh observer can understand the production process and material flow. This is because work flows are deliberately simplified and physical organisation is based around products rather than functions. . . . The result is a plant layout—a physical architecture—which offers a high degree of visibility. . . . One of the main advantages identified by management was that responsibility for quality could more easily be pinpointed: the grinder could not put the blame on the turner, etc., when the grinder and the turner were the same person. Responsibility was for an identifiable 'product' (in this case a machined component) such that the culprit for any defect could be more easily identified. . . .

Another factor in increasing the visibility of the labour process is the stripping out of stocks, particularly work-in-progress and buffers between processes. This reduces the scope for workers to 'hide' any defect or poor quality goods—detection and retaliation can take place more quickly. Further, one of the advantages of buffers to workers is the scope it gives to vary the pace of work. Synchronised production with Kanban [visual signal] control of material flow leaves little room for workers to create 'idle' time, or to 'hide' work for 'rainy' weeks, etc. . . .

TQC principles entail pushing responsibility downwards and the flattening of the hierarchy. This is a form of what [Michael] Muetzelfeldt calls 'devolutionism', where decentralisation of tactical responsibility occurs at the same time as strategic control is centralised. Most important for the purposes of this article is that 'responsibility' is devolved only under the condition of a strict monitoring of compliance with instructions. . . . At the UK Nissan plant, surveillance activities include a 'Neighbour-Watch System' (described by Nissan managers as a system for 'employee peer surveillance') and 'Vehicle Evaluation System'. These make it possible to trace faults to specific work teams and individuals on the line, and to award daily or weekly scores to each operator. This theme of surveillance is taken even further by Peugeot at their Ryton plant. They operate a similar scheme to that of Nissan, but there is even less ambiguity about its purpose as the shop floor is divided up into specific zones explicitly labelled 'surveillance areas'. Responsibility and 'ownership' under JIT/TQC regimes are presented as part of a 'customer ethos', but again the exchanges between the 'customer' and the 'supplier' are subject to central surveillance. . . .

Employees know that such information is generated by, available to, and the property of, the central power. Furthermore, employees are unaware of the extent to which even more information is generated, scrutinised and acted upon. . . . The contrast between the atomisation of scientific management and the collective approach of a JIT/TQC regime is predicated on the establishment of mechanisms of surveillance and discipline which form a superstructure of control that is able to indemnify the continuation of production against opportunistic sabotage or disruption and maximise the benefits which can be derived from such a regime. In other words, JIT/TQC regimes attempt to put the collective ingenuity of labour to work on behalf of capital. . . .

Thus, in a manufacturing setting, optimum surveillance would cover all the activities of every individual within (and, perhaps, without) the plant, providing constantly and immediately updated information to a central point commanded by an elite controlling group. Within a purely visual approach to surveillance, the capacity of the system is at once created and limited by the physical architecture of the machinery and the factory which determines the penetration of the 'Panoptic gaze'—the superstructure of control is created by the building itself and the arrangement of machinery within the space it defines. . . . It is our argument, based on observations collected during our research, that the development and continued refinement of electronic surveillance systems using computer-based technology can provide the means by which management can achieve the benefits that derive from the delegation of responsibility to teams whilst retaining authority and disciplinary control through the ownership of the superstructure of surveillance and the information it collects, retains, and disseminates. . . . To pursue the analogy of the prison, the dysfunctions of the solitary confinement of Taylorism and scientific management can now be transcended and replaced by the benefits of the open prison of the JIT/TQC work team, with discipline ensured through the means of electronic tagging. . . .

In the same way that the Panopticon relied on the subjects of surveillance being aware that they were being watched, the operators at Kay [a company researched by the authors] work in the knowledge that their basic work activity is subject to constant scrutiny, a factor which, when combined with the certainty of immediate public humiliation which will accompany the exposure of their divergences, invokes a powerful disciplinary force. Thus, the constant scrutiny of a Panoptic gaze which penetrates right to the very core of each member's subjectivity creates a climate where self-management is assured. Although the flatter hierarchy of JIT/TQC suggests that the controlling function of middle management has completely disappeared, we would argue that, rather than being dispensed with, it has simply been incorporated into the consciousness of the members themselves. In Foucault's terms, the members have become bound up in a power situation of which they are themselves the bearers.

# 51

# KIRSTIE BALL

## WORKPLACE SURVEILLANCE

An Overview

Workplace surveillance is intrinsic to labor processes in modern organizations. In her comprehensive overview, Kirstie Ball maps the many disparate elements of workplace surveillance and discusses their integration with organizational cultures more broadly. As electronic monitoring increases the breadth and depth of managerial supervision, including beyond formal workplace settings, protected spaces for social interaction and individual privacy are far from certain.

***

Any discussion of workplace surveillance begins with the idea that surveillance and business organizations go hand in hand, and that employee monitoring is nothing new. Clocking in, counting and weighing output and payment by piece-rate are all older forms of workplace surveillance. Business organizations are hierarchies, and hierarchies function by superordinate positions monitoring and controlling positions below them in the hierarchy. . . . The implication is that surveillance at work is, first, a necessity, and second, a normal, taken-for-granted element of working life. Employees expect to have their performance reviewed, objectives set, and information gathered on their activities and whereabouts—indeed, this is seen as good management practice. Controversies generally arise in three situations: first,

when employee monitoring goes beyond what is reasonable or necessary (i.e. when employers use intrusive monitoring to delve into the lives employees lead outside work); second, when they demand exacting and precise information as to how employees use their time; and third, when the application of monitoring compromises working practices and negatively affects existing levels of control, autonomy and trust. . . .

Organizations now use a raft of surveillance-based techniques that are embedded not only within specific tools, but also within the social processes of managing. Surveillance in the workplace not only produces measurable outcomes in terms of targets met or service levels delivered, but also produces particular cultures which regulate performance, behaviours and personal characteristics in a more subtle way. Surveillance in the workplace is developing in three directions—namely, in the increased use of personal data, of biometrics and of covert surveillance. The use of actual and prospective employees' personal data has grown in recent years with the widespread use of Human Resource Information Systems. Within organizations, survey evidence has indicated that electronic employee records are used in fairly routine ways and that the data are not subject to a great deal of analysis or manipulation. However, with Internet-based recruitment on the rise, some companies now engage in data-mining of CV databases and electronic snooping on potential candidates and competitors' websites. Third-party providers have now emerged who will conduct these kinds of searches for employers. Increasingly covert means are being used to search for potential applicants by accessing user chat rooms, or to gain covert access into organizations' Intranets (termed 'flipping'). . . . Recent research has highlighted that the uses of these data are not made clear to employees, policies outlining their use are not in place, and information practices are not subject to any third-party audits or checks. The same is true if biometric information (e.g. retina and iris scans, electronic fingerprinting, hand geometry, and drug and alcohol testing) is to be used for access control, recruitment, promotion or performance management purposes. Biometrics are now seen by employers as one of the ways in which the identity of employees can be authenticated, and as a way of managing health and safety in the workplace.

Informing and involving employees in monitoring practices is difficult if an organization wants to employ covert surveillance techniques to monitor Internet activity, service levels or competitor behaviour. Particularly with the emergence of the blogosphere, organizations are keen to protect themselves from defamation, and employees' web activities are checked for offensive or libellous content, sometimes even when they are posted on private servers outside company time. Cases such as that of Catherine S, who is also known as 'La Petite Anglaise', are now beginning to be heard by employment tribunals from applicants who have been dismissed for blogging about their employer. Catherine, who used pseudonyms to blog about her work experiences at a company in Paris, was eventually fired for breaching employment contract terms concerning 'loyalty to the company'. Other notable dismissals—the majority of which are female—include Delta Airlines cabin crew member 'Queen of Sky' who was summarily dismissed for allegedly posting 'inappropriate' photographs of herself in company uniform on her blog. . . .

On a very pragmatic level, there are three main reasons why employers monitor their employees. First, businesses are keen to maintain productivity and monitor resource use by employees. Second, they want to protect corporate interests and trade secrets. Email, Internet monitoring and information access control are all deployed against risks of defamation, sabotage, data theft and hacking. Finally, monitoring can protect the company from legal liabilities. The results of employee monitoring can provide evidence in legal actions, and monitoring can become a risk-management tool. Businesses therefore use employee monitoring to limit cost and risk, protect value and maintain quality. Excessive monitoring, however, can be detrimental to employees for a number of reasons—first, because privacy can be compromised if employees do not authorize the disclosure of their information, and it is broadcast to unknown third parties. David Zweig and Jane Webster, in a study of teleworkers, identified that employees felt certain information regarding their physical whereabouts was off limits to employers. The second reason excessive monitoring can be detrimental to employees is because, like all surveillance technologies, employee surveillance technologies can exhibit 'function creep'. This is because monitoring technologies can sometimes yield more information than intended, and management need to avoid the temptation to extend monitoring practice without consulting employees first. This is particularly important if the information is being used in decisions about pay or promotion. The third reason is that if employees realize their actions and communications are monitored, creative behaviour may be reduced if employees are worried about monitoring and judgement. The fourth reason is that exacting surveillance sends a strong message to employees about the kind of behaviours the employer expects or values. The organization sends a message to its workers simply by the tasks it chooses to monitor. Research finds that monitored tasks are deemed more valuable or critical than non-monitored ones, so workers will pay greater attention to the former tasks and afford greater importance to the behaviours that monitoring reinforces. Additionally, the form monitoring takes also gives messages about the importance of quality over quantity and the importance of working as a team. This can produce 'anticipatory conformity'—where employees behave in a docile and accepting way, and automatically reduce the amount of commitment and motivation they display. . . .

Finally, excessive monitoring can sometimes produce the behaviours it was designed to prevent. If workers perceive surveillance practices as an intensification and extension of control, it is likely that they will try to subvert and manipulate the boundaries of when, where and how they are measured. Studies of call centres demonstrate that intense surveillance increases resistance, sabotage and non-compliance with management. Here, workers are extensively monitored not only in terms of their quantitative outputs, but also in terms of their qualitative manner on the phone, and their overall competence.

They work their way around surveillance by manipulating measures by dialling through call lists, leaving lines open after the customer has hung up, pretending to talk on the phone, providing a minimal response to customer queries and misleading customers. Where call-centre managers are also under surveillance, they sometimes collude with workers to produce the desirable results. Incidentally, any resistance that has been observed in call centres so far has involved getting the better of monitoring (sometimes referred to as the application of 'tacit knowledge'), but not actively challenging, breaking, or sabotaging the overall practice, except for one case where resistance subverted managerial values. . . .

A more sinister facet of choice, power and empowerment arises when we step back and look at who is usually the subject of monitoring. In the early 1980s, the US National Association of Working Women conducted a survey of call-centre workers and ran a telephone helpline for stressed-out workers. They concluded that surveillance is generally (but not always) used at the bottom of organizations to cover high-volume service and manufacturing operations, and because of the nature of occupational structure, electronic monitoring is said to cover disproportionately large amounts of female and minority workers. When female workers felt unfairly treated under this technology, they frequently used images such as rape or sexual abuse to describe how they felt. Ultimately the intensification of workplace surveillance confers massive benefits on the employer, but relatively little benefit on the employee, perpetuating wider power asymmetries. . . .

From the proliferation of research findings about surveillance in the workplace emerge a number of basic points, and a number of critical issues. Before embarking on a critique of surveillance in the workplace, the following points should be acknowledged: first, that organizations and surveillance go hand in hand; and that workplace surveillance can take social and technological forms. Personal data gathering, Internet and email monitoring, location tracking, biometrics and covert surveillance are all areas of development. There is also evidence that groups of employees are appropriating information and communication technologies to stare back at their employers, exposing unsavoury practices and organizing collectively. Organizations watch employees primarily to protect their assets, although the nature and intensity of surveillance says much about how a company views its employees. Workplace surveillance has consequences for employees, affecting employee well-being, work culture, productivity, creativity and motivation.

As employees begin to discuss their work lives in public fora, either as individuals or as groups, there remains a question over how much a company has the right to 'clamp down' on employee voice away from the workplace and use information posted there to curtail the careers of specific individuals. As surveillance extends into the bodies and minds of workers, rather than simply their performance, how are they to resist it and negotiate its application? Where are the gaps? And as it polices the boundaries and internal hierarchies of organizations, how is it shaping the accessibility of work for future generations?

# 52

# GAVIN J. D. SMITH

## BEHIND THE SCREENS

Examining Constructions of Deviance and
Informal Practices among CCTV Control Room
Operators in the UK

Most surveillance is itself a form of work, and even some of the most advanced forms of technological surveillance require a significant amount of human labor. In this excerpt, sociologist Gavin Smith draws upon ethnographic research to show how control room operators employ stereotypes to simplify their tasks and engage in subtle forms of resistance to diminish the monotony of their jobs.

\*\*\*

Much of the discourse on CCTV [Closed-circuit television] has been written by both pro and anti-CCTV commentators from either a theoretical or quantitative, statistical position, and merely assumes the technology's actual operational efficacy. As such, much of the literature is characterised by a naïve form of technological determinism, whereby the 'human element' (which has always the potential to be resistive, irrational, dysfunctional and prejudicial) behind the actual operation of the cameras is largely overlooked. Most writers seem almost to forget that, by and large, CCTV cameras are neither conscious, nor autonomous, and require, in order to be effective, constant monitoring and control by human beings in a work-like situation, so that the millions of images produced can be watched, interpreted and acted upon. Indeed without this latter three way process of observation, interpretation and response, CCTV surveillance, it could be argued, is completely futile. . . .

My observations [in a CCTV control room] led me to believe that specific socio-cultural constructions of deviance were being used in the control room, so that operators perceived certain *dress codes* as being inherently deviant. The majority of the security team at Midtown College were between the ages of forty and sixty-five. My discussions with them seemed to suggest that they no longer understood contemporary adolescence in general, and youth culture and fashion in particular. Concomitantly, certain operatives seemed to link particular items of fashionable clothing to subcultures associated with crime and deviance (e.g. football casuals, ravers, drug addicts and American 'gangster rappers' etc.). Andy, for example, referring to the thieves on the campus, informed me that:

> Most of them know we're watching, so they wear 'em American base-ball caps to try an' hide their iden-tity. . . . Also you get them who wear those designer puffer jackets or jerseys with hoods on them to try an' cover up their identity. . . . Yeah, anyone wearing those sort of dodgy clothes and looking a bit shifty is a legitimate target for surveillance.

Indeed, there appeared to be a general con-sensus within the room that individuals wearing anything which remotely distorted their identity, were deliberately up to 'no good', and so justified further examina-tion. . . . Thus, it was males who seemed to warrant the most suspicion from the operators, particularly if they were wearing a certain type of clothing or appeared to be 'deliberately' resisting, hiding from or avoiding the camera's gaze. . . .

The key finding from the study was what I termed the 'boredom factor'. The boredom factor arises principally from the monoto-nous viewing of hours of routinized, une-ventful televisual images. . . . To alleviate the routine and tedious nature of their work, I noticed that the operatives adopted a number of unofficial 'time wasting' strategies. . . . For example, most of the control room staff smoked. Concomitantly, I noticed that every so often, the operator would leave his desk and head outside the room to enjoy a cigarette. Similarly, most of the staff drank either tea or coffee. Thus, the operator regularly made a new pot of tea or coffee for himself, the patrolmen

(who frequently popped in for a quick 'fly-cup') and for the duty supervisor. Toilet breaks were also a relatively regular event and again meant that the controls would be left unattended for a short duration. An ad-ditional way of fracturing the time was by reading the paper and completing the daily crossword. A tabloid newspaper was often in close proximity to the operator's controls.

The operators also overcame the boredom factor through a process of 'sec-ondary adjustment' (i.e. using the cameras for informal and unofficial ends). Secondary adjustment, I would argue, can be seen as an overt form of workplace resistance to the long hours worked, the poor wages received, and the low motivation and satisfaction levels offered by the job. Hence, adopting this strategy enabled the operatives to sym-bolically reassert *human* control over a heavily computerised, alienating system. For example, I observed the operators using the cameras to zoom in on cars that they liked. Similarly, the cameras would be used to monitor the patrolmen on the ground and to play 'hide and seek' games with them. An excellent example of this unoffi-cial, 'secondary adjustment' procedure can be clearly demonstrated through one of Jim's admissions:

> What I usually do in the evenings when I'm on duty is to swing camera 8 round on to the car park so that I can watch my own car. I jist leave it on it the whole time I'm working to make sure none of them little shits try and break in to it or vandalise it. Gives me a bit more peace of mind y'know. . . .

It would initially appear that CCTV operators hold a relative position of power over the ge-neral public due to the one-way, in-depth monitoring they can administer, and through their physically removed location in publicly inaccessible observatories. . . . However, be-fore completely accepting this view, a closer look at the operatives in my study suggests that, while they can be *empowered* by the cameras, they can also be *imprisoned* by them. The college operators—as described earlier—work very long shifts in front of often featureless televisual screens, in the confinement of a small, prison-like control room. Their task is to systematically monitor the screens for up to 12 hours at a time, and to pick out suspicious individuals and actual or potential crimes taking place on and around the campus. The pressure on the operatives to capture any crime on video and react is constant and great. There is little scope for autonomy, spontaneity or diversity in their work; they simply come in and are paid minimally to watch habitual televisual images for hours on end. Hence, their job is frequently the epitome and quintessence of routine, in that it is standardized, mundane and predictable. Nonetheless, the operatives must continue to operate the system at all times in case an incident does occur. In a sense, the operatives are the 'prisoners' of the cameras and their images, in that they are severely confined, lack autonomy and are under the complete control of the system. So whilst it is right to see CCTV operators as empowered through their role as watchers, one could argue that they are immured by it simultaneously. . . .

A key point, largely absent in the related literature, is that CCTV operation, at the present time, still generally relies on a *human element* to both monitor and control the cameras, and interpret and act upon the images produced. It is here that theory and knowledge on informal workplace practice taken from the sociology of work, becomes pertinent. . . . I would argue that [workplace resistance] strategies helped the operators cope with the general monotony, boredom and frustration of watching hours of uneventful footage. They may, however, also have been adopted as a subtle form of resistance to the wider, alienating socio-structural disparities the operators faced. Indeed, because the men were paid inadequately by Midtown College—yet held highly accountable for the crime rates on the campus, given poor workplace conditions and treated with contempt by lecturers and students alike (the very people they were supposed to be protecting)—there was no real incentive for them to monitor and operate the system efficiently. As George stated: "I sometimes ask myself, 'why should we bother'? I mean, no one cares a damn about us. We don't get any praise from anyone and we feel totally isolated". It would appear, therefore, that a potential corollary of paying operatives low wages and treating them inadequately, is that the effective functioning of CCTV is severely diminished. Thus, the efficiency of CCTV operation that is assumed by many commentators (and hence the effectiveness of CCTV surveillance in general), appeared, in this study, to be undermined not only by the realities of a 'control room culture' (i.e. the boredom, monotony and alienation endured by the operators), but also by wider economic and socio-structural factors (i.e. the low pay and general derision the operatives received).

# 53

# CHRISTIAN FUCHS

## WEB 2.0, PROSUMPTION, AND SURVEILLANCE

In this influential article, Christian Fuchs adopts a critical political economy approach to analyze the capitalist structures and logics of online social media. While social media platforms may ostensibly be free to use, they exploit the unwitting labor of users who are constantly generating valuable content and data as producers and consumers—or "prosumers." Seen from this perspective, social media sites are sophisticated surveillance apparatuses that integrate users into capitalist relations.

\*\*\*

Many observers claim that the Internet in general and the world wide web in particular have been transformed in the past years from a system that is primarily oriented on information provision into a system that is more oriented towards communication, user-generated content, data sharing, and community building. The notions of 'web 2.0', 'social software', and 'social network(ing) sites' have emerged in this context. . . .

The discussion of surveillance in web 2.0 is important because such platforms collect huge amounts of personal data in order to work. Although there is a hype about web 2.0, there is a certain truth in the claim that the Internet and the world wide web have changed: empirical analysis shows that, on the one hand, information provision is still the most important function of the web,

but that, on the other hand, co-operative functions of the web (community building, data sharing, collaborative information production) have become more important. The notion of web 2.0 might therefore be used for characterizing these changes, though at the same time there are important continuities in the development of the web. . . .

The combination of surveillance and prosumption is at the heart of capital accumulation on web 2.0. Following [Toshimaru] Ogura's and [Oscar] Gandy's argument that a common characteristic of surveillance is the management of population based on capitalism and/or the nation state, we can distinguish between economic and political surveillance as the two major forms of surveillance. [Jürgen] Habermas has stressed that the most powerful structures in modern society are money and power, which relate to the economic and political realms. Individuals in everyday life may have the ambition to transform society, but in order to bring about change they have to overcome isolation and mobilize resources. Surveillance by nation states and corporations aims at controlling the behaviour of individuals and groups, i.e. the latter are forced to behave or not behave in certain ways because they know that their appearance, movements, location, or ideas are or could be watched by surveillance systems. In the case of political electronic surveillance, individuals are threatened by the potential exercise of organized violence (through the law) if they are seen by political actors, such as secret services or the police, to behave in certain ways that are undesired. In the case of economic electronic surveillance, individuals are threatened by the violence of the market that wants to force them to buy or produce certain commodities and help reproduce capitalist relations—this is done by gathering and using information on their economic behaviour with the help of electronic systems. In such forms of surveillance violence and heteronomy are the ultima ratio. . . .

Marx highlights exploitation as the fundamental aspect of class. . . . He says that the proletariat is "a machine for the production of surplus-value," and capitalists are "a machine for the transformation of this surplus-value into surplus capital." Whereas Marx in his time had to limit the notion of the proletariat to wage labour, it is today possible to conceive the proletariat in a much broader sense as all those who directly or indirectly produce surplus value and are thereby exploited by capital. This includes besides wage labour also houseworkers, the unemployed, the poor, migrants, retirees, students, precarious workers—and also the users of corporate web 2.0 platforms and other Internet sites and applications. . . .

Alvin Toffler had introduced the notion of the prosumer in the early 1980s, which means the "progressive blurring of the line that separates producer from consumer." Toffler describes the age of prosumption as the arrival of a new form of economic and political democracy, self-determined work, labour autonomy, local production, and autonomous self-production. But he overlooks that prosumption is used for outsourcing work to users and consumers, who work without payment. Thereby corporations reduce their investment costs and labour costs, jobs are destroyed, and consumers who work for free are extremely exploited. They produce surplus value that is appropriated and turned into profit by corporations without paying wages. Notwithstanding Toffler's uncritical optimism, his notion of the "prosumer" describes important changes of media structures and practices and can therefore also be adopted for critical studies. . . .

If Internet users become productive web 2.0 prosumers then, in terms of Marxian class theory, this means that they become productive labourers who produce surplus value and are exploited by capital because for Marx productive labour generates surplus. Therefore, in cases such as Google, YouTube, MySpace, or Facebook, exploitation of surplus value is not merely limited to those who are employed by these corporations for programming, updating, and maintaining the soft- and hardware, performing marketing activities, and so on, but also extends to the users, and the prosumers that engage in the production of user-generated content. New media corporations do not (or hardly) pay the users for the production of content. One accumulation strategy is to give them free access to services and platforms, let them produce content, and to accumulate a large number of prosumers that are sold as a commodity to third-party advertisers. Not a product is sold to the users, but the users are sold as a commodity to advertisers. The more users a platform has, the higher the advertising rates can be set. The productive labour time that is exploited by capital involves, on the one hand, the labour time of the paid employees and, on the other hand, all of the time that is spent online by the users. For the first type of knowledge labour, new media corporations pay salaries. The second type of knowledge is produced completely for free. There are neither variable nor constant investment costs. . . .

That surplus value generating labour is an emergent property of capitalist production means that production and accumulation will break down if this labour is withdrawn. It is an essential part of the capitalist production process. That prosumers conduct surplus-generating labour can also be seen by imagining what would happen if they would stop using platforms like YouTube, MySpace, and Facebook: the number of users would drop, advertisers would stop investments because no objects for their advertising messages and therefore no potential customers for their products could be found, the profits of the new media corporations would drop, and they would go bankrupt. If such activities were carried out on a large scale, a new economic crisis would arise. This thought experiment shows that users are essential for generating profit in the new media economy. Furthermore they produce and co-produce parts of the products, and therefore parts of the use value, exchange value, and surplus value that are objectified in these products. . . .

The users who google data, upload or watch videos on YouTube, upload or browse personal images on Flickr, or accumulate friends with whom they exchange content or communicate online via social networking platforms like MySpace or Facebook, constitute an audience commodity that is sold to advertisers. The difference between the audience commodity on traditional mass media and on the Internet is that in the latter case the users are also content producers; the users engage in permanent creative activity, communication, community building, and content-production. That users are more active on the Internet than in the reception of TV or radio content is due to the decentralized structure of the Internet, which allows many-to-many communication. Due to the permanent activity of the recipients and their status as prosumers, we can say that, in the case of the Internet, the audience commodity is a prosumer commodity. Mark Andrejevic has coined the notion of the digital enclosure, which means that interactive technologies generate "feedback about the transactions themselves" and that this feedback "becomes the property of private companies." . . . We can argue that the contemporary Internet is a specific form of the digital enclosure that is based on the exploitation of prosumption: it is the realization of digital exploitation. Prosumers are digitally enclosed and digitally exploited. . . .

Tiziana Terranova, using the autonomist concept of immaterial labour, describes the rise of a class that works for free in the "social fabric" of the internet: "Simultaneously voluntarily given and unwaged, enjoyed and exploited, free labour on the Net includes the activity of building Web sites, modifying software packages, reading and participating in mailing lists, and building virtual spaces." Such activities are an expression of the collective productive capacities of immaterial labour. . . .

The labour that characterizes web 2.0 systems is labour that is oriented on the production of affects, fantasy (cognitive labour) and social relations (communicative, co-operative labour)—it is like all labour material because it is activity that changes the state of real world systems. The difference between it and manual labour is that it doesn't primarily change the physical conditions of things, but instead the emotional and communicative aspects of human relations. It is also material in the sense that in its current forms it is ultimately to a certain extent oriented on the economy, subsumed under capital, and oriented towards producing economic profit. . . .

The Marxian cycle of capital accumulation allows us to distinguish between workplace surveillance, workforce surveillance, and consumer surveillance. On web 2.0, producers are consumers and consumers producers of information. Therefore, producer surveillance and consumer surveillance merge into web 2.0 prosumer surveillance. Web 2.0 surveillance of workplace and workforce (producer surveillance) is at the same time consumer surveillance and vice versa. . . .

Online labour is frequently connected to ideas like entertainment, play, and fun—traditionally the realm of leisure beyond wage labour. Contemporary capitalism and contemporary web 2.0 have brought about a blurring of the boundaries between production and consumption and therefore also between leisure time and work time. No clear separation is possible. Leisure, fun, play, and entertainment have become subsumed under capital—there is the exploitation and expropriation of the online commons of communication. Labour and play intersect, they create new forms of exploitation. The main argument of this paper has been that web 2.0 is largely a commercial, profit-oriented machine that exploits users by commodifying their personal data and usage behaviour (web 2.0 prosumer commodity) and subjects these data to economic surveillance so that capital is accumulated with the help of targeted personalized advertising. . . .

There are no easy solutions to the problem of civil rights limitations due to electronic surveillance. Opting out of existing advertising options is not a solution to the problem of economic and political surveillance. Even if users do opt out, media corporations will continue to collect and assess certain data on them, to sell the users as audience commodity to advertising clients, and to give personal data to the police. To try to advance critical awareness and to surveil corporate and political surveillers are important political moves for guaranteeing civil rights, but they will ultimately fail if they do not recognize that electronic surveillance is not a technological issue that can be solved by technological means or by different individual behaviours, but only by bringing about changes of society. Therefore the topic of electronic surveillance should be situated in the context of larger societal problems in public discourse.

# SECTION 11

# POLITICAL ECONOMY

/////////////////////////////////////////////////////////////////////////////////////////////////////////////////////////////////////////

The field of surveillance studies has excelled at theorizing surveillance and examining particular examples of surveillance practices and technologies. While the economics of surveillance has not been entirely neglected, until recently it had been lacking in sustained critical political-economic analysis. Surveillance is now a global phenomenon (Murakami Wood 2013), not just in the sense of it being in every country, but in the sense of it being a part of everyday life for all the world's people, whether they know it or not. Surveillance practices, as Katja Aas has stated, form the "contours of a global polity" (2011: 332; see Section 5), but they also do much more.

There have been a few traditional Marxist analyses of surveillance, with the scholarship of Christian Fuchs (2009), for instance, offering critique of the political economy of online companies and their capital accumulation strategies (see also Section 10). Still, as Kirstie Ball and David Murakami Wood (2013: 1–2) argue: "Surveillance studies needs more serious attention to the political economy of surveillance, not just in terms of studies of particular corporate actors, or the growing 'surveillance economy' but the way in which surveillance works in and for government (in the broadest sense) at this global scale." More recently, such shifts are occurring with a growing number of studies

drawing on more hybrid approaches to the political economy (e.g., Ball and Snider 2013).

Without question, surveillance has long played a role in shaping the structure of the economy. For example, the discipline and control of workers (see Section 10), as Karl Marx noted, is central to the rise of the factory system. However, political economy goes beyond simply describing the structure of industrial organization. As Marx showed, it is the management of human society more broadly, through the appropriation of the surplus value of labor by an exploiting class. Appropriated surplus is harnessed, at least in some part, to produce the means of war and security, which are used both to expand the geographical scope of capitalism through imperialism and colonialism and to monitor and control potentially revolutionary working populations in distant parts of the empire and in the metropole. Throughout the twentieth century, techniques for disciplining workers were increasingly matched by techniques for seducing, both of the bourgeoisie and the growing numbers of the working class with disposable income and leisure time. The excerpt by Adam Arvidsson describes some of this history in its review of developments in consumer monitoring for advertising. The growth of advertising and marketing research, along with personal credit rating systems (Lauer

2010), testifies to the importance of the sur-veillance of consumption and consumers as much as production and producers. The ex-cerpt by David Murakami Wood and Kirstie Ball develops this area further, combining research from organization theory and marketing with that from architecture and human geography to develop a sociospatial theory of the "brandscape," the dream of a perfectly controlled corporate-saturated en-vironment, co-constructed with its subject population.

The field is now arriving at an awareness of the globalization of surveillance (Lyon, 2004; Mattelart 2010), a global surveil-lance society (Murakami Wood 2013; see also, Gates 2012), and even multi-layered planetary-scale surveillance (Bratton 2016; see also Section 9). These concepts repre-sent attempts to explain the role of surveil-lance in shaping complex tensions, alliances, and flows among states, corporations, and people. Across this terrain, the private sector comes to dictate security interests; govern-ment policing and intelligence agencies internalize corporate cultures and manage-ment practices; and state security functions are increasingly outsourced to private contractors (Monahan 2010). On the other hand, this is not a smooth process, but one of struggles and reversals as corporations are also called upon—and frequently fail—to meet the demands of state security (Dibb et al. 2014; Gates 2011). People also can, and do, obstruct logics of capital flow through labor movements, protest, or sabotage (Cowen 2014; Fernandez 2008; Monahan and Fisher 2011). Additionally, sometimes people can evade financial surveillance by circumventing banking institutions alto-gether, as with informal "hawala" money-transferring arrangements common in the Middle East and South-East Asia (Razavy and Haggerty 2009). In part due to concerns about financial transactions supporting crime or terrorism, many states have now mandated that banks engage in advanced forms of financial surveillance of customers. The excerpt by Anthony Amicelle describes these developments and offers a critique of how subjective biases become encoded in—or hidden behind—the software applications used to profile customers (see also, Amoore and De Goede 2008).

It could also be said that when it comes to global financial surveillance, it is states that often struggle to meet the demands of capital, as can be seen with the way that the European Mediterranean nations, particu-larly Greece, were downgraded and disci-plined not just by supranational agencies like the International Monetary Fund, the self-declared arbiter of economic surveillance, but also by private transnational credit rating agencies, like Standard & Poor's, Fitch, and Moody's (Murakami Wood 2013). This is far from the only kind of economic surveillance operating at this level.

The complexities of the global economy defy the old logic of international rela-tions and mainstream security studies. In Section 7, we saw how China's technologies and practices of internal security were not only increasingly indistinguishable from those of the West, despite being branded as "authoritarian," but increasingly built by Western corporations as much as by do-mestic companies—for example, as this book was being finished, a Danish com-pany announced a major deal for Chinese state security systems (Omanovic 2016), and it has been widely reported that the activities of unscrupulous private in-telligence providers like Hacking Team and Gamma Group have been supplying dictators and military governments with advanced security systems (see, e.g., Marczak et al. 2015).

However, technology companies, which have created entirely new models of digitally mediated, surveillance-based capitalism, have overtaken petrochemical, mining, and even banking corporations as the most highly capitalized in the world. These companies have refined the science of capital extraction, often from data generated through the "free labor" of users of online platforms or apps (Andrejevic 2013). The growth of the so-called sharing economy—with companies like Uber and Airbnb—illustrates how total control over platforms can yoke users into extractive arrangements, while companies sidestep local laws and labor practices, perhaps obliterating them in the process (Olma 2014; Schor 2014). The final two excerpts in this section analyze the capitalist surveillance logics of two powerful technology giants: Facebook and Google. The first excerpt is from Nicole Cohen's critical study of Facebook's exploitation of personal information, and the last is Shoshana Zuboff's focused and detailed, but clearly distressed, study of Google's economic philosophy. Zuboff sees in Google a totalizing model for the next reinvention of capitalism, which has surveillance as its core function. Provocatively, she highlights the supposed inescapability of surveillance under this regime by using the term "Big Other," as opposed to the clunky, authoritarian Big Brother of a former era.[1] No longer simply a mode of ordering for state and capital, surveillance itself becomes both the source of surplus value and the method of control, the brandscape identified by Murakami Wood and Ball writ global. It is a profoundly disturbing vision and should be a call to action, except that, as both sets of authors note, the means by which such calls would be generated are themselves now part of the new architecture of surveillance capitalism.

## NOTE

1. Although Zuboff makes no reference to Jacques Lacan or Slavoj Žižek, who have also deployed this term, one could easily imagine a generative psychoanalytic reading of the desire animating surveillance capitalism and critiques of it.

## REFERENCES

Aas, Katja Franko. 2011. 'Crimmigrant' Bodies and Bona Fide Travelers: Surveillance, Citizenship and Global Governance. *Theoretical Criminology* 15 (3):331–46.

Amoore, Louise, and Marieke De Goede. 2008. Transactions after 9/11: The Banal Face of the Preemptive Strike. *Transactions of the Institute of British Geographers* 33 (2):173–85.

Andrejevic, Mark. 2013. Estranged Free Labor. In *Digital Labor: The Internet as Playground and Factory*, edited by T. Scholz, 149–64. New York: Routledge.

Ball, Kirstie S., and David Murakami Wood. 2013. Editorial. Political Economies of Surveillance. *Surveillance & Society* 11 (1/2):1–3.

Ball, Kirstie S., and Laureen Snider, eds. 2013. *The Surveillance Industrial Complex: A Political Economy of Surveillance*. New York: Routledge.

Bratton, Benjamin H. 2016. *The Stack: On Software and Sovereignty*. Cambridge, MA: MIT Press.

Cowen, Deborah. 2014. *The Deadly Life of Logistics: Mapping Violence in Global Trade*. Minneapolis: University of Minnesota Press.

Dibb, Sally, Kirstie Ball, Ana Canhoto, Elizabeth M. Daniel, Maureen Meadows, and Keith Spiller. 2014. Taking Responsibility for Border Security: Commercial Interests in the Face of e-Borders. *Tourism Management* 42:50–61.

Fernandez, Luis A. 2008. *Policing Dissent: Social Control and the Anti-Globalization Movement*. New Brunswick, NJ: Rutgers University Press.

Fuchs, Christian. 2009. Information and Communication Technologies and Society: A Contribution to the Critique of the Political Economy of the Internet. *European Journal of Communication* 24 (1):69–87.

Gates, Kelly. 2011. *Our Biometric Future: Facial Recognition Technology and the Culture of Surveillance*. New York: New York University Press.

———. 2012. The Globalization of Homeland Security. In *Routledge Handbook of Surveillance Studies*, edited by K. Ball, K. D. Haggerty and D. Lyon, 292–300. London: Routledge.

Lauer, Josh 2010. The Good Consumer: Credit Reporting and the Invention of Financial Identity in the United States, 1840–1940. *Enterprise and Society* 11 (4):686–94.

Lyon, David 2004. Globalizing Surveillance: Comparative and Sociological Perspectives. *International Sociology* 19 (2):135–49.

Marczak, Bill, John Scott-Railton, Adam Senft, Irene Poetranto, and Sarah McKune. 2015. Pay No Attention to the Server behind the Proxy: Mapping FinFisher's Continuing Proliferation. Citizen Lab report, https://citizenlab.org/2015/10/mapping-finfishers-continuing-proliferation/.

Mattelart, Armand, 2010. *The Globalization of Surveillance*. Translated by S. Taponier and J. A. Cohen. Malden, MA: Polity.

Monahan, Torin. 2010. *Surveillance in the Time of Insecurity*. New Brunswick, NJ: Rutgers University Press.

Monahan, Torin, and Jill A. Fisher. 2011. Surveillance Impediments: Recognizing Obduracy with the Deployment of Hospital Information Systems. *Surveillance & Society* 9 (1/2):1–16.

Murakami Wood, David. 2013. What Is Global Surveillance? Towards a Relational Political Economy of the Global Surveillant Assemblage. *Geoforum* 49:317–26.

Murakami Wood, David, and Kirstie Ball. 2013. Brandscapes of Control? Surveillance, Marketing, and the Co-Construction of Subjectivity and Space in Neo-Liberal Capitalism. *Marketing Theory* 13 (1):47–67.

Olma, Sebastian. 2014. Never Mind the Sharing Economy: Here's Platform Capitalism. *MyCreativity*, October 16. Available from http://networkcultures.org/mycreativity/2014/10/16/never-mind-the-sharing-economy-heres-platform-capitalism/ [accessed June 28, 2015].

Omanovic, Edin. 2016. Denmark Approves Export of Internet Surveillance System to China. Privacy International, July 11. https://privacyinternational.org/node/894.

Razavy, Maryam, and Kevin D. Haggerty. 2009. Hawala under Scrutiny: Documentation, Surveillance and Trust. *International Political Sociology* 3 (2):139–55.

Schor, Juliet. 2014. Debating the Sharing Economy. Great Transition Initiative, October. Available from http://greattransition.org/publication/debating-the-sharing-economy [accessed August 26, 2016].

# 54

# ADAM ARVIDSSON

## ON THE "PRE-HISTORY OF THE PANOPTIC SORT"

Mobility in Market Research

In this piece, Adam Arvidsson considers what he calls the "pre-history" of Oscar Gandy's panoptic sort, the way in which primitive forms of consumer surveillance led to the establishment of categorical judgments about people and places, categories that persisted for a long time and influenced much of the digitized marketing that came afterwards.

***

Gathering and commodifying information has been central to the economics of the culture industry ever since the late 19th century and the establishment of a market for advertising and, consequently, for audiences. When selling and purchasing 'eyeballs', information is central to the value of the commodity traded. As [Dallas] Smythe's and [Sut] Jhally's work on the 'audience commodity' shows, the audience has scarcely any value if it can not be defined in some way (in terms of demographic make-up or at least in terms of size). Conversely, the more precise the definition, the greater the value. Indeed, information is a crucial resource for advertisers in their (not always successful) attempts to convert the 'watching time' purchased from broadcasters into actual purchasing power

(which is what they themselves claim to sell on to their clients).

Some kind of information gathering is thus crucial if media companies want to attract advertising sponsorship. While the dynamic that Smythe and Jhally describe is similar to that of today's panoptic sort, information is gathered from the activities of consumers and sold on to advertisers—there are two fundamental differences. First, in Smythe's and Jhally's models information gathering was a situated activity. Companies like Nielsen built their business on measuring people's activities in a particular setting: in their role as television audiences, in front of the set, in the living room. Today, information gathering is virtually (or potentially) ubiquitous: any kind of media or market activity can become 'raw material' for the production of an information commodity. Life itself comes to generate value. Living in a commercialized and surveilled environment also entails producing a data double that enters into the circulation of the capitalist economy as raw material for information commodities.

A second important difference is that the techniques described by Smythe and Jhally were primarily directed at placing the audience of a particular media product within a particular and relatively stable category. For example, the value of daytime radio serials derived from reliable information indicating that its audience was mainly made up of working to middle-class housewives. The knowledge interest here consisted in classifying the audience, 'containing' it within particular pre-established categories, with relatively fixed notions of taste, habits and preferences. Today, however, buyers of information are also, or even predominantly interested in the movements of consumers. It is in their surveilled *mobility* between stores, sites and lifestyles that consumers generate information that can be valorized. Neither do the techniques that are employed presuppose any *a priori* categories into which consumers are to be sorted. Rather such profiles are generated *a posteriori* through clustering and other forms of inductive methods.

Technical means that enable this kind of ubiquitous information gathering are relatively new. They are the offspring of the proliferation of computerized information systems and communication technologies during the last 20 years or so. An interest in mobility, however, goes further back. If sociologists have just recently begun to take mobility seriously market researchers have taken an interest in models that could describe and 'capture' an increasingly mobile consumer society already in the late 1950s. These research techniques paved the way for today's 'data mining' services by developing the statistical clustering techniques employed, and by establishing

new ways of thinking about consumer behaviour....

With the mediatization of social life . . . different realms of mobility tend to overlap, transforming the life-world itself into a performative realm where spatial, material and media resources can be mobilized to make and unmake particular forms of self-presentation, often of a local or temporary nature.

The emergence of such a performative attitude has worked to destabilize established social borders. Indeed, looking at the historical scholarship on the rise of consumer capitalism it seems that, apart from a certain disgust at the vulgar attempts to imitate class and style on the part of *nouveaux riches*, it has been this mobility of identity and the concomitant blurring of social boundaries that has seemed most threatening to conservative observers....

Market research developed as part of a wide attempt to control, and originally, contain, this enhanced mobility of identity. When serious research into consumer tastes, habits and buying patterns took off in the years following World War I, the main enemy was the perceived mutability and 'irrationality' of existing consumer patterns. Most early market researchers, like their marketing colleagues in general, were steeped in the then dominant paradigm of 'scientific management' and they aimed at a 'Taylorization' or even 'engineering' . . . of consumer demand. Like in the case of the 'scientifically' managed work process, this entailed the use of market knowledge to break down consumer demand into clearly identifiable segments. These segments could then be targeted by advertising that sought to educate, rationalize and shape attitudes and behaviour. The aim was to construct particular practices and taste patterns and to tie them to particular physical or mediatic places, such as the home, the supermarket or the women's magazine.

Such 'rationalizing' or disciplinary practices were deemed particularly necessary in relation to consumer segments that were thought to be prone to irrational tastes or preferences, like recently arrived immigrants—to be Americanised through advertising and market propaganda— women and youth. The segmentation of consumer demand thus worked to contain the potential diversity of consumer practice within workable categories. . . .

[S]tudies of consumer behaviour did not really come about until the establishment of mass circulating, advertising-financed weekly magazines attributed a central economic role to the commodification of audiences. . . . Research on consumer behaviour, attitudes and motivations first developed . . . in the field of advertising psychology, with experimental research on the effectiveness of this new medium of persuasion. Magazine publishers, who had sold their publications under production costs and relied heavily on advertising revenue ever since the 1890s, were the first to begin to market its readership as an 'audience of consumers'.

Originally this was done without any kind of 'scientific' backing what so ever. Based on letters to the editor or, like *Ladies World*, photographs of the homes of subscribers, they sought to market their audience to advertisers as representative of a particular kind of consumer, usually defined in terms of social class. Thus *Harper's Bazaar* was supposedly read in upper class households, *Ladies Home Journal* represented an audience of rational and frugal middle class housewives, and so on. In the immediate post war years however, big publishers like Curtis (*True Story, Love Magazine, Ladies Home Journal*) set up research departments, and a number of research consultancies, like the Eastman company, developed to service small publishers (in the case of Eastman the *Christian Herald* and *Cosmopolitan* magazine). All of these surveyed readers for data on income and demographic composition.

In the 1930s it became common for mass circulating magazines (and for radio

companies like CBS) to maintain readers' panels. *Woman's Home Companion*, for example launched a panel in 1935, consisting first of 250 and then expanding to 1500. Panellists were selected to represent different ages, occupations and income levels among the journal's readers, and they were asked to answer a survey on matters like family size, husband's occupation, type and size of home, furniture, equipment, gardens, domestic help, laundry methods, car ownership, income levels, interests and hobbies. While on the panel, members were frequently interviewed on topics like meal planning, food preparation, laundry fashions, household equipment, leisure time, home decoration and child care. The CBS panel was checked in even more detail. Through so called 'pantry checks' an interviewer visited the homes of housewives on the panel over a period of several weeks to observe which brand names had appeared and disappeared.

Much data on consumer demographics, behaviour and purchasing patterns was thus generated. However, publishers still assumed that this data could be presented as representative of a particular group of consumers, whose characteristics largely coincided with the life-world presented by the magazine itself. . . . There was a general assumption that the cultural space of a magazine was a good representation of the practices and attitudes of its readers. When radio promoted the development of nationwide ratings research in the 1930s, class differences roughly coinciding with differences between magazines were reified into a standardized typology, the so called ABCD system, used to differentiate households according to income.

As we can see from the way the J. Walter Thompson Cooperation's chief researcher Paul Cherington recommended the operationalization of the ABCD system, income differences were understood to imply a lot more about lifestyles and outlook. To him the categories meant the following:

A. Homes of Substantial wealth above the average in culture that have at least one servant. The essential point, however, in this class is that the persons interviewed shall be people of intelligence and discrimination.
B. Comfortable middle class homes, personally directed by intelligent women.
C. Industrial homes of skilled mechanics, mill operators or petty trades people (no servants)[.]
D. Homes of unskilled labourers or in foreign districts where it is difficult for American ways to penetrate.

There were no research data on motivations and attitudes that could substantiate such claims. Rather, the ABCD typology worked as a way of giving 'scientific' legitimacy to speculations about aspects of consumer behaviour on which there were no data available. Indeed, as the ABCD typology was sedimented in the 1930s through its deployment in the Cooperative Analysis of Broadcasting's (CAB) nationwide ratings research (which became the standard measure in the 1930s), and later in the Nielsen ratings index (launched in 1942), it provided a convenient ground for such speculations. Indeed, in the CAB survey much was hypothesised (or, 'surmised' to use the actual expression) about the actual behaviour of each group. The relatively small share of the radio audience pertaining to group A was supposed to be explained not only by economic factors but also by "them having [. . .] a wide range of social interests and activities limiting time for listening [and] the fact that the average program is directed to lower income groups making them of little interest for the A group." Conversely, the C group's high index of listening was explained by "lower educational standards" making listening the "preferable way of getting information."

As the ABCD typology was sedimented as the main basis for market and audience 'nose counting', it came to work as a convenient sorting device. It permitted market and audience researchers to place consumers (and listeners) in established categories based on data on income and/or residence. Once placed in such a category accompanying assumptions about relatively fixed motivations, attitudes and lifestyles made it possible to legitimately deduce further ideas about consumers. This way, the ABCD typology worked to reduce, or contain the complexity of consumer mobility into a relatively neat and simple typology that permitted a highly standardized and streamlined marketing effort. Indeed, with the ABCD typology classifications originally derived from the structure of the magazine advertising market were developed into general categories, used to contain and manage a wide diversity of consumer practices.

# 55

# DAVID MURAKAMI WOOD AND KIRSTIE BALL

## BRANDSCAPES OF CONTROL?

Surveillance, Marketing and the Co-Construction
of Subjectivity and Space in Neo-Liberal Capitalism

David Murakami Wood and Kirstie Ball's 2013 article, while founded in a detailed consideration of marketing models in theory and practice (much of which is necessarily omitted in this excerpt), is a deliberately speculative piece that lays out some possibilities for a political economy of post-neoliberal, perhaps even post-capitalist, surveillance.

\*\*\*

The brandscape is a marketing neologism that combines the concept of the 'brand', with 'landscape', the idea of total view of a place. . . . In conventional marketing discourse, the term 'brandscape' is used to refer to an imaginary market landscape, and 'site' particular brands in relation to others. The brandscape has also been defined by the UK Design Council as the 'the total experiential reach and engagement of a brand'. It is a term that encompasses 'all those who touch and interact with the brand including customers, suppliers, employees, competitors, resellers, distributors, partners, etc.', or put more simply, 'the demarcation of territory by brands'. . . .

[I]t is driven by the same goal that has haunted marketing since its conception, and one that is ultimately a problem of all political economic systems: how to align the time space of subjects with the ideologies and protocols of particular organisations. We argue that the brandscape has come to represent a climax vision, a utopia of neo-liberal capitalism, which brings together hyper-consumption, personalisation, niche marketing, lifestyle choice, just in-time production processes, the ubicomp [ubiquitous computing] revolution and surveillance practices. In order to examine this, we need first to understand how surveillance practices in marketing have attempted to recode both subject and space.

## The codification of the marketed subject through surveillance

Marketing depends upon two key developments in the modern (western) era and the surveillance techniques that flowed from them. First, the discovery of the malleability of the subject, which replaced the previous conception of bodies endowed by divine providence with an unchangeable complexion. Through new institutions, of which marketing was merely one, surveillance would build 'distinctions between incorrigible and pliant criminals and the disciplined conversion of the reformable into "useful proletarians"'. Second, the invention of statistics and the idea of the 'average man' that enabled bodies to be managed in populations—biopolitics. Thus the tools through which marketing achieves its codifications are surveillant: panel surveys, transaction data mining and population profiling are familiar tools of the marketeer. Marketing ideology does not usually, of course, mention surveillance, nor would it: the negative connotations would likely deter the consumer from aligning their interests with the organization and leave them feeling considerably 'dis-enchanted'. . . .

Dataveillance is the foundation of Customer Relationship Management (CRM). CRM is strongly surveillant and has moved marketing from the attempt to sell new products to unwilling consumers to the pre-emption and anticipation of purchase patterns through profiles generated using databases of buying behaviour and the use of consumer information to categorise and to distinguish between consumer groups. Commentators on the

emergence of the brandscape see the prominent placing and exploitation of brands in dedicated spatial settings as a corporate reaction to consumers recognising the falsehoods of traditional advertising, and the failures of more transactional forms of marketing such as CRM. Yet whilst branding may be conceptually distinct from CRM, it does not replace CRM, it builds on it. Companies now rely on such surveillant and dataveillant means of understanding their customers in order to target and pitch their brands.

As [William] Bogard and [Stephen] Graham argued dataveillance involves moving beyond representation to simulation. The captive data double can be interrogated, compared, and manipulated far more directly than the body of the subject. New 'discoveries' can be made about subjects, their transactions and tastes through Knowledge Discovery in Databases (KDD) without having to resort to intervention with the physical subject. Added value can be generated in neo-liberal capitalism by this process alone, and while the bounded certainty simulation is seductive for those seeking to manage consumer, urban, migrant and other populations, the results must at some point be played back to the subject or in other ways mapped on to it for marketing processes to have some impact on consumer choices.

## Co-constructing subject and space in brandscapes

The mapping of the simulated data double onto material subjects is a constant challenge in surveillance practice in any domain. There are three related solutions. The first is to perfect the simulation through pervasive, faster, more accurate and deeper systems of surveillance, and the joining up of separate databases to share information across technological and organisational boundaries. Pressures in this direction are strong in both private and public sectors.

The second concerns the seduction of subjects to engage them in the provision of data as a normal part of consumption practice, through loyalty schemes, social networking sites, location-based technology use and search engines to perform work in their own surveillance.

The third is to change the world to fit the simulation and to construct space to make it easier to order subjects, which we see, for example, in the creation of [what Michalis Lianos calls] Automated Socio-Technical Environments (ASTEs). ASTEs are places in which decisions on actions taken by humans are pre-determined by particular technologies, which simplify what were once opportunities for rich and complex social negotiations into a simpler menu of options, very similar to what [Alexander] Galloway has termed protocol.

For marketing, the question of how best to re-inscribe coded simulations onto material space and subjects is complicated further by mobility. M-commerce sets out explicitly to recombine simulations and the material experiences of consumers using mobile communication devices. Here CRM techniques and dataveillance are combined with locative surveillance and not just-in-time production, but just-in-time marketing. In M-commerce activities, there is significant exchange of information, involving location, identification and authentication of the consumer, a triangulation of the information with existing data on the individual, as well as with where they are, and the dissemination of a message to consumers. Processes involve the consumer voluntarily requesting data or using email services as well as the organization finding the consumer to make them aware of products and services.

Hence, although brandscaping clearly originates most immediately from brand marketing, it is the combination of branding with M-commerce built on the foundation of CRM, or at least the same dataveillant techniques that facilitate CRM, that enables its emergence.

Brandscapes come in many spatial forms. They occur within and redefine urban, suburban and rural spaces, and the object of the brand does not always refer to the corporation and its products, it can refer to the space itself, to reterritorialize it as branded and therefore as something that has an inherent experiential quality. . . .

## Securing the brandscape . . .

[T]he success of the brandscape in terms of consumer experience is premised on its security and sanitisation, so that the consumer's experience of it is comfortable, familiar and reinforces the brand appropriately. In [John] Hannigan's discussion of the 'fantasy city', an urban form constituted by Urban Entertainment Centres and branded experiences, the concept of 'riskless risk' describes the aspirations of middleclass consumers who typically inhabit brandscapes and wish to avoid contact with socially excluded or lower-class groups. Brandscapes are therefore also securityscapes.

This is most immediately obvious in the way in which the brandscaping of domestic and neighbourhood space is occurring. Gated communities are now a familiar sight in the Global North and South alike. Celebration, in Florida, originally developed by the Disney Corporation imposes a 'Disney code of ethics' on its inhabitants and is perhaps one of the more extreme examples of a brandscape permeating into domestic life. Like the *My Neighbour Tottoro* house at the Aichi Expo, the phenomenon of the Disney Town is a retroscape, but here the sense of nostalgic security is permanent rather than a temporary visitor experience. . . .

How might marketing seek . . . to turn 'flawed consumers' into willing inhabitants of the brandscape? The brandscape vision is one within which the desires of the subject are anticipated and enacted before the subject can consciously express those desires where risks are designed away. . . . This moves beyond panopticism, and also beyond biopolitics, to . . . neuropolitics—which focuses on attention, memory and ultimately the brain. Its analogue in marketing is 'neuromarketing', the use of neuroscience to inform marketing practice. The emergence of neuromarketing would seem to support observations that neo-liberal capitalism is increasingly concerned with what Nikolas Rose calls "the capitalization of human vitality" and further that control is increasingly directed specifically towards the brain, attention and memory. . . .

In this context, marketing is being directed at ever-younger children, and many online spaces of play and pleasure have a hidden marketing intent. This is clearly designed to take advantage of both the emotional inexperience and undeveloped critical faculties of children. The greater brain plasticity of younger children's brains means that brain structure itself is more open to change from outside influences. Could the new neuropolitics lead to the preconditioned acceptance of an undignified and sociospatially controlled life aligned to particular economic priorities? . . .

[B]randscapes should not be thought of so much as any kind of totalising panoptic mechanism but rather as oligoptica. . . . [Bruno Latour] defines the term as particular centres of calculation which through arithmetic action control well in very narrow or particular ways but little beyond their boundaries or direct purposes. They are apparatuses that "do exactly the opposite of panoptica: they see [much] *too little* to feed the megalomania

of the inspector or the paranoia of the inspected, but what they see, they *see it well.*" The only adjustment we would make is to argue that just as Foucault's reading of Bentham's Panopticon (amongst other apparatuses) gave rise to a generalisable theory, panopticism, so oligoptica can be generalised as oligopticism, that is a theory of fractured, contested control, in which the multiple apparatuses of tight, limited and specialized control, compete, co-constructing not some uniform new subjectivity and space but multiple subjectivities and spaces. Viewed through this lens suggests that brandscapes may simply become an element of an increasingly disordered social mosaic already patterned with the remnants of incomplete utopian schemes of previous modes of ordering. . . .

However, despite the oligoptic, fractured nature of brandscapes, one should not imagine that capitalism will not, in its continued creativity, produce new and more effective schemes to address the perceived flaws and failures in the contemporary market. There is therefore a need for ongoing political economic analysis of emerging new modes of ordering in neo-liberal capitalism, and the ways in which marketing both generates and is generated by them, and indeed emerging forms of capitalism beyond neo-liberalism. . . .

It should be recognised too that brandscapes remain both an emerging apparatus and an attractive apparent solution to risk and complexity in a world where data underpins everything from purchase to social relations, and where those data are too numerous and complex for any individual to parse. Thus, it is not so much a 'logic prison' but, if it is analogous to confinement at all, it is an affective prison, not because one openly emotionally identifies with it, but because it begins to mark the boundaries of emotional range and becomes simply too inconvenient or uncomfortable to be without. Outside the brandscape, the world might seem not just dangerous but also painful, dull, limited and lacking in content: the dead, heavy 'meatspace' of William Gibson's retired cyberspace jockeys in the Sprawl Trilogy, or the reality without compulsory drugs in [Aldous] Huxley's *Brave New World*. More research is thus urgently needed at the interface of neurological sciences, social sciences and philosophy, and there are signs that this is already occurring.

# 56

# ANTHONY AMICELLE

## TOWARDS A "NEW" POLITICAL ANATOMY OF FINANCIAL SURVEILLANCE

Financial institutions are increasingly called upon by law-enforcement agencies to monitor their customers' transactions in efforts to combat crime or terrorism. As a form of risk management, such institutions implement software to profile or blacklist customers, detect money laundering or other suspicious transactions, and generate evidence of their own compliance to avoid sanctions. In describing these developments, Anthony Amicelle also highlights the inherently subjective nature of financial profiling, which can codify biases and lead to unjust discrimination against customers.

***

From the 'war on drugs' to the 'war on terror', consensus on the usefulness of the so-called fight against 'dirty money' has been based on two distinct professional logics. The initial 1989 mandate of the Financial Action Task Force (FATF) aimed at providing 'a decisive contribution to the fight against criminal activities and above all against drug trafficking, and to improve the soundness of the international financial system'. Since then, the FATF's international recommendations have been extended to include other targeted issues (e.g. 'serious offences', terrorist financing and the financing of nuclear proliferation) in accordance with the political agendas of various FATF member-states. . . .

While professionals of security have been involved in the fight against money laundering as a way of tackling criminal organizations, professionals of finance have been focused on another objective, that of preserving the financial system and its actors. In other words, the aim of professionals of finance has been not so much to combat money laundering and crime as to prevent the use of the banking system for 'illegitimate goals'. Accordingly, various ways of defining the 'problem' and the 'solutions' have coexisted, reflecting a range of different interests and different systems of perception. Consensus on the usefulness of anti–money laundering activities is based on this assemblage of professional logics, illustrating the ambivalent foundations of interventionist policies against 'dirty money'. The fight against 'dirty money' aims at attacking criminals via the 'sinews of war' (i.e. money) but without threatening the existing economic order, since preservation of the latter is also a goal. Now, while these two goals are not necessarily antagonistic, they do exist on two different levels, and thus their juxtaposition can be a source of tensions and ambiguities between two professional worlds—that is, between professionals of security and professionals of finance.

Accordingly, current practices of financial surveillance involve a range of different actors with different interests and know-how who now have to interact with each other. The progressive implementation of FATF recommendations has generated legally binding duties and compliance policies for 'regulated institutions' (mainly banks). These have to operate within normative constraints such as 'Know Your Customer' (KYC) rules and specified standards for reporting and record-keeping. They are obliged to verify the identities of their clients, to report 'suspicious transactions', to keep detailed records of their business relationships for a specified amount of time, and to respond to enquiries from competent authorities (mainly the national financial intelligence unit [FIU] of each individual member-state). Financial institutions and other regulated actors have become 'traffic wardens' that are required to assist in regulating the flow of financial traffic. The banks hence participate in state mechanisms of security to the extent that they have not only to maximize but also to filter financial mobility, paralleling in a fashion 'the twin and apparently contradictory aims of the airport' in relation to the mobility of people and goods. . . .

According to post-9/11 regulatory developments and official discourses, being able to follow a trail of financial transactions not only allows the confiscation of illicit money after a crime, but also represents a key proactive intelligence tool for preventing acts of political violence. The UK Treasury, for example, emphasizes the 'key role' played by financial information, which is not limited to 'looking backwards' after a terrorist attack, but also includes 'looking sideways' as well as 'looking forward' in order to identify 'the warning signs of criminal or terrorist activity in preparation'. In other words the criminal police approach does not appear sufficient for security professionals to prevent erratic violence. Accordingly, their focus is on possible 'warning signs' that might enable action to be taken in relation to suspicious activities before a 'catastrophe' actually materializes. Within such an intelligence-led framework, traceability—involving a set of techniques that enable the methodical storage of information, making it possible to 'follow the money'—also means indefinite monitoring for detection of unknown associations regarding potential violent activity. This preventive and proactive move of financial surveillance has been accompanied by a regulatory and organizational shift away from a 'rule-based approach' and towards a 'risk-based approach', which in turn has been accompanied by the growth of a 'risk industry' within the financial sector.

The prioritization of terrorist financing has had a twofold impact on the practices of the regulated actors that bear the responsibility for a major part of the implementation of the institutional framework against 'dirty money'. On the one hand, the post-9/11 emphasis has radically extended the obligations of these financial 'traffic wardens'. On the other hand, risk-based regulation has given regulated actors more room for manoeuvre in terms of how they execute their due diligence. . . .

[T]he process of sorting financial flows now centres on a 'differential risk assessment' that is mostly the responsibility of financial institutions. The sorting of financial activities thus becomes a routine task for banks, which use filtering and profiling software to categorize clients and transactions, utilizing 'blacklists', data-mining techniques and specified risk criteria to automatically detect 'unusual' activities. Regulated institutions have therefore implemented internal systems that rely heavily on technological tools designed to carry out such sorting processes.

The provision of technological solutions to combat financial crime did not begin with the focus on terrorist financing, but the expansion of this risk industry has been particularly spectacular since 2001. In this context, it is interesting to note that EU-supported security research has included projects such as GATE (Next Generation Anti-Terrorism Financing Methods), which aimed at developing 'new adaptive multidisciplinary modelling techniques to detect criminal behaviour by flagging suspicious human behaviours for Anti-Money Laundering'. The ways in which such computer software functions resembles the earlier data-mining exercises that were developed by financial institutions for credit scoring and other types of customer-related assessment. The redeployment of commercial risk equipment in the surveillance technologies used in the fight against 'dirty money' has been massive. Many companies now sell 'advanced data analysis solutions' like GATE and are attempting to capitalize on the growing market opportunities of what [Wendy] Larner calls the institutionalization of 'terrorist risk as a global business practice'.

These tools are designed to enable end-users to differentiate between what is 'normal' and what is 'suspicious' for each of its business relationships, with real-time payment screening, transaction monitoring and client screening. Such profiling software aims at analysing the specific characteristics of every single customer; supporting contextual and historical analysis; recognizing risk factors (country risk, product risk, etc.) and 'known patterns' of money laundering and terrorist financing (i.e. identifying 'unusual activities'; see, for instance, the FATF's official typologies); detecting predetermined risk scenarios that can be fine-tuned by end-users; and centralizing all red flags in a single decisionmaking unit regardless of where a particular financial transaction occurred. Through the adoption of such an approach, all operations can be examined in real time by a combination of matching techniques such as behavioural profiling, list analysis and comparison with peer groups.

One of the big issues here involves the process of specifying the parameters of these tools and managing the risk categories that influence the decisions. The tasks of defining the criteria used in sorting processes and interpreting the outcomes of those processes mainly fall on financial institutions. Various studies have pointed out that profiling is not just a technical process but also a social one, in which the subjectivities of the analysts play an important role. This socio-technical process can have a real impact upon the individuals being profiled. This issue of subjectivity is especially problematic in relation to methods of terrorist fundraising that are difficult to detect owing to factors such as the relatively low value of the transactions involved or the use of ordinary financial operations to provide support for 'terrorist groups'. Given the enormous difficulties involved in detection, it would probably be better to say that regulated actors have to manage 'situations of uncertainty' rather than risks. . . .

Here, the difference between 'risk' and 'uncertainty' is not at all about intrinsic properties and calculability. Instead, the distinction depends on modalities of treatment that make regulated actors accountable for organization, management and decisions on non-measured risks, and oblige them to justify the decisions they make. These modalities of organization and decidability convert uncertainties into risks to the extent that they paradoxically routinize organizational procedures to enable daily action on low-probability/high-impact phenomena. Let me be clear here, this does not mean that the framing of terrorist financing as risk makes it possible to measure the probability of terrorist activities and/or to prevent them more effectively. . . .

The risk-management issue at stake is mainly one of means rather than one of ends. The message communicated by market leaders in anti-financial crime technologies is simply the logic of 'as if' and the suggestion that regulated actors need to 'equip themselves' to be protected from regulators. Vendors use catchy slogans such as 'it's all about accountability', 'ensure that your anti-money laundering efforts satisfy regulators', etc. Software providers emphasize the consequences of non-compliance for banks and their senior management (fines, penalties, prison, damaged reputation, decline of shareholder value, etc.). Indeed, the vast majority of the sanctions available to regulators deal not with actual cases of money laundering or terrorist financing but with cases of unjustified lack of appropriate procedures or unexplained decisions. Thus, risk management also aims at establishing auditable processes or, from a more cynical point of view, procedural alibis to avoid sanctions. Seen in this light, software providers also explicitly sell a 'form of bureaucratic insurance'. Moreover, the FATF acknowledges that by definition the risk-based approach cannot be a policy of zero risk and that regulated actors cannot stop all 'dirty money', though they do have to build and show defensible compliance systems.

Nevertheless, the uneasiness of regulated institutions and the managerial focus on technological extrapolations from data may lead to principles of action that discriminate against particular groups or individuals. As the FATF guidance document also declares:

> an over-zealous effort to counter the risks could be damaging and counter-productive, placing unreasonable burdens on industry, and act against the interests of the public by limiting access to financial service for some segments of the population.

With reference to proactive logics, profiling techniques and practices of tracing financial flows are not problem-free. Furthermore, there is growing recognition both of the inadequacy of anti-money laundering methods and tools for identifying terrorist funding and of the problems related to the applicability of risk-based approaches to terrorist financing. Although this sense of inadequacy is shared across the European level, the official discourse continues to argue that 'the fight against the financing of terrorism is aimed at preventing attacks', and that financial tools have to be proactively used to identify 'terrorist networks' and to develop counter-terrorist intelligence. The solution is then linked to new 'public–private' arrangements in the field of financial intelligence—that is, new forms of cooperation between professionals of security and professionals of finance to manage the 'risk' of terrorist financing.

# 57

# NICOLE S. COHEN

# THE VALORIZATION OF SURVEILLANCE

## Towards a Political Economy of Facebook

Nicole Cohen's piece considers the new logics of accumulation in social media. Like many of those who analyze this area, she draws on Tiziana Terranova and Maurizio Lazzarato, who have both described the "free labor" or "immaterial labor" of consumption and creative practices, which, in the context of social media, generate value when harnessed by digital surveillance.

***

Business models based on a notion of the consumer as producer have allowed Web 2.0 applications to capitalize on time spent participating in communicative activity and information sharing. In mass media models, the role of consumers has been just that, to consume, or to watch and read the product. Web 2.0 consumers, however, become producers who fulfill a critical role: without the producer-consumer—or the "prosumer"—the sites would not exist.

By uploading photos, posting links, and inputting detailed information about social and cultural tastes, producer-consumers provide content that is used to generate traffic, which is then leveraged into advertising sales. By providing a constant stream of content about the online activities and thoughts of people in one's social networks, Facebook taps into members' productivity through the act of surveillance. In this model, rather than employing workers to create content, Web 2.0 companies or large media firms that own them profit from the unpaid labour time that producer-consumers spend working on their online identities and keeping track of friends. While these sites can offer participants entertainment and a way to socialize, the social relations present on a site like Facebook can obscure economic relations that reflect larger patterns of capitalist development in the digital age. . . .

Facebook's existence depends on this aggregate of networked bodies. Web 2.0 applications are built on an "architecture of participation," their foundations depend on the creation of massive databases of user information; each new participant adding to the database and thus adding value to the site. On Facebook, almost all member activity can be conceived of as immaterial labour that benefits the company. A major task upon which Facebook is based is "adding" friends, which is the act of linking to other people's profiles and forms the basic design of the site. The work of adding friends is also Facebook's main growth strategy. . . .

[Founder Mark] Zuckerberg claims that Facebook is set apart from other social networking sites by what he calls the "social graph." He uses the term to explain the structure of the flow of information on Facebook, which happens through connections between people. The links between friends' profiles have created a massive social network with myriad connections, or lines of communication. As Zuckerberg argues, sharing information with friends through face-to-face communication or through a telephone call is inefficient, as it requires paying attention to one another simultaneously. On Facebook, however, a member can read a friend's profile and receive new information at any time. To share a photo album from a party with all of her friends, for example, a member just has to upload it once, and everyone in her network can view her photographs. . . .

Facebook pitches this approach to potential advertisers as a way of enabling "organic" and "social" promotions. At one point, advertising was limited to banner ads and flyers that were subtly integrated into the site's pared-down aesthetic. Flyers, which could be purchased for a minimum of $50 and were posted in specific networks, were used to advertise university-based events and services, while profiles could be created by any member or business to promote events or products and services. This approach was an economical way to advertise independent bands and publications, grassroots groups and organizations, or local cultural events, and was the beginning of a highly-effective form of viral marketing for large corporations. If, for example, a computer company creates a group or profile and a member adds them as a friend or joins the group a message is posted on that member's profile for their networks and friends to see, effectively enabling members to do the work of promotion for the companies, and demonstrating another way in which free labour is put to work. . . .

The addition of the controversial "Beacon" function in November 2007 signaled a dramatic intensification of Facebook's valorization of surveillance. Forty-four commercial websites signed onto Beacon, which tracks the purchases of Facebook members on certain sites (including Blockbuster.com, NYTimes.com, and TripAdvisor.com) and broadcasts messages about those purchases to their networks of friends. Facebook's press release announcing Beacon gives the example of purchasing movie tickets on a Beacon-enabled site as mutually beneficial for companies and for Facebook members. . . .

But to thousands of Facebook users, Beacon was an intrusive form of advertising that took online surveillance and targeted marketing too far. Days after Beacon was implemented, thousands of Facebook members signed a petition on the site created by online activist group MoveOn.org, asking Facebook to let them opt out of the program. A month after implementing Beacon, Facebook apologized and allowed members to opt in, or to turn Beacon off completely. This episode, including the way in which members protested, the way the protest was acknowledged by Facebook, and the way it was covered in the mainstream media, was reminiscent of the introduction of one of Facebook's staple features for surveillance and information sharing.

In 2006, Facebook added what was then a controversial feature called News Feed, which provides a running list of updates on friends' activities when members log into the site. For example, statements such as "Bob is now in a relationship with Kate," or "Sam added tennis to her interests" appear in the list, catalogued with the precise time at which the update occurred. Not only is the News Feed a means of constant surveillance of one's friends, but it provides members with incentive to log on to the site more frequently, and Facebook with an innovative and nonintrusive way to incorporate advertising into the site. With News Feed, text and graphic ads can be placed in members' feeds, appearing to be updates from friends. This strategic form of advertising was developed as a response to online users' disdain for disruptive web-based advertising and is a powerful form of advertising because of its ability to become unobtrusively integrated.

The introduction of News Feed generated negative feedback from Facebook members, who called the feature "too stalkeresque" and launched a group within Facebook itself, titled "Students Against Facebook News Feed (Official Petition to Facebook)," which attracted more than 700,000 members and was covered widely in major news media. Facebook refused to remove the service, but did make adjustments to allow members to limit what information is posted in the News Feed.

The example of the reaction to News Feed (and, to some degree, Beacon) points to the powerful manner in which Facebook accommodates resistance within its very program, while at the same time maintaining control over determining outcomes. Rather than blocking dissent, Facebook transforms resistance into productivity. It provides the tools for members to speak out against the site itself, and then responds to this dissent through the creation of new policies or amendments to current policies. The site incorporates users' knowledge into its development, which retains members (perhaps instilling them with a sense of ownership in the site, or at least a sense of the importance

of one's voice) and affirms the critical importance of an active membership. . . .

Collective intelligence, understood as general intellect, has become an important source of value creation in the digital age. Zuckerberg himself often speaks of the power of collective knowledge and aggregated information: "By taking the understanding that all the individuals have and pooling that knowledge together, you get a better set of knowledge," he has said. In fact, Zuckerberg's excitement over the power of collective knowledge seemed, at times, to trump his concern over bottom-line motivation to increase the site's numbers: "One billion page views a day is cool . . . but really what I care about is giving people access to connect and the information they want as efficiently as possible." Although this comment should be read in the context of Zuckerberg's position as a business executive promoting his company in the news media, it reveals Zuckerberg's view of Facebook as a publisher of information, again diverging from the more limited perspective of social networking sites as solely social spaces. . . .

As a publisher, Facebook does not pay a wage for the labour that produces content, and while it "does not assert any ownership" over members' content, it demands a range of rights to that content, no matter how personal. As Facebook's Terms of Service state:

> By posting User Content to any part of the Site, you automatically grant, and you represent and warrant that you have the right to grant, to the Company an irrevocable, perpetual, nonexclusive, transferable, fully paid, worldwide license (with the right to sublicense) to use, copy, publicly perform, publicly display, reformat, translate, excerpt (in whole or in part) and distribute such User Content for any purpose, commercial, advertising, or otherwise,

on or in connection with the Site or the promotion thereof, to prepare derivative works of, or incorporate into other works, such User Content, and to grant and authorize sublicenses of the foregoing.

The site's policy can be viewed as part of a larger move toward the increasing commodification of information through the extending grip of corporate interests around intellectual property and media content in general. Media companies are placing increasing restrictions on intellectual property, extending IP as a method of "protecting" the right to profit maximization. This has affected producers of content, such as freelance writers, who are faced with increasingly restrictive contracts that can demand "all rights, in perpetuity, throughout the universe," as well as participants of social networking sites, whose "data," while not necessarily transformed into private property, is loaned to private companies without compensation, for the accumulation of capital. In the so-called information age—a time in which access to information carries with it great political, economic and social weight and rights are equated with market power—asymmetrical power relations are being established between those who produce content and those who profit from it. Although it is difficult to reconcile a strict Marxist definition of exploitation with the exchange that occurs on Facebook, exploitation in this case can be more broadly conceived as "the expropriation of the common," which is to say, knowledge produced collectively or collabouratively [sic] becomes private property, which obscures the social dimension of wealth production. . . .

Much has been made in the media of Facebook's privacy policy, with concerns predominantly centered on the accessibility of user information to stalkers, or the ability of employers and teachers to read negative comments made by employees and students. Facebook does allow members to adjust profile settings to limit the amount of information that can be viewed by strangers and friends on the site, and the solutions presented to address these concerns encourage people to turn on and adjust privacy settings on their profiles. This approach places the onus on individuals to seek out and activate their privacy settings, which does not address larger issues of privacy and surveillance, nor does it acknowledge the fact that most people are unaware of website privacy settings and policies in the first place.

Critically, very few discussions about privacy have focused on Facebook's policies with regards to selling information to third parties. . . . The site's lengthy privacy policy states that information is collected not only from members inputting information into their profiles, but also as members interact with the site. Even after information is removed from a profile, it "may remain viewable in cached and archived pages or if other Users have copied or stored . . . User Content." The site also collects information about its members from "other sources, such as newspapers, blogs, instant messaging services, Facebook Platform developers and other users of Facebook". . . .

Facebook, a space where both leisure time is spent and labour is performed, is an example of how, in the social factory, general social relations become moments of production. While Facebook and its Web 2.0 counterparts may represent a break from mass media in some of the functions of its operation, a reconstitution of power relations has not occurred. Rather, we have seen the extension of processes of commodification[:] capitalist social relations and market forces extending into multiple aspects of social life.

# 58

# SHOSHANA ZUBOFF

## BIG OTHER

### Surveillance Capitalism and the Prospects of an Information Civilization

Shoshana Zuboff, best known for her 1988 book *In the Age of the Smart Machine*, was one of the pioneers in the study of workplace surveillance. In her latest work, she has expanded her gaze to encompass the characteristics of contemporary capitalism of which workplace technologies are only part. The article from which this excerpt comes performs a close analysis of two documents by Google's chief economist, Hal Varian. What is reprinted here is the foundation of Zuboff's argument about a totalizing new "logic of accumulation" enacted by Google, Facebook, and others.

\*\*\*

In the history of capitalism, each era has run toward a dominant logic of accumulation—mass production-based corporate capitalism in the 20th century shaded into financial capitalism by that century's end—a form that continues to hold sway. This helps to explain why there is so little real competitive differentiation within industries. Airlines, for example, have immense information flows that are interpreted along more or less similar lines toward similar aims and metrics, because firms are all evaluated according to the terms of a single shared logic of accumulation. The same could be said for banks, hospitals, telecommunications companies, and so forth. Still, capitalism's success over the *longue durée* has depended upon the emergence of new market forms expressing new logics of accumulation that are more successful at meeting the ever-evolving needs of populations and their expression in the changing nature of demand. . . .

[T]hree of the world's seven billion people are now computer-mediated in a wide range of their daily activities far beyond the traditional boundaries of the workplace. For them the old dream of ubiquitous computing is a barely noticeable truism. As a result of pervasive computer mediation, nearly every aspect of the world is rendered in a new symbolic dimension as events, objects, processes, and people become visible, knowable, and shareable in a new way. The world is reborn as data and the electronic text is universal in scale and scope. Just a moment ago, it still seemed reasonable to focus our concerns on the challenges of an information workplace or an information society. Now the enduring questions of authority and power must be addressed to the widest possible frame that is best defined as 'civilization' or more specifically—information civilization. Who learns from global data flows, what, and how? Who decides? What happens when authority fails? What logic of accumulation will shape the answers to these questions? Recognizing their civilizational scale lends these questions new force and urgency. Their answers will shape the character of information civilization in the century to come, just as the logic of industrial capitalism and its successors shaped the character of industrial civilization over the last two centuries. . . .

[E]xamination of Varian's combination of data, extraction, and analysis begins to suggest some key features of the new logic of accumulation associated with big data and spearheaded by Google. First, revenues depend upon data assets appropriated through ubiquitous automated operations. These constitute a new asset class: *surveillance assets*. Critics of surveillance capitalism might characterize such assets as 'stolen goods' or 'contraband' as they were taken, not given, and do not produce . . . appropriate reciprocities. The cherished culture of social production in the networked individual sphere relies on the very tools that are now the primary vehicles for the surveillance-based appropriation of the most lucrative data exhaust. These surveillance assets attract significant investment that can be called *surveillance capital*. Google has, so far, triumphed in the networked world through the pioneering construction of this new market form that is a radically disembedded and extractive

variant of information capitalism, one that can be identified as *surveillance capitalism*. This new market form has quickly developed into the default business model for most online companies and startups, where valuations routinely depend upon 'eyeballs' rather than revenue as a predictor of remunerative surveillance assets. . . .

Rather than enabling new contractual forms, these arrangements describe the rise of a new universal architecture existing somewhere between nature and God that I christen *Big Other*. It is a ubiquitous networked institutional regime that records, modifies, and commodifies everyday experience from toasters to bodies, communication to thought, all with a view to establishing new pathways to monetization and profit. Big Other is the sovereign power of a near future that annihilates the freedom achieved by the rule of law. It is a new regime of independent and independently controlled facts that supplants the need for contracts, governance, and the dynamism of a market democracy. Big Other is the 21st-century incarnation of the electronic text that aspires to encompass and reveal the comprehensive immanent facts of market, social, physical, and biological behaviors. The institutional processes that constitute the architecture of Big Other can be imagined as the material instantiation of [F. A.] Hayek's 'extended order' come to life in the explicated transparency of computer-mediation.

These processes reconfigure the structure of power, conformity, and resistance inherited from mass society and symbolized for over half a century as Big Brother. Power can no longer be summarized by that totalitarian symbol of centralized command and control. Even the panopticon of Bentham's design . . . is prosaic compared to this new architecture. . . . In the world implied by Varian's assumptions, habitats inside and outside the human body are saturated with data and produce radically distributed opportunities for observation, interpretation, communication, influence, prediction, and ultimately modification of the totality of action. Unlike the centralized power of mass society, there is no escape from Big Other. There is no place to be where the Other is not.

In this world of no escape, the chilling effects of anticipatory conformity give way as the mental agency and self-possession of anticipation is gradually submerged into a new kind of automaticity. Anticipatory conformity assumes a point of origin in consciousness from which a choice is made to conform for the purposes of evasion of sanctions and social camouflage. It also implies a difference, or at least the possibility of a difference, between the behavior one would have performed and the behavior one chooses to perform as an instrumental solution to invasive power. In a world of Big Other, without avenues of escape, the agency implied in the work of anticipation is gradually submerged into a new kind of automaticity—a lived experience of pure stimulus-response. Conformity is no longer a 20th century–style act of submission to the mass or group, no loss of self to the collective produced by fear or compulsion, no psychological craving for acceptance and belonging. Conformity now disappears into the mechanical order of things and bodies, not as action but as result, not cause but effect. Each one of us may follow a distinct path, but that path is already shaped by the financial and, or, ideological interests that imbue Big Other and invade every aspect of 'one's own' life. False consciousness is no longer produced by the hidden facts of class and their relation to production, but rather by the hidden facts of commoditized behavior modification. If power was once identified with the ownership of the means of production, it is now identified with ownership of the means of behavioral modification. . . .

The work of surveillance, it appears, is not to erode privacy rights but rather to redistribute them. Instead of many people having some privacy rights, these rights have been concentrated within the surveillance regime. Surveillance capitalists have extensive privacy rights and therefore many opportunities for secrets. These are increasingly used to deprive populations of choice in the matter of what about their lives remains secret. This concentration of rights is accomplished in two ways. In the case of Google, Facebook, and other exemplars of surveillance capitalism, many of their rights appear to come from taking others' without asking—in conformance with the Street View model. Surveillance capitalists have skillfully exploited a lag in social evolution as the rapid development of their abilities to surveil for profit outrun public understanding and the eventual development of law and regulation that it produces. In result, privacy rights, once accumulated and asserted, can then be invoked as legitimation for maintaining the obscurity of surveillance operations. . . .

These arguments suggest that the logic of accumulation that undergirds surveillance capitalism is not wholly captured by the conventional institutional terrain of the private firm. What is accumulated here is not only surveillance assets and capital, but also rights. This occurs through a unique assemblage of business processes that operate outside the auspices of legitimate democratic mechanisms or the traditional market pressures of consumer reciprocity and choice. It is accomplished through a form of unilateral declaration that most closely resembles the social relations of a pre-modern absolutist authority. In the context of this new market form that I call surveillance capitalism, hyperscale becomes a profoundly anti-democratic threat.

Surveillance capitalism thus qualifies as a new logic of accumulation with a new politics and social relations that replaces contracts, the rule of law, and social trust with the sovereignty of Big Other. It imposes a privately administered compliance regime of rewards and punishments that is sustained by a unilateral redistribution of rights. Big Other exists in the absence of legitimate authority and is largely free from detection or sanction. In this sense Big Other may be described as an automated coup from above: not a *coup d'état*, but rather a *coup des gens*. . . .

Google knows far more about its populations than they know about themselves. Indeed, there are no means by which populations can cross this divide, given the material, intellectual, and proprietary hurdles required for data analysis and the absence of feedback loops. Another asymmetry is reflected in the fact that the typical user has little or no knowledge of Google's business operations, the full range of personal data that they contribute to Google's servers, the retention of those data, or how those data are instrumentalized and monetized. It is by now well known that users have few meaningful options for privacy self-management. . . . Surveillance capitalism thrives on the public's ignorance.

These asymmetries in knowledge are sustained by asymmetries of power. Big Other is institutionalized in the automatic undetectable functions of a global infrastructure that is also regarded by most people as essential for basic social participation. The tools on offer by Google and other surveillance capitalist firms respond to the needs of beleaguered second modernity individuals—like the apple in the garden, once tasted they are impossible to live without. When Facebook crashed in some US cities for a few hours during the summer of 2014, many Americans called their local emergency services at 911. Google's tools are not the objects of a value exchange. They do not establish constructive producer-consumer reciprocities. Instead they are the 'hooks' that lure users into extractive operations and turn ordinary life into the daily renewal of a 21st-century Faustian pact. This social dependency is at the heart of the surveillance project. Powerful felt needs for effective life vie against the inclination to resist the surveillance project. This conflict produces a kind of psychic numbing that inures people to the realities of being tracked, parsed, mined, and modified—or disposes them to rationalize the situation in resigned cynicism. . . .

Nearly 70 years ago historian Karl Polanyi observed that the market economies of the 19th and 20th centuries depended upon three astonishing mental inventions that he called 'fictions.' The first was that human life can be subordinated to market dynamics and be reborn as 'labor.' Second, nature can be subordinated and reborn as 'real estate.' Third, that exchange can be reborn as 'money.' . . .

With the new logic of accumulation that is surveillance capitalism, a fourth fictional commodity emerges as a dominant characteristic of market dynamics in the 21st century. Reality itself is undergoing the same kind of fictional metamorphosis as did persons, nature, and exchange. Now 'reality' is subjugated to commodification and monetization and reborn as 'behavior.' Data about the behaviors of bodies, minds, and things take their place in a universal real-time dynamic index of smart objects within an infinite global domain of wired things. This new phenomenon produces the possibility of modifying the behaviors of persons and things for profit and control. In the logic of surveillance capitalism there are no individuals, only the world-spanning organism and all the tiniest elements within it.

# SECTION 12

# PARTICIPATION AND SOCIAL MEDIA

////////////////////////////////////////////////////////////////////////////////////////////////////////////////////////

The advent of participatory media destabilizes top-down models of surveillance in fascinating and oftentimes fraught ways. Social media, in particular, challenge the dominant idea of institutional surveillance as centralized, bureaucratic monitoring and control of individuals. Certainly, centralized and opaque forms of organizational surveillance persist, as the architectures of social media platforms are designed to encourage users to produce data that can be harnessed for capitalist gain, but the practices of individuals using participatory media far exceed the data-collection imperatives of organizations.

This raises difficult and potentially transformative questions for the field of surveillance studies: Should peer- or lateral-surveillance (of individuals watching each other online) count as surveillance? If so, where are the control dynamics? Is control, governance, or behavior modification necessary for peer observation to be considered surveillant? How should we modify our explanatory frameworks to include the nuanced complexity of micro-level influence or the subtle production of social norms through social media interactions? Can surveillance be thought of as liberating or empowering? If so, under what conditions and for whom? When social media surveillance might simultaneously include capitalist data

extraction, exploitative "free labor" on the part of users, rewarding forms of social cohesion, empowering or playful expressions of individual identity, and monitoring by myriad actors (friends, parents, partners, employers, law enforcement agents, and more), how can one begin to evaluate the overall effects—or merits—of social media surveillance?

The excerpts in this section represent a range of responses to questions of this sort. Mark Andrejevic interrogates the ways in which participatory media encourage unreflective production of data on the part of users. Such data are clearly profitable for companies, but the deeper concern for him is that robust forms of democratic empowerment are ultimately foreclosed in the emergent media ecology he calls the "digital enclosure." Hille Koskela upends typical pronouncements that exposure makes one vulnerable to external influence or manipulation. Rather, for her, participatory media, such as home webcams, can be harnessed by actors to create forms of "empowering exhibitionism." Koskela argues that such media can be liberating, allowing individuals to experiment and craft new subjectivities apart from the dictates of others. Anders Albrechtslund likewise emphasizes the subjectivity-building potential of intentional sharing on the part of users. It is important to note that both Koskela and Albrechtslund are responding to what was largely a hegemonic construct at the time of their writing: that of hierarchical models of disempowering forms of surveillance. As the field adapted to the idea of simultaneous, multidirectional, and reinforcing surveillance affordances—particularly with regard to social media (cf. Trottier 2012)—scholars placed less stress on deconstructing hierarchical models, as these were no longer presumed to be the only valid ones.

While recognizing the problematic data-extraction design of social media platforms, Priscilla Regan and Valerie Steeves explore the possibility that the very surveillance functions of social media architectures might catalyze empowering experiences for users. Especially for teenage users, the self- and group-surveillance functions of social media platforms may encourage reflexive experimentation with self-presentation, along with the cultivation of social capital and political imaginaries, all of which are crucial for identity development. Finally, Alice Marwick also attends to peer-monitoring and intentional self-presentation on social media, but she seeks to reanimate analysis of power asymmetries, with a focus on the intimate relationships among users. Borrowing from Michel Foucault's metaphor of "capillaries of power," which operate on the micro-level of everyday practices, Marwick develops the concept of "social surveillance" to visibilize power dynamics in the exchanges among users and across networks. In an important difference with Koskela, rather than emphasizing information sharing as an expression of agential exhibitionism, Marwick perceives it as being motivated by relationships of trust and intimacy, but nonetheless reproductive of disciplinary social norms.

### REFERENCE

Trottier, Daniel. 2012. *Social Media as Surveillance: Rethinking Visibility in a Converging World.* Burlington, VT: Ashgate.

# 59

# MARK ANDREJEVIC

## THE WORK OF BEING WATCHED

### Interactive Media and the Exploitation of Self-Disclosure

Contrary to continued claims about media interactivity bringing about forms of em-powerment for individuals, Mark Andrejevic flags the inherently extractive and exploit-ative dimensions of emerging digital environments. He provocatively characterizes these environments as a "digital enclosure" that uses increasingly invisible surveillance processes to turn media participation into data that are captured and commodified by pri-vate companies.

\*\*\*

Some 15 years ago [in 1986], [Sut] Jhally and [Bill] Livant, inspired by the work of Dallas Smythe, argued that communication theory needed to take seriously the notion that audiences were working when they were watching television. This paper seeks to develop their argument a bit further—to update it, as it were, for an era of new-media interactivity—by highlighting the emerging significance of the work not just of watching, but of *being* watched. The two complement each other, insofar as the devel-opment of interactive media allows for the rationalization of viewing and consumption in general, thanks to devices like interactive television that watch us while we watch. In the era of "reality" TV, wherein networks are winning ratings battles by enlisting

people to submit their lives to comprehen-sive scrutiny, the claim that being watched is a form of value-generating labor ought not to be a particularly surprising one. We are not just facing a world in which a few se-lect members of the audience are entering the celebrity ranks and cashing in on their 15 minutes of fame, but one in which non-celebrities—the remaining viewers—are being recruited to participate in the labor of being watched to an unprecedented de-gree by subjecting the details of their daily lives to increasingly pervasive and compre-hensive forms of high-tech monitoring. Their viewing habits, their shopping habits, even their whereabouts are subject not just to monitoring but to inclusion in detailed marketing databases, thanks to the advent of computer-based forms of interactive media. . . .

As an alternative to the popular portrayal of the proliferation of corporate surveillance in terms of the incredible shrinking private sphere, this essay suggests an approach influenced by the concerns of political economy and the analysis of disciplinary panopticism. Conceived as a form of labor, the work of being watched can be critiqued in terms of power and differential access to both the means of surveillance and the benefits derived from their deployment. The operative question is not whether a particular conception of privacy has been violated but, rather: what are the relations that underwrite entry into a relationship of surveillance, and who profits from the work of being watched? . . .

Foucault's discussion of disciplinary surveillance offers an approach to the question of power that seems particularly relevant to the development of the online economy since it focuses not so much on the repressive force of panopticism, but its productive deployment. The potential of the online economy that has recently attracted so much speculation—both financial and cultural—is predicated in large part on the anticipated productivity of generalized network surveillance. The power in question is not the static domination of a sovereign Big Brother, but that of a self-stimulating incitement to productivity: the multiplication of desiring subjects and subjects' desires in accordance with the rationalization of consumption. In this context, the production of ever more refined and detailed categories of desiring subjectivities serves . . . as a site for the reiteration of existing conditions and relations of power.

The starting point for an analysis of surveillance as exploitation is the assertion that just as workplace monitoring contributes to the rationalization of production, so on-line surveillance contributes to the rationalization of consumption. The attempt to extend the monitoring reach of corporate managers via the internet serves to compel personal disclosure by replacing nonmonitored forms of consumption with monitored interactive transactions. . . .

The emerging model of the on-line economy is explicitly based on the strategy for rationalizing and disciplining the labor of viewing—and of consumption in general—so as to make it more productive. The goal is to replace mass marketing and production with customized programming, products, and marketing. . . . Viewed as a strategy for promoting consumption, niche marketing is not a demand-driven phenomenon, instigated by the sudden, inexplicable volatility of consumer preferences, but rather, as Harvey suggests, a supply-side response to the saturation of the mass market.

In the media market, as well as in other segments of the economy, the promise of interactive communication technologies is to surpass the structural limitations that prevented the exploitation of increasingly compact market niches. If the advent of cable television allowed for market segmentation up to a point, the development of digital delivery allows for its extension down to the level of the individual viewer. Bill Gates, for example, anticipates a world in which not just the timing and choice of programs will be customized, but in which the content and the advertising can be adapted to viewer preferences, allowing individuals to choose the type of ending they want, the setting of the movie, and even the stars (who can be "customized" thanks to digitization). Similarly, customized advertising would ensure that every ad is tailored to the demographics of its recipient. A similar logic could be extended to products other than media programming. For example, computerization, according to Gates, will allow "Increasing numbers of products— from shoes to chairs, from newspapers and magazines to music albums" to be "created on the spot to match the exact specifications of a particular person." . . .

The attempt to develop increasingly customized programming and products foregrounds the economic importance of what might be described as the 21st century digital confessional: an incitement to self-disclosure as a form of self-expression and individuation. Interactive (cybernetic) media promote this self-disclosure insofar as they offer the potential to integrate the labor of watching with that of *being* watched. The cybernetic economy thus anticipates the productivity of a digital form of disciplinary panopticism, predicated not just on the monitoring gaze, but on the vast array of digital data made available by interactive and convergent communication technologies. . . .

The current deployment of the Internet for e-commerce may be viewed as an attempt to achieve in the realm of consumption what the enclosure movement achieved in the realm of production: an inducement to enter into a relationship of surveillance-based rationalization. The process of digital enclosure can be defined, in these terms, as the process whereby activities formerly carried out beyond the monitoring capacity of the Internet are enfolded into its virtual space. . . . [E]ntrance into what I call the digital enclosure is often voluntary (at least for the moment), but . . . consumers are compelled to go on-line for an increasing array of transactions by "the tyranny of convenience." The current trend suggests that over time, alternatives to this "tyranny" may be increasingly foreclosed. The result is that consumption and leisure behaviors will increasingly migrate into virtual spaces where they can double as a form of commodity-generating labor. If the latest work of a popular author or musical group is available *only* on-line, consumers are compelled to enter a virtual space within which very detailed forms of surveillance can take place. Electronic databases can keep track not only of who is reading or listening to what, but when and where.

The exploitation of the labor of being watched is thus crucially reliant upon public acceptance of the penetration of digital surveillance into the realm of "free" time. . . . [I]t is worth investigating the extent to which the celebration of the progressive potential of interactivity in some strands of media theory helps to promote the advantages of entry into the digital enclosure. The more we view this enclosure as a site for the potential revitalization of community and democracy, the more inviting it appears. Similarly . . . the celebration of the information age as a post-industrial resolution to the depredations of industrial society helps background the fundamental continuity of the "information era" with the exploitative relations of industrial capitalism. My intent is not to dismiss the progressive potential of interactive media outright, but rather to note how neatly their uncritical promotion lines up with the interests of those who would deploy the interactive capability of new media to exploit the work of being watched. . . .

Rumors of the death of privacy in the 21st century have been greatly exaggerated. The increasingly important role of on-line surveillance in the digital economy should be construed not as the disappearance of privacy per se, but as a shift in control over personal information from individuals to *private* corporations. The information in question—behavioral habits, consumption preferences, and so on—is emphatically not being publicized. It is, rather, being aggregated into proprietary commodities, whose economic value is dependent, at least in part, upon the fact that they are privately owned. . . .

Of central interest from a critical perspective, therefore, is the extent to which the marketers of the digital revolution continue to base its appeal upon the interpellation of an "active," empowered consumer.

As consumers start to realize that their activity feels more like labor (filling out online surveys, taking the time to "design" customized products and services) and less like empowerment, it is likely that the explicit appeal to shared control will be replaced by the emerging trend toward automated, autonomous forms of "convenient" monitoring. This is the direction anticipated by futurists like [Nicholas] Negroponte and the planners behind the MIT "Project Oxygen," whose goal is to make computers as invisible and ubiquitous as air. Their approach represents a retreat from the version of the "active" consumer associated with explicitly participatory forms of data gathering that characterized some of the early experiments in interactivity (the "design your own sneaker" or "write a review of this book" approach). Instead, the goal is the proliferation of an increasingly invisible, automated, and autonomous network. The agency of the active consumer is displaced onto what Negroponte calls "the digital butler." Interactivity will likely be increasingly reformulated as inter-*passivity* insofar as the goal is to make the monitoring process as unobtrusive as possible. The call to "action" will be displaced onto the ubiquitous technology, whose autonomy is designed to replace that of the consumer/viewer. Perhaps an early incarnation of this unobtrusive form of monitoring is the browser "cookie." Designed to increase convenience by allowing a site to remember a particular visitor so that customized settings don't have to be reconfigured, the "cookie" doubles as a digital butler for marketers, providing detailed browsing information about online consumers. It is hard not to imagine that the same would be true of other forms of digital butlers, whose allegiance remains rather more ambiguous than Negroponte implies. As these services become increasingly invisible and fade into the background, the increasingly monitored and transparent consumer comes to the fore.

In the face of the emergence of increasingly ubiquitous and invisible forms of monitoring, the appeal to privacy is often enlisted as a form of resistance. This type of resistance is rendered problematic by the fact that what is taking place—despite the recurring claim that the end of privacy is upon us—is the extensive *appropriation* of personal information. More information than ever before is being privatized as it is collected and aggregated so that it can be resold as a commodity or incorporated into the development of customized commodities. The enclosure and monopolization of this information reinforces power asymmetries in two ways: by concentrating control over the resources available for the production of subjects' desires and desiring subjects, and by the imposition of a comprehensive panoptic regime. The digital enclosure has the potential to become what [Anthony] Giddens, following [Erving] Goffman, terms a "total institution." The good news, perhaps, is that once the red-herring of the "death" of privacy is debunked, the enclosure of personal information can be properly addressed as a form of exploitation predicated on unequal access to the means of data collection, storage, and manipulation.

# 60

# HILLE KOSKELA

## WEBCAMS, TV SHOWS, AND MOBILE PHONES

### Empowering Exhibitionism

The near ubiquity of mobile-phone and computer-based recording devices raises important questions about what counts as surveillance and what the possibilities are for empowerment through surveillance. In this excerpt, Hille Koskela challenges conventional understandings of exposure as necessarily implying a loss of control. She explores the empowering potential of voluntary performances of visibility, for instance, through the use of home computer webcams.

***

There is some voyeuristic fascination in looking, but, reciprocally, some exhibitionist fascination in being seen. While being under surveillance is unpleasant for some, others are eager to increase their visibility. No longer is surveillance necessarily interpreted as a threat but rather "as a chance to display oneself under the gaze of the camera." The panoptic principle is "turned into the pleasure principle." The popularity of webcams demonstrates this clearly. . . .

While, as argued, in the televisualisation of human lives individuals increasingly "disappear," the home webcams can be interpreted as a form of "bringing back" the subject. In contrast of being targets of the

ever-increasing surveillance, people seek to play an active role in the endless production of visual representations. Their shows include a "notion of self-ownership." They seek to be subjects rather than objects. In other words, it can be claimed that what they actually do is *reclaim the copyright of their own lives*. The logic is simple: if practically anyone else can circulate one's images, why not do it oneself.

The choice to present one's private life publicly can be understood as a form of *exhibitionism*. In most cultures it is considered "normal" that you do obscuring gestures in order to protect your private life. You close the curtains when it's dark outside and light inside. You don't appear publicly if

314 SURVEILLANCE STUDIES: A READER

naked or in underwear. You don't allow anyone to see your sex life, unless you want to make pornography. In this respect it is a radical act to install a camera that shows your private life to an unknown audience. This, however, raises a question about how we understand exhibitionism? If installing a home webcam is exhibitionism, is it automatically a form of sexual perversion? Or is it possible to understand exhibitionism as a positive term? Could we reclaim the term, redefine it and de-sexualise it? Could it be cultural critique? Or perhaps an emancipatory action?

One of the first, most famous and also most examined . . . cameras has been the *JenniCAM* by Jennifer Ringley. In 1996 she installed a camera in her college dormitory room continuing her ordinary daily life under the gazes of the global audience in the Internet. While inviting the gaze of the world into her private space, she conducted her everyday tasks, did her aerobic exercises, celebrated her birthdays—and also, occasionally, had sex. This ostensibly minor change in the conventional code of what can and what cannot be shown hit deeply in the collective cultural understanding of looking and being looked at. . . . Jenni created a paradoxical stage, playing with conventional moral codes, in which she "stabilizes and yet disrupts the process of subject formation by repeating yet resisting cultural norms."

After keeping up the camera for a while Jenni received threats—more precisely, was demanded to "pose" at particular time for one of her net-admirers. In one sense her "show" was a way of creating a subject capable of resisting the traditional readings of female embodiment, however, at the same time it "would seem to offer the perfect heterosexual male fantasy." The harassment she faced was a form of cyberstalking. She closed the camera for a while, but then eventually put it back again. When she was asked *why* she chose to reinstall the camera she replied "I felt lonely without the camera." I find this statement striking. It places the camera into a position of a companion, or perhaps a pet. Or perhaps a part of Jenni herself? The camera can be interpreted as a component in an integration of body and technology, an object embedded in a "cyborg subjectivity" where the corporeal and the mechanic fuse into each other forming an entirety. . . .

I use [Jennifer Ringley] as an example of what is happening in the field of vision. She is a particular case, indeed, but she is a pioneer rather than an exception. . . .

Jenni's story made me think about something that could be called *"empowering exhibitionism."* With the cameras Jenni and others like her discuss with two fundamental regimes through which power operates. I shall call these the *regime of order* and the *regime of shame*. These can be understood as two common ways of thinking how visibility and transparency connote with power and control. By the regime of order, I mean the ways in which society regulates individuals. Gathering knowledge is seen as a form of maintaining control, a look equates with a "judgmental gaze." Everyday life is regulated, not only potential criminal acts. The regime of order was perhaps most clearly seen taking place in the former socialist countries but it also has its role in the capitalist world. . . . By the regime of shame I mean individuals' internalisation of control, in the Foucauldian sense. The idea of having or doing something that cannot be shown. The basic "need" for privacy. The regime of shame keeps people meek and obedient as efficiently as any control coming from outside. Rejecting it is unacceptable and immodest. Further, these controls coming from outside and from inside are most effective when functioning together: the combination of fear and shame ensures submissiveness.

Indeed, home webcams challenge these both. By revealing their private intimate lives individuals refuse to take part in these two regimes. If this is exhibitionism that succeeds in overcoming these two, then exhibitionism can truly work as a form of empowerment. The liberation from shame and from the "need" to hide leads to empowerment. Conceptually, when you show "everything" you become 'free': no one can "capture" you any more, since *there is nothing left to capture*. . . . Home webcams seem to be opening up *radically new subjectivities*. . . . Webcams aiming at increasing visibility rather than hiding from surveillance, can be interpreted as a form of confrontation, surveillance turned into spectacle—a form of resistance. . . .

[T]he idea of empowering exhibitionism goes quite far from the original idea of video surveillance. Why might this theme be interesting to the researchers of video surveillance? Would this have any conclusions that would be valid in "traditional surveillance" or helpful in understanding it? The reason I find home webcams interesting is the notion that they *contest* some of the conventional connections of power. First, the connection between visibility and power. Second, the idea of internalisation of control, as already mentioned. And third, the connection between power and control.

Much of the discussion around the new forms of surveillance has focused on power. . . . The traditional idea of power places those who *can see* in the position of being powerful—more powerful than those who *are seen*. This applies, I would claim, also to the Foucauldian idea of power as not possessed or exchanged but rather, exercised. The control of individuals is claimed to be the more efficient the more willing they are to submit to the overseeing gaze, the more willing they are to make themselves transparent.

Home webcams challenge this conventional conception of visibility connecting with power. People deliberately make themselves visible, but it does not follow that they would be in a position where the "automatic functioning of power" is assured. To be (more) seen is not to be less powerful. Rather, quite the opposite. The practice of presenting oneself

to the global audience "muddies our understanding of the power of watching and the privilege of sight." Exhibitionism *plays* with visibility. . . . Second, being constantly conscious of being watched by invisible overseers is supposed to lead to *internalisation of control*. The feeling of "being watched" is not depending on someone looking. People internalise the rules, regulate their own behaviour even when it is not necessary and, thus, exercise power over themselves. . . .

Home webcams challenge this understanding, too. By presenting intimate pictures of private life, their owners . . . rebel against the modesty and shame embedded in the conception of the private. They may be "normal" in some sense but they are also automatically outside some of the conventional notions of normal, exactly because of their cameras. They *refuse to be humble* which, to my opinion, is the most interesting point in the whole phenomenon. . . .

Third, home webcam owners may gain power with their cameras, by being able to overcome the regimes of order and shame, but this form of power does not head for control over others. *Power and control are not synonyms* although we easily slip to think so. The difference between these two concepts has largely been ignored in the surveillance discussion. If we think about the distinction between dominating power and resisting power, it becomes clear that not all forms of power seek for control. The empowering role of home webcams shows that there is a possibility to gain power without gaining control. Home webcams clearly break the old power relations but their purpose is not to increase control but rather to blur and mix the lines of control. They permit many interpretations, and thus, "communicate" with viewers rather than aiming to restrain them. . . .

Finally, it must be said that in practice most home webcams are extremely mundane. . . . When looking at these webcams it is difficult to see a slightest sign of resistance.

However, the point that I want to make is not that the actual pictures would show resistance. The question is not about political activism in traditional sense but about *revealing as a political act*—intrinsically. . . .

What, however, remains unanswered thus far is what makes the difference between being and not being "empowering?" I have argued that some features in the function of home webcams make them empowering. Nevertheless, what are the fundamental differences to suppressing (public space) surveillance cams remains unclear. It cannot be about who is looking: after all, when people present their private lives in the Internet the point is exactly that anyone, literally, can be looking. It cannot be about whether or not one is looked at in the first place, because the idea of empowerment is not depending of the act of looking/seeing but the act of presenting. It cannot be depending on the equipment used: the quality of both private and public cameras can vary a lot without making a significant difference to the social practices. And, it cannot be about the fact that presenting is

voluntary since one can very well be voluntarily in public space under surveillance but the deed remains without an empowering dimension.

One, but thus far very partial, answer is the role of *agency*. . . . Webcams . . . clearly support agency. What, how and when is presented is controlled by the person(s) whose images are circulated. How these pictures will be subsequently used, runs out of control. This, however, is precisely the point of the phenomenon: to reject the regime of shame means rejecting the traditional understanding of objectification. Mobile phones, although they can be used for tracking and controlling people, also seem to support active agency. From the users' perspective, shooting pictures with them just adds another function. . . . [When] it comes to the "alternative" image production loaded with resistance, mobile phone cameras clearly have their potential. Nevertheless, they obviously can be used for repressive purposes as easily as for empowering purposes. What roles may become the most important ones is a challenge for future research.

# 61

# ANDERS ALBRECHTSLUND

# ONLINE SOCIAL NETWORKING AS PARTICIPATORY SURVEILLANCE

As with some of the other excerpts in this section, Anders Albrechtslund seeks to challenge what he sees as a hegemonic, hierarchical conception of surveillance. Social media participation, he argues, should not be reduced analytically to forms of information extraction and social control. Rather, the concept of "participatory surveillance" directs attention to intentional sharing practices that can be both subjectivity building and empowering.

***

Looking at discourses in the context of online social networking and related Web 2.0 services and applications, a traditional and rather negative conception of surveillance appears. Surveillance is associated with snooping, spying and privacy invasion, and it is a prevalent view that everything related to it should be avoided if possible. This is in line with familiar frameworks such as Big Brother and Panopticon, but the problem is that they do not seem to adequately describe the actual practice of online social networking.

In the following I suggest using the concept of *participatory surveillance* to develop the social and playful aspects surveillance. . . .

## The hierarchical, vertical concept of surveillance

A conventional understanding of surveillance is that it is a hierarchical system of power. This common understanding is represented in familiar metaphors such as "Big Brother" and "Panopticon," both of which illustrate a vertical, hierarchical power relation between the gaze of the watcher that controls the watched. The hierarchical conception of this relation puts the power into the hands of the watcher while the watched is a more or less passive subject of control. In the case of hierarchies in the Orwellian sense, surveillance is also part of the destruction of subjectivity under surveillance and an effort to render life-world meaningless.

The moral panics, conspiracy theories and the difficulties in understanding why people actually would want to engage in online social networking all reflect this dystopian view on surveillance. It is the basis for the discourses of protection and education as well as for the idea that users are either performing cost-benefit analyses before creating an account on a social networking site or simply do not know enough about the lurking dangers of surveillance. In other words, it is difficult to understand the phenomenon of online social networking and related Web 2.0 services and applications when we apply this notion of surveillance.

Although the Panopticon was more or less disregarded after Bentham until Michel Foucault's *Surveiller et punir: Naissance de la prison*, apart from a few notable exceptions, it has since been the dominating conceptual framework within surveillance studies. Interestingly, students of surveillance have often tried to go beyond the Panopticon, and a number of different concepts have been introduced, *e.g.*, the *electronic panopticon* and *superpanopticon* where computerized databases are discussed as a technologically enhanced realization of the Panopticon that encompasses cultural innovations brought about by databases.

However, it still seems that writing and talking about going beyond the Panopticon—rather than actually doing it—is the case, as indicated in the recent book edited by David Lyon entitled *Theorizing surveillance: The panopticon and beyond*. In it, Lyon laconically states "[t]he panopticon refuses to go away."

The panopticon model is indeed a strong framework for discussing surveillance theoretically, and in many cases it is a fitting one. Therefore, I am not suggesting a change of directions or something similar within surveillance studies, but rather an expansion of the field of study. The many excellent theoretical, conceptual and methodological approaches are useful and necessary point of departures for any student of surveillance—and in the context of online social networking. However, if we want to better understand this and other related practices, it is necessary to challenge the hierarchical conception of surveillance.

## Surveillance as a mutual, horizontal practice

The word *surveillance* is etymologically associated with the French word *surveiller*, which translates simply as *to watch over*. The verb suggests the visual practice of a person looking carefully at someone or something from above. Both in ordinary language and within academic debate, the practice of "watching over" has become a metaphor for all other monitoring activities. Thus, the understanding of surveillance is not limited to a visual practice; rather it involves all senses—data collection and technological mediation.

The visual metaphor implies a spatial hierarchy where the watcher is positioned *over* the watched. Yet, this does not mean surveillance is necessarily a hierarchical power relation in which the watcher controls the watched. Similar to the broadening of the concept to include all senses, data collection and technological mediation, surveillance can be seen as a "flat" relationship or even in favor of the person under surveillance, either negatively as actively resisting the gaze or positively as exhibitionistic empowerment.

Further, the surveillance relationship can be mutual, as described by Mark Andrejevic who has introduced the concept *lateral surveillance*:

> Lateral surveillance, or peer-to-peer monitoring, understood as the use

of surveillance tools by individuals, rather than by agents of institutions public or private, to keep track of one another, covers (but is not limited to) three main categories: romantic interests, family, and friends or acquaintances.

Although Andrejevic does not directly make the connection, lateral surveillance seems like a useful concept to throw light on certain aspects of online social networking. However, Andrejevic brings over the power relations from the Panopticon to the peer-to-peer monitoring, arguing that these technologies actually amplify the top-down monitoring. As a consequence, law enforcement technologies are brought into social life:

> The participatory injunction of the interactive revolution extends monitoring techniques from the cloistered offices of the Pentagon to the everyday spaces of our homes and offices, from law enforcement and espionage to dating, parenting, and social life. In an era in which everyone is to be considered potentially suspect, we are invited to become spies—for our own good.

In other words, lateral surveillance makes us spies in a disciplinary society.

Although lateral surveillance is an interesting and thought-provoking concept, it does not adequately explain the practice of online social networking as described . . . above. However, I would like to hold on to the idea of surveillance being a mutual practice, as it corresponds to some of the characteristics of online social networking. I will replace the vertical relation with a horizontal, which makes it possible to understand some of the positive aspects of being under (mutual) surveillance.

## Empowerment, subjectivity building and sharing

In the following, I will call attention to two aspects of surveillance in the context of online social networking which are missing or underdeveloped in the previously discussed concepts. These are the idea of user empowerment and the building of subjectivity, and, second, the understanding of online social networking as a sharing practice instead of an information trade. Together, these two aspects, along with mutuality, makes up what I call participatory surveillance.

As mentioned earlier, a hierarchical conception of surveillance represents a power relation which is in favor of the person doing the surveillance. The person under surveillance is reduced to a powerless, passive subject under the control of the "gaze." When we look at online social networking and the idea of mutuality, it appears that this practice is not about destructing subjectivity or lifeworld. Rather, this surveillance practice can be part of the *building* of subjectivity and of making sense in the lifeworld.

An illustrative example is Hille Koskela's discussion of the use of webcams, TV shows and mobile phones. She introduces the concept *empowering exhibitionism* to describe the practice of revealing your (very) personal life. By exhibiting their lives, people claim "copyright" to their own lives, as they engage in the self-construction of identity. This reverts the vertical power relation, as visibility becomes a tool of power that can be used to rebel against the shame associated with not being private about certain things. Thus, exhibitionism is liberating, because it represents a refusal to be humble.

Online social networking can also be empowering for the user, as the monitoring and registration facilitates new ways of constructing identity, meeting friends and colleagues as well as socializing with strangers. This changes the role of the user from passive to active, since surveillance in this context offers opportunities to take action, seek information and communicate. Online social networking therefore illustrates that surveillance—as a mutual, empowering and subjectivity building practice—is fundamentally social.

Turning to the second aspect—from trading to sharing—it is expedient to elaborate on the concept of participation. To participate is to engage in something, but it is not necessarily something we do out of individual desire or pleasure. Examples could be found in all contexts of life, including work-related situations and charity efforts. However, participation as an engaging act is voluntary and must be well-defined in relation to the pseudo-participation we know from the Panopticon and Orwell's *Nineteen Eighty-Four*.

The Panopticon is set up in a way for the prisoners to take part in their own surveillance by internalizing the gaze of the watcher, and in Orwell's novel the citizens of Oceania end up taking part in their own (and others') surveillance in their "love" of Big Brother. Here, the self-surveillance is inflicted on the people watched, as they are caught up in a power relation or as a result of the brainwashing carried out by the Ministry of Love. Both of these disciplinary practices disempower and, thus, disengage the subject of surveillance. Therefore, concepts such as *participatory panopticon* are contradictory or, at best, redundant, if the internalizing of the gaze is interpreted as a form of pseudo-participation.

The practice of online social networking can be seen as empowering, as it is a way to voluntarily engage with other people and construct identities, and it can thus be described as participatory. It is important to not automatically assume that the personal information and communication, which online social networking is based on, is only a commodity for trading. Implicit in this interpretation is that to be under surveillance

is undesirable. However, to participate in online social networking is also about the act of sharing yourself—or your constructed identity—with others.

Accordingly, the role of sharing should not be underestimated, as the personal information people share—profiles, activities, beliefs, whereabouts, status, preferences, etc.—represent a level of communication that neither has to be told, nor has to be asked for. It is just "out there", untold and unasked, but something that is part of the socializing in mediated publics. One of the findings in the earlier mentioned Pew Internet & American Life Project report is that a great majority of teens use online social networking to keep in touch with friends they rarely see in real life. In this case, participatory surveillance is a way of maintaining friendships by checking up on information other people share. Such a friendship might seem shallow, but it is a convenient way of keeping in touch with a large circle of friends, which can be more difficult to handle offline without updated personal information—untold and unasked. . . .

I have tried to shed light on the social aspect of surveillance, as a form of participatory surveillance involving mutuality, empowerment and sharing. It should be stressed that my intention is not to belittle the potential dangers of surveillance on the Web. There are many threats, ranging from privacy invasion and social sorting to fraud and identity theft. Precautions must be taken to avoid these dangers.

My point is that we should not let the awareness of these threats take over when we study online social networking. When we study the actual practice, we should not be "lured" into only seeing the dangers in things. Rather, online social networking is an opportunity to rethink the concept of surveillance.

# 62

# PRISCILLA REGAN AND VALERIE STEEVES

## KIDS R US

### Online Social Networking and the Potential for Empowerment

Social media architectures may be intentionally designed to extract data from users, but their surveillance capacities might also, perhaps unwittingly, afford forms of empowerment. Priscilla Regan and Valerie Steeves carefully explore this thesis in the context of youth participation with social media. As a vital part of identity development, young people experiment with self-presentation and cultivate social capital through the nodal, multidirectional forms of surveillance that social media offer. Although top-down surveillance may still constrain or attenuate this potential, that too can become a target for empowering forms of political mobilization.

***

The bulk of writing and theorizing on surveillance adopts the perspective of what we term "one-way" surveillance where the more powerful, often the state or business organizations, watch others for purposes of control. . . . Within this perspective, some have argued that there might be a benign form of this surveillance for purposes not of outright control but of care. We would argue that care, or paternalistic, surveillance contains only a limited possibility for empowerment of the targeted individuals. For example, it may enable them to do something that they otherwise could not do, such as the elderly remaining in their home. However, the subjects of care surveillance are dependent on the surveillance and they are dependent on the operators of the surveillance—thus their empowerment is dependent and not reciprocal.

To identify the possibilities for, and the nature of, empowerment in a surveillance setting it may be more important to explore "two-way" surveillance, where there is reciprocal watching with your watching "known others" and the "known others" watching you. Mark Andrejevic refers to this as "peer-to-peer" or "lateral" surveillance and

Anders Albrechtslund refers to it as "participatory surveillance." Andrejevic sees this not in an empowering way but within the context of the war on terror and the risk society where the citizen is willingly co-opted into surveillance practices because of the "participatory promise of the market"—people learn to maximize their personal relationships by incorporating the market values of efficiency, enhanced productivity and risk reduction into social life. Reconstituting surveillance as a form of entertainment and self-expression thus becomes an important way to train people to participate on an online economy which is dependent upon the commodification of their personal information.

Social networking is based on the type of watching where individuals voluntarily reveal rather detailed information about themselves and their activities to "friends" on corporate-owned sites that seek to collect and use the information for commercial purposes. However, this "two-way" reciprocal surveillance may also offer a place where and tools with which participating individuals may empower themselves—in terms of aligning themselves with like-minded others for political or social purposes, and in terms of controlling, or at least contributing to, their identities and reputation. Albrechtslund sees this potential as well, suggesting that the building of subjectivity, the sharing practices, and mutuality in participatory surveillance open up the possibility of empowerment. . . .

However, there are at least two ways in which this "two-way" surveillance on social networking sites (SNS) compromises the possibilities of empowerment. First, the "friending" tool may provide individuals with more or less control depending on how the defaults are set. . . . Second, such information is still accessible to the corporation sponsoring the SNS and may also be accessible to "unknown others," such as future employers, educational institutions, and law enforcement authorities—and watching by such "unknown surveillance" would be part of the first "one-way" surveillance. . . .

This tension between the instrumental design of SNS and the users' social experiences and expectations is also seen in the context of a third form of surveillance as the self watching the self. This entails one's conscious monitoring of the presentation of the self allowing for the performance of identities with a reflection back to the subject. It is, in effect, identity play without another where the individual has opportunities to experiment with his/her identity, trying on different identities for a while and seeing how they fit with one's own conception of self or comfort level. This is especially important for adolescents who may use role-playing in games as a way of arriving at an identity. . . .

The surveillance encountered on SNS is therefore textured and multi-layered. Top-down surveillance is built into the sites by the corporations that own them, but, running counter to the trade-off model that would legitimate this surveillance, users are often unwilling to surrender their privacy in exchange for participation. Moreover, other forms of surveillance co-exist beside the top-down structures. Young people both watch and are watched by parents, teachers, employers and other adults within their social circle; they watch each other and themselves; they watch celebrities and appropriate and reconstitute the images of those celebrities for their own purposes in fan videos and fiction, and their videos and fiction are in turn appropriated by marketers involved in "cool hunting." Surveillance is accordingly less bilateral than it is nodal; users participate in a type of multi-directional surveillance in which the many watch the one watching the many, and in which the self watches the self. In this context, empowerment may occur in the interstitial spaces between the top-down constraints which have been engineered into the site itself, as young people interact with each other and with their online environment. . . .

We posit that there are four different models of the relationship between surveillance and empowerment in the context of young people on SNS. . . .

## Protest or Resistance Model

In general, research has shown that many teenagers are aware of the surveillance potential of websites and are less willing to give out their information. These teenagers tend to engage in several risk-reducing strategies such as falsifying information, providing incomplete information, or going to different websites that do not ask for personal information. . . . However, the corporate surveillance embedded on SNS works against this type of resistance. For example, Facebook's user agreement requires users to use their real name and contact information, and polices this requirement with algorithms that identify "fake" accounts so they can be deleted, in effect shutting out individuals who use aliases. . . .

However, one of the interesting aspects of SNS is the ability of users to organize and "talk back" to those in power. Facebook, again, is an interesting exemplar. There have been several instances of users— many of whom are teenagers and young adults—protesting about policies that they believe are surveillance-oriented in a way that decreases their control over the space and their activities on the space. This first occurred in 2006 when Facebook launched its News Feed feature whereby Facebook pushed information out to a user's friends without the user's involvement. . . . [S]ome users felt monitored in a way that made them uncomfortable, other users worried about stalking, and others were annoyed

at the amount of insignificant information they were receiving. Users started an online petition in opposition to News Feed which caused Facebook to modify the feature. . . .

## Social Capital Model

In general social capital is positive in that individuals are able to interact among others in a social network and a SNS is certainly a social network. SNS empower users to maintain existing social relationships, to find old friends and renew those relationships, and to establish new relationships. . . . Because of this, SNS can potentially empower the young people who populate them at the interpersonal level, by enabling them to establish and maintain relationships with other people. . . .

Surveillance is integral to obtaining empowerment under this model. In order to realize these social capital benefits, SNS members put themselves out there to be found, as well as monitoring what others put out there. Users thus surveil and are surveilled—and both activities can lead to stronger feelings of interconnection, in turn potentially leading to both personal empowerment (feelings of personal competence and growth) and group empowerment (greater feelings of self esteem and social belonging). . . .

## Identity/Self-Presentation Model

Within SNS youth find a space wherein they can shape and present themselves and, perhaps more importantly, where they can modify as they both see themselves in relation to others in their referent group and received feedback from that group. The self-surveillance and peer-surveillance are critical to the possibility of these empowering aspects of presenting oneself and forming an identity. Without the surveillance, the presentations would be one-way, without the feedback that is essential for there to be personal and group empowerment. . . .

## Performance Model

SNS offer youth a space in which they can perform for others and in this way try on different roles or behaviors for awhile without having to commit to that being part of their persona. . . . [T]he surveilled performance may offer them a setting in which they are empowered rather than controlled. . . . Members of the Facebook community use the website to build and enhance their social relationships through unique performances of online self, for which they invite the audience of their friends. Thus when users offer up themselves for surveillance in social networking sites, they do not do so passively. Rather, they set the boundaries, timing and form of their disclosure within the constraints of the Facebook architecture, in ways that may promote both personal and interpersonal empowerment. . . .

## Discussion/Implications

Our analysis . . . reveals that three features of the current organization of SNS, such as Facebook, act to constrain the ability of young people to use these sites in ways that would empower them. First, requiring authentic *self*-identification limits the possibility that young people will feel free to try on different identities, to join social groups whose purposes might be seen to conflict or whose members might be deemed unpopular by other groups, to engage in political speech or association, and to engage in behaviour for which there may be employment or law

enforcement repercussions. The *persistence of the identification* and record of the young person's actions and words further constrain the empowerment potential on these sites. Mistakes will not be forgotten, although they may well be forgiven at the time they occur, and are likely to be resurrected in a way that will not empower the older version of the younger person. Finally the *commercialization* of the sites is pervasive and cannot be ignored; on these sites one is always considered a consumer or potential consumer. . . .

But interestingly, our analysis also indicates that the architecture and the social character of SNS do allow for empowerment to emerge in what is otherwise a surveillance environment. . . . Our earlier examples about Facebook users forming Facebook groups to protest new privacy settings of new features illustrate this—the group feature of the Facebook architecture can be used to organize against Facebook policies. . . .

The inherently social character of SNS, which is reciprocal in nature, allows for the somewhat spontaneous, or at least uncontrolled from above, creation of or reconstitution of interstitial spaces where young people can engage with each other in ways they find to be empowering. . . .

This raises the question of whether or not the reconstituted space is created or enabled by the presence of surveillance in the first place—in other words, is surveillance empowering or do people push back to find empowerment that interrupts the original surveillance and makes it something else? It seems that young people do not change or challenge the surveillant capacities; instead, they act beside or within them. . . .

In conclusion, the surveillance that young people encounter on SNS is textured and multi-layered, and can best be understood by expanding the traditional top-down conceptualization of the panoptic gaze to take other forms of surveillance into account. Simple models that posit that young people willingly embrace surveillance in the context of a trade-off between privacy and social participation fail to account for the many ways in which they resist top-down institutional surveillance. Interestingly, it is the surveillance itself that empowers them to resist because it provides a channel through which they can collectively challenge institutional control. At the same time, the surveillance architectures on SNS are not merely uni-directional and they are not static. They are designed to be filled with social content and therefore the watching that occurs on these sites is reciprocal. The resultant visibility within and between social actors on these sites provides opportunities for young people to empower themselves by strengthening their social capital and experimenting with their self-presentation. However, the empowering potential of SNS continues to be constrained by competing corporate imperatives that seek to privilege top-down surveillance in order to mine and commodify young people's social world.

# 63

# ALICE E. MARWICK

## THE PUBLIC DOMAIN

Social Surveillance in Everyday Life

Social media present interesting challenges to traditional analyses of surveillance. If one looks at the practices of individuals using social media, rather than at the dataveillance operations of social media companies, an entirely different set of surveillance dynamics are apparent. In this excerpt, Alice Marwick develops the concept of "social surveillance" to describe the field of peer-based monitoring where the emphasis is not on vast power asymmetries but instead on subtle expressions of identity and negotiations of social relations.

\*\*\*

Typically, *surveillance* refers to an activity which enables the nation state, or capitalist formations like corporations, to manage a population. This conception of surveillance involves an asymmetry in which individuals are surveilled by structural entities, the balance of power overwhelmingly tipped in favor of the surveillor. However, individuals both comply with and resist surveillance, a dynamic referred to by Anthony Giddens as the "dialectic of control." For instance, accounts of "sousveillance" involve repurposing surveillance equipment to watch the watchers, whether by capturing video of police brutality at a Critical Mass event or tweeting about a protest march in Egypt. . . .

While both *surveillance* and *sousveillance* are good starting points with which to think about issues of power and privacy within social networks, they do not help us understand increasingly common situations in which people of relatively equal power are watching each other and acting on the information they find. While this behavior has existed throughout history, social media differs significantly from pre-digital interpersonal and mediated communication. Digital information is replicable, persistent, searchable, and scalable; it can be easily disseminated, copied, and accessed. In many communities, Facebook, with its 800 million users, is ubiquitous. Moreover, social media sites are commercial and incorporate capitalist logics, such as self-promotion and celebrity. As a result, social media users engage in self-conscious identity construction to manage impressions, taking the real and potential audience into account. The implications of enormous databases of consensually-provided information like Facebook and Twitter with their correspondingly large potential audiences are significant, and still developing.

Social surveillance clearly differs from traditional surveillance, to the point where some might question whether it is surveillance at all. . . . While surveillance is typically undertaken to manage, control, or influence a particular population, social surveillance leads to *self*-management and direction on the part of social media users. The internalization of the surveilled gaze—behavior modification as the result of being watched—can best be understood through the lens of surveillance studies. . . .

Social surveillance is the ongoing eavesdropping, investigation, gossip, and inquiry that constitutes information gathering by people about their peers, made salient by the social digitization normalized by social media. It encompasses using social media sites to broadcast information, survey content created by others, and regulating one's own content based on perceptions of the audience. It can exist either within a particular social media site (e.g. Facebook) or across a variety of sites (e.g. Twitter, YouTube, and Foursquare). Social surveillance can be distinguished from other types of surveillance by the following characteristics:

- *Power:* Social surveillance assumes a model of power flowing through all social relationships.
- *Hierarchy:* Social surveillance takes place between individuals, rather than between structural entities and individuals.
- *Reciprocity:* People who engage in social surveillance also produce online content that is surveilled by others.

## Power

In dualistic, judicial, or modernist notions of power, a large entity such as a government or corporation acts on a less-powerful actor. This hierarchical model of power is modeled after the right of the sovereign to impose his will onto his subjects, specifically the right to live or die. In this concept, power is something possessed by an authority that is "exerted over things" which can "modify, use, consume, or destroy." Michel Foucault proposed an alternate model of power as micro-level, decentralized and present in all human relationships. He theorized "capillaries of power" that flow between networks and individuals. In this model, power is ever-present, fluid, and at work in the mundane day-to-day activities that make up human life. For example, gender norms are determined not by a patriarchy seated around a table, but through millions of interpersonal moments in which "masculinity" or "femininity" is reinforced, policed, or resisted. In this model, the individual is part of a push-pull interaction in which power is negotiated.

In traditional models of surveillance, power flows from the surveyors (government or corporate actors) to the surveyed. . . . Clearly this concept does not wholly capture the dynamic in situations where individuals both have access to the same tools and are able to mutually watch each other, as in two "friends" on Facebook or Foursquare. Nathan Jurgenson and George Ritzer refer to this type of power as the "omniopticon," in which "the many watch the many." In social surveillance, social media sites are a type of capillary through which power flows not only from the site to users, but between users and across networks. Thus, while both forms of surveillance are intrinsically dependent on power relations, social surveillance incorporates the power differentials inherent in individual relationships.

## Hierarchy

Surveillance in its most commonly used form implies a significant power imbalance between the group gathering information and the group being watched. Typically, the group gathering information has *structural* or systemic power. This notion of extreme asymmetry does not capture the case of social surveillance, which is typically between peers of similar social status. However, Foucault's model of "capillaries of power" implies that power is constantly in flux between individuals. For instance, while we may idealize romantic relationships as egalitarian partnerships, at any one time one member of a couple may be wealthier, better looking, more or less jealous, in a bad mood, or far away—which can all affect the balance of power within a relationship. Although the consequences of these ebbs and flows are not the same as those between a corporation and an individual, or the state and an individual, they are no less significant to the individual. Indeed, individuals may care more about their relationships with romantic partners, family members, and close friends than they do about a nebulous corporate entity collecting personal information. Moreover, the use of the term "friends" to define connections on many social network sites flattens what may be very real power differentials based on social roles, such as boss/employee, teacher/student, or parent/child.

While traditional models of surveillance include individuals surveilled by hegemonic power structures or individuals surveilling structural entities in order to resist hegemonic power, social surveillance conceptualizes both sets of actors as individuals. This echoes the way social software flattens all relationships into a single category, and distinguishes social surveillance from other forms of surveillance that utilize social media. For instance, a Farmville-like game launched by a corporation in order to systemically gather information about people who play it does not constitute social surveillance, although the data-gathering takes place within Facebook. Rather, it falls into the category of "dataveillance" in that the corporation is an entity gathering information on individuals. Similarly, a government agent impersonating a Twitter user to investigate a drug deal does not constitute social surveillance, as the agent represents the state: the Federal Bureau of Investigation.

Social surveillance thus recognizes models of hierarchy that incorporate very real power differentials that exist beyond state/subject or corporation/consumer, based on social status, race, class, gender, social roles and so forth. While social surveillance exists between individuals, these individuals are not necessarily "equal" although they do not represent structural entities. Moreover, there are moments of slippage where a person's social role—as a parent, employee, or romantic partner—comes into unanticipated play. For instance, a Facebook user may complain about his work, forgetting that his boss is a "friend." This suggests that the division between "individual" and "entity" is not as distinct as traditional models of surveillance might have us believe. Taking social, rather than structural, hierarchy into account allows us to account for such complexity.

## Reciprocity

Social surveillance takes place between members of social media sites. People who use applications like Twitter and Facebook become part of a networked audience where participants both send and receive social information. As a user skims her Facebook feed, she may simultaneously read her friends' content, comment on it, and broadcast her own content to other people's feeds, using this information to improve her mental model of other people's identities, actions and relationships. Social surveillance thus indicates that those who practice it are simultaneously surveilled by others. This differs from the asymmetry present in social media sites when users are watched by powers that they cannot watch back, such as marketers or data-miners.

Although sharing information with others through social media is often framed as a form of exhibitionism, in reality, it is often motivated by trust and intimacy. Studies show that electronic communication is primarily used to reinforce pre-existing relationships, especially by young people. Social network sites, which require personal information, facilitate the maintenance of weak ties, strengthen friendships, and increase social capital and popularity. Many technologies, including social media, mobile phones, and instant messenger, are crucial to strengthening both individual and peer group relationships. Similarly, micro-blogging sites like Twitter encourage "digital intimacy," reinforcing connections and maintaining social bonds. Unlike user-generated content sites like YouTube or Wikipedia, where a small percentage of users create the majority of the content, social network users do not just watch: they broadcast.

Again returning to Foucault's model of *capillaries of power,* social surveillance explains how power is internalized and used for self-discipline and impression management. In social media sites, users monitor each other by consuming user-generated content, and in doing so formulate a view of what is normal, accepted, or unaccepted in the community, creating an internalized gaze that *contextualizes* appropriate behavior. Facebook users, for instance, imagine how readers will view their profile pictures and Wall posts and alter them accordingly. . . . Both broadcasting and monitoring are expected and normative parts of social media, and these processes reinforce each other. By looking at other people's content, people edit their own self-presentation accordingly.

# SECTION 13

# RESISTANCE AND OPPOSITION

///////////////////////////////////////////////////////////////////////////////////////////////////////////////////

Perhaps with the exceptions of national security or parents monitoring their children, the dominant public discourse surrounding surveillance is invariably negative. Surveillance is painted as an unwelcome intrusion, an inappropriate exercise of control, a tool of despotic or totalitarian regimes (i.e., "Orwellian") and therefore worth fighting. Because surveillance creates social orders, resistance is always a politically meaningful act, even if many of the actors involved do not see their practices as part of broader struggles. It is safe to say that when it comes to issues of surveillance, and especially state surveillance, strong affinities exist between academic and activist communities working to contest what are perceived to be abuses of power. When one adds to this the fact that many forms of resistance are incredibly creative and colorful, it is no surprise that scholars have been drawn to resistance as an area of study.

Given the myriad ways that people might challenge surveillance, it is analytically useful to differentiate between organized forms of *opposition* and improvised or ad-hoc techniques of *resistance*. John Gilliom explains, "By opposition, I refer to public efforts to block or significantly change policy. By resistance, I refer to quieter practices that seek to avoid, stymie, game, or otherwise manage a system" (Gilliom

2010: 201). Thus, when civil society groups such as the American Civil Liberties Union or the Electronic Frontier Foundation initiate public campaigns or file lawsuits on behalf of aggrieved parties, they are engaged in opposition. But when welfare recipients evade systems of surveillance by failing to report income, or people install ad-blocker programs on their web browsers, or drivers use radar detectors, they are engaged in forms of everyday resistance (Gilliom and Monahan 2012).

While the distinction between opposition and resistance is helpful, it may be more accurate to think of it as a continuum. For instance, Colin Bennett (excerpted in Chapter 64) writes of "privacy advocates" who may be engaged in formal opposition but who also often improvise and seem uncertain about how to build coalitions or create a broader social movement. Similarly, while "Cop Watch" groups may be loosely organized around shared practices and goals, as Laura Huey, Kevin Walby, and Aaron Doyle (excerpted in Chapter 65) explain, their politics are necessarily shaped by the often-unpredictable actions of police and activists, and the ubiquity of mobile phones has now moved most cop-watch practices from intentional opposition to unplanned moments of resistance when police abuse is witnessed (Simon 2012; Wall and Linnemann 2014; Wilson and Serisier

2010). In the artistic realm, a classic form of resistance by the Surveillance Camera Players (2006) involved the staging of public plays for video camera operators and effectively cast curious members of the public as unwitting actors in the spectacle of public surveillance contestation; yet even this form of resistance incorporated elements of opposition through careful planning, coordination, and media dissemination.

Ultimately, resistance and opposition hinge on power relations. As Michel Foucault (1978) observed, resistance and power exist symbiotically and co-constitute each other, implying that analyses of power must take into account forms of resistance that also contribute to the larger *dispositif*. In surveillance studies, countersurveillance serves as a zone of inquiry into these power dynamics, which manifest in symbolically expressive acts. Countersurveillance is defined as "intentional, tactical uses or disruptions of surveillance technologies to challenge institutional power asymmetries" (Monahan 2006). For instance, Finn Brunton and Helen Nissenbaum (excerpted in Chapter 66) describe techniques of obfuscation that intersperse false data amid accurate data, making identification and fine-grained classification much more difficult by dataveillance systems.

In a different vein, Steve Mann and colleagues (excerpted in Chapter 67) engage in performances that put institutional actors, such as convenience store employees, under surveillance by activist outsiders. Their goal is to spark critical self-reflection on the part of these employees and contest institutional surveillance more broadly. The technique deployed by Mann is that of *sousveillance*, or monitoring from below—turning the gaze back upon those in positions of authority. Such performance-based interventions raise a number of important questions, though. First, does not the very concept of sousveillance erroneously conflate one's status position with power? It

*One Nation under CCTV*, 2008, Banksy.

seems that the concept privileges the *direction* of the gaze over its *effect*. If surveillance is about the exercise of influence or control, then sousveillance (a view from below) would necessarily become surveillance at the moment that such influence or control were achieved, regardless of one's status position. Second, in such interventions, what are the ethics of relatively privileged, white scholars subjecting marginalized populations (e.g., African-American women working in low-wage service sector jobs) to intensified scrutiny and harassment? Is it fair, or even efficacious as a critical performance, to call such workers "totalitarianist officials," as Mann does, and treat them that way (Mann 2002)? Does this challenge or reinforce power asymmetries?

In Gary Marx's (2003) reflections on resistance to surveillance, he refers to surveillance neutralization as "an endless chess game" where each move invites another move by the adversary. Although it may seem that making any move is better than making none, there is the possibility that the adversary may simply learn to neutralize opposition more effectively. There are also lingering questions of privilege and social inequality, where activists and scholars might not accurately represent the interests or needs of the most vulnerable members of society. The excerpt by Torin Monahan challenges anti-surveillance camouflage on these grounds and questions what political opportunities might be lost when one celebrates a "right to hide" instead of seeking to challenge surveillance-facilitated discrimination and violence.

## REFERENCES

Foucault, Michel. 1978. *The History of Sexuality: An Introduction*. New York: Vintage.

Gilliom, John. 2010. Lying, Cheating, and Teaching to the Test: The Politics of Surveillance under No Child Left Behind. In *Schools under Surveillance: Cultures of Control in Public Education*, edited by T. Monahan and R. D. Torres, 194–209. New Brunswick, NJ: Rutgers University Press.

Gilliom, John, and Torin Monahan. 2012. Everyday Resistance. In *Routledge Handbook of Surveillance Studies*, edited by K. Ball, K. D. Haggerty, and D. Lyon, 405–11. London: Routledge.

Mann, Steve. 2002. "Reflectionism" and "Diffusionism." In *CTRL [Space]: Rhetorics of Surveillance from Bentham to Big Brother*, edited by T. Y. Levin, U. Frohne, and P. Weibel, 540–43. Cambridge, MA: MIT Press.

Marx, Gary T. 2003. A Tack in the Shoe: Neutralizing and Resisting the New Surveillance. *Journal of Social Issues* 59 (2):369–90.

Monahan, Torin. 2006. Counter-Surveillance as Political Intervention? *Social Semiotics* 16 (4):515–34.

Simon, Stephanie. 2012. Suspicious Encounters: Ordinary Preemption and the Securitization of Photography. *Security Dialogue* 43 (2):157–73.

Surveillance Camera Players. 2006. *We Know You Are Watching*. Factory School: Southpaw Culture.

Wall, Tyler, and Travis Linnemann. 2014. Staring Down the State: Police Power, Visual Economies, and the "War on Cameras." *Crime, Media, Culture* 10 (2):1–17.

Wilson, Dean, and Tanya Serisier. 2010. Video Activism and the Ambiguities of Counter-Surveillance. *Surveillance & Society* 8 (2):166–80.

# 64

# COLIN J. BENNETT

## THE PRIVACY ADVOCATES

Resisting the Spread of Surveillance

Throughout the world, there are civil society organizations, activists, and others fighting what they perceive to be threats to individual privacy rights. This excerpt stresses the importance of such work by "privacy advocates" and reflects on some of the obstacles to achieving a global social movement organized around privacy rights.

\*\*\*

In any one week, numerous media stories quote privacy advocates arguing this or protesting that. Privacy advocates are the people who, at least in journalistic parlance, challenge the development of the increasingly intrusive ways by which personal information is captured and processed: identity cards, video surveillance, biometric identifiers, the retention of communications traffic data, the use of cookies and spyware by Web sites, unsolicited marketing practices, data matching and profiling, the monitoring of employees in the workplace, the use of tracking devices in vehicles, the spread of radio frequency identification devices (RFIDs), and a host of other practices. There are a bewildering variety of ways that personal data can be captured, processed, and disseminated. Some people are deeply concerned about these trends and have been trying to do something about them. They tend to be identified as "privacy advocates."

The activities of civil society actors have tended to be marginalized in literature and by other actors in the policy community. Yet their activities are more important than people realize. . . . Further, they are becoming more visible and more important, partly because of online activism, but also in some respects because of the need to pull together in response to the increasing surveillance post-9/11. However, there is no concerted worldwide privacy movement that has anything like the scale, resources, or public recognition of organizations in the environmental, feminist, consumer protection, and human rights fields. In the privacy protection sector, there is a diverse, open-ended, and fluid range of groups and individuals, stretching from traditional civil liberties organizations, consumer associations, and groups established to promote freedom in cyberspace to more specialized groups involved with singles issues. When privacy conflicts arise, they tend to be waged by loose coalitions that come together for specific causes and then disband. . . .

There is a strong current of opinion in the privacy advocacy network that this issue is "different." However framed, it entails some peculiar properties that are never going to promote a broader political activism. . . . The first objection is that privacy always has to be "balanced" against a countervailing public interest that is typically more powerful. With few exceptions, there is always a justification for the capture and processing of personal information. National security arguments are invoked to justify the interception of communications. Safety is invoked to justify video surveillance. Equity is invoked to justify the collection of personal information for government services. The efficient conduct of marketing—"making sure the right people get targeted with the right ads"—is invoked to justify the collection and profiling of consumer data. The speedy and efficient access to Web sites is invoked to justify the logging of cookie technology on personal hard drives. The protection from fraud is invoked to justify the entire consumer credit industry. A desire for a productive and safe workplace is invoked to justify schemes for workplace monitoring. And even environmentalism can be invoked on occasion, for example, for the remote monitoring of home energy consumption or for the surveillance of vehicles as part of congestion charging schemes.

Privacy advocates have certainly had to struggle with a discourse that is often framed in terms of false dichotomies. They have also had to resist the very metaphor about "balancing" insisting that privacy protection is not incompatible with collective interests like security, efficiency, consumer satisfaction, and so on.

Nevertheless, there is nothing inherent in this problem that is not also manifested within other areas. Environmentalism, for example, faces arguments about the need to reconcile conservation against powerful arguments concerning the protection of productive capacity in economic sectors, be it logging, fishing, automobile manufacture, or the use of open space for governmental projects. Just because there is a battle over language and interest between advocates and powerful interests should not mean that a broader political activism is not possible.

A further argument, which also tends to be advanced in comparison with environmentalism, concerns the visibility of harm. Whereas it is possible to observe and measure the direct results of much environmental pollution, arguments against excessive levels of surveillance often have to be pitched in terms of abstract rights and fears of hypothetical consequences. To be sure, many horror stories about the inappropriate collection and use of personal information can be marshaled to the cause. However, as Philip Agre puts it: "With environmental pollution you can at least see the smoke and oily seabirds, but with invasions of privacy the information flows silently, out of sight, and then you can't figure out how they got your name, much less which opportunities never knocked because of the bad information in your file." It is true that much of the harm from privacy invasions is latent. Most individuals will therefore see the intrusive direct-marketing call, the denial of a loan, the refusal of insurance, the subjection to extra security screening at the airport, or the inaccurate tax return, and will not view these problems as privacy problems. Yet each could have been directly, or indirectly, caused by the collection and processing of inaccurate, obsolete, or incomplete personal data. The cause and effect are often hidden and circuitous. . . .

Academic research and social activism are not separate and discrete activities. The business of trying to change the way the world is run, is inherently "theoretical." Even though activists insist on their practical and down to earth approaches, they are always theorizing because they are always thinking about the underlying causes behind visible problems. They develop models of how the world works in order to change it. And they reflect deeply and consistently on how to build the kinds of organization that can make that change possible. By the same token, much of what academia treats as theoretical has been put on the agenda by social movements. There is a critical and a reflexive relationship between scholarship about and the actions of social movements. Privacy is no different . . . practice and scholarship are, and should be, inseparably intertwined.

At the same time, there is also an improvisational quality to contemporary activism. This book has also been testament to the unavoidable tendency among privacy advocates to "make things up as they go along." Some of the more traditional groups surely have more established modus operandi that produce some decision rules for campaigning. Most do not. The improvisational quality of contemporary privacy advocacy therefore means unpredictability, both for supporters and opponents. . . .

There is no agreement on whether a more cohesive movement is desirable, no agreement on what it should look like, no agreement on whether it is going to happen, no agreement on what it would do, and no agreement on the appropriate frame. No advocate has a comprehensive picture either of the issue or of the actors and groups involved. That is the nature of an open and horizontal network. No one participant has the overview. Thus, the reflections, while deep, considered, and grounded in "theory," are always shaped by personal lessons and perspectives. It is indeed striking how many advocates respond to larger questions about the network, the issue, and the movement in terms of the behaviors and characters of specific personalities.

There is also a tendency for advocates to define their positions in terms of optimism or pessimism about "the future." There are some who believe that the privacy argument will win out over those organizations who believe that they should be allowed to do whatever they wish with peoples' personal information. Chris Hoofnagle is optimistic, because of this: "I think one luxury for privacy advocates is that if you look at the issues, if you look at the facts, the privacy advocates have compelling arguments. I don't think advocates need to spin the situation. Ultimately, the privacy side is going to be more convincing." The optimists point to the greater number of privacy protection laws, the expanding policy community, the increasing fear of negative publicity that can arise from being labeled hostile to the issue, and the visible successes. . . . The "pessimists" point to the relentless set of forces, bureaucratic, corporate, political, and technological, which are increasingly aligned to produce more creative, extensive, and intrusive methods of surveillance. They despair at the cavalier way in which individuals, and especially young people, surrender their personal data without a second's thought.

I contend, however, the question of who is an optimist and who a pessimist is largely irrelevant, because there is no one trajectory by which we can measure the progress or regress of privacy protection at any one time. The variety of issues, the multiple ways in which the problem is framed, and the bewildering variety of organizational and national contexts in which it arises mean that it is misleading to derive simplified conclusions about the state of the issue. As we have concluded elsewhere, "the governance of privacy in the global economy through such multiple modes of regulation and coordination means that it is thoroughly misleading to try to observe a balance between privacy and surveillance on a global scale." It is this pluralism of issues, institutions, contexts, and actors that explain why different advocates can observe progress and regress at the same time. . . .

Even though privacy advocates may feel that they are engaging in a continual game of "whack a mole," hitting down one challenge only to find others immediately cropping up, there is much to be celebrated from this history. But the future of this network lies not in emulating other social movements, nor in waiting for the great privacy Armageddon. It lies in the persistent, relentless, and informed articulation of the very simple proposition that individuals have a right to control the information that relates to them. Few would deny this right. Everybody wants it for themselves. The cause is a just one. The issue is not going to disappear, and neither will the men and women who advocate it.

# 65

# LAURA HUEY, KEVIN WALBY, AND AARON DOYLE

## COP WATCHING IN THE DOWNTOWN EASTSIDE

Exploring the Use of (Counter)Surveillance as a Tool of Resistance

As committed as scholars and activists might be to correcting abuses of power, it is worth asking whether countersurveillance tactics might aggravate vulnerabilities or reproduce systems of exclusion. In this excerpt, the authors draw upon qualitative research on a Cop Watch program in Vancouver's Downtown Eastside neighborhood to complicate any easy conclusions about the program's value or effectiveness. Cop Watch programs could unintentionally catalyze harsher treatment of individuals by police, encroach on the privacy of local residents, and fail to represent the broader interests of the community.

\*\*\*

Monitoring by electronic and televisual means is an increasingly significant mode of governance. Surveillance, the collation and storage of information concerning a subject population and the direct supervision of that population's conduct, is usually conceptualized as an activity engaged in by elites for purposes of controlling subordinate social classes. Indeed, the usual understanding of the term *surveillance* is of an omnipresent, omnipotent, and centralized political apparatus keeping tabs on its citizens. In the present work, however, we are concerned with the more generalized, dispersed, and overlapping practices of social monitoring made possible by the proliferation of information and communication technologies in the early twenty-first century. The mass production of camcorders, cell phone cams, spy cams, and other monitoring and recording devices has, for better or for worse, put in the hands of anyone who can afford it the means of televisual surveillance.

This chapter is about the politics of surveillance and, more specifically, about the politics of resisting organizational forms of power through surveillance activities. We ask if it is possible or desirable to "reverse the gaze," so to speak. Our inquiry concerns the increasingly popular activity of "cop watching." In North America many volunteer-based Cop Watch groups have begun to organize for the purposes of "policing the police." . . .

Through the monitoring of on-duty police behavior, Cop Watch groups attempt to decrease police misconduct and brutality, which their members see as all too often directed against society's most vulnerable populations. These grassroots groups want police to be held accountable for their behavior, and they ultimately desire the realization of a reimagined relationship between police authorities and the communities they serve. Most Cop Watch groups are against all forms of oppression and are particularly concerned with racialized profiling. . . .

We analyze the Cop Watch phenomenon in light of two competing views of the use of surveillance. Cop Watch members see their work as promoting democratic accountability of a state institution that has tremendous power in the lives of marginalized citizens. This conceptualization of their work can be characterized as *sousveillance*—a term coined by Steve Mann to describe the use of surveillance technologies and tactics by the lower classes for the purposes of increasing equality through making public the hidden workings of powerful institutions and groups. The work of Gary Marx and other surveillance scholars, however, provides a second framework for assessing the Cop Watch phenomenon: as ultimately antidemocratic and thus as a reproduction of the hegemonic values that Cop Watch members claim to be at odds with. When the politics of resisting organizational forms of power through countersurveillance activities bump up against the complicated goings-on

associated with organizing dissent, the unintended result can be the undermining of democratic principles through the very means by which the movement intends to rescue them. . . .

In the summer of 2002, local activists in Vancouver's DTES [Downtown Eastside] founded a Cop Watch program. The articulated purpose of this program is as follows: "By observing, recording and documenting police abuses we hold them accountable and send a message that we will not tolerate the systematic harassment and routine physical assaults on poor and marginalized people which has unfortunately become a tool of the police trade." Modeling their activities on similar programs in the United States and Canada, Cop Watch volunteers organize street patrols to observe and document instances of perceived police violations of citizens' rights and of harassment and brutality and to help victims of abuse to complain about their treatment.

The basis of Cop Watch work is participation in "witnessing shifts." Witnessing shifts require volunteers to walk through the streets and alleys of the DTES, following police officers and recording police behaviors on Cop Watch forms or videotape. . . . While on patrols, volunteers observe police interactions with local residents from a distance of approximately twenty feet. Volunteers are advised not to interfere with police or to initiate or escalate any aggressive contact with police. . . . Witnesses who observe what they perceive to be abuses of police powers or authority fill out internal incident reports to document their findings. . . . Patrol volunteers carry "rights cards" and affidavit pamphlets. Rights cards, produced by a local legal activist organization, inform residents of their legal rights when dealing with the police. Individuals who wish to file a complaint concerning problematic police behavior, such as discriminatory treatment, verbal harassment, or physical abuse, can lodge a complaint with either the police department or the Office of the Police Complaint Commission. Members of the force's internal affairs division then investigate complaints. Affidavit pamphlets, however, advise residents on an alternative process: filing a complaint with an activist organization that promises to pursue complaints on the behalf of complainants. Formal complaints by citizens against police have quite an uneven history in general and in Vancouver in particular, which has led to extensive debate about whether it is appropriate for police to police themselves. . . .

Another possibility is for Cop Watch members to release videotaped footage to the news media, as with the Rodney King video and a number of lesser known examples. However, it is not simply the case that "seeing is believing" with home video of police activity, and there is often a complex politics of interpretation when it is given to the media. Even so, police pay close attention to the cameras as a potential source of trouble, as we discuss later. . . .

Some police officers have the view that the presence of Cop Watch cameras has an inverse effect on police performance from that desired by program participants. Cop Watch critics note that a number of the local organizations and individuals that support Cop Watch are also proponents of the decriminalization of narcotics. And yet it was felt by some of the officers interviewed that the presence of video cameras and documenting observers would make it *less*, rather than more, likely that they or other officers would be willing to exercise discretion in relation to offenses, including narcotics violations. For example, one officer noted:

The Cop Watch is ironic in itself because, if you see someone breaking the law, you can go, "If you leave the area, I'll just ignore the fact that I saw you doing something bad. But if I see you again, I'm going to have to arrest you." But if you have someone here with a video camera

following you around, as a police officer, for every little thing, you're going to get a ticket. . . .

Although Cop Watch members claim to represent their communities, many residents of Vancouver's DTES say that Cop Watch members do not represent them or their interests. Furthermore, some note that in keeping with the covert nature of their mission, Cop Watch leaders have not sought wider public input into their policies and practices or made those policies and practices publicly available. Critics also rightly note that no mechanisms for public oversight of Cop Watch's surveillance activities have been established. Thus the organization appears to be less than perfectly accountable to the community it claims to represent. Key questions thus become to what extent are the covertness and lack of public input necessarily bound up with the Cop Watch approach, and is Cop Watch simply a local phenomenon that could operate in a more publicly accountable and democratic fashion.

In interviews with DTES residents and community group members, we clearly see that the larger community is divided on the issue of Cop Watch and its tactics. . . . one area resident neatly summed the views of other critics within the community:

The people doing the Cop Watch, did they come down and ask if the seniors or the single moms down here wanted a Cop Watch? I'm sure the drug dealers would love a Cop Watch. That would be great. Are you actually talking to people who actually live here, versus people who are using this community to prey on addicts or to sell drugs?

The unintended result of Cop Watch's philanthropic activism could be the undermining of democratic principles through the very means by which they intended to save them. . . .

Although Cop Watch members and other proponents of sousveillance frame their work in democratic language, invoking concepts such as public accountability and formal and substantive equality to describe their activities, their critics offer an alternative means of conceptualizing their use of surveillance. Critics charge that, in effect, the Cop Watch program does little more than to reproduce the hegemonic values and strategies that its participants claim to resent. The flaw in the Cop Watch approach is that it speaks for the subject of police brutality (i.e., the homeless, the mentally ill, the underclass) instead of empowering the subject of police brutality to speak for herself, in effect forsaking an identity through the process of defending that identity.

The politics of countersurveillance cannot be divorced from the politics of collective action and activist organizing. The successes and failures of contentious political projects such as activism hinge in many ways on the enlisting of popular support. Enlisting such support requires the communicating of ideas and platforms to the public at large. The Cop Watch group in Vancouver has a paradoxical policy of not talking to the media about their ideas and activities. . . . The preference of the Cop Watch group in Vancouver to remain cloaked in secrecy is contradictory, however, because their mandate is public accountability and scrutiny of the police—on the grounds that the police ought not be permitted to operate in secrecy—and their antidemocratic organization disempowers the very people it purports to empower.

The particular usage of video surveillance equipment in cop watching activities also raises a number of interesting questions that might have implications for further activism in this field. Cop Watch members are not only watching over police but also more or less explicitly watching the people police come into contact with.

If a surveillance camera of any sort is used to televisually capture the events that unfold, both the police officer and the people police encounter could potentially be videotaped. . . . What happens with this information? Do Cop Watch groups have a method for the destruction of personal information? How can Cop Watch groups ensure that members of the public desire that they be watched over in such a way? What happens if police or a government agency subpoenas such a tape? Civil libertarians often raise questions about police-operated surveillance cameras in public spaces. Do the same questions about surveillance and public space apply to activists filming police interactions with local citizens on those same streets?

We by no means wish to be seen as apologists for the inexcusable behaviors that police officers sometimes engage in, but rather we suggest that the unintended consequences of using video surveillance equipment as a technique in cop watching must be weighed against potential benefits. When any form of surveillance, be it surveillance pursued by authoritative organizations or grassroots activist groups, is thought of in terms of concrete social practices instead of a priori assumptions about the relative goodness or badness of social monitoring, it is possible to raise a number of ethical questions about those surveillance and countersurveillance practices. The answers to these questions are best proposed and enacted by activist groups in their own locales. We add a caveat, however: resistance groups that employ countersurveillance tactics and technologies need to consider not only the necessity of garnering local support through a careful articulation of their political aims but moreover, in reflexive fashion, how their politics of resisting organizational forms of power through surveillance activities create ripples throughout the communities they work within.

# 66

# FINN BRUNTON AND HELEN NISSENBAUM

## VERNACULAR RESISTANCE TO DATA COLLECTION AND ANALYSIS

A Political Theory of Obfuscation

Data collection and analysis have become a big business. Through data, individuals are tracked, sorted, and controlled—typically in invisible ways. Increasingly, there are few viable options to evade such data collection without making material and social sacrifices (e.g., paying more for goods, being excluded from social networks). In this excerpt, Finn Brunton and Helen Nissenbaum propose techniques of "obfuscation" to resist dataveillance without accepting significant penalty.

*** 

We are constantly generating data and this data is not going away. It is subject to increasingly powerful tools of aggregation and analysis over time. . . . The most mundane points of contact with contemporary life involve the involuntary production of data on our part: passing security cameras, withdrawing cash, making purchases with a card, making phone calls, using transit (with a MetroCard or FasTrak tag, Oyster, Octopus, Suica, E-ZPass)—to say nothing of using the Internet, where every click and page may be logged and analyzed, explicitly providing data to the organizations on whose systems we interact. This data can be repackaged and sold, collected and sorted and acquired by a variety of means, and re-used for purposes of which we, the monitored, know nothing, much less endorse. . . . Multiple databases consolidated and cross-referenced, with incidental details linking previously disconnected bodies of information, produce a far more significant whole than any one part would suggest: identities, tendencies, groups and patterns with both historically revelatory and predictive power. . . .

One fundamental problem with the systems of personal digital data collection and analysis is asymmetry, or rather, two asymmetries. First, the asymmetry of power: rarely do we get to choose whether or not we are monitored, what happens to information about us, and what happens to us because of this information. We have little or no say when monitoring takes place in inappropriate contexts, and is shared inappropriately with inappropriate others. Second, equally important, is an epistemic asymmetry: we are often not fully aware of the monitoring, and do not know what will become of the information produced by that monitoring, nor where it will go and what can be done to it. . . .

If obfuscation is morally or politically problematic, why adopt it rather than relying on well-established mechanisms like user-opt-out, law, corporate best practice, and technology? . . . The steady rhetorical drumbeat in the discussion around data privacy is that refusal is a personal responsibility. If you're so offended by the way these companies collect and deploy your data, just don't use their services—*opt out*. No one is forcing you. To which we reply: yes and no. Many of these systems are not mandatory yet (government systems and various forms of insurance being just two exceptions), but the social and personal cost of refusal is already substantial, and growing. . . .

*Corporate best practice*. . . . Given the competitive disadvantage, any individual company going out on a limb risks losing the returns on customer, client, consumer, and even patient data. . . . Leaving it to the private sector to lead the way towards restraints on access to personal data, without at least some prodding, is like leaving it to the proverbial fox to guard the henhouse.

*Law and regulation*, historically, have been central bulwarks of personal privacy. . . . While our laws will likely be the eventual site of conversation in which we answer, as a society, hard questions about the harvesting and stockpiling of personal information, it operates slowly, and whatever momentum propels them in the direction of protecting privacy in the public interest it is amply counterweighted by opposing forces of vested corporate and other institutional, including governmental, interests. . . .

Finally, there is great interest among the technical, particularly research, community in *engineering systems* that "preserve" and "enhance" privacy, be it in data mining, surfing or searching the Web, or transmitting confidential information. . . . Tools offered to individuals directly, such as Tor and other proxy servers, are praiseworthy and valuable but the fact remains that they are not widely understood or deployed outside the relatively small circles of those who are already quite privacy-aware and technologically sophisticated. . . .

We are not questioning the ability of law, the private sector, and technology to provide relief to individuals from unfettered monitoring, gathering, mining, and profiling, only that the wait for relief from these sources is likely to be long. . . .

Obfuscation in its broadest and most general form offers a strategy for mitigating the impact of the cycle of monitoring, aggregation, analysis, and profiling, adding noise to an existing collection of data in order to make the collection more ambiguous, confusing, harder to use, and therefore less valuable. . . . Obfuscation, like data gathering, is a manifold strategy carried out for a variety of purposes, with a variety of methods and perpetrators. Obfuscators may band together and enlist others, or produce misleading information on their own; they might selectively respond to requests for information, or respond so excessively that their contribution skews the outcome. They may engage in obfuscation out of a simple desire to defend themselves against perceived dangers of aggregation, in resentment of the obvious asymmetry of power and knowledge, to conceal legitimate activities or wrongdoing, or even in malice, to render the system of data collection as a whole worthless. This diversity of purposes, methods and perpetrators is reflected in the wide range of forms taken by obfuscation tactics. . . .

Whereas some forms of obfuscation try to inject doubt into the data permanently, time-based obfuscation, in many ways the simplest form of the practice, adds an onerous amount of processing in a situation where time is of the essence. *Chaff* offers a canonical example: The radar operator of the Second World War tracks a plane over Hamburg, guiding searchlights and anti-aircraft guns in relation to a phosphor dot whose position is updated with each sweep of the antenna. Abruptly the planes begin to multiply, their dots quickly swamping the display. The plane is in there somewhere, impossible to locate for the presence of all the "false echoes." The plane has released chaff, strips of black paper backed with aluminum foil and cut to half the target radar's wavelength, floating down through the air, thrown out by the pound and filling the system with signals. . . . Knowing discovery to be inevitable, chaff uses the time and bandwidth constraints of the discovery system against it by creating too many potential targets. . . . That the chaff only works briefly, as it flutters to the ground, and is not a permanent solution, is irrelevant under the circumstances; it only needs to work well enough for the time it will take the plane to get through. . . .

The *"Craigslist robber"* offers a minor but illustrative example of obfuscation as a practice turned to criminal ends. At 11 AM on Tuesday, 30 September 2008, a man dressed like an exterminator in a blue shirt, goggles and a dust mask, and carrying a spray pump, approached an armored car parked outside a bank in Monroe, Washington, incapacitated the guard with pepper spray, and took a substantial amount of money. When the police arrived, they found 13 men

in the area wearing blue shirts, goggles and dust masks—a uniform they were wearing on the instructions of a Craigslist ad which promised a good wage for maintenance work, which was to start at 11:15 AM at the bank's address. . . . Obviously it will only take a few minutes to determine that none of the day laborers is the bank robber—but a few minutes is all he needs. . . .

Other forms of obfuscation require the cooperation of others. They have the "network effect" of becoming more valuable as more people join. . . . *Loyalty card swapping pools* provide a superb real-world example. . . . [Q]uite quickly after their widespread introduction came card-swapping networks, where people shared cards—initially in *ad hoc* physical meetings, and increasingly in large populations and over wide geographical regions enabled by mailing lists and online social networks—to obfuscate their data. . . .

Another form of collective obfuscation appears in the argument for *participation in Tor*. Tor is a system designed to enable anonymous use of the Internet, through a combination of encryption and passing the message through many different independent "nodes." . . . If you request a Web page while working through Tor, your request will not come from your IP address, but from an "exit node" (that last person who hands the message to its addressee) on the Tor system, along with the requests of many other Tor users. . . . The Tor network—and the obfuscation of individuals on the network—improves as more people join in. . . .

All of the examples thus far have been about general methods of covering one's tracks. But what if you want this data to be useful without diminishing your privacy, or to interfere with some methods of data analysis but not others? This is the project of selective obfuscation. *FaceCloak*, for example, provides the initial steps towards an elegant and selective obfuscation-based solution to the problem of Facebook profiles. . . . When you create a Facebook profile and fill in your personal information, including details such as where you live, went to school, likes and dislikes, and so on, FaceCloak offers you a choice: display this information openly, or keep it private? If you let it be displayed openly, it is passed to Facebook's servers like any other normal data, under their privacy policy. If you want to keep that data private, however, FaceCloak sends it to encrypted storage on a separate server only to be decrypted and displayed for friends you have authorized, when they browse your Facebook page (using the FaceCloak plugin.) Facebook never gains access to it. . . .

Time-based obfuscation can be quickly seen through; cooperative obfuscation relies on the power of groups to muddy the tracks; selective obfuscation wishes to be clear for some and not others. Ambiguating obfuscation seeks to render an individual's data permanently dubious and untrustworthy as a subject of analysis. For example, consider the Firefox extension *TrackMeNot*, developed in 2006. . . . TrackMeNot was designed to foil the profiling of users through their searches. . . . [It] automatically generates queries from a seed list of terms. These terms are initially culled from RSS feeds, and evolve over time, so that different users develop different seed lists. TrackMeNot submits queries in a manner that tries to mimic user search behaviors. This user may

have searched for "good wi-fi cafe chelsea" but they have also searched for "savannah kennels," "freshly pressed juice miami," and "asian property firm," to say nothing of "exercise delays dementia" and "telescoping halogen light"—will the real searcher please stand up? The activity of individuals is masked by that of many ghosts, making a pattern harder to discern, making it impossible to say, of any given query that it was the product of human intention rather than the automatic output of TrackMeNot. . . .

Obfuscation, as we have presented it here, is at once richer and less rigorous than academically well-established methods of digital privacy protection, like encryption. It is far more *ad hoc* and contextual, without the quantifiable protection of cryptographic methods—a "weapon of the weak" to take a phrase from James Scott for the modes of resistance available to those at the wrong end of the asymmetries we have described. It is often haphazard and piecemeal, creating only a temporary window of liberty or a certain amount of reasonable doubt. And it is for precisely those reasons that we think it is a valuable and rewarding subject for study. The concept can be easily understood and inventively deployed, and lets us lower the stakes of resistance, making it possible for people coerced into compliance by necessity, circumstance or demand to push back.

# 67

# STEVE MANN, JASON NOLAN, AND BARRY WELLMAN

## SOUSVEILLANCE

### Inventing and Using Wearable Computing Devices for Data Collection in Surveillance Environments

Recognition of the ubiquity of video surveillance has prompted a number of artistic and technological responses. In this piece, Steve Mann and colleagues introduce the concept of sousveillance, or watching from below, as a corrective to what they see as normalized forms of institutional surveillance that diminish personal autonomy. By staging performances that record employees in stores, for instance, as opposed to customers, the authors seek to make unequal power relationships visible and subject to debate.

\*\*\*

Surveillance is everywhere but often little observed. Organizations have tried to make technology mundane and invisible through its disappearance into the fabric of buildings, objects, and bodies. The creation of pervasive ubiquitous technologies—such as smart floors, toilets, elevators, and light switches—means that intelligence gathering devices for ubiquitous surveillance are also becoming invisible. This replacement of technologies and data conduits has brought new opportunities for observation, data collection, and sur/sousveillance, making public surveillance of private space increasingly ubiquitous. All such activity has been *sur*veillance: organizations observing people. One way to challenge and problematize both surveillance and acquiescence to it is to resituate these technologies of control on individuals, offering panoptic technologies to help them observe those in authority. We call this inverse panopticon "*sous*veillance" from the French words for "sous" (below) and "veiller" to watch.

Sousveillance is a form of "reflectionism," a term invented by [Steve] Mann for a philosophy and procedures of using technology to mirror and confront bureaucratic organizations. Reflectionism holds up the mirror and asks the question: "Do you like what you see?" If you do not, then you will know that other approaches by which we integrate society and technology must be considered. Thus, reflectionism is a technique for inquiry-in-performance that is directed:

a) toward uncovering the panopticon and undercutting its primacy and privilege;
b) relocating the relationship of the surveillance society within a more traditional commons notion of observability.

Reflectionism is especially related to "detournement": the tactic of appropriating tools of social controllers and resituating these tools in a disorienting manner. It extends the concept of detournement by using the tools against the organization, holding a mirror up to the establishment, and creating a symmetrical self-bureaucratization of the wearer. In this manner, reflectionism is related to the Theater of the Absurd, and the Situationist movement in art.

Reflectionism becomes sousveillance when it is applied to individuals using tools to observe the organizational observer. Sousveillance focuses on enhancing the ability of people to access and collect data about their surveillance and to neutralize surveillance. . . . Reflectionism differs from those solutions that seek to regulate surveillance in order to protect privacy. Reflectionism contends that such regulation is as much pacifier as solution because in a regulatory regime, surveillance information is largely exchanged and controlled by external agents over which individuals have little power. . . . By contrast, reflectionism seeks to increase the equality between surveiller and the person being surveilled (surveillee), including enabling the surveillee to surveil the surveiller.

Probably the best-known recent example of sousveillance is when Los Angeles resident George Holliday videotaped police officers beating Rodney King after he had been stopped for a traffic violation.

The ensuing uproar led to the trial of the officers (although not their conviction) and serious discussion of curtailing police brutality. Taping and broadcasting the police assault on Rodney King was serendipitous and fortuitous sousveillance. Yet planned acts of sousveillance can occur, although they are rarer than organizational surveillance. Examples include: customers photographing shopkeepers; taxi passengers photographing cab drivers; citizens photographing police officers who come to their doors; civilians photographing government officials; residents beaming satellite shots of occupying troops onto the Internet. In many cases, these acts of sousveillance violate prohibitions stating that ordinary people should not use recording devices to record official acts. At times, these prohibitions are stated. For example, many countries prohibit photographing military bases. More often, these prohibitions are unstated. For example, although many large stores do not want photographs taken on their premises, we have never seen a sign prohibiting such photography. . . .

Digital technology can build on personal computing to make individuals feel more self-empowered at home, in the community, at school and at work. Mobile, personal, and wearable computing devices allow people to take the personal computing revolution with them. Sousveilling individuals now can invert an organization's gaze and watch the watchers by collecting data on them. . . . We describe and analyze here a set of performances that follow Harold Garfinkel's ethnomethodological approach to breaching norms. We gain insight into these norms by: (a) deliberately not acquiescing in surveillance, and (b) performing visible and explicit sousveillance. By breaking organizational policies, these performances expose hitherto discreet, implicit, and unquestioned acts of organizational surveillance. More active forms of sousveillance confront surveillance by using wearable computing to surveil the surveillers reflectively, bringing into question the very act of surveillance itself. . . .

The goal of the performances reported here is less to understand the nature of surveillance than to engage in dialogues with front-line officials and customer service personnel at the point-of-contact in semipublic and commercial locations. . . . [T]he performers instigate situations in order to:

(a) gauge the degree to which customer service personnel will try to suppress photography in locations where it is forbidden;
(b) break unstated rules of asymmetric surveillance using new wearable computing inventions.

The collecting of digital images, via photographs or videos, is usually prohibited by store personnel because of stated policy, explicit norms, or unconscious norms that are only realized when they are breached. The surveilled become sousveillers who engage social controllers (customs officials, shopkeepers, customer service personnel, security guards, etc.) by using devices that mirror those used by these social controllers. . . .

The same kind of surveillance domes used by establishments can be used in wearable computing performances. These performances use wine-dark hemispheres similar to the seemingly opaque domes commonly found on the ceilings of stores. The fact that the domes may or may not contain cameras creates an important design element for the wearer because it is possible to arrange the situation such that the wearer does not know if the device contains a camera. If questioned about the wearable domes, the wearer is able to reply that they are unsure what the dome contains.

Video recordings . . . had been previously made by entering the shops with hidden cameras and asking various surveillance personnel what the domes on the ceilings of their shops were. In one case, customer service personnel explained that the domes on their ceiling were temperature sensors. In another situation, a record store owner asserted that the store's dark ceiling domes were light fixtures. By using flat panel displays to play back the recording to the customer service personnel, their surveillance is reflected back to them as sousveillance.

In practice, surveillance personnel's appeal to authority can be countered by the sousveillers appealing to conflicting authorities. To be most effective, the sousveilling camera/projector wearer needs to be operating under social control policies in the same way that the surveillance worker or official is operating under company policies about surveillance. In this way, the wearer and the employee acknowledge each other's state of subordination to policies that require them to photograph each other. While the wearer and the employee engage in what would normally be a hostile act of photographing each other, they can be collegially human to one another and discuss the weather, sports, and working conditions. . . .

The [sousveillance] performances show how certain kinds of rule violation can be deliberately used to engender a new kind of balance. They show public acceptance of being videoed as an act of surveillance in public places. When such data collection is done by ordinary people, such as the performers, to other ordinary people, it is often accepted. However, when data projectors show surveillance officials the data that has been collected about them, there is less acceptance. Organizational personnel responsible for surveillance generally do not accept sousveillance from the "ordinary people" performers, even when data displays reveal what the sousveillers are recording. . . .

Surveillance cameras threaten autonomy. Shrouding cameras behind a bureaucracy results in somewhat grudging acceptance of their existence in order to participate in public activities (shopping, accessing government services, traveling, etc.). By having this permanent record of the situation beyond the transaction, social control is enhanced. Acts of sousveillance redirect an establishment's mechanisms and technologies of surveillance back on the establishment. There is an explicit "in your face" attitude in the inversion of surveillance techniques that draws from the women's rights movement, aspects of the civil rights movement, and radical environmentalism. Thus sousveillance is situated in the larger context of democratic social responsibility. . . .

Sousveillance disrupts the power relationship of surveillance when it restores a traditional balance that the institutionalization of Bentham's Panopticon itself disrupted. It is a conceptual model of reflective awareness that seeks to problematize social interactions and factors of contemporary life. It is a model, with its root in previous emancipatory movements, with the goal of social engagement and dialogue.

# 68

# TORIN MONAHAN

## THE RIGHT TO HIDE?

Anti-Surveillance Camouflage and
the Aestheticization of Resistance

Anti-surveillance artworks that allow people to hide from automated surveillance systems have been growing in popularity. Such creations introduce an interesting paradox: hiding becomes a form of artistic expression, whereas uniqueness is cultivated by obscuring identity markers. In this excerpt, Torin Monahan argues that while anti-surveillance projects may be enticing and fun, on the whole they do not compel people to confront the legitimacy of public surveillance, the unequal application of such systems, or the root causes of discrimination and violence.

\*\*\*

A curious trend is emerging in this era of pervasive surveillance. Alongside increasing public awareness of drone warfare, government spying programs, and big data analytics, there has been a recent surge in anti-surveillance tactics. While these tactics range from software for anonymous Internet browsing to detoxification supplements for fooling drug tests, what is particularly fascinating is the panoply of artistic projects—and products—to conceal oneself from ambient surveillance in public places. These center on the masking of identity to undermine technological efforts to fix someone as a unique entity apart from the crowd. A veritable artistic industry mushrooms from the perceived death of the social brought about by ubiquitous public surveillance: irregular face paint and hairstyles to confound face-recognition software, hoodies and scarves made with materials to block thermal emissions and evade tracking by drones, and hats that emit infrared light to blind camera lenses and prevent photographs or video tracking. Anti-surveillance camouflage of this sort flaunts the system, ostensibly allowing wearers to hide in plain sight—neither acquiescing to surveillance mandates nor becoming reclusive under their withering gaze. This is an *aestheticization of resistance*, a performance that generates media attention and scholarly interest without necessarily challenging the violent and discriminatory logics of surveillance societies.

These artistic practices should be situated in the context of the state visuality projects that galvanize them. Visuality is about the normalization of state control through techniques of classification, separation, and aestheticization, which enforce a kind of reductive, exclusionary legibility. . . . Countervisuality projects may be necessary to disarm the natural logics of state visuality and confront their supposed order from nowhere. Rather than merely opposing visuality or seeking to substitute it with different totalizing regimes, countervisuality would instead challenge forms of violence and oppression, acknowledging differential exposures and effects. After all, despite popular claims about universal subjection to surveillance, it must be recognized that a host of surveillance functions are reserved for those who threaten the status quo, principally those classified as poor or marked as Other. Racialized identities of dangerousness are encoded back upon the targets through surveillance encounters that are always tied to the threat of state force (e.g., the stop-and-frisk search). These are mechanisms of *marginalizing surveillance* that produce conditions and identities of marginality through their very application.

This paper builds upon theoretical insights from the field of surveillance studies, particularly with regard to the differential treatment of populations and ways that marginality inflects experiences of surveillance. The field has had a longstanding concern with discriminatory surveillance practices predicated on "categorical suspicion" of marginalized groups and "social sorting" of populations through increasingly abstract, invisible, and automated systems of control. Perhaps because of the strong voyeuristic modalities of surveillance, scholars have further interrogated the gendered dimensions of watching and being watched and have explored possibilities for gender-based appropriation and resistance. Recently, there has also been a concerted effort to foster engaged feminist and race studies critiques that attend to intersectional forms of oppression . . . which are often enforced by surveillance practices. Feminist and intersectional approaches to surveillance studies connect the embodied, grounded nature of individual experience with larger systems of structural inequality and violence. Such approaches investigate the technological and organizational mediation of situated practice, advancing a critique of contemporary surveillance systems and power relations. The analysis presented here builds upon this orientation by questioning the values and implications of aestheticized forms of anti-surveillance. . . .

Taken at face value, anti-surveillance camouflage enacts a play of surveillance avoidance. It frames the enemy either as state and corporate actors invading one's privacy or as malicious individuals seeking to violate helpless others through voyeuristic transgressions. The gaze is always unwanted; it always individuates; it always objectifies. In this narrative, there is little room to engage the problems of categorical suspicion that undergird marginalizing surveillance because the unit of analysis is the individual, not the group. There is little room to explore complex amalgams of desired surveillance, extractive systems, and hidden effects. The provocation is one of the enlightened, bourgeois subject asserting his or her right to be left alone, which is a claim that by its very implied utterance already reveals the relative privilege of the one making it. It is also a heroic, masculinist narrative that positions women as feeble targets of voyeuristic encounters (e.g., the dreaded "upskirt" shot) who are in need of stylistic, technological shields to preserve their dignity and honor. It would seem, then, that *systems* of oppression and discrimination—racism, sexism, classism, ableism, etc.—are preserved or at least not directly contested by anti-surveillance artistic experiments. . . .

## The Thrill of "Perilous Glamour": Face Paint and Hairstyles

Bold asymmetrical marks on haughty white faces. Pointy blue and red bangs cutting dramatic lines across models' straight noses, plucked eyebrows, and parted lips. These are some of the images that comprise the fashion "look book" for the CV [computer vision] Dazzle project intended to confuse face-recognition systems. The designers proudly embrace what they call "the perilous glamour of life under surveillance" and appropriate naval tactics from a bygone era to ostentatiously "dazzle" and confuse electronic observers. As an *Atlantic Monthly* article explains:

> Dazzle takes its name from a type of naval camouflage (and otherwise) used in the world wars. Huge, jarring stripes were painted on ships, less with the intent to conceal them in the water and more with the idea of disorienting enemy weapons and maneuvering. CV dazzle applies the same concept to algorithms.

The presumed enemies in the contemporary surveillant context include any operators of automated face-recognition technology, be they state agents, advertisers, or technology companies like Apple.

To justify Dazzle approaches to anti-surveillance camouflage, artists mobilize evolutionary discourses to position their work as innovative because it is modeled on nature. A Roy Behrens quote prominently displayed on the CV Dazzle website reads: "From all

appearances, deception has always been critical to daily survival—for human and non-human creatures alike—and, judging by its current ubiquity, there is no end in immediate sight." In providing advice for makeup application, the designers make a similar comparison: "Ideally, your face would become the anti-face, or inverse. In the animal kingdom, this inverse effect is known as countershading." This conflation of natural and social systems frames surveillance from enemies as an inevitable, natural state of affairs that demands creative adaptation on the part of the would-be prey. It is a framing that—in neoliberal and social Darwinian fashion—responsibilizes avoidance of undesired scrutiny and implies that those who cannot evade the predator deserve targeting and are unfit for survival. . . .

Not restricted to evolutionary discourses, the rhetoric deployed by CV Dazzle at times seems as disjointed as the designs themselves. The discursive registers invoke the biological ("the animal kingdom"), marketing disclaimers ("results will vary"), scientific experiment ("tested and validated"), practical suggestions ("avoid enhancers"), and participatory enticements ("creating your own looks"). This disparate appeal for attention fits snugly with observations about the contemporary era of populist postmodernism, where a surplus of messages each vie for recognition and no longer rely on shared adjudication processes to determine which is more factual or true. . . .

With Dazzle designs, the face's surface may be rendered unreadable, at least temporarily, granting the postmodern primitive freedom from a radically delimited form of fixity. While late capitalist economies may thrive on the protean, the state seeks permanence and precision with respect to the identity of bodies flowing within, and beyond, its territories. Playing with illegibility allows one to flirt with, and become titillated by, the idea of deviance, all the while masking deeper inscriptions on the body, as well as on one's data doubles. . . . It is the relatively privileged and white who ride the waves of voluntary mobility and whose state-verified identity markers buoy them in their pursuits. While attention is paid to the poses of the privileged adorned with tribal-looking paint, absent are critiques of racialized threat inscribed indelibly on black and brown bodies. . . .

## Dangerous Play on the Surveillance Fashion Runway

On a raised stage in a low-lit room, soft azure lights project gyrating patterns on the crowd as male and female models strut across the stage. A mix of house music with drum loops and simulated record scratching sets the tone, creating an edgy vibe to frame the presentation of novel surveillance and anti-surveillance clothing and accessories. Most of the designs incorporate electronic sensors and circuitry, either facilitating or obstructing the flow of personal information. An MC struggles to read the descriptive text for each design, as the models too have difficulty showing off their items without dropping them or engaging in exaggerated miming to communicate their intended functions. All of this—which was the "Anti/Surveillance Fashion Show" presented by designers from the Noisebridge hackerspace in 2010—generates a spectacle of frivolity, where performers poke ironic fun at their mock serious designs while audience members look on with vague curiosity. . . . Surveillance is not challenged or resisted so much as it is manipulated or augmented to establish a façade of constrained freedom for individuals. . . .

When the fashion show turns toward issues of harassment of and violence against women, the severe limitations of this neoliberal logic of freedom become even more apparent. There are women's shoes equipped with panic alarms to "tell people to stay back

and for her handlers to pick her up." As an accompaniment to a hoodie that blinds cameras with LED lights, another design, referred to as a "rear window shade," allows women to see when someone is sneaking up on them; the MC explains: "Of course, as a soloist, no one's going to watch her back but her. . . . [The rear window shade will] allow her to surprise her surprise assailants." Finally, there is a device for dealing with upskirt photographs of women's underwear. As a woman sashays to center stage in a very short skirt and heels, the MC asks:

> But what about the common problem of the upskirt? What is a girl to do? Fortunately, she has the 'crotch dazzler'. . . . She simply need not worry. . . . [The reflector on her underwear] will show only flashes of the paparazzi's cameras rather than her privates.

The message delivered by each of these designs is a variation on the theme of not worrying about the male gaze or sexual assault. Technological gadgets are presented as exerting a form of delegated patriarchal protection (with the panic alarm shoes and crotch dazzler panties) or individual responsibility for detecting and evading attackers (with the rear window shade). The designs problematically assume both the inevitability of dangers and the vulnerability of women. Violence against women is normalized with these designs, just as is exposure to public surveillance, which effectively removes from the discussion any question about how to change the underlying cultural conditions of violence and abuse. . . .

## Conclusion

The aestheticization of resistance enacted by anti-surveillance camouflage and fashion ultimately fails to address the exclusionary logics of contemporary state and corporate surveillance. These anti-surveillance practices emerge at this historical juncture because of a widespread recognition of unchecked, pervasive surveillance and popular criticism of government and corporate overreach. The key to the popularity of these artistic efforts may be that they mobilize the trappings of radical intervention, in highly stylized form, but do so in ways that do not compel people to challenge state visuality projects. They offer hyper-individualized and consumer-oriented adaptations to undesired surveillance . . . [where] the primary message is one of accommodating pervasive surveillance and inviting a playful dance with it.

# SECTION 14

# MARGINALITY AND DIFFERENCE

///////////////////////////////////////////////////////////////////////////////////////////////////////////

Most of the early works in surveillance studies were primarily concerned with tracing the growth of surveillance practices throughout society and questioning their gestalt implications rather than their differential effects. This scholarship nonetheless set the stage for inquiry into profiling and discrimination. For instance, when Gary Marx raised the problem of "categorical suspicion" in his classic book *Undercover*, he articulated a universalist anxiety about a society where "everyone becomes a reasonable target" (Marx 1988: 219), but in so doing he drew attention to the ways in which surveillance increasingly targeted groups, beginning with categories of suspicion of which individuals were a part. Others developed this emphasis on groups to theorize the inherently discriminatory logics and uses of contemporary surveillance. For instance, Oscar Gandy (1993; excerpted in Section 1) analyzed the ways in which bureaucracies panoptically sort groups, such that poor people of color are especially disadvantaged; Clive Norris and Gary Armstrong (1999; excerpted in Section 7) documented the ways in which video surveillance operators targeted male youth as potential troublemakers and women as objects of voyeuristic desire; and David Lyon (2001, 2003) characterized modern surveillance as being fundamentally a mechanism of "social sorting" along lines of presumed risk or value.

Feminist approaches to surveillance studies, while certainly troubled by issues of social sorting, have generally taken a different tack. This line of inquiry situates surveillance in the historical context of patriarchal domination of women, minorities, and others. For instance, the male gaze is one mechanism of constructing women as passive and vulnerable objects of masculine desire (Mulvey 1975). In such instances, surveillance can serve both as a tool of objectification and control *and* as a protective, patriarchal response to gendered violence. As such, surveillance-based problems and solutions tend to reify patriarchy and the subordination of women. For example, Hille Koskela (2000; excerpted in Section 7) describes how the integration of video surveillance into traditional women's spaces in Helsinki (e.g., places of shopping and transport) had the effect of masculinizing those spaces, making women the objects of new forms of scrutiny while perhaps exposing them to intensified harassment through remote video monitoring. If attention to embodiment, context, and difference are central to feminist analysis, then most contemporary surveillance can be thought of as reproducing masculinist rationalities of disembodied control at a distance because they "artificially abstract bodies, identities, and interactions from social contexts in ways that both obscure and aggravate gender and other social inequalities" (Monahan 2009: 287).

Recently, there has also been a dynamic move in surveillance studies to cultivate feminist and race studies critiques that confront intersectional forms of oppression, which are increasingly enforced by surveillance practices (e.g., Dubrofsky and Magnet 2015; van der Meulen and Heynen 2016). Intersectionality, here, refers to the ways in which one's various identity classifications—race, class, gender, sexuality, (dis)ability, and so on—might overlap to amplify discrimination or disadvantage. As an exemplar of this work, Rachel Dubrofsky and Shoshana Magnet's (2015) edited volume *Feminist Surveillance Studies* places intersectional analysis at the forefront and calls upon scholars to connect embodied experiences of surveillance to larger systems of structural inequality and violence. Examples might include things like state identification systems that do not accommodate transgender people (Moore and Currah 2015) or battered women's shelters that report undocumented women to immigration authorities (Smith 2015). Surveillance in these cases can be thought of as having an agential, marginalizing capacity: it reproduces the conditions and subjectivities of marginality through its application (Monahan 2010). Key to such investigations is also a focus on the ways in which privilege, and especially white privilege, is encoded in surveillance and security apparatuses, such that the white body is viewed as transparent, normal, and unthreatening. Rachel Hall describes this as the "aesthetics of transparency," indicating how the white body becomes the transparent ideal, while opaque, dark-skinned bodies are translated as threatening and in need of further investigation (Hall 2015; see also Browne 2015).

It is important to note that the developments sketched here—from concerns about universal exposure to surveillance, on one hand, to critical investigations into the gendered, racialized, and classed dimensions of surveillance, on the other—are also indicative of disciplinary shifts in the field. As an oversimplification for the purpose of illustration, whereas sociologists and criminologists might concentrate on social structure, social norms, and stratification, scholars in the fields of communication, cultural studies, women's and gender studies, queer studies, and critical race studies are more likely to analyze the role of representation, discourse, and experience in materializing power relations and politics across social and cultural contexts. Thus, the turn to feminist and intersectional surveillance studies also signals the inclusion of more voices from the humanities in conversations of the field.

The excerpts in this section tilt toward such newer explorations of surveillance, marginality, and difference—ones that stress intersectionality, inequality, and power. Oscar Gandy explores how abstract systems of probabilities and statistics, upon which most organizations rely, discriminate especially against poor minority populations, creating tenacious systems of "cumulative disadvantage." Jasbir Puar critiques the racializing effects of anticipatory surveillance in the context of the "war on terror," noting how normative whiteness is constructed in opposition to the presumed dangerousness of non-white Muslims. Corinne Mason and Shoshana Magnet illustrate how everyday technologies such as mobile phones, GPS units, and websites can create new vulnerabilities for and exacerbate violence against women, especially for marginalized victims for whom encounters with law enforcement may bring about further violence. Finally, Simone Browne persuasively argues that the history of surveillance must be seen as inseparable from the history of racism. With examples ranging from the physical branding of slaves up to contemporary digital systems of biometric identification, Browne shows how race is imprinted onto bodies, even as slippages between externally imposed and self-asserted identities open up vital opportunities for resistance.

## REFERENCES

Browne, Simone. 2015. *Dark Matters: On the Surveillance of Blackness*. Durham, NC: Duke University Press.

Dubrofsky, Rachel E., and Shoshana Amielle Magnet, eds. 2015. *Feminist Surveillance Studies*. Durham, NC: Duke University Press.

Gandy, Oscar H. 1993. *The Panoptic Sort: A Political Economy of Personal Information*. Boulder, CO: Westview.

Hall, Rachel. 2015. *The Transparent Traveler: The Performance and Culture of Airport Security*. Durham, NC: Duke University Press.

Koskela, Hille. 2000. 'The Gaze without Eyes': Video-Surveillance and the Changing Nature of Urban Space. *Progress in Human Geography* 24 (2):243–65.

Lyon, David. 2001. *Surveillance Society: Monitoring Everyday Life*. Buckingham, England: Open University.

———, ed. 2003. *Surveillance as Social Sorting: Privacy, Risk, and Digital Discrimination*. New York: Routledge.

Marx, Gary T. 1988. *Undercover: Police Surveillance in America*. Berkeley: University of California Press.

Monahan, Torin. 2009. Dreams of Control at a Distance: Gender, Surveillance, and Social Control. *Cultural Studies ↔ Critical Methodologies* 9 (2):286–305.

———. 2010. *Surveillance in the Time of Insecurity*. New Brunswick, NJ: Rutgers University Press.

Moore, Lisa Jean, and Paisley Currah. 2015. Legally Sexed: Birth Certificates and Transgender Citizens. In *Feminist Surveillance Studies*, edited by R. E. Dubrofsky and S. A. Magnet, 58–76. Durham, NC: Duke University Press.

Mulvey, Laura. 1975. Visual Pleasure and Narrative Cinema. *Screen* 16 (3):6–18.

Norris, Clive, and Gary Armstrong. 1999. *The Maximum Surveillance Society: The Rise of CCTV*. Oxford: Berg.

Smith, Andrea. 2015. Not-Seeing: State Surveillance, Settler Colonialism, and Gender Violence. In *Feminist Surveillance Studies*, edited by R. E. Dubrofsky and S. A. Magnet, 21–38. Durham. NC: Duke University Press.

van der Meulen, Emily, and Robert Heynen, eds. 2016. *Expanding the Gaze: Gender and the Politics of Surveillance*. Toronto: University of Toronto Press.

# OSCAR H. GANDY, JR.

## COMING TO TERMS WITH CHANCE

Engaging Rational Discrimination
and Cumulative Disadvantage

Building upon his previous work on the unequal panoptic sorting of individuals by corporations and government agencies, Oscar Gandy's *Coming to Terms with Chance* expands the frame to critically investigate how dominant regimes of risk management, actuarial assessment, and predictive analytics solidify racialized discrimination and social inequality. Whereas discourses of "chance" imply a level of fairness among players, the current social field is one marked by inequalities that are reproduced by statistical and technical forms, such that "cumulative disadvantage" stubbornly haunts poor and racialized groups.

***

By the turn of the century, the analysis and management of risk had escaped the bounds of professional concern and scholarly expertise to claim a prominent place in the public consciousness. The information society had become the risk society, and the arcane wizardry of actuaries and statisticians became common, almost essential features of popular mass media fare. Estimates of probability based on analyses of events in the past have come to dominate decisions about the paths we should take in the future. Nothing worthy of our attention can avoid an assessment of chance. . . .

We are just beginning to understand how much initial positions play in the ways our lives develop. How well we do in the natural lottery that distributes genetic endowments at birth helps to determine how race, gender, and social class combine in unimaginably chaotic ways to move us down different paths along the unmapped roads of life. We are just beginning to appreciate the complexity in the mutually reinforcing and limiting systems that generate an array of opportunity structures or life chances that ultimately determine who, how, and what we are when we reach the end of our journey. . . .

This book is about the use of predictive technologies to shape the futures that people face in ways that no longer invite comments about misfortune or bad luck. Although we may not talk about the role of chance in many of the situations we observe, we are likely to raise questions about the role that justice and considerations of fairness have played with regard to the distribution of the outcomes that result from the choices that powerful actors have made.

Truly random or chance distributions tend not be to assessed in terms of fairness. Games of chance are enjoyed in part because of the pleasures derived from a bit of unexpected good luck. Even when the impact of chance is tempered by skill, as in card games or even in the game of golf, the unexpected arrival of good fortune still tends to be enjoyed. However, when the deck is stacked, or marked, or the dice are craftily weighted, the fun quickly leaves the room. We feel as though we have been cheated of the benefits that were supposed to come on the winds of chance.

The same is true in the game of life. If the games in which we must compete are in some sense fixed, such that the outcomes tend to favor the house, or some other group of players, moral outrage becomes the order of the day. Perhaps, this is what we really mean when we say "life is unfair." This is not simply an articulation of the view that we do not necessarily deserve everything that comes our way. It is also a suggestion that for some people, the odds may have been stacked against them, not merely by chance, but because strategic actors, informed by statisticians have changed the rules of the game. . . .

This failure to understand the meaning of difference is especially troublesome, as we have come to rely on an assumption of understanding on the part of those whose responsibility it is to develop and implement important public policies. A failure to understand the meaning of differences due to chance limits our ability to identify individual and institutional acts of racial discrimination that may have brought about these distinctions in the first place. . . .

When we think about the development and diffusion of new technologies into routine use by business and government, the primary focus of our attention is usually on the efficiency and effectiveness with which these devices and techniques can contribute to the bottom line, or contribute to the expanded production of some social good. Far too often we tend to ignore the ways in which these benefits are being distributed. And, because our traditional focus on maximization tends to emphasize benefits, the distribution of burdens is hardly considered at all.

Of course, we understand that these technologies do not drop from the sky fully formed, and ready for use. They are developed over time, and they are developed in response to the demands of institutions and actors within segments of the economy that have sufficient resources to attract the attention and dedication of developers.

Nearly all of these tools and techniques are discriminatory technologies. They are used to identify, classify, and evaluate different entities or objects. These objects are evaluated primarily in terms of their expected benefits or costs. Because their evaluation is increasingly being made in the context of uncertainty or risk, these systems are increasingly oriented toward providing guidance for actions to be taken in the future. These actions almost always involve making choices among similarly situated options, and the options that should matter the most are the options that involve choices among people, or the places where people will make their lives. . . .

[A] continuing challenge in the use of statistics in support of actions to be made in the future is the selection of the variables and data that will be used within the models. The variables that eventually come to be used in these models are not selected entirely on the basis of some unbiased, objective process that is guaranteed by some official stamp of approval, or even by a process of blind peer review. . . .

This book is concerned about the consequences that flow from the use of probability and statistics in support of discrimination, rational or otherwise. It argues that the use of discriminatory technologies contributes to the social, economic and political disparities that continue to assign African Americans and other poor people of color to the fringes of society, and condemns many of them to a life of extreme relative deprivation.

Cumulative disadvantage refers to the ways in which historical disadvantages cumulate over time, and across categories of experience. The notion of cumulative disadvantage helps to explain how a racial effect can be produced within a society that may have in fact experienced a decline in the level of animus or negative racial intent as the motivation behind critical choices that have been made.

For example, while racial animus may have been at the base of discriminatory lending decisions during the initial growth in home ownership in the US, economic rationality is sufficient to explain many of the financial barriers and burdens that African Americans still face in the housing market. Because of the ways in which racial bias shaped estimates of the present and future value of real estate in neighborhoods with a substantial black presence, contemporary estimates of loan value and risk reflect and reinforce those views, even though the incorporation of racial measures into those calculations is barred by law. . . .

Data mining is a generalized approach to the discovery of patterns in information. Often, the source information has been captured from transaction-generated data. Data mining has emerged as an important resource for the segmentation of markets into risk and value based categories. Because market segmentation involves categorical discrimination, and because the groups or categories need not be the equivalent of politically protected groups, traditional restraints on discrimination may not apply. For example, while "redlining" maybe forbidden within markets for real estate, or for associated services, such as mortgage lending, "weblining" on the basis of virtual community classification faces no such legal constraints. . . .

The same technologies that are used in support of legitimate economic and social goals are also being put to use by those motivated by criminal intent. Predictive models are used to identify likely victims in the same ways in which they might be used to identify potential customers or unacceptable risks. In markets for consumer credit, predatory lenders engage in a form of "reverse redlining" where homeowners who were at the greatest risk of default were being targeted. Consumer fraud captures a substantial part of the nation's economic resources, and the government's ability to control it lags far behind the development and spread of the new strategies and tactics being used. . . .

In 2008, a truly embarrassing status was achieved by the United States. The rate of imprisonment for adults exceeded one in 100 for the first time in American history. No other nation matched the rate, or the total number of persons behind bars. This historic rate actually increases to one in 30 for young men. For African Americans, the rate rises to one out of nine.

The differential risk of being imprisoned reflects the influence of an array of factors, including the widespread use of statistically informed predictions of dangerousness and likelihood of offending. Predictive modeling that informed decisions about which prisoners should be eligible for release became more important as the rising costs of the prison system threatened the economic stability of many state governments.

Other statistical techniques merely add to the numbers of persons at risk. Data mining and other means of computer enhanced surveillance lead to an expansion in the number of potential targets. Because of declining costs of capture, storage, and processing of transaction generated information (TGI) lower standards of potential harm become normalized, more and more people are placed at risk of arrest for a broadened array of prosecutable offenses. Administrative guidelines that once established cost "triggers" at $10,000 for heightened scrutiny of financial transactions at banks could be lowered to amounts of $500, or even $100 in the foreseeable future. When the application of these data mining and surveillance techniques moves the goal of policing beyond investigation and toward prevention, perhaps through stings or preemptive strikes, our basis for concern about systematic bias is almost certain to expand.

# 70

# JASBIR K. PUAR

## TERRORIST ASSEMBLAGES

Homonationalism in Queer Times

In *Terrorist Assemblages*, Jasbir Puar illustrates the counterintuitive ways that homonormativity supports imperial acts of violence and the war on terror: the symbolic tolerance of non-normative sexualities by the United States (through the incorporation of model, white, affluent queerness by the mainstream media, for example) is deployed to assert the comparative intolerance and barbarism of the Muslim Other and justify imperialist intervention. The passage excerpted here explores the role of surveillance in this process, particularly pertaining to the construction of threatening, racialized bodies marked for anticipatory containment or elimination.

\*\*\*

The "technological sublime" refers to the totalizing, overarching, and inflated power falsely accorded to surveillance, hyperbole that conveniently forgets that interactions between user and interface are often consensual, that security and information systems often fail in their objectives, and that control does not always espouse or shape value systems. I turn now to a preliminary sketch of surveillance technologies to construct a perfunctory understanding of intimacy and security within control societies. I am not interested in appraising the relative intrusiveness or privacy-hindering effects of surveillance. More significant is that the *perception* of an all-encompassing, impenetrable, and infallible surveillance structure affectively breeds fear, terror, and insecurity.

The private within rights discourses is overwhelmingly a "flat discourse. It largely ignores the vertical dimension and tends to look across rather than to cut through the landscape." Eyal Weizman, through what he terms "the politics of verticality," details the spatial reconceptualization of the shift from two-dimensional space—an expanse of horizontal and vertical coordinates, latitudinal and longitudinal positions, over here and over there, inside and out—to a three-dimensional space of volume, depth, and verticality. Addressing the flatness of mapping and its inaccuracy or inadequacy, the politics of verticality oscillates from representational space to informational space, from epistemological comprehensions of space to ontological presences and experiences. The variances between "looking across" and "cutting through" drive transformations in corporeal phenomena of space, territory, and occupation. Weizman's point is that the penetrative force of surveillance is also vertical rather than only lateral, unaligned and punctuated by "kissing points" (a pleasant misnomer, lending a sweetness to it all) and other momentary contacts rather than invasion or gentrification. The politics of verticality transgresses a notion of panoptic surveillance enabled through the expanse of looking from above and beyond, able to witness the visibly aberrant body in question within the prescribed sites of deviance (for queers, especially gay men, this has conventionally meant cruising zones and gay neighborhoods) to thinking about networks of contact and control, of circuits that cut through.

Networks of surveillance, in this three-dimensional, vertical setup are not removed, abstract, or cohered, but viciously intimate: unlike the apartheid of separation, these "new and intricate frontiers" invented for domination demand intimacy, not just penetration but interpenetration, matrices of scalar layers that are discontinuous yet transversal. They are discontinuous in that intimate proximities are orchestrated to produce the ephemera of nonconnection, of not-touching—not through a vacuum of distance or of severing or separation, but in the proactive, provocative swerve away from contact, the refusal of tactile knowing; the discontinuity is a deliberate rupturing, not simply a missing or a missed connection, but an intimate, brutal, *almost-but-no* kind of taunting. Intimacy in biopolitical terms is not bound to protection in the private or exposure in public. It mediates relations between transparency and opacity, waves of proximity, observation and invisibility, gazes, traces and profiles, electric and

erotic charges, passing by and bypassing, tightness, looseness, comfort, orderliness and chaos, order and disarray, rubbing and brushing against. Control networks are systems of unleashed circuitry, exuberant, fertile, that taunt the boundaries of inside and outside and, more important, beginning and end. Legislation after September 11, 2001, exacerbated an already occurring blurring of the dissimilarities between law enforcement and intelligence. The former is a reactive activity, the purpose of which is "to capture and prosecute criminals." Intelligence, on the other hand, is proactive, "collected for the prevention of, and warning about, national security threats," allowing for the "government mining of third-party private transactional data," easing barriers in obtaining "warrants for electronic surveillance," and permitting the "FBI to collect public information . . . and conduct surveillance in public places absent to a link to suspected criminal activity. What we also see is a profound sway in the tenor of temporality: the realignment from reactive to preemptive is a conversion from past-tense subject formation to future-tense subject anticipation, from the rehabilitative subject whose violated rights can be redressed through social representation and legal recognition, to regenerative populations who are culled through anticipation. . . .

These "surveillant assemblages," invested in witnessing the mobility of human and nonhuman actors, as well as affectively undulating movement itself, create the sameness of population through democratization of monitoring at the same time they enable and solidify hierarchies—in other words, the circuit amid profiling and racial profiling. Despite reports that terrorist circles are recruiting non-Arabs and non–South Asians who can pass and thus carry out attacks, racial profiling continues to be an important security measure. Yet unlike an older "masculinism as protection" model of surveillance, whereby "patriarchal logic . . . gives to protective services a right to rule over those who count on their expertise at keeping watch and apprehending," in the move from the containment and normativization of the subject to the control of populations (here we must perpetually drag ourselves from the subject as an object of inquiry, if only for a moment), self-regulation becomes less an internalization of norms and more about constant monitoring of oneself and others, watching, waiting, listening, ordering, positioning, calculating.

In statistical terms, race and sex are experienced as a series of transactional informational flows captured or happened upon at chance moments that perceive and render bodies transparent or opaque, secure or insecure, risky or at risk, risk-enabled or risk-disabled, the living or the living dead. Terrorist bodies as a "statistical population" coagulate through an imagined worldwide collectivity—the Muslim world—that perversely transcends national boundaries and is metaphorized through viral networks of contagion, infection, and the frustration generated by inaccessibility of sleeper cells that need no contact to reproduce themselves: rampant, uncontainable, spontaneous, and untraceable mimicry. The body and its color—because color and its contextual habitation and deployment still matter—both undergird the progressive accumulation of this statistical population and at times override it. The population "Muslim terrorists" comes to light not only through the Orientalist metonymic linking of Muslim and terrorist within the economy of meaning and representation. This population is made up of those caught in the violent chaotic shuttling back and forth between the statistical informational ontologies deemed "Muslim" and those that begin to bleed into "terrorist." We can say that this process of informationally creating bodies goes far beyond forms of neo-Orientalizing or racialization of religious affiliation. "The Muslim," summarily dismissed from its place as one

subject of multiculturalism, is an emergent, incipient Race, the Muslim Race. The ascendancy (rising up, evolutionary dominance) of whiteness is complemented and supplemented by the manufacture of Muslim as race.

Racialization has become a more diffuse process, not only informed by the biological body, what it looks like and what it can do, but also disassembled into the subhuman and the human-as-information. The dance between the profile that is racialized and the racial profile: a speedy (re)turn to genetic engineering technologies (stem cell research, cloning, sex selection, biological warfare, DNA manipulation, plastic surgery), informative bits and pieces encountered randomly or deliberately (the tapestry of the hand, the patterning of the iris, the motions of one's gait, the isolation of various traits and mannerisms of the body to discern trusted from untrusted: anybody can be untrustworthy until proven trustworthy, but not vice versa) interacting with the numbers and facts that matter (visa status, place of residence, country of origin, student activity, Social Security number, traveling risk status, criminal record, consumption habits, and any evidence of nonassimilative behavior). Data collection enables a mapping of race through aggregates and disaggregates that, as [Eugene] Thacker demonstrates, "becomes bifurcated along genotypic (genetic code), phenotypic (visible characteristics), and informatic (statistical) lines," while sex is removed from its associations to sex acts, sexuality, sexual orientation, and erotics and resigned to "genetic and informatic terms: *blood, sex, data.*" The profile establishes the individual as imbricated in manifold populations (not community—the designation to a dehumanizing population instead of the communalism of community is significant).

The deterritorialization of communities of belonging, those communities laboring under the identity signs of race, sexuality, gender, ethnicity, and nationality to secure the status and recognition of the subject (and its voice, history, community, intersectional coordinates), instead scrambles statistical populations. The subject is divided up into subhuman particles of knowledge that nevertheless exceed the boundaries of the body, yet it is also multiply splayed through, across, and between intersecting and overlapping populations, departing from intersectional identity paradigms insofar as compartmentalization, or analyzing components whether separately or together, is untenable. In this deterritorialization, epistemological empiricisms of statistical population are misconstrued as ontological truths about the subject and his or her culture, identity, reality. Again, a version of culture trumps or disengages itself from the circuits of capital and the political economy that produces it. Identity politics, both a symptom of and a response to these networks of control, capitulates once again to chasing the space of retribution for the subject. Control masks itself, or masks its effects, within the endless drive to recoup the resistant subject. We must instead advocate that resistance give way to delinquency. . . .

In reorienting our attention from public-private paradigms to the intimate, it seems almost ludicrous to inquire about the sector of the intimate for the suspected terrorist, the detainee, the exiled immigrant. Intimacy in its liberal fantasy form is historically the province of heteronormativity and now, as I have argued, homonormativity. . . . Therefore, when mapping the budding regimes of heightened regulation of (homo)sexuality . . . intimacy is not an object to be had or to be accorded or denied. Intimacy is a crucial part of an affective economy within surveillance systems that provoke, subsume, and muffle feelings and emotions but also sensations, hallucinations, palpitations, yearnings of security and insecurity. Further, the intimacy of the private radiates beyond an encircled physical site of disciplinary power to a form of cultural capital, a commodity circulating within power networks of control.

In control societies, surveillance imprints its presence far beyond an egregious intrusion of privacy or intimacy, as has been theorized in the case of panoptic disciplinary sites. To imply that only the privacy and intimacy of the bodies are violated through such intimate bodily practices of surveillance belies a liberal fantasy about bodily integrity, a projection of wholeness that many are not accorded, a privileged marker of liberal subjecthood as well as a marker of privileged liberal subjecthood. Experiences of intimacy are qualitatively altering due to the regularization of monitoring that Foucault speaks of. One could even argue that there is no inside of intimacy to violate, penetrate, or disturb from the outside, no depth that is safeguarded. The phantasmatic construction of this inside, this depth, or safeguarded interior intimacy is the prescriptive work of biopolitical control. That is not to say that surveillance is not violating, penetrating, disturbing, but instead that the perception of intrusion is diluted rather than concentrated, diffuse rather than focalized, multiple rather than singular. Gesturing to a biopolitical control view of contact, proximity, transparency, and corporeality entails a partial disengagement from the primacy of the self-other relay of subject formation to the regularization of quotidian affective modes of be/longing and recognition, tactility that congeals populations and distributes moments, brushings, looks, stares, and touches.

# 71

# CORINNE MASON AND SHOSHANA MAGNET

## SURVEILLANCE STUDIES AND VIOLENCE AGAINST WOMEN

Everyday technologies, from cell phones to social media sites, provide affordances for violence against women. As this excerpt shows, while there may be some meaningful forms of technological assistance for women seeking to escape abusive relationships, technology-based surveillance solutions generally push responsibility (and blame) onto women without addressing root causes of violence. The authors further argue that intersectional forms of oppression infuse the context for surveillance-based responses to violence against women, such that encounters with the criminal justice system may expose marginalized victims to additional violence and disempowerment.

*** 

Surveillance practices and their relationship to inequality have a long history, from the surveillance of slaves through a reliance on identity documents to the scrutiny of those receiving certain forms of aid from the state. . . . Scholarship within surveillance studies notes the relationship of surveillance to inequality, whether it is the scrutiny of immigrants and refugees or the policing of folks living in low-income neighbourhoods. Less attention has been concentrated on intersectional feminist approaches to surveillance that examine its relationship to racisms, sexisms, ableisms, and homo- and trans-phobias. That is, while inequalities have been paid serious attention in the field, axioms of oppression are rarely analysed simultaneously. Moreover, surveillance practices are intimately connected to stalking and have had tremendous consequences for violence against women [VAW], and yet the implications of the rise of surveillance for VAW are less studied in the field of surveillance studies, with a few excellent exceptions. . . .

The relationship between new technologies and stalking is the primary focus of anti-violence advocacy. Stalking is not a new phenomenon. And yet, new technologies complicate how women experience violence as well as how they are able to protect themselves. . . . Telephone and computer technologies used by abusers to monitor the actions and movements of victims, such as global positioning systems, electronic records, web search engines, text messaging as well as social media tools such as Facebook and MySpace, allow perpetrators to harass and track their intimate partners in new ways. Survivors report that they are increasingly experiencing stalking through 'high tech' means. For anti-violence advocates, the sophistication of stalking and harassing techniques is important to understand since women stalked by former boyfriends, husbands or cohabitating partners are very likely to be physically, emotionally, and/or sexually assaulted by the same person. Of women murdered in the U.S., 76 per cent were previously stalked by the perpetrator.

Stalking technologies complicate the ways that abusers violate victims. Global Positioning Systems (GPS) that use satellite receivers to provide real-time positioning are often used to locate and follow victims. For example, in Wisconsin in 2002, a man secretly installed a GPS device under the hood of his ex-girlfriend's car. This allowed him to track his ex-partner's exact location. One woman was followed by her ex-partner as she drove to work or ran errands. Once, she noted that her abuser tried to run her off the highway. . . . Other examples include cell phones planted in cars that are set to auto-answer, but where the ringer is turned to silent. That is, users will not hear their phone ring, but if they happen to speak while the phone is being called, they will activate their cell phone and, unbeknownst to them, take the call. Many documented cases show abusers calling phones planted in cars hundreds of times in the hopes of learning information if their victims happen to inadvertently 'answer' their phones by speaking to someone else in the car while it is 'ringing' on silent. . . .

While planted GPS and cell phone systems might be more complex and expensive, simple tracking systems used in Facebook and Twitter are highly accessible to computer users. . . . Abusers—from family members and former friends to significant others—can easily access this material through the victim's online friends. Information regarding a person's whereabouts obviously may increase the risk to their personal wellbeing. Furthermore, access to information such as email, phone numbers, and workplace information, the ability to read Facebook wall posts, to check out online friends lists, to find out the pages one 'likes' and 'group' pages one belongs to are tools that abusers can and do use. For example, an individual's friends list, their relationship status, as well as uploaded photos can anger abusers who may threaten or enact violence resulting from their desire to control the victim's communications and friendships. . . . Abusers also use SpyWare to facilitate stalking. Originally developed by companies to track consumer preferences, and then repackaged for individual users in order to monitor their children's internet use, abusers have developed SpyWare to monitor the online activities of their victims. SpyWare allows abusers to easily find out any attempts made by their victims to access information on, for example, rape crisis centres or shelters. . . .

Communicating with survivors about surveillance technologies is extremely important to anti-violence advocates. In order to increase the safety of women and children seeking their services, women's shelters have begun to take action against surveillance technologies by communicating their potential dangers. Moreover, some anti-violence advocates are beginning to explore the potential of using surveillance technologies to help victims find safety from abusers and have partnered with large corporations involved in surveillance technologies such as Google. . . .

Partnering with NNEDV [the National Network to End Domestic Violence], Google has begun to create user privacy and notification options for location-based services and worked closely with Google when the company launched 'Street View' to ensure that no undisclosed shelter appeared in Google Maps or Google Street View. NNEDV has also partnered with Verizon Wireless to provide cell phones and services to victims of violence. According to NNEDV, Verizon has been a corporate leader in domestic violence awareness and prevention for 15 years. Through Verizon Wireless' national HopeLine phone recycling programme, more than 90,000 wireless phones with the equivalent of 300 million minutes of free wireless service have been distributed to survivors across the country. . . . Although they can be helpful for individual women . . . these partnerships remain limited strategies for protecting women's safety, as companies are primarily concerned with developing tools that consumers will purchase rather than with women's safety. . . .

Most recently, the U.S. Department of Health and Human Services . . . is seeking smart phone applications that allow students on college campuses to connect with friends in real-time in order to prevent abuse by keeping track of each other's whereabouts. Bystanders are encouraged by the challenge to step up and prevent violent circumstances, but like many anti-violence initiatives, women are targeted in prevention efforts. Problematically, such applications are aimed at women as needing to be responsible for violence, rather than, for example, education initiatives that would target perpetrators of violence. That is, women are problematically expected to change their behaviour by tracking their whereabouts and 'checking in' with friends to prevent violence. While the nationwide call for these types of 'apps' encourages community support,

it does not remunerate communities nor does it provide adequate resources to help. Moreover, it asks women to give up personal information to third parties for their own self-protection. . . .

While individual privacy concerns mount, the prison system has found new surveillance technologies advantageous. . . . [I]n the U.S., African American women are now the fastest growing prison population, having outpaced African American men. The incarceration of poor women must be placed alongside the dismantling of the welfare state. The elimination of welfare programmes like Aid to Families with Dependent Children (AFDC) causes women to seek out criminalized forms of employment so that they can afford food and housing. Particularly relevant for this article is the ways in which sexual, emotional, and physical violence also propel women into the prison system. As women flee abusive situations, the lack of a social safety net means they may turn to criminalized behaviour such as sex work and the drug trade in order to meet their most basic subsistence needs. Queer people fleeing homophobic abuse and harassment in their homes, schools, and workplaces render LGBTQ folks vulnerable to the prison industrial complex. . . . [T]he relationship between homophobia and sexual harassment places queer women at increased risk of violence, and violence is a well-known factor that leads to women's engagement in activities deemed illegal by the state. . . .

We argue that the relationship of surveillance technologies to their social context and the ways that technologies reproduce and exacerbate social inequalities must be examined. In particular, while surveillance technologies may be useful to police enforcement, more policing practices result in the strengthening of a prison system that continues to overincarcerate women who are victims of violence—and particularly targets women of colour, women with disabilities and queer women for incarceration. Given the role of the prison system as an engine of inequality, we must call into question the assertion that improving existing connections between anti-violence movements, surveillance technologies, and the police is necessarily positive. . . .

Connections between anti-violence movements and the prison system have historically been and remain deeply problematic. . . . [M]andatory arrest laws in the U.S. and Canada have meant that women who call police for protection are often also arrested. A New York–based study compiled in 2001 found that a majority (66 per cent) of domestic violence survivors who were arrested alongside their abuser, or arrested as a result of a complaint lodged by their abuser, were African American or Latina/o, 43 per cent were living below the poverty line and 19 per cent were receiving public assistance. Lesbian survivors are also frequently arrested alongside their abuser since law enforcement officers frame violence within same-sex relationships as 'mutual combat'. Individuals perceived to be transgressing gender norms are often subject to excessive force upon arrest. Furthermore, undocumented women who have reported violence have often found themselves deported. To be sure, Canadian women's shelters have been raided by the Canadian Border Services Agency in order to deport 'illegal' immigrants. . . .

Pro-arrest policies and mandatory arrest laws beginning in the 1980s in the U.S. clearly demonstrate that the prison system can often undermine women's autonomy and actively disempowers them from choosing a trajectory for justice based on their own interests and wishes. In her case study on AWARE [Abused Women's Active Response Emergency alarm system] in the Netherlands, [Renée] Römkens found that women were reluctant to use the alarm, especially when it was an ex-partner that they would be involving in the criminal justice system. The women she interviewed suggested that they could not control the amount of punishment that police would inflict on their abuser. For one woman, the fact that one had to make a swift decision to press the button when an abuser appeared proved to be very difficult. Moreover, many women were afraid to press the button due to fear that the police would not take them seriously if their abuser was 'just there' and was not 'doing anything'. In the Dutch study, and a pilot study in Brooklyn, New York, Römkens found that victims avoided the direct use of surveillance systems in order to avoid a 'criminal justice outcome'. Although surveillance technologies may have the potential to provide safety for victims of violence, a complicated relationship between VAW and surveillance arises when technologies of protection are directly linked into the prison system. While mainstream anti-violence advocates continue to rely on government funding and state-based responses to violence, alternative tactics around ending violence must consider the ways that particular bodies are already entangled in systems of surveillance.

# 72

# SIMONE BROWNE

## DARK MATTERS

On the Surveillance of Blackness

In her book *Dark Matters*, Simone Browne makes a compelling case for seeing the history of surveillance as intimately linked to the racist objectives and conditions that motivated it, and that continue to do so into the present. Far from being neutral, surveillance produces and imposes race upon bodies, working to negate the experiences and agency of racialized people as equal subjects. Whether through the branding of black slaves in the eighteenth century to biometric screening systems deployed at borders today, surveillance fixes racial identities and polices bodies in discriminatory and frequently violent ways. As an important counterpoint to such racializing surveillance, Browne develops the concept of "dark sousveillance" to trace vital creative practices of resistance.

\*\*\*

Sociogeny . . . is understood as the organizational framework of our present human condition that names what is and what is not bounded within the category of the human, and that fixes and frames blackness as an object of surveillance. Take, for example, [Frantz] Fanon's often-cited "Look, a Negro!" passage in *Black Skin, White Masks* on the experience of epidermalization, where the white gaze fixes him as an object among objects and, he says, "the white gaze, the only valid one, is already dissecting me." Epidermalization here is the imposition of race on the body. . . .

[A]n understanding of the ontological conditions of blackness is integral to developing a general theory of surveillance and, in particular, racializing surveillance— when enactments of surveillance reify boundaries along racial lines, thereby reifying race, and where the outcome of this is often discriminatory and violent treatment. . . . Put another way, rather than seeing surveillance as something inaugurated by new technologies, such as automated facial recognition or unmanned autonomous vehicles (or drones), to see it as ongoing is to insist that we factor in how racism and antiblackness undergird and sustain the intersecting surveillances of our present order. Patricia Hill Collins uses the term "intersectional paradigms" to signal that "oppression cannot be reduced to one fundamental type, and that oppressions work together in producing injustice." Indebted to black feminist scholarship, by "intersecting surveillances" I am referring to the interdependent and interlocking ways that practices, performances, and policies regarding surveillance operate. . . .

Racializing surveillance is a technology of social control where surveillance practices, policies, and performances concern the production of norms pertaining to race and exercise a "power to define what is in or out of place." Being mindful here of David Theo Goldberg's caution that the term "racialization," if applied, should be done with a certain precision and not merely called upon to uncritically signal "race-inflected social situations," my use of the term "racializing surveillance" signals those moments when enactments of surveillance reify boundaries, borders, and bodies along racial lines, and where the outcome is often discriminatory treatment of those who are negatively racialized by such surveillance. To say that racializing surveillance is a technology of social control is not to take this form of surveillance as involving a fixed set of practices that maintain a racial order of things. Instead, it suggests that how things get ordered racially by way of surveillance depends on space and time and is subject to change, but most often upholds negating strategies that first accompanied European colonial expansion and transatlantic slavery that sought to structure social relations and institutions in ways that privilege whiteness. Racializing surveillance is not static or only applied to particular human groupings, but it does rely on certain techniques in order to reify boundaries along racial lines, and, in so doing, it reifies race. Race here is understood as operating in an interlocking manner with class, gender, sexuality, and other markers of identity and their various intersections. . . .

I use the term "dark sousveillance" as a way to situate the tactics employed to render one's self out of sight, and strategies used in the flight to freedom from slavery as necessarily ones of undersight. . . . I plot dark sousveillance as an imaginative place from which to mobilize a critique of racializing surveillance, a critique that takes form in antisurveillance, countersurveillance, and other freedom practices. Dark sousveillance, then, plots imaginaries that are oppositional and that are hopeful for another way of being. Dark sousveillance is a site of critique, as it speaks to black epistemologies of contending with antiblack surveillance, where the tools of social control in plantation surveillance or lantern laws in city spaces and beyond were appropriated, co-opted, repurposed, and challenged in order to facilitate survival and escape. This might sound like Negro spirituals that would sing of freedom and escape routes, or look like an 1851 handbill distributed by Theodore Parker, a white abolitionist from Massachusetts, that advised "colored people of Boston" to "keep a sharp lookout for kidnappers" who would act as slave catchers under fugitive slave laws that federalized anti-black surveillance. In this way, acts that might fall under the rubric of dark sousveillance are not strictly enacted by those who fall under the category of blackness.

Dark sousveillance charts possibilities and coordinates modes of responding to, challenging, and confronting a surveillance that was almost all-encompassing. In the *Narrative of the Life of Frederick Douglass*, Frederick Douglass carefully describes how surveillance functioned as a comprehensive and regulating practice on slave life: "at every gate through which we were to pass, we saw a watchman—at every ferry a guard—on every bridge a sentinel—and in every wood a patrol. We were hemmed in upon every side." This sweeping ordering did not, of course, preclude escapes and other forms of resistance, such as antisurveillance "pranks" at the expense of slave patrollers by stretching vines across roads and bridges to trip the patrollers riding on their horses, or counterveillance songs, for example, the folk tune "Run, Nigger, Run," which warned of approaching slave patrols. Recalling acts of antisurveillance and counterveillance, ex-slave Berry Smith of Forest, Mississippi, tells of "the pranks we used to play on them paterollers! Sometimes we tied ropes across the bridge and the paterollers'd hit it and go in the creek. Maybe we'd be fiddling and dancing on the bridge and they'd say, 'Here come the paterollers!' Then we'd put out." Such playful tricks were a means of self-defense. These oral histories of ex-slaves, slave narratives, and runaway notices, in revealing a sociology of slavery, escape, and freedom, recall the brutalities of slavery (instruments of punishment, plantation regulation, slave patrols) and detail how black performative practices and creative acts (fiddling, songs, and dancing) also functioned as sousveillance acts and were employed by people as a way to escape and resist enslavement, and in so being were freedom acts.

As a way of knowing, dark sousveillance speaks not only to observing those in authority (the slave patroller or the plantation overseer, for instance) but also to the use of a keen and experiential insight of plantation surveillance in order to resist it. Forging slave passes and freedom papers or passing as free are examples of this. Others include fugitive slave Ellen Craft escaping to Philadelphia in 1848 with her husband, William, by posing as a white man and as William's owner; Henry "Box" Brown's escape from slavery in 1849 by mailing himself to freedom in a crate "3 feet long and 2 wide"; Harriet Jacobs's escape from slavery to a cramped garret above her grandmother's home that she named as both her prison and her emancipatory "loophole of retreat"; slave spirituals as coded messages to coordinate escape along the Underground Railroad; Harriet "Moses" Tubman and her role in the 1863 Combahee River Raid that saw over seven hundred people escape

enslavement in South Carolina; Sojourner Truth's escape to freedom in 1826 when she "walked off, believing that to be alright." Dark sousveillance is also a reading praxis for examining surveillance that allows for a questioning of how certain surveillance technologies installed during slavery to monitor and track blackness as property (for example, branding, the one-drop rule, quantitative plantation records that listed enslaved people alongside livestock and crops, slave passes, slave patrols, and runaway notices) anticipate the contemporary surveillance of racialized subjects, and it also provides a way to frame how the contemporary surveillance of the racial body might be contended with. . . .

[F]or the fugitive in eighteenth-century New York, such a sensibility would encourage one to perform—in this case perform freedom—even when one was not sure of one's audience. Put differently, these performances of freedom were refusals of dispossession, constituting the black subject not as slave or fugitive nor commodity, but as human. For the black subject, the potentiality of being under watch was a cumulative effect of the large-scale surveillance apparatus in colonial New York City and beyond, stemming from transatlantic slavery, specifically fugitive slave posters and print news advertisements, slave catchers and other freelancers who kidnapped free black people to transport them to other sites to be enslaved, and the passing of repressive black codes. . . .

Lantern laws made the lit candle a supervisory device—any unattended slave was mandated to carry one—and part of the legal framework that marked black, mixed-race, and indigenous people as security risks in need of supervision after dark. In this way the lit candle, in a panoptic fashion, sought to "extend to the night the security of the day." Any slave convicted of being unlit after dark was sentenced to a public whipping of no more than forty lashes, at the discretion of the master or owner, before being discharged. Later this punishment was reduced to no more than fifteen lashes. Such discretionary violence made for an imprecise mathematics of torture. Mostly, punishment for such transgressions was taken into the hands of the slave owner. In 1734, a male slave of John van Zandt was found dead in his bed. The dead man was said to have "absented himself" from van Zandt's dwelling in the nighttime. . . .

We can think of the lantern as a prosthesis made mandatory after dark, a technology that made it possible for the black body to be constantly illuminated from dusk to dawn, made knowable, locatable, and contained within the city. The black body, technologically enhanced by way of a simple device made for a visual surplus where technology met surveillance, made the business of tea [fetching water at night] a white enterprise and encoded white supremacy, as well as black luminosity, in law. In situating lantern laws as a supervisory device that sought to render those who could be, or were always and already, criminalized by this legal framework as outside of the category of the human and as un-visible, my intent is not to reify Western notions of "the human," but to say here that the candle lantern as a form of knowledge production about the black, indigenous, and mixed-race subject was part of the project of a racializing surveillance and became one of the ways that, to cite McKittrick, "Man comes to represent the only viable expression of humanness, in effect, overrepresenting itself discursively and empirically," and, I would add, technologically. . . .

[A] longer history of biometric information technology . . . is in close alignment with the commodification of blackness. Current biometric technologies and slave branding, of course, are not one and the same; however, when we think of our contemporary moment when "suspect" citizens, trusted travelers, prisoners, welfare recipients, and others are having their bodies informationalized by way of biometric surveillance, sometimes voluntarily and sometimes without consent or awareness, and then stored in large-scale, automated databases, some managed by the state and some owned by private interests, we can find histories of these accountings of the body in, for example, the inventory that is the Book of Negroes, slave ship manifests that served maritime insurance purposes, banks that issued insurance policies to slave owners against the loss of enslaved laborers, and branding as a technology of tracking blackness that sought to make certain bodies legible as property. My suggestion here is that questioning the historically present workings of branding and racializing surveillance, particularly in regard to biometrics, allows for a critical rethinking of punishment, torture, and our moments of contact with our increasingly technological borders.

# SECTION 15

## ART AND CULTURE

The field of surveillance studies is perhaps influenced as much by literature and film as it is by social theory. It is no exaggeration to say that references to George Orwell's *Nineteen Eighty-Four* and the work of Franz Kafka are, for example, almost as prevalent as those to Michel Foucault or Karl Marx. Few articles about surveillance technology are complete without a nod to popular films from Alfred Hitchcock's *Rear Window* (1954) through Francis Ford Coppola's *The Conversation* (1974), to Steven Spielberg's *Minority Report* (2002), and beyond. Most of these references are used as a route to critical analyses of surveillance because most of these works are themselves critical, dystopian, and even paranoid.

But, as far back as the late 1990s, when Tony Scott's film *Enemy of the State* (1998) was released, it was noticed that surveillance was not simply something that caused concern but something that also tapped into the pleasures of watching and being watched. As a notorious real-world advertisement for clothing brand Kenneth Cole asked, "You are on a video camera an average of 10 times a day. Are you dressed for it?" Quoted in Mark Boal's 1998 article for the *Village Voice*, this example of "Spycam Chic" captures the cultural transformation of surveillance that had been taking place over thirty years in the United States from fear to fashion.

Surveillance has always had a close relationship to desire, and the pleasures and intensities of emotion associated with it have inspired writers and artists of all kinds, along with advertisers whose business is, of course, to create, exploit, and monetize desire. As David Bell (2009) declared, "Surveillance is sexy," or, as John McGrath noted in *Loving Big Brother* (excerpted in Chapter 73), surveillance is driven, in part, by people's love for it, or at least by a recognition that it is important to one's social being and social relations.

Voyeurism is pervasive (Denzin 1995). We like to watch. Voyeurism, in its classic form, which involves viewers who are careful not to intrude on or alter the subject of their viewing pleasure, would not in itself meet most definitions of surveillance (see Introduction to Section 1). However, surveillance products are consumed increasingly in a voyeuristic manner and have become a component of a sociocultural phenomenon that has propelled voyeurism to being a premier form of popular entertainment, with the rise of celebrity culture and in particular the dominant genre of "Reality TV" (Dubrofsky 2011; Palmer 2003). This has gone far beyond the "synoptic" surveillance identified by Thomas Mathiesen (1997; excerpted in Section 2). There is a fascination to watching, even—and perhaps especially—watching the absurd and the degrading, as sites like Chatroulette[1] have shown, and increasingly the disgusting and shocking, as the popularity of videos of killings and accidents shows. There are, of course, important political implications to increased transparency and, in particular, the prevalence of video that can hold officials and police accountable, but both the urge to record and to watch seem prior to these politics. This ambivalent relationship between desire and criticism can be seen in artworks from Agricola de Cologne's *Watch: Seconds Forever* (2001) to Mato Atom's drone fairytale, *Seagulls* (2014). And indeed, the opposite political impulse has also been significant: right from the beginning of the spread of police video surveillance in many countries in the late 1980s and early 1990s, footage was made available by operators to television shows as part of a deliberate process of normalizing visual surveillance by the state.

On the other side, as writers like Hille Koskela (2004) have noted (see Section 12), there has also been the widespread use of surveillance technologies as either narcissistic or empowering forms of display, expression, and exhibitionism. We like to be watched too. The pervasiveness of photography (Hand 2012) is also part of a culture of self-surveillance that extends into other forms of monitoring and sharing of the most intimate personal data, particularly in areas like health, where such data were previously thought of as the most private and safeguarded.

Until recently, cultural analysis within surveillance studies was limited to a focus on the kinds of watching and being watched noted above. Relatively little attention was paid to specific cultural products or how surveillance was portrayed and diffused through art and literature. David Rosen and Aaron Santesso (excerpted in Chapter 74) argue that the close relationship between literature, reading, and surveillance has been

underestimated. They posit that novels from the eighteenth century onward both represented and informed the formation of "liberal personhood," which included the development of a complex relationship with surveillance.

In a different register, with a few notable exceptions, "surveillance art" was not seen as an area for sustained scholarly inquiry until relatively recently. One major exception was the huge volume *CTRL [Space]: Rhetorics of Surveillance from Bentham to Big Brother* (2002), which was produced by ZKM and edited by Thomas Y. Levin, Ursula Frohne, and Peter Weibel. This book served as both a reader in surveillance theory and a catalog of a major exhibition curated by Levin. While artists of all types have continued to produce their own works, nothing has surpassed this magnum opus. The journal *Surveillance & Society*, through a special issue in 2010 on surveillance and new media art, sought to update the work of Levin and colleagues. From this issue, we excerpt a piece by the theorist of visibility Andrea Brighenti, which both provides a selected survey of contemporary visual and conceptual art that engages with surveillance and theorizes its importance.[2]

Like Rosen and Santesso, the excerpt by Mike Nellis interprets literature, but in the contemporary period, and argues that the "low culture" of genre fiction such as science fiction and thrillers is essential to understanding contemporary surveillance. Likewise, contemporary work on the cinema of surveillance celebrates arthouse and popular film. Several important articles and books on surveillance cinema have now been published, beginning with Peter Marks (2005) and including Sebastien Lefait (2012), Catherine Zimmer (2015), and J. Macgregor Wise (2016). We include an excerpt here from Zimmer's book, *Surveillance Cinema*.

Finally, games and gaming culture have become increasingly important, not just in themselves (for a survey, see the 2014 special issue of *Surveillance & Society* on Surveillance, Gaming, and Play), but also for the way in which "gamification" is increasingly affecting and shaping cultures of surveillance. For instance, an early example of gamification included the now defunct British company Internet Eyes, which provided a website where "players" could watch real security camera footage and were encouraged to spot crimes. Analyzing more contemporary developments, an excerpt from Jennifer Whitson concludes this section, where she notes how gamification entices users into surveillant relationships, including those of self-surveillance, but that attempts by employers to gamify tasks can create play/work dissonance that fosters cynicism and resistance.

## NOTES

1. Chatroulette is a social networking site where users video-chat with complete strangers.
2. Vibrant explorations of art and performance are also now coming on the scene, with sophisticated books like those by James Harding (2018) and Elise Morrison (2016).

## REFERENCES

Bell, David. 2009. Surveillance Is Sexy. *Surveillance & Society* 6 (3):203–12.

Boal, Mark. 1998. Spycam Chic. *The Village Voice.* Tuesday, December 8. http://www.villagevoice.com/news/spycam-chic-6422881.

Denzin, Norman K. 1995. *The Cinematic Society: The Voyeur's Gaze.* Thousand Oaks, CA: Sage.

Dubrofsky, Rachel E. 2011. Surveillance on Reality Television and Facebook: From Authenticity to Flowing Data. *Communication Theory* 21 (2):111–29.

Hand, Martin. 2012. *Ubiquitous Photography.* Malden, MA: Polity.

Harding, James M. 2018. *Performance, Transparency, and the Cultures of Surveillance.* Ann Arbor: University of Michigan Press.

Koskela, Hille. 2004. Webcams, TV Shows, and Mobile Phones: Empowering Exhibitionism. *Surveillance & Society* 2 (2/3):199–215.

Lefait, Sébastien. 2012. *Surveillance on Screen: Monitoring Contemporary Films and Television Programs.* Lanham, MD: Scarecrow Press.

Levin, Thomas Y., Ursula Frohne, and Peter Weibel, eds. 2002. *CTRL [Space]: Rhetorics of Surveillance from Bentham to Big Brother.* Cambridge, MA: MIT Press.

Marks, Peter. 2005. Imagining Surveillance: Utopian Visions and Surveillance Studies. *Surveillance & Society* 3 (2/3):222–39.

Mathiesen, Thomas. 1997. The Viewer Society: Michel Foucault's Panopticon Revisited. *Theoretical Criminology* 1 (2):215–34.

Morrison, Elise. 2016. *Discipline and Desire: Surveillance Technologies in Performance.* Ann Arbor: University of Michigan Press.

Palmer, Gareth. 2003. *Discipline and Liberty: Television and Governance.* Manchester: Manchester University Press.

Wise, J. Macgregor. 2016. *Surveillance and Film.* New York: Bloomsbury.

Zimmer, Catherine. 2015. *Surveillance Cinema.* New York: New York University Press.

# 73

# JOHN E. MCGRATH

## LOVING BIG BROTHER

Performance, Privacy, and Surveillance Space

John McGrath's fantastically rich and rewarding take on surveillance comes from a place that almost no other writer on surveillance comes from—that of a theater director. McGrath is far more interested in the affordances and libidinal pleasures of surveillance, the ways in which it functions to enact and reproduce desire, than in conventional critiques and criticisms of the surveillance state or surveillance society. His examples are multiple—from conceptual art through theater to television—but are all rooted in the same need to understand how we live in a culture of surveillance.

\*\*\*

Since the late 1990s . . . the subject of surveillance has been reinvigorated as an area of discussion. . . . While a range of disciplines and references are brought to these discussions, certain themes inevitably prevail. Specifically, discussion of surveillance is almost always framed in terms of issues of crime prevention (now very much extended to terrorism prevention) and privacy rights. . . .

I have taken as my starting point the belief that these ways of looking at surveillance are simply ideologies—means of addressing the issue that seem natural only because they are the conventional structures through which we have been encouraged to understand the profound changes that surveillance is making in our lives. Like all ideologies, the discourses of privacy and crime are as important for what they hide about our surveillance society as for what they reveal.

As a different way in to thinking about surveillance, I have developed the idea of 'surveillance space'. Drawing on a range of thinkers including [Michel] Foucault, but as diverse as [Immanuel] Kant, [Henri] Lefebvre, [Walter] Benjamin and [Judith] Butler, I have focused on the lived experience of surveillance and the cultural products that reveal our lives under surveillance to us. I hope that this different approach to thinking about surveillance may help us to deal in new and complex ways with the fact that the relevant question about surveillance today is not whether we should live in a surveillance society, but how. . . .

The dominant cultural fantasies of surveillance—the protecting eye or controlling Big Brother—equate in many ways with the fetishized figure of the twentieth-century theatre director, controlling events from which he or she is absent through the creation of a structure that necessitates and depends upon continued obedience. And yet the incorporation of representational technologies into the stage space does not necessarily support this fetishization of the director figure. At the simplest level, the failure of most theatrical uses of video, the tendency of the technology to negate the theatrical uses of video, the tendency of the technology to negate the theatrical frame, to appear much like an ill-thought-out visual aid in a shoddily constructed lecture, tends to expose the inability of the director to control anything beyond the illusory movements of play acting. The directors most accomplished in the use of on-stage video are very aware of the destruction of stage illusion that video equipment can enact, and are often actively engaged in the exploration of how this destruction relates to and undermines the production of directorial control. . . .

Given that surveillance also seemed to reflect yet distort the idea that most worried me in theatre, the idea of the director's controlling eye, I could hardly fail to look into the subject more thoroughly. So, I started to research the phenomenon of surveillance technology in contemporary life, with the instinct that theatrical space was a strange but productive place to start.

And so, much of the key evidence in this study is theatrical, from the art of The Wooster Group to the performances of New York's gay go-go boys to the theoretical texts of Bertolt Brecht, Antonin Artaud and Elin Diamond. Indeed, the key Brechtian idea of the self-aware spectator and the central Artaudian image of the 'double' were immediately relevant tools with which to start rethinking surveillance—ways to get outside of the seemingly self-evident ideologies via which surveillance was almost always seen and discussed. Theatre—and crucially the sense of space that it inevitably introduced—catapulted me into different ways of thinking about our experience of surveillance.

My approach to surveillance via theatre also had the benefit of keeping me away from an easy and lazy cliché of commentary on surveillance—the idea that surveillance is turning the whole of life into a public performance. In the case of my experiments with surveillance technology in theatrical space, it was the non-equivalence of surveillance and theatrical systems which had opened the theatre space to new possibilities, and disrupted the sense of total representational control. Equivalently, the elements of performance which can no doubt be introduced to surveillance systems do not so much theatricalize our lived experience under surveillance as open our understanding of surveillance to encompass a recognition of its productive omissions and contradictions. A sense of this interesting gap, this productive tension between theatre and surveillance made me cautious of any attempts to explain surveillance simply in terms of the way in which it puts life on show—in terms of specularization. . . .

It seemed to me that it may be more useful to separate surveillance from spectacle, or perhaps to understand the practice of surveillance as a surprisingly productive perversion of spectacle. Central to this reading is the analysis of surveillance as space.

My spatial understanding of surveillance is developed from a reading of Kant. As the canonical philosopher who most centralized space as an organizing principle—'Space is nothing other than the form of all appearances of the external sense, that is, the subjective condition of sensibility, under which alone external intuition is possible'—Kant maintains a defining position in relation to both common sense and theoretical understandings of space and perception. Obviously, a theoretically informed study written at the start of the twenty-first century is not going to take Kant's categories of intuition as immutable laws; however, the proposition that space is the fundamental *subjective* condition of perception, of knowing and understanding the external world, underlies my thinking. I have consistently returned to the question of space in analysing our understanding and experience of surveillance phenomena that may at first seem to be non-spatial by definition.

However, to discuss sound recordings, data and two-dimensional imagery—the materials of surveillance—in terms of space necessitates a complex analysis of the very areas of perception most marginalized in Kant's system. At times, particularly with respect to the key question of surveillance sound and its relations to interiority, I have teased at the edges of Kant's thought, looking for ways in which a productive contradiction between his organization of perception and the experiences of surveillance may help us understand surveillance's unexpected effects.

However, the theoretical understanding of space upon which I have most relied is something I have described as 'performative space'. . . . In beginning to think about surveillance as a space, I was able to draw upon thinkers, such as Foucault and Lefebvre, who explore the dynamic relation between psychological/representational structures and the world [through] which we move. However, my key experience of using surveillance technology in theatre was of the way in which the presence of the technology could—immediately [once] it was switched on, revealed or noticed—alter the very feel, the mood, the dimensions even, of the space that we were in: our lived experience of space changed as soon as the space became surveyed. It was to explore and explain the active change in space brought about by surveillance that I turned to ideas of performativity. . . .

For an understanding of surveillance as something other than simple representation of an event and place, the concept of performativity is crucial. Whereas Lefebvre complicates our view of space, allowing us to see the degree to which space is representational, the theorists of performativity enable us to separate surveillance from representational self-evidence, and to understand the degree to which it is spatially productive. . . .

In 'The work of art in the age of mechanical reproduction', Walter Benjamin makes the surprising assertion that individuals have a right to self-reproduction: 'modern man's legitimate claim to being reproduced'. The idea that such self-reproduction and reproduction of selves would in some way be a right, that it would be an important part of the life and values of the modern subject, has been underdeveloped in a subsequent history of media studies which emphasizes issues of objectification, simulation or representation in the demographic sense. In a world in which the scramble to appear on television in anything from talk shows to 'reality' television is exceeded in its frenzy only by the bewildered disapproval of the upmarket media, the idea that a twentieth-century thinker would locate self-reproduction in mass media as a necessary aspect of modern subjectivity puts an unfamiliar light on an overdiscussed phenomenon. Why would Benjamin consider this reproduction of self a necessary subjective tool, rather than subsuming it in a wider view of consumption (as in [Theodor] Adorno's critique of cinema, or in [Jean] Baudrillard's recent weary rant against reality television)?

Benjamin's essay famously discusses the loss of 'aura' in the world of mechanical reproduction, the loss, that is, of the sense of unique wholeness surrounding the traditional art work—held at a distance from us, self-contained and mysterious. He contrasts this traditional viewing of the art work with the experience of the architecture of a public building, which we enter, feel around us, learn in passing through it. The great buildings of the modern era, emphasizing space, not facade, are the template for understanding the ways in which twentieth-century art—mass art—can be experienced. Rather than being viewed, such work will be inhabited.

The danger which Benjamin identified was that modern subjects, rather than finding themselves in a self-aware, spatial relation to contemporary culture, would instead be manipulated into overwhelmed, self-annihilating fascination with the unapproachable excess of the mass-produced cultural artefact. The respectful relation to aura would be replaced not with an inhabiting but with a self-prostration before the might of reproductive technology. In relation to such danger (to such actuality), the right to self-reproduction—and the need to become talk show fare—makes more than a degree of sense. If technologically reproduced cultural artefacts can be understood only by inhabiting them, the rush for five minutes of fame on *The Jerry Springer Show* is perhaps a dash for survival, for a moment of placing one's own body within the space of televisual reproduction.

The 'legitimate claim' for self-representation is, then, a spatial claim. The desire to feature in talk shows or fly-on-the-wall documentaries is not, as critics usually assume, an unquestioning acceptance of the ideology of television, an assumption that any appearance in the medium associates the subject with the *Lifestyles of the Rich and Famous*. Rather, with a Benjaminian spatial understanding, we see that the impulse is a survival tactic, an attempt to comprehend televisual space from within—to replace prostration before the post-auratic object with a bodily relation to its complexities.

Such a desire for self-reproduction would not necessarily have been expected from our analysis of surveillance space up to this point. In relation to the ways in which an 'ideology of crime' functions in *Crimewatch* and similar television programmes, a desire for television representation is in some ways a contradictory instinct. . . . [T]he ideological structuring of *Crimewatch* is such that the viewer is encouraged to identify with the non-visualized position; the visualized is the black, the criminal, the other. The viewer is reassured that his or her image has been sorted through and passed as law-abiding and therefore does not need to be circulated. In examining the phenomenon of data representation we also saw that it is in this non-visual realm that the citizen-consumer feels most at ease, separated from the visualized underclass.

# 74

# DAVID ROSEN AND
# AARON SANTESSO

## THE WATCHMAN IN PIECES
Surveillance, Literature, and Liberal Personhood

David Rosen and Aaron Santesso's work *The Watchman in Pieces* is in most ways unlike much of what surveillance studies has produced and consciously so. The authors set out to remedy what they see as a serious deficiency in the field: not taking account, and certainly not the right kind of account, of literature and literary culture. It is a detailed and impressive work. In this excerpt the authors consider the cultural context in which Jeremy Bentham developed the Panopticon and find conventional scholarly treatments prone to oversimplification and anachronism.

\*\*\*

[T]he first eighteenth-century figure one associates with surveillance is Jeremy Bentham, proponent of the panopticon and a man whose psychology of incarceration is widely taken to have marked a watershed moment in the history of human interiority. In this view, Bentham's prison, with its abject inmates and unblinking observers, allowed the State to invade and rewrite the very structure of the human mind, where previously it could only exert crude pressure through physical violence. To recall Foucault's formulation . . . the prisoner's mind was now treated as "a surface for the inscription of power," with the final goal of creating an "obedient subject, [an] individual subjected to habits, rules, orders, an authority that [was] exercised continually around him and upon him, and which he must allow to function automatically *in* him." Indeed, the argument continues, in Bentham's prisons, the spread of discursive power, a process that had been under way for most of the eighteenth century, was suddenly made explicit and given overt spatial expression. The modern disciplinary State, made possible by the coupling of newly perfected human sciences with unremitting surveillance, found an early, concrete symbol in the Benthamite penitentiary.

So goes the standard account. . . . [W]e would argue that though the panopticon's importance has not been understated, it has largely been misunderstood, and that Bentham, though certainly a key figure in the history of surveillance, has been made to stand for views that have little or nothing to do with his expressed positions. To read Bentham as a prophet of "internalization" and the modern surveillance State is anachronistic— and . . . we propose to address two consequent (and related) errors in the way eighteenth-century psychological and social thought is now received. The first is a tendency to read period texts, literary and otherwise, through lenses colored by powerful developments in post-structuralist or late-Marxist philosophy; the most influential interpreters, in this tradition, of Enlightenment Europe, from Foucault to Jurgen Habermas (his early work on the public sphere rather than his later engagement with communicative rationality) to Terry Eagleton, have tended to ignore, or simplify beyond recognition, highly complex thinking about interiority and the development of the self. The idea that eighteenth-century society was "disciplinary" is used to explain the behavior of characters ranging from Robinson Crusoe to Joseph Addison's intrepid man-about-town Mr. Spectator. Blessed with 20-20 hindsight, we commonly read works from the eighteenth century as parables of internalization and mono-directional social control, in ways that anticipate contemporary discourse theory. . . .

[I]f we can correct the habit of reading Enlightenment texts as anticipatory of (a late twentieth-century) Bentham, might we not also reexamine Bentham himself and recover the way his panopticon writings are a product of their own century, the result of a new and distinctly post-allegorical way of thinking about personality? His concept of the relation between social observation and individual psychology was surely derived, at least in part, from the intellectual culture around him—and not only from

philosophy. As it happens, he was a surprisingly avid reader of sentimental literature, with one author in particular standing out:

> When I got hold of a novel, I identified myself with all the personages, and thought more of their affairs than of any affairs of my own. I have wept for hours over Richardson's "Clarissa."

Bentham the apostle of passionless objectivity is hardly visible in this remark or in his numerous other references to Richardson. He admits to his literary executor John Bowring that as a young man his "interest: [in *Pamela*] became extreme. 'Clarissa' kept me day after day incessantly bathed in tears." Rather than ask how Bentham (as he is presently understood) sheds light on Clarissa and her literary sisters, we might ask how Clarissa taught Bentham to understand everyday conduct. Could the man committed to the "suffocation of individuality," as one critic puts it, have been deeply affected by sentimentalism and its urbane understanding of sympathy? Might the panopticon itself, and the theories of surveillance underlying it, be sympathetic and respectful of individual autonomy? . . .

Those tears, had Bentham been able to anticipate his future career, should have been prompted not only by Clarissa's fate but also by the suicidal teleology of Richardson's experiment in social performance and the challenges it posed for reform. The arguments in his *Panopticon Letters* that have had the most lasting influence (via Foucault) are to be found in a handful of passages towards the beginning—and none more so than his promise, in the "Preface," that the prison would offer "a new mode of obtaining power of mind over mind, in a quantity hitherto without example." "The more constantly the persons to be inspected [were] under the eyes [of the inspectors]," we saw him reasoning in our introduction, "the more perfectly [would] the purpose of the establishment [be] attained." Especially in this obscure and ominous "purpose of the establishment" one seems to hear the prophet of modern authoritarianism, with the Powers That Be colonizing and rewriting the individual personality. Bentham, it has seemed plausible to conclude, is outlining a psychology of internalization, with the inmate, under the pressure of constant observation, slowly and unconsciously taking on the rules of the prison; eventually the rules become, permanently, part of his very identity.

And yet with the slightest further reading, it is all too clear how selectively Bentham has to be quoted for this conclusion to hold water. Bentham conceived of his panopticon as anything but an "indefinitely generalizable mechanism": although he imagined it might be employed in certain other institutional settings designed for "inspection" (such as workhouses and schools), he warned against its "perverse applications" and certainly did not consider it a model for society as a whole. Indeed, he surely would have resisted the coinage "panopticism" as altogether too abstract a concept. Whereas Foucault, very much a product of the twentieth century as well as an intellectual tradition given to totalizing claims, grandly pronounced that "there is no outside" in a surveillance society, Bentham was convinced that the effects he hoped to achieve could only occur in a discrete and controlled—indeed, a walled—environment: as he noted at the outset, his prison must occupy "a space not too large." Less a Control State, if one desires a contemporary parallel, than Caesar's Palace. Nor, while we're on this note, was Bentham sure that the psychological effects of internalization would be appropriate, let alone possible, for all classes of society. Russia, a land of "stupid people," inured to centuries of despotism, offered ready fodder for his prison houses, as did the British underclass

but one could hardly expect internalization from the better-educated, "superior ranks of life": the Michel Foucaults of this world would not be deceived.

It is worth remembering that Bentham's panopticon writings are dauntingly extensive. After the initial series of letters, published in 1787, he composed two long postscripts, each far longer than the original series, as well as a finely detailed comparison—longer still—between his prison scheme and the convict settlement in New South Wales. These last three documents are barely known today, and most of Bentham's vast correspondence, in which he pursued his panopticon scheme for the greater part of three decades before finally admitting defeat, is only now, slowly, finding its way into print. In this subsequent writing, the logic of social construction (still less internalization) is barely to be descried, but Bentham the heir to the sentimental tradition and its complex ideas about performance is evident at all points. For one thing, his intentions are explicitly philanthropic. To a modern sensibility, his plan might well seem barbaric; compared, however, to the appalling prison conditions of the time, it was a quantum improvement. Natural light, relative privacy and safety from other prisoners, indoor plumbing, no need for shackling in irons: the Newgates of popular dread could boast nothing like it.

More relevant to our point, his psychology, when examined more closely, is essentially of its age, the culmination of a century of post-empirical thinking. When Habermas remarked that "Bentham was unthinkable without Adam Smith," he was thinking primarily of economics and the immense influence *The Wealth of Nations* had on Bentham's writings about political economy. But Smith's work on sympathy was no less an inspiration—and a caution: Smith's insight that, to produce "concord," a person must modify his or her behavior to win the sympathy of his or her observers would seem to find a practical echo in the panopticon, a machine designed to promote such modifications of behavior. And yet Bentham had little interest in Smith's implication that the self could be remade: panoptic observation, Bentham made perfectly clear, was meant to encourage and *channel* the natural theatricality of inmates. Forty years earlier, Doctor [Samuel] Johnson had identified as the chief source of recidivism in jails unstructured social relations among the prisoners: "The misery of gaols is not half their evil. . . . In a prison, the awe of the publick eye is lost, and the power of the law is spent; there are few fears, there are no blushes. The lewd inflame the lewd, the audacious harden the audacious. Every one fortifies himself as he can against his own sensibility." As if in answer to Johnson's insight, Bentham asserts that the prison is meant—quite literally—to *model* right conduct. Foucault, naturally, had seen the most distinctive spatial feature of the panopticon—the central position of the inspector and peripheral, sequestered aspect of the prisoners—as irredeemably oppressive, a physical embodiment of the way State power traps the individual within limiting discourses. Bentham would have found this idea utterly foreign. . . .

Thus where Foucault makes much of Bentham's insistence on the isolation of each prisoner—the better to internalize the rules of the watchers—Bentham in fact retreats from this position almost at once. As he comments in the first postscript, "of perfect solitude . . . I know but one use—the breaking of the spirit." Isolation reduces the naturally sociable inmate to idiocy, not obedience. A few pages later, in perhaps his most startling insight, he suggests that prisoners wear masks when observed. Constant surveillance, he reasons, may well encourage sullenness and recalcitrance rather than an understanding or acceptance of the rules; so how better to encourage right behavior than dress the prisoners in costumes? . . .

In the final reckoning, Bentham was never as sanguine as his modern readers about the process of internalization itself. For Foucault, the end result of constant watching was perfect certainty on the part of the watchers: an "omnipresent and omniscient power." Bentham's concluding thoughts, in a passage that present-day commentators tend to ignore, were far more ambiguous and indeed sentimental:

> Detection is the object of [the spy]; *prevention*, that of the [panopticon]. . . . The object of the first was to pry into the secret recesses of the heart; the latter, confining its attention to *overt acts*, leaves thoughts and fancies to their proper *ordinary*, the court *above*.

Hardly the language of an authoritarian seeking to smother individuality; rather, the phrase "secret recesses of the heart" is—perhaps consciously—a near quotation from Richardson. The idea that the state could (let alone should) take over the very consciousness of its citizens could not have been further from Bentham's intentions; rather, like Richardson, he drew a sharp distinction between "overt acts," the performance that is part of everyday social behavior, and the truth of inner life, whose only possible spectator is God. With this ultimately theistic and individualized idea of personhood, Bentham's panopticon papers stake out, if anything, a residual position in the rapidly transforming culture of late eighteenth century liberalism.

# 75

# ANDREA MUBI BRIGHENTI

## ARTVEILLANCE

At the Crossroads of Art and Surveillance

Andrea Brighenti has made it his mission to bring visibility into the core of the social sciences. His work engages with visibility as categorical and as category-making, which means it inevitably intersects with surveillance. Part of this work has involved a consideration of the production of art that either uses or responds to surveillance. Here we reproduce both some of the theoretical grounding for this consideration and a few of the many examples of new media art analyzed by Brighenti.

\*\*\*

While it is probably an inaccurate tag, for the sake of brevity in the following I am going to use the term 'surveillance art' to address every contemporary artwork that in some way hints to or deals with topics, concerns and procedures that fall within the interest of surveillance studies. Clearly, at the present, surveillance art is not a recognised art current or even an art movement. Not only are there many different points of view and attitudes to approach the topic—from the overtly political, through the cynical, to the playful—but the degree of involvement various artists have developed with the topic of surveillance varies widely. Some artists have been increasingly focusing their work on surveillance, while others have evoked it only occasionally or only during a certain period of their production. Still another noticeable difference concerns the fact that, while some artists *refer to* surveillance in their work, others actually *use* surveillance technologies to make art. . . .

[M]y general argument is that surveillance art can be interpreted as an attempt to deal with issues of social visibility and invisibility and, more specifically, with contemporary *visibility regimes*. I also seek to examine how these visibility regimes are intimately related to a newly emergent social stratification of motilities, another theme that runs through surveillance art. . . .

I suggest using a distinction between three models, or paradigms of visibility: the visibility of *recognition*, the visibility of *control*, and the visibility of *spectacle*. In the first model, visibility is essential to secure one's social recognition. From this perspective, being visible is essential to obtain respect from others and being empowered as a subject. In short, visibility determines access to social existence and, conversely, social exclusion can be conceptualised as a form of invisibility. This type of visibility seems to be linked to the basic, immediate presentation of people to each other through direct eye-to-eye contact, as initially described by Georg Simmel.

In the second model visibility is, on the contrary, seen as a form of social control that disempowers the subject. Being visible means being under control by the agency that looks at us—even when that agency presents itself as 'looking after' us. Notably, new technologies extend visibility-as-control from the human sense of sight to the act of tracking and tracing apparently abstract information data. In practice, there is a shift from sensorial to intellectual seeing: a disembodied view appears that ideally resembles God's infallible vision. Whereas the first model entails reciprocal inter-visibility, the second model clearly depicts a situation of deep asymmetry in visibilities. The third model focuses instead on the degree of separation that exists between the viewer and the viewed. In practice, the spectacle exists in a regime that is utterly separate from everyday life. In particular, for critical theorists, the spectacle is a set of images detached from life and simultaneously falsely proposed as an illusory form of unity of life. The regime of visibility associated with mass media is the nearest example of visibility-as-spectacle, although clearly not the only one.

The degree of asymmetry between looking and being looked at reveals the deep, intricate relationship between vision and power. *Recognition* plays a pivotal role in this process. There are at least four types of recognition, which we may call categorical, individual, personal, and spectacular recognition. To begin with, *categorical* recognition is founded on the simple and almost always routine typification of people.

When one walks down an urban street, one encounters dozens of biographically unknown others and in order to navigate the complexity of city space one resorts to quick, stereotypical profiles to recognise people. Often, this fact generates tensions and involves the negotiation of the thresholds of what Erving Goffman first called 'civic inattention', which regulates recognition in the public domain. Second, *individual* recognition, or identification, is typically exercised by the State with regard to its own population. This type of recognition reaches its most complete form in the early 20th century thanks to instruments of classification and control like registry office records, identity cards, fingerprints—tools whose function is performed today by sophisticated biometric profiles and digital searchable databases. In practice, the individual conceived through these technologies of power is a *dividual*, a social entity that can be segmented into traits to be controlled selectively in each relevant dimension that is currently examined and which—most importantly—can be calculated in an aggregate way. Third, *personal* recognition derives from what sociologists usually call 'personal knowledge'. Goffman provided a most detailed description of the norms associated with acquaintanceship, and in particular with the 'right to initiate a direct relationship' (e.g., speaking to someone) to which only personal recognition entitles beyond a basic formalistic degree (e.g., asking for directions). Interestingly personal recognition does not coincide with individual recognition, given that it is well possible to develop an acquaintance even without knowing one's tax code or residence address. Personal recognition is a form of interaction that calls into play the moral dimension of the Self and involves a 'facework', that is a type of interaction aimed at saving the integrity and respectability of all the parties involved in the interaction itself. Facework is required when personal recognition takes place in the public domain (also in mediated public arenas: facework on Facebook). Notably, this type of recognition can also take place in the domestic domain, where it occurs in an extremely informal, often implicit way (e.g., within a family). Fourth, *spectacular* recognition has to do with the distinction between the two regimes of the ordinary and the extraordinary, or between the profane and the sacred. While celebrities are personally unknown to their audience, they are clearly different from anonymous strangers subject to categorical recognition. Indeed, people develop a peculiar sense of intimacy with celebrities that generates a tension between the ordinary setting of everyday life and the 'sacred' appearance of 'very important people'. In the model of spectacular recognition, the viewer is in fact a spectator of a spectacle that is offered to him/her, or which s/he aspires to watch. The 'spectacle of power' is very old and includes the most diverse forms of parades and *mises en scène*, in which the spectator participates precisely only as separate viewer. Clearly, also phenomena like voyeurism and scopophilia are located in the field of spectacular recognition.

It is interesting to notice that each type of recognition has a specific 'mood' attached to it and it develops specific affects. In particular, individual recognition is in some way the most impersonal and abstract form of recognition, as well as the one most closely associated with surveillance. Indeed, contemporary surveillance is based on the deployment of a technical and technological apparatus that is close to the impersonal classificatory apparatus developed by the modern state and other control agencies that form the 'surveillant assemblage'. Clearly, such apparatus also involves categorical, personal and spectacular elements, but the individualising/dividualising factor seems to remain prominent, not simply at the operative level, but also at the imaginative one. As far as the latter is concerned, in/dividual recognition typically tends to

generate a sense of *Unheimlichkeit* [uncanniness], to use the effective psychoanalytical term. . . .

The British street artist Banksy has become famous for representing in his works not simply the obsession with surveillance cameras which pervades the surveillance society, but also the very logic of surveillance. For instance, placing a surveillance camera right in the middle of a classical bucolic painting by Constable, Banksy seems to understate huge questions about, on the one hand, the real aim of the surveillance ('What is surveillance actually for?', 'Surveillance for whom?', etc.) and, on the other hand, the aesthetic quality of the surveillance society ('What type of visual landscape has surveillance created?', 'Would we push ourselves so far as to install CCTVs everywhere including a forest?', 'Where would we stop?', etc.). In another work, Banksy puts in front of a CCTV a stencil that reads 'What are you looking at?'. Here, it is the sightless vision of the CCTV that is called into question, together with the asymmetric visibility created by the practice of control. Introducing the possibility of 'replying' to the fact of being scrutinised by surveillance cameras—especially in the form of an impolite and rude but 'healthy' reaction—Banksy evokes personal recognition as a reply to or even a nemesis for the in/dividual recognition exercised through surveillance. . . .

Mukul Patel and Manu Luksch, who co-direct the London-based production centre Ambient Information Systems (AIS) and have written a *Manifesto for CCTV Filmmakers,* focus their work on issues that arise at the interface of social and technical infrastructures, including surveillance, privacy, data protection and access to data. In particular, the rules of CCTV filmmaking prescribe that it must use exclusively the 'omnipresent existing video surveillance already in operation'. In her 50-minute work *Faceless* (2007), Manu Luksch constructs a sort of psychological sci-fi narrative compiled from surveillance video footage. The plot is simple: in a dystopian society everybody is faceless; one day a woman wakes up with a face and begins her quest for a different humankind with a face, during which she is constantly thrust into a startling escape from a perpetually administered present of 'Realtime'. It is interesting to recall that the video material was recovered by the artist through the UK Data Protection Act, which gives individuals the right to access their own personal data held in computer databases. Thus, the plot of the story skillfully plays with the fact that, in order to comply with the same legislation, all other individuals beyond the main character are anonymised, that is, rendered faceless. The alienating image of a world populated by people without a face raises once again the tension between the in/dividual, subject to surveillance, and the person with all its richest moral connotations, a 'face' in Goffman's sense.

A famous case is the work by the artist and San Jose State University assistant professor Hasan M. Elahi. Coming from the traumatic experience of having been interrogated in 2002 by the F.B.I. as a suspect terrorist—an obviously absurd charge from which he was ultimately acquitted— Mr Elahi decided to transform his art into a systematic inversion of surveillance into self-surveillance or sousveillance. On his website (http://trackingtransience.net/) the artist provides overabundant details not only about his current location and what he sees just in front of him at the moment, but also about the most various aspects of his everyday life, including his finances. The endless series of pictures—more than 20,000 images—of airports, meals, and toilets posted on his website documents everything Mr Elahi does and provides the viewer with a caricatural but undoubtedly real instance of systematic surveillance.

*Faceless*, 2007, Manu Luksch.

This also connects to the theme of the emergent stratification of motilities and the dramatically curtailed freedom of movement migrants and minorities enjoy. The artist has provocatively turned himself into a high-visibility man, constantly intermingling the features of the in/dividual recognition of surveillance with aspect of categorical and even personal recognition linked to the domestic domain and the regime of the familiar (e.g., airports we've been at, food we've eaten). It has also been observed that the operation undertaken by Mr Elhai has been quite successful, not the least because he has not been detained since. . . .

[T]he indoors installation by the Los Angeles–based French artist and architect Marie Sester *Threatbox.us* (2005–2007) . . . [a]t first sight . . . looks like the screening of excerpts from war videogames mixed with real wars, including bombings, explosions, plane crashes and so on. But whenever the spectator enters the detection zone and gets tracked by the hidden video camera on the ceiling, the projector turns into a spotlight that swiftly points onto the viewer's body, a moment Ms. Sester describes as 'the attack'. A very loud, frightening noise is produced, to which people react instantly. The installation can be read as a criticism of the 'industrial-entertainment-military complex', as the artist declares. But the device exploits a very physical, instinctive reaction to motion all human beings have. Like in Moeller's and Utterback's installations, it is a reaction to the act of being seized, which is caused by the sudden shift from the state of being a detached, safe observer to the state of becoming a prey. To use the terms introduced above, it is the shift from spectacular to in/dividual recognition: people arrive as free, independent subjects who have certain expectations about the regime of visibility they are involved in, but in fact—just like Hasan Elahi—they are already the object of an ongoing surveillant scrutiny. Thus, what these installations perform is the actualisation of a virtual relationship of power that is already always present within every surveillance system.

# 76

# MIKE NELLIS

## SINCE *NINETEEN EIGHTY FOUR*

Representations of Surveillance in Literary Fiction

Mike Nellis is one of the most knowledgeable scholars around about literature and surveillance, yet he comes to literature from the position of a voracious reader and enthusiast, not as a literary scholar. Although he provides a broad overview of surveillance in popular fiction across a number of genres from conventional literary fiction to thrillers, this excerpt is drawn from the conclusion in which he reflects on the success of surveillance fiction.

\*\*\*

For better or worse, George Orwell's *Nineteen Eighty Four* still remains a touchstone . . . although the concepts it bequeathed to us—'Big Brother', 'thought police' and 'telescreen'—long ceased to be adequate for grasping the varied forms, political complexity, multiple uses, ambivalent intentions and contradictory consequences of contemporary surveillance. . . .

Literary fiction—in the broadest sense—has tackled the theme of surveillance in a way that parallels and complements (and quite possibly draws from) ideas being developed in the social sciences. It does so in a somewhat more nuanced way than cinematic fiction, and it acknowledges the increased complexity of surveillance since *Nineteen Eighty Four* appeared [in 1948]. Yet no single surveillance story has emerged to supersede this iconic novel, although the majority of the texts mentioned here are among the few to have been publicised in press reviews. No claims can be made as to how audiences have received them, and it is unlikely that any readers yet have a sense of 'surveillance novels' as a distinct literary grouping; at present, for now, that is a purely academic construction. The gist of the novels, taken collectively, is indeed that burgeoning surveillance technologies are to be feared, although if psychoanalyst Adam Philip's insightful epigram—'Paranoia is the self-cure for insignificance'—is valid, our fear is arguably functional, perhaps even agentic. In a globalized world where we occasionally sense that the control of events is beyond us, shaped by unimaginably powerful institutions, in whose machinations we might at any time be caught up, surveillance stories *both* legitimate our suspicions and also hint, rather reassuringly, that, in our fumbling quest to understand who our masters are, we are at least on the right track, even if we cannot be certain about their exact organisational forms, or their capabilities and reach.

In at least some surveillance stories, a new variant of the traditional adventure story hero is our surrogate in this quest— a person who, despite everything, still manages to live anonymously, invisibly, 'off the grid', without leaving traces, and onto whom we can project our dwindling hopes of freedom. In Ken Macleod's technothriller *The Execution Channel*, for example, a security operative frustratingly learns:

> from MI5's London HQ that all the face recognition software, all the trawling and tracking and surveillance of the British state, couldn't find a trace of the face, card transactions, or vehicle registrations of a man who evidently went by many names, only one of which was James Travis.

In broad terms, this type of character is not wholly new in Western literature. Joseph Conrad's Axel Heyst was 'invulnerable because elusive' but the Malay archipelago in the late-nineteenth century afforded more opportunities for reclusive Europeans to vanish than the present day western world affords to anyone from the Scarlet Pimpernel onwards, in traditional crime and spy thrillers, insouciant and ingenious heroes routinely stay 'one step ahead' of powerful opponents, but twenty-first century heroes require quite specific counter-surveillance skills to achieve this. Anonymity must now be worked at, via easy access to forged identity documents, the capacity to route untraceable phone calls through the net and, when necessary, an ability to anticipate and dodge the swivel and tilt of CCTV cameras. Maya and the

two young men she protects in *The Traveller* epitomise the type, but there are more mundane, realistic examples. They can comfortably take on new identities, remain anonymous despite remorseless scanning and cannot be 'mined' out of databases, at least not in real-time, not until it is 'too late' for whatever authority-subverting action the plot requires. The Harlequins' austere protocols for survival amidst the tendrils of 'the vast machine'—keep on the move, defy predictability and order, cultivate randomness—speak, in fantasy form, to the latent fears and desires of at least some late modern people.

But, for ordinary mortals, is ever greater self-diminishment before the gaze and reach of surveillance, all we have to fear? Is that the only subjectivity that surveillance produces in us? In J. G. Ballard's idiosyncratic oeuvre, the sterile, alienating domains in which the contemporary middle class lives and moves—suburbs, science parks, leisure complexes and shopping malls, in which surveillance is ubiquitous—call forth psychotic violence, before—or more precisely, at the very point at which—subjugation of their occupants is almost achieved. Such are the aggressive traits that evolution has left us with, overlain by the restless, thrill-seeking consciousness fostered by consumer society, that the discomfort of 'indisposition' is neither as passively borne (in the West), nor as easily suppressed, as Zoran Zivokovic imagined. Not everyone succumbs easily to control by impersonal systems—although the means by which it is resisted may be far from the convivial liberal understanding of rational revolt espoused, say, by Tom Paine. In much of Ballard's work psychosis is the consequence of over-control. It is invariably represented as a twisted and destructive affirmation of basic human impulses for freedom and meaning in the soulless landscapes of modernity—and given the insidiousness of the controls to which we are subject, he sees this as no bad thing. *Running Wild*—one of Ballard's masterpieces—offers a variant of this view. It begins in a luxurious gated community in southern England whose affluent parents benignly use technology to surveil every moment of their precious children's time, fatally but unknowingly eroding their capacity for affection and empathy—and are systematically massacred by them as a result. Here the childrens' psychosis is portrayed less as a *reaction against* the 'surveillance of the heart' and more as its terrifying corollary, an outworking in particularly brutal form of the same inhuman, unloving logic that misguidedly inspired the parental imposition of panoptic surveillance in the first place.

Margaret Atwood's *Oryx and Crake*, is less concerned with the consequences of what surveillance seeks to repress, and more concerned with its misapplication. Like Jonathan Raban's *Surveillance*, she insists that investment in contemporary forms of anti-terror surveillance, directed at an external 'other', deflects our attention away from far more pressing dangers, closer to home. Her novel is set at two points in the future. In the first, humanity has been rendered all but extinct by an orchestrated bioterrorist attack from within rather than without the western world. The second—nearer to us in time—depicts the police state in which the virus responsible for the man-made pandemic is first cultivated. The security services in this earlier era—the CorpSeCorp—make full use of CCTV, biometric access controls, automated motion sensors and lie-detection, but none of this hardware identifies where the real danger lies—a misanthropic scientist, emblematic of western nihilism—let alone saves the world. In the later future, the ailing lone survivor of the pandemic shambles disconsolately into the ruins of the laboratories where he had once worked:

> He passes the first barricade with its crapped out scopers and busted searchlights, then the checkpoint booth. A guard is lying half in,

half out. . . . No trees here, they'd mowed down everything you could hide behind, divided the territory into squares with lines of heat and motion sensors. The eerie chessboard effect is already gone; weeds are poking up like whiskers all over the surface. . . . He continues on, across the moat, past the sentry boxes where the CorpSeCorps armed guards once stood and the glassed-in cubicles where they'd monitored the surveillance equipment, then past the rampart watchtower with the steel door—standing forever open, now—where he'd once been ordered to present his thumbprint and the iris of his eye.

Such may be one future for the particular forms of surveillance technology with which we surround ourselves now. . . . [T]here are numerous others, and many idioms in which surveillance is being discussed. How much such fiction contributes to a critical consciousness in the wider public is uncertain, but it is of significance in itself that major novelists like Atwood, Lott, Ballard, Raban and DeLillo think surveillance is worthy of serious intellectual attention. Genre novels are important too—perhaps more important, given their mass readership—because whether surveillance is merely part of the backdrop or the specific focus of the story, they are registering its presence in the world. The distinction between genre fiction and literary fiction is in any case permeable, and increasingly spurious. Atwood, like Orwell before her, recognised that the idiom of 'speculative fiction' has much to offer as a means of engaging with the challenges of late modern life. Several hitherto literary writers e.g. Michael Cunningham; Jeannette Winterson have in fact tried their hand at science fiction (and addressed surveillance in passing) and this genre—the very first to see surveillance coming—will continue to be a key source of critical thinking on the subject. J. G. Ballard, on the other hand, famously made the transition the other way—from science fiction to literary fiction, and in *Running Wild* he produced a classic of 'surveillance literature' which has yet to be recognised as such, and which may indeed have anticipated the very neglect into which its searingly unpalatable truth about contemporary surveillance would fall.

# 77

# CATHERINE ZIMMER

# SURVEILLANCE CINEMA

Catherine Zimmer's book covers a huge range of surveillance film and media. Rather than trying to offer a "survey," which would necessarily be superficial, here we present an excerpt that focuses on one seminal surveillance film: Francis Ford Coppola's 1974 classic, *The Conversation*.

\*\*\*

*The Conversation* serves as somewhat of an *urtext* for . . . more contemporary films . . . , which centralize surveillance technology in the stylistic and thematic construction of narrative. Francis Ford Coppola's wiretapping tour de force is widely considered to reflect the explicit concerns of its historical moment around surveillance, in particular the Watergate break-ins and accompanying revelations around political surveillance within the United States. It has also been discussed in terms of how the subjectivity of its investigatory character, private detective Harry Caul (played by Gene Hackman), is structurally and politically related to surveillance practices. The film makes it difficult to separate its character-based story from a historical and technological context, and analyses contemporary to its release as well as more recent scholarship highlight this. It is thus in many ways the ground on which contemporary surveillance cinema stands, perhaps best evidenced by Hackman's casting in the role of an almost identical character in *Enemy of the State* in 1998.

In its focus on the recording and interpretation of sound, and the way that both images and narrative organize themselves around sound-recording technology, *The Conversation* clearly offers a commentary on the wiretapping practices active in the politics and cultural imaginary of the 1960s and 1970s. But if we are to read the production of a visible field as a process of surveillant narration from the origins of cinema on, then *The Conversation* provides a representation of the part that sound recording also plays in the narrative conceits of cinema as they are organized around logics of surveillance. The film is structured, both formally and in its story, around Harry's efforts to make sense out of a recorded conversation by matching image and sound. It announces its own processes of narrative signification in relation to surveillance and investigation, thus suggesting the implicit relations between cinematic production and surveillance practice. In her detailed analysis of the collaboration between Coppola, sound editor Walter Murch, and composer David Shire, Carolyn Anderson writes that "sound in film is traditionally at the service of the images, usually supporting, often connecting, rarely contradicting them. . . . *The Conversation* reverses this pattern." While many theorists of film sound have disputed (with good reason) the primacy of the image over the soundtrack, Anderson's argument highlights the negotiation that the film offers between visual and aural signification, and suggests that this negotiation is not only exemplified by surveillance practice, but that surveillance is based on similar mediations. . . .

What might initially seem to be a standard establishing shot in the film is pulled back from its seamless omniscience by a "problem" with sound: the eagle-eye view of San Francisco's Union Square, to which we are drawn increasingly close by a slow zoom until it is interrupted by distortion in the audio recording of the street noise, is revealed by a reverse shot to be the diegetic perspective of a surveillance operator on top of a building. The following shots in the sequence also become associated through perspective or focus with various characters whose positions are revealed to be either that of a sound surveillance technician or an object of surveillance. Rather than a reversal of the "traditional" system in which sound plays a supporting role to the image, this scene (and the rest of the film) actually highlights the degree to which the smooth unfolding of the images is completely dependent on the sound engineering that *The Conversation* suggests is also the work of audio surveillance: the construction and reconstruction of sound from several sources to serve as a kind of architecture without which the narrative becomes structurally *unsound*.

This film also reflects how increasingly uniform the technologies of cinema and those of surveillance were becoming: the magnetic sound recording shown in the film as essential to surveillance practice had by that point eclipsed optical recording as a far more efficient and effective means of cinematic sound production, as was the mixing of multiple tracks. And, as Mary Ann Doane has argued in her essay on "Ideology and the Practice of Sound Editing," the privileging of the image within the discourse of (and about) film is indicative not of the lack of import of sound, but of the ideological work of sound: "In an industry whose major standard, in terms of production value, might be summarized as 'the less perceivable a technique, the more successful it is,' the invisibility of the work on sound is a measure of the strength of the sound track." While the industry Doane describes is the cinematic one, the same description is apposite for the investigatory technologies and methodologies of surveillance, as *The Conversation* demonstrates. Even theories of surveillance building on Foucault's account of Bentham's panopticon have overwhelmingly focused on the visual aspects of the model, even though, as Dörte Zbikowski's history of acoustic surveillance indicates, "Part of this system were bugging lines, which supported visual surveillance with complete acoustic monitoring." The fact that, until recently, sound recording devices could be much more easily miniaturized and hidden away as "bugs" than could visual recording mechanisms is yet another measure of the possible invisibility of sound and another indication of how accounts of cinematic technologies are implicitly invested in the logics of surveillance technologies. The minimization of the visible work of sound recording practice, even as sound is produced as a defining element, is essential to both surveillance and cinematic narrative.

The rendering visible of sound surveillance technologies within the film, in such a way that the status of both image and sound is broken down and reconstructed, foregrounds how both the technical and

ideological work of surveillance and cinematic narrative are functioning along similar premises. The deconstruction of a more
expected narrative structure in the opening
sequence reemerges as the *construction* of
technological and narrative apparatuses
through which the "truth" of the story
comes out. The rest of the film follows this
same trajectory: whether Harry is actively
trying to engineer the sound on the tapes
and the film invokes a flashback image to illustrate his engineering of the narrative that
is "the conversation" or the film is exploring
the larger context of the characters and the
investigation, *The Conversation* reflexively
demonstrates that both cinematic narrative
and surveillance practice are organized not
just by the production of a visual and visible
field, but also by the seamless production
of sound recordings and dynamic relations
between sound and image. However, as the
film progresses, it becomes increasingly
clear that Harry's investigation and even
his engineered recording of the conversation are constituted by misinterpretation
of what he has heard, misrecognition of
the subject positions of both his client and
those under surveillance, and manipulation
by forces neither Harry nor the film ever
fully identify. Thus the same productions
that constitute both the sound recording
and the narrative eventually undermine
Harry's investigative authority on multiple
levels (technological, professional, and personal) and also undermine narrative coherence and psychological stability, ultimately
problematizing the epistemological foundation supporting the use of surveillance in
the first place.

Dennis Turner's 1985 analysis of the
film demonstrates *The Conversation*'s import to a discussion of surveillance cinema
as a recognizable designation. Through an
examination of the film's "ongoing drive to
constitute itself as narrative," Turner shifts
the discussion from how the film (both
technically and thematically) produces

a story through sound and image, to an
argument that it is also constructing itself through intertextual relationships to
earlier surveillance-themed films such
as *Blow-up, Vertigo,* and *Rear Window.*
Turner's choice to read the film not merely
as a reflection of its historical moment but
as a reflection on the construction of prior
cinematic narratives around investigation implies that films about surveillance
are films about cinematic history as well,
not just in terms of technology but also
in terms of narrative formation, and that
this in turn reflects back on surveillance
practice. The argument that "the film's
reworking of material from earlier texts
raises the problems of boundary and textual authority which are suggested within
its own diegesis," expands to suggest that
the problems raised by narratives of investigation are problems that exceed issues of
boundary and authority *within* narrative—
in a broader sense, the narrative's treatment
of these textual issues both addresses and
problematizes how boundary and authority
function within actual surveillance practice. Put another way, if, as Turner argues,
the film's intertextual allusions to earlier
surveillance narratives, as well as its numerous disruptions of narrative suture
through both image and sound, enact
a "drama of the disintegrating subject,"
I would posit that this subject refers not
only to the cinematic one, but to the subject
of surveillance culture as well.

However, it is important to note that the
disintegration of the viewing and speaking
subject that Turner refers to is equally de-
scribable as the *construction* of a political subject. The film's final sequence,
which presents the increasingly distraught
Harry in his own carefully guarded private space now apparently under surveillance by his former clients, demonstrates
how this disintegration must be viewed in
terms of subject position. Having realized
that the couple whose conversation he

had recorded were not in fact victims but murder conspirators, and that he has misunderstood the entire purpose and scenario of his surveillance operation, Harry receives a threatening phone call warning him not to take any action. The caller states, "We'll be listening," and a recording of the music Harry was just playing in his apartment is played back for him. Harry tears his apartment to pieces, literally, trying to locate a microphone. Unsuccessful even after ripping apart the walls and floorboards, he sits in the middle of his shredded apartment and play his saxophone. The film ends as Harry's diegetic saxophone music joins with the extradiegetic score in a kind of duet that shows that the disintegration has exceeded the space of the character and story and that even the narrative is no longer a delimited or coherent space. The camerawork in this final shot, a high-angle slow pan back and forth that imitates the automatic repetitive sweep of a video surveillance camera, also suggests that the surveillance apparatus is ultimately the film's camera, rather than a technology within the film, further eliding any distinction between cinematic and surveillant technique and technology. For Thomas Levin, the final shot demonstrates a very self-conscious example of what he describes as the "synonymous" nature of cinematic and surveillance narration: "[I]ndeed, Harry will never find the surveillant device because it resides in a space that is epistemologically unavailable to him within the diegesis: surveillance has become *the condition of the narration itself.*" The ambiguities that surround this film—Who is the victim? Who is being watched, and why? Is this a film about the pathology of a character or a culture of surveillance?—in the final scene become visible (and audible) as the way narrative is (de)structured through surveillance into a kind of fundamental ambiguity, which recurs in numerous significant ways in films that follow it.

This breakdown of boundaries between multiple spaces at the end of *The Conversation*—diegetic and extradiegetic sound intermingling, surveillance camera and film camera becoming one and the same, the destroyed space of Harry's apartment revealing the architecture within, the psychological space of reason versus insanity—is also an exposure of the tenuous boundaries between the private/individual/psychological and the public/social/political. The very rupturing of the narrative space demands that the psychological exploration of this principal character be viewed in relation to the context outside of the film—it is a formal demand of the narrative, as constructed through surveillance technologies and practices. But in exposing how impossible these boundaries are, the narrative also erects relations between those spheres: the possibility of intrusion on a private realm is what defines that space as private in the first place, and is one of the reasons why Norman Denzin posits the figure of "the voyeur" as central to the cinematic production of twentieth-century notions of privacy. The construction of Harry Caul's personal pathology is instructive in these terms—his obsession with his own privacy is not "ironic" given his job invading the privacy of others . . .: it is a testament to the structural configurations of privacy as a contiguous production of surveillance, thus connecting their formations closely. In using the narrative relations between sound and image to explore these definitionally permeable boundaries, the film also highlights how surveillance practice merges with what in another context Giorgio Agamben calls "zones of indistinction". . . .

Arguably, audio surveillance is associated in particular with the 1970s and the Watergate break-ins, while the kind of information processing seen as typical of the digital era is a more common cultural reference today, but narrative formations show that these practices have developed in tandem, with intersecting structures that build on and inflect each other. The thematization of telephone surveillance in the HBO series *The Wire* (2002–2008) demonstrates that the task of audio surveillance is not simply to record all conversations and make sense of them, but to analyze patterns of who is calling whom, process times and lengths of calls, and interpret conversations specifically encoded to avoid providing evidence. Even in *The Conversation,* with its focus on a single recording, audio surveillance and the aggregation of information are one and the same. And, as Zbikowski has noted, "The problem facing the listener when monitoring telephone calls is above all a legal one" and thus such surveillance narratives are organized around the modes in which one gains appropriate authority to listen in, as well as the technological capability. *The Wire*'s narrative arcs of surveillance (though they are not always about surveillance in particular) are often structured by the play between technology and legality, surveillance and evasion.

# 78

# JENNIFER R. WHITSON

## GAMING THE QUANTIFIED SELF

Jennifer Whitson's article considers how more and more domains of life are subject to the formal logics of gaming, and that the logics of gaming are necessarily surveillant when reproduced by digital applications that increasingly cover everything from personal fitness to workplace performance.

*** 

[G]amification is play applied to non-play spaces. Game developers and designers define gamification in terms of utilizing game mechanics, technology, and development techniques from games in non-game spaces, while those from outside of the industry generally equate gamification with adding points, leaderboards and badges to non-game activities. . . .

While the quantification of the self has commonalities with the time honoured tradition of journaling and the care of the self as an ethical practice of reflection detailed by Foucault, what is different is the precision, complexity, and the amount of the data collected, as well as the way it is ultimately presented back to the chronicler. Instead of leaving it up to us to decide what is worth chronicling, and then delegating our spotty memories to provide the details, the journaling process is automated, enabling incredibly precise details. It is also framed as playful.

The digitization of data gathering and quantification permits new kinds of accumulation and scorekeeping, detailing and chronicling the minutiae of our lives at an unprecedented level of granularity. Data-gathering is automated and feedback is near instantaneous. New technologies enable us to measure, chart, and quantify what was previously unquantifiable. It also allows us to transmit and share what was previously private. It is now relatively simple to measure and analyze patterns in our sleep, exercise, sex life, food intake, mood, location, alertness, productivity, and even our mental health and spiritual wellbeing. We effortlessly track and measure, display and share all of this heretofore unknown data using our computers, smart phones, and gaming consoles.

This form of surveillance (i.e. data collection that is then used to shape and channel users' behaviour) would have been impossible to carry out in the past. . . .

What gamification primarily leverages from games is the ways that games render space visible, from points systems to pathfinding. . . . Games excel at providing precise real-time feedback to help players chart their current progress and determine how to advance. . . . Feedback thus governs behaviour; steps towards a goal are encouraged in multiple ways and channels, while steps in the wrong direction are penalized. Feedback can be immediate (e.g. providing a *World of Warcraft* (WoW) player with real-time *per second* data on how they are faring in an attack). But feedback also takes mid- and long-range forms, providing information on how a player is progressing with goals that take weeks, months, or even years to accomplish.

Porting the feedback methods used in games to non-game activities thus makes sense. We turn to gamification to respond to a gap in our day-to-day lives, where feedback on one's progress, cues for future directions, and a place for experimentation and even failure, is lacking. For the most part, feedback in non-digitized spaces is much more infrequent and difficult to accomplish, largely because the automated cycle of data collection, compilation, analysis, and feedback is simply not established. For example, at work feedback is often restricted to annual performance reviews, whereas in academia, feedback cycles can take months and even years—as in a tenure application or journal submission.

The game involved in gamification projects is in setting challenges and goals, both short-term and long-term. Charts, graphs, and statistics are automatically compiled, transforming what is essentially a large database of meaningless numbers into something that users can quickly parse and understand. Players [interpolate] themselves in this data, seeing the messiness of everyday lives and the interiority of their selves as something that can be meaningfully collected into a database to be rendered understandable and actionable. . . .

By gamifying everyday tasks such as exercise and healthy living, users can make solitary and tedious activities more enjoyable. At the very least, users feel they are making progress, however incremental. What is important here is that this is *willing* self-surveillance. This is not institutionally-imposed disciplinary surveillance, or even the instrumentalization of hedonistic desires that fuels the consumer surveillance described by Deleuze. Gamification enrolls people into self-governance by using their highest aspirations and capacities, that of self-care and self-development.

When aggregated, this individual data becomes a statistical technology enrolled in managing large populations. Quantification, and its enrolment in games, is a process of translation, forging alignments between the objectives of authorities wishing to govern and the personal projects of those organizations, groups, and individuals who are subjects of government. This quantification becomes enrolled in a Taylorism of everyday life, in which self-help and self-improvement traditions become combined with rhetorics of managing and shaping the ideal, victorious, self-regulating body. Quantification is a pleasurable surveillance apparatus. . . .

Gamification is successfully leveraged as a form of self-surveillance by: i) exposing the minutiae of our everyday lives and delving for meaningful patterns, ii) using this data to improve ourselves, and iii) inciting and maintaining behaviour change by making this self-improvement process more pleasurable.

Take for example, gamified running apps. I loathe exercizing, yet gamified tools make this process endurable, by turning it into a game about myself. *Nike* + collects data about me (or at least the running me) on my daily exercise route. This data appears as a table, a database, somewhere on Nike's servers, with variables that change over time depending on my input (i.e. how fast, how long, and where I ran). The algorithms of the software act on this table, doing relational work. It makes a value judgement and instantly feeds this information back to me in some form of juicy aural and/or visual feedback. I adjust my input and performance accordingly (i.e. picking up my pace).

This process exemplifies what the digital does to play: the lovely sound of simulated coins clinking, or bars levelling-up, or an encouraging simulated voice, provides the feedback and support I crave, bringing me into this relation with myself and the machine, and persuading me to stay. These sounds, colours, badges, etc. let me know that the system is listening to me, that it is reading me, that its sensors are working. This feedback feels *good*. It works to mask the pain of my wheezing lungs and staggering feet. . . .

This game adds society to the otherwise solitary process of running. I am sharing with others a set of rules that I could otherwise establish and set myself. Even running alone, I am participating in a shared community of players, who all operate via the same rules and are striving for similar goals. Every time I go online I can see these players and their own progress. My pleasure is not only rooted in my individual successes, but rooted in my shared identity as a healthy subject, part of a community that embraces similar values. This is a form of being alone, together, via the shared rules that are established and upheld by the gamification software. Monitoring and sharing this data with others enables me to be part of this community. . . . [U]nderstanding how these communities are formed around the rules of play is important to understanding not only gamified self-surveillance but gamified participatory surveillance. . . .

Gamified self-tracking and participatory surveillance applications are seen and embraced as play because they are entered into freely, injecting the spirit of play into otherwise monotonous activities. . . . In contrast,

the case of gamified workplaces exemplifies an entirely different problematic. . . .

[For example,] gamification proponents Byron Reeves and J. Leighton Read . . . acquired the code from the *Puzzle Pirates* game and imagined how it could be changed to accommodate a call centre worker's daily tasks. In their ideal workplace, employees would log into the game each morning and select a team to work with. Assuming the role of pirates, each team takes a ship and quests for treasure. The interface would allow the employee to click on their teammates' avatars to automatically check on their progress, (indicated by a range of metrics such as their level, how many calls they fielded that day, and, on average, how long they took on calls). This would allow employees to check on and immediately offer aid to other workers who have encountered difficulties. Teams would receive virtual treasures and points for completing each task and meeting overarching productivity goals. Workers would select from a variety of missions and quests. They would be free to do as they will, as long as what they do consists of fielding calls.

Ideally, Reeves and Read look to create Taylorism 2.0: instead of advocating a single, most efficient method of production for every task, the competitive 'game' would provide incentive to continually improve efficiency, to innovate and find creative methods to field the greatest number of calls. As call centre employees' skill improves, the challenges to which they would be subjected also increase. The bar for achievement is constantly raised, not allowing workers to become complacent and rest on their laurels. Most importantly, workers would be told that they are free from the tightly constrained hierarchical control, and instead are 'playing' with work. . . .

Ideally, instead of resisting the monitoring of their every action, and unlike call centre workers elsewhere, workers would submit to surveillance because they are rewarded by it—being surveilled is the price of participating in the game, which replaces the dreary monotony of call centre work with a more appealing narrative of swashbuckling and pillaging pirates. Broadcasting to one's coworkers and supervisors—to the second—how long one spends on calls, or how many calls one has fielded, is not an intrusion phrased in Orwellian terms. It is a way to earn victory points and to chart one's progress as one levels up their avatar and completes quests. With minute-by-minute monitoring, gamifying the workplace results in a game that is never turned off.

And this is the problem. If workers are unable to turn the game off and are unable to choose to participate or not, this is not a game. Theoretically, the barrier for success for gamification projects is not high. Reeves and Reads' projects do not have to compete with WoW or *FrontierVille*, they simply need to show incremental improvement in the workplace, such as lower absenteeism, less churn, or slight increases to productivity and worker satisfaction. However—unlike gamified self-improvement applications—gamified call-centres have failed to gain any traction. They remain hypothetical cases.

The practical failure of gamified workplaces lies in the clashing frames, and expectations, of work and play. Frames of play are successful in opt-in gamification, but become discordant when they conflict with other competing frames (i.e. frames about work), exposing the tension between the game logic and the logic and demands of the larger social context. Pre-existing understandings of the institutional arrangement of work, and how work contrasts to play, are deeply embedded within subjects, defining their relationship with these institutions. A veneer of play is unable to hide the underlying reality of work. This effectively kills the motivation to play and instead motivates workers to thwart and resist the systems that have attempted to mislead them and take advantage of their playful tendencies. Playful frames may enable the smoothing over of potentially contentious data-gathering practices (such as sending *Nike* + a running record of my geo-positional data), but it is unable to efface the reality of work, the hierarchical and unbalanced power relations that characterize these spaces, the social expectations therein, and the fact that covert surveillance is used to judge, rank, and punish employees. When employees have no choice but to participate, the gamified call-centre can no longer be framed as a game or play, it reverts to work: 'what a body is obliged to do'. It is revealed as a thinly-veiled ploy to create ideal workers and is thus resisted.

# INDEX